Poland's War on Radio Free Europe

This book is developed as part of the international program
'European Network Remembrance and Solidarity (ENRS)'

EUROPEAN NETWORK
REMEMBRANCE AND SOLIDARITY

The Secretariat of ENRS has been operating as part of
National Centre for Culture

NATIONAL
CENTRE
FOR
CULTURE

Poland's War on Radio Free Europe, 1950–1989

Paweł Machcewicz

Translated by Maya Latynski

Washington, D.C.
Woodrow Wilson Center Press

Stanford, California
Stanford University Press

EDITORIAL OFFICES
Woodrow Wilson Center Press
Woodrow Wilson International Center for Scholars
One Woodrow Wilson Plaza
1300 Pennsylvania Avenue NW
Washington, DC 20004-3027
www.wilsoncenter.org

ORDER FROM
Stanford University Press
Chicago Distribution Center
11030 South Langley Avenue
Chicago, IL 60628
Telephone: 800-621-2736; 773-568-1550

Printed in the United States of America

Library of Congress Cataloging-in-Publication Data

Machcewicz, Paweł, 1966–
[Monachijska menazeria. English]
Poland's war on Radio Free Europe, 1950–1989 / by Paweł Machcewicz ; translated by Maya Latynski.
pages cm
Includes bibliographical references and index.
ISBN 978-0-8047-9238-7
1. Radio Free Europe. 2. Radio broadcasting policy—Poland—History—20th century. 3. Radio broadcasting, Polish—History—20th century. 4. Freedom of the press—Poland—History—20th century. 5. Poland—Politics and government—1945–1980. 6. Poland—Politics and government—1980–1989. I. Title.
HE8697.85.P7M3313 2014
384.54094—dc23

2014037399

Wilson Center

The Wilson Center, chartered by Congress as the official memorial to President Woodrow Wilson, is the nation's key nonpartisan policy forum for tackling global issues through independent research and open dialogue to inform actionable ideas for Congress, the Administration, and the broader policy community.

Please visit us online at www.wilsoncenter.org.

Contents

List of Illustrations ix
Acknowledgments xi
List of Abbreviations and Selected Government Bureaus and Divisions xiii

Introduction: The Communist Regimes and Western Broadcasting 1
1. Radio Free Europe: Its Genesis and Its Place in the Cold War 13
2. Stalinism, 1950–1956 45
3. Władysław Gomułka's Era, 1956–1970 82
4. Operation Olcha: The Security Service versus Radio Free Europe's Contacts in Poland 156
5. The Gierek Era, Détente, and a Massive Attack on Radio Free Europe, 1971–1975 181
6. From Helsinki to the Demise of Communism, 1975–1989 218
Conclusion 283

Notes 291
Bibliography 369
Index 397

List of Illustrations

Following page 200

1. *Nazi Loudspeakers:* Anti-RFE poster by Jerzey Jankowski and Stanisław Gratkowski (1955).
2. Untitled anti-RFE poster by Ignacy Witz (1955).
3. *Who They Really Are:* Anti-RFE poster by unknown author (1980s).
4. Polish Security Service plan of the RFE offices in Munich's "Englisch Garten" (*Englischer Garten,* English Garden), drawn on the basis of information provided by a secret collaborator.

Acknowledgments

Numerous individuals, especially fellow historians, were generous with their advice and help. They directed my attention to new research topics, answered questions, provided tips on archival sources, and even made available materials they had discovered in the course of their own work. I must mention Mirosław Biełaszko, Władysław Bułhak, Sławomir Cenckiewicz, Jane Curry, Wojciech Czaplicki, Antoni Dudek, Jerzy Eisler, Wojciech Frazik, Andrzej Friszke, Wanda Jarząbek, Łukasz Kamiński, Aleksander Kochański, Jacek Krawczyk, Grzegorz Majchrzak, Grzegorz Nawrot, A. Ross Johnson, Krzysztof Persak, Andrzej Paczkowski, Małgorzata Ptasińska-Wójcik, Tadeusz Rutkowski, Oldřich Tuma, Rafał Wnuk, and Janusz Wróbel. I would like to thank them all, as well as the archivists of many collections who facilitated my investigations. I would especially like to recognize Ewa Pirek and Katarzyna Zimowska of the archive of the Institute of National Remembrance. The comments offered by the editor of the Polish version of this book, Anna Równy, were extremely valuable. I am deeply grateful to Maya Latynski for her excellent translation of this book into English. She became a great expert in the linguistic nuances of the language used by the Communist Party, security apparatus, and propaganda, which was quite a challenge. Of course, I alone am responsible for the opinions expressed in this book.

List of Abbreviations and Selected Government Bureaus and Divisions

Abbreviations

BBC	British Broadcasting Corporation
BIB	Board for International Broadcasting
BND	Bundesnachrichtendienst (West German intelligence)
CC	Central Committee (of PUWP)
CSCE	Conference on Security and Cooperation in Europe (CSCE)
CIA	Central Intelligence Agency (US)
CPSU	Communist Party of the Soviet Union
FEC	Free Europe Committee
FRG	Federal Republic of Germany
GDR	German Democratic Republic
KOR	Komitet Obrony Robotników (Committee for the Defense of Workers)
KUL	Katolicki Uniwersytet Lubelski (Catholic University of Lublin)
OBOP	Ośrodek Badania Opinii Publicznej (Center for Public Opinion Research)
PAP	Polish Press Agency
PPN	Polskie Porozumienie Niepodległościowe (Polish Independence Agreement)
PRON	Patriotyczny Ruch Odrodzenia Narodowego (Patriotic Movement for National Rebirth)
PRP	People's Republic of Poland

PUWP	Polish United Workers' Party
RFE	Radio Free Europe
RIAS	Radio in the American Sector
TKN	Towarzystwo Kursów Naukowych (Society for Educational Courses)
VOA	Voice of America
ZSMP	Związek Socjalistycznej Młodzieży Polskiej (Union of Socialist Polish Youth)

Selected Government Bureaus and Divisions

Bureau of Information and Propaganda of the Central Command of the Union for Armed Struggle and, later, of the Home Army (ZWZ-AK): gathering information and conducting propaganda for the main organization of the Polish anti-Nazi resistance

Committee for Public Security: headquarters of the security police, 1954–1956 (succeeding the Ministry of Public Security)

Department of Propaganda and Agitation of the Central Committee of the Polish United Workers' Party (CC PUWP): producing political propaganda and combating ideological enemies

Directorate II, General Staff of the Polish Army: military intelligence

Ministry of Internal Affairs, Department I: foreign intelligence

Ministry of Internal Affairs, Department II: counterintelligence

Ministry of Internal Affairs, Department III: combating domestic political opponents

Ministry of Public Security: security police, 1944–1954

Ministry of Public Security, Department X: surveillance of party cadres

Poland's War on Radio Free Europe

Introduction: The Communist Regimes and Western Broadcasting

This book tells the story of the war against Radio Free Europe (RFE) that the Polish Communist regime waged relentlessly over the course of nearly four decades, from 1950 until 1989. The hostilities were part of the Soviet bloc's struggle against foreign radio stations. The events described in this book show that broadcasting became one of the main fronts in the Cold War as adversaries fought to control the flow of information and ideas. Radio broadcasting thus played a major role in the Communist regimes' ability to direct their societies and to shape them politically and ideologically.

Throughout its rule, from the 1940s until the collapse of Communism in 1989, the Polish United Workers' Party (PUWP) dedicated significant resources, focus, and energy to combating both its domestic and foreign enemies. Among the most serious of these enemies were the Western radio stations, which challenged the regime's information monopoly and sustained Poles' ties to the West and to the anticommunist émigrés who supported independent thought in Poland and, later, the activities of its political opposition. Between the time it smashed the legal Polish Peasant Party and the underground resistance in the second half of the 1940s, and the appearance of an organized opposition in the 1970s, the Polish government viewed the exile community as the sole source of organized anticommunism. Of all the émigré institutions, RFE had the largest organizational potential and the greatest capacity to sway Polish minds. Its broadcasting hours and wavelengths and its transmitters' power, not to mention its grasp of the Polish reality, made RFE vastly superior to the other Western radio stations.

The PUWP, security apparatus, armed forces, diplomatic corps, and mass media all joined in the war against RFE, other Western radio stations, and all organizations of foreign "ideological subversion" (which acquired this rubric in official Communist terminology in the early 1960s). This book explores how all these institutions and organizations operated and interacted. This information should help us understand better the roles played by the different components of the political system and the various units that together formed the apparatus of power. It also affords insight into the flow of information between these centers and their reciprocal influences, including the relationship between the party apparatus and the security organization or that between the special services and journalists and the media. The story of the fight against foreign "subversion" also has much to say about Poland's growing openness toward the West, and about the government's efforts to thwart this openness and create a closed system, one it could control completely. Finally, the battle for control of the airwaves and of the kind of information propagated by radio forms a chapter in the history of the Soviet bloc, since all its member states waged the same war against foreign radio stations and, more broadly, against Western influence. There were, however, differences as well as similarities between the Soviet bloc countries in their cooperation with and dependence on Moscow.

Over the four decades of its existence, the Communist system in Poland evolved considerably. This was evident in the extent of the party's repressions; the trends in official propaganda and the role of propaganda in mobilizing the population and legitimating the regime's rulers; the machinery of the Polish Communists' dependence on Moscow; and the Polish Communists' policies toward the Catholic Church, national traditions, and noncollectivized farming. And yet, from the early 1950s until the late 1980s, the Munich-based RFE remained one of this system's key, unwavering enemies. The system deployed a range of weapons to fight RFE: propaganda; jamming; persecution of those in Poland who secretly provided information to the radio station (and, in the Stalinist era, of those who merely listened to it); and finally, security operations to infiltrate the Munich-based staff, recruit agents from it, promote strife within it, and discredit persons of particular importance to the Polish Section. These counteroffensives varied in intensity, and some rose to temporary prominence. For example, in the first half of the 1950s, groups of people who were found listening to the radio together would be incarcerated in labor camps, but this was no longer the case under Władysław Gomułka's rule (1956–1970), when the jamming of foreign broadcasts from Polish territory ceased.

The government's determination to challenge RFE persisted for decades since fighting it was, from Warsaw's point of view, rational. Its principal motivation was RFE's importance to the Poles. The government began to conduct its own classified research into the station's audiences in the late 1960s, and some of its measurements seem quite accurate. The findings of opinion polls conducted by the Center for Public Opinion Research (Ośrodek Badania Opinii Publicznej, OBOP) are cited here for the periods covered in the different chapters of this book. To give an idea of RFE's audiences, in May 1969, 20 percent of adults listened to it; in November 1973, 7.6 percent; in November 1976, 11 percent; in November 1977, 18 percent; in May 1978, 21 percent; in January 1979, 30 percent; in 1980, 48 percent; in 1981, 53 percent; in 1982, 49 percent; in November 1984, 18 percent; in January 1987, 14 percent; and in May 1988 and February 1989, 22 percent.[1]

The listenership typically increased when crises deepened and political tensions grew. It declined in periods when the political situation stabilized and popular participation in political events decreased and interest in them declined. The OBOP research usually showed RFE as the most popular station, though at times, beginning in 1983, the Voice of America (VOA) slightly surpassed it.

The surviving OBOP data are incomplete, which prevents a full assessment of their reliability. RFE conducted its own audience research, which is discussed later in the book. Its listenership figures are much higher than OBOP's, which can be attributed largely to RFE's research methodology: the figures were derived from interviews with Poles traveling in the West, not a representative sample of the population.[2] It would seem that OBOP's figures, which are quite high, are a more accurate gauge of reality, especially considering that from 1971 on, listeners had to overcome very powerful jamming.

Because it was critical to eliminate the influence of foreign "sabotage" in the military, beginning in the 1970s the military too began to conduct its own audience research. In 1978, the Institute of Social Research of the Military Political Academy (Instytut Badań Społecznych Wojskowej Akademii Politycznej) carried out its first scholarly survey of listenership. The sample was large (consisting of a professional cadre of 836 officers, ensigns, and noncommissioned officers and 1,200 recruits). According to its authors, "the research was conducted on the basis of an opinion meter [instead of questionnaires, which would have made it possible to identify respondents—P. M.], which guarantees the greatest possible degree of anonymity." The results of the study make it clear that it was not doctored. According to its summary, "67.6% of the cadres and 64% of the recruits listen to RFE on its different frequencies. Around half of them are accidental listeners, who listen to this station very rarely." The honesty of this assessment is also noteworthy: "In designing this study, it was presumed that membership in the party organization and the ZSMP [Związek Socjalistycznej Młodzieży Polskiej, Union of Socialist Polish Youth] should have a differentiating influence on the frequency of listening to RFE, [a supposition] which is justified by the ideological-educational influence of these organizations. The results of the study did not confirm this. It turns out that members of these organizations listen to the abovementioned programs as often as nonmembers." Higher military rank similarly played no role in reducing interest in RFE's programs.[3]

In subsequent years, research on audiences of the Western radio stations used the same methods but differentiated among people who listened to the different stations. Thus, 33 percent of the professional cadre listened to RFE in 1979 and 44 percent did so in 1981. Among draftees, the numbers were even higher: 43.9 percent in 1979 and 67.1 percent in 1981. The VOA placed second, drawing more than 30 percent of listeners, and the BBC third, drawing 12 percent to 27 percent.[4]

These data further confirm that RFE's audiences grew during times of political crisis. The overall numbers of people listening to all the foreign radio stations increased, for RFE more than for the others, something that the military research shows clearly. By 1983, after the major political conflicts of the Solidarity movement and martial law periods had passed, the Military Office of Sociological Research found that RFE audiences had shrunk to 43.1 percent in the professional military and to 60.6 percent of men doing their military service.[5] A further drop was registered in 1987 (for professionals down to 14 percent, for recruits down to 26.6 percent), but by the following year, as a new political crisis came into view, the numbers started rising again (for the professional cadre to 15.6 percent, for recruits to 29.2 percent).[6] As the noteworthy précis of the 1983 study observes, "This research shows that a decisive majority of listeners do not listen to just one chosen station but most listen to both RFE and another station (RFE + VOA or RFE + BBC)."[7]

There are no reliable data on the listenership of Western broadcasts before the late 1960s. Yet the scale of the official propaganda attacks, the installation of an advanced jamming system, and the persecution of listeners in the 1950s make it clear that it must have been a very widespread phenomenon, one that the government viewed as a critical threat. The broad demand during the 1956 revolt that the government end jamming and the rebellious masses' destruction of jamming installations in Poznań in June and in Bydgoszcz in November are a gauge of how valuable the Western radio stations were to Poles living under Stalinist totalitarianism.

The importance of RFE was due not only to a listenership in the millions but also to the content and reception of its broadcasts. Countless statements testify to the fact that, especially in the 1950s but also later, for many RFE was the main source of sovereign information about the situation both in their own country and around the world, an inspiration to develop their own ideas about the reality in which they were living (as opposed to accepting the regime's slant), and a haven from the pressures of official propaganda, all of which helped them get through the most difficult times. At critical junctures, it was an indispensable source of information about protests; during July and August 1980, for example, because it covered strikes, the radio gave workers in non-striking industrial centers a sense of what their peers were doing, which provided momentum for the avalanche of strikes. After an organized open opposition came into being in 1976, RFE became the principal medium through which news about the activities and demands of this handful of courageous and determined individuals was able to reach virtually every corner of the country.

Stories about the 1950s, when listening to RFE was extremely risky, are the most moving. "In my house, we solemnly celebrated the Third of May holiday [a national holiday, banned by the Communists, which commemorated the 1791 Polish constitution—P. M.] always, even in the most difficult times," Eleonora Kosior-Zbierska reminisced in an interview with the film director Maciej Drygas. "Also on that day, May 3, 1952, my father put on an elegant suit and tie . . . and he took me into his secret little room, actually a closet, in which he listened to the radio. The window, which looked out on the forest, was not only shuttered but also insulated with an eiderdown. Sitting on a pillow was a prewar receiver with flickering colored lights. On that day in May, as the radio squealed and buzzed, I heard for the first time the voice that inspired my heart and my mind so powerfully, Jan Nowak's voice: 'And now, I speak to you, my dear countrymen, as you sit listening, on Polish soil.'"[8]

Another story from the 1950s comes from Ireneusz Haczewski: "A Phillips radio was one of the first pieces of furniture my father bought. I can remember our covered windows, the volume turned down low since we knew there were people who walked around outside and eavesdropped. The whole family huddled around this radio, as everyone tried to catch the words over the rattle of the jamming machine."[9]

For those who did not accept the reality of life in People's Poland, listening daily to RFE reinforced their opinions and created a space in which they could feel safe being themselves. "I chose internal emigration," Andrzej Kostrzewski recounted. "Free Europe's programs reinforced this choice. I listened to them every day. . . . Had it not been for RFE, I would have felt completely alone. I could only have sat in my armchair and talked to myself about how I didn't like things. But now I could find a confirmation for my views in RFE's programs. They talked about everything that irritated me in this country. And they also sustained my hopes and the certainty that all this would pass."[10]

Often, listening to RFE served as a sort of initiation into opposition activity or a developmental stage in deciding to engage politically. "The year 1976 was a phase, with its hutzpah of demonstrations against troublemakers [which were staged by the authorities to denounce workers taking part in strikes and street demonstrations to oppose price increases—P. M.]," Krzysztof Nowak of the Gorzów club of the Young Poland Movement told the journalist Piotr Zaremba. "It was then that we began to listen to Free Europe every day. We had had enough preparation, so we did not allow the system's ugly mug to take us by surprise. And what vast quantities of information there were about the opposition: we learned that there were people who were not afraid of putting their names on protest letters. We were not alone."[11]

RFE often served as the principal defensive weapon for those who engaged in independent activity and were persecuted for it. This happened in the 1970s when the radio aired news about repressions against a handful of supporters of opposition organizations, as well as under martial law, when imprisoned Solidarity activists were mistreated in an atmosphere of impunity in the many penal institutions and internment camps. According to Cracow opposition activist Adam Macedoński, "I was held in the internment camp in Załęż. Our pal Staszek Mazur set his mind on refusing to leave his cell. They brought him out by force, dragged him to some cellar and beat him up. We were in the yard at the time, and we could hear that they were torturing Staszek. We decided not to go back to our cells but to stand in the corridors until we got to see him. All of a sudden, a group of men in helmets, police batons in hand, charged in. . . . They grabbed me by the arms, and one of them slugged my face so hard that I saw stars. . . . They forced us down into the cellar, into unheated, damp cells. I jumped up to the little window, grabbed the bars and began screaming: 'They have beaten us up!' . . . It was around noon, the time when families came to visit. Some women came closer, and it was probably they who passed this information on to Solidarity. At 7 p.m., an obviously dumbfounded screw told us that Free Europe had already broadcast the news that we had been beaten up. It was thanks to this information, which traveled out into the world, that we were put back in our cells. And, surprise! We were not punished."[12]

RFE influenced not only independent thinkers but also the establishment. An example of this critical role was the series of programs broadcast from October 1954 about the compromising disclosures coming from "the heart" of the regime made by Józef Światło, a key functionary of the security police who had earlier defected to the West, which started the anti-Stalinist ferment among the party elite. Światło exposed classified information about the Communist terror, the Polish regime's dependence on Moscow, and the luxurious lifestyle of the party's leaders. RFE was even on in Security Service offices. Prison screws, a pillar of the persecution apparatus of the People's Republic, also listened to it. Stanisław Kowalski, a Radom worker incarcerated in June 1976, remembered his early days in jail: "Murderers and others with long sentences did not bother us, and neither did the guards. The latter even listened to Free Europe. They consoled me: You have your KOR [Komitet Obrony Robotników, Workers' Defense Committee], they were talking about you, don't worry, nothing bad will happen to you."[13]

The party and government elites received information from RFE's monitoring reports, which was included in various confidential materials destined exclusively for them. A small elite group also got the so-called white papers produced by the Polish Press Agency.[14] Politburo members, Central Committee (CC) secretaries, and government ministers were also given full transcripts of the radio's monitored programs, "about half a kilogram of paper per day," according to Stanisław Ciosek, a government minister, PUWP department head and then CC secretary in the 1980s.[15] Probably not all of them read everything, but Foreign Minister Adam Rapacki is said to have started every workday by reading them.[16] Władysław Gomułka, first secretary of the PUWP, received a few pages of selected RFE monitoring materials from his secretary, Walery Namiotkiewicz, every day.[17] He underlined the most important passages in red pencil.[18]

According to the top party official Andrzej Werblan, Gomułka reacted to these reports calmly, something that could not be said of the Romanian leader Gheorghe Gheorghiu-Dej. The archives of the Romanian Communist Party contain monitoring transcripts with Dej's handwritten notes, tempestuous comments on individual programs. He would write in the margins: "You fools!," "So what?," "Stop joking," "This really pains you, doesn't it," and "I have contempt for you." The transcript of a program in which RFE's Romanian Section called Dej a Soviet puppet includes a long note in his hand, which, of course, was never made public.[19]

Of all the Polish Communist leaders, General Wojciech Jaruzelski seemed to follow RFE's programs most closely. He often sent Stanisław Ciosek monitoring transcripts with notes such as "Please clarify" or "What is this about?" jotted on them.[20] A document found among the papers of the Foreign Department of the PUWP CC confirms this level of attention. It is the transcript of a program by Alina Grabowska in which she discussed a festival of Andrzej Wajda's films organized by the Soviet government in 1988, for which the director was invited to Moscow. Grabowska also contrasted Mikhail Gorbachev's openness with Warsaw's established tactics of ignoring and marginalizing the director, who was active in the opposition. Jaruzelski's note on the margin of the transcript asked CC secretaries Andrzej Wasilewski and Józef Czyrek to explain this comment. Wasilewski prepared a response, which began with a reference to RFE's programs and went on to describe discussions with the Soviets. Representatives of the PUWP leadership attempted to persuade the Russians to stop "validating Wajda in the context of the role he is playing in extremist structures."[21]

Jaruzelski himself, in an interview with the American scholar Jane Curry, said that in some cases RFE's broaching of certain topics armed the Polish leadership with arguments to use with the Soviets. He claimed he had tried to convince Gorbachev to recognize the USSR's responsibility for the 1940 Katyń massacre of Polish officers by citing RFE's programs, which millions of Poles heard.[22]

RFE appears frequently in *Dzienniki polityczne* (Political diaries) by Mieczysław Rakowski (editor in chief of the PUWP weekly *Polityka*; member of the CC; deputy premier, premier, and Politburo member). It is one of the most important sources for understanding the inside story of the post-1956 Communist elite. According to Rakowski's diaries, RFE's programs were the subject of unofficial commentaries and debates at various party meetings. By revealing subterranean conflicts or ties between individuals and groups, they played a major role in strengthening intraparty rivalries.

All this creates the impression that to the PUWP elite, RFE programs were ersatz free media, the sort that in democratic countries are a natural point of reference for the people who govern them. Already in the 1960s, a former minister of education and a Communist "dissident," Władysław Bieńkowski, was writing anxiously about this situation: "The extent of the influence of this foreign propaganda (represented mostly by Radio Free Europe) not on our society but on our government is both astounding and disturbing. . . . This propaganda (I am embarrassed to confess) largely plays the role of an opposition daily, and fighting it is becoming an important theme in the ideological life of our propaganda apparatus. What is more, these foreign sources are capable of imposing [a course of] actions in domestic policy on us, influencing evaluations of particular events and even our personnel policy. . . . The impact that these centers have on our government is much greater than their potential effect on public opinion and the public mood."[23]

* * *

In writing this book, I relied mainly on archival material. The Central Archives of Modern Records (Archiwum Akt Nowych, or AAN) and the archive of the Institute of National Remembrance (Archiwum Instytutu Pamięci Narodowej, or AIPN) hold the most important sources for reconstructing the operations of the authorities of People's Poland. I used the archives of the PUWP (deposited in the AAN), including documents of the Politburo, the CC Secretariat, and individual CC departments, as well as records of CC plenary meetings and PUWP congresses. The PUWP archive also includes the files of the Komisja Specjalna do Walki z Nadużyciami i Szkodnictwem Gospodarczym (Special Commission for Combating Economic Abuses and Sabotage), which were key to reconstructing how those who listened to RFE in the 1950s were persecuted.

Most of the documents I draw on are located in the AIPN, which in 2000 took in the great majority of documents that had been produced for decades by the Communist security apparatus and made them accessible to historians, much as its German counterpart, the Office of the Federal Commissioner for the Stasi Archives, did for the former East Germany. The documents come from both civilian (the Ministry of Public Security, Committee for Public Security and Ministry of Internal Affairs) and military structures (primarily intelligence, that is, Directorate II of the General Staff of the Polish Army).

Some of the documents produced by the Communist special services are archived in a reserved collection, a separate section of the AIPN that is inaccessible to historians and available only to the current intelligence services of the Polish state, which presumably use them for operations today or want to keep information of potential contemporary relevance classified. The documents in the reserved collection might help illuminate some of the issues discussed here, especially events from the 1980s, which I could only describe piecemeal or suggest, for lack of relevant documentation. Some issues likely will never be explained since a number of very important documents pertinent to RFE were destroyed in December 1989 and January 1990, during the political transition. Some secret services operations were never recorded in writing. This was the case with the use of violence or various "disintegration" techniques, some of which broke the law, even in People's Poland.

The destruction of some documents, the likely placement of others in the reserved collection, and the fact that AIPN has not yet finished exploring and organizing its enormous resources means that any research on the Communist secret services is inevitably carried out on a fragmentary foundation of primary sources. On the one hand, the quantity of materials is huge. The historian is obliged to wade through tens of thousands of pages of documents produced by the bureaucracy of a modern state, of which the security apparatus was just one component. This is one of the characteristics of the work of the historian of the twentieth century. On the other hand, despite the enormous quantity of material in the archives, time after time the historian stumbles on a gap or loses a trail. A thread may have no terminus because a document has been destroyed, relegated to the classified collection, or not yet found. In this case, the work of the researcher of the secret services somewhat resembles the methods used by classicists, medievalists, or archaeologists (may they forgive me for making this comparison), who at times must make assertions on the basis of very slim and incomplete documentation. At such times it may only be possible to advance a hypothesis that may be confirmed or overridden later, when previously unknown documents surface. This book is a good example of such a situation. After its publication in Polish in 2007, I came across newly located AIPN documents that pertained to intelligence and propaganda operations against RFE in the late sixties and early seventies (especially the activities of a very efficient secret agent, Andrzej Czechowicz). I then revised and rewrote parts of the work for its publication in English.

Another set of documents I used in my work on Poland's actions against RFE and the other organizations practicing "foreign ideological sabotage" were the records of the Government Press Spokesman's Office, which are housed in the Central Archive of the Ministry of Internal Affairs. They include the archives of the government spokesman Jerzy Urban, who played a starring role in the propaganda war against RFE in the 1980s, working closely with the Security Service. I also used military records, foremost among them those of the Główny Zarząd Polityczny Wojska Polskiego (Main Political Directorate of the Polish Army), which are located in the archive of the Institutions of the Ministry of National Defense in Modlin, the Central Military Archive in Rembertów, and the materials (mostly on research on the army listenership of Western stations) stored in the Military Office of Sociological Research. The Archive of the Institutions of the Ministry of National Defense adheres to a thirty-year secrecy rule, which meant that I was unable to gain access to documents from the 1980s.

It was equally important for this book to tell the story of the other side, RFE. I did exploratory research in the most important collection about its history, deposited in the Hoover Institution on War, Revolution and Peace at Stanford University, which was opened to scholars only several years ago. This archive also contains the collections of the Polish émigré politicians Stefan Korboński and Stanisław Mikołajczyk, which helped me to sketch out RFE's political context in the 1950s. The materials I found in the Polish Institute and Sikorski Museum in London were helpful for the same reason.

As I reconstructed the genesis and early days of RFE, the document collection of RFE's first chairman, Frank Altschul, at Columbia University was critical. The materials of the RFE's Research and Analysis Department, held in the Open Society Archive in Budapest, were also helpful.

I also obtained important documents from the CIA, which I requested through the Freedom of Information Act. This yielded the *Policy Handbook* of 1951, a sort of program guide for the radio.

Two personal archives, Jan Nowak-Jeziorański's at the Ossoliński National

Institute in Wrocław and Zdzisław Najder's at the KARTA Centre in Warsaw, are of fundamental importance in telling the story of RFE's Polish Service.

Of the other archives in which I conducted investigative research, not only for this book, the following must be mentioned: the National Archives in Washington, D.C., and College Park, Maryland, and two presidential libraries, the Truman Library in Independence, Missouri, and the Eisenhower Library in Abilene, Kansas. I used the documents I found there to write about US policy, especially the idea of psychological warfare, which remained a point of reference for both RFE and the Communist governments.

In writing this book, I made ample use of newspapers and periodicals published both in Poland, where they were an essential tool in the propaganda war against RFE, and in exile. The materials published outside Poland included pieces motivated by Polish intelligence criticizing RFE and other organizations, such as the Paris-based *Kultura*. I also read books and pamphlets attacking RFE and other institutions of "ideological warfare."

I collected twenty-four personal accounts. Most came through personal interviews; some were in the form of correspondence. I spoke with American and Polish RFE employees, including three directors of the Polish Section (Jan Nowak-Jeziorański, Zygmunt Michałowski, and Zdzisław Najder), the radio's helpers in Poland (including Władysław Bartoszewski and Józef Szaniawski), and representatives of the Polish intelligence services (Andrzej Czechowicz) and the PUWP leadership (Andrzej Werblan). These personal reports proved priceless as they allowed me both to confirm facts mentioned in documents, especially those created by the special services, and to hear stories missing from archival materials. I tried to make it a key rule of my research to compare the largest possible number of documents with personal accounts addressing the same issue. This, of course, is one of the iron-clad principles of the study of history, but it is especially important for research on materials created by a security apparatus, which, if used alone, can lead a researcher astray. Often I was able to reach credible conclusions or sensible hypotheses only after I had studied both Security Service and RFE documents and compared them with individual interpretations.

But using personal accounts can also be tricky, either because an interviewee's memory has been altered by the passage of time or by emotions or because a witness is making a conscious effort to mislead the historian. I decided that I would talk to actors, especially government actors, only after I had acquired enough information and documents to be able to verify their statements. For this reason, I preferred not to interview Polish intelligence functionaries who had been involved in fighting RFE in the 1980s. Because the sources available to me for that period were limited, I would not have the documents to corroborate their stories. I believe it is often preferable to go no further than a hypothesis, or even simply to pose the questions, than to take the risk that the author—and his readers with him—will fall victim to disinformation produced by former intelligence officers. This kind of caution sets the historian apart from the reporter, who is not expected to use as many sources to back up his claims.

It would be impossible to include all facts and to touch on all the relevant themes in a book that covers forty years and the activities of many individuals. I was forced to narrow down the exposition to what I thought was most important, most interesting, most representative, or best documented. Many issues will no doubt be added, completed, or developed further with new research, especially when documents whose existence was unknown when this book was being written become accessible.

For the most part, this work is organized chronologically, with chapters analyzing successive stages of the anti-RFE "warfare," starting with the Stalinist epoch and continuing on through Gomułka's and Gierek's reigns until Jaruzelski's regime came to power in the 1980s. Two chapters break this sequence. Chapter 1 describes the role of radio broadcasting in international politics and propaganda, especially during the Cold War. I discuss the origins of RFE and its place in US policy vis-à-vis the Soviet bloc, and the relationship between RFE and the CIA. I attempt to describe the radio's program line in the different periods, as well as the sphere in which the Polish desk had real autonomy from its American supervisors. Without this background, it would be impossible to understand the part RFE played in the Cold War, or the Communist governments' actions against it. Chapter 4 is a sort of case study that presents in detail—thanks to exceptionally broad and well-preserved documentation—the methods the Security Service used against RFE's associates in Poland.

I hope the huge amount of information presented in this book will help readers appreciate the picture of the Cold War that emerges from it, one that hitherto was not well known. The story combines propaganda and cultural undertakings, jamming, repression, and secret operations, all intertwined. The struggle to control the flow of information and ideas across borders turned out to be one of the most critical battlefields in the long confrontation between the West and the Soviet bloc, and this is the subject of this book.

1. Radio Free Europe: Its Genesis and Its Place in the Cold War

Radio as an Instrument of Foreign Policy and Propaganda

Radio and film are contemporaries: both were invented in the late nineteenth century. Until the end of World War I, radio played a role mostly in the military and in maritime communications. In the course of the war, however, radio increasingly was used by both sides to disseminate propaganda outside national borders. In 1915, for example, Germany began to broadcast information about the situation at the front; this information was then reprinted by newspapers in neutral countries in Europe, and on other continents. And in 1918, during the Brest negotiations between Soviet Russia and the Central Powers, the Bolsheviks used daily radio broadcasts to present their positions to foreign audiences.[1]

It was only in the 1920s, however, that radio became a mass medium.[2] The governments of many countries quickly came to appreciate it as an important political and propaganda tool, both domestically and internationally. The totalitarian regimes led the way in exploiting its potential, as they did with other methods of modern mass propaganda. The Soviet government was the first among those regimes to do so. In 1919, during Béla Kun's revolution in Budapest, Moscow broadcast programs to Hungary, and in July 1919 Radio Moscow called on British, French, and Italian workers to protest against their governments' intervention in Russia.[3] The Soviet Union opened its first station for foreign audiences in 1924, aired sporadically at first. In 1926, for the first time in the history of radio transmitting on shortwave frequencies, its broadcasts attacked Romania for engaging in a territorial dispute in Bessarabia. Also in 1926, Moscow aired programs in English in support of the striking British miners. In 1929, it began producing regular programming in German, English, and French, initially for an hour a day. The programs consisted of ideological attacks on capitalism and calls for world revolution.[4]

The Western democracies lagged Soviet Russia in both technology development and an appreciation of radio's international potential. Germany and the Netherlands launched their foreign-language broadcasts in 1929, France in 1931, and Britain in 1932. All of these broadcasts were addressed primarily to their respective country's colonies and were transmitted in the languages of the colonies. The Vatican proved to be more universal and understanding of the power of radio when in 1931 it launched its own Jesuit-run station with a speech by Pope Pius XI in Latin. The United States had no foreign-language programs between the wars. The Third Reich, by contrast, understood the importance of radio perfectly, introducing technologically and organizationally impressive broadcasting; Mussolini's Italy followed. In effect, by the end of the 1930s the totalitarian regimes' preeminence in international broadcasting was unchallenged. In 1937, Rome had programming in sixteen languages, Berlin in five, and Moscow in seven.

German foreign-language radio developed with lightning speed on the eve of World War II. In the first few weeks of the war, Germany was airing a total of 113 hours of programming in fourteen languages daily.[5] Radio propaganda had also played a key role in spreading National Socialist views among the German minority in Poland throughout the 1930s (these, of course, were not foreign-language broadcasts). Collectively listening to these programs broadcast by the Third Reich became a tradition for Germans living in Poland. The Polish government did not interfere.[6]

The British Broadcasting Corporation (BBC) began its foreign-language programming in 1938. These broadcasts were in Arabic, to counteract Italian radio propaganda in the Near East, and in Spanish and Portuguese, to compete with Germany's programs for Latin America. The BBC inaugurated its broadcasts in French, German, and Italian in September 1938 with Prime Minister Neville Chamberlain's speech as he prepared to leave for the Munich Conference. At this point, the totalitarian governments were far more advanced in waging "radio wars." Berlin began to jam some of Moscow's broadcasts, especially those that discredited prominent Nazis (such as one that discussed the Reich's propaganda chief Joseph Goebbels's extramarital affairs).[7]

World War II spurred the rapid growth of foreign propaganda by radio, with the British and the Germans excelling at it. On the eve of the war, the British were broadcasting in nine languages, and by the end of 1943 in forty-five.[8] The growth of Germany's radio programs was just as impressive. It had programming in fourteen languages in October 1939, in twenty-two in January 1940, and in fifty-three in 1943.[9] Moscow also broadcast in many languages to the occupied European countries under the auspices of the Communist International. The Tadeusz Kościuszko station, pretending to be located in occupied Poland, aired programs in Polish from July 1941 to July 1944.[10] The United States also introduced overseas programming. In February 1942 its newly created government station, the Voice of America (VOA), began its foreign broadcasts in German, English, and French. By July 1944, it was using fifty languages.[11]

The Americans would take center stage in radio propaganda during the Cold War, but during World War II they were no match for the British. The BBC was a vital source of information as well as encouragement for the peoples of occupied Europe. Its Polish-language broadcasts began a few days after the outbreak of the war, on September 7, 1939.[12] Already during Poland's defensive war in September 1939, Poland's ambassador to the United Kingdom, Edward Raczyński, spoke from London, and in subsequent years so did prime ministers and ministers of the government in exile. The BBC also retransmitted programs of the underground Błyskawica (Lightning) radio station during the Warsaw Uprising of August 1944.[13]

The Polish government in exile created Radio Polskie to replace Polskie Radio, discredited by its association with the prewar authoritarian Sanacja government, widely held responsible for the defeat in 1939. In the autumn of 1939, Radio Polskie began to broadcast official programs to Poland on Radio France's wavelengths. After France capitulated in 1940, Radio Polskie moved to England, where it used the BBC's frequencies. Its programs were intended not only to inform the Poles but also to reassure them of the continuity of Polish statehood.[14] Another important wartime station was Świt (Dawn), active from early 1942 to the end of 1944. It intended to give the impression that it was broadcasting from occupied Poland when in fact its transmitters were located in Britain. The subterfuge required the underground to relay information to London about goings-on in German-occupied Poland, including the most intricate details of everyday life, instantaneously. Unlike the Kościuszko radio station, radio Świt proved very effective, leading the Germans to invest enormous resources in efforts to locate its transmitters.[15] Świt's authority and popularity would later become a component of the model and a point of reference for RFE's Polish desk, especially in its early days, as it worked on winning credibility and trust by showing that it had in-depth knowledge about life in Poland.

Listening to foreign radio in occupied Poland was very difficult and risky. In one of their first edicts, the Germans ordered the populace to hand over all radios and antennas. "Radio receivers are a particular target of requisitions. The intention is to deprive the population of any connection to the outside world, to any news coming from there. It is only today (October 22) that the directive to relinquish radios to police stations was announced; until now they were being confiscated primarily during searches for weapons," wrote Ludwik Landau in his *Chronicle of the Years of War and Occupation*.[16] Listening to the radio or even owning a receiver entailed "long prison sentences" handed down by special courts. The Germans would later issue similar edicts in some of the other countries they occupied, including Norway.[17] Yet not everyone followed the occupying power's orders. In March 1940, Governor General Hans Frank estimated that only a little over 60 percent of registered radios had been surrendered, and that listening to foreign stations remained a real threat to the German authorities.[18]

The underground organization Służba Zwycięstwu Polski (Service for Poland's Victory) regularly monitored foreign broadcasts, especially those of the BBC, as early as October 1939; this task was later taken over by Kwatera Radiowa (Radio Headquarters), an agency of the Bureau of Information and Propaganda of the Central Command of the Union for Armed Struggle and, later, of the Home Army. Their monitoring served as the basis for the periodical *Dziennik Radiowy* (Radio Daily), the principal source of information about the war for both the leaders of the underground organizations and the underground press.[19] The clout the BBC acquired during the occupation created a very favorable foundation, one built on after the war by Western stations broadcasting to Communist-ruled Poland. Remarkably, the Soviets marching into Poland and the government of the Polish Committee of National Liberation acting under their patronage de facto upheld the German authorities' ban on owning radios. The decree for the protection of the state, passed on October 30, 1944, set the punishment for this crime as a prison term or capital punishment, and it remained in force until November 1945.[20] It was used to justify at least one death sentence, a truly shocking case. On April 5, 1945, the authorities arrested a woman in Poznań for owning a cellar in which a radio receiver had been found. After a half-hour hearing, which took place without a defense attorney on April 27, a Military District Court sentenced her to death. Her appeal for clemency was denied, and she was executed on May 1.[21]

During World War II, foreign programs were also an important source of information and a point of reference for supporters of the resistance movements in many of the countries conquered by Germany. The BBC's appeals to paint the victory symbol on walls were met with a huge response across occupied Europe. Subsequently, an audio V in Morse code (the first four notes of Beethoven's Fifth Symphony, played on a drum) was introduced and would come to be recognized across Europe as the signature tune of the BBC's programs. It became extremely popular on the occupied continent: people tapped it on doors, locomotives whistled it, and church bells rang it. The government of the Third Reich was so impressed by the BBC's success that it attempted to appropriate the V symbol: in July 1941, German radio began to air the first few notes of the Fifth Symphony.[22]

The French had the BBC's French-language programs, while General de Gaulle's France Libre radio station broadcast from Brazzaville in the Congo and later also from Algeria.[23] It was on the BBC that de Gaulle himself read his famous June 18, 1940, speech to the French people in which he promised to continue fighting.[24] But the greatest challenge to the Allies was how to reach the people of the Third Reich. The BBC's German Service delivered factual information about the situation at the fronts, the effects of Allied bombings, and shortages of supplies. The service employed more than one hundred people, including numerous antifascist émigrés from Germany and Austria, most prominently Thomas Mann. His series of programs titled *Deutsche Hörer!* became famous. Historians estimate that several million Germans listened to the BBC regularly or occasionally, despite the fierce countermeasures employed by the German government. This listenership amounted to the breaking of the Third Reich's monopoly on information. The German-language programs aired by the US-run National Broadcasting Company were less effective, since for technical reasons they were much easier to jam. So were Moscow's, which were heavily ideological and had little appeal for the Germans.[25]

The Third Reich's countermeasures were very similar to those later employed by the Communist regimes during the Cold War. As early as September 1, 1939, a special decree forbade Germans to listen to foreign radio stations. Confiscations of radios and harsh prison terms were the legal penalty, and those who disseminated information they had heard on foreign radio could even be punished by death. Each year, between seven hundred and nearly one thousand people were punished for listening to foreign radio with prison and concentration camp terms and, beginning in 1941, the occasional death sentence. Propaganda appeals and tags with warnings printed on them, which the Germans were told to attach to the wires of their radios, did not prove fully effective. The Gestapo intentionally spread rumors that the government knew how to locate radios that were set to foreign radio stations. The previously limited jamming of foreign broadcasts intensified with the outbreak of the war. Jamming was never a foolproof system because of technical difficulties and enormous cost, and because some of the jamming equipment was destroyed during the massive Allied air strikes. Also working against the Nazi government was the fact that a great majority of German homes (about 70 percent, one of the highest figures in the world) had radios. The radio was one of the principal instruments of Nazi propaganda, yet the Third Reich's rulers never took the same step as the Soviets did, once the war started, of confiscating private radios.[26]

Germany responded by airing programs addressed to the British population. They were hosted by the famous "Lord Haw-Haw," an Irishman by the name of William Joyce, who had been born in New York and was a fanatical anti-Semite and a fan of Adolf Hitler. His programs were technically excellent, lively, and ironic about the British way of life and state institutions. They became very popular. According to the BBC, in the spring of 1940 some 15 percent of the people living in the British Isles listened to them. This changed with the Battle of Britain, when Joyce as Lord Haw-Haw called on the British to rise up against their government. From this point on, he was widely perceived as a symbol of treason. Britain never instituted jamming—a sign of the fundamental difference between democracy and totalitarianism, even in moments of extreme duress—but Lord Haw-Haw was captured after the war and hanged.[27]

The eminent American poet Ezra Pound played a similar role in Italian radio programs for the United States. He warned his listeners about the Communist threat and attacked Washington for allying itself with Moscow. He was captured by antifascist partisans in May 1945 and handed over to the American military authorities, who treated him as a dangerous criminal and held him in a custom-made cage. Transported back to the United States, he was declared mentally unfit and confined to a psychiatric hospital. He wrote poetry there, and numerous international writers demanded his release. He was set free after twelve years, and he settled in Italy.[28]

The Cold War on the Air

After World War II ended, the Allies reduced their hours of foreign broadcasting. In the case of the VOA, this meant cutting its personnel by half and cutting the number of languages by slightly more than half, to twenty-four.[29] But this drawdown did not last long, as wartime cooperation gave way to growing tensions and conflicts between the United States and Britain, on one side, and the Soviet Union on the other. By early 1947, their open hostility came to be called the Cold War.[30] In broadcasting, the launch of Russian-language programming for the Soviet population was symbolic of the new era: the BBC began it in March 1946 and the VOA in February 1947.[31]

Earlier, in February 1946, the US military forces in Germany had created a radio station that broadcast to the residents of the Soviet occupation zone, Radio in the American Sector (RIAS). It quickly won a large following, and by 1949 it was reaching listeners in virtually the entire Soviet zone (which in October 1949 became the German Democratic Republic, or GDR). RIAS on the one hand adopted an aggressive tone with respect to the Communists in East Berlin and Moscow; on the other hand, it had a rich, round-the-clock program that included political news and commentary, sports, music, agricultural, and youth programs, and even contests for its listeners.[32] According to US intelligence estimates, more than 70 percent of the GDR's population regularly listened to RIAS.[33] Its success was a major factor in the creation of RFE, which was to be modeled on this German-language station run by General Lucius Clay, commander of the US Occupation Forces.

Moscow began to jam the VOA and some BBC programs in February 1948. Jamming was to become a permanent feature of the Soviet system of information control until the Gorbachev era. Its antecedents lay in both World War II—the Third Reich engaged in jamming—and earlier times. In 1932, for example, the Romanian government had tried in vain to interfere with Soviet radio programs, while in 1934 the government of the Austrian chancellor Engelbert Dollfuss had attempted to interfere with Nazi propaganda promoting the Anschluss. In Spain, from 1946 General Francisco Franco's regime jammed Moscow's Spanish-language broadcasts. (Incidentally, there is another interesting and little-known story in the "Cold War between the radios." Spanish Communists who emigrated after the Civil War also broadcast programs to Franco's Spain from Bucharest.[34]) There was also the rare instance of a democratic government's jamming of foreign radio broadcasts when in 1956, during the Cyprus crisis, the British blocked programs from Greece that could be heard in Cyprus.[35]

Perhaps not surprisingly, the December 1950 censure of radio jamming by the United Nations General Assembly had no practical consequences.[36] In response to Soviet interference, radio transmitters were made more powerful and the number of frequencies for Russian-language programs was increased (for the VOA this meant sixty-one frequencies, for the BBC forty-eight). One of the goals of President Harry Truman's Campaign of Truth, a huge propaganda offensive aimed at Communism and the Soviet bloc, was to break through Moscow's system of jamming. A significant part of the campaign's budget was devoted to propaganda by radio. The Kremlin responded by expanding and building up its network of jamming installations.[37]

At the time the United States and Britain launched their Russian-language programming, there were only about 1.3 million radios in the Soviet Union, a country with a population of more than 180 million. This small number in such a large and populous country could be ascribed not only to technical backwardness but also to the Soviet model of broadcasting, which was based on collective media, including loudspeakers in factories, collective farms, apartment blocks, and public spaces.[38] Western radios' reach was thus limited, even without jamming. There was a large number of radios in the satellite countries of

East-Central Europe, not only in more developed Czechoslovakia but also in Poland. According to Polish statistics, there were 1.46 million radios in 1950, more than 2 million in 1953, more than 3 million in 1955, and 5.64 million in 1960.[39] The foreign programs aired to the Soviet satellites could thus count on relatively large audiences and were therefore potentially more dangerous to the local Communists. According to data collected by the BBC, which are difficult to verify, immediately after the Prague coup of February 1948, half the citizens of Czechoslovakia listened to the BBC.[40]

Before RFE was created, Poles who wanted to listen to foreign radio in Polish had a choice, with the BBC consistently placing first, a position it had built up during the war. In the 1950s, the BBC's Polish Section had a staff of about a dozen. Its programming was gradually expanded from fifteen minutes to four hours daily. (In the late 1950s, RFE broadcast nearly around the clock, and the peak number of people employed by the Polish desk in Munich was nearly three hundred.)[41] The other radio stations popular among the Poles were the VOA; Vatican Radio, which had aired Polish-language programs during the war and resumed them in 1947; Radio France; and Radio Madrid. Polish-language broadcasts were also aired by West Germany's Deutsche Welle, and even by Radio Ankara, but their audiences were much smaller than the first group's, although there are, of course, no reliable data on the size of their Polish audiences in the 1940s and 1950s.

French radio began to broadcast to Poland in December 1944, and in 1945 it created a Polish section within its foreign department (émissions vers l'étranger, or EVE). André Moosmann, a journalist and Slavicist who combined his work at the radio with a position at the French Ministry of Internal Affairs, where he was in charge of matters concerning émigrés, created and led it for many years. Assisting in the organization of the Polish Section was Kajetan Morawski, Poland's prewar ambassador in Paris, who now represented the Polish government in exile in France and had excellent connections in French political circles. The radio's writers and readers, the most prominent of whom was the well-known historian and Piłsudskiite Władysław Pobóg-Malinowski, tended to be associated with the government in exile.

From 1945 to 1947, Radio France aired two quarter-hour Polish programs daily, which then evolved into a single half-hour evening broadcast, which then was extended to forty-five minutes in 1949, and later to an hour (airing from 8 p.m. to 9 p.m.). This was not much, but the station had its faithful listeners, a fact corroborated by the letters it received from them: in 1946 there were about 5,000 letters, and in 1951 more than 11,000. The broadcasts were addressed primarily to people in Poland, but, as is evident from the letters, Poles from elsewhere, including the large Polish community in France, listened to them as well. At the peak of the Cold War, the French government treated the programs addressed to the countries behind the Iron Curtain not only as a means of promoting French culture but also as a political weapon in the fight against Communism and the Soviet bloc. In the first half of the 1950s, the Polish Section used information relayed by the French Foreign Ministry, and ministry staff responsible for the different countries of Eastern Europe and the managers of the radio sections broadcasting behind the Iron Curtain met weekly at the Quai d'Orsay. The pro-Communist newspapers published in France in Polish persistently attacked the Polish programs of Radio France. On January 1, 1952, the Polish government began to jam those broadcasts too.[42]

Radio Madrid was quite popular in Poland in the late 1940s and early 1950s. At that time, Spain continued to recognize the Polish government in exile. (It would establish diplomatic relations with the People's Republic of Poland only in the 1970s, after Franco's death). Radio Madrid launched its daily half-hour broadcasts in Polish after a two-year effort by Poland's envoy, Józef Potocki, in January 1949.[43] The Spanish government covered the majority of the operating costs of the Polish Section, and the government in exile supplemented that source with its own funds. These very modest appropriations did not permit more programming, so that in the first few months, the Polish team was not even able to fill its half-hour time slot, about half of which consequently was given over to Spanish music.[44] Only two people wrote the scripts, the editor in chief and prewar radio employee Karol Wagner (who was replaced in 1955 by the journalist Wojciech Zaleski) and the poet and political commentator Józef Łobodowski.[45] At first, they attempted to coordinate the contents of their programs with the government in exile, but this proved unwieldy.[46] The editors were largely autonomous, but were supervised by the government in exile's embassy in Madrid. The Spanish authorities occasionally intervened, but never on issues of great importance to the Poles.[47] Thanks to its almost total political and programmatic autonomy, Polish Radio Madrid had a sizable audience in Poland compared to the BBC, the VOA, or RFE in its early days. An RFE report about the listenership of Western radio stations, which was based on interviews with Poles traveling in the West, ascribed Radio Madrid's popularity to its full sovereignty, its "unambiguously Polish nature," and its "critical attitude not only toward the Russians, but also US and English policies toward Poland."[48]

Radio Free Europe Is Born

In the late 1940s, Washington gradually came to believe that more decisive steps had to be taken to weaken Moscow's control over its new satellites. To meet this goal, support was needed for underground movements (in Poland's case, this meant primarily collaborating with the Fifth Command of Freedom and Independence, Wolność i Niepodległość, which was later revealed to have been a creature of the Ministry of Public Security) and anticommunist émigrés in the United States and Western Europe, and for undertaking propaganda operations aimed at the societies living behind the Iron Curtain, which were expected to sustain the spirit of resistance and slow down the process of Sovietization.[49] In the late 1940s and early 1950s, one of the key strategies used by Washington to guide the goals and methods of US policy toward the Soviet satellites was psychological warfare. According to the National Security Council, this entailed "the planned use by a nation of propaganda and activities other than combat which communicate ideas and information intended to influence the opinions, attitudes, emotions and behavior of foreign groups in ways that will support the achievement of national aims [of the United States]."[50]

Psychological warfare would serve as the field of offensive actions against the Communist bloc, which would weaken Moscow's control over the regions and nations of East-Central Europe it had recently conquered. It was treated on the one hand as a sort of substitute for a real, "hot" war, and on the other as preparation for a real war by shaping the attitudes of those people behind the Iron Curtain who preferred the West to the Soviet Union.[51]

The problem with psychological warfare was that official government institutions, such as the VOA, a constituent organization of the Department of State, had their hands tied. It was difficult to conduct aggressive propaganda that discredited Communist regimes in the satellite states while at the same time maintaining diplomatic relations with them. This problem was to be resolved by creating the Free Europe Committee (FEC) in June 1949. Formally, the committee was formed by private citizens, but in fact it had been inspired by and remained under the patronage of the State Department and the Central Intelligence Agency (CIA). One of its main champions was George Kennan, the author of the containment doctrine, who at that time headed the Policy Planning Staff of the State Department. The FEC's founders included very influential players in the worlds of politics and finance. Many of them had connections in the intelligence community, most prominently with the people who had founded the Office of Strategic Services. Some had produced radio propaganda addressed to the Europeans under the German occupation. Others were veterans of psychological warfare who had only recently served in institutions such as the Office of War Information and Psychological Warfare Division of the Supreme Headquarters Allied Expeditionary Force (SHAEF).

One of the FEC's founders was Allen Dulles, who a few years later would become the director of the CIA. Most of the FEC's financial backing came from the CIA, with the remainder coming from private sources and, beginning in 1950, from the Crusade for Freedom, allegedly an independent organization created by respectable US citizens to organize public collections for the committee to assist "captive nations." American and international public opinion was informed that all of the FEC's and later RFE's activities had their own funding.[52] In fact, the US government always provided the lion's share of the FEC's appropriations, even in the early 1950s when the Crusade for Freedom reached its high point. According to the French historian Jacques Semelin, in 1951–1952 the FEC collected $600,000 from nongovernmental sources, while the US government, primarily the CIA, contributed $28 million to its budget.[53]

The FEC could talk openly about liberating East Europeans from the "Soviet yoke." It also did not have to avoid working closely with anticommunist émigrés, which would have been a problem for the State Department. Already in its first declaration, the new organization announced that it would support democratic leaders in East-Central Europe, both in their activities in the "free world" and by reaching behind the Iron Curtain by radio. RFE, which broadcast in the satellites' native languages beginning in July 1950, became the new organization's main propaganda tool.[54] "The objective of Radio Free Europe is to prevent, or at least to hinder, the spiritual, economic and military integration of the nations of Eastern Europe into the Soviet bloc," read the first sentence of the FEC's program guidelines for the new station.[55]

The new station had greater freedom to attack the Communist regimes than did the government-sponsored VOA or the BBC, which was independent of the British government but nonetheless remained an official public institution. In its original conception, RFE was to be the station of émigrés, who were to speak through it and keep in touch with their subjugated compatriots. The Americans' initial idea was for RFE's programs to be prepared and sponsored by so-called national committees, representing émigré organizations from each country. This proved impossible because of the permanent disputes among the émigrés, not only the Polish ones.[56]

Radio Free Europe's Polish Desk

RFE programs, at first only a half-hour long, began to air in the summer of 1950 (on July 4 to Czechoslovakia, on August 4 to Poland and Hungary) from a small transmitter located in the US occupation zone in Germany. In the first two years, the programs were put together in New York, and tapes were flown to Germany. This obviously limited RFE's ability to cover current topics. The first head of the Polish Section in New York was Lesław Bodeński, a prewar employee of Poland's Foreign Ministry. In 1951, Stanisław Strzetelski, a prewar journalist, succeeded him. Strzetelski expanded the Polish staff to include about a dozen full-time employees and a diverse group of often prominent part-timers from the émigré community, among them the poets Jan Lechoń and Kazimierz Wierzyński.[57]

In 1952, the FEC activated four powerful transmitters in Portugal, radically increasing the radio's ability to reach audiences behind the Iron Curtain on shortwave frequencies.[58] Staffs preparing programs for the different satellite countries began to work in Munich, in a building on the edge of its central public park, the Englischer Garten. The Polish Section went on the air on May 3, 1952, the anniversary of the signing of the Third of May Constitution in 1791. The selection of this national holiday, whose observation had been outlawed by the Communist regime, was no coincidence. Heading the Munich bureau was Jan Nowak (his nom de guerre; his real name was Zdzisław Jeziorański), a Home Army courier during the German occupation, one of the creators of Błyskawica radio during the Warsaw Uprising, an employee of the BBC after the war, and a member of the Polish freedom movement, Independence and Democracy.[59] He came recommended by the Political Council (Rada Polityczna), which represented the most important émigré political parties.[60]

Until 1955, the Munich and New York bureaus worked on parallel tracks. The New York bureau's mandate was to prepare materials on international subjects, including Western press digests, while Munich focused on events in Poland, located much closer. This dualism, which prevented the programming from becoming cohesive, ended with the subordination of the New York office to Nowak.[61] He would spend more than twenty years, until the end of 1975, directing the station, and it owed its prominence largely to him. He was the main spokesman for the autonomy of the service in relation to the radio's American leadership, and had an enormous impact on the Polish desk's programmatic line. Nowak turned out to be the most charismatic personality in the history of RFE's Polish Section. He was rather heavy-handed in managing his subordinates, which won him many devoted supporters but also staunch enemies. Because of his role, throughout the years he was the principal target of both Communist propaganda and operations by the secret services of People's Poland.

RFE's early days were not easy, and it was not evident at the time that the radio would play an enormous role in the history of Poland. Jan Nowak was caught between his American managers and the Polish émigré community, which tried to influence both staffing and programming. Indeed, as the FEC declared, the new station was to speak in the voices of émigrés, which would make it fundamentally different from the VOA and the BBC. Émigré organizations realized from the very beginning the political advantages of having a presence on radio waves that reached Poland. "American radio is capable of 'creating' even a completely unknown person in Poland . . . and it may be the decisive tool in gaining influence in Poland. If we take the recent war as an example, Sikorski, Mikołajczyk and others, together with their politics, would have been completely unknown in Poland had it not been for the BBC's programs," wrote Stefan Korboński, a prominent émigré politician, in 1950.[62]

Clearly, the Americans, as well as Nowak, were interested in working with the main émigré parties. Nowak wrote in his memoirs that he had hired many people who were recommended by political parties in order to keep a balance among their different viewpoints.[63] The Americans also attempted to create a mechanism for program discussions, and invited the main émigré parties to form a consultative body. It was to be made up of seven representatives: three from the Political Council, comprising major exile factions; three from the Polish National Democratic Committee allied with former prime minister and Peasant Party leader Stanisław Mikołajczyk; and one who would be nominated by the government in exile. This plan failed, however, because the main émigré groups proved unable to cooperate. In the end, an advisory committee composed not of representatives of political parties but of specially invited individuals representing the parties was created in October 1952.[64] At its first meeting, it was agreed that the members would have access to guidelines for the radio and to the texts of all its programs, and that they would be invited to present suggestions in biweekly meetings with the radio station's US management.[65]

By its very nature, the actual say that this New York–based advisory body would have in the writing of RFE's programs, which went on mostly in Munich, would necessarily be limited. But it was of signal importance that neither the American management nor Nowak viewed this cooperation with the émigré community as a way to transfer decisions about editorial policy. The émigré politicians, who reached audiences in Poland by appearing frequently before RFE's microphones, saw their hopes of shaping RFE's programs, or, as Stefan Korboński had planned in 1950, even gaining a "dominant influence on the radio," dashed.

Both the Polish National Democratic Committee and the Political Council repeatedly demanded that the Polish programs be discussed with them before being aired, but this did not happen, as Korboński had observed forcefully in April 1952. "The radio uses the announcement that it is the voice of Free Poland, when the Representative not only has no influence on preparing political instructions for the Polish Section, but these instructions are also kept secret from us, and only now and then does a member of it have a chance to read them."[66] An official memorandum from the Representative Office of the Political Council sent to the chairman of the Free Europe Committee expressed similar criticism. It argued that RFE was perceived in Poland as the voice of the Polish émigré community, whereas in reality this community had no influence on the broadcaster.[67]

Joining in this criticism, which focused primarily on the radio's wrongful use of the name Voice of Free Poland, was a significant segment of the émigré community: the government in exile in London, the Union of Journalists, and the most influential publications. *Myśl Polska,* the periodical of one of the most important exile factions, the National Democratic Party, charged the station with "impersonating someone else" because "it is not . . . a Polish radio but an American one."[68] The Paris-based monthly *Kultura* also published critical statements whose common theme was the accusation, widespread among émigrés, that RFE was an American radio station speaking on behalf of Poles.[69] Zygmunt Nagórski wrote, "RFE is not an official American voice. It is even called the Voice of Free Poland. Its name shows that it has the full freedom to say to Poland what the Poles want to say. . . . But things are not so. Radio Free Europe is a radio that is American *par excellence*."[70]

The propaganda machine of People's Poland repeated the accusations appearing in the émigré press, at times by quoting texts that had been published in Britain, France, or the United States.[71] No evidence has been found that the Communist secret services inspired the émigrés' attacks on RFE in its early days. We do know, however, that such attempts were made later on. But in the early 1950s, Warsaw's ability to operate in Western Europe was limited. The reasons for the constraints included problems brought on by the reorganization and separation of the postwar government's civilian and military intelligence services.[72] It seems that the Polish government did not immediately view the new station as a major threat, though it certainly became one in 1954, from the moment it began to broadcast a series of programs by Józef Światło. It should be kept in mind, however, that the potential for Communist inspiration does not imply that Warsaw prompted all—or even most—of the voices critical of RFE, which, rather, primarily reflected actual disputes among émigrés.

Émigré politicians did not shy away from expressing their disappointment with their limited influence on the programs being broadcast to Poland. Yet it is not easy to tell who made decisions about programs and how these decisions were made, as there was little transparency in the workings of the FEC and of the radio station itself, especially in its early years. The State Department and the CIA exercised general oversight (the CIA by planning its budget), but in its daily work the FEC had significant freedom.[73] The committee's New York office prepared policy guidance for the radio station as a whole and for its individual sections. A political adviser based in Munich determined more of the overall line; in the 1950s, this adviser was the ambitious and supple William Griffith. Another key factor was the attitude of the staff and, most important, of its director. Jan Nowak managed to win a degree of autonomy unmatched by the other national directors, something that even the Americans who worked at the radio have admitted.[74] This was especially so beginning in 1955, when Nowak took over the directorship of the whole Polish desk. It was the sum of all these overlapping and changing factors that shaped the radio's political image. Obviously, it would have been difficult to exercise total control—even if the American management had wanted to—over the many daily hours of Polish programming, much of it ad hoc in response to developments, especially since the Americans did not institute preemptive censorship. The exception was the Oder-Neisse issue.

The Oder-Neisse issue arose because the Polish-German border for a long time was not officially sanctioned by the Great Powers. The Potsdam Conference in 1945 had concluded that the Oder-Neisse line would be the temporary demarcation and that a permanent border between Poland and Germany would be decided on at the peace conference, which never took place. The most important areas of programming were guided by US foreign policy interests. The Oder-Neisse border, of key importance to the Poles, was likely the most controversial issue in the Poles' relations with the radio's American management and the FEC. The United States would not recognize the line's final course until the early 1970s. In practice, it was Jan Nowak who determined how to refer to this border by reaching an informal agreement with Griffith: the writers would not be forced to take a stand at odds with Polish interests, and the Voice of Free Poland would never speak about it in its own voice. But Polish émigré leaders appearing on its airwaves would be able to talk freely about it. All statements were cleared by the radio's American management before they were broadcast, something that did not apply to any other issue.[75]

The sensitivity of the border issue did not stem solely from the fact that West Germany was becoming the United States' principal European ally. It was also linked to Germany's playing host to RFE operations. On the quotidian level, most important was the fact that Munich was a center of activity for the expellee organizations from the Sudetenland and the areas east of the Oder River. RFE's Polish Section, and even more so its Czechoslovak Section, was under nearly constant fire from the German homeland associations, which successfully mobilized support in the local government and the press. RFE's American management developed a position for the Voice of Free Poland and the Voice of Free Czechoslovakia to adhere to: questions relating to borders (and resettled populations) should be discussed on the radio as little as possible; if they could not be avoided, the radio presenters should hew to the line that all contentious issues would be sorted out in a peaceful and friendly fashion between the governments of Germany and the democratic representatives of the Poles and Czechs and Slovaks, who would be elected once these satellites became free. This was naturally the Polish desk's Achilles heel, and the Communist propaganda took meticulous advantage of it in its never-ending attacks on Nowak and his team for being anti-Polish and for supporting West German revanchism.

For the audiences in Poland, these issues were important since they affected the radio's credibility. But other factors most likely played a key role in building its position. First, RFE was on the air for eighteen hours a day (later even longer), more than any other foreign station. Its powerful transmitters and the numerous wavelengths over which it transmitted also allowed it to penetrate the barrier of jamming better than other stations. Second, RFE made an effort to reach all social groups. There were specialized programs for workers, farmers, and young people. There was even a program for party activists, *Letter to a Communist*, which sought to persuade them to stop serving the Kremlin and its representatives in Poland and to look out for the interests of the Polish people. Josip Broz Tito's Yugoslavia was an obvious model for Poland, and the radio devoted significant airtime to it. Historical, religious, and literary subjects took up a significant share of the programming and covered topics, events, and books banned by the Stalin-era dictatorship. Entertainment and music programs were also part of the fare. RFE intended to become an all-inclusive alternative to official radio, hence the broad spectrum of topics and types of programs. It even gave weather forecasts for Poland, as well as the winning numbers in the Polish national lottery.[76]

To keep in close touch with its listeners, RFE needed to have access to a comprehensive and rapid flow of information about events in Poland. For this, it conducted round-the-clock monitoring of Polish Radio and subscribed to a broad range of publications, including local ones. It also needed sources from which it could learn what was going on behind the official façade so as to be able to inform its listeners about events and issues that the Communist media passed over. After all, this was RFE's core mission. For behind-the-scenes reports, the work of RFE's offices in a dozen West European cities was critical. Their employees reached Poles traveling abroad, until 1956 mostly on work-related trips and after October 1956 increasingly also as tourists. The staff collected anonymized accounts about the situation in Poland from those who agreed to answer a standard list of questions. The questionnaires were written up by the staff of the branch offices and sent to the Research and Analysis Department in Munich. This department, which lay outside the radio's operations, had a Polish section that for many years was headed by Kazimierz Zamorski. It gauged the credibility of the interviewees and made the reports available to the program staff. The Research and Analysis Department kept an archive of information coming from all sources. It evaluated and divided materials into several categories: newspaper clippings, questionnaires, and name index cards for government functionaries and thousands of other public figures. For decades, the staff would enter data on these cards. After just the first few years, this archive, often called simply the card catalogue, had become one of the most important collections in the West of information on the countries behind the Iron Curtain.[77]

The Communist special services treated RFE's Research and Analysis Department, as well as the branch offices whose employees met with Soviet bloc citizens traveling in the West, as if it were closely controlled by the CIA. They believed it was precisely there that the heart of the "spy work" lay, work that in the Communist functionaries' imagination was as important a mission as RFE's propagandizing by radio. The Polish regime thus persevered in its attempts to infiltrate the Research and Analysis Department and gain access to its archive. This was why the propaganda machine in the 1970s exploited the public disclosures of the security police agent Andrzej Czechowicz, who had worked in that very unit, on a huge scale. (Czechowicz made public many documents that could be taken as indications of RFE's intelligence activities and close ties to the CIA.) It also attempted to penetrate the radio's regional offices, but unfortunately, little is known about this operation because the relevant documentation has been destroyed. Poland also pressured Western countries, such as neutral Sweden in the 1970s, to curtail the RFE branch offices' activities or have them shut down. The Polish secret services realized very quickly that without access to information from Poland, RFE would lose its credibility among its listeners, and therefore they did all they could to infiltrate and paralyze the Research and Analysis Department, a unit that was virtually unknown to the radio's audiences and remained in the shadow of broadcasting.

Refugees and asylum-seekers from Poland and other countries behind the Iron Curtain who had spent time in refugee camps in Germany were also an important source of information. RFE staff regularly visited these camps to seek out recent arrivals from Poland. This was how they found Czechowicz, at the time a young refugee from Poland who was employed in Munich and soon was recruited by the Communist intelligence service.

There was another category of informants used by RFE, those who on their own initiative talked to the radio. They were often representatives of opinion-making milieus, even PUWP activists, traveling in the West. Jan Nowak himself, or his right-hand man and later formal deputy Tadeusz Zawadzki-Żenczykowski, maintained contact with the most important of them. The identities of these exceptional sources, who would be returning to Poland, was guarded with special care and known to very few people in Munich (apart from Nowak and Zawadzki, and perhaps RFE's director). The system of relaying information about life in Poland contrived by Władysław Bartoszewski, which functioned for many years, was exceptional; it represented clandestine and sophisticated methods of gathering and transmitting information abroad, based on wartime conspiracy practices. The scale of the Polish regime's Security Service operation to uncover and put an end to Bartoszewski's scheme shows how much the regime feared such contacts between Poland and RFE.

From Józef Światło to the "Partisans"

In its first few years, the Voice of Free Poland won a large number of listeners and acquired the authority of a credible station that was in close touch with happenings in Poland and reacted rapidly to new developments. The new station's propaganda campaign, which emphasized Józef Światło's escape to the West and his sensational disclosures and also the station's moderate political line in supporting the anti-Stalinist thaw of October 1956, proved important in building its reputation. Its close ties to Poland and its actions aimed at influencing events directly made RFE unique. Other radio stations simply did not have the excellent knowledge of the realities of daily life in Poland, nor did they become as deeply involved in that life.

In September 1955, Jan Nowak organized a two-day retreat outside Munich for the entire program team to discuss the position RFE should take regarding the thaw under way in Poland. The team decided to support the evolutionary path of de-Stalinization and the forces within the party apparatus and opinion-making circles that favored internal liberalization and Poland's increasing autonomy from Moscow. The regime was to feel constant pressure from the masses, which favored democratization. In Nowak's summary of the discussions at the program team's retreat in a memorandum to FEC counselor Lewis Galantiere, the Voice of Free Poland was described as "the only force able to forge the disorganized masses into a common and united front for the struggle against Communism," one that could slow down Sovietization and offer the atomized society a sensible political program. Another excerpt from the memorandum shows the enormous importance Nowak vested in the radio's mission: "Had there been free radio stations broadcasting to the Soviet people between 1917 and 1945, the general outlook of people brought up after the Revolution would probably be quite different today."[78]

Nowak and the Polish desk's orientation toward evolutionary change was tested in October 1956, when Poland ran a revolutionary fever. The RFE's programs called on the Poles to behave moderately, trying to persuade them that sovereignty and democracy were long-range goals to be reached gradually and that the changes implemented after the PUWP's Eighth Plenum in October were doubtless headed in the right direction. The radio station emphasized the tragedy of the 1944 Warsaw Uprising and warned against radicalism, which could lead to the spilling of blood, a Soviet intervention, and loss of the concessions won so far.[79]

The Voice of Free Hungary opted for a completely different approach to the Hungarian revolutionary developments of October 1956. It attacked Imre Nagy, head of the Hungarian government that was not backed by Moscow, reminding people that he was a Communist and questioning his determination to attain real democracy and independence from Moscow. This editorializing weakened Nagy's authority and suggested to the Hungarians that a complete rejection of the Communist system was within reach. The Soviets' second intervention, which began on November 4, 1956, put an end to these aspirations; Nagy was deposed and arrested, and was executed two years later. Afterward, RFE was accused of sharing responsibility for the disaster of the Hungarian uprising and the accompanying bloodshed. The FEC, the US government, and even European governments publicly defended the radio station, but an internal review of the programs of the Voice of Free Hungary conducted in 1956 by RFE's principal political adviser, William Griffith, validated at least some of these charges. In recent years, Hungarian historians have analyzed the transcripts of the Hungarian broadcasts, which included information about partisan warfare and effective tactics for fighting tanks, as well as assurances of the weakness of the Soviet army. The international press digests aired by the radio suggested that armed US assistance for the partisans was very likely.[80]

The recklessness and radicalism of the Voice of Free Hungary put the calm, evolutionary attitude of the Voice of Free Poland in those critical October days in a more favorable light.[81] Yet the repercussions of the Hungarian catastrophe and the ensuing charges directed at RFE also affected the Polish desk. The least painful of these repercussions was its name change, from the Voice of Free Poland to the Polish Service of Radio Free Europe, a change intended to preempt accusations that the radio spoke on behalf of émigrés (or of any political group) and to stress its purely informative nature. The names of the radio's other national sections were also changed. In his discussions with the radio's American management, Jan Nowak opposed the change, arguing that audiences had become accustomed over several years to the original name. But he soon gave up, deciding to pick his battles, especially since this was not a priority for the Poles. Incidentally, it had not been the Poles who chose the original name, but the Americans.[82]

In any event, the change of name symbolized RFE's new role. Created as a forum for anticommunist émigrés to influence their countries, it was now ostentatiously breaking ties with them. The 1960 guidelines for the Polish desk stated that "RFE should not speak as an émigré radio station," and a similar document in 1964 said outright that programs should avoid "narrow points of view, particularly those of émigrés."[83]

The efforts of the American leadership of the FEC and RFE to set up an oversight structure for their broadcasting were much more dangerous. The State Department requested it, citing the problems that the Voice of Free Hungary programs in October and November 1956 had created for the United States. This time, Nowak and his staff offered strong resistance. They even threatened to resign collectively, something that would have presented enormous political and public relations problems for the Americans. Nowak used all his contacts and the power he had amassed over the years to convince the Americans that preventative censorship, which would amount to depriving the Poles of programmatic decision making, would disempower his team and destroy the radio's standing in Poland. The diminished stature of the Polish Service would in turn work against America's interests by weakening one of its best tools in the Cold War. It would also accelerate the trend away from the gains of October 1956, since, to Nowak, only pressure from the grass roots, supported by programs coming from a respected radio station, would restrain the Polish government from taking away the freedoms the people had won in 1956.

In 1958, Nowak took part in meetings in New York and Washington in which he testified before FEC management, Eisenhower administration officials, and the CIA. The Americans finally gave up trying to institute preemptive censorship, settling for the right to read scripts after they were broadcast and to take action when the established program line had been violated. This 1958 conflict demonstrated, on the one hand, the American management's growing tendency to tighten control over RFE's national sections and, on the other, the national sections' ability to maneuver and resist. In the case of the Polish desk, Nowak was able to draw strength from the solidarity of most of his staff and from his personal position with respect to the Americans, which resulted in part from his judicious and flexible stance in 1956.[84]

Another serious conflict arose shortly, this time over the Polish desk's presentation of the issue of the Oder-Neisse line. New guidelines introduced in January 1960 altered the modus vivendi worked out a few years earlier between the Polish desk and RFE's American management. They narrowed the Polish Section's already limited field of maneuver on this issue even further. According to the new instructions, the Polish desk could only cite governments' and government representatives' statements on this question, and then only with prior approval from the radio's Munich management. Nowak was given permission to expand the category of persons who could be quoted to include leaders of the Polish community in the United States and a dozen top figures in the émigré community, on the condition that their views not be critical of Western governments. In effect, broadcasting these views required permission to be obtained each time not only from RFE's Munich leadership or the FEC in Washington but also from the US administration itself.[85] "In accordance with the principle of objective information," Nowak wrote to the émigré political leader General Władysław Anders, "we have the duty to broadcast in our hourly news program all the most important statements on the border issue, including German pronouncements, and speeches, notes etc. by Władysław Gomułka and his government. At the same time, broadcasting nongovernmental Polish statements is being made impossible and requires that each time we ask for approval from the State Department, which as a rule denies it. We thus have a situation in which our silence helps the Communists create the impression that they are the only ones who speak out in defense of Poland's existential interests."[86]

The Communist propaganda apparatus naturally took advantage of this situation, as the unsettled status of the Oder-Neisse line dividing Poland and Germany was a convenient pretext to assault RFE. The crisis came to a head in October 1960, when the State Department refused the Polish desk permission to air either a speech by Karol Rozmarek, president of the Polish American Congress, or resolutions adopted by this most important Polish organization in the United States. In response, the staff of the Polish Section threatened to resign, while Nowak turned to RFE's key allies in the United States, as well as to all Polonia and émigré organizations, for help and intervention. The State Department eventually surrendered, which could most likely be attributed to the presidential campaign under way, in which the several million potential Polish American votes were important to the Republican administration. In the following years, the Oder-Neisse issue remained the main cause of conflicts between the Polish desk and the Americans.[87] From time to time, Nowak would write memoranda to the American management team in an effort to wrest more freedom for the Polish Service to bring up this issue, but the tide turned only after December 1970, when the Federal Republic of Germany, soon followed by the United States and the other Western powers, formally recognized the Oder-Neisse border.[88]

The steadfastness demonstrated by Nowak and his ability to mobilize not only his staff but many influential figures and groups outside the radio meant that subsequent American RFE directors and FEC officials had to take his opinions seriously. Over time, Nowak came to be recognized as an outstanding expert on Polish and East European affairs, an authority and a valuable source of knowledge about the situation on the other side of the Iron Curtain for his frequently changing American superiors, some of whom were random appointees lacking any deep familiarity with the Soviet bloc.[89]

Nowak's assessment of the Partisans, the faction in the Communist apparatus tied to Mieczysław Moczar (an influential deputy minister and, beginning in 1964, minister of internal affairs), was an example of his ability to exert a strong influence on the radio's programs, though at times not fully in agreement with the US management. In 1962, Nowak obtained reliable information from Poland that Moczar's group was growing more powerful and eliminating the more liberal "Puławy" faction of the original Communists from many positions and pushing for a confrontation over domestic policy. In July 1962, the Polish Service broadcast a series of programs exposing the Partisans.[90] In lengthy memoranda, Nowak informed his American superiors of the Moczar group's actions and argued that they represented a threat.[91]

The State Department, which initially believed there was no conclusive evidence that this faction even existed, protested strongly against discussing the potential threat of the Partisans.[92] RFE's American management was also extremely guarded on this issue. Its *Special Guidelines* asked whether the faction existed within the PUWP as an organized group and, more important, whether it was really opposed to Władysław Gomułka, the Communist leader of Poland. It recommended not overpublicizing the information about this alleged faction but instead presenting factual information about events in Poland and within the party.[93] Still, throughout the 1960s the radio's programs were dominated by the Partisan theme: warnings against them, lists of individuals close to Moczar within the power apparatus and the opinion-making circles, and speculation about their intentions. Security Service documents discuss the war that RFE had declared on the Ministry of Internal Affairs and Minister Moczar himself, a war being waged not by the station's American leadership but by the director of the Polish Section. This further underscores the powerful position that Nowak had built up over more than a dozen years. Yet rifts within his staff were a side effect of concentrating on fighting the Partisans. Some of the leading commentators, such as Wiktor Trościanko, believed that the "national Communism" promoted by Moczar's group could point to a favorable direction for the evolution of the People's Republic. This difference of opinion is discussed later in the book.

Psychological Warfare, Gradualism, and the CIA

Communist propaganda, as well as internal security apparatus documents, presented RFE as a tool of the American special services. The CIA was said to steer the radio watchfully, treating it as a sabotage tool to encourage people to engage in antistate activity and riots. Using its network of correspondents and its research department, it also conducted ordinary "spy operations." A closer look at these allegations will help to determine whether this portrayal contains a grain of truth.

As has already been mentioned, the Free Europe Committee was created by the CIA and the State Department. It seems likely that the State Department's role in the birth of the committee was greater because of the personal interest of the influential George Kennan. The CIA, by contrast, bore the brunt of financing it, as well as RFE. This meant CIA oversight of an ostensibly unofficial, private institution that in reality was implementing important US foreign policy goals. The mechanisms of this oversight were never formalized, remained confidential, and changed over time. As for the CIA, there is an additional problem, one it shares with all active secret services: its records, with the exception of those it selectively declassifies, are largely inaccessible to historians.[94]

For all these reasons, a reconstruction of the relationship between the radio and US intelligence must be incomplete and largely hypothetical. A. Ross Johnson's *Radio Free Europe and Radio Liberty: The CIA Years and Beyond* breaks new ground in outlining the relationship between the CIA and RFE. Johnson was able to gain access to the largest number of documents so far.[95] A picture of the complex relations in the FEC/RFE–State Department–CIA triangle emerges from his work. The CIA frequently defended the radio's freedom, whereas the State Department often viewed the station as too aggressive with respect to the countries of the Soviet bloc and even as standing in the way of rapprochement and normalized relations. Yet Johnson also shows that the CIA attempted to actively influence the station's program line. The CIA's influence was not uniformly strong or effective, and it usually did not pertain to the minutiae of issues and programs aired by RFE.

It is important to keep in mind a feature of the FEC in its early days. The people who created it came from the inner circle of the US political elite and had previously occupied (or, like Allen Dulles, would go on to occupy) top positions in the foreign service or intelligence agencies or in financial institutions. They were friends of secretaries of state and presidents—for example, C. D. Jackson, FEC president from 1951 to 1952, was a close friend of Dwight Eisenhower. They were an elite group who did not take orders from mid- or even high-level State Department or CIA officials. They acted with US interests in mind and intended to implement US goals in the Cold War, but they also made use of information they obtained from conversations and meetings with foreign policy decision makers. Later in the Cold War, and certainly by the 1960s, the nature of RFE's American leadership changed. But by then the radio station had become an enormous machine whose daily operations were difficult to steer from the outside; anyone who has ever worked in a large bureaucracy understands how mechanisms generated inside it shut out outside influences. Still, Cord Meyer, a CIA officer in charge of RFE from 1954 to the early 1970s, wrote in his memoirs that he edited, approved, and at times even wrote the program guidelines that the FEC officially issued in New York.[96] But other Americans who oversaw the radio do not confirm this role. Even if Meyer was right, it was a long road from guidelines developed on the other side of the ocean to the actual programs being written in Munich, generally in reaction to current, often unexpected, events.

It is much more accurate to say that the FEC and RFE worked closely with the CIA. To a certain extent, these entities, at the level of the Americans working at RFE, overlapped. Paul Henze, who in the 1950s served as the deputy political adviser in Munich and was a key figure in the early years of the radio, is a good example. After RFE, his positions included serving as the CIA station chief in Ankara.[97] William P. Durkee, who became RFE's president in 1967, had earlier spent several years at the CIA overseeing the broadcaster.[98] But this was never a one-sided dependence or close supervision by the CIA in the form of simple orders handed down. The real picture was too complex and impossible for the Communist special services, let alone the Polish propaganda machine, to fathom. To them, RFE was simply and invariably a CIA tool.

The ties that bound RFE to the CIA had their roots in the station's beginnings. Columbia University's Rare Book and Manuscript Library houses a collection of documents deposited by RFE's first chairman, the New York banker Frank Altschul. These records frequently refer to "our friends from the South," a clear allusion to the CIA headquarters in Washington, DC, to the south of the FEC headquarters in New York. "Our friends from the South" were consulted on a variety of programmatic and organizational issues and were solicited for money for specific purposes. Frank Wisner, head of the Office of Policy Coordination, appears most frequently in the documents as "F.W." Hiding behind the innocuous-sounding name of the Office of Policy Coordination is a CIA cell responsible for radio propaganda and psychological warfare, as well as for special operations behind the Iron Curtain.[99]

The available documents show that in its first years, the CIA, and especially Wisner's unit, was to exercise close oversight of the radio. The two sides accepted this simple principle, but in practice their relations were more complicated. The CIA was supposed to serve as the main source of information used in RFE's programs, but this did not happen. The information was dispatched irregularly and often was too dated for use in programs. Frank Altschul wrote in a May 1950 memorandum that after numerous reminders from the radio's staff, "our friends have been recently sending us translations from foreign newspapers"—some up to five months old. Despite early promises, the radio station received no covert information, "which was to be the spice of the program and to enable us to convince our listeners that we were in constant touch with developments in their own lands."[100] To resolve the growing problem of the shortage of materials for the radio, the CIA suggested that all programming, including commentary, be prepared at the agency, translated into RFE's broadcasting languages, and aired. The FEC management firmly rejected this idea.[101] Because the agency did not deliver current information from behind the Iron Curtain, RFE developed its own system of collecting material from correspondents in more than a dozen European cities visited by people from Communist countries. It seems that to the CIA, RFE may have been a more important provider of information about events in the Soviet bloc than the CIA's other sources. According to A. Ross Johnson, "The CIA early became a consumer of rather than a source for this information."[102]

The exchange of information and guidelines for the radio's political line initially did not look much better. RFE management wrote in August 1950: "It would be highly desirable if we could at least receive from our friends the regular indications in regard to policy which have been so often promised us. . . . Of these, we have had little more than a half dozen in all, and none of them has contained very much that was helpful. As a result, we have had to decide matters of policy as best as we could in the light of our own judgment."[103] A memorandum of November 1, 1950, articulated a similar assessment, stating that RFE had "little in the way of over-all policy guidance."[104]

The Radio Executive Committee was created in July 1950 to address some of these issues. Streamlining the collaboration between the CIA and RFE's American management, one of its major goals, proved difficult, if only because of the 200 miles separating New York and Washington.[105]

To organize RFE's program line and to eliminate the existing problems in conveying political instructions, in November 1951 a long list of programmatic goals and guidelines for all programming was developed by the Radio Executive Committee. The size and title of the publication containing the list, *Radio Free Europe: Policy Handbook*, implied that it was a sort of textbook or guide intended for RFE's US staff and its East European editors and journalists, although it is not clear whether the latter had access to it. Early on, the handbook states: "RFE cannot take a line contrary to United States Government policy."[106]

Although the handbook covered a broad spectrum of topics (including approaches to resistance movements behind the Iron Curtain; programs for youth, workers, peasants, and national minorities; and the treatment of the European movement), the guidelines remained very general and were of little help to the national staffs in writing their daily scripts. The handbook tried to sustain anti-Soviet resistance without encouraging open rebellion. On the one hand, it declared that "the purpose of RFE is to contribute to the liberation of the nations imprisoned behind the Iron Curtain by sustaining their morale and stimulating in them a spirit of non-cooperation with the Soviet-dominated regimes." On the other hand, it strictly forbade "promising armed intervention by the West." It also demanded that the radio not address groups challenging the Communist governments directly and that it not encourage active resistance or conspiracy. On the contrary, the broadcaster should warn against reckless actions that might entail brutal repressions. At the same time, the policy handbook pushed the national sections to assure "militant anti-communists that they will be given the means to fight for the liberation of their country when the time comes."[107]

Along with the lack of clarity in phrases like these, most of the guidelines stressed supporting spiritual independence and the national differences of the peoples on the other side of the Iron Curtain, who were both to maintain their cultural ties to the West and to sustain those facets of their societies' lives that would best help them resist Sovietization (such as private land ownership, the churches, or the traditions of labor's self-organization). All in all, these guidelines were sensible and cautious, calling for nothing more than an effort to hold back Sovietization by maintaining national distinctiveness in political tradition, culture, religion, and the economy.

Did the national desks adhere to these moderate guidelines? To answer this question it would be necessary to analyze all RFE program recordings and scripts, something no researcher has yet done. This task would be very difficult or actually impossible to carry out, since some of the radio's records have not survived. The CIA itself was not consistent in its relationship with RFE. There are indications that in the early 1950s, coded signals to agents and underground organizations behind the Iron Curtain were inserted into programs. Frank Altschul's papers include a memorandum dated early December 1950 that discusses the possibility of using RFE as a "channel for the sending of code messages" with instructions for conducting sabotage in armaments factories supplying the Soviet Union.[108] Mentioning this topic, so much at odds with the guidelines against encouraging premature resistance, could have been a result of the exceptionally dramatic moment at which this memorandum was written, following the huge and unexpected defeat in November 1950 of US units in North Korea by several hundred thousand Chinese "volunteers."[109]

We do not know whether such coded instructions for sabotage were ever actually broadcast. But according to Jan Nowak, Polish programs did include "various secret encrypted sentences resembling the wartime slogans aired by the BBC to the French resistance."[110] This was still at a time when the Polish programs were being written in New York. After arriving in Munich, Nowak asked RFE's main political adviser, William Griffith, to end this practice. Broadcasting encoded signals stopped.[111]

But Nowak does not mention another form of communicating with the anticommunist underground in Poland, one that predated the Voice of Free Poland's launch from Munich. Beginning in May 1951, every Friday (initially at midnight, later at 8 p.m.) RFE aired a special fifteen- to twenty-minute program addressed to the underground Freedom and Independence (Wolność i Niepodległość) movement. The program was not RFE's; it only used RFE's transmitters. According to RFE documents at the Hoover Institution, these segments were broadcast after Colonel Paul (Paweł) Sapieha of the CIA (incidentally, a nephew of Cardinal Adam Sapieha of Cracow), who served as the CIA's liaison to the Polish émigré community and, through it, to the underground in Poland, relayed this request from Freedom and Independence.

The available documents reveal that the Freedom and Independence programs contained no clandestine information or instructions, merely digests of international developments. The text of the August 2, 1951, program, which discussed the situation in Korea and political events in the United States, survives. Three Polish émigré activists in New York put together these broadcasts, which were then approved by RFE's leadership. The latter were skeptical about this idea from the beginning, questioning the veracity of the request from Freedom and Independence and the point of airing these programs for the underground if their contents resembled RFE's.[112] The broadcasts were stopped in July 1952.[113] The oddest aspect of this story is that in 1951–1952, Freedom and Independence was already deeply infiltrated by the Communist secret police and was being used to toy with US intelligence.[114] We do not know how the "special programs" fit into this plan. There are no traces of this issue in Polish archives. It also did not surface in the propaganda campaign that followed the Polish Communists' December 1952 public revelation that they had penetrated the organization's Fifth Command, when it would have been very convenient as an excuse to pounce on the American "imperialists." It is possible that the idea of the special programs stemmed from Polish émigré organizations, which were trying to gain credibility with the Americans. Showing ties to the underground in Poland was one way to achieve this goal.

The relatively cautious propaganda directed at the people of the satellites was gradually replaced by a more aggressive approach. The 1952 US presidential election influenced this evolution. The main theme of the Republican candidate General Dwight Eisenhower's campaign was adopting a firmer policy line with respect to the Communist bloc. He promised to "roll back" the Soviets from the territories they had occupied since World War II and to liberate the captive nations from behind the Iron Curtain. These promises proved to be mostly campaign rhetoric. Washington's total passivity during the June 1953 uprising in East Germany showed clearly that Eastern Europe could not count on the West to be more aggressive regarding the Soviets. Therefore, psychological warfare appeared to be the only way the Soviets could be seriously harassed without risking a "hot" war; at the same time the United States would be showing that calls for liberation were not mere campaign promises.[115]

The belief in launching a propaganda offensive, promoted in President Eisenhower's inner circle and by the CIA and the people connected to the FEC and RFE, stemmed from events that took place in June 1953 in two countries behind the Iron Curtain. The East Berlin construction workers' demonstration swiftly transformed itself into a national rebellion against the Communist regime. RIAS, broadcasting from the US occupation zone, played an important role in telling millions of East Germans about it. In the weeks leading up to this social explosion, RIAS informed its audiences about the workers' mounting demands and protests, and on June 16–17 broadcast information on the spread of strikes, demonstrations, and street clashes. According to Christian F. Ostermann, in many of the RIAS programs it was difficult to distinguish the line between information and encouragement to protest, since they even included specific instructions about how to act.[116] The importance and popularity of RIAS were reflected in the uprising's demands that the GDR government allow people to listen to the station.[117] Not willing to wait for permission, in many factories workers set their public address systems to RIAS.[118] At around the same time in Czechoslovakia, the unequal exchange of money, as a result of which many people lost their savings, resulted in strikes and stormy street demonstrations in the main industrial centers, including Plzeň and Ostrava.[119]

Although in both countries the rebellions were suppressed, from the perspective of the psychological warfare strategists they served as evidence that potent resistance was brewing behind the Iron Curtain. Moreover, the Communist governments' reactions were seen as muted and the repressions as limited, the governments apparently unwilling to disrupt the continuing thaw permeating the Soviet bloc after Stalin's death.[120]

From that point on, Washington viewed fostering bottom-up pressure on the satellite regimes as the principal goal in its policies toward the Communist bloc. A few days after the Berlin uprising, the Psychological Strategy Board developed an action program, which was adopted by the National Security Council on June 29, 1953. The program promoted expanding the activities of the stations broadcasting to the peoples living behind the Iron Curtain.[121] The FEC and RFE were assigned the main role, since they could get away with saying much more than official government institutions such as the VOA. This offensive course found its most spectacular expression not so much in RFE's programs but in the FEC's extensive "balloon operations" of 1953 to 1956, when thousands of balloons carrying millions of fliers calling for grassroots pressure on or actual passive resistance to the Communist government were released into Czechoslovakia and Hungary.[122] The public behind the Iron Curtain did not distinguish between these two organizational entities and identified the balloon operations with RFE. The project was smaller in the Polish case because of opposition from the émigré community and the Voice of Free Poland director Jan Nowak. It was limited to sending out millions of printed pieces containing information (including brochures with Józef Światło's disclosures about the Communist regime in Poland) and did not call for antigovernment actions.[123]

It is interesting that it was not the CIA that was the greatest proponent of balloon leafletting but rather the FEC's and RFE's management, supported by C. D. Jackson. Jackson had stepped down from the presidency of the FEC in 1953 to become President Eisenhower's special adviser for psychological warfare.[124] In October 1954, William Griffith wrote to Jackson about the extensive reserve of and even resistance from the State Department and "our friends" (the CIA), and promised that should the reluctance continue, the FEC would seek the backing of the National Security Council. This adds an interesting perspective to the discussion about RFE's autonomy and its relations with the agencies of the US government.[125]

In any case, the balloon operations, the culmination of RFE's psychological warfare, elicited a variety of reactions from the Communist countries. After the collapse of the Hungarian Revolution, this aggressive propaganda, which included sending out millions of fliers, became the reason for criticizing RFE's line and the policy of "liberation." Never again would such spectacular and aggressive psychological operations be staged in relation to the Communist bloc. The FEC and RFE, like the US administration, began to emphasize promoting evolutionary change, gradual democratization, and a loosening of dependence on the Kremlin in the satellite countries. The changes implemented following the PUWP's Eighth Plenum made Poland a model for the other satellites. The United States continued to place great hopes in Gomułka's team and its changes for a few years after October 1956. It hoped that the "Polish example" would be contagious.[126]

This was the main reason for the State Department's pressure on RFE's Polish programs to tone down their criticism of the Polish Communist government and, in effect, to support the anti-Stalinist and reformist tendencies within the PUWP. In September 1957, the Committee on Radio Broadcasting Policy, made up of representatives of the State Department, the CIA, and the US Information Agency (which supervised the VOA), issued new principles of radio propaganda for broadcasts to Eastern Europe.[127] Both the formalized method of developing program guidelines for RFE and their contents, which contrasted with the pre-1956 offensive line, stood out. RFE was to encourage the Poles to "seek independence from Soviet control gradually and without internal disorder." The radio "must not be narrowly and contentiously anti-Communist." The new principles endorsed airing objective and factual information about events in Poland and the world, and especially propagating the values and lifestyles of the "Western world." They stressed that the language should be very balanced and that critiques of the Communist government should avoid "sarcasm, satire and irony." RFE was not to speak to its audience as if it was opposing the Communist regime in Poland.[128]

These 1957 guidelines were a world away from the era of psychological warfare, in which RFE was to have been a principal offensive tool for weakening Soviet control over its satellites. It would be difficult to find a better example of differences in US policy toward Eastern Europe before and after 1956. The new guidelines erased the differences between the official station, the VOA, and RFE, which, as an organization nominally independent of the US government, was to enjoy far greater freedom of action and to adopt a more aggressive program line. This, after all, had been the reason for creating this institution only seven years earlier.

The next set of guidelines for the Polish desk, written in January 1960, did not invest equally great hopes in the Gomułka team and the potential for internal democratization, nor did they express a fear of a potential Soviet intervention against the "nationally-" and reform-minded government of Poland. But they represented basically the same attitude, stressing the promotion of gradual, evolutionary changes and moderation and caution in programming. They stated repeatedly that RFE's mission was to present "accurate, balanced" news and analysis and that "comment or criticism must be essentially constructive, calm and reasoned, avoiding a belligerent tone." All assessments of conditions in Poland were to remind people of the "improvements in the situation since the Stalin era." RFE "should follow the rule of avoiding a negative approach in its broadcasts to Poland. Its programs should be couched in a tone of positive and constructive thought." In any event, RFE was not to give the Poles any advice or instructions for specific actions.[129]

It is therefore not surprising that guidelines formulated thus would lead to tensions and friction between RFE and the State Department. In the second half of the 1950s the RFE's Polish desk's overly sharp tone regarding the Communist government in Warsaw exposed it to serious criticism. Its *spiritus movens* was primarily Ambassador Jacob Beam, who was under strong pressure from the PUWP and the Polish Foreign Affairs Ministry. In 1959, Beam went so far as to request that RFE's Polish Service be shut down, arguing that RFE was not broadcasting to Yugoslavia, whose status was similar to Poland's under the Gomułka regime.[130] According to Jan Nowak's memoirs, RFE's Polish desk in those years had two almost equally serious adversaries to reckon with, Warsaw's Communist regime and the US State Department.[131]

Throughout the 1960s and 1970s, the US policy toward Poland and the other satellites continued to back gradual change (hence the term "gradualism") in domestic democratization and increased autonomy from Moscow. Tightening political, economic, and cultural ties between the United States and the countries of the Soviet bloc ("building bridges," in the terminology coined by President Lyndon Johnson's administration) was expected to gradually reduce Soviet control. From the point of view of the State Department, were the RFE line too aggressive, it could only disrupt this change, hence the oversight of the radio's activities and the numerous cases of US diplomatic intervention. It was only after a democratic opposition appeared in Poland in the second half of the 1970s, followed by the Solidarity mass movement in 1980, that the United States became oriented toward more actively supporting the Poles' drive for freedom. This was the time of "promoting human rights" during Jimmy Carter's presidency and the very vocal battle against the "Evil Empire" during Ronald Reagan's administration. Now the critical point of reference was not the governing team in Warsaw but the people speaking out against the Communist system.[132]

Regardless of the changes in the United States' Poland policy, it appears that after 1956 it was the State Department more than the CIA that exercised oversight of RFE. The CIA naturally retained an interest in the radio, and former RFE employees stress that the CIA had a particular influence on internal security, which is not surprising. Yet the security procedures and protection against counterintelligence could hardly be called tight. The relative freedom of action for the Communist secret services in Munich, such as entering RFE employees' apartments (many employees lived in buildings that were wholly rented by the radio and should have been quite easy to protect) or the 1981 bombing of the radio's headquarters at Englischer Garten, were an indication of weakness in this security system.

The CIA also continued to use the information gathered by the radio's Research and Analysis Department from its network of offices and correspondents who met with people traveling to the West from behind the Iron Curtain. The questionnaire given to them included a section titled "military issues."

Kazimierz Zamorski, head of the Polish Section of the Research and Analysis Department, wrote in his memoirs that RFE's employees approached it skeptically, knowing that it would be used mostly by intelligence. It served, for instance, in the propaganda campaign that followed RFE employee Andrzej Czechowicz's return to Poland in 1971, when photocopies of several such reports about military issues were shown.[133]

But most important, the CIA continued to fund RFE. This gradually became an open secret. On being hired, US managers signed a declaration that they would not reveal this information.[134] The first time it was written about publicly, in the US leftist student magazine *Ramparts*, was in 1967. This revelation was not discussed widely, probably because of the magazine's small circulation but also because of more serious problems the Americans were dealing with then, most prominently the Vietnam War.[135] It was widely discussed only in 1971, when Senator Clifford Case brought it up in the US Congress, starting an exceptionally stormy and dramatic discussion about the radio's future that lasted several years. Some of the American public, and even the political class, led by Senator J. William Fulbright, demanded that RFE, a relic of the Cold War that had been compromised by its secret funding from the CIA, be shut down. Then the Communist special services tried to exploit, indeed intensify, RFE's troubles. In the end, RFE survived, in modified form. Beginning in 1971, the radio station openly obtained government funding and was under public control, but it retained an autonomy greater than that of the VOA, which spoke officially for the US government.[136]

In 1976, RFE was merged with the "fraternal" Radio Liberty (in Polish publications, it often appears as the Russian-language version, Radio Swoboda), which in the 1950s had used the name Radio Liberation and which broadcast to the Soviet republics. It survived in this form until the end of the Cold War and the disintegration of the Communist bloc. All of the RFE's organizational, political, and programmatic changes, implemented over the decades, had only a secondary influence on the Communist authorities' position toward it. For them, from the early 1950s to the end of the 1980s, RFE represented a first-class threat that had to be fought by any means available.

2. Stalinism, 1950–1956

Jamming

Radio Free Europe began airing programs in Polish, initially only half an hour a day, on August 4, 1950. For the first two years, a small team in New York wrote the program scripts and a fairly weak transmitter in West Germany broadcast them. Only after programming was set up in Munich in May 1952, much more powerful transmitters were installed in Germany and Portugal, the editorial staff was enlarged, and airtime was increased could there be talk of reaching mass audiences in Poland and of influencing Poles' thinking and mood. At first, both the Warsaw government and, probably, the majority of the radio station's listeners perceived RFE as only one of several Polish-language stations based in the West, the others being the BBC, the Voice of America (VOA), Radio France, and Radio Madrid. RFE built its top position step by step, competing on the one hand with the BBC, whose popularity returned to what it had been during World War II, and on the other with Radio Madrid, a Polish-run radio station affiliated with the Polish government in exile in London. In its anticommunism, Radio Madrid towered over the other stations, which needed to have their political lines approved by the governments that sponsored them.[1]

In the autumn of 1954, RFE left its competitors behind. Its rise was spurred by the programs by Józef Światło, a top functionary of the Communist political police, going on the air and immediately attracting huge audiences. These programs also led to major political repercussions. Until that time, the Polish regime had treated RFE the same way it treated other foreign broadcasters. That would soon change drastically.

One of the most important steps instigated by the Soviet regime was to introduce jamming. By September 1951, A. Zharov, head of the USSR Main Directorate of Radio Communications, was advocating the creation of a system of interference that would cover all of Poland and would rely on cooperation with the Soviet Union and the other Soviet bloc countries. RFE was ninth on Zharov's list of stations to jam, but it was singled out, along with the VOA and Radio Madrid, as being "exceptionally hostile in nature and directed against the current political system of the Polish Republic." Zharov's memorandum indicates that the Soviet Union began jamming programs to Poland in July 1950 (the jamming of radio stations broadcasting to the other Soviet bloc countries, including Hungary and Romania, started in June). But since the interference covered only a few wavelengths, it proved inadequate. In November 1950, representatives of Poland, Czechoslovakia, and Hungary agreed to work together on jamming programs transmitted on medium-wave frequencies. Since their decision was not followed by action, the Soviets stepped in. Zharov drew up a detailed plan for jamming foreign shortwave broadcasts from within the Soviet Union (for technical reasons, since sounds on these waves are transmitted over a few hundred kilometers) and on the medium waves by jammers from Poland manufactured and operated according to Soviet instructions. The use of Polish jamming equipment was "to protect certain regions of the USSR from anti-Soviet programs."[2]

On October 24, 1951, the USSR Council of Ministers adopted a decree instructing the Soviet Ministry of Communications to organize the jamming of "hostile propaganda via radio on the territory of the Polish Republic" beginning on December 1, 1951: on the short waves by jammers based in the USSR and on the medium waves by jammers in Poland, which country would receive assistance in organizing "protection from hostile propaganda" while using its own equipment. Zharov was sent to Poland with a group of "experienced specialists" to "offer assistance in organizing the Protective Service."[3] This service was created by a decision of the Polish minister of public security on December 24, 1951,[4] and the Polish system of jamming was effected by a Soviet government resolution. This edict was an accurate measure of the relations between Warsaw and Moscow at the time: the Soviet government did not even pretend to respect the sovereignty of its allies.

Czechoslovakia and Hungary also joined in the jamming of Polish-language radio stations transmitting on shortwave frequencies. Poland, for its part, interfered with foreign-language programs aired to the Soviet Union in Russian, Lithuanian, and Georgian, and to Czechoslovakia and Hungary.[5] According to Poland's Ministry of Public Security, "it would be most favorable for Poland to build transmission centers (apart from the territory of the Soviet Union) in Bulgaria, Albania and some in Romania." These centers would "protect Polish territory, while the territories of the abovementioned countries would be protected by Polish stations (Szczecin, Lidzbark, possibly Suwałki and some others).” Warsaw was even preparing a detailed plan, with a budget of about 27 million zlotys, for placing Polish-built jamming transmitters; about twenty would be in southern Romania, near Bucharest or Constanța, and the remaining thirty in two locations in southern Bulgaria, along a line from Plovdiv to Burgas.[6]

Nothing has been found in Polish security apparatus records to indicate that these plans were ever implemented. In mid-1955, there was more talk about the need to tighten collaboration with other Soviet bloc countries, especially Bulgaria, “with its exceptionally favorable geographic location,” but this continued as a phase of “experimental mutual assistance on the airwaves.” An accomplishment of Polish technical thought is worth noting here: “We are the only country that widely produces and uses special simplified protective transmitters not only for ourselves, but also for export. We are producing thirty such transmitters, as ordered by Czechoslovakia. Romania has officially applied to us in this matter, and we expect that Bulgaria and Hungary will also shortly turn to us, since in unofficial conversations representatives of these countries’ protective services have expressed an interest in these kinds of deliveries,” Lieutenant Colonel Anatol Jegliński informed his superiors.[7]

“Protection” on the medium waves was provided in Poland by a constantly expanding network of stationary centers (“K” points) equipped with jamming transmitters. In late 1953, stations covering RFE programs were operating in eleven localities: Miedzeszyn, Łódź, Bydgoszcz, Radom, Szczecin, Poznań, Cracow, Wrocław, Katowice (Stalinogród), Zabrze, and Warsaw.[8] The majority of the transmitters were working on the “long-range protection” of the whole country. Local transmitters in “centers with a heavy density of radio listeners and in especially important areas” supplemented this network. After the stationary installations were operating, beginning in June 1953 mobile units based in cars operated in Warsaw, Radom, Wrocław, and Bielsko-Biała.[9]

According to 1955 data, 374 staff jammed foreign radio programs.[10] In addition, a sizable group of civilian technical workers was employed by the Ministry of Postal Service and Telegraphs (beginning in March 1955, the Ministry of Communications); these workers serviced the jamming installations under the direct supervision of security personnel. Decades later, one of the civilian technicians described his work in a documentary film by Maciej Drygas: “A wind-up telephone was located at every transmitter with a direct line to the control desk in the Security Service. Their operators were on duty at high-class radio receivers. Each one had his own wavelength and was to seek out a station broadcasting in Polish. When the operator found a Free Europe program, he would call our operator sitting next to the transmitter and say: please turn on the transmitter to frequency x. The transmitter was quickly adjusted. The Security Service operator would call again and hold up the receiver to the voice. Then our man on duty would set the transmitter's generator to drown out that station's frequency all the way, i.e., to silence, in other words he covered the resonating wave with his wave. Then the Security Service employee would turn on the tape recorder with a tape of noise."[11]

Indeed, the expansion of the jamming network progressed at an impressive pace. In December 1951, nine transmitters with a total power of 62 kilowatts worked less than eight hours per day; in August 1953 "29 transmitters (a 223% increase) of 355 kw (a 472% increase) are working 468 hours per day (a 60-fold increase)." In this period, the scale of "hostile radio propaganda" also increased from 45.5 hours of programs in Polish in December 1951, when the Polish jamming system was installed, to 198 hours by August 1953. In the same period the number of wavelengths being used also grew, from twelve to forty, as did the power of the transmitters. What is more, in 1953 "the adversary" began to use "tactics of concentrating a major part of his means for new countries at different times," which of course made it difficult to respond.[12] This was one of the reasons why Warsaw promoted the idea of closer cooperation among the countries of the Soviet bloc.

The people at the very top were interested in the project. In a memorandum to Bolesław Bierut, president of Poland and first secretary of the PUWP, another key member of the Polish Politburo, Jakub Berman, wrote that improving jamming would guarantee the peaceful progress of the parliamentary election campaign in October 1952.[13] In May 1952, Berman also brought up jamming in a conversation with the Soviet ambassador, Arkadii Sobolev. He asked the Soviets to send over a specialist (Zharov or someone from his group) because the Polish specialists were not managing on their own. According to Berman, the audibility of the "hostile" radio stations had recently improved and, what was more, on May 3 a new station had begun to broadcast on shortwave frequencies, which was all the more troubling because of the impending elections to the Sejm and the campaign that would precede them.[14] We also know that Bierut discussed "fighting hostile propaganda" with the Soviet leadership in Moscow in July 1953.[15]

As a thaw appeared across the Soviet bloc after Stalin's death on March 5, 1953, and after the Polish Ministry of Public Security was dissolved in December 1954, the build-up of the system of jamming continued. The Protective Service was merged with the Office of Radio Communications in the Ministry of Internal Affairs but continued under the management of Lieutenant Colonel Andrzej Jegliński. In September 1955, there were 249 jammers with a total power of 1,766 kilowatts (a sevenfold increase in two years). According to Andrzej Paczkowski, it is likely that in 1955, jamming used more energy than broadcasting.[16] It is therefore not surprising that in some areas of the country, jamming would have interfered with the Polish Radio program, something that listeners complained about in letters sent to various institutions.[17] And this was not yet the planned maximum "radio protection." The government expected to open an "enormous transmission center in the Szczecin region, whose mission will be mostly to protect the USSR," in 1956. In return, it hoped for "a significant increase in the USSR's assistance and significantly enhanced effectiveness of protection for our country."[18]

This enormous expansion of the jamming network entailed serious costs, and not only financial ones (which in 1956 were estimated at about 83 million zlotys annually).[19] The several hundred staff who monitored foreign programs day and night were "exposed to the permanent, systematic effects of hostile propaganda," which was bound to erode the morale of even the most loyal ministry staffers. "The moral and political state of the Office of Radio Communications apparatus is not satisfactory," Lieutenant Colonel Jegliński maintained in September 1955. "There are too many cases of drunkenness, brawls, violations of work discipline, gossiping and matrimonial fights, which go as far as divorce."[20]

The key question, of course, is, how effective was the jamming? The Ministry of Public Security kept exceptionally detailed statistics by decade, radio station, wavelength, broadcast times, and areas of the country. They cannot be cited at length here, but the overall figures are revealing. In March 1953, the ministry calculated that "the approximate effectiveness of (our and our friends') protection is about 82%, and in Warsaw and Silesia (mostly in the Stalinogród area) this effectiveness is about 97–99%. This is the case with all programs except Free Europe's, concerning which effectiveness in some areas of the country is about 60% (this happens mostly because of its long programs, from 8 to 16 hours)."[21] Interestingly, beginning in February 1953 the effectiveness of the jamming of RFE is measured in the Protective Service's ten-day reports separately from all the other stations. This special concern confirms that less than a year after the Voice of Free Poland began to broadcast from Munich, the Polish government already saw it as an unrivaled adversary.

These figures on the effectiveness of jamming are probably exaggerated, but it is impossible to know by how much. The director of the Protective Service, Lieutenant Colonel Andrzej Jegliński, himself admitted some proneness to error in November 1953 as he modified the methodology used for the ten-day reports.[22] Later reports show a drop of a few percentage points in the effectiveness of the jamming. A March 1953 document (found by Lechosław Gawlikowski) sets the effectiveness of jamming much lower, at 30 percent of "hostile broadcasts." But since it is not signed and its author is unknown (we know only that one of the document's addressees was Jakub Berman), its credibility is lower.[23] It should also be kept in mind that these figures are global and that there were differences, at times quite significant, between regions, times of day, and wavelengths. For example, in late March 1953 the jamming of 60 percent of programs between 4:54 a.m. and 9:15 a.m. was effective on most wavelengths, while between 8 p.m. and 2 a.m. only 45 percent of programs on some wavelengths were jammed. These were the hours, before and after work for the majority of Poles, when the radio's audiences were the largest. Jamming had much better results (80 percent to 95 percent) in the middle of the day, between noon and 3 p.m., but people with jobs tended not to listen to the radio then.[24]

In general, jamming was more effective in large cities than in small towns or rural areas. There were also significant differences between cities. Jamming was most effective in Warsaw and in heavily populated Upper Silesia. According to data for March 1–10, 1953—that is, the time when all stations were broadcasting news of Stalin's death and speculating on its consequences—in Warsaw and Stalinogród, "overall protection" (from all "hostile" programs) was about 95 percent, and in Zabrze, Silesia, it was as high as 99 percent; but for the same period in Szczecin and Poznań it was about 50 percent, and in Wrocław, Łódź, and Cracow it was just under 60 percent.[25]

The huge expansion of the jamming network in 1953–1955 seemed not to have significantly improved its effectiveness. The "hostile" radio stations responded by boosting the power of their transmitters, adding program hours and wavelengths. According to data for September 1955, which unfortunately are not as detailed as those for 1953, nationally the average effectiveness of the jamming was 75 percent, while in areas with supplementary local transmitters it was 95 percent. Insofar as the number of radios in the latter area, comprising twelve cities, was estimated to be 740,000, out of 1.75 million for the whole country, the average effectiveness of the "protection" for all listeners was 83.5 percent.[26] In autumn of 1956, the effectiveness of shortwave jamming was estimated at almost 70 percent, and at 90 to 99 percent for large cities.[27]

Producing Receivers with a Reduced Range of Frequencies

Because the Ministry of Public Security did not believe that jamming was thoroughly effective, it became interested in a new method of fighting what it considered hostile programs. Radios would now be produced to transmit on a narrower band of shortwave frequencies. In May 1953, in a letter to Minister Stanisław Radkiewicz, General Juliusz Hibner suggested limiting the short waves to 31 to 49 meters. "All the foreign radio stations that may and should interest the Polish listener (Moscow, Kiev, Leningrad, Prague, Budapest, Bucharest, Sofia, Berlin) broadcast mostly on the 49-m and 41-m frequencies, less often on 31 m and very rarely on 25 m. Only the capitalist countries' radios work on the shorter wavelengths," contended the commander of the Internal Forces, which supervised the Protective Service.

Hibner attached great hopes to this plan, which in a few years could bring a decisive victory in the war against "hostile radio propaganda." "In 1953–1954," he maintained, "our industry is planning to manufacture nearly half a million radios, and probably many more in the following years. If we take into account the fact that, on the one hand, the majority of radios owned by our citizens are old, frequently post-German, they will 'die' naturally in the next few years, while on the other hand the continuously rising standard of living will influence the excellent growth in the number of radios being bought by the population, it will become clear that in the next few years, if we make an appropriately quick decision, the majority of radios will naturally make it impossible to listen to a decisive majority of hostile programs on the wavelengths that are the most difficult to protect."[28]

The decision was indeed made very quickly. On June 6, 1953, the government Presidium adopted a resolution in accordance with the Ministry of Public Security's ideas, about starting the production of radios with a limited range of medium waves (31 to 50 meters). The Ministry of Machine Industry immediately implemented the changes in construction and began to produce the radios serially. Every radio produced in 1954 was to adhere to the adopted specifications. But the vigilance of Ministry of Public Security functionaries stopped the Polish government from making a very serious mistake. A few months later someone realized that the radios being manufactured would make it impossible to listen to "programs broadcast on 25 m in Polish by the Soviet Union." General Hibner was forced to ask the government to amend its resolution, extending the permissible wavelength to 25 meters.[29] This resolution was in force until November 10, 1956, when, in response to the population's post-October demands, the law was repealed.[30] This period was likely too short to fulfill General Hibner's hopes that the war against "the enemy's radio propaganda" would take a decisive turn.

Harassment of People Listening to Western Radio

Failing to block the reception of foreign broadcasts or to produce limited-range radios, the Polish government turned to a method that was socially much more painful: singling out people who listened to Western radio. The security police now focused on combating the practice of collective listening among neighbors and friends and, of course, at work. It considered the act of setting factory public address systems to the "hostile" wavelengths a particularly serious offense. It was a "counterrevolutionary" act, carried out and inspired by "imperialist" agents. Even persons heard commenting on news heard on Western radio or talking about it to others were persecuted. The Special Commission for Combating Abuses and Economic Sabotage sentenced those charged with taking part in these group listening sessions or of disseminating "whispered propaganda" (usually according to Article 22 of the June 13, 1946, decree, commonly known as the Small Criminal Code) to six- to twenty-four-month terms in labor camps (this was the longest sentence the commission was authorized to hand down).[31]

An overview of just a few cases conveys the atmosphere of this period and the government's perception of the dangers lurking in Western radio. Persecution touched people who lived in big cities and in the countryside, university-educated people and those who had completed only a few years of elementary school.

In October 1952, functionaries of the District Office of Public Security in Bochnia arrested Julian Dominik, a farmer from Lipnica Dolna. He was accused of organizing collective foreign-radio listening sessions with neighbors in his house. Witness accounts discuss the effort it took to hear a program through the jamming. One told the investigator, "He set the radio to Free Europe, but it was impossible to hear what the foreigners were saying because there was noise and crackling on the radio. But Dominik tried to remove these obstacles in the apparatus, and he turned the knob, and then we could hear what the Americans were saying, but not everything was understandable." The District Office of Public Security requested a twenty-four-month sentence in a labor camp for Dominik; the Special Commission gave him twelve months.[32]

After being arrested in December 1952, Jerzy Stepaczenko, a waiting room attendant (*świetlicowy*, a function that the modern reader may have difficulty understanding) in the Central Train Station in Białystok, was sentenced to eighteen months. He was charged thus: "after hearing the last Warsaw newscast, at 23.05 he set the radio to the foreign station, Free Europe, and allowed the travelers in the waiting room, who numbered about forty, to listen to a program maligning the USSR and the countries of democracy. . . . After he listened to the whole program, he did not turn off the radio until the moment he was taken in."[33]

Grzegorz Świtalski, a maintenance worker for a radio broadcasting system in Warta, Łódź Province, was sentenced in April 1953 to a slightly shorter term of twelve months in a forced labor camp. This member of the Union of Polish Youth, detailed to work for the radio on the recommendation of the District Committee of the PUWP in Sieradz, together with some friends, set the receiver to RFE and some other Western stations. His friend Włodzimierz Świtalski, a member of the Volunteer Citizens' Militia and an Industrial Guard officer in a factory in Sieradz, was handed an identical sentence for listening with him to foreign programs and spreading the news he had heard, which "presented the economic and political situation in the USSR and People's Poland in a false light, to spread to his colleagues and acquaintances at his place of work."[34]

In July 1953, Władysław Dub, a village leader in Dańczów, Kłodzko District, who kept a community-owned radio at home, received the maximum sentence of twenty-four months of forced labor. Villagers had listened to RFE, the BBC, and the VOA in his house. He was also accused of "spreading false information that could inflict fundamental damage on the interests of the Polish state." One of the witnesses recalled, "Dub Władysław came to my house where . . . he stated whether I listened to the radio, to which I responded that I did not, to which he stated to me that I should listen to Free Europe in the evenings, so that I would learn, because we no longer have a Poland, he was using indecent language because Poland had been added to the Soviet Union and is a republic of the USSR."[35]

A few other cases did not involve using state or "socially owned" equipment or such brazen actions as that by the train station waiting room attendant. The discrepancy underscores the random nature of the verdicts, which were out of proportion to the political weight of the misdeed. Thus, twenty-four-month labor camp sentences were handed down to two inhabitants of Sokołów, who had been arrested by the District Office of Public Security in Wysokie Mazowieckie. Stanisław Kobyliński ("a collector of recyclables . . . has no education") allegedly organized regular ("three times a week") sessions of listening to foreign programs in his apartment. Aleksander Samulski, a local teacher, allegedly played the main role by commenting on their contents. In February 1953, a handful of people listened to RFE's programs about the collectivization of agriculture, and a lively discussion ensued. "Next spoke," wrote the District Office of Public Security to the Special Commission, "Samulski Aleksander and, as the most enlightened person he 'explained' to those present, speaking about the current government, that it wants to turn people into riff-raff because when the cooperative system of management takes over the whole Polish countryside, the people will be going around barefoot and unclothed."[36] Were it not for the lengthy sentences given the two accused men, this incident could serve as a very inspiring story about representatives of various social strata listening to RFE and a local member of the intelligentsia explaining the programs to others.

The forester Zygmunt Szpet also received the highest possible sentence for listening to foreign radio in his forester's house in front of clients. In March 1953, as he was listening to Radio Madrid, two individuals entered his office and after a few minutes asked what station he was listening to. When they heard his truthful answer, the men, plainclothes secret police officers, searched the house and seized him.[37]

Another person sentenced to twenty-four months in a forced labor camp was a student at the Medical Academy in Łódź. Lech Szutenbach was a member of the Union of Polish Youth and of the PUWP. Several people listened to foreign broadcasts in his apartment. The following fragment of the indictment presented by the Łódź Security Service to the Special Commission illustrates well how the security apparatus viewed foreign radio stations: "Fed antagonistic propaganda by the radio 'yappers,' he then spread false information about the sovereignty of the Polish state and the reasons for the temporary difficulties with supplies; he also anticipated the American aggressors' alleged victory in Korea. It is the mission of stations of the Free Europe, Voice of America etc. kind to entangle the Polish nation in a net of lies about the goals of our peace policies, about our socialist construction, so as to steer it into the war that the imperial countries are preparing against the Soviet Union and the people's democracies. Hence, anyone who repeats any of the information being aired by these imperialist countries' radios or enables others to hear them . . . is committing a crime against peace."

This indictment had a grotesque touch. The image of the "enemy of the people" clearly needed to be painted black, so listening to foreign radio was logically linked to other transgressions: "Szutenbach Lech's hostility to our system is also visible in his attitude toward his duties as a health supervisor at a children's summer camp organized by the Barlicki Cotton Factory in Justynów. The children were dirty and neglected, not properly fed, as Szutenbach Lech busied himself with totally different activities," wrote the investigator of the Office of Public Security in Łódź, Władysław Paderewski.[38]

The Security Service often placed people who were arrested for listening to foreign radio in temporary detention for many months before the detainees could appear before the Special Commission. Jan Król from Dębnica Kaszubska was apprehended in January 1952; nine months later his wife, who had been left alone with three children, wrote a desperate letter to the authorities. The accused did not confess, and the documentation of his case includes no witness testimony. In October 1952, the Special Commission sentenced him to nine months of hard labor, including the period of detention, implicitly legalizing the actions of the secret police.[39]

Secret Service functionaries treated listening to foreign radio as evidence or a symptom of a hostile attitude, which was bound to lead to other political misdeeds. Władysław Ozór from the village of Marciszów was sentenced to twelve months in a labor camp for listening to foreign programs with his neighbors. After a program ended, he would allegedly try "to convince others not to participate in the elections to the Sejm of the People's Republic of Poland." The investigators also tried to make a connection between those who listened to foreign radio and cases of torn-up electoral posters in the village.[40] In July 1953, the organist Henryk Ciesielski was arrested in Podedwórze village in Włodawa District and sentenced to eighteen months in a labor camp for "organizing" group listening sessions for members of the church choir. The District Office of Public Security was able to point to a particular "enemy": "It was determined in the course of the investigation that in Podedwórze . . . enemy activity of the kulak-speculator and hostile clergy elements has increased, assuming the form of the dissemination of false information directed against the current regime of People's Poland, aiming to prevent the collectivization of the countryside and to introduce a wartime mood among the peasantry. It has been determined that the collective listening to radio programs from capitalist countries, which disseminate hatred for the countries of people's democracy, is a source of acquiring false information."[41]

The Special Commission's materials are an extremely valuable historical source as they portray not only government oppression but also listeners' perceptions of foreign broadcasts, which did not always correspond to those stations' intentions. The witnesses who testified in the forester's cottage case remembered an RFE program describing how "in Russia, Jewish doctors poisoned three Communists . . . and they would even have poisoned Stalin himself but didn't manage to because they were caught."[42] They were clearly referring to the steadily mounting anti-Semitic campaign in Russia and the persecutions in the last months of Stalin's life, specifically the "Doctors' Plot"—interestingly enough, interpreted not according to what RFE broadcast but in line with the Stalinist propaganda.

About 4,400 people were sent to work camps for disseminating "enemy propaganda" between 1950 and 1954, most of them in 1952–1953; in 1954, the number clearly dropped.[43] We are unable to tell exactly how many of them (certainly the figure was very high) were punished for listening to foreign radio stations or for talking about the news they had heard. Such an analysis would require researching the documentation of all the cases of the thousands of people sent to labor camps for such infractions.

It appears that the persecution of people who listened to Western radio occurred in waves, with the security police becoming more active at times of important political developments or of increased scrutiny by the Ministry of Public Security. From time to time the ministry's leadership would call on its field offices to intensify their struggle against "hostile propaganda." Thus, in an October 1952 memorandum from the ministry to the heads of provincial security offices, Western radio stations were blamed for spreading "hostile, warmongering propaganda" during the election campaign, as well as "inciting people to practice sabotage and murder" and "airing directives for illegal organizations, spy networks and bands." "Imperialist radio programs have become the main source of inspiration for the underground. Enemy, reactive elements, who often lack directives on how to act during the elections, have been trying to organize group listening to programs and spreading information obtained in this way," read the memorandum.[44]

The security police was accused of not being appropriately vigilant, as evidenced by, for instance, its failure to make any arrests linked to the collective listening to Western radio since the end of the previous year. The minister instructed the force to fight energetically against "hostile propaganda": "You must immediately begin to establish who the people are who are organizing the collective listening, as well as those who listen to hostile programs and who are suspected of disseminating the information they hear. In villages where there are radios, you must recruit agents, with the goal of exposing the sources of the hostile gossip and eliminating them." Radkiewicz recommended arresting both "the organizers of listening to hostile programs and those who themselves listen and disseminate hostile propaganda," and handing the cases over to the prosecutor's office.[45] In a memorandum of February 27, 1953, the minister of public security again instructed the secret police to beef up their struggle against collective listening to RFE—this time the station was singled out and listed first—and other "imperialist" stations.[46]

The battle against listening to "enemy" stations was also waged in the military. That the authorities continued to issue orders to put an end to this practice is proof that the orders were not obeyed. On October 12, 1951, the head of the Main Political Directorate of the Polish Army ordered "decisively thwarting listening to and repeating the lies of the imperialist radio stations." More instructions were issued on November 30, 1951, and July 7, 1952. The head military prosecutor backed the head of the Main Political Directorate when on December 9, 1951, he instructed the organizations answerable to him to "request the harsh punishment of those who organize collective listening to the programs of foreign radios that spread enemy propaganda and build up an atmosphere of war." It has not been possible so far to find documents about punishments for troops accused of listening to Western radio stations. Aleksander Kochański has been able to establish only that in 1952, a lieutenant colonel of the Ninth Łużycki Tank Regiment was downgraded to warrant officer.[47]

Propaganda Attacks

For RFE, Communist propaganda attacks were always a gauge of its effectiveness.[48] Had the Poles not wanted to listen to its programs or had interference been successful, the official press and radio would have had no reason to criticize RFE. Instead, propaganda assaults on the Munich station continued without cessation from its early days almost to the end of the People's Republic of Poland. The press clippings of these attacks, along with the drawings, caricatures, and posters, especially those from the Stalinist era, all classics of Communist visual propaganda, would fill several volumes.[49] The language and rhetorical devices the Communist propagandists used evolved over the decades, but the most important themes from the 1950s persisted through the years.

The most powerful piece of criticism, which recurred like a mantra, was that RFE served German interests. This charge was pushed most brutally in the Stalinist period, a time when it was also most likely to appeal to the Poles, who had not forgotten the atrocities of the war. Just a few months after the Voice of Free Poland was introduced, the popular afternoon paper *Express Wieczorny* began an article titled "From a Neues [New] Europa to a Freies Europa" with these words: "So, what an amazing opportunity. We will now be able to listen to the voice of the same Gestapo men who so zealously conducted interrogations on Szucha Avenue [the Gestapo headquarters—P. M.] in Warsaw, performed executions in the Montelupi Prison in Cracow and tortured people in the 'Clock' building on Uniwersytecka Street in Lublin. You will remember that some of these gentlemen spoke fluent Polish. Today, these same fellows have been hired by radio Freies Europa (Free Europe)."[50]

Another popular daily, *Życie Warszawy*, went even further: "And now we have a little riddle: Why is Free Europe, Freies Europa, called . . . Free Europe? Because the gates to Hitler's concentration camps, the gates to Auschwitz, Treblinka, Stutthof etc., etc. always bore a sign that read 'Arbeit macht frei,'" the author, who went by the name SŁAW, asked, and then answered himself.[51]

It would be difficult to find an equally dramatic text in the rich history of propaganda assaults on RFE. By comparison, constantly mentioning the radio's

German name, Freies Europa, or explaining that the Voice of Free Poland really should be called the Voice of Free Germany, emphasizing that its headquarters were in Munich—the city where Hitler's movement was born and where a 1938 conference allowed the Third Reich to carry on with its conquests—were simple and relatively innocent operations.

Of the countless statements discussing the radio's alleged subordination to the Nazis, one more is worth citing; it was written by Wanda Odolska, probably the best-known radio voice of the Stalinist era. Her style was inimitable, even by the language standards of that era's propaganda. "Free Europe is an American-Bonn organ, paid for in dollars and marks, in absolute harmony with the murderers of Warsaw, with the torturers from the concentration camps, with the Nazis who managed to escape the noose, which emits venom through its microphones. The Nazified ex-Poles who have found cushy little jobs at RFE must love this politics of warmongering. Everybody knows."[52]

Communist propaganda consistently struck at the radio's real Achilles heel, its inability to state its own position on the question of the Oder-Neisse border, a delineation not officially recognized by Western countries until the 1970s. Because many of the inhabitants of the Recovered Territories, taken over by Poland from Germany after World War II, continued to be convinced that their situation was provisional and feared both another war and the Germans, criticism of the radio on this issue touched an acutely raw nerve for millions of Poles. The Stalinist propaganda machine used this theme in dozens of different ways, also in satire. Here is a sample from *Żołnierz Wolności*, the military's daily: "An employee of the Voice of Free Poland, which by an odd twist of fate is broadcasting from Muenchen (Munich), his hair disheveled, rushes into the office of his editor in chief, and shouts: 'Boss, for Heaven's sake, we have a special program, "We will make you beautiful and independent, O our homeland," going on the air in 10 minutes, and we still have no script.' 'What do you mean, we don't have a script,' bristles Mr. Trądzik, M. A., 'what happened to it? Oh, damn it,' he suddenly remembered, slapping his forehead, 'it hasn't been approved yet.' Whereupon he nimbly grasped the receiver: 'Herr Obersturmbannführer Puffke? Hier spricht Trądzik. Good morning! Have you kindly approved the text for 'Let's make . . . ' or 'Let's make our homeland . . . ,' something like that?' 'I have not and will not approve it,' a voice grumbled on the line, 'because there is too much beating around the bush and shame in it, when you talk about the old German cities, Danzig, Posen, Kattowitz and the others.' 'But, Herr Puffke,' the editor exclaimed, whining, 'we can't do it too brutally. You've known us for a long time, you know very well that we have no claims on those cities, we're only thinking about our audience in Poland.'"[53]

Compared to this, other recurrent themes in these condemnations of RFE—including its subordination to US intelligence (which of course needed to merge seamlessly with the theme of serving the Germans), it sending signals to agents in Poland, warmongering, or simple lack of journalistic integrity (for instance, the accusation that letters from listeners in Poland were manufactured)—seemed ordinary, even feeble. At times the various accusations were mutually exclusive. On the one hand, all program scripts were allegedly approved by Nazis in Munich; on the other, as Wiesław Górnicki wrote about instructions from across the ocean, "every morning councils of RFE's language sections meet . . . to listen intently to their master's voice, i.e., the daily orders from New York. The well-known [British] Labour Party politician [Richard] Crossman confirmed this fact that daily instructions are sent to Munich in the English publication *The News* [*sic*] *Statesman and Nation*."[54]

When necessary, the writers cited not only the Western "imperialist" press but also Polish émigré publications. The PUWP daily *Trybuna Ludu* took pleasure in quoting attacks on the Voice of Free Poland, of which there were many in its early months: "Its Polish programs," said the Sanacja mouthpiece *Orzeł Biały* about the Munich-based radio—which resembled a Nazi public megaphone, according to the Communist *Trybuna Ludu* editors—"are American, not Polish, shows."[55] This, incidentally, was one of the first articles in the Polish press about the Voice of Free Poland after its inauguration on May 3, 1952.

Another characteristic motif of Stalinist propaganda was exposing the "class" profile of the editors in RFE's Polish Section. The caricatures appearing in newspapers and on posters showed figures of plump men in top hats, fat cigars in their mouths, or of individuals wearing monocles. The June 4, 1952, *Trybuna Ludu* article quoted above sneeringly described "refined gentlemen with their expensive wives in furs and diamonds." Another article exposed the writer of programs addressed to workers who used the name Jacek Śniady as "Count Michał Tyszkiewicz," then added in passing that he was an "agent of the Intelligence Service,"[56] which must have made less of an impression. The identification was certainly false: it was Jerzy Szyszko-Bohusz who used the pseudonym of Jacek Śniady, while Tyszkiewicz worked on the news desk. This error underscores the fact that in this early period, Polish propaganda and intelligence knew very little about the personnel of the Polish Service.

One of the ways in which propaganda works is to introduce new facts that reinforce an image that was created earlier. These facts must become increasingly dramatic, or else the audience will lose interest in repetitive, familiar content and rhetorical devices. In April 1955, Warsaw Radio accused RFE of causing the death of the Polish sailor Stanisław Talarek. When his vessel sailed into the port of Stockholm, "seasoned intelligence agents and collaborators of the Free Europe yapper persuaded Talarek to jump ship. This was how this Polish sailor's tragedy began." Talarek was so honest that he did not want to work for Western intelligence, thereby condemning himself to a refugee's destitution and homelessness. Remembering who had persuaded him to defect, he turned to RFE, but RFE also refused to help. In despair, the sailor committed suicide. Warsaw Radio's announcer told his listeners, "The suicide's body was found outside the door of the RFE office."[57] Before the year was over, the Ministry of National Defense had published a fictionalized story about Talarek.[58]

The propaganda of the Stalinist period about RFE also included rhymes, and not only in satirical publications such as *Szpilki*. They were not highbrow efforts. The following sample gives a flavor of the era. *Gazeta Białostocka* published a poem by Józef Prutkowski entitled "Radio Free Europe." Three stanzas of the longer work read:

> Free Europe booms: In Poland there's no food
> Your capital lies in ruins . . .
> The editor rubs his hands: sehr Gut.
> The editor's boss murmurs: okay.
>
> The "Polish" announcer is thrilled as a child
> As he hurls buckets of slops at Poland,
> The editor praises him in German.
> With a . . . Nazi accent.
>
> And for trying so hard,
> For his hateful shouts
> He is given a bonus in dollars, D-marks,
> That is, so many silver coins of Judas.[59]

But the propagandists clearly realized that, despite all their efforts, people continued to listen to RFE. On the one hand, they branded and mocked listeners as naïve fools: "An ass's ears and an ass's face expression," wrote the farmers' paper *Nowa Wieś*, "this is how caricatures that appear in our newspapers customarily portray these dupes who still occasionally want to listen to Free Europe's baying."[60] On the other hand, in many cases writers engaged in relatively factual—for the era—discussions, using more than insults to argue with particular programs. This was the case with Józef Światło's broadcasts, for which he was accused of being a provocateur and a US agent in the Ministry of Public Security. Editorialists also rejected the radio's allegations that the 1954 elections to the People's Councils were not free and democratic. "No one from higher up imposed the candidates, as their commentator, the kulak Lasota, would have it. And if some eager beaver popped up somewhere, the community itself would bring him to heel," the *Wave 49* radio program assured its listeners.[61]

Warsaw Radio's *Music and Current Events* program debated the details of RFE's allegation that the Soviet Union was not giving Poland economic assistance but only imposing a forced build-up of its heavy and armaments industries, which were working for the Soviet empire. Warsaw Radio first quoted an RFE program (including its musical signature, the May 3 Constitution song "Witaj majowa jutrzenko") and then went on to list all the reasons why RFE was not telling the truth: "As you sit eating your breakfast roll, do you know that most rolls, especially in 1945–48, were baked with flour milled from grain delivered from the Soviet Union? Did you know, as you look at the beautiful shirts in a store window, that we produced nine out of every dozen shirts from cotton delivered by the Soviet Union? Did you know, when you bought five meters of fabric for a new dress for your wife, that four of these five meters were woven from fibers that our textile mills produced out of Soviet raw material?"[62]

Attacks against RFE were one of the most constant, omnipresent motifs in Communist propaganda. Their protagonists changed over the decades. The figure of the "kulak," the rich farmer who exploited poorer peasants, no longer appeared after 1956. The "Zionist"—"the Jewish nationalist"—was one of the main enemies between the mid-1960s and the early 1970s, but later receded into the background. Even the "reactionary clergy"—those Catholic bishops and priests who wanted to preserve their autonomy with respect to the Communist state—were not targeted by equally powerful invectives in the different periods. But the Communist propagandists remained interested in the "Munich baboons" (this was the title of a 1980s television program)—RFE lackeys of Washington and Bonn—as figures and rhetorical devices evolved and key motifs changed.

"Free Europe did not merely have the status of a so-called hostile radio, as it was also displaced into a different sphere of reality with symbolic meanings," wrote the most eminent expert on the language of propaganda in Communist Poland, Michał Głowiński. "In this resistance, it was not merely a question of rejecting this or that view, of disqualifying this or that piece of information or even of simply oppressing an institution viewed as adversarial. Hiding behind this was a certain deeper intention: in Communist propaganda, Free Europe became a symbol of evil, like the CIA or particular persons; for example, during martial law, President Reagan or the [German expellee activists Herbert] Hupka and Herbert Czaja. Indeed a symbol, since this was no longer a question of particular actions or viewpoints, but of a peculiar institution to which to attribute everything that is the worst from the point of view of real socialism."[63]

"Behind the Scenes in the Secret Police and the Party"

It was as a consequence of the defection to the West of Lieutenant Colonel Józef Światło and the airing of programs based on his revelations, *Behind the Scenes in the Secret Police and the Party*, that RFE was able to exert its greatest direct influence on the situation in Poland in the first half of the 1950s—and perhaps in its entire history. The programs began in October 1954 and aired daily for several months. They developed into real political dynamite, one of the key factors that sped up Poland's farewell to Stalinism. Światło, who had served as the deputy chief of Department X, charged with watching over the party cadres, was one of the best-informed functionaries of the political police, the Ministry of Public Security. He took part in many important operations, including the arrest in August 1951 of the former PUWP secretary general Władysław Gomułka and in September 1953 of Cardinal Stefan Wyszyński, Primate of Poland.[64] (Both were regarded as enemies and threats to the ruling Stalinists; neither was executed.)

Światło spoke about the criminal methods of the secret police, the role of Soviet advisers, the Polish leadership's close dependence on Moscow, and the Communist elite's luxurious lifestyle. Hundreds of thousands of people listened to these programs, and the office of the minister of public security kept a special bulletin to record the reactions of both the public and the ministry's own staff. The bulletin took note of cases of secret police informers' and agents' refusal to collaborate, dictated by the fear of being found out in the wake of Światło's defection. "According to the Provincial Office of Public Security in Wrocław, 10 agents (including five priests) have reported to us, alarmed by the abovementioned fact, putting it this way: what guarantee is there that Światło knows nothing about their collaboration, or that he has not passed on information about their collaboration with the organs of public security," read the first note prepared after the programs began airing.[65] Incidentally, it turned out that even the ministry's functionaries listened to RFE. Some of them discussed Światło's disclosures and even listened to his programs at work, including in the office of the deputy chief of the City Office of Public Security in Zakopane.[66]

The party leadership consulted Moscow (General Secretary Bierut spoke on the telephone with Russian premier Georgi Malenkov) and was forced to make quick decisions to defuse at least some of the effects of Światło's admissions.

The director of the investigation department of the Ministry of Public Security, Colonel Józef (Jacek) Różański, was arrested on charges of using exceptionally brutal interrogation methods; Światło's boss, Colonel Anatol Fejgin, was expelled from the party; and Minister Radkiewicz was removed from his position. The ministry was dissolved and its work was divided between the Committee for Public Security and the Ministry of Internal Affairs. Some employees of both the central and local offices were also dismissed, and agents who had been registered en masse in earlier years were "unregistered." Public criticism of the "mistakes and deviations" of the security apparatus was allowed so that it would never again regain the cohesiveness and aggressiveness that preceded Światło's appearance in the RFE broadcasts.[67]

The Balloon War

Reorganizing the security ministry in no way ended the troubles stemming from Światło's revelations after he went over to the Americans. The Free Europe Committee (FEC) had since the early 1950s attached considerable weight to the so-called balloon actions, viewing leafleting from afar as one of the best methods to break through the Iron Curtain and to limit the effects of jamming. As early as 1951, the FEC sponsored the dispatching from West Germany of a flotilla of balloons with containers full of propaganda leaflets. Driven by the wind, the balloons were expected to reach Prague and Pilsen around the time people were on their way to work. A similar operation was staged in July 1953, shortly after the Berlin uprising and the worker unrest in Pilsen, and again, on a much larger scale, in the spring and autumn of 1954. Thousands of balloons carried fliers to Czechoslovakia and Hungary, calling on people to take up various forms of resistance against their regimes. The suggested means ranged from crossing out candidates' names on trade union ballots and writing in alternative candidates, to sabotaging compulsory deliveries of food products (which peasants were obliged to submit to state agencies), to organizing strikes and street demonstrations.[68]

RFE's American management planned a similar action for Poland. This idea, however, triggered protests from both Polish émigré groups and the head of the Polish desk, Jan Nowak. Nowak posed to his American bosses that using this unusual method would give rise to unrealistic hopes that the United States was planning to act more decisively with respect to the Soviet bloc, and that such hopes would inevitably lead to disillusionment with the West. Nowak most vehemently opposed the idea of calling for resistance to the Communist regime from abroad. If the Americans insisted on using balloons, he asserted, they should carry only information, not political propaganda.[69]

Nowak's reasoning won, and the radio station decided to send brochures with the text of Światło's radio programs to Poland. The action began on February 12, 1955. Altogether about 800,000 brochures titled *Behind the Scenes in the Secret Police and the Party* were sent out in Operation Spotlight. A short time later, other printed pieces were dispatched by the same method. They included *I Chose the Truth* by Communist defector Seweryn Bialer; translations of the Vatican decree of the Holy Office condemning the pro-Communist Catholic PAX weekly *Dziś i Jutro* and Bolesław Piasecki's book *Zagadnienia istotne* (The real issues); Nikita Khrushchev's "secret" speech at the Twentieth Congress of the Communist Party of the Soviet Union (CPSU); and even George Orwell's *Animal Farm*. Between November 1955 and August 1956, seven issues of the bulletin *Wolna Europa* (Free Europe), with a circulation surpassing a million copies of each issue, were also sent out by balloon. The bulletin contained information about world events, discussed topics covered in RFE's programs, and devoted considerable space to issues censored in Poland, such as the detention of Poles in the Soviet Union after World War II. The scale of the operation was impressive: in less than two months, between April 24 and June 13, 1956, over a million and a half items were sent to Poland.[70]

From the very beginning, the Polish party and state leadership treated this propaganda by balloon, which projected and complemented broadcasts, as a major menace. In February 1955, the Secretariat of the CC PUWP began to react. "The recent balloon drops and mailings of slanderous and provocative materials, which aim to stir up chaos and undermine the masses' trust in the party, its leadership and the people's government, are a manifestation of American-Nazi sabotage. The shamelessly mendacious network of American-Nazi yappers and the rowdy gangs of dollar-paid Judases, provocateurs, agents, spies, and all kinds of mercenaries funded by the United States are still trying, albeit in vain, to hurl abuse at, spit at, tarnish with vile and lowly lies, repulsive gossip, [and] criminal smears the most precious leaders of the working class," read a circular for the executives of the PUWP provincial and district committees. Its fierce, Stalinist tone was extreme, considering that these were the beginnings of the thaw.[71] During party meetings, members were urged to locate balloon drops and to resist the "enemy" propaganda. To assist them, the CC Department of Propaganda and Agitation prepared special instructional materials that presented the FEC and RFE as tools of "Hitlerite revanchists" who wanted to start another war, take back the Recovered Territories from Poland, and "turn the whole globe into a new Oświęcim [Auschwitz]." It stressed that the very name of the institution that wanted to implement these base goals was "identical to the notorious 'Neues Europa,' Adolf Hitler's pride."[72]

Communist propaganda naturally reacted vehemently to the balloon operations. Of the hundreds of articles and radio programs, an editorial by Wanda Odolska stands out as a true classic of Stalinist propaganda: "A Pole finding this garbage will perhaps ponder the lowliness of these traitors. But that's not all! Let him think for a moment about the real authors of this whole action. . . . American gentlemen are capable of anything: air drops of toxic lice and Colorado potato beetles, parachuting spies and saboteurs. They couldn't send us their airplanes in 1939, or in 1944, as the naïve ones gazed into the sky waiting for American assistance. They refused to help then, but now they are generous with all sorts of poisons."[73]

The Polish government mobilized the security apparatus, party activists, and members of the Union of Polish Youth to clean up the fliers and balloons. In every district security office an employee was designated to coordinate the battle against the enemy from the air. The population was encouraged to hand in the drops they found, and cash rewards (20 zlotys per brochure, 100 zlotys per balloon envelope) were paid out by local security offices. Yet most people, even employees of the party and security bureaucracies, kept the balloons, often to make raincoats out of them. Security officers followed tips from their networks of informers and searched homes for hidden fliers and balloons.[74]

To stop the balloon actions, the region's Communist governments launched a coordinated diplomatic campaign, one of the largest in the decades-long war against the FEC and RFE. During Chancellor Konrad Adenauer's historic visit to Moscow in September 1955, which initiated diplomatic relations between West Germany and the Soviet Union, the Soviet leadership demanded that Germany put an end to the balloon campaign.[75] The governments of the satellite countries targeted by the drops all delivered protest notes to the US government (Czechoslovakia had been first, in July 1953).[76] Warsaw protested on February 11, 1956, to the US embassy, then to the other members of the United Nations. Its note described the balloon actions as "a blatant violation of the principle of territorial sovereignty" that also endangered air traffic and caused numerous accidents, such as skin burns, fires, and explosions of the gas inside the balloons. The note cited specific cases of injuries to people who came in contact with the balloons, as well as fires.[77] It is impossible to verify the information collected by the Committee for Public Safety, so it may be that some of these cases were true.

The crowning argument used by Communist diplomacy and propaganda was the February 1956 crash of a Czechoslovak passenger plane, allegedly because of a collision with the balloons. At the United Nations, Prague demanded compensation from Washington. The American government and the FEC rebuffed the charges, claiming that the likely cause of the accident had been bad weather.[78] The Hungarian government made similar accusations, which were less well known internationally. In January 1956, there allegedly took place a "collision of two airplanes as they chased after a sabotage balloon that had crossed into Hungarian territory from Austria." A Hungarian pilot allegedly perished.[79] Another accident reportedly caused by balloons occurred in Poland. On August 3, 1956, a plane crashed during a training flight near Sochaczew, and two pilots died. "The detailed investigation into the causes of the catastrophe, the downing of a MiG 15, was caused by its collision with a balloon filled with hydrogen and weighed down by leaflets," read the Polish government's statement on September 5, 1956.[80]

The news story about balloons causing the crash seems even less credible than the earlier cases of burns and fires.[81] In fact, neither Polish diplomats nor the propaganda bureau took up the case of the Sochaczew accident, which seems to confirm that the allegations were fictitious. But it is interesting that earlier, in a February 1956 note, the Polish government claimed that in October 1955, balloons had endangered the Canadian minister of foreign affairs, who was flying over Poland to Moscow. This news, alleged the Polish Foreign Ministry, became a sensation that was widely discussed in the American media.[82]

The Polish government's statement of September 5 demanded that the US and West German governments stop dispatching the balloons and repeated the earlier contentions. Poland's Foreign Ministry intended to use an additional threat, curtailing the exit permits for Germans who were being allowed to leave Poland as part of a family reunification program. "If in the coming months the balloons continue to be released from the FRG [Federal Republic of Germany] into Polish airspace, the pace of sending out transports to the FRG will slow down further. The staffs of the local-level People's Councils will begin to explain, letting it slip out as an indiscretion, to people seeking permission to leave for the FRG within the family-reuniting operation that the slowed pace of dispatching transports is related to the hostile action of releasing balloons from the FRG," Foreign Minister Adam Rapacki wrote to the party leadership. Warsaw intended to respond to the anticipated intervention by the West German Red Cross that "in the conditions of the FRG government's hostile actions vis-à-vis Poland, it is difficult to implement the principles of reuniting families that have been agreed on by the Red Crosses." The Poles assumed that this would push the German Red Cross to "exert pressure on the Bonn government to suspend the balloon action."[83]

Yet these plans to stop the balloons amounted to nothing. The balloon operations were halted on October 20, 1956, during the Eighth CC PUWP Plenum, not because of anything the Polish government did but largely because of the exceptionally tense situation: Władysław Gomułka's fate as party leader was being decided, and an armed Soviet intervention loomed as a real possibility.[84] American decision makers, the FEC, and the leadership of RFE's Polish desk concurred that under the circumstances, the most important goals were to keep Gomułka in power and to reduce tensions in Poland.[85] The balloon actions targeting the other countries were stopped as the Hungarian Revolution began, principally because of the criticism of RFE from the West that it was worsening the conflict in Hungary and supporting unfounded hopes that the United States would come to the aid of the revolutionaries.[86]

Incidentally, the balloon action was described in a book published in Poland. Władysław Kisielewski, a well-known pilot and balloon enthusiast, wrote in his memoirs about the June 1957 inauguration of the balloon season, the first since the war. After a few hours in the air, pouring rain forced his recreational balloon to land in a field. "I gathered up the balloon's envelope, thoroughly soaked, then set out for the nearest village to ask for help," reminisced Kisielewski. "As soon as I reached the tree line along the road, a drenched man emerged and called out to me: 'Gentlemen from Free Europe, get out of here because our activists have just called the militia.' . . . It took me a long time to convince him that Free Europe's balloons are not the only ones sailing over Poland."[87] Because he mentioned this incident, Kisielewski was able to have his book published by an official publishing house only during the brief post–October 1956 thaw.

Launching Intelligence Operations

Intelligence operations—collecting information, recruiting agents, conducting inspiration and disinformation actions—seemingly played only a minor role in the war on RFE in the 1950s and would become a key component in this engagement only in the next decade. The earliest known evidence that information about RFE was being collected by operational methods dates to 1952. It concerns "Cezary," the largest and most successful operation of the Ministry of Public Security in the first half of the 1950s. It created a fictitious leadership, the so-called Fifth Command, for the underground organization Freedom and Independence (Wolność i Niezawisłość, or WiN), which it had broken up earlier and now entirely manipulated. The operation successfully involved a large group of people in both Poland and the émigré community in the West, as well as US intelligence.[88] In 1952, an emissary from WiN's foreign department went to Poland, and the Ministry of Public Security monitored all his contacts. "As a result of the exposure under way we obtained: . . . information concerning American stations, such as the Voice of America, Radio Free Europe," reads a report from the ministry's Department III, responsible for fighting political enemies. And further: "The funding for spying activity is appropriated by US intelligence through the so-called Free Europe Committee."[89] We know today that FEC obtained funding from the CIA not for espionage but for operations that included the radio station and the political activities of political émigrés from Eastern Europe. Thus, the CIA's relations with the FEC and RFE, as well as the flow of funds between these organizations, were very different from how the Ministry of Public Security imagined things.

This perception of the radio stations' role is symptomatic. Department III's report for 1952 begins: "In the course of 1952, the enemy attempted to disturb our peaceful construction and the calm in our country. The activities of the hostile, reactionary circles of all types are basically being directed by foreign centers, which have conveyed instructions to Poland, by courier or through radio programs (Voice of America, Free Europe)."[90]

Training materials for Ministry of Public Security functionaries, developed in connection with a much publicized trial of a group of clergymen in Cracow in 1953, paint a similar picture of foreign radio stations. They present RFE literally as a US intelligence sabotage tool: "The yapper has been trying to find a recruitment base for US intelligence and for Political Council centers in Polish territory, it tries to facilitate the work of spies dispatched to Poland. This yapper also serves as a go-between, spreading political sabotage and propaganda to assist economic sabotage." It was also typical of the Stalinist mentality to depict all indications of dissatisfaction and resistance as having been caused by hostile propaganda and the "reactionary clergy": "Polish society is becoming increasingly homogeneous. It is only the dregs of the ownership classes, which are under the influence of the hostile propaganda of the American yappers, and the reactionary clergy that are sabotaging the uniform will of our people by creating fertile ground for exploitation by American espionage centers and their agents."

The authors of the training materials demonstrated very limited familiarity with RFE's Polish Section. A small part about RFE's political profile is based on the opinion of an émigré newspaper. It also shows how closely the Ministry of Public Security was watching émigré attacks on the station: "The American yapper that is Radio Free Europe in Munich has a Polish section, which is headed by an NiD [Niepodleglość i Demokracja; Independence and Democracy] man, Nowak, and which, in the opinion of Mikołajczyk's *Narodowiec* organ, is completely dominated by the Political Council and the 'Sanacja.'"[91] This was the only relatively specific, if untrue, piece of information about the Voice of Free Poland.

A few years later, Poland's intelligence was much better informed about the FEC and RFE, both through agents and through open sources, including the press and FEC publications. During the post-1956 thaw, more journalists, writers, and academics traveled from Poland to the West, and some went to Munich, where they were generally welcomed as people who had stories to tell about the atmosphere and accelerating developments in Poland. That group included Polish intelligence agents.

The earliest agent's report that could be found in documents archived at the Institute of National Remembrance was written in July 1956 by agent "Paweł." In it, *Trybuna Ludu*'s Bonn correspondent Marian Podkowiński wrote about his meeting with the staff of RFE's Berlin office and about a conversation he had had in Munich with the deputy director of the Voice of Free Poland, Tadeusz Żenczykowski. According to "Paweł," Żenczykowski spoke about RFE's difficulties since the beginning of the thaw and relaxed censorship: "Zawadzki [Żenczykowski's RFE pseudonym—P. M.] is astounded by the open criticism in our press, which 'deprive[s] him of a living because you are writing more than we are, and when we want to return to a subject, it turns out that Warsaw has already grabbed it.' Zawadzki was open about the difficulty of being in a situation when [Stanisław Cat-]Mackiewicz and others are going back to Poland and writing."[92]

The information gathered from a variety of sources was used not only for operations but also to prepare more general analyses of "adversarial centers." In 1956, Department I (foreign intelligence) of the Committee for Public Security (the successor agency to the Ministry of Public Security as of December 1954) prepared a large study of "centers of psychological warfare run by the United States." It said of the FEC that "it is seemingly a private organization, but actually it was created and is being directed by the State Department" but mentioned nothing about the CIA overseeing or funding it. It described in detail RFE's internal structure, including its information evaluation department, which it deemed "an ordinary intelligence unit." The materials it collected were "used by American intelligence stations." In discussing the methods RFE used to gather information, the report noted that refugees and all those who left Poland, such as sailors, were a very important source. It gave the locations and methods of functioning of RFE's offices ("information centers") in various European countries and even reproduced the questions in the survey that RFE used to interview people from Poland. The report also included brief factual descriptions of more than twenty employees of RFE's Polish desk, including Jan Nowak-Jeziorański and his closest co-workers. In discussing the procedures for preparing programs, the report noted that "every program . . . passes through censorship and is approved by RFE's American management"—which was not true.[93]

Research in Ministry of Public Security and Committee for Public Security documents for the 1950s uncovered no evidence of attempts to recruit agents from among the radio's staff, apart from Zbigniew Brydak (his case is discussed below), or to infiltrate it with agents from the outside. It is also not possible to confirm Józef Światło's assertion that in 1953 he traveled to East Berlin (from where he crossed over to West Berlin and surrendered to the Americans) with his boss, Anatol Fejgin, to discuss the liquidation of Wanda Pampuch-Brońska with the head of the East German secret police, Erich Mielke. Pampuch-Brońska, a prewar Communist who had been imprisoned in Soviet labor camps in the 1930s, was a member of the Polish Workers' Party after the war, then defected to the West, where she went on RFE to talk about her experiences in the Soviet Union, Stalin's elimination of the leadership of the Communist Party of Poland, and the Great Purges. Światło claimed that key Politburo member Jakub Berman himself had ordered him to "shut up" Brońska, following instructions from General Secretary Bierut, who in turn was acting under pressure from Moscow.[94] In his report, which was written shortly after Światło's disappearance, Fejgin mentioned operating against Brońska and potentially getting help from the East German secret police as the main subject of his talks with Mielke, but did not mention an assassination plot.[95] There is also no trace of it in the five Ministry of Public Security volumes on exposing Brońska.[96] These, of course, are not conclusive arguments because as a rule plans of this kind were only discussed orally, not written down. Operational activities against Brońska may have been considered the indispensable step to more radical action. But it is also not out of the question that the plan was a confabulation created by Światło or an element of the CIA's psychological warfare.

The Case of Zbigniew Brydak

As already noted, the Ministry of Public Security and the Committee for Public Security operations documentation about RFE from the first half of the 1950s is fragmentary. In his memoirs, Jan Nowak-Jeziorański writes about the three attempts by the Communist intelligence service to infiltrate RFE at that time. He does not give the name of the young man who was "brought from Poland by his parents, and [whose] stepfather found him secretly communicating with Security Service counterintelligence." The youth confessed, and spent a year and a half in a German prison. No mention of this case has been found in either the Ministry of Public Security documents or in Jan Nowak's papers, or in the RFE archive at the Hoover Institution.[97] The second agent was named Jabłoński (Nowak does not give a first name); he was recommended by Wiktor Trościanko for a job at the radio in 1953 and contributed to some programs as a freelancer.

He was caught red-handed just as he was sending information to Polish intelligence.[98] There is also no trace of this case in available documents.

It is only the third of Nowak's cases that can be partly reconstructed, by comparing documents from Nowak's archive and the incomplete archive of the Polish security police. "Early on at the radio, a young refugee, Zbigniew Brydak, came to me for help," writes Nowak in his memoirs. "I felt an instinctive animosity toward him, and Brydak did not get a job with us, but was hired as a reader by the Munich office of the Voice of America. His Polish girlfriend discovered that he was an agent of the Polish secret police . . . and Brydak was arrested in his apartment. He decided to use the truth to save himself. Not only did he confess to everything, but on his own initiative wrote a long report that described in detail Polish secret police methods, all in the hope that the Americans would employ him as a double agent."[99]

According to Nowak's memoirs, which concur with the documents in his archive, American intelligence stopped working with Brydak after obtaining information from him.[100] A few months later, in the spring of 1955, he was released and left to his own devices. Discredited in the émigré community, Brydak returned to Poland, where he was used in propaganda attacks against RFE and the émigré community as a whole. His story is still full of ambiguities, and the report he wrote for the Americans is probably only partly true. The management of RFE's Polish Service, which was permitted to read the report, asked Światło, who was in New York, to verify the information about Brydak's work for the secret police and its methods. Poland's most famous defector said it did not look credible and that he had never come into contact with the top-secret police functionaries Brydak mentioned.[101]

The documents in the Institute of National Remembrance archive in Warsaw allow us to verify in part Brydak's report for the Americans. The four volumes of his so-called working file confirm that he really was an agent, working under the code names "B-15," "O'Henry," and "Nagórski."[102] To Poles he met outside Poland and to the Americans who questioned him, he claimed to have been a prewar Scout, a member of the Gray Ranks during the German occupation, and an activist of the Polish Scouting Association after the war, affiliated closely with the Scouting Headquarters and, after the Communists took over the Scouting movement, with the semi-underground Program Commission. He also belonged to the Polish Socialist Party. He confessed to the Americans that he had informed on Scouting activists who tried to keep their organization independent, and allegedly many were arrested as a result of his denunciations.[103]

Brydak really was a Scout.[104] His Security Service working file includes his reports about the Scouting movement beginning in 1947. In 1952, he probably attempted to follow orders from the Ministry of Public Security to stage a provocation that would draw in Scout activists: "an underground channel to West Berlin for people fearing arrest in Poland."[105] According to Brydak's account, in June 1952 the secret police conducted a sham search of his apartment and "found" underground publications. He went into hiding, allegedly to avoid arrest. In reality, he was being groomed to work as an agent outside Poland and to be transferred to West Berlin.

The plan was put into effect in November 1952. Once in the West, Brydak presented himself as a defector from Poland—where he was in danger of being arrested—who had found his way to a refugee camp. After leaving the camp, he was employed in the guard units (Polish auxiliary formations) in the US occupation zone, then moved to Munich and attempted to get a job at RFE. Despite Nowak's caution, he managed to make contact with some of the editors of the Voice of Free Poland, including some former Scouts, and gave them a paper on the situation of the Scouting movement in Poland. He also sent the paper to the leadership of the émigré Scouting movement in London. "I coordinated and agreed on this paper with Warsaw, and a copy was handed over to them at the appropriate moment in Paris," he recalled in his report for the Committee for Public Security after returning to Poland.[106] In the memorandum written for the émigré Scouting movement, he offered to establish radio contact with Poland "via the Scouting programs being broadcast by the Polish sections of the radios fighting Communism, such as Free Europe or the Voice of America or the BBC. These programs would be new food and nutrition for the Scouting youth who are waiting for them."[107] All the facts point to this offer as being an attempt to create a new regular program on the Voice of Free Poland, one that would be controlled by the secret police.

In 1953, Brydak did record a few programs for RFE about Scouting. He did establish a closer and more regular working relationship with the Munich section of the VOA, and in 1954 he hosted a series of youth programs for it. He also appeared on Radio France. In all these broadcasts he used the texts about Polish Scouting he had developed in collaboration with the Ministry of Public Security.[108] His correspondence with the émigré Scouting leaders in London, which has been saved in Jan Nowak's papers, shows that one of Brydak's missions was to infiltrate the émigré Scouting movement. He attempted to draw Scouts living in the West into preparing programs for the VOA with him. Nothing came of these plans, since the Scouting leadership distrusted Brydak.

After he returned to Poland, Brydak appeared on Polish Radio on the Kraj (Our country) channel for Polish émigrés in the West, in August 1955.[109] He also took part in Polish Radio programs, including *Music and Current Events* (*Muzyka i aktualności*) and *On the Youth Antenna* (*Na młodzieżowej antenie*).

He took the name Stefan Michalski, which he had already used on the VOA. He also published three long texts about his experiences as an émigré in the popular periodical *Świat*. Their titles, "The Berlin Traps," "Guards," and "The Microphone and the Files," speak for themselves. In the first one he presented the epic tale of a naïve young refugee from Poland who falls prey to the West's mirages and, after arriving in Berlin, finds nothing but destitution, drifting, and total exploitation by espionage services, which try to take advantage of his gullibility. Working as a guard, he is approached by a "peddler from RFE's Berlin office," who tries to extract espionage-style information from him, including places where it is easiest to cross the Polish-German border illegally.[110]

The second article describes the émigré's ordeal as he tries to stay in the West at any price and agrees to serve in the American guard companies in Germany. "The companies . . . drag themselves behind the army like camp followers and live on leftovers from the American kitchen and the American uniform warehouses. . . . Venereal diseases have decimated them, and even created hotbeds of epidemics. Nearly all of them suffer from varicose veins and gastric diseases. . . . Another kind of human loss is the mania for suicides, which happen almost daily," wrote Brydak, a.k.a. Michalski.[111] A dozen years later, Andrzej Czechowicz would also caution the Poles about the guard companies, in which he too had served before being hired by RFE and then recruited by the Ministry of Internal Affairs.[112]

Even though Brydak had closer ties to the VOA and had appeared on other Western radio stations, his third article attacked and vilified RFE alone. This shows whom the authorities of the People's Republic of Poland considered their worst enemy. Brydak persistently called it by its German name, Freies Europa, making it absolutely clear to his readers whose interests (in his opinion) the radio served. The article picked up themes common to Communist propaganda in hundreds of attacks on RFE for years to come. Brydak wrote that RFE's branch offices were working for Western intelligence and underhandedly extracting information from refugees from Poland. Many of RFE's employees in Munich were also allegedly paid by various intelligence agencies, and the radio itself was "simply a form of the American intelligence services." Employees of the Polish security apparatus were convinced that the Evaluation (or Research and Analysis) Department and its files were at the heart of this espionage organization.

Another typical rhetorical device Brydak employed was to denounce RFE's staff for its "neo-Nazi sympathies" and ties to the "most reactionary circles of revisionists and neofascists in Munich," even for collaborating with the Gestapo during the war. Brydak also claimed that the RFE's American management approved all programs before they went on the air—though this was the case only for materials about the Oder-Neisse line. Brydak emphasized that "everything is being done at Freies Europa to avoid irritating the West German revisionists. This is why RFE is forever silent about the question of the Recovered Territories." He touched the Polish desk's weak spot, since its hands were tied on this important issue. He also reiterated the usual charges of dishonesty and manipulation in the programs. Here Brydak (and no doubt his mentors on the Committee for Public Security) came up with something original. To quote a grotesque fragment of his article: "The evidence for how the Voice of Free Poland lies to its listeners includes the programs prepared by Wiktor Budzyński. Every other week, he records an artistic program in studio no. 1, with 'audience' participation. This audience is made up exclusively of RFE employees and their families and an invited claque of convalescents from a tuberculosis sanatorium in Gauting near Munich."[113]

The Voice of Free Poland responded with programs exposing Brydak's intelligence mission. They cited his report to the American authorities and quoted his confession that he had worked for the Communist secret services.[114] Jan Nowak maintained in his discussions with William Griffith that the Brydak case was "one of the best opportunities for propaganda" since RFE had used Światło precisely because he could be exposed as an agent. To Nowak, it could even create antagonisms between the secret police and the propaganda office, since the latter likely knew nothing of Brydak's ties to the special services.[115] But there is no indication that Nowak's ambitious plan was successful in this respect.

When he arrived back in Poland, Brydak prepared a sizable study for the Committee for Public Security in which he included the sum total of his knowledge about RFE, Radio Liberation (the earlier name for Radio Liberty) broadcasting to the Soviet Union, the VOA, the émigré Scouting movement, Russian and Ukrainian émigrés in Munich, and the organizations assisting refugees from behind the Iron Curtain. His information about RFE's Polish Section was rather superficial, since he mentioned only a handful of editors' names. His list of the home addresses of Radio Free Poland employees might have been of value to the secret police, although by then they may have already acquired this information from other sources. It is interesting that in his articles, Brydak reproached the Voice of Free Poland for its pro-Nazi sympathies and connections, whereas in his report to the secret police he argued that the Poles mingled little with the Czechoslovak and Hungarian staffs because they employed many "former collaborators."[116] We do not know whether Brydak sent more exhaustive reports about RFE from Munich, but there is nothing of this kind in his working file.

One of Brydak's key successes as a spy was to bring out of the VOA office "a phone book containing the full personnel listing with addresses and office and home phone numbers. The Americans had confiscated it."[117] This says a lot about the modus operandi of an intelligence agency that also used open sources. In the 1960s, the Ministry of Internal Affairs similarly attempted to obtain a copy of RFE's staff address book.

Brydak was getting ready to write a propaganda book attacking RFE. Its detailed outline indicates that he intended to deploy the same themes as in the three articles he published in *Świat*.[118] This book was never written, perhaps because the intelligence system was reorganized and experienced serious problems in 1956. It is also not out of the question that RFE's propaganda counteroffensive, which exposed Brydak as a Communist agent, was a factor. In any event, Brydak's case foreshadowed the case of another agent, Andrzej Czechowicz, which a dozen years later led to a much grander propaganda campaign.

The last notes in Brydak's folder are a dreary and grotesque (it is difficult to shake off this impression) epilogue to his spying story. In 1981, Brydak reported on every group of people he was in contact with: invalids employed by the Świt cooperative, Polish Tourist and Country Lovers' Society guides, members of the Polish Scouting Association, and the Union of Fighters for Freedom and Democracy veterans organization. He continued to harbor literary ambitions: his file contains a report titled "Scenes from ambiances," in which he lists signs he has seen at bus stops and conversations he has heard in a laundry in Smolna Street in Warsaw. The recipient of his reports was another veteran of "secret police work," Colonel Feliks Dwojak, who had headed the Provincial Office of Security in Poznań in 1956 during the workers' anticommunist revolt.[119]

The Repatriation Campaign

Using Brydak for propaganda not only served Warsaw's war on RFE, but was also an element of its huge action in 1955–1956 directed against the émigré community as a whole. The official goal of the so-called repatriation campaign was to encourage as many émigrés as possible to return to Poland.[120] A no less important (if undeclared) goal was to divide the émigré community by stirring up antagonisms and infiltrating it with agents. Coordinating, or at least inspiring, these actions, which took place not only in Poland but also in other countries of the Communist bloc, was Moscow. They were modeled on the successes of the Soviet special services in the Russian émigré community in the West in the 1920s. The Committee for Public Security played a key role in the Polish repatriation campaign. Its employees and agents were active aggressively and widely abroad, while in Poland the Polonia Association for the Development of Relations with Poles Abroad was formed.[121] The Kraj radio station broadcasting to Poles in the West, a sort of mirror image of RFE, also served as an important tool.[122] It was nowhere nearly as successful as RFE, and not only because of its content. According to a February 1956 evaluation by the committee's Department I, "the audibility of Kraj outside our borders is very weak. One can listen to it only at certain times and not on all the frequencies on which it broadcasts."[123]

Appearing on the Kraj radio station, Brydak tried to persuade émigrés that there was no point in political emigration and to discourage defections. His articles implied the same, as he described the poverty and humiliation he had experienced in the refugee camps and guard companies. His references to RFE's uncertain position in Germany were also intended to foster uncertainty among the staff. Brydak argued that after the occupation of Germany ended, the Bonn government would expel the radio. "The whole building gives the impression of being temporary, no one has thought it worthwhile to invest much in it," he wrote in *Świat*. "This presumption was right in that Freies Europa's status in West Germany really is provisional. Freies Europa perched itself in Bavaria taking advantage of its occupation status. Already, then, the Free Europe Committee had to sign an agreement with the government of Bavaria, which, under pressure from the American authorities, granted it a protective license and signed a five-year location agreement. This agreement expires in 1956. Rumors have long circulated among Freies Europa employees about RFE's planned move to Portugal, Crete, Cyprus or another Mediterranean island."[124]

It is noteworthy that the Communist secret police would spread very similar rumors about RFE's looming eviction from West Germany in the late 1960s and 1970s, when Willy Brandt's Social Democratic government adopted a policy of normalizing relations with Eastern Europe. In both cases, the intent was to press RFE employees to return to Poland or to become more receptive to collaboration with Polish intelligence.

In RFE's calculation, Brydak's appearance on Kraj radio had an impact on the Poles in the West. RFE's correspondents reported that asylum seekers in West German refugee camps and crews of Polish fishing vessels discussed his descriptions of the awful conditions of life for refugees from behind the Iron Curtain.[125] This, incidentally, indicates that the evaluation made by the Committee for Public Security about Kraj's limited reach was overly pessimistic. The responses to Brydak's programs about RFE stressed very firmly that his case revealed the real goal of the actions targeting the émigré community: "The moment that agent Brydak stepped in front of the Radio Warsaw microphone and began to publish in the Communist press, playing the assigned role of the disillusioned refugee who returned home . . . clearly revealed the methods used by Communist propaganda."[126]

For RFE, this was a battle in a very important war. One of the main themes in its programs in 1955–1956 was debunking the repatriation campaign. RFE contrasted it with the demand to allow Poles living in the Soviet Union to return (or rather to come, since many of them had never actually left Poland, as the borders changed in the wake of World War II) to Poland.[127] After October 1956, 224,000 Poles were repatriated from the Soviet Union. The Voice of Free Poland played a role in this success, though one that is difficult to measure, by incessantly reminding the world about these exiles.

The duel between RFE and the Communist propaganda remained a motif in the "struggle over the émigré community." Kraj Radio denounced RFE for being a tool in the hands of "German revanchists." Remarkably, it did not use the radio's Polish name in these pronouncements but usually its German translation, Freies Europa. Here is a sample of the rhetoric Kraj used about RFE: Commentator Kazimierz Golde asked a question that he, of course, answered himself: Do RFE's employees care "about Poland or about Adenauer and his army? About things improving in Poland or about proving themselves to those who pit them against Poland, finance them and, of course, direct them?" Zbigniew Mitzner addressed the director of the Voice of Free Poland: "It must be supremely shameful to give oneself to foreign, hostile propaganda that is the enemy of one's own country and to pretend that this point of view is Polish and not that of an enemy of Poland. *Nicht wahr, Herr Nowak?*"[128]

It is interesting that to Kraj, RFE was the bête noire of the émigré world, while, for instance, the Paris *Kultura*, even though it too was criticized, could be engaged in debate. In April 1956, Zbigniew Florczak said that *Kultura* "is not just a shoddy and gutless function of Anglo-Saxon intelligence like, for example, Free Europe."[129]

The assaults on RFE would resurface during the most spectacular incidents in the repatriation campaign, for example when Stanisław Cat-Mackiewicz returned to Poland in mid-June 1956. Already in his first press conference, at the airport, this prominent writer and former émigré prime minister took on RFE, accusing it of being an American tool in sowing ferment behind the Iron Curtain. He bundled RFE together with the Berg affair (the collaboration between some émigré circles and the CIA, uncovered in January 1953), saying that Washington's only interests in Poland were propaganda and intelligence operations. He labeled the deputy director of the Voice of Free Poland, Tadeusz Żenczykowski, a "Bergist" and "ozonowy Goebbels"—an allusion to his role in the 1930s as head of propaganda for Ozon (Obóz Zjednoczenia Narodowego, National Unity Camp).[130]

Cat-Mackiewicz's philippics against RFE were an extension of his émigré writings, in which he had been one of the most outspoken critics of the balloon leafleting program. Polish intelligence was interested in egging on this opposition. As an émigré, Cat-Mackiewicz had long maintained contacts with intelligence agents working for the Ministry of Public Security and the Committee for Public Security. He had allowed them to pay him, which is of course not to say that his writings about RFE in the émigré press did not express his own views.[131]

Kultura's columnist Juliusz Mieroszewski predicted that once Cat-Mackiewicz went back to Poland, he would disparage RFE. He wrote to *Kultura*'s editor, Jerzy Giedroyc, a few days before Cat-Mackiewicz's return: "They fund fellowships for all kinds of mediocrities in that America of theirs. It would be much cheaper for F[ree] E[urope] to have Cat on this side of the curtain and to pay him, a lot if necessary, than to have him sitting in Warsaw arguing with them. If Mackiewicz wants to blast FE, there is no one at all in Munich who can match his talent, bite and drive. And he will definitely do it because he is seething with hatred for that institution."[132]

* * *

The watershed year of 1956 was important not just from RFE's point of view but primarily for what was happening in Poland. In June 1956, crowds in Poznań destroyed equipment jamming Western radios located on the roof of a government office building. As the equipment was being thrown down into the street, the demonstrators chanted: "We want freedom!", "They will finally stop their buzzing!", and "We want to listen to the outside world unjammed!"[133] In October 1956, at the peak of the de-Stalinization movement, many rallies and demonstrations demanded an end to jamming, as did resolutions adopted by the crews of factories and offices.[134] It would be difficult to find better proof of the importance of foreign radio to the Poles at that time.

Under pressure from these demands, on October 26 the Politburo decided to continue jamming only those stations "whose programs are evidently slanderous and hostile toward Poland and which sow premeditated confusion, and this applies above all to Free Europe's programs."[135] Since Radio France and most BBC programs had not been jammed since 1955, this really meant that only the jamming of the VOA would stop.[136]

Gomułka spoke at length about jamming during a meeting with editors on October 29. The first secretary spoke openly about many important and touchy subjects, and so it is not surprising that his remarks were not included in a printed collection of his official speeches from this period. Referring to the demand for an end to jamming, he said that "it was wrong, it was completely erroneous to begin jamming these programs." But an end to interference should be tied to talks with Western governments and to "the promise that propaganda that is rooted not in reality, but in untrue facts, will be stopped. He noted that such talks were being planned with the British government, but "encouragement, demands that are frequently made by our comrades, often make it very difficult to settle these or other questions that could have been settled." At the same time, Gomułka stressed that RFE must be treated differently from the other stations: "Concerning some programs, especially Free Europe's programs, we will never stop jamming programs that have absolutely no relation to the truth, that distort that truth."[137] He clearly saw no contradiction between this declaration and his previous one that the decision to introduce jamming had been wrong.

The government delayed the announcement of its decision to suspend jamming in part, and we do not know whether it was implemented as early as October 1956. The October 29 speech by Gomułka suggests that jamming continued not only in regard to RFE. The press communiqué about the end of jamming was not published until November 25. The short note that appeared on the front page of *Trybuna Ludu* with the headline "We have stopped jamming" informs: "The government has decided that the stations jamming Polish-language programs by foreign radio stations have ended their work. The equipment and technical installations used for jamming will be used for Polish Radio communications and radio. Eliminating the jamming stations will make it possible to launch other undertakings, including starting several of our own regional stations. Let us mention that the incidents of jamming that still occur originate from stations outside Poland. The talks that have begun with the governments of our neighboring countries should shortly lead to a further improvement of reception."[138]

Earlier, on November 18, crowds demonstrating in Bydgoszcz had destroyed jamming equipment. The proximate cause of the incident was the militia's assault on several people outside the local cinema. The irate crowd challenged the guardians of order and attempted to enter the militia's Provincial Headquarters, and then moved on to the building with the jamming equipment on its roof. The marchers shouted "Enough of the jammers!", "Down with the Communists!", "Down with the reds!", and "Down with the Russians!" Despite a guard's warning shots, the crowd destroyed the equipment and set it on fire. When firemen arrived to put out the fire, the crowd threw rocks at them and slashed their rubber hoses. People observing the fire sang the national anthem and patriotic songs, including "Rota," "Boże coś Polskę," and "Bogurodzica." Never again as long as the People's Republic of Poland existed would such dramatic events occur in connection with the jamming of foreign radios, which underscores their importance during the information blockade and isolation of the Stalinist era.[139]

The day after the Bydgoszcz events, Minister of Communications Jan Rabanowski wrote to Premier Józef Cyrankiewicz: "Even though our jamming stations have stopped their work, the USSR's, Czechoslovakia's and other friendly countries' stations are still jamming Polish-language programs. Even though they have been notified about the decision on this issue in our territory, they have intensified the work of their stations in Polish territory. In this situation, the Polish population is still convinced that jamming stations are working in Poland." The minister requested that the decision to cease jamming be announced as soon as possible. "The absence of such a decision is causing growing dissatisfaction among the population to this day, and the attempts by groups of demonstrators to enter the grounds of stations, and even to wreck them, prove it. Such incidents have occurred in places that include Poznań, where a group of persons entered the grounds of an installation to check whether the installation was really working; in Cracow, where a correspondent of *Echo Krakowskie* was granted an interview to calm down the voice of the population; in Lidzbark Warmiński, where an action to destroy the installation was planned and where putting the transmitter to work for Polish Radio partly calmed the situation."[140]

Minister Rabanowski claimed that the jamming equipment destroyed in Bydgoszcz had already been switched off, as had other jamming installations across Poland. But this would contradict the Politburo's position quoted earlier, as well as Gomułka. Testimony by participants in the Bydgoszcz events also indicates that the installations they had damaged continued to be used.[141]

The minister of communications expressed his fear that "the news of the Bydgoszcz incidents may bring about similar behaviors by irresponsible elements also in other localities." He demanded: "In case of a definitive decision to liquidate the jamming service, it is absolutely necessary to call on the governments of the USSR, Czechoslovakia, Bulgaria, and Romania to end their jamming of programs in Polish."[142]

It is likely that it was the events in Bydgoszcz that finally pushed the government to stop interfering with all stations, including RFE. On December 14, 1956, the minister of internal affairs issued instructions to "stop radio protection in Poland," and the Ministry of Internal Affairs Office of Radio Communications was dissolved.[143] The Soviet Union and Czechoslovakia continued to jam, but their effectiveness was significantly diminished by the lack of cooperation from the Polish installations.[144] No documents have been found to indicate that the Polish government requested, as the minister of communications had suggested, that the governments of the other countries of the Soviet bloc stop jamming foreign programs intended for Polish audiences.

The Polish authorities resumed their systematic jamming in March 1971 and continued it until 1988. In the other countries of the Soviet bloc, decisions on interference reflected phases of liberalization and deliberalization in both domestic policies and relations with the West. The Soviet Union would jam all of Radio Liberty's programs until 1988. There were periods when it interrupted its obstruction of the BBC and the VOA, including the spring of 1956, in the wake of the Twentieth Congress of the CPSU and Khrushchev's "anti-Stalin" speech, and in 1959, during Khrushchev's visit to the United States. A longer, five-year break followed the signing of the Nuclear Test Ban Treaty in 1963. The Soviet Union resumed interfering with the VOA and the BBC during the Prague Spring; it stopped again in 1973 during the East-West détente and the preparations for the Helsinki Conference on Security and Cooperation in Europe. Soviet jamming resumed after the August 1980 events in Poland and lasted until Mikhail Gorbachev's perestroika in 1988.[145] In July 1963, Romania stopped jamming all Western radios as one of its gestures of introducing a more liberal domestic policy and distancing itself from the Soviet Union. It is noteworthy that even during Nicolae Ceauşescu's most repressive period, jamming was not restored.[146]

In January 1964, Hungary followed in Romania's footsteps. The Politburo of the Hungarian Socialist Workers' Party passed a resolution that simultaneously stopped jamming and guaranteed that installations would be kept in a state of readiness, so that interference could be resumed within forty-eight hours.[147] Czechoslovakia gradually suspended its obstruction of Western broadcasts between 1961 and 1965, with the exception of RFE and West German radio, but after the Prague Spring was suppressed it went back to full jamming.[148] Bulgaria stopped jamming the VOA in 1974 and restarted it five years later. Indeed, Bulgaria would maintain interference the longest of all the Communist countries, until March 1989.[149]

3. Władysław Gomułka's Era, 1956–1970

A Semi-Thaw

The security apparatus became much less active after the watershed events of October 1956. Triggering this retreat was outspoken public criticism of its methods, the dissolution of the Committee for Public Security and its regional offices, and the dismissal of more than nine thousand of its officers (nearly 40 percent, as of September 1956).[1] The very cautious and restrained style adopted by RFE's Polish Service in the fall of 1956 also contributed to the hiatus in Warsaw's political and propaganda assaults on it, helping to stabilize the situation in Poland, consolidate First Secretary of the PUWP Władysław Gomułka's power, and dodge a Soviet intervention.[2]

A meeting between Jan Nowak-Jeziorański and some of his associates and a delegation from the official Polish Students' Association in early March 1957 was a sign that the situation had changed. The delegation was made up of journalists writing for *Po prostu*, the popular and feisty weekly that called on the government to continue on its democratic, liberalizing course. Nowak would write in his memoirs that the *Po prostu* people admonished RFE for being too deferential toward Gomułka and for failing to request forcefully that the Polish government continue to democratize and increase its autonomy from Moscow.[3] An account of their discussion by delegation member Wiesław Adamski, deputy chairman of the Polish Students' Association Leadership Council, written for the party authorities (and copied to members of the Politburo and the CC Secretariat), indirectly corroborates Nowak's account. According to Adamski, Nowak and his people expressed the fear "lest some publications (*Po prostu*, *Przegląd Kulturalny*) and some Radio Warsaw programs and discussions among intellectuals become too radical and lead to 'aggression' (an intervention by the Soviet armed forces). . . . Everyone agrees that the tone of our press, especially *Po prostu*, challenges the Soviet Union, the people's democracies and the party conservatives, that *Po prostu* and groups close to it helped Gomułka at the right moment, but that currently they are getting in his way and doing 'anti-Polish work.' They claim that every country controls its press, and consider the attacks by *Po prostu* against it to be harmful. In their arguments, the appeals, or even pleas, for a milder tone and less radical demands were tangible."[4]

Polish intelligence also considered RFE's line to be moderate and not intended to weaken Gomułka's position or to put strains on the situation in Poland. A study from Department I (foreign intelligence) of the Ministry of Internal Affairs in February 1958 became aware of a new element in RFE's programs, "the belief that the PUWP and its predecessors, the PPR [Polska Partia Robotnicza, Polish Workers' Party] and KPP [Komunistyczna Partia Polski, Communist Party of Poland], are not foreign agents but a Polish national revolutionary current that requires help in its attempts to shed its foreign tinges and influences, because for now the Communists on top are unavoidable."[5] RFE's goal, in keeping with the State Department's beliefs, was gradually to promote Poland's independence from the Soviet Union, to underscore the differences in the Polish and the Soviet regime models, and to broaden internal civil liberties—and to do all this without removing Gomułka and the PUWP from power and without breaking openly with the Soviet bloc, at least in the short term. Certainly the Ministry of Internal Affairs interpreted the main intentions of US policy correctly.[6]

According to a February 1958 Ministry of Internal Affairs analysis, after October 1956 RFE had deferred its goal of regime change to an unspecified future date, and for the time being it intended to act as the "constructive opposition." It noted RFE's appeals to its listeners to remove antidemocratization officials from their positions, to engage in intraparty disputes (against Natolin, the more conservative Stalinist faction, and in favor of Puławy, the more liberal and anti-Stalinist faction), to cross out the names of candidates heading party lists in the January 1957 elections (actually, RFE appealed to people to cross out only the names of those candidates who were known for their Stalinist views),[7] and to support independent candidates who favored decollectivization and the private ownership of land, as well as to create independent student and worker associations and unions. Still, this otherwise quite sober, balanced, and nonideological analysis ended with the statement that RFE remained a dangerous adversary: "The above-mentioned does not of course mean that Free Europe has drastically changed its fundamentally hostile attitude toward our country: these are merely tactical moves, which, incidentally, have recently led to disputes and interpellations in the reactionary émigré activist circles. We must consider it vital to counteract RFE's ongoing hostile, destructive activities in Poland."[8]

It is remarkable that the Ministry of Internal Affairs report used almost the same term as Jan Nowak had in a 1957 programmatic memorandum to his American bosses. The Security Service mentioned a "constructive opposition," while Nowak viewed the radio as a "responsible opposition." Nowak emphasized the evolutionary scenario of changes in Poland and viewed RFE's support to both the population and those forces within the PUWP that promoted further democratization as RFE's most important goal.[9] The strategy he outlined roughly corresponded to Warsaw's analysis. There is no indication that Polish intelligence had laid its hands on Nowak's confidential memorandum, something it did not have the operational capacity to do then.

The Ministry of Internal Affairs authored two other extensive studies of RFE in this period. The first, dated August 1958, discusses the organizational structure of RFE's Polish desk and the responsibilities of its various units and staff, and includes more detailed biographical sketches of employees than in earlier documents. It summarizes Nowak's position thus: "He favors the Polish Section's autonomy with respect to its American patrons. He describes the radio's tactics toward Poland as serving as a 'constructive opposition' and as having the ability to say what Poland cannot because of geopolitical conditions."[10] This newer and better understanding of the Polish desk largely stemmed from the fact that RFE's contacts with visitors from Poland had increased since October 1956, and there was no shortage of secret agents among them.[11]

The second ministry paper focused on RFE's information analysis section (with its changing name of Evaluation, Evaluation and Research, and finally Research and Analysis), which provided materials for programming. "Experienced individuals who are familiar with other installations of this type and understand this type of work claim that no other archive exists with information about the Eastern countries to match this one, in terms of the quantities of materials, the archive of RFE's Department of Evaluation and Use of Information. . . . The main suppliers of these materials are the 16 outposts subordinated to Radio Free Europe," assessed the Security Service.[12] We know now that in 1958, the ministry was conducting operations not only among the Munich staff and against the Free Europe Committee (FEC) in New York, but also in RFE offices in Berlin, Paris, and Stockholm.[13]

The operation to expose Bogumił Brydak serves as evidence that the ministry's interest in the radio's Research and Analysis Department, and especially the materials it collected, continued to grow. Until July 1957, Brydak headed RFE's Frankfurt office, whose work included collecting information from refugees from Poland; he then moved to Munich, where he was employed in the archive. In 1955, the secret police attempted to contact him through his wife and sister living in Poland. It contemplated recruitment by luring him to East Berlin to meet with his wife. It also considered bringing him there by a ruse (his wife's sudden illness during her stay in Berlin) or by force. The ministry knew from a secret collaborator using the alias Górski, a good friend of Brydak's in Munich, that Brydak had had a drunk-driving accident and that he had not informed his superiors at the radio about it. In 1959, Górski suggested the following course of action: "Fearing a major sentence and subsequent difficulties, we could offer to sneak him into Poland with this arrangement: material compensation and guarantee of a job in return for some part of the file collection."[14] There are no available documents to confirm that the ministry actually did anything to launch either of these options, but Brydak's case is a good illustration of the importance to Warsaw of gaining access to the section of RFE's archive containing information about its sources in Poland. This would continue to be a focal goal of Polish intelligence over the next dozen or so years.

The Rusty Nail in US-Polish Relations

For a few years after October 1956, the Ministry of Internal Affairs made no major moves against RFE. But Poland's Foreign Ministry remained active as it tried to take advantage of the temporary warming in relations between Warsaw and Washington to weaken the "hostile" radio's position. It put pressure on Ambassador Jacob Beam, who believed that the United States should support the post–October 1956 Polish government. Warsaw issued its first protests as early as January 1957, when RFE's Polish Service appealed to its listeners to cross out the names of more than a dozen candidates on ballots for the Sejm elections, those who were most discredited by their Stalinist pasts. These protests led the State Department to issue a stern reprimand to the radio's leadership and to threaten to introduce preventive censorship.[15] Nowak had to succumb to this powerful pressure, and evening programs on the eve of the election and on voting day warned listeners at the last minute that crossing out the names of official candidates would weaken Gomułka's position and increase the possibility of a Stalinist comeback or even of a Soviet intervention.[16] The French ambassador Éric de Carbonnel wrote to his ministry that RFE's words may have had a real influence on voters' choices.[17] This incident confirms the importance of RFE, but, even more important, it provides an example of the effectiveness of an intervention by the Polish government.

Polish foreign minister Adam Rapacki complained about RFE during his visit to the United States in October 1957. In a conversation with Secretary of State John Foster Dulles, he stressed that the Polish government had abandoned jamming, but in return expected that foreign radio stations would not interfere in Poland's domestic affairs. Rapacki compared RFE's existence to the other unresolved issue lingering after the Cold War, the division of Germany.[18]

Rapacki's statement about RFE may have served as an additional reason for various government agencies in Washington to subject the radio station to close scrutiny, which brought on the problems discussed in the first chapter of this book: program limitations and outright closing. But it appears that the main reason for Washington's focus on the station now was the shock of the Hungarian tragedy and the general interest in reorienting US policy toward the Communist bloc.

The government of Poland maintained its pressure, no doubt realizing that some people in the US government viewed RFE unfavorably. First Secretary Władysław Gomułka himself criticized RFE during Vice President Richard Nixon's visit to Warsaw in August 1959. This criticism was preplanned and part of a larger, more comprehensive strategy that had been devised jointly with the Foreign Ministry.[19] "We must shut down, finish off this repulsive work. It's a rusty nail being used to split open the promising fruit of bilateral Polish-American relations. Such propaganda is immensely harmful," the first secretary maintained—in vain, since Nixon showed no sympathy for this argument. For his part, the vice president talked about how, when he had visited Caracas, Venezuela, in May 1958, he had been attacked by a crowd incited by Radio Moscow.[20] Jan Nowak came to view Nixon, after his trip to Warsaw, as one of RFE's biggest champions in Washington. Contributing to Nixon's perspective was probably also the welcome he had received from Warsaw's enthusiastic crowds, whose information about his route through the city could only have come from RFE since Poland's official media did not mention it.[21]

But the Warsaw government did not give up. In the autumn of 1959, Foreign Minister Rapacki met with Secretary of State Christian Herter and accused RFE of upsetting US-Polish relations. Herter responded that Washington was trying to impose tighter control on RFE.[22] The Foreign Ministry took this as confirmation that the Polish strategy was correct. A note written in October 1959 assessed that "even though we must not expect Free Europe to be closed down quickly, the talks we have conducted clearly indicate that the Americans will impose a change of tone on these programs, leaving the final decision as a bargaining chip in potential broader agreements on cultural exchanges—and with the Soviet Union as well."[23]

The controversies about RFE's future reached American and European newspapers. Warsaw had additional information from intelligence sources. In January 1960, the Ministry of Internal Affairs prepared a study about RFE's future. From the Polish government's perspective, it must have looked promising: "The question of Radio Free Europe's future remains a topic of discussions and deliberations for various Western actors. Because of developments in the international situation in the wake of Vice President Nixon's visit to the USSR and Poland and Premier Khrushchev's to the USA, as well as the expiration in 1960 of the FRG government's license for the radio's operations in Munich, there has been talk in political and émigré circles in the West of the possibility of shutting down RFE. According to information we have, in October 1959 American decision makers, after long deliberations, approved the RFE Polish Section's budget only until July 1960."[24]

In the same document, Polish intelligence cited details of the discussions between the US State Department and the Vatican Secretariat of State. The US government had allegedly offered to transfer RFE to the Vatican. No evidence of these plans and discussions has been found, so the issue remains an enigma. Did Department I of the Ministry of Internal Affairs really come across traces of confidential discussions, traces that are now buried? Or was this a misunderstanding, or a case of false information? The latter explanation seems more likely.

Pressure picked up in early 1960 during a visit to the United States by Vice Premier Piotr Jaroszewicz. The Polish Foreign Ministry believed there was a chance that the radio would be shut down. In his conversation with the secretary of state, Jaroszewicz accused RFE of interfering in Polish domestic affairs and thereby disrupting US-Polish relations. After the visit, Poland sent a memorandum with a list of examples of RFE broadcasts critical of Gomułka's government.[25]

Attempts to take advantage of RFE's difficult position in the second half of the 1950s and the beginning of the 1960s ultimately failed, despite the many signals from Washington that had inspired hope in Warsaw. After several years of negotiations and occasionally very serious disputes between the State Department and RFE, a modus vivendi was established that allowed the station to operate in relative calm for the next ten years. Within a few years of October 1956, the Polish government's ability to exert pressure on the United States diminished significantly. Gomułka's team was treated less as anti-Stalinist, "schismatic," and interested in gaining autonomy from Moscow. Washington was no longer afraid that harsh criticism of the Gomułka government would harm ties between Poland and the West and weaken US influence on the situation in Poland.[26] The Polish government would not have another opportunity to launch a political and diplomatic offensive until the late 1960s and early 1970s, with the double complication of Willy Brandt's *Ostpolitik* and RFE's serious new problems in the United States.

In the period immediately following the Polish October, Warsaw's diplomatic offensive was not accompanied by stepped-up propaganda against RFE in Poland, certainly not on the scale of what had occurred in the first half of the 1950s. Perhaps the only publication matching the viciousness and deceit of that earlier time was a three-part series of articles about RFE in October 1959 in *Polityka*. Its author, whose byline was the initials D. P., accused the radio and its staff of all possible crimes and misdemeanors, these accusations styled along the lines of Stalinist propaganda: spying for the United States, serving German interests, collaborating with German revisionist circles, abandoning the Oder-Neisse line, "pathologically chasing after dollars and US passports," engaging in "orgies," and "squealing on colleagues to the Americans and to the dictator Nowak."[27] Nowak appeared in this trilogy as the villain: "Let's take the example of their boss, who, guided by the last bits of shame he has left, appeared everywhere (also on 'the Voice of Free Poland') under the pseudonym Jan Nowak, but whose name is in fact Zdzisław Jeziorański, and who comes from Poznań Province. His officer's career ended in 1929 when he was removed from the army by General Zając because of mental illness and certain unattractive habits that should not be mentioned in polite society."[28]

In his memoirs, Jan Nowak-Jeziorański wrote that Daniel Passent, who in the 1970s and 1980s became a well-known Polish journalist, was the author of these articles.[29] Passent later confirmed that he had initialed the "edited materials that he had received officially via his Editors."[30] The three texts were a mélange of lies, insinuations, and minute details of events, some of which had taken place many years earlier (in the early days of the radio, the "balloon war"). They even used excerpts from articles in the émigré press critical of RFE. Only the Ministry of Internal Affairs possessed this information, and the *Polityka* articles smacked of having originated there.[31]

The End of the Thaw: Sanctions against "Sabotage" Partners in Poland

The war against RFE resumed in the early 1960s, ending the few years of diminished hostilities in which the Ministry of Internal Affairs had limited itself primarily to the first phase of operational investigation of the Munich staff and freelancer reporters. This was part of the PUWP's post-October policies aimed at eliminating or limiting the areas of autonomy wrested by Polish society in 1956, when the system was in deep crisis. After the government had restored full censorship to publications and culture, extensively purged editorial offices, and folded the most brazen publications, foremost among them the weekly *Po prostu*, it turned to persecuting individuals and groups who maintained contacts with "hostile centers" in the West, especially those who, in the opinion of the secret police and party leadership, sent information and documents abroad.[32] This became, in historian Krzysztof Persak's words, a "peculiar obsession" for Gomułka and some of his associates. It probably also originated from Nikita Khrushchev's reprimands of the Polish Communists, on occasions that included a meeting in May 1957. At that meeting Khrushchev very sternly admonished Gomułka, saying that secrets, including military ones, entrusted to Poland were being leaked to the West.[33]

It did not take long for repercussions, arrests, and trials to begin. Hanna Szarzyńska-Rewska, accused of distributing copies of the Paris *Kultura*, was arrested in January 1958 and in July was sentenced to three years in prison. In September 1961, Anna Rudzińska was arrested and sentenced to a year in prison for translating a book on sociology that the *Kultura*-affiliated Institut Littéraire in Paris was planning to publish. Regardless of the details of the charges in the indictments, both cases were intended to serve as a very solemn warning to all those who maintained contacts with foreign organizations and relayed information about the situation in Poland to the West.[34]

In December 1961, the secret police arrested the journalist Henryk Holland, an associate of the party "revisionists." He was accused of relaying news about the Twenty-Second Congress of the Communist Party of the Soviet Union that was making the rounds in the Warsaw party elite to a journalist with *Le Monde*. Holland died (a suicide, according to Krzysztof Persak) by falling out of a window. He was widely declared a victim of the secret police and his death by defenestration a symbol of the brutality that the government was yet again resorting to. His funeral became a demonstration for intellectuals and party activists opposed to bringing back repressions, which would overturn whatever remained of the October reforms. In response, the government staged hearings before a committee put together by the party leadership, which were often chaired by Gomułka himself, and harassed some of the people who had attended Holland's funeral. At one of the hearings, Gomułka charged the funeral participants with "helping Free Europe" practice hostile propaganda.[35] In this atmosphere, RFE, which commented on all important events in Poland and strived to acquire as much information as possible about government policies and the moods among the party elite and the creative intelligentsia, was yet again becoming an important enemy.

Gomułka harshly attacked groups that maintained contacts with "hostile centers" in the West during the so-called ideological plenum of the CC PUWP in July 1963. He began with the assertion that the center of gravity in the competition between the capitalist world and the socialist camp (in official terminology, this was the phase of "peaceful coexistence") had moved toward ideological confrontation. It was the West's intention to weaken the socialist regime gradually by using propaganda conducted by "centers of sabotage" and through "penetrating" culture, learning, and the arts. "Because of our country's key strategic and political location, because of the specific nature of our historical development, we have long been exposed to the cumulative and especially intensive propaganda attacks by imperialist forces, which extensively take advantage of the services of the reactionary émigrés," Gomułka explained to the plenum's participants.[36] He decried the relaying of information about goings-on in Poland to the West. "The information and political gossip that hostile foreign centers have acquired," the first secretary warned, referring chiefly to Holland's case, "were neatly exploited for activities that included practicing sabotage propaganda aimed against our party and against Poland. Articles and radio programs about group divisions and contests within the party were cooked up on the basis of these materials, intending to stir up confusion and distrust in our ranks."[37]

In the ensuing discussion, Mieczysław Moczar, vice-minister of internal affairs, who oversaw Department I's foreign intelligence work and whose duties included fighting RFE, attacked the radio. He accused the US embassy in Warsaw of gathering information about Polish attitudes toward its broadcasts and thereby "fine-tuning RFE's programs." He argued that the war's main front ran differently from the 1950s: "We have long stopped focusing on the spies who photograph our distinguished ships *Błyskawica* or *Grom*. . . . In their fight with the socialist camp, the imperialists make it their main mission to organize ideological sabotage and to spread it by any means and capacities." Moczar also challenged RFE's assertions that writings by journalists in the socialist countries were "made to order."[38]

The prominent writer Jerzy Putrament then argued that "we are under incredible pressure from hostile propaganda. We are the target of the enemy's incessant mangling by radio."[39] Michalina Tatarkówna, first secretary of the Łódź Committee of the PUWP, wrote that RFE took advantage of every demonstration of even constructive criticism that appeared in the Polish press. She used the example of Hanna Krall's article in *Życie Warszawy*, which discussed how factories in Łódź abided by labor laws; the article was then quoted in a radio program by Jacek Śniady (the radio name of Jerzy Szyszko-Bohusz) to attack the executive committee of the Łódź PUWP.[40]

The Letter of the 34

The next phase of attacks on RFE came with the Letter of the 34, which was delivered to Premier Józef Cyrankiewicz on March 14, 1964. All available evidence indicates that the government would not have reacted so violently to the intellectuals' protest against the tightening of censorship and limitations on book publishing had it not been for RFE's broadcast of the contents of the letter, references to it, and discussions of it in many of its programs. Gomułka accused the signatories not so much of writing the letter but of informing "sabotage radio stations" about it even before the government could respond to their demands.[41]

The protest against RFE's and other foreign organizations' use of the letter was the focus of the Polish government's propaganda campaign, which included the so-called counterletters: the Letter of the 10, which was signed by some of the same persons who had signed the Letter of the 34 and was published in the *Times*, and another, much more aggressive letter. The authorities compelled some six hundred writers to sign the latter, a significant number insofar as the membership of the Writers' Union was less than one thousand. The signatories declared: "We, the undersigned writers, are expressing our firm protest against the organized campaign maligning People's Poland that is being cultivated in the Western press and on the radio waves of the saboteur Free Europe."[42]

As signatures were being collected for the counterletter, Gomułka received members of the governing council of the Polish Writers' Union. He conveyed his views of the intellectuals' protest and the role RFE was to have played in it very emotionally. Since this was not a public statement, it is a faithful rendition of the man who at the time ruled Poland. "We must ask: What was it all about? Is it a coincidence that over 30 intellectuals have nothing to say in their letter to the head of the government but a handful of unkindnesses?" Gomułka posed this rhetorical question only to answer it himself a moment later: "No, it is no coincidence! Because their action was not intended as a letter to the premier but as a letter to Free Europe, to anti-Polish sabotage-intelligence centers. There is no doubt about this whatsoever, even if we had absolutely no other evidence. But we do have evidence."

The conclusive evidence he referred to was the writer Antoni Słonimski's role as the protest's *spiritus movens*. According to Gomułka, Słonimski was taking revenge for the embargo on his articles in the satirical weekly *Szpilki*. "Is this really in the least proportional to the dimensions of the smear campaign being pursued by Free Europe?" Gomułka asked again. He also grieved that Słonimski had refused to denounce RFE and to sign the counterletter: "We did ask Mr. Słonimski to declare that Free Europe had spat on his country, to take a stand as a citizen of this country, to declare that this is his country and that he is cutting himself off from this slanderous campaign being pursued by Free Europe. And how did Mr. Słonimski react? He does not wish to cut himself off from Free Europe. So as long as Mr. Słonimski views Free Europe as his pulpit, there can be no discussion."[43]

It would be difficult to consider this statement to be fully rational. It confirms the first secretary's aversion to discussing any real problems that might have been the source of the intellectuals' protest and his obsessive focus on RFE's "antagonistic" inspiration.

The Trial of Melchior Wańkowicz

The arrest on October 5, 1964, of Melchior Wańkowicz, one of Poland's most prominent writers, was a direct consequence of the Letter of the 34. Wańkowicz was accused of sending the text of a speech he had not yet given, which was prepared for the June meeting of the Warsaw chapter of the Polish Writers' Union, to RFE. He had indeed sent its text, which discussed the chicanery against the signatories of the Letter of the 34, to his daughter, Marta Erdman, living in Washington, D.C., via the US ambassador. RFE broadcast excerpts from it in July without revealing its author's name. It was the CC PUWP Secretariat that made the decision to arrest Wańkowicz, on the one hand to rein in the willful creative intelligentsia and on the other to intimidate all those who had been delivering information to "hostile centers" abroad.[44] The writer was sentenced to three years in prison, even though the authorities had no evidence that he had intended to send his speech to RFE. He was released from jail in November 1964 because of poor health. An amnesty cut his sentence by half, and he never served it.[45]

It seems that the government did not realize all its goals by staging Wańkowicz's show trial. Intelligence reported that "more intensive listening to Free Europe among all social strata, and especially among the intelligentsia, is a very typical reaction to the trial."[46] According to Nowak, the consequences of the attacks on RFE relating to the Letter of the 34 included an upsurge in RFE's contacts with Poland and a greater influx of information.[47] Minister of Internal Affairs Franciszek Szlachcic confirmed this in a 1971 meeting of propaganda secretaries of the provincial committees of the PUWP when he said that "the greatest flow of information and correspondence to the centers of sabotage occurred in 1965, when tens of thousands of items of information were sent to these centers from Poland."[48]

The question remains, how did the secret police obtain Wańkowicz's speech, which it used as evidence in his indictment? Witness Major Tadeusz Cibor, an intelligence officer and earlier an employee of the Polish embassy in Washington, testified that he had acquired the incriminating material "while performing work functions."[49] According to Wańkowicz's daughter, Gomułka told Wańkowicz in January 1965 that the secret police had photographed a copy of the writer's speech at the US embassy in Warsaw before she had managed to send it to Munich, as was her father's wish.[50] A clue confirming this interpretation is a memorandum from the Ministry of Internal Affairs to Gomułka on the eve of his meeting with the Writers' Union. Because Wańkowicz had distributed copies of his speech to some of his friends in Warsaw and also denied sending the text to RFE, the ministry suggested that he should be warned "that should he distribute the mentioned materials any further, the Ministry of Internal Affairs will announce publicly the real route he had used to send these materials abroad."[51]

Portraying the Enemy

The Ministry of Internal Affairs shaped and coproduced Gomułka's and other top leaders' views and decisions as it supplied information about threats to the socialist system. Beginning in the early 1960s, the roles played by RFE, the Paris *Kultura*, and other "imperialist" centers continued to grow. The feedback naturally went in both directions: reacting to the impulses flowing from the seat of power, the security apparatus notched up its war against the foreign "ideological-political sabotage" organizations (in 1962–1963, the party and the secret police began to use this term regularly), increasingly focusing on the "hostile centers" that inspired the system's opponents in Poland; it also attempted to find and cut off the channels through which information was being sent to the West.

One of the earliest comprehensive assessments of the dangers coming from the foreign centers was written in late June 1963 by the Security Service Unit at the Ministry of Internal Affairs, a body most likely made up of representatives of the main operational departments. Some sections of this document largely match what Gomułka said about foreign sabotage at an ideological plenum in early July. It is very likely that his speechwriters used the Ministry of Internal Affairs study.

The first sentence of the study reads: "In conducting the uncovering of antagonistic activity over the last 2 years, one can observe facts pointing to the broadening and intensifying of penetration by the intelligence services, as well as an intensification of activity characterized by ideological-political sabotage against Poland and other socialist countries." It goes on to present the mechanisms and goals of this "sabotage" and stresses the new aspects of the threat: "The strategy and tactics of imperialism's political struggle against our camp have fundamentally changed. . . . Intelligence and political sabotage used as methods in the struggle against the socialist countries have been elevated to the rank of the United States' and other NATO countries' state policies. . . . The state leaders take part in directly leading and supervising intelligence and sabotage activity. They have excavated and exposed various forms of struggle of the ideological-political sabotage type that aim to sow ideological confusion, to stir up disbelief in the ideals of socialism, to shatter the unity of the socialist camp, to cause quarrels among the workers' parties, to prop up revisionist and liberal-bourgeois tendencies in the countries of the socialist camp. . . . They take the stirring up of a 'psychological war' as one of the key means aiming to 'shatter Communism' from the inside, to transfer from the 'politics of liberation' to the road of the strategy of 'softening Communism,' calculated to develop so-called ideological ferment."[52]

The Ministry of Internal Affairs believed that outside factors had inspired the writers' protest. "RFE and *Kultura* played a key role in preparing the Letter of the 34. . . . We are observing antagonistic and harmful political activity by some Warsaw writers whose contents coincide with the opinions pronounced by RFE. They are fanning antiparty sentiments from antisocialist positions, using the arguments of the anticommunist foreign centers, attacking the party mostly for its cultural policies," read the report about the situation in Poland by the Office of the Minister of Internal Affairs.[53]

Yet in the opinion of the Ministry of Internal Affairs, neither the propaganda campaign about the Letter of the 34 nor the harassment and repressions directed at its signatories reached their goals. A meeting of the ministry's leadership concluded that "to summarize the outcome of the action relating to the Letter of the 34, the leadership organs of the psychological war have decided to expand their activity related to organizing collective actions in Poland, which in their opinion were to be an excellent method of putting pressure on the party and state apparatus."[54] Accordingly, the main focus chosen by the "saboteurs" were the creative intelligentsia and young people.[55]

In the mid-1960s, as the situation in Poland stabilized, the Security Service determined that the external "sabotage" centers constituted the principal threat to the system. The 1965 annual report from Department III (responsible for combating internal political opponents) affirmed that there had been "a decrease in expressions of unfriendly activity within our country" and that attempts to disturb political peace had occurred only because of "anticommunist centers' clamoring for a boycott of the elections" and efforts to "bring about states of tension and matters to a boil in Poland."[56] A May 1966 document formulated this thesis even more clearly: "in the area of class warfare, the front has clearly moved to the abroad–at home axis."[57]

This provocation of antisystemic behaviors from abroad supposedly influenced not only the intellectuals' protests but also the formation of conspiratorial youth groups. This charge appears in the 1964 report from Department III: "Some of these groups had 'programs' with slogans calling for speaking out against the state authorities. The contents of these slogans were frequently similar to Radio Free Europe's antagonistic propaganda."[58]

Statements of this type, and even more forceful ones about people who started illegal organizations as a direct result of listening to RFE, made "hostile" signs, or distributed anonymous letters and fliers, and even "groups amassing arms and ammunition" who attempted to contact the radio, were repeated in the ministry's writings in subsequent years.[59] Some reports used astonishingly precise data. For instance, in 1962, under the influence of so-called foreign saboteurs, thirty-five groups allegedly were created, with a total membership of 197, and in 1966 there were six groups comprising forty conspirators. In 1967 in the town of Łowicz, a "6-person illegal organization called the Military Anticommunist Organization created as a result of listening to RFE" was allegedly exposed.[60] To confirm all this information would require studying dispersed documents from investigations of youth conspiracy groups. But it is also possible that the assertion about encouragement by RFE is less a reflection of reality than of the mentality of Security Service employees, something that is crucial to our understanding of the way the Ministry of Internal Affairs waged war against RFE.

From the ministry's point of view, RFE also played a role in encouraging the March 1968 student revolt. Typically, as Jerzy Eisler points out, fliers distributed at the University of Warsaw in the days prior to a rally on March 8 warned students that "Michnik, Blumsztajn, Szlajfer and their band are trying to create unease among us. . . . In fact, they are expressing the interests of their patrons, the Zionists and RFE. . . . They care about brawls, scuffles and publicity on RFE."[61]

The conceptual and even linguistic clichés propagated by the ministry are also reflected in a flier titled "Whom do you support?," which appeared on the grounds of the university in the morning of March 8 before the rally began. It exposed those who had inspired the rally: "Adam Michnik, son of Ozjasz Szechter. He took lessons in provocation and political brawls from Kuroń and Modzelewski, the group's well-known leader. Permanent and distinguished Radio Freies Europa informant. . . . Henryk Szlajfer . . . activist of the 'Babel' club, valued by Western correspondents, supplier of information to Freies Europa."[62]

According to the Ministry of Internal Affairs, slogans relating to RFE appeared during the demonstrations and street unrest in Warsaw. The Department III list has "The press is lying! Listen to Free Europe!" in first place. It was allegedly accompanied by equally or more radical ones: "Let's not spare stones and bricks for militiamen and other sons of bitches," "Down with Gomułka's and the USSR's rule," "Down with Communism," "We will avenge Katyń. Let's throw off the Soviet yoke," and "Beat the PUWP. Grab our weapons."[63] This list of slogans is included in the collection of materials the ministry distributed to the party leadership. The materials were intended to impress on Gomułka the ministry leadership's perspective on the events under way and to sustain him in the conviction that it was necessary to use force. Reports prepared by local Security Services offices, which were not intended for use by the PUWP's leadership, are more credible. For example, a report from Nowa Huta argued that "an unhealthy atmosphere . . . dominates in the worker hostels. Seventy-five percent of their inhabitants are outspoken in their praise for the events, malign the party and the government and listen individually or collectively to Free Europe's radio programs late into the night."[64]

In another case, in Lublin, someone set the public radio in the Student Housing Complex to Free Europe, and by "leaning a cupboard skillfully against the door, blocked it from the inside after leaving the room. The broadcast of Free Europe's programs was stopped by switching off the fuses located outside that room. Because of the above, the appropriate steps were taken: an operational-investigative group was created with the goal of uncovering the perpetrators."[65]

One of the most important documents of the mass movement, the proclamation adopted on the first day of the strike at Warsaw Polytechnic, mentioned RFE. The students demanded: "We request truthful information in the mass media. We do not want to obtain our information from sources such as the Free Europe station, which, even though it is currently telling the true version of the events in Poland, is basically antisocialist and anti-Soviet. Our requests include having public information in Poland that will not lie."[66]

Here it is interesting that the students both criticized the Polish mass media, contrasting them with the truthful RFE, and subjected RFE to ritualistic criticism, in the same way as it was presented at the time in official propaganda: as a primary enemy of socialism, a true political and ideological monstrosity. It is difficult to tell whether this language represented the stereotypes lodged in the young people's minds or was a tactical device that the strikers used in an effort to enter into a dialogue with those in power.

The goal of foreign "sabotage," in the eyes of the Ministry of Internal Affairs, was not only to motivate the declared enemies of socialism but also to influence the party itself, to create conflicts and divisions inside it. Such sabotage allegedly used two methods. The first entailed supporting the "revisionists," primarily intellectuals who called themselves Marxists, were former or current members of the PUWP, and were demanding further liberalization and reforms. To achieve this, these external centers abandoned their openly anti-communist, Cold War rhetoric. "This is an expression of the 'fine-tuning' with which hostile centers reacted to the new situation in Poland, where those who speak up in a hostile way today do not use slogans aimed directly at the socialist regime but are playing from a position of 'socialism's healers.'"[67] The second method was exemplied by RFE's attacks on Deputy Minister (from 1964 Minister) of Internal Affairs Mieczysław Moczar's Partisans, a nationalist faction including elite party members, who were trying to win power in the party and the state. The Security Service assessed the anti-Moczar campaign being waged by RFE's Polish desk as libelous, but its documents presented it—for the first time since 1963—as a serious threat to the party's cohesion.[68]

One of the reasons why the Ministry of Internal Affairs fought RFE with such great zeal in the 1960s was likely RFE's consistent unmasking of the Partisans, which began in 1962 with Jan Nowak's decision to attack Moczar's faction, prompted by information Nowak had received from people at the top of the party leadership, including Foreign Minister Adam Rapacki and the well-known economist and PUWP CC member Oskar Lange.[69] Indeed, the Security Service realized fairly quickly that the leaks to Munich came from high up. It had received information from Polish intelligence that RFE's first program about the Partisans had used sources "delivered by a person who occupies a top party position in Poland. Texts or minutes of Politburo meetings also reach Munich from the same source via London or New York."[70]

The party elite also reacted vigorously to RFE's attention to the Partisan theme. *Dzienniki polityczne 1958–1962* [Political diaries 1958–1962] by Mieczysław Rakowski, editor in chief of the weekly *Polityka*, who was in close contact with many PUWP leaders, testify to this. The August 14, 1962, entry reads: "About two months ago, Radio FE broadcast two programs about the relationship of forces in the Polish party's leadership team. They devoted a lot of space to the so-called partisan group, i.e., Moczar, Korczyński, etc. FE claims that this group wants to take over the key positions in the party, that it is fundamentally anti-Gomułka, but even more anti-intelligentsia. The programs caused much mayhem in the apparatus in the so-called political circles in Warsaw."

Rakowski spoke with Zenon Kliszko, the number two man in the party, about conducting press interviews with CC secretaries. Kliszko expressed a reservation lest this flaunt divisions in the party leadership. "'You know, comrade,' he said, 'interviews on different topics may expose differences. Yes, there are differences, there even should be differences, but what is the point of displaying them in public, especially now, after the FE programs?' Then we talked a lot about these very programs. . . . This whole issue clearly interests him. When I spoke with Loga [Ignacy Loga-Sowiński, Politburo member and chairman of the Central Council of Labor Unions—P. M.], I had the same impression. Loga did talk about this a lot. He also wondered who had transmitted them."[71] What an excellent example of RFE's influence on the situation in Poland, of the degree to which the party leadership paid attention to it!

Beginning in 1967 a very important new element appeared in the "picture of the enemy": RFE was presented as an institution prompted or even directed by Jews and "Zionists." There were several reasons for this theme. First was the presence of people with "pro-Zionist" views on the editorial staff. Second, because "persons of Jewish nationality, who immediately after leaving Poland began to collaborate or make contact with these centers, have played an essential role as informants [about the situation in Poland]. We received information in 1967–68 telling us that revisionists and Zionists from Poland were keeping the centers of political and ideological sabotage, including RFE, apprised of the situation there, and they explained political problems there with a bias," read a Ministry of Internal Affairs report in January 1969.[72]

Third, RFE was presented as being predisposed to the influence of Israel and of an unspecified "leadership of a Zionist organization." A July 1969 Ministry of Internal Affairs Department I document written in openly anti-Semitic language describes RFE (and the Paris *Kultura*) as an organization that was manipulated by Jews: "Jewish émigrés from the People's Republic, who back in Poland as a rule held exposed positions in the party apparatus, the mass media, scholars, writers and so on, are the main engine for creating a broad front in the battle against Communism. Their gradual gnawing and constant inciting of hatred for the Polish nation through a variety of channels accessible to them in Israeli government circles and the local leaderships of Zionist organizations create a climate that favors adopting the idea of creating a broad front in the battle of an anticommunist nature. Elements in the Israeli government are also not indifferent to engaging such centers as RFE or *Kultura* for its sabotage and to using these centers to do Israel's job; at the same time, this creates an opportunity to remove the blame from itself and to shift the burden onto the 'Polish' sabotage centers."[73]

A similar attitude appeared not only in analytical documents written for the ministry's top officials but also in strictly operational actions, and even in the "elite" foreign intelligence of Department I. The resident spy in Vienna, Henryk Wróblewicz, established a system of communication with a freshly recruited agent code-named "Kondor," a young Pole who traveled in émigré and refugee circles. They agreed on five key words to use on postcards and in letters between the agent and his case officer. The first three referred to the institutions and milieus to which "Kondor" was to gain access: "Karol" was RFE, "Agata" the Paris *Kultura*, and "Róża" denoted "Zionist organizations." The remaining two were "Norka" (little burrow), for Jews, and "marriage—contacts with Jews," Wróblewicz informed the central office.[74]

The anti-Zionist obsession of the ministry that for many years was the main nursery of anti-Semitism in Poland survived until the early 1970s—in other words, at least a few years after Minister of Internal Affairs Mieczysław Moczar left office, in July 1968. As late as 1971–1972, the majority of the ministry's studies of RFE stressed its "Zionist" orientation.

Scouts, Athletic Competitions, and "a Socialist Anti–Free Europe"

The Ministry of Internal Affairs was the main organization responsible for combating what was deemed Western sabotage, both analytically and operationally. Yet beginning in the mid-1960s, other institutions became increasingly focused on this subject, and they adopted the perspective of the security apparatus. The production of a long paper titled "Imperialism's Activities in the Areas of Foreign Propaganda, Psychological Warfare and Ideological Sabotage and Our Counteraction" by an interagency committee made up of representatives of the CC PUWP, the Ministry of Internal Affairs, the Ministry of Defense, and the Foreign Ministry reveals the importance of the threat from the "sabotage" forces to top government officials.

The report, which took several months to write, following a resolution of the National Defense Committee in January 1966, analyzed the workings of the most important Western information and propaganda institutions, including RFE and other radio stations. It began with the assertion that since the early 1960s, "psychological warfare," "ideological-political sabotage," and propaganda (it treated these concepts as synonymous) had become increasingly important weapons for the United States and other Western countries to use in their war against the Soviet bloc. "The 'doctrine of softening,' which was in force during Kennedy's presidency, has been replaced by Johnson's policy of 'building bridges' to Eastern Europe, which is based on the concept of so-called selective coexistence," posited the paper. "It is the nature of this policy to try to shatter the unity of the socialist states—using this method—and to shift the balance of power in the world in favor of imperialism. The policy of 'building bridges' strongly ties forms of achieving its goals to the activization of the American ideological front. The new term 'the United States' ideological offensive,' which reflects the increased interest in this front and its growing role in the USA's foreign policy, has appeared in official American statements."[75]

Poland was to be the main target of the West's "sabotage-ideological" attack "because of its key strategic and political location, its political role in the Socialist system," while the most important "channel of activity" was propaganda by radio. The paper pointed out that the "sabotage radio stations" broadcast the most in Polish (thirty-eight "program hours, i.e., original programs," whereas the Czechoslovak program, for example, was only twenty-seven hours). RFE was most important because of its "extremely offensive type of activity" and because it had the greatest volume of broadcasting of the offending stations. The study estimated that RFE's "Polish-language programs make up 85 percent of all the time devoted to sabotage and propaganda aimed at Poland by all the Western radios."[76]

A proposal to take up a long-term competition with RFE by creating new domestic and international radio stations was an interesting feature of this interagency report. It began with a recommendation to "start a domestic program of a highly attractive, argumentative and antisabotage nature on the short waves." The program would consist of "selected, most attractive positions of the First, Second and Third Programs" and broadcast "on a range of frequencies close to Western radios, especially RFE (aiming to create a sort of unique 'jamming' of the program)." The proposal to "create a program structure that would be an attractive alternative to Western radio programs" and "over time as far as possible also to guarantee a similar chronological schedule of programs" pays a distinctive homage to RFE's radio abilities.

The first stage of the plan for the new program was to use low-power transmitters that the armed forces were phasing out (the Scout radio station operated similarly), and in the long term the report proposed "conducting the necessary international discussions within the Warsaw Pact on the issue of broadcasting to Poland on the Fourth Program by stations of friendly countries, the USSR and the HSR [Hungarian Socialist Republic] (Poland can be completely blanketed with short waves only with added help from outside its borders)."[77] The plan covered a multiyear period: it considered that the broadcast of a full, twenty-four-hour Fourth Program, announced to start during the Eighth Plenum of the CC PUWP in May 1967, could begin no earlier than 1973.

The launch of this program was promised repeatedly, but it suffered from delays. It was finally begun in January 1976.[78] Earlier, the method of offsetting RFE, as conceived by the party decision makers, had consisted of the programs of Scout Radio, which had begun in 1957 with transmitters donated by the army. A few years into its activity, the radio obtained new, more powerful transmitters and a new, much better frequency, this time from the Ministry of Internal Affairs. The initial euphoria of Scout Radio's people gave way to an understanding of the reasons for this unexpected attention from the government. As one of them reminisced, the new frequency "varied by only a few millimeters from the frequency on which . . . Radio Free Europe's Polish Service had broadcast. Because this was a time when the jamming of this station was being reduced, our 'benefactors' probably came up with the idea that the size of its audience would shrink if right next to it a more powerful station aired an attractive program with a large segment of Western music, also in Polish. Maybe someone looking for Free Europe will come across a Scout Radio program that is interesting and has music that is very rarely broadcast by Polish Radio, but very often by Radio Luxembourg and in Louis Connover's [*sic*—Willis Conover's—P. M.] programs on the Voice of America, and he will look no further."[79]

This Machiavellian plan turned out to be double-edged. Listeners to a radio station that became quite popular because of good music and because it avoided stiff, "wooden," ideological language would sometimes accidentally be caught in the enemy's net. "If it's a question of the working Scout Radio," a speaker worried during a meeting with the head of the CC Press Office at the University of Warsaw Journalism Studies Department, "which is intended not just for young people, we need to remember that these programs are broadcast on a frequency right next to Free Europe, that these are frequencies operating next to it and, looking for the Scout station, youth comes across Free Europe, and we all know that programs are being broadcast from there with an attractive form, and at the same time are of a very political nature."[80]

The second proposal formulated in the interagency report of June 1966 went well beyond creating a new Polish Radio program in direct response to RFE. It recommended "researching the possibility of taking up joint investments, the construction of radio centers in Europe and Cuba equipped with a complex of powerful transmitters. . . . These centers would become the foundation of joint radio propaganda to the West conducted by a special radio organization (as a grassroots organization created ad hoc, a sort of anti–Free Europe). This organization would have access to personnel from all the socialist countries participating in it."[81] The idea of creating a socialist anti–Free Europe station resurfaced many times, and in the other countries of the Soviet bloc as well, but it was never implemented.[82]

The Polish government was seriously concerned not only about the scale of RFE's programs but also about the radical increase in their number over only a few years. According to the Ministry of Internal Affairs, in 1963 RFE broadcast around a thousand programs (it is not clear whether it meant only original programs). In 1965, the number was 1,776; in 1966, 2,000; in 1967, more than 3,400; and in 1968, more than 3,700.[83] At about the same time, the Security Service informed the party leadership that "in many areas of Poland, the audibility of Polish Radio is very faint, while RFE can be heard very well."[84] The situation was worst in the south and the west, where in many areas "Polish programs are more difficult to hear than the programs of enemy stations."[85] In March 1966, the head of the press office of the CC, Stefan Olszowski, was alarmed about this problem: "If we consider that all of Poland lies within the range of powerful Radio Free Europe and several other stations, such as German radio and even partly (in the Western Territories) Spanish Radio Madrid, that all the time, 24 hours, they are leaking various kinds of disinforming news, that at the same time the Polish Radio program is not audible across the whole country—then this situation calls for some drastic measures."[86]

The threat came from the facts that the "hostile" stations broadcast nearly twenty-four hours a day, their transmitters were powerful, and they used many frequencies, but it could also be attributed to the attractiveness of their programs, and not just the political ones. The audiences appreciated RFE's sports coverage, which was based on reports from correspondents sent to all important events and competitions. Polish Radio reporters did not attend as many of them, if only because they were constrained by meager foreign currency reserves. "Our coverage of foreign athletic events in which Polish competitors take part requires a detailed analysis," said Stefan Olszowski in a meeting with sports journalists. "It is absolutely necessary to have our own coverage, not only because we need to guarantee that they are evaluated from the socially most important perspectives. . . . It is also necessary because sports are becoming more popular, and the lack of our own, competent information causes fans to listen to other, including hostile, sources of information, foremost among them Radio Free Europe, which currently has extensive sports coverage."[87]

Olszowski's words not only recognized the quality of RFE's programs but also confirmed the effectiveness of RFE's so-called replacement concept, adopted at its birth. The idea was to offer programming on both political and neutral topics, about all issues and areas of life that Polish listeners would find interesting, including sports, music, and weather. RFE was supposed to—and did, essentially—become a surrogate Polish Radio.

The Eighth Plenum of the CC PUWP in May 1967 devoted a significant amount of time to so-called foreign sabotage, primarily by Radio Free Europe. This was the first "ideological" plenum since the memorable one in July 1963, when Władysław Gomułka presented a comprehensive review of Polish culture and the dangers threatening it. His address to the Politburo sustained the thesis of the "USA leadership" ratcheting up its ideological warfare against the socialist camp. "Radio war occupies the central place in the arsenal of psychological warfare," stated the Politburo. "Free Europe's agents and its anti-Soviet branch, Liberty, have become the main tool in psychological warfare. They are conducting broad radio and publishing propaganda, as well as activities of the intelligence-sabotage type, mostly from the territory of the FRG and with the support of anticommunist émigrés from the different socialist countries."[88]

A very interesting vision of RFE's importance came from Zenon Kliszko, a key Politburo member and First Secretary Gomułka's right-hand man, in his opening speech at the plenum. RFE's role allegedly consisted of publicizing all protests staged in Poland, which gained political weight only thanks to the radio. "A small group of young people from the University of Warsaw, who have been poisoned by revisionism, who tried to launch illegal antistate activity there two years ago, could only count on using their own forces to disseminate their views among a few hundred people. But foreign antisocialist forces came to their rescue, and Free Europe devoted quite some time to publicizing this group's tract [Jacek Kuroń and Karol Modzelewski and their "Open letter to the Party"—P. M.]."

Kliszko continued: "The secretary general of the Provisional Central Committee, the so-called PCC [he meant Kazimierz Mijal and his "pro-China" group—P. M.], a character out of an operetta, even if the Albanian embassy helped him, could reach a maximum of a few hundred people with his proclamations. But Free Europe, which is not put off even by the fact that he is ardently defending 'Stalinism,' spends hours transmitting his proclamations, on the assumption that everything that attacks our party is good for [Free Europe's] sponsors. Without this help from the imperialist centers of sabotage and psychological warfare, all kinds of little antiparty and antisocialist groups would be insignificant, or almost insignificant, in the political life of our country."[89]

Other speakers also brought up RFE and various centers of foreign "sabotage." The first secretary of the CC PUWP in Lublin, Władysław Kozdra, declared that "302 inhabitants of our province have attempted to make direct contact with Free Europe radio, and 113 citizens with Voice of America radio."[90] Such detailed figures could only have come from the Security Service. Adam Kruczkowski from the East-West Center demanded that cooperation on fighting sabotage in the socialist camp take place through "regular consultations at the level of central committees of our parties."[91] The head of the Committee for Radio and Television, Włodzimierz Sokorski, and the head of the CC Press Office, Stefan Olszowski, informed the gathering of the preparations for the launch of Polish Radio's Fourth Program, portraying it as an antidote to Radio Free Europe.[92]

Security Service Pollsters: Public Opinion Research

The Security Service conducted what was likely the first semi-scientific opinion poll about the listenership of Western radio stations in the mid-1960s. In

1965, "information was collected in a confidential manner from persons representing a variety of social groups" in Wrocław, Poznań, Cracow, and Warsaw provinces and in the city of Łódź. It showed that about one-third of Poles (7,738 of the nearly 23,000 people polled) listened to Western radio, "mostly RFE."[93]

Detailed reports from two of the urban centers provide greater background for the poll. The Wrocław Security Office included the city and twelve selected counties in its analysis. It used 204 "sources of information" (current and former secret collaborators and "citizen contacts," a looser category of collaborator). These individuals gave the Security Service the names of everyone they knew who listened to foreign radio, and they asked listeners for their reasons for listening, evaluations of programs, favorite programs, and times when they were most likely to listen. The analysis also used archival materials. It examined about four hundred cases for listenership to foreign radio, including two hundred personal files and work files of secret agents who had been eliminated from the intelligence network, and the same number of operational cases for the years 1964–1965. Furthermore, it took into account 111 current cases being studied by the Investigations Department of the Provincial Office of the Citizens' Militia.

The scale of this research operation is striking. On the one hand, it shows the threat the government saw in foreign radio stations; on the other, it underscores the relative public calm of the mid-1960s, which permitted the Security Service to devote significant effort and resources to it. The Wrocław secret police attempted to tabulate the audiences of foreign radio stations according to age, education, social stratum, and area of residence. The researchers were handicapped by the very large margin of error that resulted from recording unrepresentative data, something they themselves were aware of.

More interesting are the evaluations and the concrete examples given in the report, which showed RFE's decisive primacy on the airwaves. "It was established in the course of research that the largest number of people listen to the Free Europe station. In some social groups, the interest in these programs is universal. . . . The people who spoke about this subject assessed FE's programs as 'attractive,' 'interesting,' enticing to listeners. What is more, this station broadcasts to Poland, and it is very easy for all receivers to find it." It was also clear from the report which programs were the most popular: "The sources agree that there is most interest in the news, and the commentaries on various topics that succeed them."

Equally interesting are the conclusions about the tangible effects of listening to foreign radio, even though, as was mentioned earlier, it is very difficult to confirm them. They reflect the mentality of the secret police rather than reality.

The Wrocław Security Service noted that "young people whose parents were known for their hostile attitude, and in homes where FE programs were regularly listened to, have taken up activity that is primitive in form, but still antagonistic and harmful, such as distributing antistate and anti-Soviet appeals and leaflets (in Krowiny, Świdnica District, in Karpniki, Jelenia Góra District, and in the city of Wrocław) and the attempts to found an illegal organization in a mechanical technical secondary school in Jelenia Góra." The distribution of information heard on foreign radio allegedly caused lower productivity in some factories. Even worse was the fact that "the agitation by hostile radios, especially FE, against candidates for the Sejm on the Front of National Unity list in the pre-election period has been reflected by crossing out [their names] during the elections. It has been ascertained that persons listening to such programs have also tried to convince other voters to cross out the names of candidates from among central activists."[94]

The Łódź secret police conducted its research with even greater flair, using as many as 257 personal "sources of information." This is the picture that emerges from its data: "Among workers, 50% listen to RFE's programs regularly. In the group of 'free professions and private business' this percentage is 70. . . . One can also venture that in some closed groups (journalists, writers, lawyers, clerics), listening to RFE and to other Western radio programs is a permanent phenomenon and encompasses ca. 80% of the number of these groups."[95] It seems that the Łódź Security Service estimates were highly exaggerated, since not even RFE's internal studies indicated such high listenership.

Despite their unscholarly methodology and inflated numbers, the overall picture that emerges from the Security Service studies is surprisingly credible. The first study conducted by the Center for Public Opinion Research (Ośrodek Badania Opinii Publicznej, or OBOP) to use much more scientific methods (this and OBOP's subsequent studies, which were carried out sporadically until the end of the Communist era, were confidential, distributed only to members of the state and party leadership) did not differ significantly from those conducted by the Security Service, although it did show higher listenership figures.

According to the first study by OBOP, in February 1969 some 48 percent of adult Poles listened to Western radio. In May 1969, the second study introduced a question about specific stations. Of the 41.2 percent of those polled who admitted to listening to foreign radio, about half named RFE, corroborating the earlier Security Service study.[96]

The OBOP data show that in the first half of the 1970s, the percentage of listeners to Western radio decreased significantly, with the percentage listening to RFE declining the most. This drop can be attributed to the calmer atmosphere and a decline in the population's interest in politics during the first years of Edward Gierek's rule. The listenership figures picked up again—and, again, the most for RFE—beginning in 1977. The period of stability and hope for a socialist "economic miracle" was ending; the economic crisis could already be felt, and an organized opposition had come into being. The listenership trajectory shows clearly that people listened to Western radio the most in times of political tensions, and RFE was the station to which they were most likely to turn, primarily in search of political news.

The Ministry of Internal Affairs Goes on the Offensive

Top-level Ministry of Internal Affairs documents (including reports from operations departments and evaluations and projections from the minister's office) throughout the 1960s invariably brought up "ideological-political sabotage" as either the most important or one of the most important threats to the socialist system in Poland. For this reason, combating this threat became one of the ministry's principal tasks.

The first large-scale operations began in 1962. According to the 1963 report discussed above, "the activity of Western and émigré centers of propaganda and sabotage has for about 1 year been a subject of active interest to Department I of the Ministry of Internal Affairs. In accordance with the guidelines of the ministry's leadership, a special group has been created in Section VIII of Department I and has begun to work out these issues. The work of our unit has made it possible to learn about the problems, the mechanisms of activity, the organizational structure, personnel composition and so forth of the most important Western and émigré centers, organs and institutions of 'psychological warfare.'"[97]

The 1963 Department I report mentions "the most valuable" information acquired through operations and passed on to the "party leadership," other ministries, and the Soviet, Hungarian, and Czechoslovak secret services. Of the eighteen subjects listed, five concern "sabotage." They are "anticommunist institutes," "the Paris *Kultura*," "list of names of persons engaged in the activity of the organs of 'psychological warfare,'" "Radio Free Europe," and "Radio Free Europe's sabotage polling action." As an aside, it is noteworthy that the Soviet services were cited, following the custom in Ministry of Internal Affairs documents, as "PR." This mysterious initialism meant "*przyjaciele radzieccy*" (Soviet friends).[98]

For now, these were only "advanced preparations for a more thorough and multifaceted exposure" of the adversary and "the launching of appropriate counteractions." The latter were to consist of "quickly discovering information leaks from Poland," as well as uncovering attempts by the so-called sabotage centers to contact Poles traveling abroad. Disinformation and propaganda actions were planned to compromise hostile institutions and persons, both in Poland and abroad. The latter goal was to be assisted by "increasing the action of ridiculing political sabotage centers in Polonia circles and stigmatizing their activity in émigré publications that we [the Ministry of Internal Affairs—P. M.] sponsor."[99]

The document mentions no titles, but we know that the Polish government subsidized *Nasz Znak* published in Sweden (some of its texts were actually written in Warsaw) and *Oblicze Tygodnia* and *Kronika* in London.[100] The Foreign Affairs Ministry published *Tygodnik Polski* in Paris.[101]

Krzysztof Tarka recently exposed the Ministry of Internal Affairs subsidy to *Horyzonty*, which was published in Paris and represented an extreme faction of the nationalist movement. Witold Olszewski was its editor in chief and Jędrzej Giertych its principal commentator. Its anti-German, pro-Russian profile was the basis of its understanding with the Polish government. The security services also expected it to criticize RFE and the Paris *Kultura*.[102]

Writing in *Horyzonty* in August 1966, Giertych criticized the entire émigré "camp of fighting with Russia," which to him was the "camp of foreign espionage." The FEC and RFE formed its core and were not only supported by the Americans but also supervised by the Germans. "And let's remember that the Free Europe Committee is dependent not only on America. Its main transmission equipment is located in Munich. Is it conceivable that today's Germany would allow this enterprise to exist if it were unable to exert some influence and some pressure on it?" was Giertych's rhetorical question. He also disparaged RFE's acceptance of foreign subsidies: "I use the term 'foreign spies' metaphorically, but also literally. The life and functioning of the Polish anti-Russian camp outside Poland is based largely on foreign monetary subsidies. These subsidies give it strength and resources." *Horyzonty* was conspicuous for its independence and national character.

In the context of this periodical's financing by Department I, the foreign intelligence department of the Ministry of Internal Affairs, Giertych's declaration takes on an unintended irony: "It would be interesting to see the various émigré publications and organizations if their subsidies were stopped and if they, like *Horyzonty*, had to start supporting themselves only with the money they receive[d] from subscribers and supporters."[103]

The Ministry of Internal Affairs was also plotting much more offensive operations than inspiring attacks against "sabotage centers" in the émigré press. It was planning sabotage and coercion: "Further progress in penetrating the abovementioned institutions will make it possible to initiate operational moves, which will complicate the activity of the center[s] of psychological warfare by, for instance, destroying their files and archives, destroying or intercepting anticommunist literature, disorganizing radio propaganda, [undertaking] sabotage actions in technical equipment, physical sanctions against émigrés who continue their exceptionally antagonistic activity, intrigues and stirring up disputes among its employees etc." It posited creating "a political center for coordinating, inspiring and documenting, which would collect and develop the needed documents, prepare materials to undermine the trust of American elements toward émigré staff and toward émigré centers, prepare assessments of the effectiveness of the work of the FEC, *Kultura,* etc. vis-à-vis Poland and organize preventive moves toward citizens of the PRP [People's Republic of Poland] traveling to the West who might serve as an uncontrolled source of information for the FEC."[104] Another document written at roughly the same time raised the need to coordinate activities of the Polish and Soviet security organs, "joint work in the sphere of recognizing and discrediting centers and persons practicing sabotage and unmasking their intentions, goals and methods."[105]

This outline of the plan for fighting what was labeled sabotage was being implemented bit by bit, and two departments of the Ministry of Internal Affairs carried the burden. A key task for Department I (it included the crucial Section VIII, which in 1978 was renumbered as Section XI), intelligence, was to expose "sabotage-propaganda centers conducting actions against the PRP" through operations. It is remarkable that this mission was determined to be of equal importance to "identifying the central offices and links of the intelligence services of the main capitalist countries."[106]

Department III's work was to find people in Poland who collaborated with the sabotage centers (its Sections III and IV were assigned RFE and *Kultura*) and the channels through which information was passed abroad. Ministry of Internal Affairs documents constantly mentioned this last task as a priority, emphasizing that without the flow of credible and detailed information from Poland, both RFE and *Kultura* would lose much of their importance and influence. In October 1963 the Ministry of Internal Affairs admitted that it had had no successes in this domain. "We have not yet succeeded in effectively identifying and seizing the threads connecting the hostile elements from Poland to the foreign centers. We are encountering significant difficulties in determining the sources who smuggle harmful news."[107]

The data in the Department III report for 1964 show how much it focused on destroying contacts with those it deemed foreign saboteurs. Of the 643 cases of operational verification being researched in the central office, 106 concerned "suspicious contacts with hostile and anticommunist centers."[108]

This is a significant share if we take into account the fact that Department III had a very broad range of responsibilities, which included counteracting all oppositional behaviors, supervising the cultural milieus, and overseeing the entire economy. It is noteworthy that fighting sabotage was first on the list of tasks assigned to this key department of the ministry. In 1966 its focus was "Activities of centers of ideological-political sabotage in the PRP:

- contacts made by Polish citizens with these centers,
- transmitting information to these centers,
- distributing propaganda materials in Poland."

"Illegal organizations and groups," "political terror," and "enemy written and oral propaganda" were further down the list.[109]

Department II (counterintelligence) assisted Departments I and III in combating sabotage. It observed Polish citizens' contacts with foreigners and diplomatic personnel, a potential route for sending information to "sabotage centers." Office "W" and its regional equivalents (sections "W" in the provincial commands of the Citizens' Militia) for their part inspected correspondence, confiscating letters to RFE written from Poland and handing them over to Department III, which subjected their senders to operational control; at times this led to detentions and trials, usually on charges of "disseminating false information."[110]

In 1963, Department III launched an operation to find everyone in Poland who maintained contacts with RFE, both those based on personal acquaintance with its employees and those consisting of a letter from a listener intercepted by the Security Service. All provincial offices of the Security Service were assigned this task in November 1963. The central office would ask the regional branches whether they had their "secret agents with access to Radio Free Europe." As a result, a circular ordered all provinces to create lists of persons in contact with RFE and even of those who might potentially be in contact. Lists of agents who would be suitable as contacts with RFE were made, and various operational scenarios were planned for getting to members of its staff.[111]

In 1965, Department II—counterintelligence—used eighty-six secret collaborators (including individuals with the status of operational contacts) "who during their travel in the West reached persons from the enemy centers of political emigration, employees of the Paris *Kultura* and the Free Europe station and organizations of Ukrainian nationalists." In the same period, it was determined that 405 Polish citizens had maintained or attempted to make contact with the "enemy centers," including 109 who had made contact with RFE, 38 with *Kultura*, and 39 with other émigré organizations. In this reporting period, Department III functionaries conducted "574 preemptive conversations with citizens of the PRP departing to capitalist countries (43 persons conveyed information to us that would have operational value after their return)."

According to Department III, all this activity "significantly influenced the drop in the number of materials sent abroad that maligned the PRP." This assessment, as well as all the statistics given here, should be taken with a grain of salt. Interestingly, Department III considered Jerzy Giedroyc, the editor of the Paris *Kultura*, as the ultimate authority on this issue. The 1965 annual report cited what he had said in the presence of a secret collaborator: "He did not expect the activities of the Polish organs to be capable of having such a great impact on the intelligentsia, and would become the reason for them to avoid and break off contacts with the periodical's staff."[112]

The Security Service obviously was interested in the passage of information to the West not only by ordinary citizens but also in the form of leaks from the ruling team. The ministry's attempts to trace the sources of RFE's information about divisions within the PUWP and the doings of the Partisans, the nationalist faction consisting of party elite, were discussed earlier. The propaganda campaign after Andrzej Czechowicz returned to Poland in 1971 attempted to exploit this theme. Even before RFE began to attack Moczar, the Ministry of Internal Affairs examined every indication that any of the party's inside secrets had reached Munich. A Department I agent had reported in 1959 that "the radio's employee Tadeusz Katelbach possesses a copy of the minutes of the Twelfth Plenum of the CC PUWP. The copy bears the stamped number 0030 or 00030 on the original. The agent saw this document by chance when he visited Katelbach's home."[113] Department III checked with the Central Committee, but the report proved false, because only thirteen unnumbered copies of the minutes of the Twelfth Plenum had been made."[114] (In other words, the agent's claim was implausible because all copies were unnumbered.)

The Ministry of Internal Affairs reports continued to request that all units of the Security Service that were taking part in the battle against RFE coordinate their plans and operations.[115] The 1964 Department III report states that "joint plans for undertakings were developed together with Departments I, II, and V against the main centers of sabotage."[116]

Despite such declarations, a coordinating office for all antisabotage actions was never created. But much was done to make the exposure of such institutions abroad and their collaborators in Poland one of the main missions of both the security apparatus and other institutions, especially the "ideological front." In 1963, the Security Service introduced a "new discipline, the problem of ideological-political sabotage," into operations training.[117]

In the new phase, propaganda activity was very actively encouraged. "Department I has recently submitted to the press various materials on the hostile activities of the centers of psychological warfare. The materials were used in some publications," read a report prepared in 1963 by the Security Service Unit of the Ministry of Internal Affairs.[118] This initiative also reached outside Poland. "We continued to publish articles aimed against *Kultura* and Free Europe in the controlled émigré press," wrote Department I in its report for 1965.[119] This method was routinely used by Communist intelligence. In its 1964 report, Department I wrote that "Section VIII inspired the publication in Sweden of a brochure entitled 'The History of the Sins of Stanisław Mikołajczyk' [Dzieje grzechu St. Mikołajczyka; Mikołajczyk was a prime minister of the wartime government in exile and leader of the émigré Peasant Party—P. M.], which debunked his political activity from 1939 to the present moment."[120]

It would be impossible to make a comprehensive list of the writings that Department I placed in publications in the West. An article by Andrzej Stefanowski in *Nasz Znak*, a periodical published by one of the factions of the émigré peasant movement, was most likely one of them. It contained a polemic (a word that is probably too elegant for this kind of text) against a response by Juliusz Mieroszewski in the Paris *Kultura* to a series of articles against RFE by Janusz Kolczyński that had been published in the Warsaw *Kultura*, a Communist weekly. Judging from both the importance to the Ministry of Internal Affairs of Kolczyński's pieces and the line of reasoning and vocabulary used in *Nasz Znak*, there is no doubt about who had instigated them, or probably also about who was their actual author. "The articles published in the Warsaw weekly were long: they contained a huge number of facts, documentation, names, figures, lists and a number of other pieces of information. In a word, the inner workings of this institution and its goals were exhaustively bared and deciphered in these articles," argued Stefanowski. "For the émigré reader, this was no great revelation, but to the reader in Poland, the publication was certainly very instructive and useful because this was the first time that he saw an analysis of the true face of the 'free European' operation, as it has been conducted for over ten years under the banner of the supposedly 'free' world and under the pretext of 'disinterested' service to Poland."

Stefanowski argued that Mieroszewski had not written his article by himself. "The stretch of time between the series published in the Warsaw *Kultura* and Mr. Mieroszewski's response clearly indicates that its supervision reached the very top of the hierarchy and Free Europe's central decision-making office and was 'discussed' and worked over at numerous conferences and by more than one 'expert' on both sides of the Ocean." According to the *Nasz Znak* author, this did not translate into high quality in Mieroszewski's polemics: "The substance of Mr. Mieroszewski's school essay was exceptionally clumsy, as is always the case with a communal creation by too many authors. It was clumsy in the first place because it did not respond to the key and most important issues brought up by the Warsaw *Kultura*, which point by point justified Free Europe's foreign, anti-Polish stance—in effect, it was harmful to the Polish national interest. And as if that were not enough! Mr. Mieroszewski in his enunciation neither contradicted arguments and documents nor even questioned them once. Nor would this have been very easy for him, since the material and supporting evidence cited by the Communist weekly did not operate in generalities, slogans, and empty words but solely on the basis of documentation drawn from publications and various multifaceted sources or from Free Europe itself." In conclusion, the authors attacked both RFE and the Paris *Kultura*: "But maybe it's good that we finally have proof that Mr. Juliusz Mieroszewski, a man who is always full of vigor and absolute 'sovereignty' and a flawless knight of the 'freedom of speech,' in reality plays the modest and ordinary role of an 'apparatchik,' but at Free Europe, hence a foreign center of anti-Polish festering."[121]

In Poland, writings by Dr. Janusz Kolczyński, an instructor in the Administrative Department of the CC who worked closely with the Ministry of Internal Affairs and used information acquired from operations, stood out most prominently. He published a series of articles in the Warsaw *Kultura* in 1963 aimed against RFE (it was to these articles that Mieroszewski had responded), the book *Dywersja* (Sabotage) about RFE and *Kultura* in 1964, and in 1969 a book devoted exclusively to the FEC and RFE.[122]

The same Kolczyński became the head of Ośrodek Wschód-Zachód (East-West Center), created in 1965, at first within the Polish Institute of International Affairs and later as part of the PUWP's mass-media company RSW "Prasa–Książka–Ruch." In 1975, it was enlarged and renamed Instytut Badania Współczesnych Problemów Kapitalizmu (Institute for the Study of the Contemporary Problems of Capitalism).[123] This institution, which worked closely with Department I in the war against political-ideological sabotage, acted as the main expert-analytical center for both the Ministry of Internal Affairs and the CC PUWP.

Security officers, too, conducted information-propaganda actions aimed at so-called foreign sabotage by organizing lectures and training for party activists. In a way, they were pioneers. The issue of fighting "sabotage" became a fixed component of party lectures and training in the late 1960s. In 1969, an "action of party meetings . . . devoted to exposing RFE" was organized.[124]

We know the least about the activity of the cells engaged in the disinformation campaign, which aimed to disgrace adversaries, spread false information both inside and outside Poland, and stir up conflicts. The activity of these cells varied over time and was probably greatest in the first half of the 1970s. Jan

Nowak-Jeziorański has written exhaustively about the campaign, which was also directed against him.[125] We know that at least two units in the Ministry of Internal Affairs conducted such operations. One of them was Inspectorate "I" (which was also called the Self-Contained Section I, Samodzielna Sekcja "I," and, from 1978 on, Department XII), which operated within Department I.[126] Its duties included organizing "active inspirational-sabotage and disinformation operations and other special operations connected with selected institutions, organizations and the adversary's plans and intentions in capitalist countries." The key directions and action methods of Inspectorate "I" included "paralyzing the activity of the centers of anticommunist sabotage and psychological warfare and their employees; discrediting particular parties, political groups, special services, organizations and institutions and their leaders and activists who conduct antipeace and hostile activity (the NATO countries, the Vatican, Free Europe, *Kultura* and other sabotage organizations)."[127]

Also, Group "D" was created within Department III in the early 1970s "to program inspirational-disinformation activities against anticommunist centers."[128] No documents created by these two units have been found. (In the case of Inspectorate "I," only a protocol for the destruction of documents in September 1989 has been found.) The rule for such extralegal actions must have been to leave behind the fewest written traces possible.[129]

Everything points to the fact that a brochure titled *Monachijska menażeria* (The Munich menagerie), distributed in the West in the 1960s, was the product of the disinformation cells in the Ministry of Internal Affairs. It contained extensive information about the internal workings of the Polish desk, information that of course was distorted and mixed up with blatantly false statements. Its author claimed to be an RFE employee who was dissatisfied with Nowak's "dictatorial" rule and the "anti-Polish" style Nowak had imposed on the staff. To make the brochure credible, the author implied that it had been published in exile: it expressed very favorable opinions of some émigré institutions, such as the Libella bookstore in Paris, and lamented that, even though a dozen copies had been sent to Poland, no publisher wanted to print it.

A careful reading of the brochure reveals characteristic themes used both in earlier Ministry of Internal Affairs propaganda and disinformation campaigns and in operations that would emerge more prominently a little later, in the 1970s. It begins by claiming that RFE's field offices were espionage cells that exploited gullible visitors from Poland and drove them into serious trouble: "The gentlemen called RFE correspondents are ordinary spies who cast their nets to catch our compatriots coming from Poland, and especially our friends and relations visiting us. They scrupulously note the names of many naïve people from Poland who receive visits from spies from Free Europe." This would be the leitmotif of the propaganda campaign that followed Andrzej Czechowicz's return to Poland.

Accusing the most important employees of RFE's Polish Service of working for Western intelligence services was a regular theme. Yet the brochure provided details that the propaganda machine would only fully exploit in the 1970s. For instance, it claimed that British intelligence had "passed [Jan Nowak] on to the CIA." He had earlier allegedly served as a "German agent in the Home Army, and before the Warsaw Uprising was defeated, German intelligence ordered him to leave for London." The same allegations would later appear in Czechowicz's spurious memoirs, published in Warsaw in 1973.

Propagandists also tried to discredit Nowak by writing about his authentic passion for collecting antiques and adding fabricated details. As one brochure's anonymous author claimed, "He deals in antiques, especially Polish ones. He uses his agents, officially called the radio's correspondents, for these shenanigans. He often travels to auctions, pretending that they are work trips. He is very greedy for precious gifts, so his employees, just to be left in peace, must give him presents twice a year, i.e., on Zdzisław's and Jan's name days [for both his real name and RFE pseudonym—P. M.], just as in feudal times."

If the episode were not so sordid, this detail would reveal that the author of the brochure had a sense of humor. It resembled another allegation made against Nowak, one that would never be repeated since even the Ministry of Internal Affairs must have realized that it had gone too far. The *Munich Menagerie* brochure accused Nowak of having been forced out of the cadet academy in Vladimir-Volynsky in the interwar period for sodomy, specifically for having sexual relations with a mare. To make this allegation credible, the brochure named the émigrés who allegedly knew about this disgrace and who had covered it up.

Calling Nowak's deputy, Tadeusz Żenczykowski, "Goebbels's student" was a rerun of a propaganda motif from the Stalinist period. This claim was based on two allegations. In the 1930s, Żenczykowski had indeed worked as the propaganda chief of Sanacja's National Unity Camp (OZON) and allegedly had kept "a photograph of Goebbels on his desk as a relic, with an emotional handwritten dedication." Second, on RFE's airwaves he "spoke not, in fact, from Berlin but from Munich, the city in which his preeminent guru had given speeches on numerous occasions."

Bringing up Nazi connotations with the Bavarian capital was one of the most typical tricks in Polish Communist propaganda attacks on RFE. But the very frequent accusation of Zionism in *Munich Menagerie* was a sign of the times. It was used against both the Poles and the Americans working at RFE. The brochure unambiguously suggested that those of the radio's editors who were most antagonistic toward People's Poland were not Poles but Jews. Its author asserted that he had decided to speak up because "recently, the influence of Zionism and of Bonn on the radio has become unbearable to a Pole's dignity." Nowak and Żenczykowski were accused of threatening the handful of editors who opposed the alleged Zionist bent of the radio with the "revenge of the espionage network."[130] In this context, the brochure's author named Wiktor Trościanko and Józef Ptaczek as positive figures. These two editors were indeed opposed to Nowak's policy of frontal attacks against the "nationalist" faction, the Partisans. Naming them no doubt helped deepen the conflicts and distrust between them and their supervisors.

Nowak was aware that the Ministry of Internal Affairs was stepping up its operations and disinformation campaign directed against his team, since there were people among his contacts in Poland who knew Polish government secrets. In January 1969, Nowak wrote a memorandum to RFE's American director warning that the Ministry of Internal Affairs was preparing a massive disinformation campaign. He began by describing the memo as "one of the most important I have written in my 17 years' association with RFE." He requested additional security for the radio's offices at Englischer Garten and in other cities to protect the most valuable and most confidential documents, especially those concerning the identities of informants from behind the Iron Curtain. He warned that Communist intelligence would try to obtain original RFE documents to manufacture hoaxes, which would then be distributed among émigrés and among RFE's employees.[131] Nowak's predictions were to come true shortly. Most of the security measures he proposed were not implemented until the Czechowicz affair.[132]

Nowak's information was confirmed by Henryk Birecki, a top Polish diplomat who defected to the West in the wake of the March 1968 events. The two men met in Paris in November 1969 and spoke for many hours. Birecki warned that Warsaw had decided to spend significant sums of money to escalate its intelligence and propaganda activities against RFE, the Paris *Kultura*, and other émigré organizations. It intended to spend as much as $100 million, which Nowak, in a written account of the conversation, considered implausible.[133] One may doubt the accuracy of Birecki's information, but it did convey the general direction the Polish government was taking, as it had consistently been bolstering its efforts against what it dubbed foreign sabotage, especially that promulgated by RFE, since the first half of the 1960s.

Cooperation with the KGB

It appears that the goal of tightening cooperation between the Polish and Soviet secret services to fight foreign "political and ideological sabotage" was also achieved. This is an extremely difficult issue to research since only a few Polish documents are available (it is possible, of course, that some are stored in the reserved collection of the Institute of National Remembrance, which is off-limits to historians), and the materials of the Soviet security apparatus are totally inaccessible. Nonetheless, even the handful of available Ministry of Internal Affairs documents allows us to reconstruct some aspects of the secret services' cooperation and to propose some hypotheses.

A list of information items that Poland received from the KGB in 1957–1960 allows the conclusion that one of them was related to RFE. Department III, however, already knew it "from other sources."[134] The first signs of cooperation between the Ministry of Internal Affairs and the KGB to fight sabotage appear in 1964 and 1965. The leaders of the two bureaus met in Moscow. Sabotage was one of the main topics in the materials prepared for the conference by the Polish side; of the twelve detailed memoranda, three addressed it. The relevant memoranda are headed "The ways in which sabotage centers affect Poland," "RFE's impact," and "The Paris *Kultura*'s paths of impact." They stress that "undermining the Polish-Soviet alliance and the socialist community by promulgating slogans about Poland's alleged 'dependence on the USSR and loss of sovereignty'" was one of the main goals of sabotage.[135] This anti-Soviet activity included RFE's discussion of Polish citizens remaining in the Soviet Union, especially programs mentioning that "allegedly 200,000–250,000 deported Poles are living in the territory of the Soviet Union" and that "allegedly, there are Poles in 56 concentration camps."[136]

In Paris *Kultura*'s case, the Poles shared information acquired through joint operations with the Soviets. A note reads that Giedroyc, *Kultura* editor in chief, had "suggested that one of our secret collaborators go to Kiev with a tour group or on a business trip and write an extensive report about the 'development of revisionist currents among the creative intelligentsia, and find separatist tendencies in this group in Ukrainian society.'"[137]

A paper prepared for the Moscow meeting also stated that "the problems of operational work related to defending our country from penetration by foreign intelligence services and by anticommunist centers of ideological-political sabotage were also the object of close cooperation with the security organs of the Ukrainian SSR, the Belorussian SSR, and the Lithuanian SSR. In 1964 and 1965 . . . working meetings with representatives of the security organs of the USSR were held, at which the implementation of joint undertakings was assessed, plans for operational exposures and combinations were developed, [and] tasks for each unit of s[ecret] c[ollaborators] were agreed on. Constant contact was also maintained through the exchange of information."[138]

This last piece of information points to very close cooperation between the Ministry of Internal Affairs and the KGB in the mid-1960s, including cooperation on issues such as operations or the use of spies. A document dated a few years earlier shows that there was also cooperation in the recruitment of agents. In discussions of joint undertakings between Polish and Soviet intelligence in West Germany, plans were made for the "mutual exchange of materials concerning persons with potential for recruitment when one of our intelligence services has a greater capacity to perform the successful recruitment of those persons."[139]

Cooperation between the Polish Security Service and the KGB was not limited to the top managerial level. A document prepared in March 1965 for a meeting in Kiev indicates that "contacts on the levels of department directors and heads of sections have been broadened, which has led to cooperation becoming more concrete and taking on the form of a working relationship. This form of cooperation makes it possible to exchange information directly, to undertake actions on particular issues and simplifies the solving of complex tasks."[140]

Throughout the 1960s the battle against foreign sabotage invariably ranked at the top of the list of issues discussed in meetings with the Soviet security police. In a May 1966 document titled "Issues for a Meeting with the Vice-Minister of the USSR" (probably a vice chairman of the KGB), the first question that the Polish side planned to ask was, "How can one respond so as to paralyze the activity of the sabotage centers' offensive?"[141] The list included detailed notes about various issues the Polish side wanted to bring up. Again, the first was a paper titled "The Effects of the Main Ideological-Political Sabotage Centers on Poland"; the section on RFE was the longest.

Cooperating with the KGB was the work of not only foreign intelligence (Department I) but also Department III, with its responsibility for combating internal political opponents. According to a note written by Department III, between 1965 and 1967 "the two sides held five working sessions in Kiev, Ternopol, Białystok, and Warsaw, at which the main areas of work and of cooperation were discussed and operational combinations in the joint operations were agreed on."[142] One of the main areas of cooperation was "responding to and destroying the political-ideological sabotage being conducted against our countries by Western centers."[143]

Department III prepared a long list of topics to discuss in meetings with the Soviet partners. These included "organizing operational actions aimed at preventing confidential information of a political nature from penetrating to the hostile centers, which may use them to conduct political-ideological sabotage against our countries"; "locating and cutting off direct contacts between the employees of those centers in our countries and the sources and channels of relaying information"; "forms of limiting contacts with the hostile centers, such as passport policy, warning conversations, confiscations of correspondence sent to the centers"; "operational control of persons who are connected to the centers and who visit our countries"; "the operational securing of travel to the capitalist countries for persons from the creative milieus, who may be of interest to the hostile centers, such as RFE, the Paris *Kultura*"; and "organizing disinformation efforts and inspiring actions aimed at unmasking the centers of sabotage."[144] In the 1960s, these were the priorities for the Ministry of Internal Affairs, both domestically and in foreign intelligence. A ministry document developed in February 1969 for a meeting with the Soviet comrades repeats the list of areas of cooperation almost word for word.[145] This use of earlier versions of documents points to a bureaucratic routine, as well as to the constancy of goals set by the security apparatus.

It was probably Department III that prepared this last document for a meeting that took place in Moscow on March 10–15, 1969. Significantly, it lasted six days. It was likely the most important meeting of the leaders of the two services in the late 1960s. Taking part on the Polish side were Minister of Internal Affairs Kazimierz Świtała, the director general of the Ministry of Internal Affairs, the director of the Minister's Office, and the directors of Departments I and II (intelligence and counterintelligence); on the Soviet side were KGB chairman Yuri Andropov, his deputy, and the heads of units I and II of the KGB (intelligence and counterintelligence). The minutes reveal that the group decided to "continue and broaden the exchange of intelligence information," including the areas of "centers of ideological and economic sabotage, [and] reactionary émigré organizations." Plans were made to "conduct joint, active intelligence operations and disinformation-uncovering undertakings in justified cases."[146]

Following the meeting in Moscow, the Polish minister of internal affairs ordered individual departments of his ministry to prepare detailed two-year plans for implementing the decisions that had been adopted. Department III thus intended to broaden the "exchange of operational information about the adversary," especially information on the "radio stations, including RFE, and the Paris *Kultura* and eastern and Sovietology institutes" listed in the first item. They also planned to "undertake joint operations to:

a. identify the ties between centers of ideological-political sabotage in the West and persons in Poland seeking contacts with Soviet citizens and attempting to have an impact on regions of the Soviet republics lying on the Baltic;

b. prevent leaks about the situation in Poland or the USSR to hostile information centers and the penetration into Poland of hostile émigré publications targeting Poles or for conveying to the USSR; and
c. separate from the intelligence-reconnaissance operations, to assume joint undertakings with the goal of starting quarrels and disgracing individual employees of the centers of sabotage and their operating methods."

It also planned "trips by representatives of Sect[ion] IV to the USSR for consultations, and vice versa."[147] This section of Department III was charged with destroying contacts between Polish citizens and the "hostile" centers of ideological-political sabotage abroad. The document goes on to list the pseudonyms of the covert collaborators of the Ministry of Internal Affairs who could be used for operational actions conducted jointly with the Soviet services. I have not managed to link any of these names with those of the people charged with anti-RFE activities. There are also no traces of cooperation with the KGB in the documents concerning attempts to penetrate RFE described in the next section. The failure to turn up such links does not mean that such cooperation did not exist. The cited documents may lead us to deduce that, at the very least, the Poles gave the Soviets information obtained through operations.

Propaganda and disinformation operations were a natural area of cooperation. They were conducted on a large scale in the 1970s and included the return to Poland of Ministry of Internal Affairs agent Andrzej Czechowicz and the enormous media campaign that accompanied it in Poland and in other Communist countries. But this cooperation had no doubt begun earlier. In October 1969, the KGB had asked the Polish Ministry of Internal Affairs to help prepare "a film about the subversive activities of organizations from capitalist states." The request continued: "The production of this film intends to heighten Soviet citizens' political vigilance. We plan for the film to reveal the forms and methods used by the adversary to implement ideological sabotage." The KGB, "together with employees of cinematography," collaborated in its production. The Poles were asked to share "documents, film tapes, and photographs," preferably with written commentaries.[148]

Operations Abroad: Spies

One of the Security Service's main goals was to launch operations targeting RFE in order to gain the maximum amount of information about the station, which it would then use to recruit agents from within the Polish Service and to initiate actions against the radio. An analysis of surviving documents, especially work on individual editors, shows that the collection of materials about the staff began on a large scale in 1962–1963. Many files were started, in some cases resuming earlier work that had been interrupted, some of it from many years before. This corroborates information in the documents quoted earlier about the priority the ministry placed on fighting RFE and what it dubbed political-ideological sabotage. Significantly, this activity took place at a time when Poland's intelligence activities in the West were being rebuilt after the serious losses stemming from the defection of Michał Goleniewski, a top Department I functionary who had worked as a CIA agent probably as early as 1958 and in January 1961 went over to the Americans in West Berlin. After his desertion, a large part of the spy network was eliminated, many employees of Department I were let go, and the department was restructured.[149]

In the initial phase of its work, the Ministry of Internal Affairs used relatives and friends of RFE employees to learn about their views and to gauge who might be willing to collaborate or to collect information to assist in recruiting others, to learn about the situation inside the Polish Service, and to acquire information on potential conflicts and individuals' weaknesses. According to RFE security, in November 1967, Poland's intelligence was by far the most active of all the Communist special services. Czechoslovakia's was second.[150]

Ministry of Internal Affairs officials frequently used blackmail, threatening not to issue a passport unless its recipient agreed to report on his conversations in Munich. In other cases, passport officials would appeal to family feelings, trying to convince the petitioner that it was in the interest of his relative working for RFE to cooperate with the Polish authorities (a frequent euphemism for the Security Service). This could pave the way for his return to Poland, where he was promised a stable life, a professional career, and so on. At times, officials would use the employee's known partiality to the Polish state or his patriotism, arguing that weakening RFE was in the interest of Poland and of the socialist camp. The passport applicants' strategies also varied, ranging from evasion and pretending to cooperate all the way to actively taking part in the Security Service operations or agreeing formally to serve as an agent.

Jerzy Lovell, a Cracow journalist and writer, was an example of an agent who willingly agreed to collaborate and who performed his tasks with full commitment, even enthusiasm. His sister was the wife of Tadeusz Chciuk, a wartime courier of the government in exile, who operated under the nom de guerre Marek Celt. Chciuk authored regular RFE programs for farmers under the byline Michał Lasota. In November 1951, before he was formally recruited, Lovell delivered to the Ministry of Public Security extensive data on his sister's family living outside Poland and on her contacts with relatives in Poland. His first report concluded: "It is possible that I have missed some facts that seemed insignificant to me, but which to you would be important. This is why I am waiting for your questions, which I will answer immediately if I know the answers. With party greetings. . . ."[151]

The first mission assigned to "Tokarz" was a trip in August 1952 to West Berlin, where he tried to invite his sister and brother-in-law from Munich. He was to ask his brother-in-law to collaborate with the Ministry of Public Security. In the detailed recruitment plan prepared by Department VII of the Ministry of Public Security, he was to mention the existence of "compromising materials" as the main persuasive threat.[152]

Tadeusz Chciuk, who had worked closely with Stanisław Mikołajczyk and another eminent émigré politician, Józef Rettinger, in the 1940s, had been arrested in Poland in March 1946. The price he paid for his release was signing an agreement to collaborate, to supply information about Rettinger and the structure of the Ministry of Internal Affairs of the government in exile in London, which he knew very well from his work as a courier, and to prepare biographical sketches of émigré politicians.[153] After his release from prison, he told Mikołajczyk and other leaders of the Polish Peasant Party about the document he had signed and what he had told his interrogators. In September 1948, assisted by an émigré courier, Wacław Felczak, he fled Poland with his wife and children. One of the main reasons for his flight was to escape the Security Service, which intended to transform the pledge he had signed in prison into real collaboration.[154]

Lovell did not succeed in his mission because his sister and brother-in-law did not travel to Berlin to meet him. The security apparatus did not use his services in subsequent years, but it remembered him in 1959 as it began to plan an almost identical mission. In December 1959, Lovell did meet his sister and her husband in Paris. Chciuk vehemently refused to collaborate. He rebuked the attempt to blackmail him by saying that "immediately after arriving in the West he had told 'those who needed to know' about the fact and extent of his collaboration, and the people in charge know, and had always known when they were hiring him at Free Europe."[155] One more attempt to enlist Chciuk was planned for 1963, but a projected meeting in Germany between Lovell and his sister and brother-in-law did not take place.[156]

Another example of the Security Service's use of family members was its attempts to reach Zygmunt Michałowski, who in the 1950s worked in RFE's Paris bureau, and later served as the deputy director of the Polish Service in Munich and, after Nowak's departure, as its director. Intelligence sources indicated that Michałowski was favorably disposed to the October 1956 de-Stalinization changes in Poland, which—in the eyes of Department I—created an opportunity to "win him over." His brother, Krzysztof, a Benedictine monk in Tyniec, approached him first during a visit to Paris in September 1957. The available documents do not recount their conversations but do include a description of the papers Zygmunt kept in his desk at home.[157] The same file includes subsequent reports from Krzysztof, in which he tells the Security Service about their communications, Zygmunt's views and his personal life, and a detailed description of his house in Munich. Krzysztof (who used the aliases "Włodek," "Franek," or "Michał") also advised the officers on ways to persuade his brother to collaborate, since they realized fairly quickly that an open offer would be rejected.[158] Even though in Zygmunt Michałowski's case the agent's efforts yielded nothing, the Security Service was very pleased with his assistance: "TW [*tajny współpracownik*—secret collaborator] 'Michał' . . . prior of the Benedictine abbey, has for many years collaborated with Dep[artment] IV of the Security Service of the Provincial Command of the Citizens' Militia in Cracow. In the course of his cooperation so far, he has proved to be a valuable agent, who loyally and keenly performs the missions assigned him."[159]

In his research into the surveillance of the Catholic Church in Cracow, Marek Lasota found eighteen volumes of the monk's reports, which cover the period from the early 1950s to the 1970s. Michałowski also reported on Bishop Czesław Kaczmarek, who had been imprisoned in 1951 and later became the main defendant in a show trial, and on the Benedictine sisters in Vilna, for which he received thanks from the KGB.[160]

The Security Service also attempted to get to Zygmunt Michałowski by using his nephew, the prominent journalist Ignacy Krasicki, who was "won over to collaborate on the principle of willingness, by the Sec[urity] Ser[vice] of the Provincial Command of the Citizens' Militia in Cracow,"[161] in 1960. Secret collaborator "Witold" prepared a detailed profile of his uncle, passed on information about his private life, and suggested scripts of conversations that could lead to recruitment. They met for two days, September 17–18, 1963, in Sardinia. Michałowski, who, in cooperation with Nowak, frequently conducted interviews with travelers from Poland, questioned Krasicki about the balance of power in the PUWP leadership. He emphasized that he was treating their meeting as "a beginning of a serious political dialogue," and that "he would like to meet with a responsible political personality from Poland."[162]

But "Witold" had a different goal. He wanted to organize a meeting between Michałowski and a "recruiter" from the Ministry of Internal Affairs. He recommended to Department I that "the person who is sent should be not only intelligent, but also socially at ease. Z. M. is not an easy conversationalist and he needs to be approached in the right way."[163] The central office designated the proper officer, Edward Jankiewicz, the head of Section VIII of Department I, but Michałowski rejected the offer of a meeting. Over the next year, the Polish desk broadcast warnings about Ignacy Krasicki, presenting him outright as an operative who was gathering information in Rome during the Vatican Council.[164]

All the Ministry of Internal Security efforts to reach Michałowski proved futile. In 1973, his file was moved to the archive, with the justification that "further work on this target offers no hope of concluding the case successfully. The attempts so far to make contact with the target made in 1956–70 have yielded no positive results."[165]

This does not mean, however, that the Security Service did not exploit reports from its secret collaborators, especially about Michałowski's private life. It used information provided by Krasicki about Michałowski's personal tragedy, his wife's suicide. In his misleadingly named memoirs (confected by the Ministry of Internal Affairs), Andrzej Czechowicz accuses Michałowski of nothing less than taking part in her murder. She had allegedly asked for a divorce, to which her husband did not agree. "At that point, the Scotswoman began to threaten that she would reveal her husband's secret relations," wrote Czechowicz, or rather his ghostwriters at the Ministry of Internal Affairs. "On one occasion, a little tipsy, she began to talk about it out loud in front of witnesses. There was a great commotion, but no more such incidents occurred. The Scotswoman was locked up in a psychiatric hospital. After returning home, she was no longer alive. The official version: suicide. Very few people believed it."[166]

It is not easy for a historian to write about the personal affairs of people who were persecuted by the security apparatus. One is often torn between trying to present the most comprehensive picture possible of events and wanting to respect the protagonists' privacy, which has already been violated by the Security Service. This information about Michałowski is included here because it shows the ministry's modus operandi and the significance of seemingly neutral facts submitted by agents, which, when twisted and cooked, could be turned into a tool for slander.

Another thread in the case of Zygmunt Michałowski that demonstrates how Polish intelligence worked was an operation planned in Department I after the initial efforts to recruit Michałowski had failed. "On 24.10.1960 a plan was developed for an operational undertaking intended to discredit 'P' ['Posłaniec,' messenger, the code name assigned to Michałowski as the target in this case—P. M.]. With this in mind, it planned to send out a flier to collect money for 'Posłaniec,' who was allegedly incurably ill (with Buerger's disease). There is no information about the results of the undertaking or whether it was implemented," wrote the Department I functionaries who took over Michałowski's case in 1963.[167] Incidentally, this would confirm that Michał Goleniewski's defection caused major disruptions and a break in the continuity (also the personnel continuity) of many intelligence operations.

The accessible documents indicate that the Ministry of Internal Affairs likely had no secret collaborators inside RFE in early 1963. Department II hoped to infiltrate the Polish desk via agent "Kryspin," an announcer's brother-in-law.[168] Department III could rely on a few secret collaborators who were in contact in person or by letter with Polish desk staff.[169] It is likely that the two departments attempted to reach some radio employees independently of each other's intelligence, as well as of Department I's intelligence. This shows that the coordination of activities endorsed by the ministry's leadership had its flaws.

It was Department I that scored the first operational success by signing up a radio announcer, Jerzy Bożekowski.[170] Money, paid by intelligence officers at every one of their meetings, which always took place outside Munich (in Vienna, Geneva, or The Hague), was his only motivation. Bożekowski was not a player and had limited access to information and inadequate opportunities to interact with the management of the Polish Section. Still, the ministry considered the information he provided to be of operational value.

Its collaboration with "Fonda" (Bożekowski's code name) confirms the ministry's interests in the radio's plans and its intentions toward it. In their first meeting, Bożekowski agreed to collect the originals of RFE documents, as well as information about cooperation between RFE and the Paris *Kultura*. From the very beginning, Department I wanted to know in particular about RFE's contacts in Poland. "Fonda" was to obtain the originals of letters from listeners in Poland and the names of RFE people who interviewed Poles in the West, both those traveling as tourists or on business and those remaining there permanently as refugees or asylum seekers. This was its constant interest, since in the years that followed, the Ministry of Internal Affairs would continue to focus on infiltrating the network of interviewers.[171]

Department I also expected "Fonda" to deliver intelligence about the activities of Western intelligence services, especially about "the contacts and cooperation between FE and the German side, focusing especially on the FRG's intelligence organizations and the eastern institutes working on Poland." The latter request would probably be used for propaganda attacks against the Polish Service, which traditionally presented RFE as serving the German revisionists. From this point of view, the information collected by "Fonda" was not very encouraging: "It must be emphasized here very emphatically that there exists no cooperation between RFE's Polish staff and the Germans," reported the new agent in his first paper. "The Germans' attitude toward RFE is very unfriendly, which can be felt all the time and which is expressed in the frequent attacks against RFE in the German press, and also in some official statements by Bavarian politicians."[172]

These attacks were for the most part inspired by organizations of German expellees from Poland, who were especially influential in Bavaria. The case officer saw an opportunity to play the German card in a new way, using the information from "Fonda." "The issue that in my opinion is worth noticing is the fact that the Germans barely tolerate, or even oppose, FE's activity aimed against the countries of the Communist bloc. Of course not because they are our friends, they would have nothing against such activity, but on the condition that this not take place in their territory. This, as the Germans claim, interferes with their ability to implement a flexible policy and form relations with us the way they would like. . . . In these circumstances, it seems appropriate to take advantage of this moment and, wherever it suits us, to set the Germans on FE, pointing out that it is the cause of the problems. This creates worse conditions for the existence of FE and demoralizes its employees," the case officer for "Fonda" proposed to his supervisors, sensing the future direction of relations between Warsaw and Bonn. During negotiations over the border treaty, signed in December 1970, the Polish government repeatedly demanded that RFE be removed from West German territory, as is discussed below.

A lengthy report by Lieutenant Colonel Mieczysław Schwarz, who had engaged "Fonda," illustrates what interested the Ministry of Internal Affairs the most and in which direction its planned operations against RFE were headed. One motif is especially interesting. "In my conversations, I inquired of 'Fonda' in an exploratory way about the possibility of performing an act of sabotage at the station, more precisely of blowing up the station, immobilizing it for a longer period of time or completely destroying it," he wrote. There was also the possibility of sabotage on a smaller scale, for instance substituting tapes and broadcasting a program prepared by the ministry. "Fonda" thought that would be possible, but emphasized that "the technician would hear it after a few minutes and stop the broadcast." But he did suggest destroying the master control room, "which is the heart of the station. . . . For the appropriate compensation, which needs to be agreed on, 'Fonda' is prepared to take on the role of organizing this operation based on a small amount of explosive materials, which we will deliver. 'Fonda' will look around the building before we meet again, from the perspective of the technical side of the issue, the possibility of placing the material."[173] One of Lieutenant Colonel Schwarz's supervisors wrote a question mark in the margin next to this passage. It may be that the case officer was showing his own initiative, but we must keep in mind that sabotage was one of the potential methods of fighting RFE mentioned in earlier documents, and also that an act of sabotage would later be committed in Munich, though not against the Polish Service. In 1981, a bomb placed outside the building's external wall exploded next to the wing housing RFE's Czechoslovak Service, wounding several employees.[174]

"Fonda's" handwritten report for Schwarz covers basic information about RFE, such as the responsibilities of the different departments and methods of editorial work, American management, security, and so forth. For the ministry, the profiles of the Polish employees must have been the most valuable. A note scribbled by one of Schwarz's supervisors on the first page of the report about hiring "Fonda," which specifies the expectations of the new agent as providing "people's characteristics and relations," is evidence of this. At that time, the ministry clearly had very limited knowledge about them, something that is evident in Kolczyński's 1964 book, which until the end of the 1960s was the most important piece of propaganda about RFE. It mentioned the names of only a few employees of the Polish Service, without the kind of personal details that later publications indulged in. A second Kolczyński book, published in 1969 and wholly devoted to the FEC and RFE, has much more thorough portraits, undeniably deformed by propaganda and probably based on information gathered through operations.

The new recruit provided brief but at least partly new material about the Polish staff: their real names (many of the writers appeared on the air under pseudonyms), views, private lives, legal status (type of passport or residence document), relatives in Poland, and relations with Director Jan Nowak. This material would be used for both propaganda, in appropriately modified form, and operations, for example to reach relatives living in Poland. Warsaw wanted to know who had bad relations with Nowak so that it could use this information to attempt recruitment, or at least to feed internal disputes and antagonisms. In several cases, "Fonda" openly suggested "exploiting" several people.

The most important clue that "Fonda" delivered was about Kazimierz Zamorski and the unit he directed, a Polish section in the Research and Analysis Department, which was independent of Nowak and answerable to the radio's American management. In Polish government propaganda, this was the "central link in the espionage work."[175] Zamorski's domain included reports and questionnaires prepared from interviews with people from Poland who met with RFE employees or those who answered questions asked by RFE interviewers in other cities in Western Europe.[176] Subsequently, reaching the filing cabinets containing these reports would become one of the ministry's principal ambitions.

Intelligence work on Zamorski (code-named "Morski") officially began on January 12, 1965. His file includes an earlier note that reproduces the profile "Fonda" had sketched out in the first meeting with his case officer: "K. Zamorski is not an anticommunist but instead an earnest Poland enthusiast, and here one can clearly see his wife's influence, since she cannot stand RFE and cannot stand the so-called old émigrés, as she does not share a common language with them. They are both very intelligent and pleasant, not blinded, and they think rationally."[177]

The security police subsequently tried to take advantage of the antagonism between Zamorski and Nowak. "These sentiments were inflamed as a result of our inspirational-operational undertakings," reads a report for the director of Department I.[178] Yet efforts to recruit "Morski" (the ministry used this code name for both him and his case) or to convince him to return to Poland and to use his return for propaganda failed. Still, the secret police scored a success by contacting this highly placed person, first with a letter offering collaboration, which was given to him by a niece who obtained a passport solely for this purpose, and then in a meeting with agent "Lucis."[179]

Department I was very interested in the effect that the propaganda appearing in Poland had on the Munich staff. "The appearance in the Warsaw *Kultura* of articles discussing the role and activities of the Committee and Radio FE by Janusz Kolczyński caused a great sensation at RFE," Schwarz reported on what he had heard from Bożekowski. "It was a good shot. . . . According to 'Fonda' and others, the article's only flaw was the description of Karol Marek and Pampuch-Brońska as leading German revisionists. . . . There is a general perception among RFE employees, especially after these articles appeared, that Warsaw understands RFE's problems very well and that everything it knows was covered in them."

The importance that the ministry attached to Kolczyński's writings suggests that they had collaborated on them closely. Intelligence checked their accuracy and effects, clearly thinking about new propaganda themes. In the book version of Kolczyński's writings (almost identical to his earlier articles in the Warsaw *Kultura*), the fragment about Karol Marek and Wanda Pampuch-Brońska was changed, probably according to information provided by "Fonda." The book no longer accused these staffers of being "known for their pro-German sympathies, their collaboration with West German revisionist publications, for their contacts with revisionist organizations in the FRG."[180]

A new section appeared that accused émigrés connected to RFE and the Paris *Kultura* of collaborating with the "revisionist" monthly *Der Europäische Osten*. "One of them is Wanda Brońska-Pampuch. The same one who, after I published my article about Free Europe, ardently protested that she had never collaborated with any revisionist German publication," wrote Kolczyński.[181] This shows clearly the coordination and efficient flow of information between intelligence operations and the "ideological front."

From that point on, the collaboration with "Fonda" bore no more fruit. He provided nothing more of any value; for instance, he did not manage to get an imprint of a key to the offices of the Polish section of the Research and Analysis Department. His handlers thought his hand-drawn plan of its offices had too few details and was unhelpful, which again reveals what interested the ministry the most. "Fonda" continued to ask for money, and sold the miniature camera he had been given to photograph documents. Their relationship broke off in December 1964, and Warsaw's attempts to restart it in 1967 failed.[182]

In the second half of the 1960s, the Ministry of Internal Affairs had new agents in RFE's Polish Service, ones who were more disciplined than "Fonda." The ministry had talked Andrzej Czechowicz, a new émigré from Poland, into collaborating. After staying in a refugee camp and serving for a short time in a guard company of the British army in Germany, in April 1965 Czechowicz was hired by the RFE Research and Analysis Department, a key target for the Security Office.

Most of the materials about Czechowicz have likely been destroyed, and so we are reduced to making assumptions and analyzing circumstantial evidence about many aspects of his case. His personal file, begun after he was brought back to Poland in 1971, includes his handwritten letter dated September 8, 1964, to the Polish Military Mission in Berlin. In it he asks for permission to return to Poland. Serving in the British guard company, he declares that he is "ready to be subjected to any punishment" for illegally remaining abroad and proclaims that he can "still do a lot for Poland" to "repair the harm he has inflicted on . . . his motherland."[183]

This letter does not mention working for intelligence or trying to get a job at RFE. Czechowicz only wanted to be allowed to go home without suffering any consequences. Other documents reveal that it took so many months for a new passport to be issued and for permission to return to Poland to be granted that the young refugee began to work at RFE, something the secret police clearly decided to exploit. A short handwritten note of September 6, 1965, reads: "Andrzej Czechowicz, do not let him know about the authorization to issue a passport, but wait for a decision."[184] This is most likely a trace of the pressure being put on the new RFE employee. Czechowicz himself admitted after 1989 that he had been forced to collaborate with the secret police shortly after taking a job with RFE. Polish intelligence was to have used the letter he had written to the Polish Military Mission, the disclosure of which may have compromised him at RFE.[185]

Czechowicz talked about his work for the Ministry of Internal Affairs in a 2005 interview. A few months after he started at RFE, a man he did not know appeared in his apartment and bullied him into turning his television and radio all the way up and running the water in all his faucets. In the bathroom, he told Czechowicz, addressing him roughly with the informal "you," that he was to work for Polish intelligence. "We have iron discipline," he warned. He also gave him the time and place for a meeting in Vienna, where Czechowicz was to appear holding the German weekly *Quick* in his hand.

There were meetings like this every two or three months in various towns in Austria, France, the Benelux countries, Denmark, and Switzerland, but never in Germany, where the Poles feared the West German and US intelligence. Czechowicz was given assignments. He would also hand over materials he had acquired (which included photographs of documents taken with a miniature camera) to the Ministry of Internal Affairs courier, with whom he would exchange briefcases in busy places in Munich.

Like the other agents, Czechowicz prepared profiles of RFE's employees and reported on conflicts among the staff and about opposition to Jan Nowak. This information was used to recruit new agents. Czechowicz confessed that he himself had suggested a dozen or so people who in his opinion would have been receptive to such offers or pressures. He also reported on his colleagues' trips, including vacations, and their habits. This enabled the secret police to lie in wait for an unsuspecting RFE employee at a hotel in Spain or Italy.

Attempts to recruit agents, or simply to obtain information, could be dramatic at times. Czechowicz told his case officer about a colleague who usually spent his vacations on the Spanish coast, where he would go for solitary swims far out to sea. The next time the man went swimming, two operatives followed him in a boat, pretended to push him under with their oars, and then pulled him out, only to demand a report about a Polish desk program conference. They warned that if he refused, he would not return to shore alive, and if his information proved false, they would find him again and then they would not even bother to talk to him.

Most desirable were tips about Jan Nowak's planned trips, especially to countries bordering the Soviet bloc, such as Austria or Finland. According to Czechowicz, the Ministry of Internal Affairs made plans to kidnap Nowak.[186] It was only Edward Gierek, who became first secretary of the PUWP in December 1970, who put an end to these—allegedly advanced—plans, fearing an international scandal. Czechowicz was also tasked with finding out who on the Polish desk and among the American management was Jewish. This request is of a piece with the massive escalation of anti-Semitism at the ministry from the mid-1960s to the early 1970s and the invocation of this theme in the public attacks on RFE. Perhaps the most eccentric task given Czechowicz was to find out whether RFE knew who had murdered a son of Bolesław Piasecki, the leader of the PAX pro-Communist Catholic organization, who was kidnapped in 1957. This request inadvertently recognized RFE's expertise and acknowledged the ministry's own powerlessness, for its own investigations had failed to turn up an answer to this question for years.[187]

Like Bożekowski, Czechowicz held an insignificant job. But he did have access to reports of conversations with people from Poland. It was probably copies of these materials that made up the lion's share of what he sent to Warsaw. According to Minister of Internal Affairs Franciszek Szlachcic, his office received some five thousand reports from Czechowicz.[188] There are more than four hundred RFE reports submitted by him in the Institute of National Remembrance archive. They cover a variety of topics: the economy, the military, church-state relations, internal PUWP matters, the personnel situation in the Foreign Ministry and the activities of Polish diplomatic missions, the political émigré community, and the journalism, academic, and artistic circles in Poland. Czechowicz was successful in determining at least several dozen names of people in Poland (many of them PUWP members or journalists trusted by the government) who met with RFE employees during their travels abroad and talked about the situation in Poland, especially within their professional and social groups. Because of such contacts, RFE treated many of these individuals as "sources" and assigned them index cards, which Czechowicz then managed to copy and send to Warsaw. These materials would become the foundation of the propaganda campaign after Czechowicz went back to Poland in March 1971 (discussed in chapter 5).[189] But prior to his return, Warsaw used the information from Czechowicz about the people and internal relations in RFE's Polish Service for propaganda and for further intelligence operations.

Information from Czechowicz probably helped the ministry find another RFE employee who agreed to collaborate.[190] Janusz Koryzma was a young actor who had left Poland in 1963 and remained in the West. He began to work for RFE as a reader, but after some time was demoted to in-house messenger, someone who carried correspondence and documents. According to agent "Gama" (we do not know his identity, but it is possible that this was one of Czechowicz's code names), Koryzma became extremely bitter and talked openly about wanting to return to Poland. "He is very susceptible to recruitment because he misses Poland very much, and he has had enough of traipsing around the world, he hates RFE and especially Nowak and his despotic manner," reported "Gama" during a meeting with a Department I functionary.[191]

In July 1966, a Department I officer showed up at Koryzma's home unannounced. "Going to 'K's' apartment entailed a certain risk, since the target inhabited a building occupied exclusively by RFE employees," acknowledged the final evaluation of the case.[192] The success of actions like this one

(Czechowicz's work for Polish intelligence began in a similar way) does not speak well of RFE's internal security or of West German counterintelligence.

Koryzma was happy to collaborate and to have the Ministry of Internal Affairs decide when he would return to Poland. He supplied documents (or their photographs) and notes about materials that passed through his hands. They seem not to have been of great value to the Security Service. They included "files of various informational reports for the period 1965–May 1967 . . . a telephone book with the personnel and structure of FEC–RFE–RFE field bureaus, certain financial documents."[193] We can assume that the ministry had received the same or similar documents from Bożekowski and Czechowicz.

The Security Service was somewhat disappointed with "Kamera" (the code name given to Koryzma). "The agent's aptitude as a spy is lesser than we had expected," concluded the final report for his case.[194] His personal characteristics made him additionally troublesome. "The agent sees himself in a way as a real intelligence employee, and he would like to play an independent role, to make various decisions and moves by himself. He demonstrates that he has an imagination, probably because of the films he has seen and the spy books he has read," wrote his case officer after one of their meetings.[195]

His behavior caused practical problems. "Kamera" would not appear for appointments, he would arrive in places (Rome in one case) without an appointment, or he would send too many postcards with a coded text to a contact address he had been given. He implied that he could take on special missions. One of his handlers' reports noted that "'Kamera' had declared that he could blow up or burn rooms at RFE, that he would finish off Nowak. He finds it irritating that Nowak presents himself as a hero. (He cannot stand it when the abovementioned hums the Home Army hymn almost every day after arriving at work.)" On another occasion, Koryzma "offered to help with a plan to kidnap Nowak."[196]

The intelligence officers did not treat these words solely as a sign of fervor and bitterness on the part of "Kamera." "We tried to analyze the truthfulness of his declarations. . . . If the need arose, as he said, I could undertake something," read a report about a meeting with Koryzma.[197] It is worth remembering that Department I had quizzed another agent, Jerzy Bożekowski, about a possible bombing.

In October 1967, Koryzma was told that he had not been performing his duties at RFE, and he was suspended from work. The Security Service took advantage of this situation to deepen the internal divisions among the Polish staff. "We supported the agent's idea of suing the director of the Polish Service, J. Nowak, in a civil court for groundless release from work. The RFE labor union also supported his case. This caused ferment among the personnel of the Polish Service," read a note summarizing Koryzma's collaboration.[198]

When it became clear that "Kamera" would not win his lawsuit, the Ministry of Internal Affairs decided to bring him back to Poland and to use him in its propaganda. The operation was planned very carefully. The central office sent instructions to the officers in charge of the operation: "When you discuss the issue of his return, make sure that 'K' takes all possible documents that we could use to compromise RFE (decide: whether there are realistic conditions for 'K' to create favorable circumstances in Paris, which we could use to compromise RFE or *Kultura*, for example, if he could organize a meeting with RFE employees he knows, visit bookshops distributing hostile literature, such as Libella)."[199]

Even more interesting is the suggestion made by the case officer to the director of Department I, handwritten on the first page of a report dated February 6, 1968: "It would be useful to conduct consultations in the meantime with the friendly services of Czechoslovakia, Bulgaria and Hungary with the suggestion to bring out or even kidnap someone from their RFE sections to intensify the counterstrike and thereby to distract USA's CI [counterintelligence—P. M.] from our people at RFE."[200] This daring plan was not implemented, but it is a good illustration of both wanting to protect another agent who remained at the radio (at that moment it was Andrzej Czechowicz) and coordinating the special services of the Communist countries to fight RFE, at least to the point of exchanging information and discussing operations.

Using Koryzma for propaganda, which would probably have resembled the campaign of Czechowicz's return in 1971, did not work out because of an unexpected turn of events. Koryzma was fired from his job, and the German authorities deported him to France. He suffered a nervous breakdown and required hospitalization. Even then, the Security Service did not abandon its plan to transport him to Poland. "The attempts we have undertaken with the goal of bringing the agent to Poland did not have a positive result. According to the management of the hospital, the health of the abovementioned person does not permit the execution of repatriation," wrote Czesław Kozubski in November 1969.[201]

After spending over a year in the hospital, Koryzma returned to Munich. But the Ministry of Internal Affairs decided that maintaining its relationship with him would be too risky. All in all, his was a tragic story of an unbalanced man who allowed the secret police to take advantage of him. It demonstrates how seemingly insignificant information about human frailty and antagonisms reaching the secret police could be put to destructive use.

Czechowicz's ministry-written memoirs tell Koryzma's story and, even compared to everything else in that book, make an exceptional caricature of it. They allege that Nowak began to despise Koryzma after his wife became interested in the young actor. Nowak removed him duplicitously: "In Strasbourg, West German police transferred Koryzma to French officers, and they also handed over a medical report according to which he was mentally ill, suffering from symptoms of a dangerous persecution complex. He was therefore placed in a mental institution. The story of the Scotswoman, Michałowski's wife, was beginning to repeat itself."[202] Thus, any lie, no matter how absurd, could be used in a propaganda assault on RFE. The only thing that mattered was connecting it by any means available to actual events (a firing, a commitment to a mental institution, a suicide).

In August 1968, Department I succeeded in placing Mieczysław Lach, who had left Poland illegally in 1965 and had been recruited a few months earlier in Vienna, at RFE. The Polish secret police hired him with the help of his friend, an RFE pollster who used the code name "Freda." In both cases a financial incentive played the main role, and in Lach's case there was the additional argument that intelligence work would allow him to return to Poland in the future. "Kumor" was hired by the Audience and Opinion Research Department. Lach's was the first and only known case of an agent hired by the radio in Munich after having been recruited by Polish intelligence. His main mission was to "uncover the Poland-based sources of RFE's information."[203]

Unfortunately, even fewer documents survive about Lach's collaboration than about Bożekowski's. There is no detailed description of the materials he delivered, which were probably mostly studies written by his unit. "Beginning in December 1969, the agent began to supply original documents from the facility and beginning in March 1970 secret and confidential documents. . . . The agent's information was very useful for the operational work on the facility. After Captain Andrzej Czechowicz was pulled out of RFE, 'Kumor' became the key source located in the facility," read the concluding evaluation of Lach's work.[204]

Another document admits directly that after Czechowicz's return to Poland, Lach "remained our only active source in the facility," and emphasizes his significant contribution: "In documenting the facility by acquiring studies, reports, recording conversations with employees, photographing them, fragmentarily operating an 8mm camera, the agent has demonstrated significant personal initiative, resourcefulness and engagement."[205] In working with the Ministry of Internal Affairs the agent took advantage of his two personal passions, photography and skiing. "Kumor" and "Freda" took part in "excursions organized by the labor union."[206]

At least some of Lach's photographs of RFE employees were reproductions of those used in propaganda publications (and also in Czechowicz's memoirs) that appeared in the 1970s and 1980s. Lach was also a co-author of one of them, a fictionalized narrative, *Ufam ci Kilroy* (I trust you, Kilroy), which outdid most such publications in its heavy use of calumny and slander, for the most part moral, aimed at RFE employees.[207]

Both Lach and Czechowicz were of secondary importance to the functioning of RFE's Polish Service. Everything points to the fact that Warsaw did not manage to recruit any high-level employees through whom it could influence either the internal situation in the Polish Service or its programs. But we must remember that the surviving documents are incomplete, and that this statement is merely a research hypothesis that may be revised in the future if more materials become available.

Polish intelligence observed and attempted to recruit or intimidate not only staff members of the Polish Service in Munich but also full- and part-time employees of RFE's field bureaus, believing that these bureaus worked directly for Western intelligence. A smattering of surviving documents about the case of Andrzej Chilecki gives an insight into the ministry's activities of this type. As an RFE freelancer in Vienna, Chilecki met with many Poles and drew on his interviews with them for material to use in reports for the Research and Analysis Department in Munich. He also published articles in the Paris *Kultura* and the London *Dziennik Polski* and *Orzeł Biały*.

In early December 1966, Section III of Department I prepared a plan to recruit Chilecki. The person chosen to serve as intermediary was a journalist from the Warsaw publication *Nowa Wieś*, Stefan Jakobs, whom Chilecki knew well and trusted. He was a secret collaborator of Department II, working under the code name "Bar." Polish counterintelligence agreed to lend its agent to intelligence for this mission in Vienna. It was assumed that financial gain would entice Chilecki and, if this was not enough, threats.[208] They knew that Chilecki was concerned about his safety, as the secret agents who had infiltrated the Polish émigré community in Vienna reported that he had talked about kidnappings by Communist secret services.

Agent "Bar" went to Vienna according to plan, using an invitation sent to him by Chilecki, who also paid for his trip.[209] Chilecki questioned "Bar" about the situation in the PUWP, among journalists, and in agriculture, and did not conceal his intent to write a report based on their conversation. At some point, "Bar" mentioned that Chilecki should work for Polish intelligence. When the financial incentive did not do the job, Jakobs moved on to the next argument prepared by the Ministry of Internal Affairs. "Listen, Andrzej," he said during their late-night chat in Chilecki's apartment in December 1966, "you have a car, you often drive in the streets of Vienna, have you ever thought that you might have an accident? You could simply, unknowingly, die in a car crash. Remember, don't underestimate the methods of the Security Service."[210] But the Security Service did not predict Chilecki's reaction: he phoned the Austrian police, who arrested Jakobs on the spot. During his interrogation, Jakobs initially admitted that he had tried to recruit Chilecki, but then during the trial backed out of his confession. He spent more than two months in jail. After the trial, he was released and expelled from Austria.[211]

But this was not the end of the ministry's interest in Andrzej Chilecki. In April 1969, it prepared a plan to kidnap him, perhaps as revenge for the trouble he had caused Department I with his reaction to the recruitment attempt. It was the intelligence resident in Vienna, who went by the name "Konrad" and worked as a diplomat in the Polish embassy, who developed a plan to kidnap Chilecki. He suggested "during a meeting administering sleeping tablets in 'Hil's' coffee or wine," and then transporting him in "Konrad's" car, which had diplomatic license plates and therefore would be subjected to only a cursory inspection at the Austrian-Czechoslovak border. The plotters considered transporting "Hil" in the car's trunk or even in the back seat. In the latter case, a passport would have to be produced for him. A doctor would take part in the kidnapping, "to check constantly how the sleeping drugs were working."

"Konrad" projected that if Chilecki agreed to collaborate once he was in Warsaw, he could be used in a large disinformation operation. "If 'Hil' breaks down, we will have an opportunity to confirm the belief that he had been an agent of the East after all. This would cause so much confusion. It is worth implementing the case if only for this fact. The costs of implementing the case will not be high. The risk [is] very slight," he reasoned to his superiors.[212]

We do not know what decisions were made. Had a kidnapping been attempted and failed, it would certainly have become public. The Chilecki case was closed in October 1970, since "continuing this work holds no promise."[213] Despite the fragmentary surviving documentary evidence and Department I's failed attempts, this case is unique in that it discloses the inner workings of Communist Poland's intelligence. It also shows the ease with which the Communist secret services could operate in Vienna. Infiltrating the émigré and refugee communities was commonplace, as was hiring agents inside them (for instance, Mieczysław Lach). Documents about Chilecki reveal that several agents observed his every move.

Another story playing out in Vienna at roughly the same time was that of Stanisław Wawrzyńczyk, a psychiatrist from Poland who had arrived in Austria in September 1966. During World War II, Wawrzyńczyk had served as the chief of Home Army intelligence in the Vilna region. With the Soviet occupation, he was sentenced to ten years in a camp in Vorkuta, where he worked as a doctor. Once in Vienna, he wrote a paper for RFE and the Paris *Kultura* about the gulag. Persons with whom he met included Kazimierz Zamorski, from

RFE's Research and Analysis Department, and Wacław Pomorski, who headed the Polish Section of RFE's Vienna bureau.[214] It was probably at this time that Department I agents met with him to persuade him to return to Poland. In late August 1967, he disappeared suddenly and resurfaced in Warsaw, having traveled through Budapest. His homecoming was used as propaganda against RFE and the Paris *Kultura*.

On September 17, 1967, the party daily *Trybuna Ludu* published Dr. Wawrzyńczyk's somewhat mysterious declaration, in which he recounted how a year earlier he had gone to Vienna to take a job with a hospital to improve his professional qualifications to benefit his patients in Poland. But envoys from "sabotage" centers stood in his way. "Unfortunately, before long my vision of this promising scientific work was disrupted by gentlemen representing Radio Free Europe and the Paris *Kultura*, who harshly attempted to engage me in political activity that assailed Poland's interests," alleged Dr. Wawrzyńczyk. "Throughout my stay in Vienna, this thought, which stemmed from my sense of a Pole's and a patriot's dignity, disturbed me. Finally, after I [had] thoroughly examined the total picture of the new situation in which I found myself, and the fact that my passport would be expiring soon, I decided to interrupt my professional work and to move up my return trip to Poland. Today, addressing the authorities of the PRP, I am loyally reporting on the circumstances of my stay in Vienna and asking for understanding and for help in finding my way out of this situation."[215]

Janusz Kolczyński, whom one could always count on in such situations, shed more light on this mysterious story in an article in the weekly *Przekrój*. "Radio Free Europe's agents, who have recently not been burdened by a surplus of successes, desperately clung to this Polish doctor-scientist," explained Communist Poland's most eminent expert on foreign sabotage. "To convince Dr. Wawrzyńczyk to 'choose freedom,' to exploit his name in provocative propaganda, would finally have given them their long-awaited success. . . . They therefore grabbed various methods they had crammed during their briefing in RFE's Munich central office, from blackmail and intimidation to sketching miraculous mirages of a brilliant scientific career in the West. This concentrated psychological attack lasted several months."

The desperate doctor found no other way out than to flee to Poland, and his story was to serve as a warning to all who traveled to the West. "There is a broader backdrop to Dr. Wawrzyńczyk's case," warned Kolczyński. "It reminded us once again of the existence and activities of Free Europe's agents, who take advantage of every opportunity to catch fish in murky waters. They are active in all the larger cities in Europe, in Vienna, Paris, Rome, London, Stockholm and others. . . . A 'countryman' of this sort approaches every single tourist group from Poland. These 'compatriots' especially try to make contact with persons who come from Poland for fellowships, internships, practicums, work missions. It happens that persons of good will fall into the nets set by these cunning agents. They are disoriented and inexperienced. After all, the agents do not appear with their visors up. They penetrate their victim gradually, like stone on water [*sic*—trans. note]. It begins with reminiscences. A common acquaintance, sometimes a minor favor, a loan etc. Only later, after they have managed to entangle their victim in their net, do they begin to use different, brutal language."[216]

In a memorandum about Dr. Wawrzyńczyk's case, Department II director Mikołaj Krupski wrote about "bringing" Wawrzyńczyk to Poland, without being more specific about how exactly this would be done. According to Krupski, "as a result of a search conducted on August 29 of this year in Wawrzyńczyk's apartment in Vienna, materials were found proving his collaboration with the Paris *Kultura* (letters to Giedroyc) and RFE, a copy of a paper titled 'The Psychology of Terror in the USSR,' with handwritten notes, and a paper addressing some aspects of the political situation in Poland."[217]

The account of the search, which was conducted by the Polish Security Service in Vienna, the capital of a neutral country that does not share a border with Poland, is shocking. Both Krupski's memorandum and another unsigned document stress that Wawrzyńczyk had given RFE and *Kultura* information about Katyń.[218] This would confirm Kazimierz Zamorski's hypothesis that "bringing" Dr. Wawrzyńczyk to Poland was intended primarily as a way to ward off publicity about Katyń in the West. It is possible that Polish intelligence had acted under pressure from the KGB, but no documentary evidence of this has been found.[219] The secret police interrogated Wawrzyńczyk about his work with RFE and *Kultura*, but his case was dismissed.[220] The price he paid was being forced to participate in a propaganda campaign against these two émigré institutions.

The Case of Wiktor Trościanko

Perhaps the greatest success of Poland's intelligence was not the recruitment of any of the RFE employees discussed so far but the "operational dialogue" with the editor Wiktor Trościanko, who never agreed to formal collaboration. It was an achievement not so much of Department I of the Ministry of Internal Affairs as it was primarily of military intelligence.[221]

Trościanko was one of the station's top political commentators, a prominent activist in the National Party in exile and an idealistic anticommunist. He had a flawless record under the German occupation and then as an émigré. Before the war he had been a journalist, during the war he oversaw the National Party's press and fought in the Warsaw Uprising in battalion "Gustaw," and after defeat he spent time in a prisoner-of-war camp for officers. In exile, he published several books (novels and memoirs), and—most important—he was one of RFE's brightest writers (or rather voices), hosting the popular opinion program *Odwrotna strona medalu* (The other side of the coin). "Trościanko was born to debate, he had a sharp tongue and an excellent pen. But he could mercilessly ridicule and destroy an adversary with one perfect word," wrote Jan Nowak-Jeziorański, who considered him one of the most important figures on the editorial staff and assigned him political commentaries at many key junctures.[222] In the indexes to both volumes of Nowak's memoirs, Trościanko's name is among the ones most frequently mentioned.

Trościanko often challenged Nowak. He emphatically opposed broadcasting Józef Światło's confessions, considering him a Communist criminal. After Czechowicz was revealed as a spy in 1971, Trościanko was one of Nowak's chief critics, reproaching him for being inexcusably careless with regard to Polish secret police scheming. In the 1960s, together with Józef Ptaczek and Jan Krok-Paszkowski, he headed a group of editors who increasingly disapproved of RFE's anti-Moczar line. They believed that it was a serious mistake to treat the Partisans as the principal threat to Poland and saw an evolution in a more "national" direction as in fact favorable, promising greater autonomy in relations with Moscow. They rejected arguments advocating the promotion of the more liberal forces within the PUWP who were being marginalized by Moczar and his people. The group also reacted with indignation when Nowak hired journalists who had left Poland after the anti-Zionist campaign of 1968 and who had earlier worked on official publications of the PUWP, and in many cases had been members of the party.[223] Quarrels over such political and human differences in the Polish Service help to explain the evolution of Trościanko's story.

Between 1965 and 1971, Trościanko met with officers of the Military Internal Service (Wojskowa Służba Wewnętrzna) several times. This might seem surprising, since this service was charged with using counterintelligence to provide security for the armed forces and was active mostly domestically; foreign intelligence, especially of a political rather than military kind, was not its mission.[224] This connection shows the relativity of the formal division of labor in the universe of the special services.

Beginning in 1969, a high-level Department I functionary began to take part in these meetings. Because Trościanko vehemently refused to work with civilian intelligence, viewing it as closely dependent on the PUWP and not serving the nation's interests, the man introduced himself as a military intelligence officer. Trościanko wanted their contacts, which had been initiated through a family friend, military intelligence agent "Bogdan," to be purely political and to have nothing to do with intelligence. National Party leaders Tadeusz Bielecki and Antoni Dargas knew about these meetings, and Dargas took part in two of them, in 1966 and 1969.[225]

In the second half of the 1960s, the National Party came to believe that the developing Soviet-Chinese conflict and the growing centrifugal tendencies in the Communist bloc, including the Romanian schism and the Prague Spring, were creating an opportunity for Poland to move into a more partnerlike relationship with the Soviet Union. In this new international situation, however, it was West Germany, becoming stronger and more independent, that was a mounting threat. The nationalists' views, which carried on the pro-Russian and anti-German orientation of the prewar National Democrats, set them apart from the majority of political parties in exile. Also distinguishing them was their failure to denounce the anti-Zionist campaign of March 1968, which they viewed as merely an intraparty conflict that was harming Poland.[226] Witold Olszewski's and Jędrzej Giertych's *Horyzonty* actually joined in the anti-Semitic campaign by publishing articles about "Jewish scheming" against Poland.[227]

From the perspective of the National Party leaders, nationalism was gaining a voice in the Communist countries, changing the nature of their regimes. "The national current is so powerful that even the Communists have been using national slogans and ideas, wanting to gain popular support or to strengthen the influence of their factions in the party leadership," Tadeusz Bielecki wrote in June 1968.[228] Antoni Dargas further developed Bielecki's concept in the same issue of *Myśl Polska*: "A new phase in the evolution of Central and Eastern Europe has begun, despite the limitations and lines set by membership in the Communist bloc. It is expressed by the fact that nationalism, defined as the preeminence of the national interest and the demand for a modern socioeconomic structure with a high technical level and sizable productivity to guarantee material prosperity, is marching into the arena in Central Europe, replacing the ideology and doctrine that ruled unquestioned in Stalin's time, and in weaker form under his successors. The Communist governments have been appealing individually or collectively to these new authentic forces or trying to reach out to them, wanting to win at least some support in their societies or to gain a stronger position in public opinion."[229] Dargas gave this speech at the opening of the Third Central Conference of the National Party in May 1968. It is an expression of the National Party's official views and, at the same time, an explanation of the reasons why its activists had begun to talk with exponents of the allegedly "national" forces in the Polish government.

In their conversations with military intelligence in late May 1969, Trościanko and Dargas mentioned wanting to start joint activities to oppose "the FRG's militarism" and "Zionism," in the name of "defending the whole nation's interests." They admired the Polish government's drive to affirm the Oder-Neisse border, as well as its removal of officers of Jewish origin from the armed forces (in 1967–1968, these numbered about 150). "The fact of purging the leadership cadre of the Polish Army of antinational elements is known in the West and uniformly positively assessed," was the comment on Trościanko's and Dargas's statements in a report to the head of the Military Internal Service, General Teodor Kufel. Their discussions included having Trościanko publish a book "showing the Zionists' anti-Polish role since World War II" with an émigré publishing house in England or France. Polish intelligence would furnish the materials and funding necessary for such a publication. Dargas, in turn, promised to write articles for the National Party's *Myśl Polska* challenging the Paris *Kultura*'s interpretation of the March 1968 events in Poland, especially the special volume its Institut Littéraire had put out. Again, Poland's intelligence would deliver the appropriate materials.[230] No such articles appeared in *Myśl Polska* in 1969 or at any other time.

In their meetings, Trościanko talked at length about the influence the "Zionists" had within RFE. To him, they dominated the radio's programmatic line, with their inspiration coming from two main sources. First, as he made the case to a Ministry of Internal Affairs officer in April 1969, "the Israel sympathizers and the so-called liberals hiding inside the party leadership are behind the currents of RFE's propaganda attacks. They have been in contact with RFE for years. . . . On the basis of his most recent observations, [Trościanko] is convinced that most of the information about the situation inside the party travels through hidden Zionist circles, who incite the incessant attacks against the M[inistry of] I[nternal] A[ffairs] and Comr. Moczar." The second source was allegedly persons who had left Poland because of the "anti-Zionist" campaign provoked by the regime. "There has never before, as long as RFE exists, been such an inflow of information from Poland as there is now. This avalanche is coming primarily from Vienna. Jewish émigrés and RFE's other fans, informants, who are capable of saying or writing more, are brought to Munich, and Nowak funds their stay in coordination with Jewish organizations. RFE's management has set aside significant sums of money for this."[231]

Available materials indicate that Trościanko's interlocutors lapped up his anti-Zionist assertions, which only validated the vision of the world that held sway in the security apparatus in the second half of the 1960s and early 1970s. Numerous Ministry of Internal Affairs studies from this period cited in this book repeated his evaluations almost verbatim.[232]

Yet Lieutenant Colonel Zbigniew Mikołajewski of the ministry's Department I, Section VIII, was not satisfied with reflections on the international situation and Zionism's threat preached by "Medal" (Trościanko and his case were assigned this code name in an obvious reference to his radio program; it was used interchangeably with "Tuba" and "Mentor"). The agents tried to extract as much factual information about the Polish desk from him as possible. Their goal was clear: "We must gradually transform the existing contacts with 'Tuba,' in which he serves as the National Party spokesman for talks with army representatives in Poland for the purpose of combating the FRG's militarism, into an intelligence contact. This will allow us to learn more about the facility."[233]

"Medal" consistently refused to formalize his collaboration in any way, declaring his anticommunism and his desire to reach an understanding solely in order to defend national interests. He heard an offer that "as an employee of a sabotage-intelligence center who understands national interests he become 'our consultant' on the topic of the defense of the national interest of the PRP." He was enticed with the promise of having his books published in Poland. "'M[edal]', a disappointed political activist of a very ripe age, has literary ambitions. He was impressed with our promises," Mikołajewski assessed the situation.[234] They also tried to persuade "Medal" to return to Poland, an offer he allegedly listened to with a kindly interest.[235]

The offer from Department I disclosed the huge hopes being attached to working with Trościanko. "As part of interference-political undertakings, in view of 'M[edal]'s' active involvement in RFE, he was advised to reduce his political-propaganda engagement ag[ainst] the PUWP's political leadership. It was also suggested that 'M[edal]' oppose Nowak's extreme aggressiveness-obsessiveness in the political meetings of RFE's Polish staff," Mikołajewski informed his superiors after a meeting in August 1971.[236] No other suggestions of this kind, which meant de facto Ministry of Internal Affairs efforts to influence the radio's program line, were ever presented (or at least no traces of them have been found so far) to the other RFE employees with whom the special services were in touch. Indeed, none of the earlier agents had as prominent a position at RFE as "Medal."

Trościanko did not become an agent, nor did he return to Poland. There is also no indication that he followed the political instructions he received from the Ministry of Internal Affairs. But he did gladly supply extensive information about the atmosphere and relationships in the Polish Service (his handlers were interested, for example, in reactions to Czechowicz's defection) and programmatic tactics and plans. He sketched out profiles of his colleagues (for instance, speculating on who was working for Western intelligence) and American managers. Most upsetting is his own initiative suggesting how best to discredit particular RFE employees, especially Nowak, toward whom he was openly hostile. A report after a meeting with Trościanko in May 1969 reads: "As for discrediting the most important RFE employees, 'Mentor' now claims that our political attacks against them do not harm their patrons' image of them but, on the contrary, often have the opposite effect. Discrediting them in the press should focus on moral-ethical aspects, possibly criminal activity, connections and so on. Thus, Trościanko proposed concocting a story about Nowak being a drug dealer."[237]

There is a trace in intelligence documents that this suggestion was taken up. In the autumn of 1970, Lieutenant Colonel Czesław Kozubski gave a new assignment to agent "Kondor," an art dealer who also smuggled art in the West and took drugs, which got him into trouble with the Danish police. "Nowak is buying up antiques, he is especially interested in *polonica*. 'Kondor' will find something of this type in antique shops in Copenhagen and offer it to the above-mentioned," Kozubski instructed his agent. It is difficult to tell whether the secret police was planning to build a closer relationship with Nowak or to create an incident to discredit him. "Kondor" did not fulfill his mission: "he has been corrupted, and the pedagogical methods we applied have yielded no positive results." This episode shows the importance to the Security Service of every piece of information about the private lives of the people it was studying that it could lay its hands on.[238]

Another of "Medal's" candidates for humiliation was Aleksandra Stypułkowska, radio name Jadwiga Mieczkowska, who was Trościanko's rival for primacy as political commentator; incidentally, she was also a supporter of the National Party. During World War II, Stypułkowska had been imprisoned by the Nazis in Pawiak prison and the Ravensbrück concentration camp. After the war, she was greatly respected in émigré veteran organizations and served as a member of the council of the Association of Former Political Prisoners. In 1969, Trościanko came up with the idea of alleging that she had served as a *Kapo*—a privileged prisoner functionary—in a concentration camp. "The attack should have a serious tone and not sound like an opinion piece. Only documented assertions will have an impact," he recommended.[239]

Department I became very interested in this idea. I have found no documents or people to confirm the charge—but how could there be any about this person whose wartime past was widely known and who had been entrusted with important functions since the war? Polish intelligence still put this accusation in Czechowicz's mouth when he said in an interview that Stypułkowska was "now representing herself as a member of the resistance movement in Ravensbrück. In fact, she was a *Kapo* in that camp, and because she had played this role, being a Jew, she came out of that hell unharmed."[240] During a meeting with his keepers, Trościanko praised Polish intelligence for their hard and precise hit. Very pleased, he talked about the shock this caused Stypułkowska:

"her health failed (heart), her activity diminished and she did not come back to normal for 3 months. She became bitter and apathetic."[241]

"Medal" either forgot that he had been the one who had suggested this idea to the Polish special services in a meeting two years earlier or found it hard to believe that his suggestion alone had been at the core of this brutal accusation. Lieutenant Colonel Mikołajewski used it to convince Trościanko that he was already deeply involved in actual collaboration and that, because of it, the next step in the direction of tightening it would not change much: "Our conversations were intertwined with many 'delicacies.' E.g., 'M[edal]': So what's the story behind discrediting Stypułkowska, where did the materials come from . . .? Me: What will you say if I tell you that the materials came from you—you informed us about Stypułkowska as a *Kapo*. . . . 'Medal' did not say a word."[242]

From the point of view of the Ministry of Internal Affairs, the most productive of Trościanko's suggestions was one concerning the director of the Polish Service. Disappointed that the attacks on Nowak in the propaganda campaign about Czechowicz's return to Poland did not weaken his position at RFE, Trościanko recommended in a meeting in August 1971 that the secret police use Nowak's wartime past. He suggested accusing Nowak of having served as an administrator of Jewish property confiscated by the Nazis. He told Lieutenant Colonel Mikołajewski that the writer Józef Mackiewicz had been spreading such rumors.

Everyone in the émigré community, as well as in the Ministry of Internal Affairs, was familiar with the conflict between this émigré author and the director of RFE's Polish Service. "Germanophile, anticommunist, in conflict with Nowak" was Mikołajewski's terse description of Mackiewicz.[243] Nowak consistently refused to work with Mackiewicz, who during the war had been sentenced to death by an underground Home Army court for writing for the collaborationist daily *Goniec Codzienny* in Vilna. To this day, people argue whether he really did.[244]

Trościanko advised Warsaw that an attack on Nowak needed to be prepared well, since it would yield results "only if it is supported by documents." Mikołajewski wrote in one of his reports that "Inspectorate 'I' was alerted to this case."[245] Preparations for a broad "disinformation operation" took the specialists at the ministry quite some time. In 1972, as the future of RFE was being discussed in the United States, two US senators received copies of a statement written by a *Volksdeutscher* from the town of Żyrardów, Johann Kassner. He claimed that between 1940 and 1942, Jan Nowak-Jeziorański had administered confiscated Jewish property on behalf of the occupying authorities. In 1974, the statement also appeared in the second edition of Czechowicz's cooked-up memoirs, *Siedem trudnych lat* (Seven difficult years). It was also then that various personalities in Western Europe received copies.[246]

It is not clear whether it was actually Trościanko who first suggested that the secret police exploit these wartime charges, as Mikołajewski's note suggests. Czechowicz claimed that an editor in the Polish Service had told him about it earlier.[247] Kassner's statement, published in Czechowicz's book, is dated April 22, 1970, while Trościanko made his suggestions in a meeting with the secret police in August 1971. The fact that the original of Kassner's declaration was never shown publicly (only copies of it were sent out) makes it impossible to confirm its date and therefore to resolve the question of who came up with this idea first.

"Medal" was no longer able to support the ministry with his ideas during its disinformation operation. The August 1971 meeting was their last, and ties were severed because of a serious botch by the secret police. After lengthy negotiations, military intelligence agreed, however reluctantly, to hand the case of "Medal" over to civilian intelligence. The Department I position that "the dialogue between representatives of the M[inistry of] N[ational] D[efense] and 'M[edal]' (his political group—N[ational] P[arty]) should be considered a serious political mistake" won.[248] From then on, conversations with Trościanko were to be used to obtain information about RFE and in the long term to recruit him, and not to seek a political understanding between the National Party in exile and the Polish secret police. Already during their meeting in Spain, Trościanko was to be shifted to the exclusive use of Mikołajewski, of Department I, who continued to present himself as a Defense Ministry officer; "Bogdan," whom "Medal" trusted, was to continue serving as the intermediary.

From the very beginning, relations between the Ministry of Internal Affairs and military intelligence were not good. Mikołajewski arrived safely in Spain by airplane, where he met Trościanko. "Bogdan," on the other hand, despite Department I advice, chose to drive his own car. As he was crossing the German-Swiss border, West German counterintelligence detained him for reasons unrelated to "Medal." To the surprise and shock of the Ministry of Internal Affairs, "Bogdan" had other important spying missions for military counterintelligence and Directorate II of the General Staff that Department I had not been informed about.[249] After a few months in prison, he was exchanged for a West German spy captured in Poland. Trościanko, his acquaintance, was interrogated by the German prosecutor's office, where he testified that the agent was innocent. Department I, fearing exposure, decided that maintaining contact with "Medal" was too risky.

Trościanko retired in the 1970s and moved to Spain, where he died in 1983. He had cooperated with Polish Communist intelligence not for personal gain. It would appear that he was guided by two motivations, a desire to combat the German threat and "Zionism," and an obsessive dislike of Jan Nowak.

A Report from Munich

Andrzej Brycht, born in 1935, one of the best-known Polish writers in the second half of the 1960s, also contributed to attacks on RFE. Critics gave a favorable reception to his 1966 novel *Dancing w kwaterze Hitlera* (A ball in Hitler's headquarters) and short stories, most of them about the war and German crimes. On the one hand, they appreciated the young author's genuine literary talent. On the other, his work fit excellently into the political and ideological mood of the time, which was marked by anti-German propaganda (which included an offensive against the Polish episcopate for its "Pastoral letter of the Polish bishops to their German brothers" in November 1965) and reminders of the Poles' wartime martyrdom. Some writers considered Brycht to be aligned with the nationalist Partisans, and he was also associated with Bolesław Piasecki's PAX (a group of nationalist Catholics who cooperated closely with the Communist regime), which published his books. For a few years in the late Gomułka period he was a key figure in the literary world, his books were published in unimaginably high print runs (*Dancing w kwaterze Hitlera* went through seven editions in four years), and he incessantly appeared on television and took part in countless meetings with large crowds of readers across Poland. His exceptionally colorful life—he had been a boxer, soldier, miner, and a deserter from the Military Mining Corps, and had been convicted several times for hooliganism—made him an icon of mass culture and an attractive character for the young generation. He was frequently compared to another famous writer, Marek Hłasko, with the difference that Brycht was the regime's pet, a real treasure for the government, as his unique style and authentic popularity allowed it to influence a diverse public.[250] Despite all this, he was respected in the émigré community. The Paris *Kultura* praised *Dancing w kwaterze Hitlera*, and RFE rated it one of the three best books to appear in Poland in 1966.[251]

In 1967, Brycht published a series of stories in the Warsaw *Kultura* about his two-week stay in Munich, where his German publisher had invited him. Also in 1967, the stories were compiled and published together as a book. In the next two years, *Raport z Monachium* (A report from Munich) was reissued three more times, the total number of copies in print reaching almost 400,000.[252] Ryszard Filipski toured Poland with his Teatr Jednego Aktora to perform a stage adaptation of *Raport z Monachium*. The Warsaw education authority instructed schools to host its performances. The production received the Janek Krasicki Silver Medal as "a complement to civics instruction."[253] The book was even placed on school reading lists.[254]

The highest party authorities praised Brycht, presenting him as a model for other writers. "So how many party members, people of the pen, have recently visited the FRG?" First Secretary of the Gdańsk Provincial Committee of the PUWP Jan Ptasiński asked at a CC PUWP plenum in May 1967. "Can anyone remember the reports they wrote about their travels, were they imprinted in our memories? None of them has had the courage to write bold and passionate political reportage like the non-party member Brycht. The series of Brycht's articles, his numerous meetings on the coast were met with enormous interest. And this publication, which coincides with the FRG's proclamation of its new eastern policy, has helped very much to expose it."[255]

The main theme of Brycht's book was West Germany as a country overrun by revanchists, neo-Nazis, and war criminals, who had American help in preparing a new war and planning to take back from Poland the Recovered Territories. RFE came up in many places. As Brycht drove by the radio's building, the appropriate associations immediately popped into his head: "This radio, whose announcers have awful diction, which is simply unbearable. . . . So it is from here that these coarse little sentences, paid so well with German marks, float into the Polish air: 'God bless the Polish peasants . . . Jacek Śniady on the microphone.' . . . Or: 'The end of Communism in Poland is near, Wiktor Trościanko wrote this program.' If he could, he would write it, this Trościanko, this serious capitalist, for five hundred dollars per month."[256]

When Brycht meets someone at a reception, his first reaction is to fear that the person may be an RFE reporter, dispatched to make a covert recording of their conversation, which will then be appropriately manipulated: "Oh my God, don't let him be some clown from Free Europe with a tiny tape recorder in his lapel because I've heard stories here about what they did to some foolish little engineer: private discussions about science and . . . love turned into a shrill political interview: because the one thing they can do pretty well is cut tapes and reglue them. . . . The silly man said: we are now working in an atmosphere of total freedom to experiment. Half an hour later he was saying: life is not worth living without love. Then he said: we don't have some instruments in Poland, so we will import them. . . . The montage added up to a full quarter hour and sounded something like this: Without freedom, life is not worth living, and we don't have freedom in Poland. . . . This was three years ago. Now maybe their work is less primitive . . . but, really, we don't know anything."[257]

The motif of manipulating naïve Poles who talked to RFE reporters or pollsters when traveling abroad was a permanent feature of propaganda campaigns against "sabotage" centers. It occupied a prominent place in Andrzej Czechowicz's ghostwritten memoirs, which appeared a few years later. Another method traditionally used by propaganda and the secret police was to show émigrés as bitter people aware of the fiascos that were their lives and of serving the wrong cause, but unable to find a way to return to Poland. Providing the names of particular individuals served the additional function of discrediting them among the people they knew, of stirring up distrust and conflict. Brycht's *Raport z Monachium* features Tadeusz Nowakowski, a well-known émigré author, who wrote cultural programs for RFE. He allegedly confessed to Brycht: "As for me, if I could relive everything from the start, I would be in Poland now, no matter what bad things might happen. Can you even begin to imagine what happens to me when my son says 'earthberry'? Not strawberry but earthberry! Because he thinks in German, *Erdbeer*, and translates it literally into Polish!"

In response, Brycht demands that Nowakowski return to his homeland. "So why do you want to suffer? Pack up your things right now, button up your family's coats and go back to Poland! People are right to appreciate those so-called prodigal sons, always and everywhere, because their existence confirms family rules. So I don't think that anything bad will happen to you, only your earnings will certainly get worse, so this is the one thing you need to think about. But with what you know about things that most people don't know anything about, you can write a book that the whole world will read, and so there will be money there. So what are you waiting for?"[258] This last appeal resembles the luring of many émigré figures, also RFE staff, that Polish intelligence officers and agents specialized in, which has been described repeatedly in this book.

When he published *Raport z Monachium*, Brycht was working for the Security Service. In November and December 1966, before he left for Germany, two Department II functionaries had "operational conversations" with him. Not only did Brycht agree to collaborate, he shocked them by immediately declaring his enthusiasm. "It is interesting that the above-mentioned tried very insistently to learn about any plans we may have for his person for the future, making it clear that he was always ready to serve and that we can be sure that whatever he is assigned he will perform conscientiously," Lieutenant Colonel Andrzej Dudziński noted. Just before he left, "A. Brycht phoned me," Dudziński reported to his superiors, "on his own initiative, motivating the call with his desire to say good-bye, but also to ask whether I might have any other things to discuss about his trip."[259]

It is possible that Brycht wanted to reassure himself that in exchange for his willingness to work for the Security Service he would be able to continue to travel to the West. A few years earlier he had been denied permission to visit Switzerland, where he was to receive the literary Kościelski Prize. But the story of his collaboration gives the impression it was voluntary. He did not resist reporting on people he met, he completed his assignments, he brought typed reports signed by hand with his code name "Gerard" to meetings in secret locations. In 1967, the Security Service treated him as a "covert contact" (it also used the terms "work contact" and "operational contact" for him) and beginning in 1968 as a secret collaborator.

Surviving files contain handwritten receipts for the money paid him, not huge sums (altogether about 8,000 zlotys). They alone would hardly be a significant incentive for Poland's top-earning writer of the era. It is a challenge to understand why a writer—who was applauded by top state officials and official propaganda, for whom Minister of Internal Affairs Moczar himself could be a partner, or at least people from his immediate entourage, and not a lieutenant colonel of the counterintelligence—would collaborate with such passion. There are no hints in the secret police documents to assist us in interpreting his motives. Perhaps what explains it was a lack of any moral constraints, not viewing collaboration as reprehensible, and the desire to use the secret police to settle personal accounts with other writers.

There is no evidence in surviving documents that Brycht planned the contents of *Raport z Monachium* together with the police. But one would not expect the mid-level counterintelligence officers who recruited him to be Brycht's partners in conversations about a book. If such conversations did take place, they would have been with altogether different people, propaganda specialists, of whom there were plenty among Moczar's trusted people. The book's convergence with the official propaganda line, even some motifs (for instance, RFE) identical to those regularly present in the Ministry of Internal Affairs repertoire, suggests there may have been such cooperation. In any event, immediately after his return, Brycht wrote an exhaustive account of his stay in Munich. He included profiles of the RFE editors he had met (including the writer Tadeusz Nowakowski) and information about others he had come in contact with in Germany.[260] For example, he reported on the activities of two other Polish writers with whom he was in touch there, Wiktor Woroszylski and Witold Wirpsza.[261]

In the following months, Brycht supplied information, either on his own initiative or as ordered by the functionaries he met with, about the views and statements of writers, journalists, and others he had come across. Thus, after a meeting at the Student Discussion Center at the University of Warsaw, he reported on his clash with a group of pro-democratic, antigovernment students called the "commandos." "Its main leaders, Henryk Szlajfer and Józef Dajczgewand, reproached the author of *Raport* for his bias, nationalism, and even directly building the foundations of fascism in Poland. . . . During the very stormy discussion, Szlajfer spoke, and his statements included: 'Why are you telling us this nonsense, that 5 million people died in Auschwitz? Twenty million people died in concentration camps in the USSR, what do you have to say about that?'" he reported, outraged, to his case officer.

Brycht evidently took the whole affair very personally, like a writer whose pride has been hurt, and not like an agent charged with writing a detailed report. "Our contact, talking about his literary event, did not hide his outrage at the representatives of the 'commando' group who spoke there, he used condescending terms for them, believing that life is treating them too well. . . . He stated that punks of their ilk should be used for physical labor," noted Dudziński. Brycht made sure to report that "this group allegedly has close contacts by letter with the . . . Free Europe station. It is probably also from there that materials about the case of L[eszek] Kołakowski [a philosopher who in 1966 gave a speech at Warsaw University critical of the party leadership and subsequently was excluded from the PUWP—P. M.] have seeped in."[262]

RFE, which on many occasions spoke critically about the author of *Raport z Monachium*, quickly became the writer's primary enemy. In October 1967, Brycht asked the secret police to let him see the monitoring materials of RFE's programs in which he had been attacked. After consulting with his bosses, Dudziński agreed. The Ministry of Internal Affairs hoped that this would enable it to "decipher some of Free Europe's information sources from 'Gerard's' circle of acquaintances."[263]

These hopes soon proved justified. That very same month, after RFE aired a program in which Brycht was quoted and information about him was provided, he turned over to the secret police the names of four people he knew who had spent an evening with him at the Journalists' Club in Foksal Street in Warsaw and had heard him talk about matters that were then broadcast by RFE. Brycht told Dudziński which of the four was the most likely RFE informant and why he thought so.[264]

Brycht's uncontrollable temper got him in trouble at the very pinnacle of his success. He clearly stopped controlling himself during meetings with readers. Information began to reach the CC PUWP and the Ministry of Internal Affairs that the writer had mocked Gomułka, the GDR (where he had been sent to write a book about the "good" Germans), the Vietnamese Communists, and the Vietcong (from his time as a special correspondent in Vietnam).[265] As a result of his openly expressed opinions, in May 1970 the Culture Office of the CC PUWP forbade Brycht to appear in public, and Department II suspended their collaboration. The officers charged with this secret collaborator, however, considered this decision not only an overreaction but actually unfair since it "was made in a way that did not allow 'Gerard' to defend himself or even to clear up and explain the charges against him." Department II continued to see Brycht as a loyal agent and resumed their collaboration in February 1971.[266] Soon the ban on his public appearances was lifted.[267]

The secret police then were all the more surprised when in June 1971 Brycht got off a Polish excursion ship in Italy and asked for political asylum in Belgium.[268] Before he left Italy, he sent two telegrams, to RFE and to the Paris *Kultura*, informing them of his decision and asking for help.[269] "Chosen freedom, awaiting money" is how Janusz Marchwiński, who worked for RFE's Polish Service at that time, remembers the gist of Brycht's message.[270]

Brycht explained the reasons for his decision and defended himself against the charges directed at him in the September 1971 issue of the Paris *Kultura*. "First, I am not a colonel of the Ministry of Internal Affairs of the People's Republic of Poland. This ministry has never asked me to take any full-time jobs with them," he wrote, and in this case he was truthful. He also denied the rumors that his last book, *Raport z Monachium*, "had been written by General Mieczysław Moczar." He claimed to have left Poland because he no longer wanted to "write the untruth" and "every few months to sniff out the way the winds were blowing in the new era, which in any case always stank of old military foot wrappings, the rotting teeth of the peasant who rules the district and the nauseating smell of exhaust fumes of the tanks rolling into city streets."[271]

Attempting to understand the causes of Brycht's "desertion," the Security Service analyzed his latest literary output. To their amazement, it turned out that probably the last piece of work he had submitted to Wydawnictwo Łódzkie publishers less than a month before he traveled to Italy was a story titled "Fen" (*Föhn*). "It tells the story of a sports journalist," wrote Lieutenant Colonel A. Lesner, "who is spending time in Munich and is recruited by people connected to RFE. The author reveals the mechanisms and methods used by the CIA people who recruit Poles who are there temporarily. Andrzej Brycht is critical of RFE's activity, and in the case of his protagonist shows the CIA's revenge for disloyalty (the protagonist is killed by a time bomb)."[272] In the mind of the Security Service, the story's hero, the journalist murdered by the CIA, was the alter ego of Brycht, who "at times lent him some of his own characteristics."[273]

The idea of exploiting Brycht's last story written in Poland in their operations occurred to the functionaries. "In view of the fact that Brycht is staying in the West, it seems useful to implement his publishing proposal in the form of a book, which should serve to maintain and deepen the uncertainty at RFE and other centers vis-à-vis A. Brycht."[274]

Brycht's decision to defect disoriented the Ministry of Internal Affairs, whose functionaries thought it possible that he wanted to collect attractive reporting experiences on his own, and then use them in a book that would bring him even more popularity. Major Z. Rybacki speculated that "perhaps he made the adventurous decision on his own to reach the sabotage centers with the intention of returning to Poland and publishing the sensational materials (Capt. Czechowicz's example) here."[275]

This supposition came true, in a way, and only years later. Brycht spent a long time in Canada, returning in 1988 to Poland. Before long he had published a book, *Azyl polityczny* (Political asylum), a lampoon of seemingly everyone he had come across as an émigré, including the editor in chief of the Paris *Kultura*, Jerzy Giedroyc, who was the first person to help him outside Poland. He complained that RFE, unwilling to forget what he had written about it, did not want to assist him when he stayed in the West.

The Polish Army in Combat with Radio Free Europe

Battling the alleged foreign sabotage was also entrusted to noncivilian institutions. Military intelligence made a significant contribution to fighting the "invisible enemy." In 1963, the mission of military intelligence (Directorate II of the General Staff) was broadened to include "reactionary emigration." This work was to be conducted in cooperation with the "Ministry of Internal Affairs, Main Political Directorate, and the Office of the Chief of the Military Internal Service."[276]

It appears that it was only at this time that military intelligence expanded its operations against the Polish émigré community in the West, including RFE. This was the result chiefly of the decision by many Polish state institutions to step up the fight against foreign sabotage (this decision was described earlier in this book with the example of the Ministry of Internal Affairs, which played the main role in this realm). Second, military intelligence had earlier experienced significant problems, which would have made it difficult to initiate actions against the émigré community and RFE, had such plans been formulated. At a time when the radio was beginning to broadcast from Munich, military intelligence had only just (since 1950) been separated from civilian intelligence, and it was going through a serious crisis. To quote from a 1961 Directorate II study, "in 1952–54, it became necessary to eliminate a significant part of the agent network because of exposure or of their total unproductivity. As a result of putting order into the spy network in the field and directing it to gather information of a military, military-political, and military-economic nature, of the 402 agents active in 1952, their number was brought down to 55. At the same time, it needs to be stressed that many agents with a great intelligence potential refused to continue to collaborate. . . . The years 1955–60 are characterized by beginning to work almost from the ground up, for the most part with a young cadre lacking intelligence qualifications."[277]

The late 1950s brought new setbacks when several high-ranking intelligence officers, including Colonel Paweł Monat, Lieutenant Colonel Jerzy Bryn, Lieutenant Colonel Henryk Trojan, and Captain Mieczysław Skorupiński, defected and went over to Western intelligence agencies.[278] "These circumstances made it necessary to freeze a significant part of the endangered spy network in the territories of the more important countries (FRG, France, and the USA)," read the Directorate II annual report.[279]

Despite these difficulties in operations abroad, in the mid-1960s military intelligence scored an important victory in the "emigration area," launching an "operational dialogue" with Wiktor Trościanko and Antoni Dargas. Again, it is noteworthy that this was a success not for Directorate II of the General Staff but for the Military Internal Service, military counterintelligence, which was supposed to operate domestically. This shows that frequently the division of labor and interests between the different branches of the special services existed only on paper. Indeed, a special cell within the Internal Military Service was charged with fighting ideological sabotage. This was Section III of Directorate I.[280]

To return to the Trościanko-Dargas case, it is significant that a representative of civilian intelligence (that is, Department I) became involved in the operation. The choice may have been made on the principle that operations vis-à-vis the émigré community are not—or at least were not then—a priority for military intelligence and would not be run by it alone. This hypothesis is also confirmed by the fact that no military intelligence materials have been found for any other equally serious case concerning the émigré community and RFE. It is not out of the question, however, that this is because military intelligence documents are less easily accessible to historians than civilian intelligence materials. An analysis of the documents of Directorate II of the General Staff confirms that its main interest were military issues (often technical ones, such as NATO armaments, organization, mobilization plans, and so on).

Much more is known about the political and propaganda activities conducted by military organizations, mostly the Main Political Directorate of the General Staff, against what it perceived as sabotage. Already in 1958 it was regularly monitoring RFE's and other foreign stations' programs and analyzing émigré publications. The information bulletin prepared for the leadership of the Ministry of National Defense was based on these analyses.[281]

The army's political propaganda department was also affected by this growing interest in "ideological sabotage" and in RFE from the early 1960s, discussed earlier in this book in the context of the Ministry of Internal Affairs and other civilian institutions. In 1962, the Main Political Directorate prepared a study that viewed psychological warfare and ideological sabotage as key imperialist weapons for fighting socialism. "Western radio stations are one of the main instruments used to implement propaganda against the socialist countries," the military specialists in ideological warfare asserted. "Radio Free Europe plays the main role, as it airs programs in Polish 18 hours out of 24. It has a powerful technical and personnel base at its disposal. It comments on almost every important political, economic, and cultural event in our country rapidly and falsely."[282]

According to the Main Political Directorate, propaganda and ideological work by civilian and military institutions should fight the effects of the enemy stations. It considered restoring jamming, which had been suspended by the Polish government in 1956. But it assessed that "it is a very costly undertaking. We would need to expend a few hundred million zlotys for the purchase and operation of jamming devices, including salaries for ca. 5,000 employees." Furthermore, this great expense would not guarantee full effectiveness: "We know from the period when the Jamming Service existed in Poland that the results of its work were insufficient. Despite cooperation with the countries of our camp, full jamming was not achieved. It was possible to hear the hostile programs aired on various frequencies in different places in Poland, and the use of various systems of directional antennas and neutralizers on receivers significantly improved the reception of the jammed stations."[283] What an interesting assessment of the huge effort and expenses invested in the 1950s to create Poland's powerful jamming system after the fact!

Significantly, the Main Political Directorate viewed not only RFE but also the Paris *Kultura* as very dangerous adversaries. "It operates in its own way," the study reads, "behind a mask of 'sympathy for the Polish road to socialism,' emphasizing its oppositional and not its counterrevolutionary nature. It fulfills its mission—ideological warfare against Communism—in a more refined way than do other émigré publications and radio stations."[284]

A study conducted in 1964 researched the effects of Western radio stations on the officer cadre and soldier recruits. It was not quantitative (this methodology would be introduced in the 1970s) and focused on how the contents of programs by the "hostile" stations penetrated the military ranks, with RFE considered the greatest threat. The Main Political Directorate believed that, in the military, "direct and regular" listening to foreign programs was very limited. But their contents seeped into the army differently: "There are many more cases, though not on a massive scale, when various types of commentaries, rumors, and information from Western radio sources, from civilians, families, and so on, come down to the soldiers, including the professional cadre. This occurs especially in periods of serious political and other events, when the need for political information clearly increases. For example, we observed an increase in the troops' interest in Western programs in the first half of April of this year, after the first rumors appeared about the letter from the 34 intellectuals to the prime minister."[285] Commentaries heard in foreign programs were repeated most often in garrisons in Warsaw and its immediate vicinity and near other big cities. "The contents and tone of statements in some cases could be mistaken for the tone of Free Europe's commentaries," the Main Political Directorate assessed.[286]

The paper ended with this conclusion: "We must put a lot of work, both across the whole country and in the army, into developing a methodology and a system for distinguishing geography and intensification of hostile propaganda activity and its influence on the attitudes and views of members of our society. Our understanding of this matter is still superficial, and in many cases based on intuition and speculation rather than on facts and precise reasoning."[287]

According to this report, listening to foreign broadcasters was a marginal occupation in military units, but in some locations its threat appeared to be quite serious. During an inspection of the Saxon Tank Division, Lieutenant Colonel Eugeniusz Samsel uncovered a looming menace: "it has been removed to a forest garrison (Gubin-Komorowo), which is located far from any large urban centers, which deprives the cadre and the soldiers of the basic service of political information by radio. In the case of Gubin, Polish stations are very difficult to hear, but Free Europe can be heard very clearly."[288]

Regardless of the actual reception quality of the "sabotage" radios in the army, its political-propaganda department devoted great attention and energy to fighting this threat. This can be seen in the number of lectures and trainings devoted to it. Thus, for example, in the "training year 1966/1967," in the operational air force alone, meetings devoted to ideological sabotage were held in thirty-five units.[289] In the Pomeranian Military District in September and October 1967 alone, eighty-two lectures on "centers of hostile propaganda and anticommunist sabotage" were presented.[290]

The place of sabotage in ideological training is illustrated well by the list of "lecture initiatives" conducted in the navy in 1967. The biggest subject, taken up in twenty-three meetings, was "the Polish Workers' Party fight for the national front and social reforms." Sixteen meetings addressed "50 years of the Soviet economy," fourteen discussed "the social achievements of the Soviet nations," and eighteen focused on "the current problems of anticommunist ideological sabotage."[291] What an outstanding outcome: only the Polish Workers' Party was more popular than sabotage!

After the June 1967 Six-Day War between Israel and its neighboring Arab states, the military, like civilian institutions, added a new element to the enemy's portrait, "Zionism," allegedly one of the main inspirations for sabotage. In the case of the military there was also the especially painful motif of the defeat of the Arab armies, which had received Warsaw Pact equipment and organized and fought according to its models. "The propaganda of the imperialist radios, which twists the recent events to their advantage, is attempting to undermine faith in the stability of our defensive alliances and in our military equipment," warned a Main Political Directorate paper written a few weeks after the war in the Middle East ended.[292]

It is significant that it was in June 1967 that the Main Political Directorate began to prepare its weekly analyses of the "monitoring of hostile radio stations." These were distributed to the members of the Politburo and the CC PUWP Secretariat.[293] In the late 1960s, the Main Political Directorate aspired not only to expand its antisabotage activities in the armed forces, but also to play an important role both in the national front of fighting the ideological threat coming from foreign centers and in cooperation with the other countries of the Communist bloc. In February 1970, it developed a plan to organize a symposium in which representatives of the Warsaw Pact would discuss their experiences in fighting what the party called ideological sabotage and launch closer coordination. It argued that "our practice so far shows that in the community of Socialist countries and within the Unified Armed Forces of the Warsaw Treaty, no appropriate common directions, forms, and methods of challenging the psychological warfare and ideological sabotage have been developed."[294]

Since no documents about such a symposium have been found, we do not know whether it took place. In early March 1970, the Political-Defense Department of the Committee for National Defense conducted training on "ideological sabotage."[295] At around the same time, the Main Political Directorate was promoting tighter cooperation with the Ministry of Internal Affairs in fighting ideological sabotage. It would consist of joint training for the employees of the two institutions and cooperation "in the fields of permanent recognition, assessment, and analysis of the directions of ideological sabotage against our country and proposing political means to counteract it."[296]

Soon enough, such close cooperation would happen in the propaganda campaign constructed around the return of Andrzej Czechowicz. It would be the Ministry of National Defense that would publish the most important propaganda materials, including the brave captain's trumped-up memoirs.

4. Operation Olcha: The Security Service versus Radio Free Europe's Contacts in Poland

Beginning in the late 1950s, it became a priority for the Security Service to limit contacts between Polish citizens and RFE, the Paris-based *Kultura,* and other émigré publications and organizations. As was mentioned in chapter 3, in 1958 Hanna Szarzyńska-Rewska was sentenced to three years in prison for distributing copies of *Kultura*. In 1961, Anna Rudzińska was arrested, charged with translating a sociology book for publication by *Kultura*'s Institut Littéraire, and sentenced to a year in prison.[1] Also in 1961, Andrzej Markiewicz, an employee of the Catholic organization PAX, was arrested and sentenced to three years in prison for publishing some articles in *Kultura*.[2] Other writers, among them January Grzędziński, Jan Nepomucen Miller, and Stanisław Cat-Mackiewicz, were also punished for making contact with émigré publications, foremost among them the Paris-based *Kultura* and the London-based *Wiadomości*. The Security Service conducted investigations, read the suspects' correspondence, and eavesdropped on their conversations. Grzędziński was arrested, but his case was dismissed because of his advanced age and ill health. Indictments were brought against the other two writers. In September 1965, Miller received a three-year prison term, which was reduced to a one-and-a-half-year suspended sentence. The preparations for Mackiewicz's trial were interrupted by his death in February 1966.[3]

The story of Władysław Bartoszewski and his associates fits into this political and ideological context. For many years, this group of people relayed information about Poland to RFE, and its members were therefore subjected to a scrupulous investigation, a broad spectrum of operational moves (including "disintegrating" ones), and repressions by the political police. A close analysis of their case sheds light on both the nature of the later Gomułka years and the methods used by the Security Service. The surviving materials of Operation Olcha (which means alder) are exceptionally detailed. They permit us to reconstruct step by step nearly all the secret police moves, including forgeries—something that is extremely rare, since most materials of this kind were carefully destroyed. Olcha serves as a case study, allowing us to examine in greater detail than elsewhere in this book the operations of the security apparatus vis-à-vis the people who collaborated with RFE from Poland.

Conspiracy, Continued

The secret police had a long-standing interest in Władysław Bartoszewski. An Auschwitz inmate, a member of the underground Council for Aid to the Jews (Rada Pomocy Żydom) during World War II, and a staffer of the Bureau of Information and Propaganda of the Headquarters of the Home Army (Biuro Informacji i Propagandy Komendy Głównej AK), in 1945 he became involved in the conspiratorial activities of the Armed Forces Delegation for Poland (Delegatura Sił Zbrojnych na Kraj), as well as in the legal opposition, the Polish Peasant Party (Polskie Stronnictwo Ludowe, PSL). Arrested in 1946, he was freed after a one-and-a-half-year investigation without charges being filed. He was rearrested in 1949 and sentenced to eight years in prison, this time charged with espionage for the underground organization Freedom and Independence Association (Zrzeszenie Wolność i Niezawisłość, WiN); he was released in August 1954. Beginning in 1956, he wrote for the Catholic weekly *Tygodnik Powszechny* and conducted research on the occupation, including assistance to Jews in hiding. His best-known work on this subject, co-authored with Zofia Lewinówna, *Ten jest z Ojczyzny mojej. Polacy z pomocą Żydom 1939–1945* (He is my neighbor: The Poles who came to the Jews' rescue, 1939–1945), was published in 1967.[4]

In 1957, the police again became interested in him. Surveillance became intense in the early 1960s, both because of Bartoszewski's contacts with the Israeli embassy and his travel to Israel to research Polish-Jewish issues and because of his activity in Home Army associations. In February 1963, observation (which included interception of correspondence, bugging of his home, and outdoor monitoring) was turned into Operation Bonza (Big Shot).[5] This was also the code name assigned to Bartoszewski, alternating with "Szatan" (Satan), "Bartek," and others. The first two monikers show the peculiar respect that the Ministry of Internal Affairs had for this experienced target.

But what the political police did not realize for a long time was that Bartoszewski had been in regular contact with RFE. He initiated this connection in

1963 during the first foreign trip he was allowed to take, to Israel, after being released from prison. As he changed planes in Athens, he sent a letter to Tadeusz Żenczykowski, deputy director of RFE's Polish Service and an older colleague from the Home Army's Bureau of Information and Propaganda. Żenczykowski phoned him daily at his hotel in Tel Aviv, and on Bartoszewski's journey home they met in Vienna.[6] This launched a lengthy and productive collaboration in which Bartoszewski would pass on information he had gathered in various milieus (especially the media, culture, and the Catholic Church), developments within the government, and the regime's plans, repressions, and harassment. RFE used it in many of its programs, including Wiktor Trościanko's *The Other Side of the Coin*, which specialized in exposing secrets of the Communist system. Bartoszewski also delivered complete papers, which were then aired by RFE and published anonymously in the radio's publication *Na antenie* (On the air). Not coincidentally, one of his most important papers addressed the crimes committed by the security apparatus in the first ten years of People's Poland.[7] Bartoszewski reminisced many years later that this idea of working with RFE was born during a conversation with another Stalinist prisoner, Mieczysław Pszon. "As we remembered the slammer, the prison screws and their methods, we thought about what to do so that people who had not been through it would learn this truth and many other truths. I believed that since a muzzle had been placed on information, we had to do everything to help true information reach people," he told an interviewer for *Tygodnik Powszechny* in 2002.[8]

Bartoszewski passed on information gathered from conversations with hundreds of members of the intelligentsia, among whom he spent most of his time, mostly in Warsaw, where he lived, and in Cracow, where *Tygodnik Powszechny* was located. The most interesting facts came from Wiesław Chrzanowski, Jan Józef Lipski, and the lawyers Witold Lis-Olszewski and Kazimierz Ostrowski. He told no one about his contacts with RFE, although some could certainly have guessed. He did not pass on information from the *Tygodnik Powszechny* community so as not to endanger the weekly, which the regime was already watching closely.

At their first meeting, he and Żenczykowski agreed on a few addresses in London to which Bartoszewski would send his letters for RFE. But the main route was Vienna, through Kurt Skalnik, head of the Austrian president's press office, who had earlier served as editor of the Catholic weekly *Die Furche*. Bartoszewski would also often give letters to Western diplomats for Skalnik, who then mailed them to Munich. Serving as regular go-betweens were the directors of the Austrian Cultural Institute in Warsaw and sometimes Dutch and Swedish embassy employees, but never American or German diplomats, who were the most closely watched by the secret police.[9] RFE's American management, told by Jan Nowak about the Bartoszewski connection, feared that if this link to the foreign diplomats was discovered, the Polish government would use it for a propaganda attack on the radio, charging it in particular with espionage. It seemed to be potentially very dangerous, especially when in the late 1960s reports about close ties between RFE and the CIA appeared in public. They even tried—without success—to dissuade Bartoszewski from his enterprise.[10]

In the second half of the 1960s, Bartoszewski traveled to the West several times, using every occasion to meet with Żenczykowski for hours or even days at a time. Jan Nowak sometimes went along. The meetings never took place in Munich, for reasons of security, and Bartoszewski never even crossed the threshold of the radio's headquarters. He talked about everything he knew about Polish domestic issues, answering many questions.[11] The third person in the RFE's Polish Service who knew about this connection was Father Tadeusz Kirschke.

Bartoszewski had an assistant, Danuta Bańkowska, also a lifelong underground activist (the Home Army and Freedom and Independence), who was on the staff of the Main Office of the Association of Polish Librarians. She typed materials for Żenczykowski and mailed them from various cities in Poland or from foreign locations during her travels. Her work in the 1960s reminded her a little of her contributions in the immediate postwar period. According to the Security Service, she had been "the main messenger and distributor for the central region of WiN . . . she made copies of secret documents. . . . She would then pass these materials on to particular boxes." She was arrested in 1946 and sentenced to ten years in prison, from which she was released in 1955.[12] Later, Ewa Drężepolska, employed by the Ministry of Domestic Trade, who during the war had also worked in the Bureau of Information and Propaganda and had known Jan Nowak (Zdzisław Jeziorański) as a student in the economics department of Adam Mickiewicz University in Poznań, also joined Bartoszewski's team.

It is difficult to dispel the impression that their work was a sort of collusion of former Home Army members and activists in a postwar conspiracy, people who were continuing their struggle for a free Poland in a new era and with new methods. But their point of reference was the same ethos and mutual trust based on shared experiences. The story of Stanisław Salmonowicz, a younger lawyer and historian at Nicolaus Copernicus University in Toruń who also joined this group, confirms this observation. When he was in Paris on a fellowship in 1966, Salmonowicz spent a few days talking with Żenczykowski. He had been too young to take part in the 1940s underground, but he had been raised on the rhetoric and thinking of the Home Army and Freedom and Independence. He had an uncle, Colonel Ludwik Muzyczka, from whom he learned about these organizations, and he devoted much of his academic work to them.[13] Two others who worked closely with Bartoszewski, the attorneys Kazimierz Ostrowski and Witold Lis-Olszewski, had also been in the Home Army, and the latter also in Freedom and Independence, for which he paid with a prison term of several years.

Operation Olcha demonstrates that the Secret Service's enormous distrust of the 1940s underground activists, which lasted well into the 1970s and even the 1980s, was not merely an ideological obsession but was actually justified, not only because these people evidently disliked the Communist regime but also because their underground experience presented a threat to the political police. The caution and self-discipline they had acquired in much more difficult times allowed Bartoszewski and his friends to operate for several years without attracting secret police attention. The Security Service itself recognized this when a biographical report about Bartoszewski it prepared in December 1966 remarked on his "excellent familiarity with the rules of conspiracy."[14]

The First Traces: The Legal Profession

The secret police came across Bartoszewski's trail by accident, or at least through information that did not directly concern him or his closest associates. Their investigation began simultaneously with a detailed examination of the émigré press and RFE programs and surveillance of the Warsaw legal community, one of Bartoszewski's main sources of information for RFE. According to a memorandum from Colonel Henryk Piętek, the director of Department III of the Ministry of Internal Affairs (responsible for combating political opponents), this is how agents first picked up his trail: "Our analysis of Radio Free Europe programs and some article appearing in the émigré press devoted to political trials and the justice system gave us reason to suspect that these programs and articles had been written on the basis of information from Poland. Because of the details included in them, this information could only have come from the legal profession."[15]

Beginning in June 1965, a series of articles about events in Poland appeared in the émigré weekly *Tygodnik Polski* in London. They covered the situation in the Polish Writers' Union but focused mostly on the political trials of the so-called Trotskyites, Ludwik Hass, Kazimierz Badowski, and Romuald Śmiech; the writers Melchior Wańkowicz and Jan Nepomucen Miller; and the attorney Karol Głogowski, founder of the illegal Union of Young Democrats, as well as the investigations of the writers Stanisław Mackiewicz and January Grzędziński. The Security Service intercepted two anonymous letters, mailed in Poland to an address in London, that "demonstrated a high level of concurrence" with published texts. The service decided that the articles in *Tygodnik Polski* demonstrated such deep familiarity with this subject that they must have been written using sources supplied by the defense in the political trials. Three lawyers were chosen as potential leaks, Witold Lis-Olszewski, Jan Olszewski, and Stanisław Szczuka. Later, Władysław Siła-Nowicki was added to the list. The men were subjected to surveillance, which consisted primarily of placing spies among lawyers. Lis-Olszewski was singled out as the most suspect, and bugs were planted in both his home and office.[16] On May 5, 1966, Department III launched an operational investigation code-named "Olcha." Its principal target was Lis-Olszewski; beginning in 1967, Władysław Bartoszewski also came under intense scrutiny.

Another link to Lis-Olszewski was found in August 1966 during a search of the home of the elderly writer Szymon Szechter and his assistant, Nina Karsov.[17] The suspect materials included a lawyer's arguments presented during Ludwik Hass's trial and other court documents. The Ministry of Internal Affairs decided that it had been Lis-Olszewski who had helped Szechter and Karsov prepare materials to send to London for publication in the émigré press.[18] The political police took the next steps mostly using information gathered from the bugs installed in Lis-Olszewski's and Szechter's apartments, and also in Danuta Bańkowska's and Władysław Bartoszewski's.[19]

Department III acquired several recordings from the summer and autumn of 1966 in which Lis-Olszewski and Bartoszewski talked about sending materials abroad and "expressed great satisfaction with the camouflage RFE had used in a program about the trial of [Mieczysław] Zawistowski and Głogowski." They were referring to the fact that RFE had not mentioned the verdict, even though one had already been announced, wanting to create the impression that it had incomplete information because it was not in contact with the lawyers. Thanks to a bug, the police also knew that "Danuta Bańkowska had picked up materials of unknown content from Lis-Olszewski meant to be sent abroad on Bartoszewski's orders."[20] People who suspected that their conversations were being bugged often communicated in whispers "with a radio playing loudly" in the background, so that in many cases the secret police were incapable of reconstructing the whole sequence and had only a very general notion of what the conversations were about.

The Security Service made a list of RFE's programs on the political trials in Poland that aired from August to November 1966.[21] It knew in December 1966 that Władysław Bartoszewski, assisted by Danuta Bańkowska, was playing a central role in sending information to RFE and that the main source of materials about the political trials was the Warsaw lawyer Witold Lis-Olszewski. But it was still looking for an answer to the question of how exactly this information was being transmitted to the West, and it attempted to gather evidence that would allow it to launch legal proceedings. In subsequent years, these two goals would determine the secret police actions, which gathered momentum. Significantly, the issue of materials being sent to the Polish-language London press, to which readers in Poland had negligible access, receded into the background, while RFE, heard by millions of Poles, came to dominate Operation Olcha.

Searching for the Smuggling Routes

In 1967, the Ministry of Internal Affairs made two attempts to arrest persons traveling out of Poland who were suspected of being associated with Bartoszewski. Each time, the ministry hoped that searching them would yield material evidence that it could use to arrest them and put them on trial. The documentation for both cases shows that the secret police force was using information it acquired primarily through bugging and secondarily from intercepted correspondence. Retracing the sequence of circumstantial evidence accumulated by the Security Service reveals the service's operational methods. In February 1967, a letter from Kurt Skalnik to Bartoszewski was intercepted. It read: "Everyone liked the Christmas cake very much." In a March 7 phone conversation, Bartoszewski asked his friend Jan Zaborowski, who worked at the Interpress news agency, to take some "baked goods, namely a gingerbread, which he would bring to him just before his departure" on a trip abroad. The secret police took this as an indication that materials were being prepared for RFE ("perhaps they were actually to be hidden inside a gingerbread"). It planned to detain Zaborowski at Okęcie airport and to search him thoroughly. There was even a backup plan: "In case, despite everything, the outcome of the search is negative, we have prepared an anonymous letter to show to Zaborowski that alleges that he is a major diamond smuggler."

The search, which was conducted by a customs official and a Department III functionary dressed in a customs official's uniform, yielded no gingerbread and no materials to compromise Bartoszewski. The officials did find Kurt Skalnik's letter, but its contents appeared to contain no incriminating evidence. At the same time, there was an unpleasant slipup. The Security Service also searched the famous violinist Wanda Wiłkomirska, not realizing that she was married to Mieczysław Rakowski, editor in chief of *Polityka* weekly and a deputy member of the CC PUWP. The officers thought her a suspect since a person named Wanda had been mentioned several times in the "Olcha" case, including in recorded conversations.[22]

The trail was false, since Bartoszewski never sent information to Munich via Interpress journalists.[23] The Security Service did not realize that it had accidentally come across the most important foreign go-between in his contacts with RFE, Kurt Skalnik. But the airport fiasco did not discourage the secret police from trying again. In early May 1967, it inferred from a bugged conversation between Lis-Olszewski and Bartoszewski that they were planning to send new information to RFE, including some on the trial of Szymon Szechter and Nina Karsov, the banning of Karol Głogowski from practicing his profession, the harassment of Władysław Siła-Nowicki, censorship, the situation inside the Ministry of Internal Affairs, relations between the state and the Catholic Church, and the pro-China actions of a group within the PUWP opposed to First Secretary Władysław Gomułka (who had returned to power during the de-Stalinization in October 1956). Bartoszewski allegedly mentioned that a person traveling abroad by train from Warsaw's Gdańsk Station on May 10 would be carrying these materials. The secret police knew that this was the day Danuta Bańkowska would be leaving for Italy. She was observed very carefully on the train, and after it left Katowice, Department III functionaries dressed in customs agents' uniforms subjected her to a body search. Like the March search, this one yielded no results.

Section II of Department III, in charge of Operation Olcha, declared Bańkowska's search an unmitigated failure and the result of a false approach, which, like the search of Zaborowski's luggage, revealed what the ministry was interested in. But it also affirmed that "despite the great meticulousness of the search, it is not out of the question that Bańkowska may nonetheless have been carrying materials for RFE in the form of a microfilm hidden inside an object, a suitcase handle, a figurine etc., something a customs search being conducted on a train is incapable of finding." In conclusion, it was decided that in the future similar searches should be avoided, and in exceptionally justified cases they would be "so thorough that they would preclude the possibility of materials not being found." It also adopted the hypothesis that "materials are taken out of Poland partly memorized and partly in the form of microfilms . . . which are transported very well hidden inside props."[24] Both suppositions were partly correct. Bańkowska had memorized all her information and wrote it down only when she reached Rome, in a letter she sent to Żenczykowski. Bartoszewski sometimes sent microfilms "the Austrian way," through the Austrian Cultural Institute. They included documents and wartime newspapers, which RFE used in its historical broadcasts.[25]

The Security Service launched extensive operations (also using secret collaborators) to determine who among Bartoszewski's acquaintances had access to facilities for making microfilms, but these investigations yielded no results. Attempts to persuade Danuta Bańkowska to collaborate also failed, even though a close relative of hers had been recruited to convince her to view the Security Service favorably. The Security Service exerted exceptionally brutal pressure on her during a two-day interrogation in an isolated location in Nieporęt near Warsaw, where she was taken without warning.[26]

The secret police also attempted to break the lawyers it suspected of giving information to Bartoszewski and Karsov and Szechter. On November 20, 1967, it searched Lis-Olszewski's and Siła-Nowicki's apartments.[27] In Lis-Olszewski's home, they found a typescript in French about the trial of Karol Głogowski; an English-language text about the Wańkowski and Miller trials and the investigations of Cat-Mackiewicz and Grzędziński; and a copy of Eugeniusz Żytomirski's poem "Odebrano mi Polskę" (They have taken Poland away from me), published by the émigré paper *Wiadomości*. In Siła-Nowicki's apartment, the secret police found numerous research papers about church-state relations in Poland and documents from the trials of Nina Karsov and Jacek Kuroń and Karol Modzelewski.[28] Both attorneys appeared before the disciplinary committee of the bar association, which then suspended them from their professional activities in March 1968.[29]

On December 11, 1967, Lis-Olszewski was charged with storing "papers containing false information about the sociopolitical situation, which may cause substantial harm to the interests of the Polish state."[30] The secret police knew much more about Lis-Olszewski's work with both Szechter and Karsov and Bartoszewski through a bugging device, but it clearly did not want to reveal this knowledge in the investigation or in the trials that were being planned. The Investigation Bureau of the Ministry of Internal Affairs questioned Bartoszewski on numerous occasions in the months that followed.[31] He answered so skillfully that this evidence proved insufficient to put him on a trial. The case was dismissed.[32]

Round-the-Clock Observation

Over the next few years, Bartoszewski was placed under constant surveillance. As he planned to travel to East Germany in 1967, the Polish secret police asked the Stasi for help.[33] All foreign nationals with whom Bartoszewski came in contact, both Western journalists and diplomats, were also shadowed. All his acquaintances traveling abroad, dozens of people, were placed under investigation. Thanks to the interceptions of letters by Office "W," and probably with the help of bugs, the secret police determined that Ewa Dreżepolska was working with Bartoszewski, since postcards from England with coded information from Tadeusz Żenczykowski came to her address.[34] The secret police tried to recruit three housekeepers in a row working for Bartoszewski, but each one left his employ shortly after being approached. Bartoszewski believes they were honest women who did not want to be forced to report on him.[35] The police also recruited his neighbors so that it could install bugs in an apartment he moved into in 1967.[36]

Despite this enormous operation, the police failed to determine how Bartoszewski sent information abroad. In July 1970, Department III in effect admitted defeat. In a report on this operation, it stated clearly that "working out Bartoszewski has so far not permitted us to uncover the route by which he sends materials to RFE." Six potential scenarios of a "smuggling route" were named: the US and Austrian embassies, the Austrian Cultural Institute, the West German trade mission, and West German journalists accredited to Warsaw. The secret police had good intuition here, since it decided that the trail leading to the Austrian Cultural Institute was a good probability.[37] It continued to seek out more information about Kurt Skalnik. In March 1969, it asked the KGB for help. The deputy director of Department III turned to his Soviet comrades to "ask to be informed whether the security authorities of the USSR know the person of Skalnik and, if so, are they able to check his potential connections to anticommunist centers in the countries of Western Europe."[38] An evaluation of the principal suspect, created after many years of intensive work, served as a sort of justification of this limited success: "Bartoszewski has significant conspiratorial experience, he works craftily, astutely and appreciates the capacity of our apparatus."[39]

In July 1970, the Ministry of Internal Affairs decided that if it was to score new operational successes, isolating and neutralizing Bartoszewski and his associates would be the main method to use: harassing them with arrests, searches, and warning conversations, dismissing them from work, forbidding them to travel abroad, "preventively cutting them off from all organizational and social connections," and "creating family complications for the targets in the case."[40]

A breakthrough in Bartoszewski's and his associates' case came about quite by chance. In May 1970, Department III became interested in Stanisław Salmonowicz. The secret police knew that the two historians were in touch over their shared interest in the wartime Polish Underground State. Secret police functionaries asked the Bydgoszcz Security Service about Salmonowicz, an associate dean at Nicolaus Copernicus University in Toruń, which was located within their jurisdiction. It turned out that they had been watching

Salmonowicz for about two years; in 1968, the secret police had opened a so-called evidence questionnaire for him because of his oppositional mindset and his family connections to the Home Army and the Freedom and Independence group.

At about the same time, freshly recruited secret collaborators at the university alerted the Security Service that for a few years now, RFE had been airing news about their institution that was known only to insiders. But since there had been no coordination between the Bydgoszcz and Toruń Security Services and Department III, the transcript of a telephone conversation between Salmonowicz and Bartoszewski that had taken place on March 16, 1970, was not sent to the central office. Only after Department III asked the Provincial Command of the Citizens' Militia in Bydgoszcz on May 20, 1970, did it make a connection between the two cases.[41] The police put Salmonowicz under close surveillance, placed a bug in his apartment, and conducted a secret search (Salmonowicz found a key that the secret police had copied in the files now being kept at the Institute of National Remembrance, Warsaw).[42] Of pivotal importance was the arrest of Salmonowicz shortly before he was due to leave for a historians' congress in Salzburg in late September 1970. The secret police suspected that he would be carrying materials from Bartoszewski to RFE, having observed a meeting between the two men in Warsaw a few days earlier.[43]

Arrests

This time, the secret police were right on target. On the evening of September 24, they arrested Salmonowicz as he was leaving Bartoszewski's apartment. He was trying to catch a taxi to take him to the airport and was very happy when a car drove up immediately. But instead of a taxi driver, there were Security Service functionaries inside, who took him to the Ministry of Internal Affairs. They found a piece of paper with handwritten notes in his coat pocket and later determined that it was a list of the issues Salmonowicz was to discuss with Żenczykowski when they would meet in Vienna. The issues included Bartoszewski being denied a passport, the harassment of the writer and composer Stefan Kisielewski, the writer Antoni Słonimski's trip to the West, and Professor Kazimierz Wyka's departure from the post of director of the Institute of Literary Studies of the Polish Academy of Sciences.[44]

Bartoszewski had asked Salmonowicz to destroy the piece of paper before he left his apartment, but Salmonowicz decided to look at it one more time at the airport to remember it better. During the secret police interrogation, he initially denied having talked with Bartoszewski and claimed to have no idea how the piece of paper had found its way into the pocket of a coat he had put on for the first time in months. The officers first tried to talk him into collaborating. If he agreed, he would continue on his way to Vienna and Salzburg. "Your plane will wait for you," they initially tried to tempt him by giving him time to decide. After an all-night interrogation, during which he absolutely refused to cooperate, the prosecutor filed charges, and Salmonowicz was transported to jail.[45]

As their next step, the security policemen in charge of the investigation planned to search the apartments of several people they suspected of working with Bartoszewski and to interrogate them. Yet Minister of Internal Affairs Kazimierz Świtała, who appears to have been personally interested in the case, decided to trim this plan and to search only Ewa Drężepolska's apartment.[46] Some handwritten notes were found there, which, as she later testified during her investigation, were a list of the topics that Żenczykowski had given her a few months earlier in Paris to research for RFE. They included detailed questions that included the situation in the legal profession, the intellectual and artistic communities, and the official veterans' association, Union of Fighters for Freedom and Democracy.[47]

Drężepolska was arrested on September 25 and Bańkowska on September 30.[48] Over the next few months the two women and Salmonowicz were subjected to intensive interrogations. They were placed in cells with agents who tried to encourage them to start talking with the investigators and to stop denying charges or refusing to testify. The agents argued that from the point of view of the final outcome of the investigation, this would be the most favorable strategy. They warned that persons who refused to testify would be burdened with a disproportionately large share of the guilt. They also attempted to get information out of them that they had not given during their interrogations.[49] All this was used to "soften" the prisoners gradually and to obtain testimony that could be used as the foundation of not only their own but also Bartoszewski's trials.

The secret police decided not to arrest Bartoszewski because of his academic position and presence in the press at home and his widespread contacts abroad. But the method chosen for him was exceptionally treacherous, aiming first to recruit him as a secret collaborator and then to isolate and discredit him among the people he knew. The police also tried to sow distrust among the three prisoners and between them and Bartoszewski by emphasizing that he was free, while his three associates were risking serious punishment for acts that he had persuaded them to commit. This secret police strategy is interesting not only in the context of Operation Olcha but also as an illustration of secret police methods in general.

The Investigation

The prisoners were charged with relaying information to RFE, a crime under article 132 of the criminal code, "acting to harm the political interests of the PRP." Because the material evidence gained through operations and searches was limited, statements by the accused would be key to bringing criminal charges. Ewa Dreżepolska admitted during her interrogation that Bartoszewski had asked her to allow encoded postcards signed "Irka" with information and questions from Tadeusz Żenczykowski to be addressed to her. The name used for her, "Kasia," was her wartime underground name. She also testified that during a stay in Paris in May 1970 she had had long conversations with Żenczykowski and with Marian Czarnecki from RFE's Paris office, and that she had given them information from Poland and written down a list of new topics of interest to them (the list was then found in the search of her apartment). She confessed that they had also discussed the details of a trip to Paris being planned for May 1970 by another of Bartoszewski's associates. She did not know the person's identity, and Żenczykowski had mentioned only his code name, "Łosoś." Bartoszewski and Żenczykowski were using a principle of conspiracy of not allowing their two associates to know each other's identities, but the Security Service had an easy time guessing that the other person was Salmonowicz. Even without this play on words (*łosoś* means salmon), the secret police knew that he was planning to attend an academic conference in Paris in May.

Bańkowska also divulged her role in Bartoszewski's group of associates. The written account of how the secret police broke this elderly woman who had already spent nearly ten years in prison is exceptionally moving. Let it suffice to quote from a report by the female prison cell informant "Piotr": "This morning Bańkowska said that she has completely given up, that she is going to let her hair grow out because with the sentence she expects (and she expects a long one), it will be good if her hair is long. . . . For two nights now, Bańkowska has been shouting in her sleep: 'Mama, save me, I'm dying.' In the morning, Bańkowska is tired from sleep, she talks about how she has very exhausting dreams and that she dreams about her mother, that they are standing over a precipice."[50]

Bańkowska initially confessed to having been in contact with Żenczykowski, but she refused to give the name of the person with whom she collaborated in Poland. It was only during later interrogations, after realizing that the secret police already knew it, that she confirmed it was Władysław Bartoszewski. After some time, Salmonowicz also stopped denying that he had agreed to hand over materials from Bartoszewski to Żenczykowski in Vienna. But he argued throughout that he did not know what these were and that he had not consciously engaged in collaboration with RFE.[51] But this confession did not save him from further pressure. Toward the end of the investigation, Security Service functionaries who had not taken part in questioning him appeared in his cell and offered freedom in exchange for collaboration.[52]

The Security Service made an effort to impress on the three arrestees that the information it had (which it had acquired from them or from the agents sharing their cells) had come from Bartoszewski. In fact, during his many interrogations at the Warsaw Citizens' Militia Command, he had consistently denied being in contact with RFE or having worked together with any of the three.[53]

The historian reading the protocols of the testimonies, reports from the cell agents, and notes about the Security Service's plans (which were mostly written in dry, bureaucratic language) should not come away with the impression that these were weak, isolated, and besieged people incapable of resisting the secret police machine directed at them. The materials are foremost an indictment of the Security Service and of its methods, brutality, and perversity.

A Battue Hunt

A note from October 23, 1970, summarizes the first stage of the investigation, following the submission of the most important testimony by Dreżepolska and Bańkowska. In the note, Director of the Investigations Bureau Colonel Józef Chomętowski requests the arrest of Bartoszewski and the same indictment for him as for the three other arrestees.[54] Then, on November 6, members of the PUWP leadership received information about the key decisions made in the operational investigation and the interrogation (including excerpts from the testimonies). These party members were Mieczysław Moczar, who oversaw the Ministry of Internal Affairs as a deputy Politburo member and CC secretary; CC secretaries Stefan Olszowski and Jan Szydlak; chief of the Administrative Department of the CC Stanisław Kania; head of the Department of Culture Wincenty Kraśko; head of the Education Department Andrzej Werblan; and First Secretary of the Warsaw Committee Józef Kępa. The Ministry of Internal Affairs suggested charging Bartoszewski with a crime and beginning proceedings against him without taking him into custody or arresting him temporarily.[55] It is likely that the party leadership chose the first option, but no documents have been found to confirm this. But we do know that the prosecutor, Maria Pancer, notorious for her role in numerous political trials, favored arresting Bartoszewski.[56]

To the Ministry of Internal Affairs, Bartoszewski had been the principal figure in "Olcha" all along. On October 1, 1970, eighteen Security Service agents strode into his apartment, carrying food supplies. The search took twenty-seven hours. They took several hundred books, as well as newspapers, notes, and documents, most of them related to the wartime occupation, which Bartoszewski needed for his work—this was practically Bartoszewski's whole archive, "about half a ton of paper."[57] Within days, all intellectual Warsaw knew about the search. "They searched Władek B.'s apartment," Stefan Kisielewski wrote in his diary on October 7. "The victim was his library, one of a kind in Warsaw, simply made up of rare books about the occupation and the Uprising, printed in Poland and abroad, which he had been collecting for years. What a huge scandal. . . . They allegedly suspect B. of collaborating with the 'hostile radio station,' allegedly they asked about me, Jasienica, and Lipski."[58]

As the interrogations of Bartoszewski were beginning, operations were being conducted to discredit him. Already on October 14, the Security Service planned "to spread a version about Wł[adysław] Bartoszewski's ambiguous situation, since he has not been arrested, through our network of secret collaborators in groups in which Bartoszewski and the people who work with him spend time."[59] This plan was launched very energetically. Secret collaborator "A-Wiktor" reported that in his conversation with Bartoszewski on October 20, Bartoszewski complained that "some publishers have been getting anonymous letters about me and Danka [Bańkowska—P. M.]. They are typed and include the question, why is Danka in prison and I am free? . . . Security wants to disgrace me under the pretext of commiserating with Danka."[60]

A copy of one of these anonymous letters sent out by the secret police survives in files—an exception, since most such forgeries were scrupulously destroyed so as not to leave any material traces of the regime's illegal activities. Its author, who calls himself "Prawnik" (lawyer), writes in a letter to the editors of numerous newspapers that "for unknown reasons," Bartoszewski, in contrast to his three associates, has not been arrested. He also asks whether "it is true that nowadays collaborating with Radio Free Europe is not subject to prosecution" and asks the editors for an explanation of this whole case in their paper.[61] But no copy of an anonymous letter allegedly written by Home Army veterans, who expressed their outrage at Bartoszewski's "hypocrisy," survives. To make it appear credible that the letter had come from former Home Army soldiers, copies were also sent from abroad, including Vienna.[62] Stefan Kisielewski noted in his diary on November 3: "a disgusting anonymous letter signed by an alleged 'Znicz,' a Home Army officer (this was to have been one of Bór-Komorowski's noms de guerre) is circulating around town, and this letter accuses Bartosz[ewski] that his 'partners' are in prison for FE, and he's fine, travels abroad whenever he likes and is married to a 'party activist.' In a word, a classic provocation à la tsarist Okhrana or Stalin."[63]

The secret police arsenal related to Bartoszewski also included the anti-Semitic theme, which in the second half of the 1960s and early 1970s was a key component of the ministry's operations. According to secret collaborator "Jot," "letters have been sent to radio, television, Interpress, editors, and the Chief Prosecutor's office and signed 'Znicz'—Home Army, according to some, and 'Znicz' group according to others. The letters say that Bartoszewski . . . used to write books about how he had saved Jews during the occupation, and today he is a servant of Jewish intelligence, both Wiesenthal and Free Europe, which survives on Jewish-American subsidies."[64]

Bartoszewski's books were withdrawn from bookstores, and the censorship office removed his name from all publications, even footnotes.[65] On December 7, 1970, he was officially charged with crimes. Secret collaborators confirmed that Bartoszewski was suffering from the actions taken against him, especially being unable to research and write. It was only after preparing the ground in this way that the Secret Service began to try to implement its principal plan of recruiting Bartoszewski. A detailed strategy was prepared by Major Janusz Łabęcki, who played the main role in Operation Olcha. It was based on agents' reports that the operations so far had softened up Bartoszewski. "Bartoszewski assessed the confiscation of his book from bookstores in September of last year as a very serious move by the authorities against him because in the period of the greatest troubles with Jasienica and Wańkowicz their works were not removed from the shops. Last fall, talking about his situation, Bartoszewski said that some people have begun to avoid him. He assessed the anonymous letter signed 'Znicz' as aiming to make him socially and intellectually repulsive. Bartoszewski is in a very unpleasant situation in the Association of Polish Librarians, where lady colleagues who had been very helpful until now do not want to make a glass of tea for him or pack books he wants mailed and are not speaking to him."[66]

Łabęcki assumed that during the recruiting conversation with Bartoszewski, the Security Service would present the evidence collected against him, including the testimonies of his three partners. This was to convince him that "an honest connection to the Security Service will give him a chance. Otherwise, we will do everything to eliminate him as a human being and an activist." Were Bartoszewski to agree to collaborate, his three associates would be freed and the court would give them suspended sentences. So as not to arouse suspicion with this finale to the case, the plan was to "spread a version in his circles via S[ecret] C[ollaborators] that the accused had been treated leniently because of the change in party leadership, which clearly does not want to inflame the situation." Were the attempt at recruitment to fail, Bartoszewski and his colleagues would be tried in a criminal court, and "all publishing and writing activity would be blocked."[67]

The crucial talk took place on January 7, 1971. Taking part alongside Major Łabęcki was the deputy director of Department III of the Ministry of Internal

Affairs, Colonel Karol Pawłowicz. The conversation ran according to the exhaustive scenario prepared ahead of time by Łabęcki. After the men showed Bartoszewski what they knew, they made an offer that—one might think—he could not refuse. "It was stressed to Bartoszewski that the Security Service is able to direct his case in any direction, i.e., bring it to trial with sentences and causing his civil death or concluding the investigation in a way that was favorable to him. Creating an honest connection to the Security Service is an opportunity for him, and the starting point for this could only be a statement about his connections to anticommunist centers."[68]

This last point was characteristic of recruitment methods. The Security Service began by asking for a minor act—as long as it was in writing. This statement would be a tangible link connecting the two sides, a first step in drawing a person into actual collaboration. Bartoszewski's response proved that secret police documents show more than just human downfall and depravity: "You, gentlemen, are seeking a platform for an understanding outside this investigation to allow me to get out of this. But there is one factor here that you, gentlemen, have not taken into account: perhaps this man who is in danger (Bartoszewski) is not the man who, being over 50, would agree at any price to wipe out the previous 30 years of his life and to take a completely different path. He may prefer to go to prison."[69]

The next meeting with Bartoszewski took place on January 13, and the one after that on January 16 in Harenda Café off Krakowskie Przedmieście. Major Łabęcki talked Bartoszewski into the latter meeting with the promise that they would discuss the list of books confiscated during the search of Bartoszewski's home, to make it possible for at least some of them to be returned. During this meeting the secret police officer only asked Bartoszewski to "write and give the Ministry of Internal Affairs profiles of people he knew in the émigré community, for example, General Pełczyński, Garliński, Ciołkosz." This was also a very typical trap set by the security people. But Bartoszewski consistently refused. Łabęcki's report concludes with bureaucratic precision that the only option that is left is the second one.[70]

On February 12, 1971, Department III developed an exceptionally precise plan of operations aimed at discrediting and isolating Bartoszewski. Secret collaborator "A-Wiktor" was to "arouse" suspicions of Bartoszewski (including citing the letter from "Znicz") in the lawyer and former Polish Socialist Party activist Ludwik Cohn. Operational contact "J-M" was to spread similar rumors among Warsaw lawyers ("in the court snack bars"). It did not forget another milieu that was important to Bartoszewski: "Operational conversations being planned by Section IV of Department III of the M[inistry of] I[nternal] A[ffairs] with two persons from the historians' milieu to mention

Bartoszewski in passing in a favorable way, so that the persons will interpret it as a slip-up on our part and become suspicious of Bartoszewski's connection to the Security Service." It also planned to use information gathered from bugging devices in these conversations "so as to make the interlocutors believe that the Security Service acquired this information from Bartoszewski." It also planned to "write and send out an anonymous note undermining trust in Bartoszewski among the opposition intelligentsia." The plan was not limited to Poland. Department III, together with Department I (foreign intelligence), was to "implement an operational combination with the goal of 'leaking' information about Bartoszewski's collaboration with us to RFE and from the West back to Poland."[71]

We do not know whether all the plans were put into effect and to what extent they succeeded. Naturally, knowing Bartoszewski's subsequent story, they were entirely ineffective, and yet this after-the-fact perspective may be deceptive. "A-Wiktor's" and other secret collaborators' surviving denunciations reveal that at least some former Home Army activists bought the rumors about Bartoszewski's collaboration with the secret police.

Some hints at other secret police actions not mentioned in this plan also survive. The attempt to use the March 1971 return to Poland of Andrzej Czechowicz, an RFE employee who had been recruited by Department I, provides an interesting motif. The enormous propaganda campaign tied to Czechowicz focused on RFE's informants in Poland, whose names Czechowicz had allegedly found in Munich. In another meeting, again at Harenda Café, Major Łabęcki tried to persuade Bartoszewski that, now that Czechowicz was back, the secret police could use the evidence he had brought with him, which in order to protect him had not been revealed earlier in the investigation. Bartoszewski was to have replied that "this does not concern him, and the only thing that could be done is a provocation."[72] His intuition was right on the spot. In his television appearances, Czechowicz was told by the secret police to mention the initials of citizen "W. B." as one of the main, he believed, informers for RFE, whose criminal activity had been uncovered by this courageous spy.[73] Czechowicz's reports clearly indicate that he did not manage to find evidence in RFE files that Bartoszewski was passing information to Munich, which speaks well for the security measures Jan Nowak used to protect this exceptional collaborator.[74]

Another significant trail survives in the "Olcha" files. It is a memorandum from the deputy director of Department III, Colonel Karol Pawłowicz, to the deputy director of Department I, Colonel Józef Osek. It asks him to "rewrite the enclosed text as a report prepared by Tadeusz Żenczykowski for RFE from a meeting in Vienna with a Polish citizen in May 1970. Please give the source of information as a historian who is in regular contact with RFE."[75] The text prepared by Department III was a biographical sketch of Dr. Zygmunt Śliwicki, an acquaintance of Bartoszewski's who had been held in Pawiak prison during World War II. It included a few pejorative phrases, such as "after the war he served the Communists," and also charged him with plagiarism.[76] This is a blatant trace of the secret police attempts to forge RFE reports from its informants that Czechowicz had allegedly acquired in Munich. It is likely that the secret police used blank forms, which Czechowicz had sent to Poland. During his press conferences, Czechowicz showed such reports and also had them reproduced in his 1973 "memoirs," titled *Siedem trudnych lat* (Seven difficult years). Some of them may have been created on these blank forms. This particular case probably aimed to provide "evidence" of Bartoszewski's work for RFE, and it also may have been another effort to discredit him among the people who knew him, as someone who maligned decent people to RFE.

Another characteristic topic of the ministry's interest was Bartoszewski's wartime past. The "Olcha" files include an unsigned and undated note listing Bartoszewski's incarceration in the Auschwitz (September 1940–June 1941) and Prądnik (January 1945) camps. The Security Service planned to locate some of his fellow inmates, and possibly documents ("We are interested in their photographic copies"), and also to determine why he had been released from Auschwitz. As for the Prądnik camp, the functionaries wondered whether it had been possible to be released "for a bribe."[77] This is a very clear trace of a search for information that—after being properly doctored—could serve in future attempts to discredit Bartoszewski, this time by using his widely known honorable wartime past. It is important to remember that in the early 1970s, the Security Service was conducting a massive campaign to malign another hero of the Polish Underground State, Jan Nowak-Jeziorański, the director of RFE's Polish Service. Nowak was accused of collaborating with Nazi intelligence and of serving as a *Treuhänder*, an administrator of seized Jewish property. The Security Service apparently sent out anonymous letters and copies of documents to prove this.[78] In Bartoszewski's case, it is worth noting that the ministry was interested in "photographic copies," which can be altered.

The "disinformation" and "disintegration" operations connected to Bartoszewski's work for RFE were conducted with remarkable persistence. In late June 1972, an envelope that allegedly contained a statement by Bartoszewski was found in the hallway of the building in Starynkiewicz Square in Warsaw that housed the publications *Trybuna Ludu*, *Chłopska Droga*, and *Dokumentacja Prasowa*.[79] In it, Bartoszewski confessed to working for RFE, having been hired by Tadeusz Żenczykowski, whom he had known from their work together for the Home Army's Bureau of Information and Propaganda. That experience was also one of the reasons why Bartoszewski had developed a "worldview unfavorable to socialism." But he did see the light, and now regarded his work for RFE as a serious mistake. "I will not discuss the details of this work here because I have done it in another document, which I have conveyed to the proper authorities," he declared. But he did give reasons for his disillusionment with RFE: "for some time now, doubts came up whether RFE's activity agrees with the interests of the Polish nation. The more the radio's VIPs, Tadeusz Żenczykowski and Jan Nowak, let me in on the secrets of their activity against the Polish reality the more these doubts grew stronger. Over time, they have been transformed into the certainty that the Polish Service of Radio Free Europe does not represent the interests of the Polish state, and the people who work for it have long stopped feeling and thinking in Polish. I can say on the basis of my personal experiences that Radio Free Europe is implementing a policy of sowing chaos and sabotage toward Poland, in accordance with the principle, about which Jan Nowak once told me, that the worse things go in Poland the better." The author concluded with the promise that he would inform people about the real role being played by RFE in "a series of articles in the press." His declaration was accompanied by a cover letter addressed to "Dear Editor" and asking for its publication in "your paper." Both texts had Bartoszewski's forged signature on them. The envelope also contained another sheet of paper with a handwritten note. "Kazik" was informing "Jureczek" that the editor in chief had put off publishing "Mr. B's" declaration: "I have no idea why. This case has been going on for quite a long time, so this is why it might be good to bury it behind the scenes. So you can see that I was telling the truth, but you didn't want to believe me."[80]

Of course, these seemingly Aesopian formulations referred to Bartoszewski's purported collaboration with the secret police, which the Warsaw journalists and intellectuals, among whom such rumors had been spread for nearly two years, would be able to read clearly. It should be stressed again that the surviving documents for this case are unique. Current research has not yielded another instance in which traces of the Security Service's provocative, "disintegrative" actions (to use the ministry's jargon) could be seen so clearly.

Bartoszewski sent out a letter to the editors of press agencies and printed publications, as well as to many prominent people, informing them that the declaration had not been written by him. In July 1972, he informed the General Prosecutor about the forgery. He emphasized that the harm it was inflicting on society was all the greater since, as an officeholder in two institutions, the Polish PEN Club and the Book Lovers' Society, he had the right to sign checks on their behalf.[81] The prosecutor's office referred the case to the Warsaw Command of the Citizens' Militia, which commissioned a graphological analysis of the signatures from the Office of Criminality of the Main Command of the Citizens' Militia. The office concluded that both were without a doubt not authentic.[82] Because of this, the Warsaw Command was forced to launch an investigation. It interviewed several people, including Bartoszewski and the individual who had found the envelope with the declaration.[83] It drew up a thorough plan to determine who had been the author or authors of the texts.[84] What a grotesque situation: it had been Section II of Department III of the Ministry of Internal Affairs that had developed and intended to implement this plan, and now it was conducting operations against Bartoszewski. The same office had prepared all the previous provocations, including, most likely, the declaration. This demonstrates the sham nature of at least some bureaucratic procedures used by the Security Service and the documents it produced—were one to take them literally.

Of course, the investigation did not reveal the counterfeiters. But the secret police did try to use this incident to create disagreements between Bartoszewski and the people he knew. In a conversation with the former commander of the sabotage organization of the Home Army, Józef Rybicki, a functionary of Section II of Department III, hinted meaningfully that "Bartoszewski suspects all his acquaintances who have an antagonistic attitude toward him of forging his signature."[85]

Wasted Efforts of the Security Service

Edward Gierek's regime, which came to power in December 1970, wasted all of Major Łabęcki's and his Department III comrades' hard work by not wanting to try Bartoszewski and those who assisted him with his contacts with RFE. It had clearly decided that a trial would not be in the interest of a government wanting to present a new, more liberal face after the December massacre of workers, especially since several dozen activists of the underground Ruch organization were already in jail awaiting trial.[86] Their attempt to set the Lenin Museum in Poronin on fire could not go unpunished; collaborating with RFE was a less spectacular and scandalous offense, if no less of a threat in the long term. The government still had problems terminating the case of Bartoszewski and his associates satisfactorily. In January 1971, the Provincial Prosecutor's Office in Warsaw declared that "because of the nonemployment of temporary arrest for Wł[adysław] Bartoszewski, a position needs to be expressed about the illegitimacy of maintaining arrest in relation to the remaining suspects, whose role in the uncovered activity was clearly secondary." It also argued that the material evidence gathered so far (statements from those who had been provisionally jailed and notes and correspondence found during searches) was so rich that releasing the accused would not have a negative impact on the continuing criminal proceedings.[87] The Ministry of Internal Affairs was opposed to this decision, but it was not successful in imposing its position.[88] Bańkowska, Drężepolska, and Salmonowicz were released in the second half of January.

Still in January, in the first weeks of Gierek's rule, the decision was made that the investigation would not lead to a criminal trial, despite the collected evidence. "Even though the offenses committed by Wł[adysław] Bartoszewski exhaust the provisions of Art. 132 kk [Criminal Code—P. M.]," the directors of Department III and of the Investigations Bureau of the Ministry of Internal Affairs wrote in a joint memorandum, "in view of the current situation, it is not recommended to put him and the other persons on trial; therefore the decision was made to dismiss the case conditionally."[89]

For legal reasons, a dismissal proved more difficult than either the Ministry of Internal Affairs or the Prosecutor General's Office had anticipated. The problem lay in the amount of convincing material evidence. The prosecutor's office delayed making a formal decision, which Stanisław Salmonowicz protested since, as a lawyer, he knew the regulations as well as his rights.[90] There was a long discussion in the prosecutor's office about how to close the case most properly. As late as August 1971, Prosecutor Pancer admitted that "the current state of evidence for the investigation allows us to state that substantially the most appropriate way of dealing with the case would be to file charges against all the suspects. . . . The material evidence that has been collected is sufficient to justify this decision, especially in view of Drężepolska's and Bańkowska's confessions." According to Pancer, dismissing the case "because of the slight danger to society" of collaborating with RFE "would create a very dangerous precedent." However, accepting the classification that there is insufficient evidence of a crime would lead to questioning all the material evidence. Choosing the second option would also mean that the regime was taking responsibility for the months that the suspects had been jailed, which may have brought on civil suits. Pancer referred to the trial under way, instigated by Drężepolska's lawsuit to restore her right to work and to award her compensation.[91]

The next round of discussions in the Prosecutor General's Office also led to the conclusion that because of the "exceptionally complete and convincing material evidence," the case should end by referring the indictment to a court, and each potential method of dismissal "would be touched by legal and substantive flaws."[92] This was the recommendation that Prosecutor General Kazimierz Kosztirko received from his deputy, Henryk Cieśluk, who referred to the positions of all the prosecutors charged with or supervising the case, as well as the staff of the Prosecutor General's Office who had been consulted on this case. He noted that if the case was referred to a court, it would be possible to resolve the situation on the model of the "well-known precedent of the trial of the accu[sed] Wańkowicz, who had been lawfully sentenced [in 1964 for giving a manuscript to RFE—P. M.], but did not serve his sentence." Cieśluk recommended further consultations with the chairman of the Supreme Court and the minister of justice.[93]

To this day, it remains a mystery who decided to stop the dance: did the prosecutor general make the decision alone, or was he following orders from a higher-up? In either case, on September 29, 1971, Prosecutor Pancer issued the decision to terminate the investigation. Her justification was quite odd from the point of view of the government and the legal system of People's Poland. It states that the suspects "had entered into an agreement with representatives of Radio Free Europe, acting on behalf of a foreign organization in order to harm the Polish state, and then, as part of their agreement, gave that station false information about sociopolitical and economic conditions in Poland." But this act, "in view of its minor threat to society, does not constitute a crime."[94]

Such dilemmas faced by the prosecutor's office are a good illustration of how the security apparatus of People's Poland functioned in the post-Stalinist period. On the one hand, it was evidently at the beck and call of the regime and did not resist serving as a repressive tool against people viewed as the regime's enemies. On the other hand, it needed to act within the confines of "socialist legality." This on occasion brought on troublesome limitations, especially when a sudden political turn forced the prosecutor's office to perform real legal balancing acts.

As the prosecutor's office sought the best way to close his case, Bartoszewski was engaged in an epic attempt to recover his requisitioned books, papers, and notes. He was finally successful in August 1972. It may have helped that Stanisław Stomma, a member of the Sejm, intervened in writing.[95] Until then, the secret police used the library as leverage in its conversations with Bartoszewski.

Bartoszewski was not given a passport for several years, and until 1974 the censorship office blocked his publications. In December 1974, he did publish *1859 dni Warszawy* (Warsaw's 1,859 days), a chronicle of life in the capital under the German occupation, with the Znak publishing house in Cracow. The following year, the Polish PEN Club awarded the book the Mieczysław Lepecki Prize. The main censorship office made sure that not too many reviews and discussions of it, or even information about the prize itself, appeared; it allowed them only in "cultural periodicals" and in *Tygodnik Powszechny*.[96] Censorship's intervention in Juliusz W. Gomulicki's bibliographic essay was an example of such grotesque harassment. In the essay's references to

Bartoszewski's writing, the censors removed phrases such as "widely known" historian and writer, "excellent" documentarian, or "best" expert on Warsaw's occupation-era history.[97]

The Security Service placed Bartoszewski under surveillance until the end of People's Poland, both at home and also when he traveled abroad. But neither the ministry's operations nor the prosecutor's investigation interrupted his work for RFE, with the small difference that he no longer sent materials to Munich via Polish citizens but only used the help offered by Western journalists or diplomats.[98] Surviving documents do not tell us whether the secret police knew about this. His cooperation with RFE was quite intensive until Jan Nowak's departure at the end of 1975. Bartoszewski's main contact, Tadeusz Żenczykowski, had retired a few years earlier. Then the ties loosened, which only confirms the thesis that the activities that the Security Service followed so systematically for so many years using such great resources were largely the conspiracy of former members of the Home Army, mostly the Bureau of Information and Propaganda, whose cooperation was based on trust, loyalty, and a system of values dating back to the occupation. Stanisław Salmonowicz, fired from Nicolaus Copernicus University, had difficulties in his academic career because of this affair.[99] Danuta Bańkowska was able to return to her job at the Association of Polish Librarians.[100] Ewa Drężepolska won the right to go back to work at the Ministry of Domestic Trade.[101]

The regime clearly viewed Operation Olcha as one of its most important security operations, and it used a photocopied case study of it in its training.[102] It was written by the two officers of Section II of Department III in the Ministry of Internal Affairs who had played the largest role in it, Janusz Łabęcki and Jerzy Podolski. The former, who was born in 1931 and graduated from the law faculty of the University of Warsaw (a rarity in this ministry), was promoted several times thanks to this case and could have embarked on a big career. His first task in the case of Bartoszewski's collaboration with RFE was surveillance of the Warsaw prosecutor's office, and he was especially well prepared for it. During Operation Olcha, he was promoted to deputy head of Section II of Department III, from captain to major, and he also received a "high monetary reward" (the documents do not give the amount) from his minister. Yet his brilliant career was crushed by a disciplinary transgression, a dramatic abuse of alcohol, which lost him his managerial positions. But he must have continued to enjoy his superiors' trust, since in 1972 he was moved to the "D" Group of Special Tasks.[103] In the early 1970s "D" cells were created in Departments III and IV for so-called disintegrating operations, a broad range of extralegal, usually criminal, moves against the opposition and the Church (threats, anonymous letters, forgeries, kidnappings, beatings, and even murder).[104]

* * *

The story of Władysław Bartoszewski and the other people who together helped RFE shows the growing repressive tendencies in 1960s Poland. Only a few years after October 1956, when a significant opening in the system in terms of both politics and culture was allowed, the regime began to act consistently, often very brutally, to "discipline" the intellectuals, to limit their contacts with the West and with the political émigré community. RFE and the Paris *Kultura*, as well as anyone in Poland who stayed in touch with them, were at the top of the list of the regime's enemies. The regime viewed the relaying of information to RFE as particularly dangerous since without it the "enemy" radio, which reached millions of Poles, would have a much more difficult task. The scale of the means used to implement Operation Olcha is a good indicator of the importance attached to this case, as well as of the Security Service methods used in the late Gomułka and early Gierek periods.

An analogous case was that of the so-called Mountaineers, a group of young people who in 1968–1969 began to work closely with *Kultura*. They sent important materials about events in Poland (such as documents from the March 1968 student movement) to Giedroyc and brought back publications of its Institut Littéraire. In early 1970, Maciej Kozłowski, Jakub Karpiński, Krzysztof Szymborski, Maria Tworkowska, and Małgorzata Szpakowska were sentenced to multiyear prison terms (from three to four and a half years). The trial's propaganda was turned against Giedroyc and *Kultura*.[105] It was reasonable for the Ministry of Internal Affairs to imagine that Operation Olcha would have a similar finale. To sentence a well-known historian who had widespread international contacts and had been awarded a Righteous among the Nations Medal would no doubt have been more difficult than to persecute the young, unknown Mountaineers. But it is possible that had the secret police managed to achieve a breakthrough in Operation Olcha even a few months earlier, there probably would have been a trial and sentences for Bartoszewski and his associates. The workers' rebellion in the Baltic cities and the new Gierek regime's desire to show its more liberal face got in the way of the meticulous preparations by the secret police.

5. The Gierek Era, Détente, and a Massive Attack on Radio Free Europe, 1971–1975

New Leadership, Old Enemy

Władysław Gomułka's downfall in late December 1970 changed nothing in the PUWP leadership's view of Radio Free Europe. Edward Gierek's team, which declared it would govern differently and made an effort to win society's support, emulated its predecessors in fighting "ideological sabotage." RFE was on the agenda of the Eighth Plenum of the CC PUWP, the first plenum in the new reality, in early February 1971. The plenum's main goal was to settle scores. "At this very moment, the Free Europe center is simply working 'round the clock as Polish revisionism's main assistant. Every day we receive many kilograms of paper covered with the texts of Free Europe's programs. Especially recently, as its ranks were strengthened by cadre revisionists from Poland such as [Zygmunt] Bauman, [Artur] Kowalski, [Juliusz] Katz-Suchy, Plater,[1] [Stanisław] Wygodzki, [Lucjan] Perzanowski, [Krystyna] Miłotworska, [Eugeniusz] Żytomirski, and hundreds of others who are spewing hatred of socialism, hatred of Poland," said Mieczysław Moczar, using colorful imagery to remind his listeners how the party leadership perceived RFE's programs.

It was exceptional and yet typical of this government to focus so much on RFE at such an important time, immediately after the tragedy of the bloodily suppressed workers' revolt on the coast in mid-December 1970. Former minister of internal affairs Mieczysław Moczar, in 1971 a member of the Politburo and CC secretary in charge of the security apparatus, had a personal interest in RFE, somehow justified by the radio's anti-Partisan campaign (the Partisans were a nationalist faction among the Communist elite). "You know, comrades," complained one of the most powerful men in Poland, "that Free Europe has been harassing me for many years, fiercely and brazenly. I must confess that I have lived through more than one occasion, more than one moment, when things were difficult for me, I've lived through these kinds of moments especially because the party did not offer a challenge; on the contrary, some comrades have been spreading all kinds of nonsense and they sometimes do it through official channels. Others, for a variety of reasons, even premeditation. I am not even ruling out inspiration here. You, comrades, of course know, some of you hear, others read bulletins, that Moczar was the leader who organized taking power from Gomułka, so he must be against Gierek. This is more nonsense, of course. But nonsense that is repeated hundreds of times leaves a residue, even among serious comrades." Moczar's accusations went beyond contemporary affairs: "Free Europe has aired thousands of programs about how during the occupation I killed Home Army people and Jews." He added to these personal grievances—which also confirmed the importance of RFE's programs for the party elite—a ritualistic reference to the authority of the first secretary as a "classic" in fighting the "sabotage" radio. "I believe that the position Comr. Gierek took at one of the CC Secretariats was very right when he said that we should not and may not remain inactive in regard to the Free Europe center and its hostile activity, that we must discuss response options," stressed Moczar.[2]

The Eighth Plenum, which took place a few weeks after the power switch, was dominated by the settling of scores. Speakers pointed out mistakes made by the previous team, which had brought on the dangerous crisis. Jan Czapla, first deputy head of the Main Political Directorate of the Polish Army, accused it of nothing less than neglecting the fight against foreign sabotage, which thus became a major reason for the serious troubles of December 1970. "This defensive attitude created a vacuum, immobilized any possibility of prevention," argued Czapla. "As a result, a stronghold of enemy sabotage has been created in our country, tainting the political awareness of sizable social groups. This was a time (1956), you can remember this, comrades, when mechanisms jamming RFE were put away, and at the same time the basic forms of party, ideological training were cut or eliminated. We in the military experienced it painfully and for many years, and probably to this day we are feeling the effects of these reckless decisions. This disability, created by the absence of a counteroffensive . . . touched our whole country's organism, and the army's efforts in this area were necessarily at the ministerial level, so they were unable not to have a broader external influence." Czapla requested strengthening the fight against foreign sabotage, systematizing and coordinating the counteractions: "There must also . . . be an efficient, functioning central command center to link the counterpropaganda operations. It might also be useful to integrate some actions of the countries of our camp, which in the case of our alliance's armies, as can be seen in practice, is bringing useful results."[3]

The Free Europe theme was also prominent in the preparations for the Sixth PUWP Congress in December 1971 and during its sessions. At a meeting of the first secretaries of the provincial committees that preceded the congress, Stefan Olszowski, CC secretary in charge of ideology and the mass media, "discussed the situation among journalists and an action plan for the mass media before, during, and after the congress." He went on to "outline . . . the main directions of FE's sabotage and our responses."[4]

At the congress, it was not only party and government people responsible for fighting sabotage (such as Chairman of Polish Radio and Television Włodzimierz Sokorski or Janusz Kolczyński, head of the East-West Center) who addressed the threat from the hostile centers of sabotage because it was their responsibility, but also ordinary delegates. Jan Postoł, who represented Łódź-Brzeziny, said: "It is an issue that encompasses the possibility that we could make our political work more offensive. For example, information intended for regional party organizations, which was given to us in the pre-congress period, about tendencies that will, for example, come up in Free Europe, was valuable. This was immensely valuable information for us, [for it] enabled us to launch offensives."[5]

It is difficult to escape the impression that at this time, what the PUWP deemed foreign sabotage, and especially RFE, appeared as a ritualistic enemy, one that the party needed to mobilize its rank and file. After the student movement was broken up in March 1968 and the workers' rebellion was crushed in late 1970 to early 1971, it became all the more important to serve up an external enemy.

A paper prepared by the Press Office of the CC PUWP immediately after the December crisis made an interesting contribution to the impression the party apparatus had of RFE. The radio had been the main stimulus for the coastal explosion: "For several months, an antagonistic campaign persisted in this radio's programs intending to take advantage of our economic difficulties to create and incite moods of dissatisfaction in our society. In the last days, this campaign was transformed into virtually open calls for disturbances and excesses. For as long as it has existed, and whenever Poland has been the venue of controversial events, Radio Free Europe has been the first to try to sow anxiety and to support society's excitement. This time, too, without regard for what the burning of houses, the destruction of factories, and the robbing of stores might bring, in the spirit of 'the worse, the better,' RFE has tried to reap anti-Polish benefits for itself from events that are painful to all Poles."

This document inadvertently recognized the impact of RFE, in the most curious party Newspeak. It wrote that the enemy "was rubbing his hands with glee, hoping for a fire that would devour our land. These enemies include, first and foremost, the Munich radio station."[6] The style of this document drew heavily on worn-out associations and schematic reasoning. That it had been written by the Press Office suggests it may have been used as instructional material for newspaper editors, supplying a readymade scheme for portraying the December crisis and RFE's role in it.

In April 1971, Minister of Internal Affairs Franciszek Szlachcic presented a somewhat more sophisticated assessment of RFE's role in the December events: "The tactics used by the sabotage centers consist of so-called mirror imaging to varying degrees," he said at a meeting in the offices of the Ministry of National Defense. "Thus, individual groups of workers or employees made certain demands in this period. The sabotage centers heard about these, and they had only one goal: to refine them appropriately, multiply them, and relay them to Poland. And so a circular feedback of demands was created. Afterward, it was difficult to tell what had come from Free Europe and what Free Europe had transferred to Poland."[7]

From his very first day in office, First Secretary Edward Gierek received information from the Ministry of Internal Affairs highlighting the looming dangers emanating from RFE. On January 5, he received a memorandum (a digest of the most important intelligence distributed regularly to the top tier of the party-state leadership) from Department I (foreign intelligence) of the ministry that included extensive data about RFE. It warned that "on the basis of information that it has collected, RFE will broadcast special libelous programs about the new party-government leadership, its 'ties to former members of the authorities,' [and] particular comrades' attitudes toward the USSR."[8]

Over the following weeks and months, several other reports from Department I to the Politburo and Secretariat of the CC PUWP also discussed RFE. Thus, the March 8 report announced that Andrzej Czechowicz had been brought back to Poland.[9] The March 31 report warned about the growing threat from the enemy radio station: "RFE is going to pick up every piece of news about signs of dissatisfaction, protests, or workers' or other groups' demands. The anti-Soviet touches will be emphasized, as well as, in this context, personal attacks on those members of the leadership who (according to RFE) have been 'groomed and placed in their positions in Poland by Moscow.'" It also reported that RFE was preparing a series of programs about Władysław Gomułka, going back to the German occupation.[10]

In early 1971, the Propaganda and Agitation Office of the CC PUWP developed a programmatic document that proved that the existing view of foreign sabotage had not changed: "It was a characteristic of the confrontation between socialism and imperialism in the 1960s that the focal point of this confrontation moved to the ideological level. The stepped-up ideological battle on an international scale has been a direct outcome of this process, as has the activation of psychological warfare, which imperialism is waging on socialism." The document also restated the thesis that foreign organizations had been motivating the opposition's activity in Poland, or that at least a tight link and alliance existed between these external and internal enemies: "The content of the sabotage campaigns launched and conducted by anticommunist psychological warfare organizations in the West is (as was demonstrated by the experiences of the CSRS [Czechoslovak Socialist Republic] and March 1968 in Poland) being connected more closely to the requirements and activities of the anti-socialist forces inside the socialist countries or else focused on inspiring and organizing oppositional tendencies."

The most important demand made in the programmatic document was the creation of a "team for fighting anticommunist ideology" in the CC PUWP, which would be charged with preparing evaluations and recommendations for fighting sabotage for the Politburo and Secretariat of the CC, and also with coordinating the implementation of the party leadership's resolutions. The team would be made up of representatives of offices within the Central Committee, the Ministry of Internal Affairs, the Foreign Ministry, the Main Political Directorate of the Polish Army, the Ministry of Communications, and the Center for the Study of East-West Relations (or East-West Center).[11]

The proposal to coordinate the battle against what the PUWP deemed sabotage had come up repeatedly in the 1960s. In early 1971, the Main Political Directorate of the Polish Army also suggested it, independently of the Propaganda and Agitation Office of the CC, and sent a long memorandum about this issue to the PUWP leadership.[12] On June 3, 1971, the CC Secretariat put together "a team to coordinate the directions, methods, and means of fighting hostile propaganda" and adopted the principles developed by the Office of Propaganda and Agitation.[13] The group was to meet once every two months, and "a 1–2 person sector in the Office of Propaganda and Agitation of the CC and the Center for the Study of East-West Relations would be put in charge of the practical implementation of the Team's decisions and recommendations."[14]

There are no archival materials available documenting the team's activities. According to Andrzej Werblan, deputy marshal of the Sejm and a member of the CC Secretariat in the early 1970s who had been involved in action on the ideological front, the team did not actually do anything. One reason for this was the political marginalization of its patron, Stefan Olszowski, who in December 1971 left the office of the CC secretary and became the foreign minister.[15]

As before, the struggle against foreign sabotage was the domain of a variety of institutions. Leading it was the ever-expanding East-West Center headed by

Janusz Kolczyński, since the 1960s a key figure in the fight against sabotage, working closely with the Ministry of Internal Affairs. The East-West Center published and distributed a monthly analysis of foreign-instigated sabotage to numerous institutions. It was largely devoted to RFE's programs, articles in the Paris-based *Kultura* and other émigré periodicals, and the political activities of the émigré community. It also organized national and international conferences on fighting sabotage and published numerous papers on psychological warfare. The size of its personnel points to the center's rapid growth: starting with seven employees in 1966, it grew to fifty-two by 1972.[16] This originally small unit of the Polish Institute of International Affairs was soon transformed into the Institute for the Study of the Contemporary Problems of Capitalism.

The post–December 1970 leadership also reinstituted interference with RFE's programs, which had been suspended in 1956. On January 16, 1971, the government presidium authorized the minister of communications to start talks with Moscow about coordinating jamming.[17] Under Gomułka's regime, until December 1970, RFE's Polish programs were jammed only from the Soviet Union and some other bloc countries. During the dramatic events of December 1970, the Polish government used transmitters for Polish Radio's foreign-language programs to jam RFE. But preparations to resume jamming had been made earlier. In 1969, the Ministry of Communications had created a detailed plan based on the guidelines prepared by the Main Political Directorate of the Polish Army, the Secretariat of National Defense, and the Ministry of Internal Affairs. It included both the airing of Polish programs on the same wavelengths as those used by RFE and the more primitive method, which had been used before 1956, of emitting a signal interfering with the programs aired by the "hostile centers."[18]

A permanent system of jamming was launched on March 17, 1971. Yet it did not bring fully satisfactory outcomes, at least initially. According to an evaluation by the Main Political Directorate of the Polish Army, "the system of interfering by airing Warsaw II Radio on the same frequencies as RFE's programs on the medium wave and of FM programs on the short wave, and interfering with buzzers, does make it more difficult to listen to their programs, but it is not effective in completely neutralizing the audibility of the Munich station in all of Poland's territory."

The effectiveness of jamming varied across the country and according to the kind of frequencies on which RFE was airing its programs. According to the Polish Army assessment, "interfering with RFE's programs on the medium waves by using the Warsaw II program is most effective in the vicinity of Warsaw, in the area where this program can be heard well. Traveling away from Warsaw, the effectiveness of jamming decreases quickly. Interference in the southwestern part of the country is especially ineffective." Jamming medium-wave programs was even more difficult, for technical reasons. RFE's broadcasting at various times on a few different frequencies "makes it practically impossible to jam all the frequencies in the whole country's territory." Jamming RFE on the short waves was "most effective in central Poland (Warsaw region) and partly in the northwest. It is least effective in southwestern Poland (Wrocław)." From the army's point of view, this was not a desirable outcome. "It needs to be mentioned," emphasized the Main Political Directorate, "that the areas where jamming RFE is least effective cover the majority of army garrisons."[19]

An interesting thread about jamming by the neighboring Communist countries has surfaced in a document of the Main Political Directorate. According to it, at least in the early 1970s, these operations were not coordinated. Also, "RFE airs Czech programs on the same frequency of the medium wave until 19:00. In southwestern Poland, these programs are effectively jammed (probably by Czechoslovakia). The instant RFE ends the Czech program and begins the Polish program, the jamming stops, and the jamming system we turn on then is not as effective as the Czech one."[20] We can assume that it was only the agreement with the Soviet Union signed on April 17, 1971, that regulated the coordination of jamming between the Polish government and the other bloc countries.[21]

In subsequent years, jamming could also be more successful because of the expansion of the technical base of Polish broadcasting. Beginning in 1976, RFE's medium-wave programs were covered by Program II of Polish Radio, with transmitters in Wola Rasztowska, Katowice, Wrocław, and Szczecin. We also know that the Third Regiment of Radio Interference stationed in Lidzbark Warmiński broadcast signals interfering with RFE.[22] The jamming of RFE would last until 1988.[23]

Czechowicz Returns

The Polish government organized its most massive campaign against RFE in the first few months of Gierek's rule, centered on Andrzej Czechowicz's return in March 1971. This campaign was planned jointly by the Ministry of Internal Affairs, the Press Office and the Propaganda Department of the CC PUWP, and the especially active Main Political Directorate of the Polish Army.[24] Even before Czechowicz's return, the Main Political Directorate had developed a complex plan for fighting what it deemed foreign sabotage, which included a propaganda offensive against RFE.[25] Copies of the plan had been distributed among the party leadership and in the Ministry of Internal Affairs.

A few weeks after Czechowicz's appearance in Warsaw, Minister of Internal Affairs Franciszek Szlachcic outlined the origins of this enormous campaign in a meeting with Polish Army commanders: "The Main Political Directorate of the Polish Army has shown significant initiative in launching the coordinated and offensive operations against the sabotage centers. The Main Political Directorate comrades have developed an initiative for an offensive and coordinated operation against centers of sabotage. Comrade minister of national defense presented this initiative to Comrade Gierek. I was present during their conversation. Comrade Gierek responded to this initiative positively and said that under the conditions of psychological war, the role of the military in fighting political-ideological sabotage should be significant and large. And this is why the Main Political Directorate's initiative has been adopted as the foundation for developing a coordinated and active counteroffensive against sabotage centers, and why as part of this activity we planned to deal a so-called heavy blow to Free Europe. The Czechowicz case was this heavy blow."[26]

Newspapers were the first to announce the news of Czechowicz's homecoming on March 9. Quoting the Polish Press Agency (PAP), they reported that "on March 8, 1971, a Polish intelligence officer from the Ministry of Internal Affairs returned home after completing his special mission in Munich. For many years, until the day he came home, he was an employee of the so-called Polish Service of Radio Free Europe in Munich. In the next few days, the public will be informed comprehensively by the press, radio, and television about the details of his work at RFE."[27]

The media reported extensively on the press conference that took place the next day. In the following weeks, newspapers published numerous interviews with Czechowicz, often accompanied by excerpts of documents he had brought with him (or which the Ministry of Internal Affairs had acquired elsewhere), discussions of his "achievements," or simply attacks on RFE. Interviews with Czechowicz appeared in *Trybuna Ludu*, *Żołnierz Wolności*, *Perspektywy*, *Express Wieczorny*, *Kulisy*, *Sztandar Młodych*, *W służbie narodu*, *Panorama Śląska*, *Trybuna Opolska*, *Itd.*, and *Panorama Północy*. Polish Radio aired a six-part conversation with Czechowicz titled "The Captain Returns" (Powrót kapitana) by Janusz Kolczyński, chief expert in fighting sabotage and the host of a television program on which Czechowicz also appeared.[28]

Czechowicz's direct "chaperone," who prepared him for these numerous press conferences, television and radio appearances, and interviews, was an officer of the Ministry of Internal Affairs, Jerzy Kudaś-Bronisławski, incidentally also the author of many attacks on RFE in the press as well as of large-print-run quasi-spy novels, for which he used his knowledge of the ministry's operations.[29] One could not fail to notice how carefully the journalists were chosen for this campaign, which was so important to the party and to the Ministry of Internal Affairs. Ignacy Krasicki, who commented on Czechowicz and RFE on television, had been an agent whose missions included RFE. Editor in chief of *Express Wieczorny* Zbigniew Sołuba had since 1947 served as an agent for the Ministry of Public Security, the Committee for Public Security, and the Ministry of Internal Affairs under the code names "Nawrócony" (Converted) and "Zbyszewski." In 1965, Department II of the Ministry of Internal Affairs (responsible for counterintelligence) decided to remove him from its list of active agents because "he is now a well-known party activist and journalist. Because of these functions, he meets with members of the government and CC secretaries."[30] But the secret police continued to rely on his help, though in a different way. The Czechowicz campaign disclosed the overlap of propaganda and special services.

Czechowicz was presented as an intelligence captain who had been placed at RFE by the ministry, but earlier information about his recruitment in 1965 contradicts this claim. The propaganda campaign also used documents and accounts from other sources, including Mieczysław Lach.[31] Czechowicz's statements, which were meticulously prepared by the secret police, focused on a handful of themes. Confronting RFE's informants living in Poland was a leitmotif present in almost all his oral and written pronouncements. Czechowicz claimed that he had made a list of persons in Poland who either themselves sent information to RFE or agreed to interviews with RFE's pollsters when they traveled abroad, often believing that they were discussing neutral subjects and not spilling secrets. He gave the example of two young men who wrote to RFE from Poland asking to hear particular music but, without realizing it, also wrote about topics that RFE then exploited for its "hostile propaganda" or even spying.[32]

Minister of Internal Affairs Franciszek Szlachcic emphasized during meetings with propaganda secretaries of the PUWP's provincial committees that the most important goal of the Czechowicz campaign was to sever the connections that allowed information to travel from Poland to RFE. He mentioned that there were about three hundred Polish citizens "who consciously or recklessly, but methodically, did it. In some cases it may be necessary to file charges, but in most it has been decided to have the leaderships of their institutions and factories and the secretaries of party organizations summon these people for conversations. The informants include well-known names." Szlachcic considered the whole campaign a great success, one that would make RFE's life very difficult. "Its old, years-long sources in Poland have been cut off, some foreign publications are no longer cooperating with Free Europe, which is now a compromised institution. . . . I believe that this is not the last hit, though one right on target," declared the minister.[33]

Materials found in the archive of the Institute of National Remembrance in Warsaw reveal that Czechowicz did indeed succeed at finding the names of individuals from Poland who had met with RFE people and discussed the situation back home.[34] In its system of recording their names on index cards, RFE treated many of them as sources, which Czechowicz was able to find. Some of these records were reprinted after his return to Poland in publications, including his book, *Siedem trudnych lat* (Seven difficult years). Czechowicz also sent in a large number of reports based on information given by these individuals. RFE's reference system allowed select staff to link a name card in the archive with a particular report and to find the source of a particular piece of information. Czechowicz claimed in his memoir that he had gained access to some of these materials with a key to the closed-off room that he had copied illegally.[35] Many people who spoke with RFE representatives probably did not realize that what they said might be used in research papers and that their names would be noted on lists accessible to only a handful of employees. These discussions may also have been social conversations with acquaintances they knew from Poland or earlier trips abroad. RFE, interestingly, listed as its sources prominent Polish journalists who traveled abroad for work, scholars trusted by the Polish government who held important positions at universities and in the Polish Academy of Sciences, or even Sejm deputies. Sources included many party members, sometimes even secret police collaborators. This situation illustrates another important phenomenon: the dense network of contacts, at least in the post-Stalinist period, between members of the Communist elite and anticommunist political émigrés. Outside Poland, the regime's most trusted journalists could talk openly with people from the "hostile" radio station, which they fought fiercely in their writings back home.

These findings suggest that one of the main reasons why many of the RFE sources went unpunished after Czechowicz delivered this information to his handlers was that they belonged to the Communist elite. Disciplining or even publicly criticizing these trusted people would have been problematic; it could even have discredited the government. The authorities confined themselves to much more restrained and discreet actions. Another reason must have been the new Gierek government's attempts to avoid worsening the already tense public mood only a few months after the massive strikes and demonstrations of December 1970, which the army and security apparatus had suppressed by force. Therefore, information Czechowicz found out about individuals who had been in contact with RFE was conveyed to their supervisors, newspaper editors, university deans, or directors of the Polish Academy of Sciences institutes. In the case of journalists, the Ministry of Internal Affairs also supplied materials about them to the Press Office of the CC PUWP. Furthermore, all these individuals' local Security Service offices and provincial committees of the PUWP were instructed to observe the lawbreakers. Individual disciplining and warning conversations with supervisors were their basic penalty. In cases of especially important or trusted persons, the Ministry of Internal Affairs would deliver the file to the person involved as a warning to indicate what "failure to be cautious" in contacts abroad could lead to and imply that the secret police agency was "omniscient." One of the people who received this treatment was Zbigniew Sołuba, editor in chief of the very popular *Express Wieczorny* daily.[36] His enthusiastic participation in the Czechowicz propaganda campaign could therefore also be attributed to this notice, something that would not have been evident to outside observers.

One of the most interesting aspects of these RFE analyses was the attempt by the secret police to use them against the Catholic Church. A Ministry of Internal Affairs document discusses giving Cardinal Stefan Wyszyński some RFE studies based on conversations with Catholic activists, including Sejm deputies from the semi-oppositional ZNAK group. Its obvious intention was to spoil the primate's relationship with them. This internal Security Service document stressed that the studies contained "piquant" statements about Wyszyński.[37] Surviving documents in the Institute of National Remembrance archive do not indicate clearly whether this folder was eventually delivered to the primate, although there are many indications that it was. This cannot be confirmed by examining Church records either, since those are not accessible to researchers.

This operation of disciplining persons who had been in contact with RFE was conducted so discreetly that neither the public nor RFE, which generally had an excellent grip on the goings-on in Poland, knew much about it. Hence, it appears that the government was successful, at least for a time, in intimidating Poles traveling abroad and thereby disrupting the flow of news from Poland to RFE. Only three names of people who were sanctioned in this way surfaced, informally, in Warsaw gossip: the literature expert Professor Wacław Kubacki, the journalist Marian Podkowiński, and Feliks Widy-Wirski, who had served as minister of information and propaganda in the late 1940s.[38]

Kubacki was indeed charged with making contact with RFE in 1971.[39] Podkowiński was a journalist with the party daily *Trybuna Ludu* and its correspondent in West Germany, as well as a secret police collaborator. As has already been mentioned, he also reported on his contacts with people who were close to RFE. It is not out of the question that they treated their conversations with him, a player in the party establishment, as a source of useful information about the situation within the PUWP and in the media milieu in Poland. The only evidence for this, and an interesting one, is a note made in 1963 on an index card in RFE's archive about Mieczysław Moczar. Podkowiński is mentioned as the source of information about Moczar when he was deputy minister of internal affairs and led the Partisan faction. After Podkowiński's name are the letters "s.ltd.," which meant "source" and "limited" (limited access to the information and to the identity of the source).[40] This was one of the RFE archive's designations for its informants. Czechowicz claimed that it was thanks to such notations in the documents to which he had access that he was able to identify RFE's sources from Poland.[41] Rumors about Podkowiński's contacts with RFE may have been an internal party intrigue in 1971.

Widy-Wirski, who spent the 1960s in Paris as the director of the Polish Academy of Sciences Research Outpost, allegedly served as the intermediary in Jan Nowak's contacts with Zenon Kliszko, Politburo member and Gomułka's closest associate.[42] Kliszko had reportedly provided Nowak with information that could be used against the increasingly powerful Minister of Internal Affairs Moczar and his Partisan group. Both Nowak and his deputy, Zygmunt Michałowski, who was often sent to speak confidentially with people from Poland, denied having been in touch, even through an intermediary, with Kliszko. Maciej Morawski, RFE's Paris correspondent, also did not confirm the rumors about Widy-Wirski as a liaison to Kliszko. Morawski did say that Widy-Wirski met with another employee of RFE's Paris office, Tadeusz Parczewski, but there is no mention of Kliszko in the notes from these conversations.[43] There is also no trace of Widy-Wirski's contacts with RFE in the materials the Security Service maintained on him while he worked in Paris.[44]

The theme of Widy-Wirski allegedly serving as Kliszko's go-between with RFE may also prove that another, hidden motif of the Czechowicz campaign was to discredit Gomułka's entourage. In Jan Nowak's view, the witch hunt being planned by the Ministry of Internal Affairs was stopped by Edward Gierek, who was afraid it might spread to his own people.[45]

The intentions of the organizers of this propaganda campaign were not clear even to the power elite. Mieczysław Rakowski, at the time the editor in chief of *Polityka* weekly and a deputy member of the CC, a few days after Czechowicz's return noted his hypotheses in his diary: "All of it is quite mysterious. It's basically not clear what security wants to achieve. . . . There may be different motives, for example: 1. wanting to intimidate our countrymen so they don't get too chatty with foreign correspondents; 2. making us cautious when we go abroad; 3. creating a bad atmosphere around FE internationally, since the main goal of my government is to shut that station's trap; 4. eliminating some people in Poland."[46]

In all his statements, Czechowicz stressed that RFE was fully controlled by the CIA and that many of the Polish émigrés who worked in Munich were salaried US agents (Nowak, for example, in Czechowicz's pronouncements had been taken over by the Americans from British intelligence). Individuals providing even seemingly insignificant information, for example in conversations with pollsters, also became de facto participants in these espionage operations. The scraps of information they delivered were compiled into reports, which were then used by the CIA. Thus, an unaware and unsuspecting average citizen who happened to say a few sentences too many while spending time abroad became an actual collaborator with US intelligence. Newspapers and Czechowicz's ministry-prepared memoir were illustrated with photocopied RFE analyses based on conversations with travelers from Poland on military issues, including command structures, moods in different garrisons, and arms production. This was undeniably intelligence material, and even those who sympathized with RFE may have questioned the station's intentions.

Czechowicz's description of the inhumane conditions in the German refugee camps in which he had spent some time himself, Zirndorf and Münster, was another of his themes. The Western intelligence services, which infiltrated the camps and recruited people who had no chance of returning to a normal life, exploited desperate refugees, he said. This aspect of the propaganda campaign was obviously meant to discourage all Poles who might be thinking about fleeing to the West.

This "ace spy of People's Poland" from the very beginning tried to persuade the public, in accordance with the ministry's then-prevalent view, that RFE was serving not only the CIA but also the Jews (although this word was not spelled out either here or in the propaganda campaign in March 1968) and the "Zionists." During his first press conference, Czechowicz said, "the materials collected by the intelligence cell [RFE's Research and Analysis Department—P. M.] are used by others, for example that notorious Wiesenthal and his collaborators."[47] In his interview with *Trybuna Ludu*, Czechowicz left no doubt which RFE employees should be considered Poland's worst enemies and traitors: "Finally, there is the group that is so viciously anti-Polish that only Nowak's shrewdness, as he watches to make sure they don't cause too much trouble, forces them to stick to the rules according to which this place calling itself the 'Polish Section' works. It is a group of escapees and émigrés from the last three years, obviously connected to the anti-Polish and anti-Soviet Zionist centers."[48]

To make Czechowicz seem credible and likable, the campaign stressed not his Marxist views and devotion to the socialist cause (it did not claim, for example, that he was a member of the PUWP) but his patriotic family roots. It emphasized that he came from a landowning family, that his grandfather had been a anti-Russian insurrectionist in 1863 and his father a cavalry officer in September 1939. It was not by chance that he was said to have spent the war years "together with his mother in the territory of the Soviet Union," which in that era's Aesopian official language clearly meant that his family had been deported by the Soviets.[49] This mélange of background material, so characteristic of the period's propaganda, also included a comparison to Captain Kloss, the hero of the wildly popular television series *Stawka większa niż życie* (Stakes higher than life itself) about the adventures of a Polish (actually, Soviet) World War II agent in German uniform.[50] There were even plans to make a film about Czechowicz, to be co-authored by Andrzej Konic, the director of the series.[51]

Opinions about Czechowicz among his closest Munich colleagues are an interesting addition to his propaganda image. Immediately after he surfaced in Poland, they said: "He hated Gomułka, was violently anti-Russian and also anti-Jewish. He claimed to be a fan of socialism with a human face. He believed that our station demonizes Moczar, his importance and his politics. He was resolutely critical of US policies and always spoke negatively about America. He was also contemptuous of the Germans, even though he moved in German circles."[52] But perhaps the most interesting aspect is his attitude toward Moczar, since Czechowicz belonged to the group of Nowak's critics on the staff who believed that the Polish Service devoted too much time and energy to attacking the Partisans, Moczar's nationalist faction in the Communist elite.

The Czechowicz propaganda campaign served as a model for a similar operation in Czechoslovakia a few years later. In 1976, Prague gave enormous publicity to the homecoming of an employee of RFE's Czechoslovak section, Pavel Minařik. This campaign, directed by the secret police, contained the same elements as Czechowicz's. It began with a huge press conference, which was followed by endless interviews in the press and on radio and television, and later the publication of a book, *Captain Pavel Minařik: The Spy Returns*. According to the historian Petr Cajthaml, the two agents were made into stars of the Communist mass culture of the 1970s.

Like Czechowicz, Minařik was presented as a cadre intelligence officer. After the opening of the Czechoslovak Security Office (Státni bezpečnost) archives, documents surfaced making it clear that Minařik had worked as a secret collaborator at RFE and only became a cadre member once he was back in Czechoslovakia. The only difference between Minařik and Czechowicz was that the former had been recruited before leaving Czechoslovakia and was hired by RFE after posing as a refugee who went to the West after the Warsaw Pact invasion of his country in August 1968.

The two agents' Soviet counterparts were the Radio Liberty employees Yuri Marin and Oleg Tumanov. Marin's return home was announced in Moscow in

1976, and it followed the same pattern. Marin was presented as an experienced officer who had spent many years working inside the enemy institution. Interestingly, he was identified as a major, to convey the KGB's "seniority" over the "fraternal" services represented by Captains Czechowicz and Minařik.[53] In 1986, the KGB "evacuated" another Soviet spy from Radio Liberty. Oleg Tumanov, who had worked in Munich since 1966, was most likely recruited by the KGB while he was still a Radio Liberty employee, although the Soviet propaganda claimed that he was an intelligence officer who skillfully infiltrated the hostile institution. His tasks were similar to those of Andrzej Czechowicz: collecting information about the radio's staff and their contacts with émigrés and travelers from the Soviet Union.[54]

If we are to believe Ion Pacepa, the head of Romania's foreign intelligence who defected to the United States in 1978, Nicolae Ceauşescu also yearned to have his own Czechowicz. Apparently, Ceauşescu was impressed by the story that Edward Gierek told him during a visit to Bucharest. After Gierek left, Ceauşescu summoned Pacepa and demanded that Romanian intelligence come up with an operation modeled on the Polish one: "We must compromise Free Europe once and for all. . . . The way Gierek did." Ceauşescu brought this up many more times. The Romanian secret service was close to bringing home an agent it had had for many years, "Ionescu," in RFE's Paris office, but after long negotiations he refused to return to Romania.[55]

Assisting *Ostpolitik* and Senator Fulbright

While cutting off RFE's information sources in Poland was the key goal of the Czechowicz campaign, it was certainly not the only one. Its masterminds wanted to worsen the radio's problems both in Germany and in the United States. When the Social Democrats came to power in Germany in 1969 and launched their new eastern policy, *Ostpolitik*, aiming to normalize relations and limit tensions between West Germany and Poland and the other Communist countries, RFE's continued operations out of Germany became questionable. During negotiations over the Polish-German border treaty in December 1970, Warsaw demanded RFE's removal from Germany. The issue resurfaced during later discussions aimed at increasing political and economic contacts and—something that was especially important to the Bonn government—setting conditions for the release to West Germany of Germans living in Poland.[56]

RFE was certainly not the most important point in these negotiations about issues that mattered the most to the Polish government. Wanda Jarząbek, an expert on Polish-German relations, puts RFE in sixth place, after the border,

Germans leaving Poland, economic cooperation, cultural and scientific-technical cooperation, and reparations for Polish Nazi victims.[57]

In any event, the Polish regime repeatedly brought up its demand to have RFE removed from Germany, including in top-level talks. Just a few weeks after the signing of the Polish-German agreement, Premier Piotr Jaroszewicz discussed the issue of RFE in a meeting with Rainer Barzel, a Christian Democratic Union (Christlich Demokratische Union Deutschlands, CDU) opposition politician.[58] Significantly, this was one of the new premier's first international meetings since the end of Gomułka's rule. In October 1971, Deputy Minister of Foreign Affairs Adam Willman brought up RFE during a visit to Bonn. He heard that RFE was a very sensitive issue in German-American relations and that therefore the Poles should not expect quick solutions.[59]

In some instances, West German politicians' reactions seemed more promising. In February 1972, Herbert Wehner, chairman of the Social Democratic Party (Sozialdemokratische Partei Deutschlands, SPD) parliamentary group in the Bundestag, visited Warsaw, and during a conversation with Gierek reacted to the Poles' demands more favorably: "As for the activity of the Free Europe station, Wehner assured us that he personally supports our position and presents it actively in various public statements. He does not share the view of other members of the SPD group that Free Europe has changed its methods and become sort of more civilized. . . . Wehner declared that he would continue to push for the removal of Free Europe from the FRG's territory. He asked for further materials to use for this purpose."[60] Accounts of Wehner's talks in Warsaw, including those on the subject of RFE, appeared in many German newspapers, including *Frankfurter Allgemeine Zeitung* and *Die Welt*, and *Süddeutsche Zeitung* carried an interview with Wehner. Therefore, the Polish regime could have some influence on the West German public and get it used to the demand to remove RFE from Germany.[61]

At the same time, RFE's fate was being decided across the Atlantic. Following the revelation that the CIA had been secretly financing it since its creation, RFE came under severe criticism in the US Congress. It was portrayed as an institution lying outside democratic control, a Cold War relic standing in the way of international détente and improved relations with the Communist bloc. The battle for RFE's future opened with a speech by Senator Clifford Case on January 21, 1971, in which he raised the issue of its CIA funding. Case demanded a new institutional solution that would guarantee RFE's sovereignty and appropriate funding and give the US government oversight. This began a nearly three-year period of uncertainty about the radio's future. New legal solutions were discussed. The US Congress would agree on RFE's budget only provisionally and always after fiery debates. Various administration and congressional committees evaluated its work. The exceptionally influential Democratic senator J. William Fulbright, chairman of the Senate Committee on Foreign Relations, led a dynamic campaign to close it down.

In the end, RFE survived, and the state of impermanence ended in October 1973 with the creation of the Board for International Broadcasting. This body, whose members were appointed by the president, was to exercise general oversight of RFE and Radio Liberty and to guarantee the stations' freedom from direct administration pressure.[62] Now it became clear that the SPD government would not rescind RFE's license to operate out of West Germany, despite the Polish government's hopes, which had at times seemed vaguely realistic.

Warsaw used this period of uncertainty about RFE's future to step up its offensive, which had its synchronized propaganda, diplomacy, and intelligence dimensions. It also carefully chose times at which to attack. The timing of the Czechowicz campaign was to supply ammunition to anyone in the United States and West Germany who viewed RFE as an obstacle to international détente, as it portrayed the radio as an institution engaged not only in aggressive propaganda in the "spirit of the Cold War" but also in espionage. This charge also helped to increase anxiety among the staff about the radio's future, making them more vulnerable to pressures from the Communist secret police and offers to return to Poland. This message was present in the first press articles containing Czechowicz's disclosures. "Free Europe's position in the FRG has recently become increasingly difficult. Adding to its employees' mutual suspicions is this nervous uncertainty: are we staying in the FRG? Some West German press is critical of the feats of these slanderers. More and more people in the West admit that the activities of this espionage-propaganda organization are getting in the way of international détente," wrote Bohdan Roliński in *Trybuna Ludu*, reporting on the first press conference given by the "ace spy of People's Poland."[63]

Another excerpt of Czechowicz's confessions about "RFE conducting espionage against countries in whose territory it is active" obviously intended to suggest arguments to the radio's German challengers.[64] Information about how RFE's pollsters allegedly skewed data about the size of the radio's audiences and opinions about the programs collected among travelers from Poland fed Senator Fulbright's arguments in his polemics against the radio's backers, who pointed to the radio's popularity in its target countries.[65]

In a session of the Senate Foreign Relations Committee, Fulbright did refer to Czechowicz's "revelations" when he spoke about the unmasking of RFE's spy network in Poland.[66] Furthermore, Czechowicz's implications that he had not been Poland's sole spy on the radio's staff were intended, on the one hand, to deepen the shock and distrust in the Polish Service, and on the other, to convince the American public that this institution, which was spending so many US taxpayer dollars and was being defended so fiercely by "Cold War circles," had been deeply penetrated by Communist agents.[67]

A note survives in the Institute of National Remembrance archive in Warsaw about a conversation between a Polish intelligence officer and "Senator Fulbright's consultant" on the Senate Foreign Relations Committee.[68] There are also accounts of discussions between the same officer (who appears as agent "Cedro" in internal Department I records) and employees of the US Information Agency and a member of the Presidential Study Commission on International Radio Broadcasting, chaired by Milton S. Eisenhower, which was to determine the future of RFE. This demonstrates Warsaw's understanding of RFE's situation and the plans Washington was making for the station, as well as the attempts to influence staff and politicians who played a role in decisions about RFE and Radio Liberty.

The controversies over RFE, which heated up during the Czechowicz propaganda campaign, gave Warsaw a convenient backdrop for a diplomatic move. On May 26, 1971, the Polish government sent notes to the US and West German governments demanding that the radio station be shut down. Its arguments were a precise replica of what Czechowicz (or rather the Security Service, which prepared his statements very carefully) had been saying: "Irrefutable evidence in the possession of the Polish authorities leads us to believe that RFE conducts not only propaganda operations but also activities of espionage, sabotage, and subversion, in large part using its network of offices and branches located in several European countries. Some 80% of the materials it acquires through various channels are transmitted as reports to the central office of American intelligence."[69] In his conversation with the US ambassador when he delivered the note, Deputy Minister of Foreign Affairs Józef Winiewicz stressed RFE's "sabotage-espionage" activity.[70]

The diplomatic offensive continued for several more years. Polish officials brought up the issue of RFE during the first visit by a US president to People's Poland. Richard Nixon stopped in Warsaw from May 31 to June 1, 1972, on his way back from Moscow, where General Secretary Leonid Brezhnev had also discussed RFE.[71] "We pointed out that the activity of centers of American propaganda such as the Free Europe station not only poisons the atmosphere of good relations but is also contrary to the spirit of détente," reads a summary of the talks with Nixon the CC prepared for the secretaries of the PUWP's provincial committees.[72]

Most outspoken about RFE was Minister of Foreign Affairs Stefan Olszowski in his meeting with his US counterpart, Secretary of State William P.

Rogers. According to the Polish minutes of their meeting, Olszowski presented a set of solid arguments for closing down the station: "Both sides should strive to eliminate issues that do not serve bilateral relations. The activity of Radio Free Europe, which poisons the atmosphere of mutual relations and represents a destructive factor, is a blatant example in this respect. We presented our stand on RFE more broadly on the basis of concrete examples from its programs. We demonstrated its attempts to oppose Poland to the USSR, personal attacks on Polish politicians and members of the government. We stressed that Free Europe does not have the right to call itself a Polish radio station or to use the Polish national anthem in its programs."[73]

These arguments appear to have had no significant impact on the other party: "Rogers restated the US government's position that RFE is a private organization and that the Administration has no control over its programs, even though it is funded with American money." Because nothing concrete was decided on this issue, it could only be noted that Rogers "raised the possibility of continuing the discussion about RFE's activity, suggesting that this issue be included in the European Conference as part of the question of exchanging information and ideas."[74]

It is noteworthy that the pressure on the US president about RFE was a joint, coordinated Warsaw-Moscow action. Edward Gierek revealed this in a meeting with the first secretaries of the PUWP's provincial committees. "In terms of ideology and politics, we have treated our talks with Nixon as a continuation of the Moscow talks," he explained. "They took place on the same platform and aimed in the same direction: the struggle for peaceful coexistence. . . . This is of fundamental importance and allows us to act more offensively against the ideological and political sabotage of the imperialist centers. I also have in mind the Free Europe station, on whose subject we have currently been exerting pressure together with our Soviet comrades."[75]

RFE came up again a few months later, during Gierek's official visit to Paris from October 2 to 6, 1972. To the Polish regime, this visit was extremely important both for its expected economic benefits and for its general strategy of building good relations with the most important countries of the West. "The heart of the matter is that the issue of the Paris *Kultura* and Radio Free Europe and other centers of hostile political sabotage was raised extensively for the first time," Gierek later informed the Politburo.[76]

Gierek first brought up these issues in a meeting with French president Georges Pompidou, and then Foreign Minister Stefan Olszowski discussed it with French foreign minister Maurice Schumann. Their hosts were obviously surprised: "The French side was not prepared for these subjects, and further talks are absolutely necessary."[77] The French record of Schumann's reply is more emphatic: he said that RFE is primarily a US and West German problem, and RFE's Paris bureau does not broadcast from France.[78]

Then, in January 1973, Olszowski brought up fighting RFE at a meeting of the Warsaw Pact foreign ministers in Moscow. He proposed a joint "energetic attack against the centers of sabotage propaganda, and especially against the most aggressive radio stations among them, Free Europe and Freedom [Radio Liberty—P. M.]." He informed the gathering, "We have spoken and acted many times through different channels, including diplomatic ones, about the activities of sabotage radio stations."[79]

The Polish government, and especially its Ministry of Internal Affairs, considered the closing of the RFE bureau in Stockholm in 1973 an international success in its fight against RFE. Department I documents show that the office had been spied on since 1963, and pressure on the Swedish government with the intention of shutting it down was increased in the Czechowicz campaign. The only trace of this case found to date is a document closing the case of the Stockholm bureau. Captain Paweł Raczyński of Section XI of Department I wrote: "The operations information that was acquired was also used for the talks conducted in the diplomatic way with the Swedish F[oreign] A[ffairs] M[inistry]. As a result of the occurrence of the qualitatively unfavorable situation of the Stockholm office after the return to Poland of Captain Czechowicz and the intensification of political and diplomatic procedures, RFE's Stockholm bureau was closed down in October 1973."[80]

There is no information in surviving documents about Polish secret police activity aimed against the Stockholm office. There is also no evidence in the archive of the Polish Foreign Ministry of any Polish diplomatic initiatives in Sweden.[81] Jan Nowak and Maciej Morawski have said that the Stockholm bureau was shut down not as a result of Warsaw's pressure. They justified it with budget cuts, which led to eliminating some outlying offices.[82] The closing was thus most probably a case of the Ministry of Internal Affairs giving itself credit for something it had not done.

Gierek also brought up the issue of RFE during his visit to the United States in October 1974. The Polish delegation presented its arguments in a meeting with President Richard Nixon and Secretary of State Henry Kissinger: "We described Radio Free Europe's activity as an anachronism that harms mutual Polish-American relations. We emphasized that this radio's programs interfere in Poland's internal affairs, attack the government of People's Poland. They vilify our country's activists. They also strike anti-Soviet notes and present Polish-Soviet relations in a distorted way." It appears that this time the Americans showed no more understanding than on previous occasions. Kissinger

Nazi Loudspeakers: Anti-RFE poster by Jerzy Jankowski and Stanisław Gratkowski (1955). From left to right, the microphones are labeled "Voice of America" (*Głos Ameryki*), "Free Europe" (*Wolna Europa*), and "Radio Madrid" (*Radio Madryt*).

Untitled anti-RFE poster by Ignacy Witz (1955). The text on the microphone reads "Free Europe," while the liquids being poured into the funnel include "lies" (*kłamstwo*, *łgarstwo*), "blackmail" (*szantaż*), "gossip" (*plotka*), and "slander" (*oszczerstwo*).

Who They Really Are: Anti-RFE poster by unknown author (1980s). The text on the hat reads "Voice of America" (*Głos Ameryki*) and "Radio Free Europe" (*Radio Wolna Europa*).

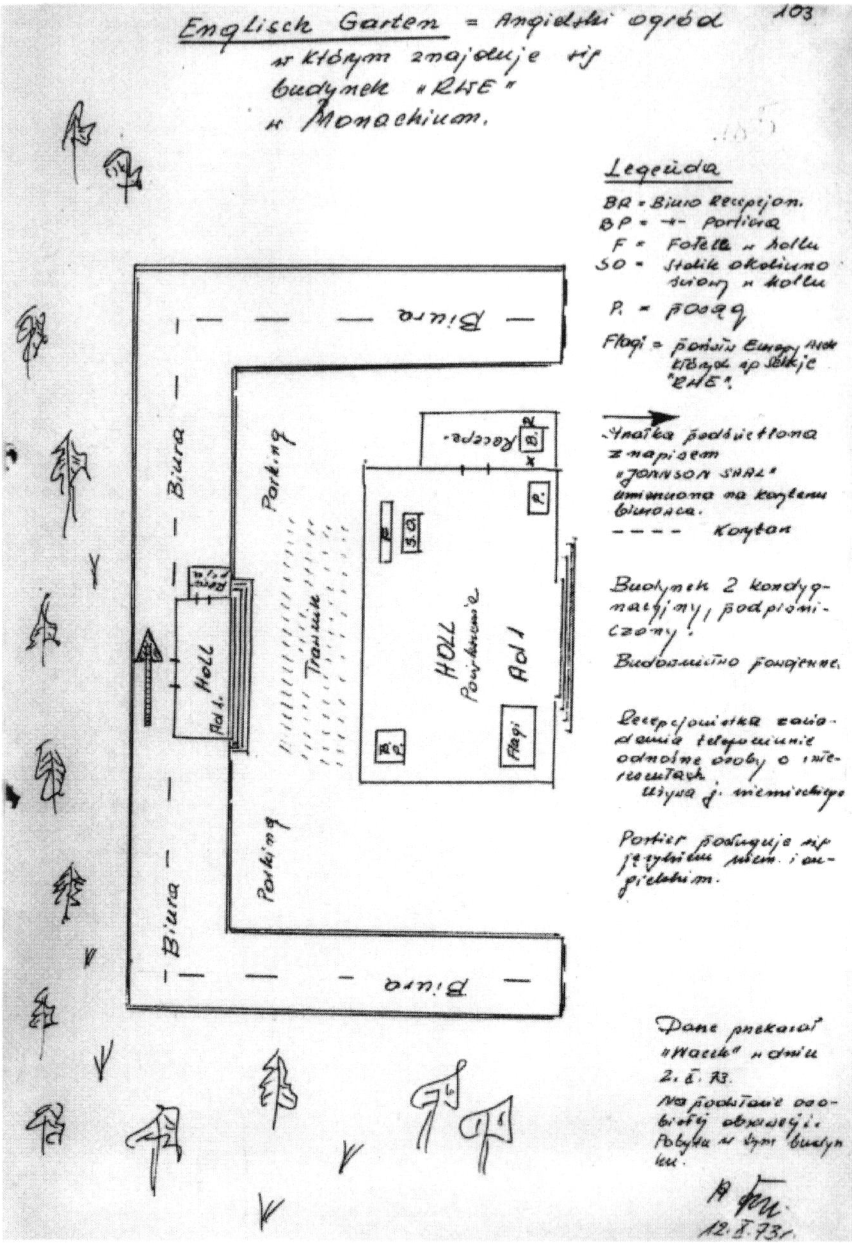

Polish Security Service plan of the RFE offices in Munich's "Englisch Garten" (*Englischer Garten*, English Garden), drawn on the basis of information provided by a secret collaborator. Notes written on the document explain that the receptionist in the entrance hall speaks German and announces visitors by phone, which may suggest that the Security Service contemplated infiltrating RFE's premises. A note at the bottom states that the plan is based on information obtained in 1973 from agent "Wacek," who spent some time in the building. (Archive of the Institute of National Remembrance)

"expressed his reservations that the activities of Radio Free Europe are not the domain of the State Department, but he would nonetheless look into this issue. . . . He also accepted our offer to provide documentation illustrating the harmfulness of RFE's activity in recent months."[83]

The fight against RFE never played as important a role in Warsaw's foreign policy as in the first half of the 1970s, when the radio's future was being decided. Its dynamism made it stand out prominently among the countries of the Soviet bloc.

Propaganda Attacks, "Disinformation," and "Disintegration" Operations

In reviewing the Czechowicz propaganda campaign in July 1971, the Press Office of the CC PUWP concluded that it had achieved its fundamental goals. These included "discrediting RFE's informants stemming from among . . . émigrés and citizens who visit Western countries . . . warning all those who consciously or by accident may deliver materials for RFE programs. . . . In relation to abroad, the main task was to present RFE's true face as a relic of the Cold War, an institution whose goals and activity are contrary to the principles of peaceful international cooperation." According to the Press Office, which coordinated the propaganda use of Czechowicz's so-called revelations, it had succeeded in proving "RFE's ties to American intelligence" to both the Polish and foreign publics, as well as the fact that "RFE's bureaus in individual Western countries conduct intelligence activity and harm not only s[ocialist] c[ountries] but also the countries in whose territories they are located. [This has] given our diplomacy significant arguments enabling it to resolve the issue of RFE's intelligence connections to the CIA in the international arena and in individual Western countries."

According to the Press Office, it was an equally great achievement to "begin the active and coordinated joint operations of s[ocialist] c[ountries] against RFE and other sabotage centers." East German and Czechoslovak television ran films about the Polish Ministry of Internal Affairs agent and the information he had gathered. The Soviet Union began making a similar film, in which Czechowicz participated. *Népszabadság*, the Hungarian Socialist Workers' Party daily, published a ten-part series titled "The Captain Served in Munich." East Germany, Czechoslovakia, Bulgaria, and Hungary prepared to publish a translation of *Captain Czechowicz Fulfilled His Mission*, a collection of his public statements for Polish newspapers, radio, and television.[84]

Another research paper prepared by the CC PUWP Press Office, likely with materials furnished by the Ministry of Internal Affairs, is even more interesting.

It stresses that one of the greatest benefits resulting from the staging and publicity of the agent's "return" was the "legalization and ability to give the appropriate institutions access to materials acquired by both A. Czechowicz and our other operational sources." This confirms the hypothesis presented earlier that the information delivered by the agents recruited among the Munich staff in the 1960s was useful not only from the point of view of operations but also for propaganda. This Press Office study points directly to another of the campaign's goals, which, it believed, had been largely achieved: "introducing confusion, disorientation, and disorganization into the sabotage centers, especially RFE, and thereby making it difficult for them to conduct their propaganda and sabotage-espionage efforts against our countries, cutting them off from many of their sources of information."

The Czechowicz case was also supposed to initiate close cooperation in fighting RFE among the special services of the Soviet bloc countries. Talks were held from March 23 to April 24, 1971, in Department I of the Ministry of Internal Affairs with delegations from the special services of the Soviet Union, East Germany, Hungary, Czechoslovakia, and Bulgaria. The goal of these meetings was to agree on jointly combating RFE. The following methods were enumerated:

> —to strive jointly by all channels and means to remove RFE from the territory of the FRG and to eliminate it. In order to realize this mission effectively, periodic meetings have been agreed upon in order to exchange views and goals and to coordinate operational undertakings;
>
> —legalization of documents and materials acquired and possessed by the services of the interested countries, which so far could not be used because of the possibility of giving away their sources;
>
> —systematic exchange of information conc[erning] RFE, its national services and bureaus in the countries of Western Europe, and the mechanism of collecting intelligence materials, areas of interest, sources of information, structure, goals and directions of action, people who work there etc.;
>
> —joint inspirational undertakings toward RFE employees.[85]

It is likely that the leadership of the Ministry of Internal Affairs considered the Czechowicz case its great achievement, one that allowed the Polish security apparatus to play the main role in the Soviet bloc's struggle against RFE. Unfortunately, it has been impossible to find any documents about the talks with the "fraternal" services in March and April 1971 or about any further coordination of operations. We do not know whether such cooperation took place or whether it was limited to using the Czechowicz case in other Communist countries' propaganda attacks on RFE. But there were signs that the case built up the Polish secret services' position as most familiar with RFE of all the bloc countries. In August 1971, the KGB gave the Polish Ministry of Internal Affairs an evaluation of RFE's legal status in West Germany, which was prepared in view of actions that could help remove the radio from Germany. Moscow was asking Warsaw to evaluate the study and, most important, to "acquire additional information about RFE's legal situation in the FRG."[86]

The Czechowicz-related assaults on RFE continued for months, even years. As early as 1971, a collection of the "captain's" most important pronouncements came out as a book in a 100,000-copy run with an introduction by Janusz Kolczyński. His ministry-written memoir, *Siedem trudnych lat* (Seven difficult years), published in 1973, featured expanded forms of all the earlier themes. The author (or rather authors from the Ministry of Internal Affairs, who were using information the ministry had gathered earlier) devoted numerous pages to portraying individuals working for the radio. He described most of them as American agents who hated socialist Poland, cynical go-getters, or simply weak, defeated people ready to commit any lowly act for money. The anti-Zionist motif was also pervasive: the book addressed actions taken on behalf of and under the influence of Simon Wiesenthal, "Zionist centers," the state of Israel, or simply Jews who had left Poland after March 1968. The spurious memoir was manufactured by a well-known reporter appointed by the ministry, who taped the agent's confessions. After it was transcribed and edited a little, the top echelons of the ministry gave the text its final form.[87]

A new theme, one that had been absent from the first attacks in 1971, also appeared in the memoir: the allegation that Jan Nowak, a legendary Home Army courier, had collaborated with the Nazi occupier. In the first edition of *Siedem trudnych lat*, Nowak appeared as a German intelligence operative ("and not even military intelligence but the one that Himmler's SS apparatus had led"), while his last assignment to London, transmitting information about the Warsaw Uprising, was allegedly carried out in cooperation with the Germans.[88] The second edition, released in March 1974, included a copy of the statement, already mentioned, by the *Volksdeutscher* from Żyrardów, Johann Kassner, who claimed that between 1940 and 1942, Jan Nowak-Jeziorański had administered Jewish property seized by the Nazis. As noted earlier, it was Wiktor Trościanko who came up with this idea. The Czechowicz memoir did not mention Kassner's accusation, which may imply that at the time, even the Ministry of Internal Affairs was not fully convinced it should be publicized.

Czechowicz stated in 2005 that the Ministry of Internal Affairs had paid Kassner well for his statement. Czechowicz also claimed that he had been the one to make the connection to Kassner, who lived in Munich. He was to have received his name not from Trościanko but from another anti-Nowak RFE editor, whose name Czechowicz did not reveal.[89] This claim cannot be confirmed. While the date on the photocopy of Kassner's statement is April 22, 1970, and Trościanko gave his information in a meeting in August 1971, the statement was first used in 1972 in the United States and then in 1974 in Europe, after publication of the second edition of *Siedem trudnych lat*. The original of the document was never shown publicly, only a copy. Hence it is impossible to determine either when it was made or who gave it to the secret police, Trościanko or another editor via Czechowicz.

Czechowicz also explained why Kassner's statement had not appeared in his book's first edition. Jerzy Łukaszewicz, CC secretary in charge of propaganda, did not permit it to, considering it not credible enough. It had been Franciszek Szlachcic, the second most important figure in the party leadership and the one who oversaw the security apparatus, who decided to include it in the second edition of the memoir.[90]

Using documents that included some from Simon Wiesenthal's Jewish Documentation Center, Jan Nowak was able to determine that Kassner had been responsible for turning Polish Socialist Party activist Anna Golde in to the Gestapo. Nowak concluded that since People's Poland did not hunt Kassner as a war criminal and since he had been able to travel to Poland after the war, he must have worked for the Polish secret police.[91]

Documents in the Institute of National Remembrance archive in Warsaw give us some clues. The brothers Alfred and Johann Kassner, Germans living in Poland, had signed the *Volksliste* during the war and were appointed receivers of numerous Jewish enterprises and administered some formerly Jewish properties in central Warsaw. Since the documents indicate that they lived in Żyrardów for some years, everything points to the likelihood that one of them had given the Security Service the statement it used against Nowak. In testimony before the Ministry of Public Security in 1948, Alfred Kassner stated, "I . . . employed solely and exclusively Poles who . . . were active as members of political parties in all the enterprises I took care of."[92]

The Ministry of Public Security investigation documents show that in 1943, the Home Army determined that Alfred Kassner had been a Gestapo informer; a Home Army man attempted to execute him, but only wounded him. The investigation materials also include information on how Anna Golde had been handed over to the Gestapo. Johann Kassner escaped to Germany in 1945 ahead of the Red Army and, according to his brother, settled in Bavaria. Alfred Kassner remained in Poland, where he was arrested by the Ministry of Public Security in 1948. After a year-long investigation, he was handed over to Soviet authorities, which sentenced him to ten years in prison on charges of spying on the Soviet Union. The reason for this charge is unclear but is probably related to the time he had spent in Russia before World War I, something put forward as evidence that he had been a German spy. Yet materials from this kind of investigation should be viewed with extreme caution, since it would have been conducted according to Stalinist rules, which had nothing to do with seeking the truth. Its goals included attempting to show that Zygmunt Zaremba, leader of the underground Polish Socialist Party—Freedom Equality Independence, who had lived abroad since 1946, had been a Gestapo agent. The documents show that Kassner was released from a Soviet prison before he had served his full sentence and was back in Poland in 1957.

A "control card," which is to be signed by every person who reads a file, is an important source of information. Between 1965 and 1973, this file was used by functionaries of Department II of the Ministry of Internal Affairs (counterintelligence) and of Office "C," the ministry's archive. Between February 1969 and February 1973, the materials about Kassner were located in Department II. It was at this time that the Security Service was preparing and executing the operation aimed against Nowak, using a Kassner—Alfred's brother, Johann. During the war, Jan Nowak had worked in the Receiver's Office of Secured Real Estate and administered two Jewish tenements in Królewska Street in Warsaw. This job gave him foolproof work papers, which were very useful for his work for the Home Army.[93] It is possible that his and one of the Kassners' paths crossed and that, years later, the Security Service found them.

Historians know of other instances of the Ministries of Public Security and Internal Affairs using former Gestapo functionaries and agents. This was the case with an agent couple, Ludwik Kalkstein and Blanka Kaczorowska, who turned Home Army commander Stefan Grot-Rowecki in to the Germans.[94] In Pomerania, there was the well-known case of Johannes Kassner-Kaszubowski (no relation to the other Johann Kassner), a Gestapo functionary who worked on the Polish underground during the war and was personally responsible for crimes against its activists, and who then served as a Polish Ministry of Public Security agent in West Germany in the second half of the 1940s and the early 1950s.[95]

The charges against Jan Nowak were disseminated in the United States for quite some time. In 1972, as RFE's future was being decided, Kassner's declaration found its way to two senators, Clifford Case and James Buckley.[96]

After the second edition of *Siedem trudnych lat* with Kassner's statement was published in Poland in September 1974, the Cologne daily *Rheinischer Merkur* wrote about the charges against Nowak, citing Czechowicz's bogus memoir. Nowak sued the author of the article, Joachim Goerlich, a German who had emigrated from Poland in the late 1950s. The court dismissed the case, ruling that Goerlich had merely repeated Czechowicz's allegations and was not responsible for their credibility.[97]

After the lawsuit was over, many important émigré figures received letters with a distorted explanation of its ruling, claiming that the court had recognized the truthfulness of what Czechowicz and Kassner had written.[98] In late 1974, another "document" was distributed to incriminate Nowak. A copy of a letter dated August 8, 1940, and signed SS Obersturmführer Dr. Zahn, according to which Zdzisław Jeziorański was applying for the job of administrator of a confiscated Jewish-owned brickyard in Radzymin, was sent out to numerous individuals and institutions in the West.[99]

The goal of these letters was obviously to discredit the creator and longtime director of RFE's Polish Service, both in the émigré community and to his American management and, most important, to audiences in Poland. The accusations first appeared in Czechowicz's memoir in the spring of 1974 and were restated a year later in a television program featuring Andrzej Smoliński, an RFE employee recruited by Polish intelligence in Munich and brought back to Poland in another Ministry of Internal Affairs operation.[100]

In countering these charges, Jan Nowak explained that he had never managed a brickyard in Radzymin—had never even been to the town—and had been instructed by his Home Army commanders to take a job in the Receiver's Office of Secured Real Estate. Tadeusz Żenczykowski, Nowak's superior in the Home Army, vouched for him. German police experts concluded that the document was most likely a postwar forgery; it had been written on a typewriter without German diacritical marks and included inaccuracies in Nazi phrases and titles.[101]

In this era, forged letters intending to discredit Father Tadeusz Kirschke, who wrote the Polish Service's religious programs, as well as Andrzej Chilecki, who worked as a RFE freelancer, were sent to many people in Western Europe.[102] There is clearly a connection between all these events and the Ministry of Internal Affairs documents from this period announcing intensified disinformation and "disintegration" operations against RFE and the Polish émigré community.

Nowak learned that Kassner's statement had been distributed in the United States by Karol Sitko and Aleksander Ostoja-Starzewski, while in Germany Janusz Kowalewski sent out copies of Goerlich's article. The men were Polish émigrés who worked for German expellee organizations, which for many years had been attacking the Polish Service for its support of the Oder-Neisse line as the permanent border between Poland and Germany. These organizations were especially influential in Bavaria and in Munich. They considered Nowak a Germanophobe.[103] The attacks on him were reprinted by extreme right-wing neo-Nazi publications, such as *Intern-Informationen*, which appeared in Switzerland and was distributed in West Germany by mail.[104]

There is no conclusive evidence that these actions were influenced by Department I of the Ministry of Internal Affairs, but, from what we know about the disinformation operations of the early 1970s, this is highly likely. It does not mean that any of the émigrés who opposed Nowak were necessarily Polish Security Service agents, as no documents to support this claim have been found in the Institute of National Remembrance archive. Often a suggestion was enough, such as slipping Kassner's statement (which, as we know, the ministry had paid for) to the right people who disliked Nowak. To Polish intelligence, using extreme right-wing groups in Germany that opposed the Oder-Neisse border and reiterated German claims to the eastern territories lost in 1945 may have made the charges more credible and also covered up any traces leading to Warsaw as the source of this operation.

Interestingly, the persons who played an important role in the anti-Nowak campaign were connected to Juliusz Sokolnicki, who appeared in London in the 1970s as the self-appointed president of the Republic of Poland and who stood in the way of efforts to create a united front of the broadest spectrum of émigré organizations.[105] In 1977, Sokolnicki appeared alongside Edward Gierek at the wreath-laying ceremony at the Tomb of the Unknown Soldier in Paris. He also issued statements attacking the democratic opposition in Poland.[106] The historian Krzysztof Tarka established recently that Sokolnicki had collaborated with the Committee for Public Security.[107]

The facts of the charges against Nowak's collaboration with the Germans are clear. Yet because even today some people believe them, it must be emphasized in closing that the accusations are based on just two documents, at least one of which is a forgery.[108] First is Kassner's statement, for which he was paid by the Ministry of Internal Affairs. When the statement was distributed in Germany, Kassner was no longer alive, and so Nowak could not ask him to testify at his trial. There was nothing in the statement to discredit Nowak since Nowak had explained on many occasions why he had worked for the Receiver's Office. The second piece of evidence was a copy of an SS document considered a forgery by the West German police. Significantly, it was mailed out anonymously, and the Polish government never showed it publicly in the West. Had the secret police really had an original document in its possession, it would no doubt have used it to destroy the man whom the party leadership and the Ministry of Internal Affairs considered one of their worst enemies.

Psychological pressure on Nowak and his wife, as well as on his American superiors, was yet another disintegration method. They received anonymous letters from alleged former Home Army soldiers who were "outraged" by his collaboration with the Nazis. Some of these letters are in Nowak's archive at the Ossoliński National Institute in Wrocław. An example: "Treuhänder Komisar Nowak. You finished off others, and now justice has come to get you, you Nazi property manager. Like a hyena, you fattened yourself up on the property of gassed victims. Now, the ground is slipping out from under your feet, and you have to brown-nose swindlers to save your skeen [*sic*]. If you were honorable, you renegade, you would put a gun to your head. Heil Johann. Skoryna."[109]

Most of the anonymous letters were in the same handwriting, which was strikingly clumsy, probably to make it difficult for a graphologist to analyze. Many were written on identical postcards with a reproduction of an Otto Ottler painting of a vase of flowers and were mailed in Munich. Polish intelligence officers were obviously Art Nouveau fans. But they also used less sophisticated methods. When Nowak was in the hospital after an operation, an anonymous caller told his wife: "Your husband, you wh---, the enemy of People's Poland, has just died."[110]

These incidents were a component of the Communist secret service disintegration and disinformation operations of the first half of the 1970s. In 1972, two original letters from Jan Nowak were stolen from the offices of a Polish newspaper in the United States and used to prepare forgeries, which were then published in *Życie Warszawy* in February 1973.[111] Their "added" section accused Senator Fulbright of being a pro-Communist and called on the Polish community in America to stop his reelection. The letter was sent to the senator, who read it at a session of the Foreign Relations Committee. It represented an all-out success for the secret police. It was discussed in very fierce terms and included Nowak's and his American superiors' explanations.[112] Earlier, in 1971, forgeries were used to worsen the mood of uncertainty among RFE's Polish staff: they would receive forged letters from RFE's American management, which claimed to be thinking about relocating the station to Turkey because of West Germany's unfavorable attitude.[113] Maciej Morawski found one such letter under the door of his apartment in Paris.[114]

No documents about these events have been found in the Institute of National Remembrance archive. As a rule, the Ministry of Internal Affairs left behind no traces of its forgeries. Presumably, two ministry units, Inspectorate I and Group D of Department III, engaged in this activity. Both the circulation of fake documents and the Czechowicz campaign were implementing directives to intensify operations and the disinformation and disintegration plans, which were formulated in the early 1970s by the ministry's leadership and in the Security Service documents guiding its work. As Minister of Internal Affairs Wiesław Ociepka said in January 1972, "The fundamental intelligence mission for the whole ministry is to develop our offensive, to concretize operational undertakings with the goal of reaching hostile centers of sabotage, sites of political interest to us and the special services of our main adversaries. We expect intelligence to strengthen its disinformation-inspiration activity and other operations units of the ministry to adopt this form of action."[115]

It was primarily Departments I and III that were to realize this mission. "Implementing fundamental changes in the style of our work and moving to an offensive type of action requires instituting operational games and combinations to a much greater degree than we have done so far," decided Department III at its national meeting. "This will give us the possibility of going more deeply into the hostile groups we are working on, especially centers of external sabotage, and also groups connected to these centers." Concrete steps were taken to support this direction of activity: "The department, aware of the importance of this type of action, has created group 'D,' which will serve as a real laboratory working out the principles and most effective methods of implementing such undertakings."[116]

It is important to remember that at roughly the same time as "disinformation" operations aimed at Jan Nowak were under way, similar methods were being used against RFE's Polish associate, Władysław Bartoszewski. The Security Service was spreading rumors, anonymous letters, and forgeries aimed at undermining trust in him. There is evidence in the archives that the Security Service was looking for information about Bartoszewski's liberation from Auschwitz in 1941 and for surviving witnesses who had been incarcerated with him. The Ministry of Internal Affairs was probably trying to charge him with collaborating with the Germans, just as it would shortly do in Nowak's case.[117]

Similar methods were used in the early 1970s with respect to Simon Wiesenthal, head of the Jewish Documentation Center in Vienna. Ministry of Internal Affairs documents present him as an agent of Zionism and of Israeli intelligence, a leading enemy of People's Poland. Its hatred for this relentless Nazi hunter was all the greater since he had revealed facts discrediting figures in the Polish government. Thus, Wiesenthal accused Kazimierz Rusinek, deputy minister of culture and secretary general of the veterans' Union of Fighters for Freedom and Democracy (ZBoWiD), of having served as a *Kapo* (a trusted prisoner functionary) in the Mauthausen concentration camp, and Deputy Minister of National Defense Grzegorz Korczyński, a commander in the People's Army in Lublin Province during the war, of murdering a group of Jews in hiding.[118]

In 1972, the Ministry of National Defense published a book by Wacław Szafrański (Jan Nowak believed that this was the aforementioned journalist Ignacy Krasicki's alias) titled *W sieci Szymona Wiesenthala* (In Simon Wiesenthal's net). In it, Wiesenthal is accused of having been a Gestapo agent during the war, a member of a Jewish network led by Abram Gancwajch in the Generalgouvernement (General Government, a part of occupied Poland not incorporated into Germany).[119] The book restates these charges repeatedly, without citing any documents or eyewitness accounts that would in any way substantiate them. The same applies to statements about RFE's close cooperation with the Jewish Documentation Center, which was allegedly steered by the CIA, Israeli intelligence, and Jewish organizations. Soon after the book appeared, a statement claiming that Wiesenthal had collaborated with the Gestapo in Bucharest during the war, written by two Nazis living in Argentina, traveled in neo-Nazi circles in West Germany. Nowak believed that Krasicki himself had obtained this statement on a trip he had taken to Argentina with two Security Service functionaries. West German Nazi publications also quoted from Szafrański's book.[120]

In keeping with the rule not to leave written traces of such controversial activities, however, surviving documents in the Institute of National Remembrance archive notably do not mention these operations or the operation against Nowak. Materials concerning the secret police investigation of Wiesenthal include a single document describing the way forged letters were mailed out by the Polish intelligence resident spy in Vienna with the goal of starting a quarrel between the Jewish Documentation Center and the local Jewish community.[121]

It was not only Polish intelligence that specialized in fabricating charges about collaboration with the Gestapo. The same accusation was spread in Britain about the Czech émigré Josef Josten, publisher of the *Features and News from behind the Iron Curtain* bulletin, which covered news inconvenient to the Communist regime. Josten had served in the Czechoslovak units of the British Army during the war, returned to Czechoslovakia in 1945, and then escaped after the 1948 coup. Josef Frolik, who defected from the Czechoslovak intelligence service to Britain, revealed in 1974 that Czechoslovak intelligence had used the Abwehr and Gestapo archives that had survived in Prague for its disinformation campaign. False documents were made from surviving ones to show that Josten, who had spent the war in Britain, had worked for the Gestapo.[122]

It appears that in the 1970s, Czechoslovakia's state security was the second most active in the émigré community in the West after the Polish. It also often used disinformation. Apart from the cases of Josten and Captain Minařik there was the widely known activity of its agent Erwin Marak. He left his country with thousands of other Czechs and Slovaks after the Warsaw Pact invasion in August 1968. Passing for a political émigré, he lived in West Germany. In December 1974, Prague Radio broadcast a program of Marak's fabricated telephone conversations with employees of RFE's Czechoslovak Service, which intended to show that émigrés were hoping for a World War III.[123]

The number of attacks on RFE in the mass media was also a measure of the security services' interest in the radio. Figures kept by RFE's Research and Analysis Department indicate that, for instance, in the first quarter of 1975 there were forty-nine such attacks in the Czechoslovak media. Poland ranked second, with ten attacks on RFE, and the Soviet Union third, with eight.[124] The Czechoslovak Communists' motivations in fighting RFE and other émigré organizations were fully rational. About 140,000 people had left Czechoslovakia in 1968–1969 and become an important part of the émigré communities created by the first, even larger exodus of 1948–1949. Like the earlier emigration, the second wave included many individuals who had belonged to the political and intellectual elites. After the suppression of the Prague Spring and the massive purges called "normalization," Gustáv Husák's government saw the politically minded and well-organized émigré community, expert on the situation back home and trying to maintain close contact with it, as its main challenger.

Détente and Fighting "Sabotage"

Instructions from the very top of the Polish government guided the offensive against RFE and the external sabotage organizations. A joint session of the Politburo and the Presidium of the government on November 16, 1972, recommended that the Ministry of Internal Affairs step up its operations. "More offensive and effective operations need to be aimed against the sabotage centers, especially RFE and all opposition," stated Edward Gierek.[125]

The build-up of the fight against RFE in the early 1970s intended not only to worsen RFE's already serious problems in the United States and West Germany, exploiting them to the max to weaken RFE, but also, if everything were to line up perfectly, to deal it the death blow. At least two other motives guided this strategy. First, it was the assumption that after the splintering of the intelligentsia's opposition in March 1968, when student strikes were suppressed with brutal force and opposition intellectuals were purged, along with the bloody pacification of workers in December 1970, outside sabotage (so deemed) remained the main threat to the regime. In the words of the director of Department III, Colonel Henryk Piętek, spoken at a Ministry of Internal Affairs leadership meeting in September 1971, "we are seeing the growth of the penetration of the political-ideological sphere by foreign centers. In revisionist centers at home, there is lethargy and a lack of ideas on how to proceed."[126]

The second motivation had to do with the specific interpretation of détente by the party leadership and the Ministry of Internal Affairs. The relaxation of relations between the capitalist countries and the socialist camp, a liberalized passport policy resulting in a much higher volume of travel, and the economic and cultural opening up to the West jointly brought new threats to the political system. "In the current line-up in the international situation and the progressing stabilization of the socioeconomic situation at home, we are seeing a shift in the confrontation front between the socialist and capitalist camps on the ideological-political level. The forces that are conducting activity directed at the consciousness of the societies of the socialist countries are very important in this situation," asserted the Ministry of Internal Affairs in October 1972.[127] Opening the March 1974 "Council of the National and Foreign Ideological Front" of the PUWP, Jan Szydlak, a member of the Politburo and a CC secretary, pointed to "the new international situation, which is shaping the process of détente and popularization of the principles of peaceful coexistence. It increases the role and weight of the ideological struggle between socialism and capitalism."[128]

It was not only the Polish leadership that defined détente in this way but also the "comrades" responsible for the propaganda-ideological front in the "fraternal parties." A May 1974 Moscow meeting of CC secretaries responsible for ideology was convened to discuss fighting ideological penetration from the capitalist countries; another, in March 1975 in Prague, was a working session for representatives of their ideological and foreign departments.[129] In the early 1970s Hungary, like Poland, enlarged the units within the Central Committee of the Hungarian Socialist Workers' Party and the Foreign Ministry charged with monitoring and combating the influence of foreign radios and other forms of ideological sabotage. These efforts intended to create a mechanism for coordinating the work of the various party and state organizations.[130]

The security police appreciated the dangers stemming from détente similarly. The materials about fighting the Soviet Union's enemies, which the KGB supplied to the Polish secret services, devote significant space to the operations of "special services, enemy centers of ideological sabotage and foreign anti-Soviet centers" that had been conducting "ideological sabotage against the USSR, adjusting it to the situation stemming from the peace policies of the socialist countries, the conditions of reduced tension in their international situation and the further broadening of trade, economic, and cultural contacts between the USSR and the capitalist countries."[131] A multiday seminar on ideological sabotage took place in Havana in March 1974, with delegations from the security agencies of the Soviet Union, Poland, Hungary, Czechoslovakia, East Germany, and Mongolia taking part. They recounted their experiences in the fight against foreign sabotage and discussed the need for better coordination of actions on this front.[132]

In Poland, a "symposium on the subject of the current state of threat from ideological-political sabotage and the political-operational system of response" was organized by the Ministry of Internal Affairs in September 1974 for various institutions to share experiences. Apart from the hosts, representatives of the CC PUWP (including Jerzy Łukaszewicz), Foreign Ministry, Main Political Directorate of the Polish Army, and the East-West Center were present. They received materials from the Havana meeting.[133]

In operations, a plan to fight the most important center of sabotage, RFE, was prepared by Department I of the Ministry of Internal Affairs in June 1974. It was based on the premise that existing diplomacy, propaganda, and Ministry of Internal Affairs operations had significantly weakened the sabotage centers, especially RFE. Uncertainty and fear for the station's and its staff's future now dominated its leadership's and employees' thinking, the report held. "The exponents of the sabotage centers fear a new wave of coherent Polish diplomatic actions aimed at the administrations of the main capitalist countries concerned, especially the USA. With equal anxiety, these exponents await special actions by our apparatus that will discredit their actions. . . . Their fear stems not only from the possibility that the popularity of the sabotage undertakings in Polish territory will weaken as a result of our actions, but primarily from the effects 'in their own territory' and the strengthening of the opponents of Cold War forms of sabotage, which also exist in political and government circles in the countries of their patrons, especially the USA," argued Colonel Leszek Guzik, deputy director of Department I.[134]

This argument confirms the thesis that the previous propaganda campaigns had been addressed not only to the Polish public but also to RFE's foes in the United States. According to Department I, maintaining the existing battle lines with RFE could deal it the death blow. "Our tested operational data show," claimed Colonel Guzik, "that every new powerful strike at RFE may make the essential difference in tilting the scale in favor of those who oppose its existence, who are demanding the station's liquidation for a variety of reasons, many of which are very different from ours. We know that the proponents of RFE's existence await the return of the next man to Warsaw with trepidation and, for some, fear of it simply borders on psychosis."[135]

Polish intelligence was certainly too optimistic, since RFE's most difficult period was behind it and the new laws Congress passed in October 1973 assured the radio's continued existence. The ministry's leadership nonetheless approved the plan of action developed by Department I (to be overseen by Deputy Minister Mirosław Milewski), as did the political leadership, although we have no information about the precise level of government that discussed this plan.[136]

The plan's key component was to bring the next two agents working in RFE's Polish Service back to Poland and to build a propaganda campaign around their return. The first was Mieczysław Lach, who has already been mentioned, and the second Andrzej Smoliński, code name "Kryza," who wrote economic analyses in the Research and Analysis Department. The ministry's interest in Smoliński lay in "unsettling the American patrons' trust vis-à-vis those on the staff of the Polish section of RFE with whom Captain Czechowicz maintained social relations."[137] The ministry probably intended to make contact with individuals whom US intelligence might suspect of conspiring with Czechowicz and recruit them, or, if they refused, discredit them by revealing their contacts with Polish intelligence. This would contribute to worsening the mood of uncertainty and distrust among the staff.

Smoliński had worked in the Office of the Council of Ministers and defected in 1965. In September 1973, his father visited him in Munich, serving as a messenger for the Ministry of Internal Affairs, which asked him to return to Poland and promised that he would not be punished for working for the Americans. Smoliński hesitated for a few months and then accepted the offer. "Classified information leads us to believe that he was disillusioned with the Americans and resents them for creating formal obstacles (for having been a member of the PUWP in Poland) to obtaining US citizenship and settling in the USA. He also felt that his patrons did not give him the proper care during an illness. He is also not good at languages, which is another obstacle to getting used to life in the West," analyzed Department I.[138]

The ministry's initial goal had been to "keep 'Kryza' on site as a regular source with the ability to pull him out when the situation suits us." Smoliński's work for Polish intelligence was to be the "price of rehabilitating him from the hostile activity he had practiced so far against his country and making a future return to Poland possible."[139] In the few months he worked for Polish intelligence, "Kryza" supplied information to his case officer mainly about the mood of the staff, reactions to Czechowicz's return to Poland, and changes at RFE after the new regime governing its operations was approved by the US Congress. After "Guzik's plan" was adopted, however, his handlers decided to bring him back to Poland, together with his wife, who also worked for the radio, in late August 1974, and then, in November 1974, to bring back the "'Kumor'-'Freda' espionage duo," the names given Mieczysław Lach and his life partner.

Department I worked out the details of the propaganda campaign, including the texts of Polish Press Agency (PAP) press releases.[140] It is noteworthy that in both cases there was no mention of the ties of "Kryza," "Kumor," or "Freda" to Polish intelligence—in contrast to the Czechowicz case. This was intentional. According to the author of the PAP press releases, Colonel Henryk Wróblewicz of Department I, "the phrase 'as PAP has learned' allows a variety of commentaries about their return to develop, including the assumption that a collaborator of our apparatus who had been introduced into RFE has returned, without officially burdening us." Another phrasing was also not random: "The word 'next' can be interpreted to mean that there will be others. This is very important in disorganizing the station's work and deepening the existing slackening there."[141]

Smoliński's and Lach's returns were publicized significantly less than "Captain" Czechowicz's. This was most likely because the secret police believed that to repeat the earlier campaign on an equal scale would bring no new tangible benefits. Also, Czechowicz's public statements had used up all the materials collected about RFE, including those from other sources, such as Lach. Warsaw probably also realized, on a level higher than Department I, which was in charge of "Guzik's plan," that RFE's greatest difficulties were behind it and that a new propaganda campaign would not lead to its closing.

But Warsaw did not stop trying to convince several other RFE employees to return. Publicizing such cases, especially were they to involve important and well-known figures, would have been the best way to exacerbate the mood of uncertainty on the Munich team, compromise it before the Americans, or undermine the position of Jan Nowak, whom Warsaw consistently saw as its number one enemy. Not only Kazimierz Zamorski and Wiktor Trościanko but also Paweł Zaremba, one of Nowak's most trusted colleagues, heard such offers, in Zaremba's case through his brother. Zaremba was promised an appropriate material situation in Poland and an opportunity to publish his books and continue his academic career.[142] He naturally engaged in these discussions with his boss's full knowledge, and they prepared questions together to help them understand the other side's intentions.[143]

Offers of returning to Poland were the Communist special services' tested method of fighting the political emigration, "disintegrating" it. It was employed widely in the so-called repatriation campaign of 1955–1956, when Warsaw managed, with the appropriate propaganda framework, to bring back several prominent figures, including former prime ministers in the government in exile Hugo Hanke (who had been recruited earlier by the Ministry of Public Security) and Stanisław Cat-Mackiewicz, as well as the eminent writer Melchior Wańkowicz.[144]

* * *

The first half of the 1970s saw the high point of Warsaw's anti-RFE activity. At no other time did Warsaw conduct such a vast offensive, which consisted of a mix of diplomacy, propaganda, and special operations by the security apparatus. It failed to reach its principal goal of eliminating the station. But neither did it manage to have the station moved out of Germany. People still argue about how much the attacks against Jan Nowak contributed to his resignation from the directorship of the Polish Service in December 1975. The main reason for Nowak's departure was the American policy of limiting the capacity and scope of RFE's activity in the era of détente, with many in Washington seeing the radio as a Cold War relic and an obstacle on the road to the full normalization of relations with the Soviet bloc. For the Polish desk, this meant, first, increased interference in its broadcasts to reduce content that might irritate the Polish regime, and second, deep personnel cuts, to adjust its size to this new era in East-West relations. The role of the station was to diminish as, it was assumed, barriers to the flow of information and exchange of ideas began to be lowered.[145]

Another reason for the decision to replace Nowak was the growing disagreements among the staff, which was becoming increasingly difficult to manage, as Nowak writes in his memoirs. He could no longer count on the support and full loyalty of its great majority, something that had been key in the fight for the Polish desk's autonomy in the second half of the 1950s and the early 1960s. On the one hand, the tensions stemmed from the dissatisfaction and slights caused by Nowak's autocratic leadership. But on the other, they were also grounded in real political and ideological differences. Thus, some of the staff were increasingly opposed to focusing on fighting the Partisans, a nationalist faction within the Communist elite, or to hiring people who had left Poland after March 1968, many of whom had worked in the Communist media and some of whom had been members of the PUWP.

The Ministry of Internal Affairs fed all these disputes. In this way, then, the grand secret police campaign against Nowak did contribute to spoiling the mood and relations among the Polish staff. It is a sad paradox that many of the people who were not enamored of their director tended not only to believe in the charges of collaboration with the Nazis leveled against him but often also to sustain them and pass them on with open delight. This was even the case with some eminent personalities with unblemished pasts, including Kazimierz Zamorski and Stefan Wysocki, both of whom published their memoirs many years after Nowak's departure.[146]

A memoir by Danuta Mierzanowska, who worked as an announcer, captures the atmosphere in the Polish Service in the last months under Nowak's leadership: "The litigation against German newspapers continued. Nowak could not get enough of shouting in it nor, as it turned out, win them. This must have been the greatest calamity of his life. Meanwhile, the rift in the team became unfathomable, and the bitterness grew daily. People who were hurt and insulted began to speak up: 'enough.' The number of grievances submitted to the Americans grew. Every day, guessing, gossip, inquiries, 'guilty or not guilty' discussions became the most important topics of conversations, and the toxic atmosphere was unbearable."[147]

The Polish political police checked off Nowak's departure at the end of 1975 as its own huge success, accomplished over long years. Andrzej Czechowicz remembered the words of his supervisor in Department I, uttered at the news of Nowak's departure: "We are square now. He finished off Moczar, we've dispatched him."[148] This insider opinion that RFE's attacks had greatly contributed to the downfall of the very influential minister of the interior can be seen as the highest recognition of Jan Nowak's work.

The appointment of Zygmunt Michałowski, who for several years had served as Nowak's deputy, to succeed him as director guaranteed the continuity of the radio's political line. Nowak's exit, however, marked the end of an era for the Polish Service. He had created a voice that for millions of Poles was an invaluable source of information about events in Poland and abroad, an institution that knew more about Poland than anyone else in the West. No director after Nowak would have as strong a position with respect to the Americans or the Polish émigré community. He had done this for nearly a quarter of a century, and at many junctures and on many issues had played a decisive role in shaping the radio's program and the operations of the Polish team. Now, from the point of view of the Polish regime, a very dangerous adversary was leaving the scene; Warsaw had invested huge resources and effort in his removal. But the station survived, and the Polish regime's war against it continued for as long as the Communist system existed.

6. From Helsinki to the Demise of Communism, 1975–1989

Helsinki versus Radio Free Europe

The Final Act of the Conference on Security and Cooperation in Europe (CSCE), signed by the leaders of thirty-three European countries, the United States, and Canada in Helsinki in August 1975, crowned the process of détente between the West and the Communist bloc countries that had been launched in the early 1970s. It was the most important international treaty since the Potsdam Conference of 1945. The Final Act of the CSCE was, in a way, a surrogate peace treaty that formally and legally ended World War II and sealed its political and territorial consequences. For the Soviet Union, it was the long-awaited sanctioning by the West of the postwar frontiers and political order, that is, the validation of Soviet dominance in Central and Eastern Europe. To reach this goal, Moscow even agreed to include in the Final Act the so-called third basket, which guaranteed respect for human rights, freedom of movement, cultural exchanges, and the free flow of information.[1]

Opposition and dissent movements in the satellite countries and the Soviet Union itself, as well as the Carter administration, which made human rights a pillar of its Soviet bloc policy, repeatedly brought up the third basket.[2] It is noteworthy that in the period immediately following the conference, the governments of the Communist countries presented the signing of the Final Act as an enormous success, claiming that the Eastern bloc had achieved full recognition of its borders and its system of government.[3] They also maintained that détente meant not a relaxation of their ideological struggle with the West but, on the contrary, the creation of an important new field on which they could compete. Numerous top-level party documents proclaimed that it was necessary to intensify the political and propaganda campaign against foreign centers of sabotage (so deemed), which the Communist bloc countries believed were attempting to influence the internal situation in the socialist countries. Notching up the propaganda campaign was to be based on a unique interpretation of the provisions of the CSCE Final Act (as well as of the third basket), according to which the agreement ruled out interference in the domestic affairs of the countries that had signed it, including the continuation of foreign radio broadcasts and other means of conducting sabotage. "As part of the demands for increasing the responsibility of our Western partners for information and cultural activity, we must intensify our activity opposing the surviving 'Cold War' imperialist propaganda institutions, such as Radio Free Europe or the [Paris] *Kultura* publisher. Their further existence indeed contradicts the spirit and the letter of the Helsinki Final Act," read a document adopted in January 1976 by the CC PUWP Secretariat.[4]

Another document produced by the CC Secretariat a few months later restated these theses and sketched out the necessary moves to oppose "propaganda that is hostile to us." Specifically, two paths of action were proposed:

> —strengthening diplomatic-political actions in the direction of eradicating typical sabotage organizations, such as RFE and others, which absolutely requires political cooperation between Poland and all the socialist countries;
>
> —continuing the diplomatic-political activities aimed at neutralizing the moves of émigré milieus hostile to us (and their organizations, such as *Kultura*, *Aneks*, and *Jedność*), especially by exploiting the resolutions of the CSCE and influencing those capitalist countries from whose territory they are exercised, to put an end to practices that are hostile to Poland and by isolating the above-mentioned groups from the broad masses of Polonia.[5]

All these documents restated that the worst sabotage organization was RFE, "the most blatant Cold War instrument of anti-Polish activity."[6] The CC Department of Ideological-Educational Work also mentioned other foreign radio stations, among them the Voice of America (VOA), BBC, and Deutschlandfunk. "But we do not in any way place them in the same category as Radio Free Europe," emphasized the authors of the department's study, titled "Anti-Polish Propaganda: A Threat to the Nation's Vital Interests."[7]

The unpublished study mentioned the agreement signed in Helsinki as the reason why RFE's activity could be declared to be at odds with international law: "Every country has the right and the duty to defend itself from revolutionary and sabotage activity, and this is in accordance not only with its domestic laws but also with the norms of international law. As we understand it, [Radio]

Free Europe's pursuits are illegal, violating fundamental international norms but also the CSCE Final Act. Because of this, all cooperation between this spy agency and our citizens is illegal."[8]

This last statement is an excellent illustration of the attitude of a faction within the party apparatus and the secret police that would have liked to have seen Poland introduce penal sanctions for any contact with RFE and other "sabotage" organizations in the West into its legislation, or at least use existing laws more often, as in the past, against people collaborating with RFE or with the Paris-based *Kultura* (such as Władysław Bartoszewski or Hanna Szarzyńska-Rewska and Anna Rudzińska). Similar suggestions appeared later as well but were never consistently implemented, lest they complicate Poland's relations with the West.

Cooperation within the Soviet Bloc in Fighting Radio Free Europe

Many CC PUWP documents created after the Helsinki conference demanded closer cooperation among the socialist countries in fighting RFE. Such cooperation already existed—between both the ruling parties and the secret police—by the early 1970s. Judging from the available documents, it tightened in the second half of the 1970s. In any case, the subject of fighting Western propaganda and sabotage, especially that promulgated by RFE, came up in many meetings of representatives of the ruling parties, as well as of their special services. They tried to agree on political and propaganda moves, or at least on individual operations.

A conference of Communist and Workers' Party Central Committee secretaries charged with ideology and foreign affairs took place in January 1976 in Warsaw. The PUWP CC secretary Jan Szydlak presented "a conception of undertaking joint actions aimed at shutting down the sabotage radio stations."[9] His proposal was adopted, and the PUWP was charged with preparing a program of joint actions against RFE and Radio Liberty. The Foreign Ministry coordinated its development, and the CC PUWP Department of Ideological-Educational Work, the Ministry of Internal Affairs, the Institute of Research on the Contemporary Problems of Capitalism, and the army's Main Political Directorate also took part.[10]

But before another meeting could take place, the Soviet bloc scored a major political and propaganda victory. In February 1976, the accreditation of RFE's sports reporters, who had arrived in Innsbruck to cover the Winter Olympics, was revoked. This was the result of "a fierce protest from the leaderships of the teams from the socialist countries (with the exception of Romania)."[11] The

Olympic authorities' surrender evoked a sharp public reaction from Secretary of State Henry Kissinger and protests in the US Congress. Indeed, the situation seemed to repeat that of 1972, when RFE correspondents had been denied accreditation at the Munich Olympics. In both cases, however, the radio reported on the games. In 1972, Wojciech Trojanowski and Tadeusz Nowakowski provided commentary on the competitions as they watched them on television in an RFE studio at Englischer Garten.[12] In Innsbruck, RFE's Polish newsmen aired their programs from a hotel room. They were so professional and so lively that audiences in Poland could easily believe that they were listening to reporters watching and reporting from the competition sites in real time.[13]

At the next meeting on ideological issues, held in Sofia in March 1977, the Poles presented a plan of joint actions.[14] This plan has not been found in Polish archives, but its main parts can be reconstructed by consulting related documents. At a June 1976 Moscow meeting of representatives of the socialist countries' ministries of foreign affairs, the director of the Press and Cultural and Scientific Cooperation Office of the Polish Foreign Ministry had explained that the action plan aimed at RFE and Radio Liberty should be ready before the 1977 Helsinki review conference in Belgrade. The West was expected to bring up human rights, which were protected by the third basket. The Soviet bloc would counter with a demand that the saboteur radio stations be closed since, according to Moscow and its allies, they were violating the provisions of the Final Act. By then the socialist countries should have been able to resolve important tactical issues, such as whether to demand the immediate shutting down of RFE "or perhaps first a change in tone and content (putting an end to their interference in our internal affairs), which might make it easier for us to gain support from influential Americans who are opposed to RFE."

The top-level officials at the March 1977 Sofia meeting considered it a priority to "form a special 'anti-RFE lobby' in the Congress, State Department and other organizations in the USA, and in the FRG. Each socialist country should [attempt to] sway different influential personalities with whom it already has a friendship or good contacts." A similar operation was to be conducted in Spain, where Radio Liberty transmitters were located. Plans were crafted to "influence journalists in the USA and FRG to publish articles opposing RFE." There was also to be opposition to "the participation of RFE reporters in international conferences and events (UNESCO conferences, Olympics, congresses, etc.)," which, if it was not always effective, would at least raise on the stage of world opinion the question of the legality of RFE's actions. The socialist countries were to coordinate their diplomatic and propaganda statements with the initiatives of other members of the bloc, and use similar arguments in them.[15]

The Sofia meeting adopted the PUWP's proposal as its preliminary plan, and the PUWP was asked to coordinate further stages of cooperation in anti-RFE and anti–Radio Liberty actions. Subsequent meetings of representatives of the ideological and foreign departments of the bloc's parties discussed these topics. At a May 1978 gathering in Leipzig, after the PUWP delegation had spoken, the representative from the Communist Party of the Soviet Union (CPSU) stated that "our proposed operation of unmasking RFE/RL and refusing to recognize and respect it is needed especially today and may play a major role in the preparations for the Olympics in Moscow in 1980. The Americans have opted for blackmail and are making the accreditation of RFE/RL correspondents to the Olympics a condition of their sports teams' participation in the Games."[16] In response to the Soviet invasion of Afghanistan in December 1979, the United States and several Western countries, as well as a group of pro-Western developing countries, did not take part in the 1980 Moscow Olympics.

The PUWP-coordinated program of joint actions by the Communist countries against the radio stations identified as practicing ideological sabotage brought no breakthrough or even the development of new forms of action. In many meetings with US leaders and members of Congress, the Communist countries repeated their demand that RFE and RL had to be shut down, for they considered these institutions to have violated the CSCE Final Act and endangered détente. Leonid Brezhnev also raised the prospect of shutting down the stations in his talks with German chancellor Helmut Schmidt in May 1978.[17] But this demand received a less favorable hearing than it had in the early 1970s, when the radios' fate was being decided after their CIA financing had been revealed in an atmosphere of scandal, and the Brandt government had remained open to the possibility of starting talks about their expulsion from West Germany.

Cooperation between the special services of the Soviet bloc countries seemingly improved in the second half of the 1970s. A meeting of intelligence representatives from Czechoslovakia, Bulgaria, Hungary, East Germany, Poland, and the Soviet Union took place in Prague in February 1976. The attendees adopted an "action plan" to oppose RFE and Radio Liberty, both the stations' propaganda and their operations. The action plan adopted as its minimum goal the removal of the radios from the European continent, and shutting them down altogether as its maximum goal. The plan included publishing books and articles in the socialist countries as well as in the West using information and documents acquired by the agents who had been active in Munich, Andrzej Czechowicz and Pavel Minařík. English- and German-language brochures modeled on Soviet publications uncovering the saboteur radios as tools of the US intelligence services would also be distributed in the West. Documentary and feature films would be produced. All these planned projects were intended to mobilize the international public to support "putting an end to RFE's and Radio Liberty's criminal activities . . . which violate international law and the CSCE Final Act." Operation Pająk (Spider) in Austria would discredit the radios in the eyes of the government of Austria and others who had signed the Final Act. In Germany, the effort was expected to inspire Bundestag members' speeches, statements by "progressive groups," and letters addressed to the US government demanding that these centers of radio sabotage be shut down.

Plans were also laid for a great propaganda initiative, namely, creating a tribunal in a socialist country that would put RFE and Radio Liberty on trial. The "court" proceedings would use documents acquired by the Communist bloc's intelligence services. Testifying before the tribunal would be former employees of the radios, among them Andrzej Czechowicz, Mieczysław Lach, Andrzej Smoliński, Pavel Minařík, and Pavel Marin.[18] No such spectacle starring secret service agents and functionaries ever took place, even though the KGB continued to bring it up.[19]

During this period a similar but larger plan was discussed in Soviet bloc party meetings. The Leipzig conference of May 1978 debated setting up an international tribunal, to be called "Imperialism in the dock," in "one of the progressive Third World countries." Representatives of Western Communist parties and "progressive" intellectuals would also be participants. The tribunal would serve as a sort of response to the Western countries' invocations of human rights in their relations with the Soviet bloc. The tribunal would publish and disseminate internationally "indictments" against "imperialism's most important actions."[20] According to Andrzej Werblan, PUWP CC secretary in the 1970s, the plan failed because of opposition from the Italian and French Communists.[21]

Other proposals made by the Soviet bloc's special services in the action plan resulting from the March 1977 Sofia meeting included instigating and deepening internal divisions and conflicts at RFE and Radio Liberty (through promoting rivalries between the two stations, tensions between RFE's national sections, and resentment of Jewish colleagues), embarrassing some employees, and trying to force others to go back to their countries. The special services strategized about sharing tips on issues and staffers in the different national sections who could be used in operations. Intelligence and counterintelligence services were to step up their "penetration" of the radio stations by introducing agents who would speak up "from nationalistic émigré positions, Zionists, and dissidents." "Spy games" would be organized, with the goal of uncovering and taking over channels through which information and documents traveled between citizens of socialist countries and the radios.[22]

At least some of the ideas listed in the action plan were implemented. Operation Pająk included the publication of an article by Emil Hoffman in the Vienna newspaper *Volksstimme* arguing that RFE's and Radio Liberty's activities were illegal. The article was picked up and republished by Moscow's *Izvestia*. The Stasi (East German intelligence service) wrote it, as we know from drafts of the article found in Berlin by the office of the Federal Commissioner for the Stasi Archives. Czechoslovak intelligence wrote and published a pamphlet presenting RFE employees as Western spies and distributed it in English, French, German, Spanish, and Slovak translations in many countries.[23] We also know that in the late 1970s, the KGB and Bulgarian intelligence services conducted a joint operation code-named "Nord." Bulgarian agent "Ivan" worked on exposing two Radio Liberty freelancers in West Germany. These two intelligence services allegedly also introduced an agent into RFE's Bulgarian Section.[24]

The second half of the 1970s and the early 1980s saw the two most dramatic events in the history of anti-RFE plots. In September 1978, the Bulgarian writer and journalist Georgi Markov was jabbed with the tip of an umbrella on a street in London. He died a few days later, poisoned by the ricin in a pellet that had been ejected from the umbrella. Before taking up permanent residence in the West in 1969, Markov had been a well-known writer who moved in the Bulgarian Communist leader Todor Zhivkov's social circle and hunted with him. He had also worked for Bulgaria's Committee of State Security, writing propagandistic novels and film scripts. He had thus acquired an expert understanding of Bulgaria's Communist elite, which he then used to expose its members by writing for RFE, the BBC, and Deutsche Welle. Bulgarian security documents reveal that Sofia viewed Markov as a first-class enemy, and his series of programs on RFE was seen as the most ferocious propaganda attack on the Bulgarian government.[25] The Bulgarians asked the Soviet secret police for help; they obtained from the secret police the poison and the weapon (umbrella) for the assassination.

An attempt was made to kill another Bulgarian RFE freelancer, Vladimir Kostov, using the same weapon. Before defecting to the West in 1977, Kostov had worked as a representative of the Bulgarian press agency in Paris, but he was in fact an intelligence operative. Like Markov, he was attacked with an umbrella in the street, in Paris, but the poisonous pellet was removed in time.[26]

In February 1981, a bomb exploded outside the offices of the Czechoslovak desk in RFE's main building in Munich. Four staffers were wounded. The investigation revealed that the terrorist group led by the notorious Carlos the Jackal (the Venezuelan Ilich Ramirez Sanchez) was responsible for the attack. Documents released after the fall of Communism show that Romania's Securitate had ordered the attack and delivered the explosives. It is not clear why the bomb was placed outside the Czechoslovak and not the Romanian Section. It may have been a mistake.[27] The Communist special services tried to use the bombing to fan a mood of endangerment among RFE's staff. Anonymous letters warning about new attacks arrived at the station.[28]

Romanian intelligence worked autonomously and therefore did not take part in the Prague special services meeting or in any other such meetings. The RFE bombing was only one of several exceptionally violent acts ordered by Nicolae Ceauşescu against RFE Romanian desk employees and freelance reporters. Three Romanian émigrés in Paris received letter bombs in February 1981, immediately before the Munich bombing. Threats were sent to others. Emil Georgescu, one of the main editors in the Romanian Service, was brutally beaten in January 1981 in Munich (a detailed report about this attack was found in Romanian secret police archives), and in July 1981 two French criminals stabbed him more than twenty times with a knife.

The Romanian Securitate's actions against RFE were only one manifestation of Ceauşescu's repressive policies directed against his real and imagined enemies. In Romania, the secret police would find and persecute any citizen suspected of listening to RFE. The Romanian dictator ordered the Securitate to find the author of every letter sent from Romania to the radio. It is paradoxical that Ceauşescu never chose to restore the jamming of RFE's programs, which had been abandoned in the 1960s. Doing so would no doubt have worsened his image in the West, which continued to view Romania favorably—as a Communist country, but one that was independent of the Soviet Union. The attacks organized on the orders of the Romanian dictator are an illustration of the long road his regime had traveled since the mid-1960s, when shortly after coming to power Ceauşescu had signaled new, more open policies and invited the director of RFE's Romanian Service to visit.[29]

After the meeting in Prague in February 1976, gatherings of representatives of the special services devoted to fighting RFE and other organizations deemed to be practicing sabotage took place in Budapest (1977), Warsaw (1979), Moscow (1980), Sofia (1983), and Prague again (1986).[30] The intelligence agencies repeatedly exchanged documents about RFE, including some acquired through operations.[31]

At the Budapest meeting, Poland's deputy minister of internal affairs, Mirosław Milewski, gauged that since the signing of the Final Act of the CSCE, the Western "sabotage" organizations and émigré groups had increased their anti-Polish government activities. He also discussed which countermeasures were the most efficient, in the opinion of his ministry: "The fundamental effort is spy work aimed at gaining advance information about the long-term plans of the enemy's headquarters. With the help of espionage and special undertakings, activity in the direction of disintegration, compromising, isolation, and neutralization of the most active sabotage centers and groups and leading activists."[32] In the vocabulary of secret police functionaries, "special undertakings" generally meant using extralegal methods that left minor, or even no, traces in documents: fanning conflicts by spreading false rumors, intimidation, beatings or attacks, and assassinations. The meeting's Hungarian hosts called for "joint actions against sabotage and ideological sites." They suggested conducting "operations on the principle of joint, bilateral, and multilateral plans" and "joint operational uncovering of targeted sites and planning the penetration of these organs."[33]

The repeated calls for common Soviet bloc operations on the one hand show that they were aiming to improve their cooperation and on the other indicate continued shortcomings. Because of limited access to these most protected secrets of the special services, it is hard to know whether this example of the KGB-Bulgarian connection in eliminating opponents was an exception or the rule in relations between the Communist intelligence services.

From the Birth of the Opposition to Martial Law

Another watershed in Poland's contemporary history came in June 1976. Worker protests, which exposed the disaster that was Edward Gierek's strategy of "accelerated development" and the magnitude of society's dissatisfaction, led to the creation of organized, open opposition movements.[34]

In this new reality, as RFE acquired a new role, the Polish government changed its perception of it. Illustrating this change are references to the threats from RFE found in Ministry of Internal Affairs documents from the months leading up to the explosion. In a Department III report about the conditions in Poland in April 1976, there is only one mention of RFE. It refers to a "six-person, informal group of students of Polish philology at the Jagiellonian University in Cracow, who disseminated information heard on RFE and found in Western publications [émigré publications smuggled into Poland—P. M.] among students in Cracow."[35]

The next monthly report, from June 1976, mentions RFE several times. In Szczecin, in an Otex shop, "an RFE program about the December [1970] events recorded on a magnetic tape was broadcast on the internal [house] radio system." The Security Service determined that the shop's manager was guilty and arrested him. Department III also reported on the discovery of a "4-person illegal youth organization called New Poland's Army." It was allegedly founded by four students from Comprehensive Secondary School No. 1 in Warsaw who planned to produce and distribute "hostile fliers." "The RFE programs they had listened to, and a rumor about opposition elements starting fires in Warsaw in the autumn of 1975, were the impulse for the formation of this conspiratorial group."[36] Also in May 1976, the Security Service reported that informal groups of workers existed in the Lenin Works in Nowa Huta and that they "viciously criticize the policies of the central authorities, often using slogans heard in RFE programs."[37]

The image of RFE as an "inspiring" and "inciting" organization was typical of both party and Security Service thinking in the 1960s and the first half of the 1970s. A change in this perception occurred only after organized political opposition came into being. This shift was tied to the strategy adopted by the Committee for the Defense of Workers (Komitet Obrony Robotników, KOR) and later by numerous other opposition organizations. One of the founding principles of this strategy was openness in most of the groups' activities (printing and distributing underground publications was the most important exception). Their effectiveness, as measured by their ability to reach the greatest number of people, and the relative safety of their activists depended on how well informed the Polish and international public were about these groups. Here, too, RFE's role proved invaluable, something both the opposition and the Communist government understood very well.

In his memoirs, Jacek Kuroń went into great detail in describing this system: "The police were breathing down our necks and arresting us on every available pretext. The rule was that when they did it in the street, people were supposed to shout out my phone number and their name as loudly as possible. Very quickly, 39-39-64 became accepted as the number to call every time the authorities broke the law. When the police stopped anyone anywhere, I would almost always get the news. . . . Free Europe broadcast information about arrests and releases immediately. This could work efficiently only when we all adopted a basic discipline. And we did because it was Radio Free Europe's broadcasts that were the most effective method against arrests. After the radio broadcast the news, one could almost always expect a release."[38]

The usual channel for passing information to RFE was Britain or France. Jacek Kuroń or someone else from the KOR circle—Grażyna Kuroń, Anka Kowalska, Ewa Milewicz, Halina Mikołajska, or Ewa Kulik—would phone Eugeniusz or Aleksander Smolar. The Smolar brothers had been active in the student movement at the University of Warsaw in the second half of the 1960s, were arrested in 1968, and in the early 1970s left for Sweden. They published the *Aneks* quarterly, at first in Uppsala and then in London.[39] People from other opposition groups also relayed information to the West by way of the Smolars. Kazimierz Janusz from the Human and Civil Rights Protection Movement (Ruch Obrony Praw Człowieka i Obywatela, ROPCiO) often called them, too.

Eugeniusz Smolar also spoke on the phone with the leader of the Confederation for an Independent Poland (Konfederacja Polski Niepodległej, KPN), Leszek Moczulski. But the bulk of the information came from KOR. According to Eugeniusz Smolar, the information obtained through KOR was the most precise and concerned events that had usually been verified before news about them was sent to the West. Other groups most often sent only their own announcements.

The Smolars would tape these telephone conversations on a cassette recorder and then type up the most important information. They then would phone the RFE Polish director's secretariat. His secretaries would call them back and tape what the Smolars were telling them. According to Eugeniusz Smolar, before August 1980, RFE got about 80 percent of its broadcast material about the opposition's activities through this method.[40]

News from Poland was transmitted to RFE in this circuitous way for several reasons. Chiefly, at the time there was no automatic dialing from Poland to West Germany (though it was introduced at some point to France and Britain), and calls had to be placed through an operator. There was also caution. Since the Polish government treated RFE as a sabotage and spy organization under the CIA's control, passing information from Poland to the Smolars was less dangerous in terms of potential penalties.

The news conveyed to RFE was not only about repressions but primarily about the opposition's initiatives. People read even lengthy statements from KOR and other groups on the phone.[41] Thanks to them, millions of RFE's listeners in Poland, as well as the Western public, could learn about the actions of dozens of individuals, and in the late 1970s up to a few hundred, who were being constantly watched and pitted against the secret police. News aired on RFE about opposition activities also played a very important role in enlarging the circle of people who engaged in opposition activity. Bogdan Borusewicz, one of KOR's earliest collaborators in the Baltic Tri-City area, reminisced about the early days of his activism: "In 1977, Staszek Śmigiel, a student in the Electronics Faculty of Gdańsk Polytechnic, came to see me. He had heard my address on Radio Free Europe. Together with Antek Mężydło, they pulled in friends from their dormitory. They were a large, very active group."[42]

The Polish government was well aware of RFE's publicity mechanism for the activities of a small group of opposition activists. The Security Service was even familiar with KOR activists' statements, which admitted directly that RFE's help was a major boost for the opposition. The Warsaw Security Service determined that in June 1977, Wojciech Onyszkiewicz had met with a Swedish citizen and told him about the dramatic events that had followed the murder in May 1977 of the Cracow student Stanisław Pyjas, including the student demonstration, the boycott of the Juwenalia student festival, and the creation of the

Student Solidarity Committee in Cracow. Onyszkiewicz had allegedly said that "Radio Free Europe played a huge role in helping these events happen, as it informed the people of Cracow about his and his associates' initiatives as they evolved, which made it much easier for them to organize antistate activities."[43]

A report from Department III of the Ministry of Internal Affairs in April 1978 reads: "RFE is kept apprised of the deeds of hostile groups and of developments in Poland, as they develop and in detail through indirect channels. There is a concentrated propaganda attack from the Western mass propaganda media related to the creation of the Society for Educational Courses [Towarzystwo Kursów Naukowych, TKN] and the countermeasures in the area of the functioning of the 'flying universities,' which presents the ongoing phenomena in a tendentious light, which it receives from Poland. The contacts with foreign centers are maintained in telephonic form (for example, 24-hour shifts in J[acek] Kuroń's apartment) and through direct trips by people from these circles for temporary stays in the West."[44]

Exemplifying the conviction that the struggle was not merely against a handful of "enemies of socialism" but with a much more powerful and outstandingly organized hostile machine, which backed them and opened mass propaganda fire at their every move, is a letter to the chairman of the Polish Academy of Sciences from the Warsaw Council of the Federation of the Socialist Unions of Polish Youth. Writing on behalf of members of "activist youth" organizations (de facto hit squads created by the Security Service), the letter complained that the "discussion" with speakers from the TKN did not bring the expected results. The letter alleged that "from their first contact with opposite views, some TKN lecturers became impatient, began to sneer at those whose opinions differed from theirs. After almost every such discussion, Radio Free Europe immediately aired information that was untruthful and offensive to the young students who took part in these discussions. During subsequent discussion at TKN lectures, tensions increased since, on the one hand, the opponents of the discussion were systematically maligned by RFE on behalf of TKN, and on the other, the lecturers, foremost among them J[acek] Kuroń and A[dam] Michnik, began to incite brawls, at first verbal and then physical."

The authors of the letter went on to describe the invasion of Kuroń's apartment just before a TKN lecture was to take place and the severe beating of several of those present, including the host's teenage son. In the federation's version it was the opposition who beat up the students in order to discredit the "activists": "They provoked an anti-Polish campaign in Western propaganda, [and] began to vilify the young people, who, in a physical sense, fell victim to the provocation in order that they would then fall victim morally." The senders asked the chairman of the Polish Academy of Sciences to "help defend our classmates' good name, as their pure intentions and actions could not protect them from the carefully and skillfully prepared vilification campaign."[45] It would be difficult to find greater praise for RFE's effectiveness as a key player in publicizing the violent crushing of TKN.

We are left with the important question, why did the government not act more decisively to cut off or at least reduce the flow of information from the opposition to the West by, for instance, cutting off Kuroń's phone service? It had been suspended several times, including during the period following the death of a student at Jagiellonian University in Cracow, Stanisław Pyjas, who was presumably killed by the Security Service (opposition activists switched to phone booths), but was always eventually restored. A very general answer would be that the authorities feared a negative Western reaction to their repression of the opposition. They decided it was not worth paying such a high political and propaganda price for the persecution of a small group of people who in no way threatened their system's stability—something the government believed almost until the end of the Gierek era. It assumed that the opposition represented a small group, isolated from the rest of society, and that using harsher repressions might alienate the much larger neutral intelligentsia from the government.[46]

Historian Andrzej Friszke answered the question of why the government did not simply cut off Kuroń's telephone service more exhaustively in a book published in 1994—that is, before historians were granted access to Ministry of Internal Affairs documents. It is likely that the Security Service preferred to use this connection and bug it to keep track of KOR's contacts with the West.[47] Documents found after the creation of the Institute of National Remembrance in Warsaw and the opening of its archives housing Ministry of Internal Affairs files to historians confirm this hypothesis. The Security Service often preferred to have so-called operational control, to keep track of activities that were illegal from its point of view, to disrupting or destroying opposition organizations and activities.[48]

From the beginning, collaboration with sabotage organizations in the West was an important component of the charges the Security Service prepared against KOR's members and helpers, waiting for the moment the party leadership would authorize a tougher policy against the opposition. In November 1976, in the early days of KOR, the secret police searched the homes of Kuroń and Jan Józef Lipski because they disseminated "false information." The Investigations Bureau of the Ministry of Internal Affairs launched an investigation of Kuroń, Lipski, and Adam Michnik that focused on their contacts with RFE, the Paris *Kultura*, and *Aneks*. In April 1977, Prosecutor

Wiesława Bardonowa presented the charges against Kuroń and Lipski based on article 132 of the criminal code; the charges included entering into an understanding with representatives of hostile foreign organizations, RFE and *Kultura* among them (the same article had been used in 1970 for Władysław Bartoszewski, Danuta Bańkowska, Ewa Dreżepolska, and Stanisław Salmonowicz). At this news, Adam Michnik, who was traveling in the West, returned to Poland and was indicted on the same charges. After Pyjas's death on May 7, 1977, and the resultant student protests, eleven KOR members and collaborators were arrested and accused of the same crimes.[49]

It was at this time that Gierek's team came closest to using force to fight the opposition. Minister of Culture Józef Tejchma wrote in his diary on May 21, 1977, a few days after KOR members had been arrested, "The power group in our leadership has developed a formula of three threats: a. ideological pressure from hostile organizations in the West, b. the activities of the domestic opposition, c. the position of the liberals in the party."[50]

Two months later the government backed off its repressive course. On July 22, 1977, the Sejm passed an amnesty, which sanctioned the release from prison of the KOR members and the workers who had protested in June 1976. Western reactions influenced this decision.[51] RFE also contributed to negative Polish and international public opinion as it broadcast extensive news about the ongoing hunger strikes being staged to protest imprisonments, with the most famous one taking place in St. Martin's Church in Warsaw. In many cases, it was solely thanks to RFE that both Poles and Westerners learned about what the opposition was doing, since the government would immediately interrupt its activities or at least try to prevent news about them from spreading. In June 1977, three Gdańsk Polytechnic students began a hunger strike. According to a report from Department III of the Ministry of Internal Affairs: "The university tried to treat the hunger strike incident as 'an internal university matter' that was doomed to fail right from the start in view of the foundation and actual goals of this initiative, as was proven, e.g., by the fact that on the 17th of this month at 20:10 RFE broadcast the first information about the hunger strike and promised extensive future commentaries."[52]

Because of the emergence and growth of these domestic opposition movements, the security apparatus focused increasingly on this internal enemy. It viewed RFE as an exceptionally strong bolster, even a fundamental tool, for KOR and the other groups that were challenging the system. The Ministry of Internal Affairs described the radio's role during a meeting of the Soviet bloc countries' security services in Moscow in April 1980: "RFE's activity directed at Poland is closely correlated with the activity of the antisocialist groups active in our country. RFE propagates the actions undertaken by these groups and informs in a biased way about the counteractions taken by the state authorities on the basis of accounts sent to it from Poland."[53] But despite these threats, the Polish Ministry of Internal Affairs reassured the "fraternal" services that it was fully in control of the activities of the "antisocialist forces": "We are assuming in the prognosis for the development of the socioeconomic situation in 1979–85 that it will not significantly change the situation [of the political opposition]; hence on the basis of experiences to date we predict that the antisocialist groups will not grow quantitatively in a significant way but that there will be an attempt to improve further the methods and forms of hostile activity."[54]

This prediction missed by a mile. Only a few months after the Moscow meeting, a wave of strikes rolled over Poland. The protests would lead to the creation of Solidarity, a movement of millions. RFE played an important role here, as it aired information about strikes and workers' demands. From the very first day of the strikes in July 1980, the demand grew for radios with shortwave reception, the best for listening to Western stations.[55]

Addressing a Politburo meeting on August 15, 1980, the second day of the strike in the Gdańsk shipyard, Premier Edward Babiuch said, "Free Europe and gossip have been shaping people's knowledge about the strikes."[56] Edward Gierek's words at another Politburo session the next day reveal the importance the government saw in this encouragement from RFE: "We must inform some Western diplomats about the situation in Gdańsk . . . that it is a result of putting order in the economy and, in some instances, of Free Europe's sabotage."[57]

The government then introduced an information blockade in the three coastal cities, Gdańsk, Gdynia, and Sopot, which included cutting off telephone connections to the rest of the country, to prevent the strikes from spreading. But its plan was thwarted by RFE and other Western stations. The Western broadcasters were also very valuable to the striking crews. "It was thanks to Free Europe that people in Gdańsk, in all Poland and across the world found out that we were on strike. They learned our names, which gave us some assurance of safety," reminisced Bogdan Borusewicz, the main organizer of the strike in the Gdańsk shipyard.[58] This was the same system of overcoming anonymity that had protected the opposition in the 1970s. Thanks to RFE, the members of the Inter-Factory Strike Committee who were negotiating with the government learned about the situation in all of Poland and about the growing support for their demands.[59] It was not just the members of the negotiating committee who listened to Western radio but most of the workers locked in their sit-down strike at the shipyard. Many years later Jarosław Sellin, a Young Poland Movement activist, said that what he remembered most about the strike was "straining to hear Free Europe."[60]

At this time, RFE would appear—at times almost laughably—in the settling of accounts that swept the Politburo as its members began to understand that they would be forced to surrender to the growing flood of strikes. Thus, during an August 23 meeting, General Wojciech Jaruzelski accused the Gierek team of hiding information about the deteriorating economic situation: "Two years ago, we said that our debt has reached 17 billion, but we knew about it from Free Europe," said the minister of defense and Politburo member.[61]

RFE's audiences grew tremendously after the strikes began and the Solidarity labor union was created, confirming the observation that interest in Western radio programs increased in moments of crisis and political stress, only to drop off as stability returned. According to data gathered by the Center for Public Opinion Research (Ośrodek Badania Opinii Publicznej, or OBOP), in January 1979, 30 percent of Poles listened to RFE. In 1980, the number grew to 48 percent, and in 1981 it reached the highest point in the history of People's Poland, 53 percent. It remained high throughout 1982 (49 percent), but in May 1983, after more than a year of martial law, it dropped significantly, to 17 percent.[62]

The OBOP studies were not publicized but were reserved for the Polish government, which could use them to gauge the effects of radio sabotage somewhat rationally, and party and police cited the data from these sociological studies in their documents. For example, Deputy Minister of Internal Affairs Władysław Ciastoń informed his bloc counterparts in a special services meeting in Sofia in October 1983 that in Poland, "in the second half of 1980, the interest in RFE programs grew dramatically as a result of the explosion of the strike crisis."[63]

In the sixteen months of Solidarity's legal existence, the security apparatus focused on exposing the union and other independent groups and on preparing for the huge operation of martial law.[64] In these circumstances, attacking RFE and other Western radios was no longer a priority. But propaganda attacks on Solidarity continued to accuse it and the opposition groups of coordinating their actions closely and even of acting on the orders of foreign centers of sabotage, most prominently RFE.

Countless newspaper articles exposed Solidarity's true motivators and patrons.[65] The titles of these articles speak for themselves: "Vain Calculations," "Bad Intentions, Saboteurs' Pens," and "Who Is Responsible for the Incitement and Interference."[66] In the last article, Ignacy Krasicki, an old hand in the war against RFE as both a secret police agent and a writer, argued that it had been RFE that served as the patron for KOR's "excesses" and created a favorable atmosphere for the "creeping counterrevolution." Jerzy Dziadul declared in *Trybuna Robotnicza* that the relationship between the Katowice Steelworks Solidarity chapter and RFE was obvious since the union's bulletins ran excerpts of RFE's programs.[67]

False Prophets, a high-print-run book by Jerzy Kudaś-Bronisławski—a Security Service officer, a leading writer for the Ministry of Internal Affairs, and the author of several publications about fighting Western intelligence and so-called sabotage—also exposed foreign "inspirators" and "patrons." A large section of the book was about RFE. Kudaś-Bronisławski restated facts and charges from earlier publications, including Janusz Kolczyński's writings in the 1960s and the 1971 book by Kazimierz Kąkol titled *Na szlakach dywersji* (On the trail of sabotage).[68] It is logical to assume that these authors used the same information and documents that could be found in the special services files.

Kudaś-Bronisławski's book was conspicuous in frequently quoting criticism of RFE that had appeared in the West, especially in the Polish émigré community. On the one hand, it quoted Józef Mackiewicz, who had written that Jan Nowak was an "agent in the service of the Americans."[69] It was immaterial that Mackiewicz disparaged not only RFE and the United States but even the Catholic Church in Poland for its insufficient "anticommunism." On the other hand, Kudaś-Bronisławski included numerous references to articles appearing in émigré publications that were subsidized or even run by the Ministry of Internal Affairs, such as *Kronika*, *Oblicze Tygodnia*, and *Nasz Znak*. Some articles in these publications were actually written in Warsaw. Department I began by placing its texts in émigré publications to discredit—at least among less-informed readers—its most dangerous adversaries, namely, RFE and the Paris *Kultura*. The accusations that were thus "validated" were used in publications appearing in Poland for Polish readers.

Kudaś-Bronisławski quoted from the article in *Nasz Znak* discussed earlier (in chapter 3), in which Andrzej Stefanowski attacked Juliusz Mieroszewski for his polemics with Janusz Kolczyński's publications, which had appeared in the Warsaw *Kultura* in 1963. The Ministry of Internal Affairs first supplied Kolczyński with all its information about RFE and then used its agent in the Polish Service in Munich to check the staff's reactions to this information and to catch errors and inaccuracies, which could then be corrected in the book based on these articles. Next, an article was placed in *Nasz Znak* praising the writings by this Poland-based specialist on "ideological sabotage." The circle closed when Kudaś-Bronisławski's book, *False Prophets*, published in 1981, quoted the article that had appeared in the émigré publication.

Unmasking the opposition's and Solidarity's Western "inspirators" and "patrons" belonged to the permanent repertoire of more than just propaganda attacks. It also featured in statements by government officials, even high-level ones, and not only when they addressed external audiences, which revealed the real thinking of at least some in the Communist power apparatus. For example, there were the pronouncements made by Leonid Zamyatin, head of the International Information Department of the CC CPSU and member of the Politburo Committee for Polish Affairs (the so-called Suslov Commission), in Katowice in January 1981. Zamyatin alerted his Polish comrades to the nature of the threats they faced in meetings at the PUWP's Provincial Committee, in the editorial offices of *Trybuna Robotnicza*, and in the Katowice offices of radio and television: "They (the imperialists) know that they are incapable of defeating us militarily," Zamyatin explained, "that they are incapable of physically violating our frontiers because they would meet firm resistance. So they have opted for a different (undeclared) war, the war of ideological sabotage." He twice quoted President Jimmy Carter's reported statement that the United States "today needs not so much missiles as new methods to conduct psychological warfare. Today, 3 radio stations are more important than 10 missile complexes." Zamyatin warned his audiences that "recently over 6,000 well-prepared specialists, clever enemies employed by RFE, are working against us."[70]

Zamyatin's speech was authoritative in that his January 1981 visit was intended to encourage the PUWP leadership, apparat, and activists to fight the "counterrevolution" with greater energy. On his return to Moscow, he presented his evaluation of the situation in Poland to the Politburo of the CC CPSU.[71]

Martial Law and "Normalization"

RFE's American management observed increased jamming of its Polish programs beginning in spring 1981, a foretaste of the even more powerful interference that would accompany martial law a few months later. These measurements were based on a study the radio commissioned from a West German telecommunications company, which also revealed that the majority of the jamming devices were located in the Soviet Union.[72]

According to RFE's data, the intensified jamming made listening to its programs significantly more difficult. Thus, in November 1981, 46.5 percent of the programs reached Polish listeners without any interference, but by January 1982 that figure had dropped to 36 percent, and in July 1984 it was only 24 percent. The effectiveness of jamming in the first few weeks of martial law was increased by redirecting some of the Soviet devices that had earlier interfered with Czechoslovak programs. Now, for a while, the Czechs and Slovaks could hear RFE more clearly.[73] Propaganda attacks also multiplied at this time. Whereas prior to martial law about twenty were recorded monthly in Soviet bloc newspapers and electronic media, in December 1981 there were forty-six (twenty-two in the Soviet Union and twenty-four in the satellite countries). This trend persisted for several months.[74]

For the Polish government, after it had interned and arrested Solidarity activists, suppressed strikes, and successfully shattered the legal mass movement, the opposition, which was organizing underground, became the main enemy. For more than a year after December 13, 1981, the date of the imposition of martial law, the opposition repeatedly mobilized Solidarity's supporters for mass protests ranging from symbolic commemorations on the thirteenth of each month to street demonstrations, the most spectacular manifestation that Solidarity was alive.[75]

Under martial law, especially in the first months when telephone connections were cut off and freedom of movement was restricted, support from the West—especially from RFE—for the Poles' freedom aspirations was an even greater threat to the Polish authorities than it had been prior to December 13, 1981, when the government's opponent was a well-organized mass movement with its own mass media and communications. "In this period, when their contacts and ability to act together were seriously limited by martial law, sabotage radio propaganda played an important role in inspiring. It became the main source of information, opinions, suggestions, and instructions for those who favored antistate activity," said Deputy Minister of Internal Affairs Władysław Ciastoń in a special services meeting in Sofia.[76]

A study by the Institute for the Study of the Contemporary Problems of Capitalism presented RFE's role in the early 1980s thus: "The main center of inspiring antisocialist activity has moved outside Poland. . . . From the moment Solidarity was created, Radio Free Europe has been trying to play the role of the union's radio station. Very often, even before the Solidarity leadership's information and decisions could be copied and distributed, they would find their way to Radio Free Europe. . . . The introduction of martial law meant suppressing the main opposition organizations that were taking advantage of Solidarity's networks and apparat. Free Europe adopted the mission of being an inspirator in creating strongholds for the political underground. With this goal in mind, it both had widespread influence on sustaining the agitated mood in Poland and also tried to serve as a surrogate for the nonexistent opposition leadership in Poland. It issued orders regarding resistance to the authorities. Immediately after December 13, 1981, Free Europe activated the propaganda machine to organize a general strike."[77]

Yet these were not mere propaganda clichés that the specialists in fighting foreign-instigated sabotage were using out of habit and without great conviction. Available documents imply that at least some in the government, including those at the top of the ruling elite and the leaderships of the power ministries, really believed that RFE's programs played an actual motivating role. In a meeting of the Directorate II, Department of the General Staff, the leadership of military intelligence evaluated the situation in Poland a few days after the first large street demonstrations under martial law, in early May 1982: "In several cities, the adversary wants to show that he has support. We expect that people will be going out into the streets, blockades. On May 13 we expect strikes, the Provincial Headquarters of the PUWP and the Citizens' Militia are to be attacked, and the Western radios are sending coordinating signals."[78] It is remarkable that military intelligence not only misattributed the guiding role to Western radio stations but was also wrong in its predictions: the demonstrations and strikes that took place on May 13, 1982, were much smaller than the protests of May 1 and 3.[79]

Minister of Internal Affairs Czesław Kiszczak, General Jaruzelski's right-hand man and the principal architect of martial law, believed firmly in RFE's inspirational or even causal role. In a Politburo meeting on May 4, 1983, he argued that the radio had joined in the preparations for the previous few days' street demonstrations and had played an "instructional" role.[80] Even twenty years later, in a conversation with American researcher Jane Curry, Kiszczak maintained that RFE on its own initiative had called for street demonstrations and determined where and when they should take place.[81]

It would be difficult to find a better example of mythmaking, or even of demonizing the enemy, than such statements coming from the man who commanded the special services and was likely the best-informed person in the country. In fact, neither RFE nor any other Western radio station called for antigovernment demonstrations; they only relayed information about underground Solidarity's plans and appeals. From the time Zdzisław Najder took over as the Polish desk's director in April 1982, RFE regularly read out the texts of documents or fliers published underground, something that stations such as the BBC did not do.[82] But this had nothing to do with promoting unrest.

The Polish government treated the Western radio stations as a top threat not only because it believed that RFE was steering the population's resistance to martial law but also because of the Reagan administration's position. The propaganda offensive against the martial law government and support for Solidarity were the cornerstones of Reagan's Poland policy.[83] Hence, the struggle over the "sabotage" stations became an important battle in the conflict between the Soviet bloc and the West, which was heating up again at the beginning of the 1980s.

In the first years of martial law, protests against US policies, and especially against the activities of the US radio stations, were frequently to be found in the speeches of Polish party and state leaders and in the declarations and notes sent to US diplomats. General Jaruzelski protested against economic sanctions and RFE and VOA programs in a January 4, 1982, letter to President Reagan.[84] On September 1, 1982, a day after the largest street demonstrations of martial law took place, the National Council of the Patriotic Movement for National Rebirth (Patriotyczny Ruch Odrodzenia Narodowego, PRON) declared that "the external and internal inspirations of this unrest are well known. The

American radio station Free Europe especially excels at it, simply employing gangster methods to encourage people to commit antistate acts, and then disseminates their false version with a bias."[85] PRON's feisty language contrasted with the dry tone of most official documents and speeches. On December 3, 1982, General Jaruzelski gave a speech in Jastrzębie in which he accused RFE and the VOA of inciting unrest and anxiety and held Washington responsible for their behavior.[86]

During a September 27, 1982, session of the United Nations General Assembly, Polish foreign minister Stefan Olszowski accused the United States of conducting an anti-Polish propaganda campaign. "The majority of these actions, and especially radio programs in Polish," he said, "are propaganda attacking our domestic order, pushing for a change in Poland's sociopolitical regime. In recent months, this activity has acquired all the characteristics of propaganda aggression against Poland. This contradicts the principles lodged in the charter of our organization and violates the established norms of international cooperation in the areas of information and mass communications, especially in the fora of the United Nations and UNESCO."[87]

Polish officials spoke up against RFE's and VOA's programs in nearly every meeting with US diplomats, including Foreign Ministry talks with US ambassador Francis J. Meehan (January 22, 1982), another US embassy official (August 22, 1982), and a political affairs counselor (January 27, 1983). The last official was given a protest note about RFE's and VOA's programs, "which included personal attacks on the chairman of the Council of Ministers, Army General Wojciech Jaruzelski."[88] On April 27, 1983, in a note to the US deputy chief of mission, the Foreign Ministry demanded the immediate closing of the embassy library in direct response to RFE's and VOA's "anti-Polish deeds."[89]

The diary of Mieczysław Rakowski, General Jaruzelski's close associate and Poland's deputy premier from 1981 to 1985, is a good source of information about RFE's significant presence in the life of the ruling elite. RFE appears in it very frequently, as members of the leadership reflect on RFE's reactions to their decisions, to the actions of Solidarity leaders, and even to the rivalries within the PUWP. Many speeches at the Eighth Plenum of the CC PUWP in February 1982 appealed for intraparty unity, while the resolution adopted by the plenum condemned "factionalism." Rakowski was initially surprised by the unmissable presence of RFE in the lives of the Communist elite, but soon came up with an explanation: "I came to the conclusion that this may come from Free Europe's daily crowing about factional battles in the Polish party, and CC members listen to it attentively."[90] In August 1982, Rakowski noted that the secretaries of the PUWP provincial committees invited to a Politburo session reported that in their regions' factories "there is great susceptibility to the West's propaganda, especially Free Europe's."[91] When in October 1982 RFE aired the text of a letter from Tadeusz Grabski, a leader of the hard-line faction, in which he criticized Jaruzelski's team for its overly liberal policies, Rakowski thought that "it was our guys who had planted it at FE through their channels because publicizing the letter may make the Poles realize what lies ahead if the current team collapses."[92] On November 17, a few days after Lech Wałęsa was released from internment in Arłamów, Rakowski noted in his diary, "Evening, phone conversation with W[ojciech] J[aruzelski], also talked about Wałęsa. Wojciech is fearful that he may now speak to the nation almost every day via Free Europe."[93]

In January 1983, Rakowski recorded another conversation with Jaruzelski: "WJ himself brought up views of him and also of me that Free Europe has been airing. 'There was a time,' he said, 'when every opinion like that upset me. . . . Now, I don't give a monkey's.' I've always known that he is very thin-skinned, that he easily gets hurt, wounded. But we'll see if he really doesn't care about what they are barking from Free Europe."[94]

In March 1983, the Sejm voted on changes in the composition of the Council of Ministers. Over a hundred deputies voted no or abstained when Minister of Agriculture Jerzy Wojtecki was being recalled. Rakowski noted that it "really was a setback for WJ. . . . I watched the TV news that night. Some moron, probably Główczyk or someone like him, did not give the results of the vote. I'm certain that later tonight Free Europe will air them." He was right. Next morning he arrived in Poznań for a meeting with press, radio, and television editors in chief from western and northern Poland. "One of the editors asked me why the papers had written nothing about the results of the vote," noted the deputy premier. "Free Europe broadcast them last night. I went through *Głos Wielkopolski*. Sure enough, not one word about them. And we are planning an offensive propaganda! This is idiotic. Sometimes I really no longer believe that our system can be reformed."[95]

This and other examples show the constant, almost obsessive references to RFE in the 1980s not only as an external adversary but also as an important factor in current decision making, even in intraparty disputes. Only the Gomułka government, and especially Minister of Internal Affairs Mieczysław Moczar, who was a focus of RFE's criticism, had paid as much attention to RFE's programs.

Counterpropaganda: Jerzy Urban versus RFE

In May 1983, the Council of Ministers prepared a document declaring that Poland had become a target of RFE's "propaganda aggression." The document considered it absolutely necessary to stiffen sanctions against people maintaining contacts with this "hostile radio station": "we recommend publishing the formula that 'collaborating with Radio Free Europe and with institutions and persons working on its behalf or in its name, a foreign organization acting to harm the interests of the People's Republic of Poland, is, according to Polish criminal law, a punishable crime.'"[96]

This note, which was distributed to all the ministers, did not mark a new stage in the war against RFE but instead reflected the recurring tendency to increase penalties for Polish citizens who stayed in touch with the centers of foreign sabotage. The Jaruzelski government was not able to take any radical steps in this direction, if only because of its policies toward the West, which aimed to convince Western states that Poland was becoming more liberal, lifting martial law's restrictions and abandoning repression. For this reason, next to jamming, counter-propaganda appeared to be the best method for fighting radio sabotage. From the very beginning of martial law, various units of the party and state apparatus developed plans for adopting extensive countermeasures against RFE and other Western radio stations.

In late January 1982, the CC PUWP began to make plans to neutralize the effects of the huge propaganda campaign of the Reagan administration, which culminated in "Let Poland Be Poland," a television program featuring appearances by Western statesmen and prominent artists. Poland responded with radio and television programs that used Ministry of Internal Affairs materials, "including film materials made in Munich," and a series of newspaper articles about "American propaganda sabotage against Poland" and "about the way Western radios accompanied the activity of KOR, KPN [Konfederacja Polski Niepodległej, Confederation for an Independent Poland], Solidarity, NZS [Niezależne Zrzeszenie Studentów, Independent Students' Association], what tendencies they supported, what they passed over in silence, what they openly encouraged."[97]

The early period of martial law saw the publication of a propaganda leaflet by Ignacy Krasicki about RFE. He described the radio as "the main tool in the psychological warfare being conducted by NATO staff officers against the socialist countries." This well-known regime journalist argued that "during the August events and later, RFE instructed the opponents of socialism in Poland in exploiting the crisis and the deformation of the system in order to bring about a final reckoning with the PUWP, our political system, and class alliances." He used information no doubt acquired from the Security Service, which the reader would be unable to verify but whose level of detail was meant to make a big impression. For example, Krasicki wrote that Bogdan Lis, a Solidarity leader, was in Munich in 1981 and twice contacted CIA officers.

Repeating a standard Security Service–party propaganda theme, Krasicki "revealed" which of RFE's employees had been PUWP members or had written for official publications before leaving Poland. Krasicki devoted a whole chapter, titled "Renegades," to them. He also reiterated the charge against RFE—namely, that it was encouraging underground Solidarity—being made frequently by Jaruzelski, Kiszczak, and other government officials: "Despite the suspension of this union's activity, there is unquestionably an internal link and coordination between RFE's propaganda endeavors and the intentions of the system's and the government's opponents who continue to be active in Poland. Some of these endeavors, as we wrote earlier, concern various forms of active and passive resistance against martial law, which includes coded instructions."

The only original motif in Krasicki's pamphlet was criticism of the Gierek government, whose "technocratic" and too "liberal" attitude RFE allegedly liked: "In 1970–1980, RFE supported the technocratic-bureaucratic tendency, which at the time was the typical embodiment of the revisionist orientation, which led to such serious degeneration of the system and laid the foundations of the critical crisis in the early 1980s." Also, according to Krasicki, the Gierek team was responsible for tolerating contacts between the native opposition and RFE, with disastrous consequences: "The situation in 1976–1980 in which various 'antisocialist' organizations in Poland, foremost among them KSS-KOR, were able to use RFE's microphones and multifaceted support with impunity created a great opportunity for this station's patrons. From the Radom events in 1976 to the August social explosion in 1980, RFE consistently set the course of the Polish counterrevolution."[98]

Using this style and these arguments, Krasicki's brochure was addressed primarily to party activists—preaching to the converted. The book *Ufam ci Kilroy* (I trust you, Kilroy; mentioned in chapter 3), conversely, was an attempt to go beyond this group to reach a mass public, people who were not necessarily interested in politics. It had been co-authored by Mieczysław Lach, a Ministry of Internal Affairs agent in Munich who had been brought back to Poland in 1974. This book was a mixture of spy story and comedy of manners that used appropriately deformed information stolen by Ministry of Internal Affairs agents, as well as photographs of the radio's employees acquired in a similar way (Lach was an avid photographer).

Ufam ci Kilroy stands out in the treasury of Communist propaganda works, though its attacks on RFE place it firmly in the gutter. It presents the Polish Service as a lair not only of spies and Nazi collaborators (which had already been done) but also of various species of degenerates, embezzlers, sexual deviants, and prostitutes. Kilroy is a CIA agent assigned by headquarters to uncover other Communist agents at RFE after the outing of Czechowicz. The failure of his mission suggests that Polish intelligence could effortlessly penetrate the Polish Section. It all added up to a mixture intended to make the book attractive to the Polish reader, who was growing increasingly resistant to ideological Newspeak but thirsted for contacts with the West, even in this degenerate form. The novel, written by Mieczysław Lach and Zdzisław Uberman, or at least published under their names, came out in a 30,000-copy edition.[99]

The Ministry of Internal Affairs, as well as the Central Committee, discussed the development of the proper strategy to respond to RFE and the other presumed centers of sabotage. In December 1983, the Academy of Internal Affairs hosted an academic conference, at which a dozen papers addressed various institutions of sabotage and options for neutralizing their influence. Andrzej Czechowicz appeared as a scholar and, together with Colonel Henryk Kopczyk, presented a paper titled "The Inspirational Role of the Centers of Sabotage in Programming Opposition Activity in the PRP."[100]

In March 1984, the CC Secretariat began to fight against sabotage. Its staff commented anxiously on the results of an OBOP poll according to which 24 percent of Poles listened to Western radio regularly or sporadically.[101] The Information Department of the CC PUWP believed that this figure was actually lower than the poll responses indicated because of the touchy nature of the question, and thought that the correct proportion of listeners was a few percentage points higher.[102] This is yet another example of the "enlightened absolutism" of the Jaruzelski team, the first to consider public opinion polls important.

The plan adopted by the CC Secretariat posited escalating the propaganda response from the government and the mass media and creating the Counterpropaganda Unit, to be made up of representatives of all the institutions engaged in fighting sabotage (CC departments, the Ministry of Internal Affairs, the army's Main Political Directorate, television, the Institute for the Study of the Contemporary Problems of Capitalism). The document from the Information Department of the CC PUWP reads: "Radio stations broadcasting Polish-language sabotage programs 37 hours a day are the most important instrument in the enemy's propaganda effort versus the Polish population."[103] Of these thirty-seven hours, twenty were RFE's.[104]

There was nothing new in either the proposed response methods or the goal of coordination. The 1960s and 1970s had witnessed much talk about the need to combine the efforts of the government apparatus and the propaganda office, and appropriate committees were created to tackle this challenge. Yet neither then nor in the 1980s did the ambitions to synchronize actions lead to a breakthrough. Greater efforts, however, were exerted and organizational structures proliferated. In the mid-1980s, for instance, the Central Committee put out detailed weekly analyses of the sabotage radio stations' programming,[105] when monthly studies were all that the other institutions concerned (the Ministry of Internal Affairs, the Institute for the Study of the Contemporary Problems of Capitalism) wanted.

The real novelty in the Jaruzelski era was the role of the government spokesman, who took on the burden of the anti-RFE propaganda polemics. Jerzy Urban, the government's leading showman and previously a well-known journalist, brought up RFE's programs at virtually every one of his weekly press conferences. These were not ritualistic accusations of "propaganda aggression" against Poland but mostly challenges directed at specific programs or even anticipatory attacks focusing on particular issues or pieces of information that Urban would receive from the Ministry of Internal Affairs. Western correspondents' questions to Urban also often referred to RFE programs, their main source of information about Poland, especially in the early months of martial law, when journalists' ability to gather news was limited.[106]

Surviving Government Press Office files include many materials about RFE that were used by Urban to prepare for his press conferences. The materials included both monitoring transcripts of particular programs and memoranda he received from the Ministry of Internal Affairs and other ministries. For example, the Ministry of Culture prepared a note on "making library materials available," which Urban used to deny RFE's claims that school libraries had been instructed to put away books in their collections that had been written by authors involved in the opposition.[107] When RFE reported that Podbeskidzie Solidarity activist Grażyna Staniszewska's health was deteriorating after several months in prison, Urban countered with information prepared for him by the Ministry of Health.[108] Likewise, the CC PUWP's Social Sciences Academy developed profiles of RFE's Polish editors for him.[109]

In January 1985, Urban found a reason to roll out the heavy guns. The entertainment program *Radio Youth Weekly* quoted a text that had appeared in a Paris émigré lampoon of the satirical weekly *Szpilki*. The publication dedicated its parody of Hitler's speech at the 1939 Nationalsozialistische Deutsche Arbeiterpartei (NSDAP) Congress in Nuremberg to General Jaruzelski. Urban charged RFE with "propaganda gangsterism." He boomed: "The idea was to suggest that General Wojciech Jaruzelski says the same things in his speeches as Hitler did, that he is a Hitler-like politician. This radio station, which is overseen and directed by the US government and financed by American government money, has perpetrated the greatest affront imaginable against the head of government of a country with which the United States maintains diplomatic relations, a Polish officer who spilled blood fighting Nazism."

The most interesting aspect of Urban's philippic is that he spent most of it not expressing outrage at this insult but rather exposing the alleged manipulation and mistakes committed not only by the article's authors but also, implicitly, by the station that broadcast its text. "Hitler's speech is a forgery created by Free Europe's editors, made to resemble our party's speeches," revealed Urban. Citing an author of books about the Third Reich, Franciszek Ryszka, Urban painstakingly constructed the argument that no NSDAP congress had taken place in 1939 in Nuremberg or in any other German city. "It had been scheduled for that September, but it was cancelled," contended the government spokesman. "RFE is thus operating with an invented speech by Hitler made at an event that never took place. Free Europe is putting words into Hitler's mouth that he never used. Hitler did not use the term 'comrades,' he did not talk about the Reich's secure and fair borders because he believed that its borders were unfair. . . . Hitler did not use the term 'Zionism,' he could not have promised to end food ration coupons since there were no such coupons in the Third Reich before the war."[110]

Urban's historical erudition must have amazed the Western journalists at his press conferences. His speech was likely one of those instances that reassured the Ministry of Internal Affairs that "we can effectively counteract sabotage propaganda . . . and undermine RFE's credibility with a fast and skillful response."[111] After the press conference, the State Department issued a statement distancing itself from the text broadcast by RFE and expressing regret that Jaruzelski had been compared to Hitler. This in turn caused unfavorable commentaries to appear in the Polish émigré press.[112]

Urban's press conference of October 13, 1985, again focused largely on RFE. This time he did not discuss a particular radio program but informed the gathered journalists of conflicts inside RFE's Polish desk. He talked about disputes and troubles between individual employees, and especially about those between Director Zdzisław Najder and a group opposing him. Urban supplied details intended to enhance the credibility of his account. He introduced tabloid-worthy specifics, such as the seduction of a wife as the source of enmity between two men. He claimed that his information came from a letter he had received from an RFE employee.[113] His was a classic move straight from the repertoire of "disintegrating" actions by the special services, aiming to fan suspicions among the people working in Munich. Official newspapers picked up Urban's story. As early as October 15, *Trybuna Ludu* published an article, its headline in large type: "Quarrelsome RFE."

To the knowledgeable observer, the nature of Urban's information, some of which was true, left no doubt that it stemmed from espionage sources. The materials used by Urban included an unsigned note with the heading "Concerning: conflict situation in RFE Polish Section," whose text he repeated verbatim. Zdzisław Najder's collection, now at the KARTA Centre in Warsaw, includes another copy of the note among the documents Najder received after 1989 from Colonel Henryk Piecuch,[114] who had been given them by Deputy Minister of Internal Affairs Władysław Pożoga, head of Polish intelligence, whom Piecuch had interviewed for a book.[115] A handwritten note in the margin of Pożoga's copy reads: "The contents of this information do not give away Sect. XI sources." (Section XI of Department I of the Ministry of Internal Affairs fought what was considered foreign sabotage, primarily on the part of RFE.) This confirms not only that Urban abundantly used Ministry of Internal Affairs materials, which is well known, but also indirectly that in the mid-1980s, Polish intelligence had a spy in RFE's Polish Section.

Another piece of news that must have come from a spy was Najder's dismissal, which Urban announced at his February 12, 1987, press conference, several weeks before RFE management made it public. Urban's announcement had two goals: to show the degree of penetration of RFE by Polish intelligence and to contribute to aggravating the discord between Najder and his American bosses.[116] This operation, of which the press conference was only a piece, must have been prepared meticulously by the secret police. The same day's *Express Wieczorny*, the popular afternoon paper, ran an article titled "Najder Is Shown the Door," which restated Urban's words.

During his press conference, Urban interpreted the departure of Najder, in the 1970s a creator of the underground Polish Independence Agreement (Polskie Porozumienie Niepodległościowe, PPN) and in exile an official adviser to the Brussels office of Solidarity, as the US government's withdrawal of support for the Poles' drive for independence. "I would like to express the hope," said Urban, "that dismissing this man, who has been sentenced to death in absentia for working for foreign intelligence, will convince RFE to abandon aggression and aggravation, and that it is a sign that the American authorities intend gradually to adjust RFE's program to reflect the intention expressed by the government of the USA gradually to improve relations with Poland." Other statements by Urban reflected the familiar tricks the Polish government had frequently used to sow conflicts among RFE's Polish staff: "I have been informed that some of RFE's Polish staff and freelancers are now considering the possibility of returning to Poland, and have begun research in that direction. I wish to declare that Poland is for everyone, that there is also a normal life and work for everyone in Poland."[117]

Urban's disclosure resonated, and not only in Poland. RFE President Gene (Eugene) Pell issued a statement in which he denied that the American authorities had decided to fire Najder, and at the same time declared that a change of directors would not affect the radio's program line.[118] Leading newspapers worldwide wrote about it.[119] When Najder's departure was officially announced in early March, Urban exulted at his next press conference about what had been going on inside the Polish Service in Munich in recent weeks and how people had reacted to his statements over the preceding month.[120]

The Death Sentence for Zdzisław Najder

The trial of Zdzisław Najder, which concluded with a death sentence, was distressing, even by the standards of martial law. It was presumably intended to serve both as a serious warning to all those who collaborated with RFE and as payback for the actions of a man who as early as the mid-1970s had co-founded an underground organization that published programmatic papers on important political, social, and international issues and who, despite extensive surveillance, had managed to slip out of the hands of the Security Service.[121]

On December 13, 1981, Najder was in Oxford, on a fellowship to work on his area of specialty, the author Joseph Conrad. When the news of martial law broke, he decided to accept an offer to become the director of RFE's Polish Service. This possibility had first been raised in April 1978 and was restated on several occasions during his trips outside Poland. Najder came to Munich for the first time in late January to early February 1982 and met unofficially with the staff. He became the director in April 1982, succeeding Zygmunt Michałowski, who had retired.[122] Surviving Security Service files do not reveal whether the agency had been aware of the plans for this personnel change at RFE earlier.

On May 10, 1982, at the request of the Ministry of Internal Affairs, the Head Military Prosecutor's Office began its investigation of Najder. This confidential request to start the investigation was dated April 29, 1982, the day the new director's inaugural speech was aired by RFE. The author of the note, Lieutenant Colonel H. Połeć, wrote that the Security Service had obtained "confirmed information that . . . Zdzisław Najder . . . has for at least a few years been collaborating with political sabotage centers and other anticommunist organizations in the West. . . . Z. Najder's criminal activity in this area has been expressed especially by the regular conveying of tendentious information about the sociopolitical situation in Poland, foremost the mood in intellectual circles, to representatives of the Institut Littéraire in Paris and of Radio Free Europe, and this information was used in various propaganda campaigns waged against the PRP by these sabotage centers."

Lieutenant Colonel Połeć went on to charge Najder with initiating the PPN and taking part in its activities. Najder's RFE appointment was to crown this "criminal activity to harm the PRP's political interests." The note does not mention charges of espionage and treason, but it does end with the statement that Najder had for a long time been in contact with employees of the US embassy in Warsaw, "with whom he discussed issues related to undertakings directed against the Polish state."[123] The ministry had clearly decided to present Najder with the bill for his many years of activity as an "enemy of the system," using all the available information about him. The RFE theme was only one of the "load-bearing elements" in the construction of the investigation, although Najder's RFE appointment served as its catalyst.

Only two months later the investigation took a turn when Najder was charged with espionage. Asking for its legal reclassification in a memorandum of July 2, 1982, was Colonel Zdzisław Pudysz, head of Section II of the Investigations Office of the Ministry of Internal Affairs, who was soon to be promoted to head the whole office and in 1985 would become a deputy minister.[124] The investigation materials clearly reveal the rushed and clumsy preparation of evidence for the show trial. This "unmasking" of RFE's spy face was to compromise the radio to its Polish listeners, intimidate its potential collaborators, and put the US government in a difficult situation.

Two types of "evidence" of Najder's spying were collected during the investigation and used in his trial. The first type consisted of objects and documents that had allegedly been found during a search of his summer house in Czarny Bryńsk near Brodnica; these items were intended to prove unequivocally that Najder was a CIA agent. According to Ministry of Internal Affairs Lieutenant Colonel Andrzej Dudziński's testimony, "after pushing aside the coal crate in the cellar, I found a piece of the kind of container that American intelligence used frequently. They used such containers to send money, instructions, and equipment to their agents."[125]

The other key piece of evidence was Najder's desk, a search of which revealed a well-concealed secret compartment holding a letter clearly showing the prominent Conradist's true occupation. A passage from the letter shows that it would fit perfectly into a second-rate spy movie. In it, Najder's "friends" thank him for the "personnel and political information" they received from him, and ask him to be careful and to "stop coming to our embassy because we really care about your safety." It also mentions "1,500 dollars" enclosed "in the parcel." Another passage explains why Najder had remained abroad and taken the new job: "We would like to discuss the details of our offer and to implement them gradually. We can guarantee high pay and full compensation for the property you left behind." The letter is riddled with professional terminology straight out of the world of espionage: "We are closing down pine point," his "friends" wrote.[126] According to an expert opinion by the Office of Criminal Affairs of the Headquarters of the Citizens' Militia, the letter had been written on paper "used for special purposes, when the document needs to be destroyed quickly."[127]

Other evidence of Najder's spy contacts was circumstantial. Colonel Józef Chomętowski, director of the Office of the Minister of Internal Affairs, informed the prosecutor's office that the very fact that Najder had accepted the job at RFE should serve as evidence: "Zdzisław Najder, while illegally remaining outside Poland, has taken a job in the position of director of the Polish Section of RFE/RL, a position that has uninterruptedly been occupied by CIA cadres. Najder's predecessors were Jan Nowak-Jeziorański and Zygmunt Michałowski. Z. Najder's direct supervisor is James Brown, a CIA staffer. . . . The information we have leads us to believe that Najder's promotion is a reward for his previous CIA service.[128]"

The ministry clearly decided that more empirical evidence had to be found to support these general statements. It submitted a report from a functionary performing operations abroad, who then testified at the trial. According to Colonel Sylwester Flak, "we mobilized intelligence sources in the United States. We received information that Najder had been summoned to Washington for special CIA training."[129] Polish intelligence allegedly was able to determine that the training had been conducted at the end of November to the beginning of December 1982. This was not the first trial for which the Ministry of Internal Affairs was using an agent who "revealed" secrets acquired through operations. In 1964, Major Tadeusz Cibor had played the same role in the trial of Melchior Wańkowicz, who was similarly charged with collaborating with RFE.

Najder's contacts with US and British diplomats in Poland were another piece of evidence. The Ministry of Internal Affairs made a list of their names, together with short profiles showing that most of these diplomats had worked in Poland as spies, which in itself was held to prove that Najder was employed by Western intelligence. Yet the prosecution presented no evidence for this. This line of reasoning, which was repeated in both the indictment and the verdict, was a sensation, even by the standards of legality in People's Poland.

The prosecutor also commissioned an expert opinion on the Paris *Kultura*'s and RFE's connections with the CIA. The Institute for the Study of the Contemporary Problems of Capitalism, the intellectual aid in the CC PUWP's and the Ministry of Internal Affairs' fight against foreign ideological sabotage, was entrusted with this task. The resulting report, written by Małgorzata Dehnel-Szyc, MA, who (according to the enclosed invoice) spent 274 hours working on it, reads: "The available sources do not allow us to reach a clear conclusion about the connections between Radio Free Europe and the special services of the NATO countries. We can generally conclude that such connections must exist."[130]

During the trial, some of the witnesses were asked about Najder's German roots. A document dated September 1982, which outlines the investigation, devotes significant attention to it: "The investigation so far has established the following: Zdzisław Najder comes from a German family (on his father's side), which, as he says himself, 'was thoroughly Polonized in one generation.' Still, during the interwar period, there existed certain connections between Zdzisław Najder's father and the Germans. Every year in the 1930s, the Najders went to the village of Marianka near Mińsk Mazowiecki. The village was inhabited by German colonists, who manifested an anti-Polish attitude before the outbreak of the war. . . . Zdzisław Najder was interested in the situation of the indigenous population in Opole Province. An awareness of his German origins may have been the main factor that significantly influenced the totality of Najder's behavior."[131]

The investigation also repeated the standard martial law theme that Najder, as RFE Polish Service director, encouraged unrest and violent upheaval in Poland. According to the Ministry of Internal Affairs, this was precisely the mission the CIA had assigned him before he assumed his new job. "It was a question of creating groups of correspondents in Poland whose job was to inform RFE about the situation in Poland, but in order to prove themselves at work they were to become sabotage groups," Colonel Flak argued during the trial.[132] On the one hand, such thinking naturally served to charge Najder. On the other, it was a reflection of the ministry's stereotypical view of RFE: as early as the 1960s, internal documents were accusing the radio of inciting underground antistate groups.

The court concurred with the majority of the investigation's findings and the charges listed in the indictment. On May 28, it sentenced Najder to death, while admitting in the very same sentence that there were gaps in the evidence. Its wording is shocking when we realize that it affects a person being handed the death sentence: "It has been decided unanimously that the defendant Zdzisław Najder has maintained contacts with American intelligence for a long period of time. The impossibility of establishing the period of time when this collaboration began in no way affects the existence of the crime. . . . The fact that it could not be established what information the accused had given to American intelligence also does not in any way alter the existence of the crime."[133] It is blatantly conspicuous that the Stalinist show trials had been prepared more meticulously than this one, and that the judges and prosecutors available to the regime then had performed their roles more convincingly.

Even the Ministry of Internal Affairs must have questioned the evidence used in the trial. The anonymous author of the document titled "Theses for the speech for the trial of Zdzisław Najder" wrote that "we have been unable to ascertain the concrete nature, weight, and importance of the information Zdzisław Najder gave to foreign intelligence" and hence demanded a prison term of only fifteen years. Another anonymous hand (most likely high up in the ministry) crossed it out and wrote at the bottom of the page, "I request . . . the death sentence."[134]

The first chairman of the Supreme Court in July 1989, when the Communist system in Poland was collapsing, focused on these obvious weaknesses and gaps in the evidence to prepare an appeal. It was discovered that the "evidence" for Najder's spying had been found during a search conducted by the Security Service without a prosecutor. Furthermore, witnesses had testified that "before the date of the official search, unidentified individuals, probably Security Service functionaries, entered the . . . house." The prosecution did not have the same faith in the letter found in Najder's desk, which was to serve as the principal piece of evidence against Najder, as it had seven years earlier. "As a letter addressed to a spy, this form of communication between agent and agency headquarters shows incredible carelessness. Furthermore, it contains too many details, an almost complete accumulation of the typical elements needed to charge someone with espionage. In the situation described here, one may suspect for good reason that this piece of evidence was forged," assessed the head military prosecutor in January 1990.[135]

According to a carpenter's testimony, Najder had paid him to build the secret compartment in his desk to protect valuables from theft. Najder told this author that he had used it to hide alcohol. He was well aware that the Security Service was watching him: it had erected a temporary shack near his summer house (many witnesses remembered it as the "green hut"), from which ever-present civilian functionaries observed the goings-on inside the house. Najder remembers that before he went to Oxford in 1981 he had hidden PPN typescripts in the roof beams, which eluded the searchers.[136]

Colonel Flak from Department I of the Ministry of Internal Affairs also changed his testimony: "There was no evidence that Zdzisław Najder had collaborated with foreign intelligence," he testified in January 1990, clearly unconcerned about contradicting his earlier words.[137] The prosecutor's office considered the possibility of starting criminal proceedings "on false charges," particularly the suspicion that "evidence had been forged and planted." But it quickly abandoned this idea because of the "improbability that this issue could be cleared now, because of the significant passage of time," and also because "Z. Najder himself has shown no interest in moving in this direction."[138] This is a good example of the prevalent attitude toward setting straight the old system's crimes in the early years after the 1989 revolution.

It has been impossible to find documents about Security Service operations conducted against Najder outside Poland. They have probably been destroyed. It is also difficult to confirm US and Western intelligence reports that an assassination was being planned. RFE's security was put on alert three times by signals of an approaching attempt to kill or to kidnap him, and for several weeks Najder was under the Americans' round-the-clock protection.[139] After 1989, Henryk Bosak, a high-ranking Polish intelligence functionary, told Najder that there had been plans for "special operations."[140]

Since employees of RFE's other national sections had been assassinated, and the RFE building had been bombed in 1981, it is not out of the question that the Polish Security Service did indeed make similar preparations.[141] But it is also possible that Polish intelligence spread these rumors intentionally, as psychological warfare to torment Najder. The rumors about a planned assassination were confirmed by a friend of Najder's from his youth, Andrzej Madejczyk, who was thought by the Polish émigré community to be working for West German intelligence, Bundesnachrichtendienst (BND), which Madejczyk did not keep secret. In his conversations with Najder, Madejczyk would reveal things he knew from his BND work.[142] The recently opened files of Father Konrad Hejmo, a Dominican monk who served as a secret collaborator of the Polish security apparatus in the Vatican, indicate that Madejczyk operated for a long time as a Communist agent code-named "Lakar." He was assigned the Polish Catholic Church and the émigré community, which probably did not prevent him from working concurrently for the BND. Meeting with Najder may have been one of his assignments, and the two men saw each other privately in Munich and in Najder's house in Burgundy. Najder is also mentioned in Father Hejmo's file: "Lakar" questioned the monk exhaustively about Najder's visits to Rome as director of RFE's Polish Service and about his relationship with Primate Józef Glemp.[143]

Najder recorded his meetings with Madejczyk in his diary. It is interesting that on one occasion Madejczyk "warned" Najder about Nowak, who, he said, had served as a Nazi recipient of Jewish property during the war. This would indicate consistency in the Security Service's disintegration operations.[144] Warsaw sustained the charges that Nowak had collaborated with the Nazis for over a dozen years after he had resigned from his position at RFE.

It has been impossible to find out whether during Najder's directorship the Security Service instigated or encouraged the conflicts in RFE's Polish Service. This method was in the special services' emergency arsenal, and it was used with some of the other directors. Najder remains convinced to this day that at least some of his adversaries on the staff were conscious or unconscious tools of the secret police. He cites Henryk Bosak, who claimed that during his directorship the Security Service had four agents in RFE's Polish Service.[145] It is impossible to confirm this today because no documents have been found about espionage at RFE in the 1980s. But we must keep in mind that conflicts were an inseparable part of the functioning of a staff made up of people coming from different milieus, holding different political views, and being from different generations, who met under conditions of emigration, in which context it would be more difficult to find employment elsewhere.

Chapter 3 discussed the older editors' challenges to Nowak over hiring and supporting people who had worked in official institutions or editorial offices in Communist Poland. Some of the newcomers hired after March 1968 met with antipathy from some of the older staff. Najder was criticized for favoring the Solidarity emigration, as well as for his authoritarian, conflict-generating management style.[146] Several senior editors (paradoxically, some of those who had left Communist Poland in the 1960s and 1970s) protested that some of the newcomers had worked in Communist radio and television and called them "maciusiowcy," from the name of Maciej Szczepański, chairman of Gierek's committee for radio and television.[147] These critics ignored the fact that many of these people had been active in Solidarity and some had been interned under martial law.

It would definitely be a mistake and an exaggeration to suspect Najder's adversaries on the staff of primarily following Polish secret police orders or being encouraged by it. There is no denying that an acute conflict existed under Najder's management. One piece of evidence is the anonymous texts criticizing Najder that his opponents distributed at the radio. Copies of many of them are included in his papers in the KARTA Centre archive. The growing internal discord, which was making the functioning of the Polish Service extremely difficult, was one of the main reasons why in March 1987 American management dismissed Najder. Another reason was Najder's involvement in the activities of the Solidarity organization outside Poland and, most important, his position as adviser to Solidarity's Brussels office, which to the Americans represented a conflict of interest between the position of Polish Service director and political activism.[148] As he left the radio, Najder charged the American directors with violating the established principle of partnership, which consisted of respect for the Polish desk's autonomy and noninterference in the content of its programs.[149]

Tensions among the staff, even if they had nothing to do with the actions of the Ministry of Internal Affairs, were carefully exploited and publicized by the Polish press. For instance, *Trybuna Ludu* wrote about the conflict between the senior editors and those who arrived in Munich in the 1980s. It cited an interview in the London émigré daily *Dziennik Polski* with Alina Grabowska, a prominent RFE commentator and, incidentally, one of the radio voices most frequently attacked by Polish propaganda.[150]

According to Najder, some of his opponents on the staff accused him of serving as an active agent of the Polish secret police, even of the KGB, whose mission was to destroy the Polish desk from the inside.[151] Echoes of these charges appeared in the press attacks against Najder organized by the Security Service. The article in *Express Wieczorny* that was discussed earlier, "Najder Is Shown the Door," was one such example. Again quoting an émigré opinion —a favorite Security Service trick—the article reported that "there have been discussions in the émigré clubs, at first vicious but recently quite serious: whom is Najder really working for? The malicious ones added that it's obvious: for those who want someone in this position who will break up the radio's work, just as Najder has done. The program is now the pits; he has triggered quarrels among the entire staff and created a situation in which the RFE editors are spending their time arguing instead of working, actually suing each other over libel and money."[152]

At around the same time, the Soviet satirical periodical *Krokodil* presented Najder as a diabolical enemy of socialism. It published a series of three long, multicolumn articles about him under the single title, "The Four Faces of Agent X." What a distinction! No other Polish oppositionist or émigré activist had ever been given this treatment. The articles included detailed information not only about Najder's life but also about the Ministry of Internal Affairs investigation of him in 1982–1983.[153] This is indisputable proof of the cooperation between Polish and Soviet intelligence, even though there is no evidence of this case in the Polish archives.

We do not know whether the Ministry of Internal Affairs fed the accusations that Najder was working for the Communist secret police. Warsaw never officially spoke about Najder's contacts with the Security Service in the late 1950s to early 1960s. To reveal them even decades later would have gone against the fundamental principles of the special services, even when a former secret collaborator had transformed himself into a dangerous "enemy." According to Jerzy Morawski, this information was used confidentially during Najder's 1983 trial to sway hesitant jurors. "Najder is a Security Service collaborator . . . he betrayed them and stayed abroad. And we have our people there who are now in mortal danger because of him," reminisced a juror who was finally convinced that the death sentence was the right price this "traitor" should pay.[154]

Ministry of Internal Affairs Disintegration Operations

The available documents on the Ministry of Internal Affairs' operations against RFE in the last decade or so of People's Poland are less extensive and detailed than those for the earlier decades. It is most likely that many of the most recent files were destroyed in 1989–1990. It is also possible that some materials about espionage and operations abroad have been stored in the so-called reserved collection at the Institute of National Remembrance (according to the law, for cases "vital to the security of the state"), which is not accessible to historians.

The materials that have been found, however, show that in the 1970s and 1980s the Ministry of Internal Affairs continued to employ its old methods. One of them was to persuade émigré writers to publish texts attacking RFE and other organizations held to be engaging in sabotage. Beginning with the birth of the organized opposition in Poland in the mid-1970s, this often also involved persuading these writers to criticize people and groups acting against the Communist system. Now the Communist press could reprint criticism appearing in the West or at least cite it, making official propaganda more credible.

It is instructive to retrace this method using the example of Jędrzej Giertych, a well-known National Party writer and activist in London, who had earlier criticized RFE as an "American spy network" in various publications, including *Horyzonty*. In 1976, on his own initiative, Giertych published an "Open Letter to Polish Society in Poland" in which he cautioned against the actions of the opposition (he named PPN and the campaign protesting constitutional changes that strengthened the PUWP and its links with the Soviet Union). He argued that under the influence of the West, including some people in the émigré community, the opposition wanted to push the Poles into suicidal insurrections, which would lead to the spilling of blood and a Soviet intervention.[155] Giertych personally mailed his open letter to nearly eight hundred addressees in Poland.[156] Thinking him an ally, the Security Service decided to try to persuade him to use some of its materials in his attacks on KOR, the Paris *Kultura*, and RFE.[157]

The secret police made contact with Giertych through his son Maciej, who lived in Poland. In 1977, Lieutenant Colonel Janusz Mazurek, in charge of foreign sabotage in Section VIII of Department I, met with Maciej several times. He emphasized that for all their ideological differences, the Polish government appreciated Jędrzej Giertych's patriotism and hinted that it would only be possible to distribute his open letter in Poland with Security Service approval. He charged RFE with presenting a forged letter to compromise Giertych. "Talking about émigré intrigues vis-à-vis my father and their inspirational role in acting ag[ainst] the PRP, I mentioned that the appropriate answer and an expression of proper patriotism would have been publications with critiques of émigré leaders. I mentioned *Kultura*'s inspirational role. I mentioned to him that Zionist elements, with whom *Kultura* and RFE collaborate, are playing a role in this," read Lieutenant Colonel Mazurek's report about his first conversation with Maciej Giertych.[158]

Giertych's criticism was to focus on Adam Michnik, "who is fêted . . . and paraded all over Europe by various émigré organizations and whom RFE and *Kultura* present as the protagonist of the 'opposition.'"[159] The Security Service offered to give Giertych materials (including a report from the post-1956 Rehabilitation Commission) about his half-brother Stefan Michnik, who had worked as a military judge in the Stalinist period and had been responsible for death sentences for political prisoners. If Giertych publicized this information, it would hit KOR and the émigré groups that supported it, primarily *Kultura*, in which Stefan Michnik published under the pen name Karol Szwedowicz.[160]

In April 1977, after returning from London, Maciej Giertych gave his father's reply to his handler. Jędrzej Giertych was very interested in the theme the Ministry of Internal Affairs had suggested, and "he would like to publish it, but for that he would have to obtain from us copies (Xerox) of the document we had shown 'Maciej' (it was a photocopy of the report from the commission that examined the responsibility of prosecuting and court organs, which mentioned Captain Michnik as one of the judges charged with passing wrongful death sentences) or another document or newspapers from the period of the trials. . . . J. G. wants to have it 'in writing' in case he is taken to court for libel. He need not reveal where he got this information; it will be sufficient if he receives such a document from Poland."[161] Giertych suggested to Polish intelligence, through his son, that it could put the materials about Stefan Michnik in his home mail box in London.

There is no confirmation in the surviving documents that this operation was carried out. Jędrzej Giertych did write about Stefan Michnik in the periodical *Opoka*, which he published, but only after the émigré daily *Narodowiec*, published in Lens, France, broke the story. The author of the piece about Michnik was Tadeusz Borowicz; then a letter signed by a Michał Podgórski from Britain appeared in the column "Readers' Voices."[162] At least the letter clearly shows its secret police provenance, if only because of its phrasing and rhetorical devices, which are evident to any researcher familiar with the products of the Ministry of Internal Affairs.

In June 1978, Jędrzej Giertych published a long article titled "Michnik" in *Opoka*, which began with a discussion of Adam Michnik's *Kościół, lewica, dialog* [The Church, the Left, a dialogue], which had recently been published in the West in Polish. Giertych "uncovered" Michnik's Jewish roots and "Trotskyite" connections. He also wrote about Stefan Michnik. He used this occasion to attack not only the opposition in Poland but also the Paris *Kultura*, which published Michnik-Szwedowicz's articles, and "Free Europe's propaganda," which, according to Giertych, publicized the harmful activities of the opposition and of Adam Michnik in particular.[163]

A sort of epilogue to the attacks on the Paris *Kultura* for publishing Stefan Michnik's articles was the publication in *Zeszyty Historyczne* (also a Giedroyc periodical) of the so-called Szerer Commission report from June 1957, probably the same materials that the secret police had tried to give Jędrzej Giertych.[164] Stefan Michnik was one of the judges on the panels that handed out death sentences. The publication of this report was the best way to put an end to the Ministry of Internal Affairs game. Stefan Michnik was mentioned not only by the Szerer Commission, which examined military courts, but also in the report of the Mazur Commission, which examined not only the courts but also the prosecutor's office and military counterintelligence.[165] We do not know which report the Security Service gave to Giertych, perhaps both.

Just as in earlier periods, the special services of People's Poland attempted to introduce agents into RFE's Polish Section. In 1977, they banked on Father Stanisław Wielgus, an assistant professor at the Catholic University of Lublin (Katolicki Uniwersytet Lubelski, or KUL). According to Security Service files, Wielgus began to meet with officers of Section IV of the Provincial Command of the People's Militia in Lublin, who treated him as a secret collaborator, in 1967. Since he had spent time in Western Europe on academic fellowships, in 1973 he was transferred to Department I, specifically its Section VIII.[166]

Polish intelligence learned that Father Tadeusz Kirschke, the author of RFE's religious programs who had been with the Polish Section from the very beginning, was preparing to retire. "The information about the 'Szerszenie' [Locust] site we have obtained recently indicates that the director of the Polish Service, Michałowski, is looking for a new employee to replace Father Kirschke. . . . This employee should, apart from the political aspect, meet certain criteria, namely: come from Poland, be a cleric and know current Polish issues, have a higher education, preferably be a KUL alumnus. . . . This situation creates an opportunity to conduct an operational combination, with the goal of introducing our agent into RFE's Polish desk in Father Kirschke's place. We have pinpointed agent 'Grey' for this combination," read the action plan prepared by Department I.[167]

Stanisław Wielgus, who according to the Security Service was a reliable and trustworthy secret collaborator, as well as a "very intelligent man, cultured, with broad intellectual horizons," in the judgment of Department I, had a good shot at taking over the position vacated by Father Kirschke. Polish intelligence assumed that during a half-year academic fellowship at a university in Munich, Wielgus would be able to make the appropriate contacts with employees of RFE's Polish Section, primarily through pastoral work among the local Poles. It was then very likely that he would be offered a job at the radio.[168]

In a meeting with Wielgus in October 1977, Lieutenant Colonel Janusz Mazurek, the same officer who had talked with Maciej Giertych, presented his idea of penetrating RFE. He even gave Wielgus one of Father Kirschke's last programs to read and evaluate. "When I asked him whether he could do better, 'Grey' replied in the affirmative," Mazurek wrote in his report.

To Mazurek, several important decisions were made during his conversation with Wielgus: "I told him that it is possible that Father Kirschke will retire, and for that reason it would not be good for us if his place were taken by someone who will use the religious platform to conduct sabotage, anti-Polish activity on a religious basis. We would like him to take his place and to head the religious section at RFE. 'Grey' said that he would have no professional difficulty heading such a section. He has the appropriate education and experience in publishing (he works on KUL's editorial team). But he does not think that he could get into RFE easily, especially since he would not like to sever his relations with Poland, and a longer stay abroad would be very tiring for him. After a long discussion and much convincing, 'Grey' agreed to take on our mission. But he was adamant that he would not cut himself off from Poland. It was agreed that for our part we would direct his movements in the FRG in such a way as to place him in the orbit of interest of RFE's leadership. He will set the condition that he will appear incognito (under a pseudonym) so as not to break off his ties to Poland. . . . 'Grey' is certain that he will get favorable recommendations from KUL's leadership and the church hierarchy, in case RFE should ask."[169]

In February 1978, a few days before his departure for Munich, agent "Grey" signed so-called departure instructions, a commitment to perform specific tasks for Polish intelligence.[170] Most of them involved RFE. The instructions reveal which of the aspects of the radio's activities interested the Security Service the most. Wielgus's assignment included acquiring the American management's programmatic guidelines, establishing the "long-term action concepts" and "the Polish Section's directions of interests," and also learning its "assessment of the current situation in Poland, including the condition of Church-state relations." He was also assigned tasks on more specific issues, such as identifying "communications channels with Poland" (which were of never-ending interest to the secret police), the Munich club where radio employees met, and even the radio's "entry pass regime."[171] This information could come in handy if outsiders, probably secret police agents or functionaries, tried to enter the building.

In a statement made in January 2007, then Archbishop of Warsaw Wielgus claimed that he had been forced to sign the departure instructions by a "very brutal intelligence functionary's" "screaming and threats." The files indicate that Colonel Stanisław Kubat of Section XI of Department I also took part in the meeting, and he allegedly warned Wielgus that if he said no, Kubat would "destroy" him.[172]

Wielgus did not meet the expectations of the Security Service. He did not get the job at RFE and did not acquire the information from the radio that he had been assigned. He only managed to meet Father Kirschke, and he reported on their two conversations. These have not survived in the accessible files.[173] Department I assessed that "Grey" demonstrated "complete passivity in the area of getting to know people in the sphere of our interests." Wielgus agreed with this assessment. He explained himself: "the objective conditions lined up in such a way that he counted 'on a lot, but it turned out that this is not so easy.'"[174] Department I made no more attempts to use him.[175]

A sociologist couple from Łódź, Andrzej and Jolanta Gontarczyk, were entrusted with the mission of infiltrating RFE. "Yon" and "Panna" had been working for the Security Service since the 1970s. In Łódź, they informed on opposition groups with which they were vaguely associated and then reported on Solidarity structures in which they were active, both legal and (after December 13, 1981) underground ones.[176] They were both chairmen of the Solidarity committees in their places of work, as well as advisers to Solidarity of the Łódź region.

In 1982, the Gontarczyks were transferred to the Ministry of Internal Affairs Department I. They moved to West Germany in late 1982 and got to know émigré groups such as the Polish Socialist Party, and some RFE editors. Jolanta Gontarczyk did some freelance work for the radio as a West German correspondent. The couple's greatest success was infiltrating the group organized by Father Franciszek Blachnicki in Karlsberg. This creator of the anti-alcohol Abstention Crusade and of the Light and Life religious movement had been one of the most persecuted and monitored priests in Communist Poland. After he left Poland in December 1981, the prosecutor's office opened an investigation, charging him with entering "into an agreement with persons acting on behalf of foreign organizations, including the saboteur Radio Free Europe, the Paris Club, the so-called Aleksandr Solzhenitsyn Fund, with the goal of acting to harm the PRP's political interests."[177] A warrant was issued for his arrest.

In Karlsberg, Father Blachnicki directed the International Light-Life Evangelization Center. He also founded the Christian Service for the Liberation of Nations, which was to help Poland and "the other nations enslaved by Soviet Communism." He established contacts with Czech, Slovak, Ukrainian, and Russian dissidents.[178] From then on he became a target of vicious attacks that appeared not only in the Polish press (*Żołnierz Wolności* called him the "Polish Ayatollah") but also in Soviet publications (*Pravda* wrote about this "saboteur in a cassock").[179]

The Gontarczyks won Father Blachnicki's full trust; "Panna" became the chairperson of the Christian Service for the Liberation of Nations and "Yon" a consultant to its council. This was no doubt one of the most successful infiltrations of the political émigré community in the 1980s by the Ministry of Internal Affairs. The agents were uncovered a few years later. According to surviving secret police files, it was the underground Fighting Solidarity that found information about their real roles, probably through a leak from the Provincial Section of Internal Affairs in Łódź.[180]

On February 26, 1987, Father Blachnicki informed his staff in Karlsberg of the Gontarczyks' espionage activities. The next day he engaged the couple in a stormy discussion, after which he fainted and died.[181] There have been suspicions that he did not die of natural causes.[182] In November 1987, a general meeting of the Christian Service for the Liberation of Nations charged the Gontarczyks with espionage.[183] It was only then that they resigned from their positions, and in April 1988, fearing arrest by the West German Office for the Protection of the Constitution, they returned to Poland via Belgrade and Budapest.[184]

The Ministry of Internal Affairs decided to exploit the Gontarczyks' return in its propaganda. Jerzy Urban announced their arrival during a press conference on April 26, 1988, and devoted a large part of it to attacks on RFE. He inaccurately referred to Andrzej Gontarczyk as a "Radio Free Europe journalist" and his wife as an "announcer at the same radio station." He treated their homecoming as the beginning of a wave of repatriations of RFE employees: "I said some time ago that some of Free Europe's personnel have been making confidential contacts with Polish officials, feeling them out about the possibility of coming back. I think that the Gontarczyks' arrival in our motherland is only the beginning. You are all welcome here." He also encouraged the radio's employees to come to Poland as tourists. "Let them compare the real image of Poland, which they so often malign in their programs, with the realities of our life and the real conditions in Poland," said Urban.[185] This was typical disinformation. Urban must have known very well that security regulations at RFE forbade its employees to travel to Communist countries, even though many of them would certainly have liked to visit their homelands and their families.

This was only the beginning of the exploitation of the Gontarczyks in propaganda. Ministry of Internal Affairs press spokesman Major Wojciech Garstka drew up a months-long plan for press publications and radio and television programs, and Deputy Minister Władysław Pożoga signed off on it. Jerzy Urban took part in two meetings of the ministry leadership devoted to it, in June and August 1988, and helped to establish the guidelines for this propaganda campaign.[186] According to Major Garstka, his team intended to implement the campaign "via fully trustworthy journalists," and the Ministry of

Internal Affairs would deliver materials to their editorial offices. The group even wrote the questions for the journalists to ask at the Gontarczyks' press conference at the Interpress agency. The Ministry of Internal Affairs press spokesman was to oversee and check the materials prepared for publication.[187] This is an example of the osmosis between the worlds of the secret police and the official media in People's Poland. In summarizing the campaign in December 1988, the Ministry of Internal Affairs presented Urban's first statement at his weekly press conference, two half-hour television programs, and articles in the *Polityka* and *Walka Młodych* weeklies as its most important components.[188]

In the *Polityka* article, Wojciech Markiewicz introduced the Gontarczyks as the victims of, first, the repressive policies of martial law (they had lost their jobs in 1982), and, second, the soulless Polish émigré community, which hounded the couple with baseless charges of working for Communist intelligence. He used both the Gontarczyks' statements and materials that he could only have obtained from the Security Service, such as internal documents from RFE security and analyses of the Polish Service written in 1987 by Jakub Karpiński, Aleksander Smolar, and Waldemar Kuczyński. Markiewicz represented the Polish Section as a collection of old émigrés who had long ago lost contact with their homeland and recent arrivals unable to adapt to the radio's atmosphere. They therefore all the more eagerly enjoyed the comforts of life, such as the radio's subsidized restaurant, where "a liter bottle of Johnnie Walker" cost "5–6 marks (outside, it costs ca. 20 DM)."[189]

Walka Młodych, a weekly publication of the Union of Polish Socialist Youth (Związek Socjalistycznej Młodzieży Polskiej, ZSMP), published an interview with the Gontarczyks by Jacek S. Jóźwiak. Like other publications, it highlighted the RFE theme and presented both Gontarczyks as the radio's correspondents in West Germany. "Their salaries, even by German standards, are excellent," Andrzej Gontarczyk said about RFE employees. "The new émigrés are awed by them because they hand out money and are capable of destroying anyone. But something is troubling them, they drink a lot, most of them don't leave the Polish ghetto. You know, these are people who went from being unidealistic conformists to radical anticommunists. For some good chow, for a chance to shine."[190] Apart from attacking the radio, the interviewees pointed out that Poles who decided to stay in Germany illegally were doomed to rootlessness and had no future.

The propaganda campaign surrounding the Gontarczyks' return was a repeat of Czechowicz's, but in the different circumstances of the fading Communist system. The "spy duo," like Czechowicz, planned to publish their memoirs. The title was ready: "On Their Knees: A Study of Today's Emigration."

Unfortunately, unforeseen events got in the way: "In view of the new socio-political situation [the 1988 strikes and the negotiations between the government and Solidarity—P. M.], these undertakings went unrealized, and at the present moment and in the near future, their realization seems unlikely," wrote Major Wiesław Bednarz, head of Section XI of Department I in the Ministry of Internal Affairs.[191]

Much as had happened during the Czechowicz propaganda campaign, now the Ministry of Internal Affairs not only encouraged the writing of articles and television programs, it also took advantage of materials it had acquired through operations, in this case by other agents. Warsaw Radio broadcast excerpts of a speech given by Jan Nowak-Jeziorański in the autumn of 1987 (in two programs, on May 7 and 9, 1988) during a closed-door meeting of the Polish Service in Munich, which was probably either recorded by one of the participants or stolen from the director's office.[192]

Archival materials contain no specific information about agents working on the Polish desk in the 1980s. The documents cited earlier indicate that after Mieczysław Lach and Andrzej Smoliński returned to Poland in 1974, the secret police had no spy in the Polish Section. The assignments given to Stanisław Wielgus in 1978 appear to confirm this. What would be the point of giving a cleric the task of identifying "RFE's entry pass regime" if the Security Service had a spy, a radio employee who entered the building daily? But it is not out of the question that this was a way to test an agent's loyalty and skills.

The available documents show that many attempts were made to introduce agents into the radio, as was the case with Father Wielgus, or at least into the Polish community in Munich. The Security Service vested some hopes in Zygmunt Krok-Solorz, who was recruited in 1983. As the owner of a transportation company in Vienna, he delivered parcels from many Polish émigrés to their families in Poland. The Security Service hoped he would get to know RFE employees and, especially, that he would acquire their relatives' addresses in Poland. This would have had real operational significance, since coaxing RFE staffers' family members to collaborate, or at least to serve as go-betweens, was a standard Security Service method. Krok-Solorz did not meet the Security Service expectations. He did provide information about a shipment of printer's ink to the underground in Poland, which was useful to the ministry, but he did not gain access to RFE. A report from his case officer shows that Krok-Solorz supplied data about Father Stanisław Ludwiczak, who took over the religious programming from Father Kirschke, but what he provided must have been very vague since the agent did not even meet him in person. After drawing benefits from his collaboration with the secret police, a "consular" passport, and privileges for his business activity, Krok-Solorz began to avoid his Security Service contacts. The ministry recognized this in June 1985 and shut him out of their agents' network.[193]

There is no doubt, however, that in the 1980s, and certainly under Najder's directorship, Polish intelligence had agents inside RFE's Polish Section. Attesting to this are the acquisition of the already mentioned recording of Nowak-Jeziorański's speech made in a closed meeting in Munich, detailed knowledge about internal conflicts (which government spokesman Jerzy Urban used in his press conferences and which the ministry took advantage of in many publications), and documents from the Polish desk. According to a note written in April 1988 for the propaganda campaign focused on the Gontarczyks' homecoming, the Security Service had a stenographic record of papers written by Karpiński, Smolar, and Kuczyński from the Polish editors' program discussion, three of Najder's memoranda, documents concerning Najder's departure, and "satirical materials written by employees of the Polish Section of RFE illustrating the internal conflicts and the ongoing battle between former director Z. Najder's backers and opponents."[194] These materials included fliers and satirical poems prepared and distributed at the radio by staffers at odds with Najder.

It remains a mystery who delivered these materials to the Polish secret services. Colonel Henryk Bosacki, a high-ranking functionary of Department I (and for some time head of Section XI, in charge of fighting sabotage), told Najder in 1993 that "all the way to the end he had four people at RFE."[195] Because it is currently impossible to confirm such claims, I must resort to quoting them.[196]

Some documents about the operational game that the Ministry of Internal Affairs ran in 1987 against RFE's Polish Service and other émigré organizations, especially Solidarity's Brussels office, do survive.[197] Its protagonist was an underground Solidarity activist from Konin, who appears in the secret police materials as "Bogumił." People interviewed for this book have identified him by his first and last names. A young worker, he was probably recruited by the secret police in Konin after being arrested.[198] Because of circumstantial evidence that he had been forced to collaborate during a very violent investigation and because of his tragic death, I have decided not to reveal his name.

The Security Service assigned "Bogumił" a variety of tasks, including intercepting the communications between the Brussels office and the Solidarity underground in Poland, taking over some of the smuggled printing equipment from the West to Poland, and identifying contacts between RFE employees and underground organizations in Poland. He was also told to start "disintegration" to exacerbate the conflicts among the Polish staff. I have only been able to reconstruct those aspects of this still unexplained, exceptionally complicated, and multitrack case that directly affect RFE.

"Bogumił" arrived in Munich in 1986 as an emissary of the Konin underground Solidarity. He was well received, since his recommendations included the Catholic Church in Konin. When he returned in March 1987, he was treated as someone trustworthy. His hosts were Franciszek Drzewiński, a Solidarity activist in 1980–1981 and a member of the Intervention Commission for Mazovia Region, and his wife, Danuta, a journalist working at RFE. He stayed with them, and in their absence photographed documents, as well as addresses and phone numbers he found on notepads and in diaries. He met other RFE employees, among them Father Stanisław Ludwiczak, Piotr Załuski, Konrad Tatarowski, Witold Pronobis, and Aleksander Świeykowski, all supporters of outgoing director Zdzisław Najder.

"Bogumił" arrived in Munich at a very dramatic time, a few days after the change at the top of the Polish Service had been announced. He was invited to the farewell party for Najder at Załuski's house, later delivering a detailed and quite accurate account of it.[199] He met mostly those who were close to the departing director and who remained bitter about the situation (Father Ludwiczak resigned in protest). Most of these people had been living outside Poland for only a few years and were closely connected to Solidarity; many of them had been interned under martial law. This would explain both their commitment to working closely with underground Solidarity and their outrage over the way in which Najder had been treated, which "Bogumił" and the Security Service exploited.

A group of RFE editors, including Piotr Załuski and Konrad Tatarowski, made plans to publish a bulletin by the name *Przeciek* (Leak), which would be produced outside Poland and distributed both in the West and in Poland. They believed that this would be a very good way to share information and materials available in the West with readers in Poland. The Konin underground, and specifically "Bogumił," was their main partner. "Bogumił" promised to print and distribute *Przeciek* through "Solidarity" networks. He was to receive two mimeograph machines in Munich. The Security Service placed great hopes in this endeavor. The operational game prepared after the return of "Bogumił" to Poland was as follows: "After we receive the printing equipment from the FRG, the Secret Collaborator will begin to print and distribute the illegal *Przeciek* bulletin under close operational supervision. The operational interests of our service will determine its circulation. We will use the texts we receive to identify the current directions of RFE's propaganda activity in relation to the political underground in Poland."[200]

Aleksander Świeykowski had two mimeograph machines in Munich. He worked out with "Bogumił" that he would use his channels to smuggle them into Poland. One was to go to Konin.[201] The Security Service did not have a grip on this trafficking, and "Bogumił" first heard that the machines had been sent out in September 1987. The transport was also to include packages of *Przeciek*. "Finally, on November 4, after many adventures, the Secret Collaborator received the equipment, two identical Gestetner 466 mimeographs, a lubricating machine for an offset printer, and two tables for two different printers," stated a Security Service report in January 1988.[202] From then on, both machines were under Security Service oversight, and one of them was sent to Rozwadów in Zamość Province.

But the Security Service did not manage to intercept the parcels containing *Przeciek*, even though it had prepared a drop box just for this purpose. "*Przeciek* appears in the FRG and is sent to Poland. The parcels containing this bulletin are allegedly sent to the drop box in Konin. This box was organized by Section V of the P[rovincial] O[ffice] of I[nternal] A[ffairs] in Konin and is under ongoing operational control. Not a single mailing has arrived there," the Konin Security Service informed Deputy Minister Henryk Dankowski in January 1988.[203]

Przeciek was edited and printed in Munich. Six issues appeared between May and October 1987. Most of its authors were RFE editors, including Aleksander Świeykowski, Danuta Drzewińska, Konrad Tatarowski, Piotr Załuski, Witold Pronobis, Andrzej Świdlicki, and Lechosław Gawlikowski. Zdzisław Najder wrote one article for it. Receiving no response from Poland, no information that it was being read or cited in underground publications, the group abandoned the project.[204] No Security Service documents other than the one quoted above have been found to indicate whether it had intercepted *Przeciek*.

The other area in the operational game that recruited "Bogumił" as participant was more productive for the Security Service. Najder's friends asked him to find articles that Alina Grabowska had written for official publications. A journalist from Łódź who had left Poland in the wake of the March 1968 events, in the 1970s and 1980s Grabowska was one of RFE's best-known political commentators, and one of those most viciously attacked by Polish propaganda. She also clashed intensely with Najder and was seen as the leader of the "anti-Najder" group at the radio.[205]

Much earlier, Najder's associates had asked various people from Poland, especially Łódź, who were visiting Munich to try to uncover information about Grabowska's activities in Communist Poland.[206] "Bogumił," or rather the Security Service, was the first to respond to this request. From today's perspective, the actions of Najder's associates may seem shocking, but we must remember how extremely intense the emotions and conflicts within the Polish Section were in the 1980s. It was entirely commonplace to disseminate charges of spying (for the Security Service or even the KGB) and to cite opponents' actions or texts dating back to People's Poland. A flier distributed at the radio by the "anti-Najder" group contained a comparison of Danuta Drzewińska's text for RFE in 1983 with a commentary she had allegedly read on the air in 1978 as a journalist with Warsaw Radio.[207]

Were the Security Service operations, which consisted mostly of library research, not a grim story about the abuse of human antipathies, they would be almost grotesque. In June 1987 Warrant Officer M. Traciłowski went to the Ludwik Waryński City Public Library in Łódź. He told his supervisors in the Konin Security Service office that he had ordered bound volumes of publications, including *Głos Robotniczy*, for which, so he had been informed, Alina Grabowska had written. Traciłowski prepared short précis of individual articles. He came to the conclusion that Grabowska had "mostly been in charge of cultural issues and the errors occurring in them." He concluded by informing his superiors about possible next steps: "I learned from the person servicing the photocopying machine at the C[ity] P[ublic] L[ibrary] in Łódź that there exists the possibility of obtaining photocopies. To do this, one must submit a request to the management of the C[ity] P[ublic] L[ibrary] in person or in writing on a special form, which I am attaching to my note. In the description one must list: the publication's catalogue number, year (newspaper issue, date of publication), page numbers, title and author and number of copies. 1 copy costs 10 zlotys."[208]

In this case, even the Security Service became a victim of the very restrictive use of photocopying machines in People's Poland. So as not to divulge the operational game, "Bogumił" himself had to come to the library and use the information provided by the scrupulous officer and personally order photocopies of Grabowska's articles. A relative delivered the photocopies to Munich, also bringing a letter from "Bogumił" to Franciszek Drzewiński in which he declared that he could also look for materials to discredit other members of the "anti-Najder" group (even though this was a few months after Najder's departure from the radio) and that he would need more information about what to look for and where. "In view of the absence of the abovementioned information, the S[ecret] C[ollaborator] has interrupted his search for other documents. The likely reason why Franciszek Drzewiński did not send them was the stabilization of the internal situation inside the Polish Service at RFE and the weakening of existing internal tensions," the Konin Security Service gauged in January 1988."[209]

Danuta Drzewińska remembers that a photocopy of an article by Grabowska was pinned to a bulletin board in RFE's Polish Service—an established method in the internal underhanded battles.[210] A complete set of photocopies of Grabowska's articles landed in Piotr Załuski's hands. He thought at the time that they must have come from someone in the Solidarity underground movement who had visited the radio station.[211]

Załuski provided a thick wad of photocopies of Grabowska's articles from the Polish press, which he had kept for nearly twenty years. It is an exceptional experience for a historian to be able to recreate a sequence of events step by step thanks to recovered documents and witness accounts. At the same time, these documents illustrate very eloquently the disintegrative actions of the Security Service, which took advantage of every opportunity to create or deepen internal conflicts—but, of course, not only in the 1980s, since it had conducted similar large-scale operations during Jan Nowak's directorship.

The story had a tragic ending. In 1988, "Bogumił" was killed in Germany by a truck, whose driver the police have never found. After he died, officers of the West German Federal Office for the Protection of the Constitution appeared at RFE. They interviewed people who had known "Bogumił" and revealed that he had been a Polish agent and was being shadowed by German counterintelligence.[212] Later, the news was circulated at the radio station, whose source none of the interviewees for this book could recall, that "Bogumił" had severed his ties to the Security Service and demanded that his wife and three children be allowed to join him in Germany. If the Security Service did not meet his demand, he threatened to make his collaboration public. Hence, this interpretation has the Polish special services murdering "Bogumił" to eliminate a former agent who had begun to present a risk. But because of a lack of documentation, this supposition cannot be confirmed.

The Arrest and Trial of Józef Szaniawski

On June 29, 1985, in broad daylight in Aleje Jerozolimskie, a Warsaw thoroughfare, seven Military Internal Service (MIS) officers in civilian clothing arrested Józef Szaniawski, a historian, journalist, and part-time employee of the Polish Press Agency (PAP). After they shoved Szaniawski into their car, one of the officers pulled out his gun and threatened to shoot him if he tried to escape. Szaniawski was transported to the MIS headquarters at the corner of Chałubińskiego and Oczki Streets, where the military prosecutor charged him with espionage and warned that he might be sentenced to death.[213]

Szaniawski had been working for RFE since 1973, sending information and materials he had access to at PAP, where he wrote classified analyses. These were published in PAP's Special Bulletins intended for members of the party leadership, or even as so-called white papers, which were limited to an even smaller group. An acquaintance, Janusz Roszkowski, vice chairman of PAP, had recommended Szaniawski for this job. Most of his papers analyzed the

Soviet Union and were based on articles from local Soviet newspapers, not on clandestine sources. According to Szaniawski himself, not many people at PAP were interested in writing about these issues, which explains why an outsider was hired to do it. Stefan Olszowski, at that time a very influential figure in the party leadership, had reportedly ordered these analyses of the Soviet press, wanting to have his own source of information about the situation in the Soviet Union.[214]

Szaniawski's arrest and trial were obviously for show. Much like the earlier trial of Zdzisław Najder, which ended with a death sentence, the Szaniawski case aimed to intimidate Polish citizens maintaining contacts with RFE and other foreign organizations conducting sabotage. A few months before Szaniawski's arrest, the newspapers published an announcement from the Prosecutor General's Office warning the public not to collaborate with RFE, the Paris-based *Kultura*, the Solidarity Coordinating Office in Brussels, *Kontakt* publishers in Paris, or the US-based *Pomost*. "We have determined definitively their various degrees of veiled cooperation with the espionage services or other agencies of countries whose policies are hostile to Poland. Their common goal is to harm our state with various available methods aiming to destabilize our domestic situation, [and] weaken our international position, as well as the defenses and security of the People's Republic of Poland. These organizations' publications and radio programs strike at our state's constitutional order and its main organs, disseminate false, slanderous information, and instruct people in undertaking disruptions of the public order," warned the Prosecutor General's Office. The concluding words of the announcement sounded even more threatening: "Many Polish citizens have informed us that when they were outside our country they were pushed into collaboration to harm Poland. It has also been ascertained that some persons, some on their own initiative, guided by a variety of motivations, often material ones, themselves participate in these kinds of activities. The Prosecutor General's Office reminds citizens that collaborating with foreign organizations hostile to Poland violates the law and is subject to punishment as prescribed by law, and it warns citizens about the charges, which, in order to protect the interests of the state and of its citizens, will be severe and put into effect with full ramifications."[215]

No documents have been found from Szaniawski's operational inquiry, and we only have access to his investigation and trial records. Many issues remain unresolved, including the most important question: how did the secret police learn about his work for RFE? The MIS documents indicate that military counterintelligence "acquired operational materials and information" about Józef Szaniawski's "espionage activities" in November 1984, more than half a year before arresting him.[216]

The only material evidence of Szaniawski's collaboration with RFE was his correspondence with Wiktor Trościanko. The MIS found letters from Trościanko during a search of Szaniawski's apartment. It remains unclear how it acquired Szaniawski's letters to Trościanko; it was most likely during a burglary of Trościanko's vacation home in Spain in 1984, after his death. Several sources, whose reliability is very difficult or even impossible to verify, concur in this interpretation. In 1990, Lieutenant Colonel Franciszek Sznajder of the MIS told Szaniawski that after Trościanko's death, two cars carrying military counterintelligence officers went to Spain and entered the locked, temporarily uninhabited house (Trościanko's widow was in England).[217] This is a likely explanation, since it was the MIS that had conducted an "operational dialogue" with Trościanko in the 1960s and 1970s. Deputy Minister of Internal Affairs Władysław Pożoga reportedly told Henryk Piecuch that the Security Service had broken into the house.[218] Andrzej Madejczyk, of Department I and perhaps also a BND agent, told Najder in 1986 about the break-in.[219]

The secret services may also have used these versions as disinformation to protect the real source of Szaniawski's letters. In any case, the burglary did indeed take place, and the director of RFE's security, Richard Cummings, let on that he knew about it when Najder gave him the information he had received from Madejczyk.[220]

The intelligence that the MIS and the prosecutor's office had about Szaniawski's collaboration with RFE was limited to the contents of his correspondence with Trościanko. This decisively confirms the "Spanish trail." The MIS did not have the letters that Szaniawski had written to others at RFE, Józef Ptaczek and Zygmunt Michałowski. It was also unaware of the full spectrum of Szaniawski's work for RFE. The indictment marked 1974 as the beginning of his collaboration, the year Szaniawski wrote his first letter to Trościanko, which was in the hands of the MIS, on August 8, 1974.

Yet Szaniawski had contacted RFE a year earlier, telephoning Munich from West Berlin, where he spent every summer working in a restaurant. He found RFE's number in a telephone book, phoned, and asked to speak to Jan Nowak, who happened to be on vacation. He then asked for Trościanko, whose program *Odwrotna strona medalu* (The other side of the coin) he liked to listen to. From that moment on, Trościanko became his main contact at RFE, and over time their collaboration turned into friendship. After Trościanko retired in 1976, Józef Ptaczek took over. Szaniawski occasionally came to Munich, where he also spoke with Michałowski, and once with Nowak. He mailed his materials to various addresses in Germany provided by Trościanko, both from his annual stays in Berlin and from Warsaw. The mailings were usually papers he had written for PAP about the situation in the Soviet Union, mostly on the basis of the dozen Soviet local papers he read and analyzed daily, as well as articles on Polish-Soviet and Sino-Soviet relations and the situation in Poland (topics included the strikes and protests of June 1976, books withheld by the censorship office, and the controversy over the nineteenth-century patriotic painting of the Racławice panorama, which the authorities considered to be anti-Russian).[221]

Investigation and trial documents indicate that the MIS knew about only a small part of Szaniawski's collaboration with RFE. The Security Service's interest in Szaniawski in the first half of the 1970s is puzzling and has not been explained. In September 1974, Department I of the Ministry of Internal Affairs sent a tip to Department II that in August of that year an anonymous caller had told the Polish embassy in Cologne that Józef Szaniawski, who had access to classified information at PAP, had "made connections in W[est] Berlin, where he provides information for remuneration." The caller "stated that he is in the FRG for work and had learned about Szaniawski from third parties."[222]

The August 1974 report about Szaniawski's contacts with RFE was true (including the fact that he had given materials about the situation on the Sino-Soviet border to RFE), but Szaniawski claimed that none of the people with whom he was acquainted in Berlin could have known about it.[223] The story about the call to the embassy is strange. It is not out of the question that Department I invented the anonymous caller to withhold its source at RFE, a common practice in information-sharing among the ministry's units. Counterintelligence had learned earlier that Szaniawski's analyses at PAP's Center for Press Documentation "catches and exposes . . . elements pointing to errors, differences and national conflicts in the USSR." Reporting this was Szaniawski's supervisor, Jerzy Barszczewski, the Ministry of Internal Affairs' clandestine contact "Baj."[224] Szaniawski was subjected to surveillance in the operational inquiry code named "Szaniec." Having revealed nothing, the inquiry was terminated in November 1975.[225]

The surviving files show no traces that the secret police knew anything about Szaniawski's collaboration with RFE in the 1980s. Perhaps the anonymous caller to the Polish embassy really had been an agent inside the Polish desk who may have heard about Szaniawski's relationship with Trościanko when they met in Munich in the summer of 1974. If we follow this trail, explaining the interruptions in the flow of information from RFE were the reappearances in Poland by Andrzej Smoliński in late August and Mieczysław Lach in November 1974. From what we know today, in the following few years Department I had no secret collaborator at the radio.

During the half-year investigation, more than a dozen men, both MIS officers and, most likely, Security Service functionaries in civilian dress questioned

Szaniawski. Only some of the interrogations were recorded, and Szaniawski later remembered something that the investigation documents do not show. The interrogators tried to make him confess (he was even given a statement to sign) that he had met Stefan Bratkowski and Dariusz Fikus in Munich. This was probably intended for use in a much larger show trial, in which these very well-known journalists, who were involved in the opposition and in underground publishing, would be sitting in the dock with Szaniawski.[226]

Szaniawski's wife, the famous singer Halina Frąckowiak, managed to reach Minister of Internal Affairs General Czesław Kiszczak. Kiszczak would habitually receive well-known artists and intellectuals and respond to some of their requests to obtain a passport or to release someone from an internment camp or jail. He liked to talk about it in the many interviews he gave after 1989.[227] Frąckowiak asked Kiszczak to free her husband and assured him that the charges of espionage could not be further from the truth. The minister told her, "If you help us, we will help you." Frąckowiak agreed to take part in the Soldiers' Song Festival in Kołobrzeg, which many well-known artists had been boycotting since the imposition of martial law. This led some of her colleagues to ostracize her. But her sacrifice was for naught, as the general did not keep his side of the bargain.[228]

The investigators tried different methods to break Szaniawski. After a few months of questioning, head investigator Colonel Andrzej Glonek persuaded Szaniawski to write a letter to the head of the MIS, General Edward Poradko, and gave him precise instructions about what to write. According to Szaniawski, the version surviving in the investigation files is the last of several he had written that Glonek dictated. Glonek promised the despairing prisoner, charged with spying and threatened with the death sentence, that he might be allowed to walk free if only he could convince the head of the MIS of his good will.[229] In the letter, Szaniawski admitted to his contacts at RFE but denied being a US spy. He expressed "regret and remorse" and asked for a chance to redeem himself. "I want to atone for my actions not by passively sitting in prison, but by wiping out my activities with the help of the MIS," he wrote to the head of military counterintelligence. "And this is why I am writing to Citizen General to give me this chance. I ask you from the bottom of my heart not to submit my case to a court. I want to 'arise' in the exact place where I 'fell.' I want to act, and I think that I know how to do it against Radio Free Europe, if possible in Munich or, if not, in Poland. And if this, too, is impossible, I want to collaborate with the M[inistry of] I[nternal] A[ffairs] against the enemies of People's Poland, especially against American intelligence and the domestic opposition."[230]

There is no indication in the surviving documents that either the MIS or the Security Service intended to use Szaniawski as a secret collaborator. Instead, the evidence points to this method of "softening" him before the trial, to make him confess and fully cooperate with the prosecution. Even after the collapse of People's Poland and after his release from prison in December 1989, the letter would be used against him and even published.[231] Thus, a piece of evidence that should have been employed to denounce the methods of the Communist secret services was, paradoxically, used against Szaniawski.

Szaniawski was tried in January 1986 by the Warsaw Military District court. The trial was closed, and the "public" consisted of dozens of MIS and Security Service officers. Szaniawski's wife and brother were not allowed into the courtroom and had to await the sentencing in the hallway. Two television crews filmed the trial, with Marek Barański, a prominent television journalist who collaborated with the Security Service, leading one of them.[232] Polish Television broadcast fragments of the trial immediately after the main evening news in October 1986 on Citizens' Militia and Security Service Day. This unmasking of an "American spy" was portrayed as one of their greatest accomplishments.[233]

Because the correspondence between Wiktor Trościanko and Józef Szaniawski was the only evidence submitted by the prosecution, it needed to "prove" that RFE was in fact an agency of the CIA and that the editors who were in touch with the accused were US agents. In response to a question from the MIS, the director of the Office of the Minister of Internal Affairs submitted a letter in which he described the RFE-CIA relationship. According to Colonel Czesław Żmuda, "there exists a personal union between the Central Intelligence Agency and Radio Free Europe and—in the decision-making aspect—the CIA has influence on the station's program of activity . . . it has been determined that those considered to be CIA cadres are: Z[dzisław] Kołodziejski, J[ózef] Ptaczek, W[ładysław] Poncet, Z[ygmunt] Michałowski, Z[dzisław] Najder, and the late Trościanko."[234]

Testimony by Lieutenant Colonel Andrzej Czechowicz, however, served as the decisive evidence. This veteran of anti-RFE operations asserted that the radio was under CIA control and that many of its employees were US intelligence staff or, at least, agents. Czechowicz profiled the two RFE editors with whom Szaniawski collaborated concisely, but in sufficient detail for the prosecutor: "When I was in Munich, both Wiktor Trościanko and Józef Ptaczek were persons known to me from the station. They both worked in the broadcasting department, were certainly CIA collaborators."[235] During the trial, Czechowicz supplied further details charging Trościanko, and consequently Szaniawski. "In the '50s, Trościanko was expected to become RFE's director, and this position can be occupied only and exclusively by a CIA employee. . . . Furthermore, Trościanko was involved in the Berg affair [cooperation between

Polish émigrés and the CIA in the early 1950s—P. M.], he was trained to smuggle people across the border as agents," said Czechowicz.[236]

The court ruled that "Wiktor Trościanko was and Józef Ptaczek was and remains an employee of American intelligence. This fact should be declared as existing objectively."[237] Thereby, Szaniawski's contacts with both RFE editors were determined to amount to collaboration with foreign intelligence. The court considered an excerpt from Trościanko's letter to Szaniawski of August 1974, which was quoted as material evidence in the justification of the sentence: "I consider you a colleague, since our conversations and letters lead me to believe that we are working for the same cause."[238]

The trial of Szaniawski was almost identical to Zdzisław Najder's a few years earlier. Here, too, the opinions about RFE-CIA connections coming from the Ministry of Internal Affairs and from experts in fighting sabotage, as well as forged evidence, were used as the deciding arguments. The only difference was that Najder had been tried in absentia, while Szaniawski waited for his sentence in an MIS jail. Prosecutor Zbigniew Szawłowski asked for a fifteen-year prison term.[239]

On January 27, 1986, the Warsaw Military District Court, made up of Lieutenant Colonel Zbigniew Matacz (chairman), Colonel Jerzy Przygodzki, Colonel Jerzy Kowalski, Lieutenant Colonel Mieczysław Wiatr, and Lieutenant Colonel Janusz Michalczak, handed down a sentence of ten years in prison and confiscation of the property and of the illegal publications inspected during a search of Szaniawski's home.[240] After Szaniawski's sentencing, Halina Frąckowiak was forced to buy her own furniture back from the court. As it searched their apartment, the MIS had confiscated not only underground and émigré publications but also a book that had been published legally in Poland, *1859 dni walczącej Warszawy* (The 1,859 days of fighting Warsaw), an account of life in Warsaw under the German occupation, which had been published in 1974 by Znak publishers.[241] Thus, in a way the authorities could never have intended, a link was created between Szaniawski and the book's author, Władysław Bartoszewski, another person persecuted for collaborating with RFE.

In April 1986, the Military Chamber of the Supreme Court reduced Szaniawski's sentence to eight years.[242] He was moved to Barczew, an old Prussian strict-discipline prison, where he spent twenty-two months in solitary confinement.[243] Neither the roundtable negotiations of spring 1989 nor the June 4 elections, nor even the formation of a Solidarity-led government, changed his situation. As late as August 17, the Garrison Court in Olsztyn rejected his motion for a conditional release.[244] The same court waited until December 16, 1989, to let him go, and cut his sentence by half, in accordance with the amnesty of December 7.[245] Two days later, Szaniawski walked free.[246]

In April 1990, Minister of Justice and Prosecutor General Aleksander Bentkowski petitioned the Military Chamber of the Supreme Court to review Szaniawski's sentence.[247] But the military men who had accused him and sentenced him would not admit defeat. The head military prosecutor added a letter Szaniawski had written by hand to the head of the MIS from jail in October 1985 to the evidence being prepared for his appeal. He also gave a copy of the letter to the minister of justice. "It appears that the enclosed document provides an exceptional description of the personality of its author and remains relevant to the initiated exceptional appeal proceedings," wrote General Henryk Kostrzewa.[248] The minister's reply does not make him look good: "I am shocked by this letter, completely thrown off balance. How many more times will I have to witness instances where the ideals of honesty and loyalty have become completely foreign to people?"[249] Bentkowski was not shocked by the actions of the MIS functionaries or of military prosecutors and judges, but by a letter from a prisoner with the death sentence hanging over his head.

In October 1990, the Military Chamber of the Supreme Court invalidated the 1986 sentence and cleared Szaniawski of all charges.[250] Still, this did not mean that the military judges and prosecutors had changed their attitude. Szaniawski was denied access to his investigation and trial records and managed to obtained them only thanks to an intervention based on the principles of human rights from the Helsinki Committee.[251] In 1993, following instructions from the deputy head military prosecutor, the Pomerania Military District prosecutor's office initiated explanatory proceedings to learn "whether there had taken place a criminal activity by the former Military Internal Service."[252] The proceedings did not penalize any of the MIS functionaries or prosecutors, or military prosecutors or judges.

The Final Years of the People's Republic of Poland

In September 1986, the Polish government released more than two hundred political prisoners. This marked the beginning of a limited, government-controlled liberalization of the system, aimed primarily at winning public suport—including that of some independent and opposition groups—for the economic reforms necessary to respond to the deepening economic crisis.[253] The changes in the Soviet Union, perestroika and glasnost, initiated by Mikhail Gorbachev and gathering momentum in 1986, assisted the new political line.

The new strategy of the Jaruzelski team—alongside fighting domestic opposition and the institutions and groups in the West supporting it—increasingly featured an element of persuasion and propaganda aimed at convincing the population of its "new opening," its willingness to talk. Now, RFE was no longer being presented primarily as encouraging mass street demonstrations, which were virtually nonexistent in the second half of the 1980s. But it continued to be treated as a major adversary in the struggle for the minds of the Poles, especially over interpretations of the processes under way in Poland. As Mieczysław Rakowski noted in his diary in September 1986, "freeing all political prisoners is still one of the main topics. The whole opposition is now wondering what to do. Thrilled at being released, it waits for the next step. And, most important, union pluralism. The West and the Church support it. Free Europe (they are listening to it) is cramming information and commentaries that imply that Solidarity really exists into the Poles' heads."[254]

In early October 1986, Rakowski gave General Jaruzelski a memorandum outlining the necessary new political strategy. He stressed the weaknesses of official information and propaganda, which, he believed, were incapable of interpreting important political events convincingly: "We should be taking advantage of the new energy and keeping up a daily dialogue with society but, instead, there is the proverbial radio silence. In the meantime, RFE and the other stations broadcasting in Polish are devoting a large share of their programs to information and commentary on the state of Polish affairs, propagating the belief that the opposition is on the offensive."[255]

On January 31, 1987, Wojciech Jaruzelski received US deputy secretary of state John C. Whitehead. Their meeting was an important step in the gradual normalization of relations between People's Poland and the United States following the release of political prisoners in the autumn of 1986. The first secretary of the CC PUWP told the US diplomat that "Poland is the target of mass propaganda campaigns, especially by RFE and the Voice of America, whose aggressiveness resembles methods used in wartime."[256]

This was a repeat of the traditional accusations against the Western radios that had been voiced since December 13, 1981. Soon, however, the Polish government put into action an important new strategy toward RFE. Its new, more liberal policies were to include ending the jamming of Western radio stations. In early March 1987, Warsaw decided that it would do it on January 1, 1988. In April 1987, a meeting took place of representatives of the institutions responsible for the political and propaganda preparations for this date: the Foreign Ministry, the Ministry of Internal Affairs, the Main Political Directorate of the Polish Army, and the CC PUWP's Propaganda Department. The group resolved to make this decision an item in negotiations with the US and British governments to win political and economic concessions. It also anticipated multilevel talks with Moscow. The Ministry of Communications was to open negotiations with its Soviet counterpart about ending the jamming of Polish-language programs with Soviet equipment. Jan Główczyk, a member of the Politburo and a CC secretary, was to bring it up in his meeting with the head of the Propaganda Department of the CC CPSU, Y. Shklarov. CC Secretary Włodzimierz Natorf was to meet with CC CPSU members and win their approval to "bring 2–3 experts from Poland [to discuss] this issue."[257]

Winning the approval of the "Soviet friends" to stop jamming took much more time than did negotiating with the Western countries. This was an accurate gauge of Poland's subjugation even in this era of advanced perestroika. Moscow's unilateral decision had introduced the jamming of Polish-language programs in the early 1950s, and now, thirty years later, Jaruzelski's team was forced to engage in difficult negotiations to end it.

The Soviet bloc governments publicly maintained their stand on the rationale and legality of the jamming. At the Helsinki review conference in Vienna in June 1987, the Soviet, Polish, and Bulgarian governments defended their actions, stressing the "anti-establishment" nature of the Western programs.[258] But in the course of 1987, a breakthrough occurred in the Polish government's official position on RFE. Confirming it was Marshal of the Sejm Roman Malinowski during a visit to Washington as the head of a parliamentary delegation. A VOA reporter asked him about jamming, and he replied, "Personally, I listen to Western radio stations and I haven't noticed that they are jammed." "Also Free Europe?," the reporter continued. Malinowski: "I also listen to Free Europe, and there is no interference, even though I have a small radio."[259] Even though Malinowski was not telling the truth about jamming, and despite the unintended comedic quality of his words ("a small radio"), his statement showed a departure from the venomous attacks of the first half of the 1980s.

Current research has not found any transcripts of Polish-Soviet discussions about the cessation of jamming. But it is possible to recreate Warsaw's stand in its negotiations with the Western countries. Two weeks before the scheduled end of jamming, in December 1987, members of the Board for International Broadcasting (BIB), which oversaw RFE, met with Polish diplomats in Washington. The Poles requested that, in view of improving US-Polish relations, the US government wield a moderating influence on RFE's Polish programming. Stefan Staniszewski, director of the Foreign Ministry's Press, Cultural, and Scholarly Cooperation Department, presented a litany of charges against the radio, drawn from the 1980s emergency propaganda arsenal: insulting top state officials (he gave the example of the Jaruzelski-Hitler comparison), remaining under the influence of "extremist émigré organizations," supporting the underground in Poland with money and deliveries of duplicating equipment, and "attempting to create new underground organizations."[260] The last charge most likely reflected the accusations appearing in official newspapers at the time, according to which RFE was trying to create a peace movement in

Poland, something that did not exist until then, by speaking on the airwaves about the opposition Wolność i Pokój (Freedom and Peace) movement.[261] The BIB representatives emphatically refused to influence RFE's program line.

The two sides also argued about the size of RFE's audience in Poland. According to the Americans, more than half of all Poles listened to it. The Poles provided data for 1987 showing that about 22 percent of Poles listened to all the foreign broadcasters, and only 2 percent regularly listened to RFE.[262]

Both estimates were most likely exaggerated, in opposite directions. There was no question that the audience for RFE was shrinking. While, according to Poland's OBOP data, in May 1983, 49 percent of Poles listened to RFE, in June 1985 the figure was only 20 percent, and in October 1986 it was only 14 percent. In May 1989, the audience grew again, to 22 percent. BIB's figures, based on interviews with Poles traveling in the West, also showed a drop, but a much smaller one. In the period October 1983–September 1984, 66 percent of Poles reportedly listened to RFE, and for the period October 1987–September 1988 the figure was 51 percent.[263]

RFE's management was most concerned about losing listeners to the VOA. According to data generated by the Americans, in 1987 the two stations had nearly equal listenership.[264] Were this trend to persist, there would be no reason to continue financing RFE. The data, especially OBOP's, confirm that the RFE's listenership would increase in times of tensions and conflicts and decline when the mood became calmer and the political situation stabilized. This pattern could be attributed to RFE's more political nature, focusing as it did on the situation in Poland, and especially the opposition, more broadly and deeply than did the VOA or the BBC.

Warsaw's attempts to win concrete benefits in exchange for ending jamming yielded nothing. Still, on January 1, 1988, as had been decided earlier, the jamming of RFE's Polish programs by equipment located in both Poland and the Soviet Union ended. A short time later, in November 1988, the Soviet Union stopped interfering with the Radio Liberty programs addressed to its citizens.[265]

A few months later, the Jaruzelski government may have regretted terminating its jamming. In April and May 1988 a series of strikes took place, sparked by the February 1 price rise, the largest since the martial law.[266] The Ministry of Internal Affairs believed that RFE had played a major role in bringing on the protests. "An analysis of RFE programs in April reveals," reads a Security Service paper, "that this station's earlier programs undeniably suggested that strike actions should begin. On April 6 of this year, for instance, an economic program about economic issues encouraged—directly—fighting for wage increases (because their increase 'only marginally affects the rise of costs and prices'), reassuring potential strike participants ('the authorities and the management are really afraid of the workers')." Once the strikes began, RFE played a very important role in sustaining and spreading them: "The massed sabotage propaganda campaign (in which RFE played a leading role) was evidently directed at popularizing the existing strikes, supporting the strike actions under way, disseminating, stimulating, and initiating the striking mood (or moods of protest and dissatisfaction) among the working crews."[267]

The last anti-RFE propaganda offensive in People's Poland originated from an idea presented by government spokesman Jerzy Urban. During his June 21, 1988, press conference, he offered to go to Munich and take part in a public debate with commentators from RFE's Polish desk. He also invited them to Warsaw, where they would take part in an on-air discussion on Polish Radio's Program V, which broadcast abroad.[268]

Urban's proposal came a few days after Polish Television had aired a film about the Gontarczyks. On the one hand, Warsaw was continuing its propaganda assault on RFE, while on the other it was making a show of Jaruzelski's "new" attitude, unafraid of discussion. Polish propaganda publicized Urban's offer. *Życie Warszawy* wrote about submitting RFE to "a test of truth,"[269] while *Sztandar Młodych* asked, "Will RFE pick up the gauntlet?"[270] *Żołnierz Wolności* made no effort to coin a new type of polemics in its attack on RFE and responded to Urban's suggestion in traditional martial-law style. The soldiers' daily thus named RFE "a dinosaur of McCarthyism" and accused it of being paid in dollars to conduct "anti-Polish activities": "basically encouraging anxiety among the population in late April–early May [the workers' strikes—P. M.], attempts to stick political characteristics onto economic events, propagating scenarios of events that had been invented in Munich and elsewhere."[271]

RFE/Radio Liberty president Gene Pell responded to Urban on the very same day. In a statement broadcast by RFE, he accepted the offer and invited Urban to Munich. Pell did not consult the Polish desk before doing it, which ignited a conflict.[272] Polish propaganda then spent the next three months publicizing each new development in this saga and exposing the internal disputes at the radio, which it presented as a symptom of weakness and fear of discussion.

Pell's positive response to Urban's offer generated a true rebellion among RFE's Poles. People pointed out in stormy discussions that Jerzy Urban was the personification of martial law's worst lies and manipulation and that he therefore could not be treated as a discussion partner. Staffers charged management with violating the principle of partnership, which presupposed a joint discussion of the most important issues concerning Poland. The government in exile in London and chairman of the Polish American Congress Alojzy Mazewski were among the émigré and Polonia authorities backing up the Polish desk.[273] "To the Poles, Jerzy Urban is what a red rag is to a bull. He has no right to challenge anyone to a duel since the honor code in Poland does not allow people to shake hands with him because he has taken himself out of society," wrote *Dziennik Polski,* the most important émigré paper in London.[274]

As a result of these stands, RFE's management toned down its position. Pell stopped inviting Urban to a studio discussion and instead suggested meeting somewhere in Munich. This gathering would include invited representatives of the Polish opposition, and a transcript of the discussion would be aired by RFE and Polish Radio. Pell also rejected Urban's suggestion that the discussion be aired by Polish Radio's overseas program. "Reciprocity demands that any visit of RFE representatives to Poland include a radio discussion to be broadcast in its entirety on Warsaw's domestic service," read Pell's letter to Urban.[275]

To Warsaw, the confusion that Urban's offer introduced into the enemy camp was very convenient, and the government tried to use it for propaganda. The top officials, including General Jaruzelski, developed a strategy. In early July 1988, Urban informed Jaruzelski of "the growing conflict between RFE's American management and the Polish Section's team." He explained his intentions: "I therefore want to worsen this conflict, as well as sustain the atmosphere of an offensive vis-à-vis RFE."[276]

The party leadership created a team to plan and coordinate actions toward RFE. The team was made up of Urban, Jan Bisztyga (also an intelligence officer), and Jarosław Pachowski from the Propaganda Department of the CC PUWP, Stefan Staniszewski of the Foreign Ministry, Colonel Aleksander Makowski, head of Section XI, Department I, of the Ministry of Internal Affairs charged with fighting RFE, and Janusz Kolczyński, an associate professor at the Academy of Social Sciences of the CC PUWP. In its inaugural meeting, the team agreed that Urban's proposal was "a manifestation of a shift from fighting the sabotage radio defensively to offensively and reducing its influence. These actions are needed especially since the end of jamming and RFE's adoption of the practice of freely telephoning people in Poland and in this way acquiring interviews, statements, and information."

The team remarked on the possibility that Urban's initiative could lead to disorientation or even opposition from party activists: "RFE has been and remains defined by us as a sabotage-espionage organization whose activity violates international law, journalistic integrity, and the principles of the free flow of information, as well as Poland's national interest. A visit to RFE by an official representative of the Polish government would therefore unexpectedly ennoble this radio station and recognize it as a de facto partner . . . it needs to be explained right away, through intraparty channels, that this action is an offensive against RFE and not its recognition or ennoblement."

The team expected Urban's visit to Munich to yield important political and propaganda benefits. It would intensify the conflict between the American management and the Polish staff and give ammunition to those people in the West who were questioning the purpose of RFE's further existence in an era of warming East-West relations and progressive dialogue. Their plan foresaw Urban meeting in Munich "with RFE's American leadership . . . without the participation of representatives of the Polish Section, so to speak over the heads of the Munich Poles." At this meeting Urban would present "documented argumentation on the question of RFE's activity for Poland, including legal arguments, BIB guidelines in Washington, and RFE's actions defying American guidelines." Urban was to present not only the stick of the traditional charges against the Polish Section but also the carrot of allowing an RFE correspondent to be accredited in Warsaw, on the condition that RFE "begin to lose its sabotage character."

The most important assumption in the Munich debate scenario was that "J. Urban alone should go into the dispute with the entire journalistic collective of the RFE Polish Section, on the principle of 1 against 100. This placement for Urban will win him sympathy in the Polish public opinion and the international opinion." The group assumed that a television crew led by the editor Tadeusz Zakrzewski would record the discussion. The government spokesman's main task was to steer the discussion in such a direction as to concentrate fully on RFE's activity. "Examples of RFE's negative activity should be selected in such a way as to present its morally repulsive and professionally reprehensible deeds in contrast to the norms in force in the West and in the definition of the part of society that is politically unfriendly to us. . . . In his initial statement, J. Urban will also aim to confront RFE's line with East-West policies and Washington's official line. Perhaps by proving that RFE's line contains a hidden attack against the Democrats, we will succeed in causing a conflict between RFE and the Congress."

The team also developed an idea that would give the government spokesman the last word on every question: "We need to negotiate up front that because J. Urban is facing some 100 RFE journalists alone he has the right to respond to every one of their statements. The tactics of his responses should lie in constantly returning to RFE's activity as the subject of the meeting and preventing the meeting from being transformed into a mass attack on the situation in Poland."[277]

General Jaruzelski responded to the team's strategy with handwritten comments and corrections. His remark on the planned response to RFE president Gene Pell was "Good."[278] The team focused mostly on the benefits of accrediting an RFE journalist to Poland. In a separate letter to General Jaruzelski, Urban argued that "the accreditation of an RFE correspondent in Warsaw would have a calming and restraining effect on RFE's program line, it would impose on them the obligation to confirm various news with us, make it easier to keep an eye on some of their contacts, and so on."[279]

But despite these very careful preparations, the Munich debate continued to be pushed into the future. Urban used the next few press conferences to talk about his correspondence with RFE's American management and charge it and the Polish Service with being afraid of a debate. "I can guarantee that I will not do anything to anyone on the Polish staff, I will not insult anyone, bite anyone, so there is no reason to be so terribly afraid of the Polish government spokesman," he said in his distinctive style on August 9, 1988. He also cited the findings of public opinion research, according to which 39 percent of Poles approved of the idea of Urban's trip to Munich, while 10 percent opposed it.[280]

In the end, Urban declined Pell's offer to meet only with the American managers and, instead of a general debate, to have a discussion with a small group of invited persons, which would be taped outside RFE. "I can therefore declare that Free Europe is afraid of a public discussion and is shirking it," Urban charged in his statement, which was picked up by the mass media. "This fear and this unwillingness by Free Europe to engage in a dialogue and in a confrontation of views are dressed up in beautiful statements about the freedom of speech and the willingness to exchange ideas freely and openly. Free Europe claims that it represents the free world, while we put a muzzle on the flow of ideas. But it is only facts, not verbal declarations, that testify to the real openness and freedom of this American radio in Munich."[281]

Yet not even the deftest moves by Jerzy Urban could stop the flow of events unfavorable to the Polish government or push RFE onto the political defensive for long. During the roundtable talks and the campaign for the June 4 parliamentary elections, RFE's Polish Service telephoned opposition activists and Solidarity Citizens' Committee candidates daily. On May 9, 1989, the new government spokesman, Zbysław Rykowski, attacked RFE, saying that the "Citizens' Committee has got its own station." On May 29, a few days before the elections, the Government Press Office criticized RFE for interfering in the election campaign by choosing its candidates.[282]

After considering it, the Polish government decided not to accredit an RFE correspondent for the election campaign.[283] But already in mid-June, an RFE man came to Warsaw for the first time in the history of the radio. It was Maciej Morawski, who obtained accreditation to cover French president François Mitterrand's visit. A short time later, *Tygodnik Powszechny* published a long interview with the director of the Polish desk, Marek Łatyński,[284] who arrived in Poland on July 7 as one of the journalists reporting on President George

H. W. Bush's visit.[285] In August, the *Polityka* party weekly published excerpts from a very long interview with former director Zdzisław Najder, who had been sentenced to death in 1983.[286] Also in August, Jan Nowak-Jeziorański, whom People's Poland had fought for years with great energy and perseverance, arrived in his homeland for the first time since World War II.[287]

Yet despite all these signs that RFE was being treated as a "normal" radio station, the Ministry of Internal Affairs continued to perceive it as a political enemy. As late as September 5, 1989, the Security Service prepared another one of its regular studies of RFE's programs, with analyses of its scripts critical of the PUWP.[288] This is the last record created by the Communist security apparatus about RFE—apart from the log of destroyed documents—that current efforts have been able to locate.

RFE director A. Ross Johnson and BIB representatives came to Warsaw in early October to discuss the opening of an official RFE office in Warsaw with representatives of the new government of Tadeusz Mazowiecki.[289] As preparations were being made to open it in May 1990, the Ministry of Internal Affairs, still headed by General Czesław Kiszczak, had its paper shredders running twenty-four hours a day.

Among the papers destroyed on December 12, 1989, were Department I documents about RFE's interview office in Paris (code-named "Natręt"), RFE's London office (code-named "Wembley"), RFE's interview office in Brussels (code-named "Xurb"), RFE's interview office in Washington (code-named "Kant"), RFE's New York office (code-named "City"), and RFE's Paris office (code-named "Stol," the RFE correspondent's office, which was separate from the interview office), RFE's Rome office (code-named "Colosseum"), RFE's interview office in Bonn (code-named "Mobus"), RFE's interview office in Copenhagen (code-named "Parcel"), and RFE's Audience and Public Opinion Research Department (code-named "Trzmiel"). A day earlier, documents relating to the observation of Jan Nowak (code-named "Dygnitarz" [Dignitary]) were destroyed, and nearly three months earlier, on September 21, those of Inspectorate "I," charged with disinformation and disintegration actions aimed against the émigré community, were made to disappear.

Because these last two sets of records were wiped out, a reconstruction of the special actions conducted for many years against the longest-serving director of RFE's Polish Section can only be built on very patchy documentation. The destruction on January 15, 1990, of four volumes documenting the operations against RFE as an institution, code-named "Szerszenie" (Hornets), which could have been key to recreating the Ministry of Internal Affairs' actions against RFE, was the greatest loss. The day after Jan Nowak's papers were annihilated, documents about the operational inquiry of Jerzy Giedroyc (code-named "Proust"), the creator and longtime editor of the most important émigré periodical, *Kultura*, were sent to the shredder. On September 21, materials about the *Aneks* quarterly, another important émigré publication, were liquidated. A committee made up of three Department I employees determined that the records "were of no operational or historical value, and were therefore slotted for destruction."[290]

Historians may disagree. This book could have been quite different had these records survived. Instead of having to resort to questions and hypotheses, it would have been possible to reconstruct the story of the Polish Communist government's war against RFE much more comprehensively.

Conclusion

The story of the Polish Communist government's battles against RFE and other Western radio stations plays into two historical processes. First, it constitutes part of the narrative of the Cold War, the confrontation between the West and the Soviet bloc, in which rivalries in the fields of information, ideology, and culture were a crucial element. As the Communist ideological offensive rolled out in the West and the totalitarian states in East-Central Europe were being molded in isolation from outside influences in the second half of the 1940s and the first half of the 1950s, the competition over information and ideas became significant to the Western world. The powers in the Kremlin and its satellites appreciated the importance of this confrontation. It would last, with varying intensity and conducted by varying methods, until the end of the Cold War.

The second historical process took place inside the world of Communist dictatorship, which fought to win and maintain control over the minds of its citizens and the channels of information and ideas, to reduce or eliminate the external influences it viewed as a threat to its system's stability, and to sustain the mechanisms that guaranteed its grip on its citizens' lives. The universe of a dictatorship is by its very nature closed, as it aims to isolate its people from rival political, ideological, and sometimes even cultural models. The Communist parties' and regimes' totalitarian ambitions strengthened this tendency. They viewed RFE and other Western radios not only as an external enemy but also as a real internal threat, one that offered considerable support and actual inspiration to the opposition at home and to ideas that challenged the political and ideological orthodoxy.

The Communist regime was defeated in both these intertwined respects, the Cold War and the internal competition over information and ideological monopoly. The contribution that RFE and the other Western radios made to its defeat cannot, of course, be quantified. But if we take into account the size of their audiences and the magnitude of the measures put in place to combat them, these stations were more than marginal. One indicator we know of is that in the mid-1950s, more electric power and funding may have been appropriated for jamming Western radios than for broadcasting Polish Radio programs. Indeed, the Communist system's lengthy and exorbitant spending on its war with RFE, just one of its enemies, makes it clear that this political system was incapable of functioning efficiently and of guaranteeing its citizenry a decent standard of living.

People who could not come to terms with the reality of People's Poland and sought alternative sources of knowledge about their own country and the rest of the world listened to Western radio. At the pinnacle of Stalinism, RFE and the other foreign broadcasters were, together with the Catholic Church, their principal source of ideals and values, constituting a crack in the body of official information and the ideological order. In moments of crisis, such as December 1970 or, especially, the summer of 1980, RFE's programs were a crucial source of information for protesters and strikers. Without these programs, the spread of strikes in August 1980 and the concurrence of demands made by workers across the country would certainly have been more difficult to achieve. Yet it was not only people who viewed the Communist system unfavorably who listened to RFE, but also members of the ruling group. The best evidence of this are the revelations made in Józef Światło's broadcasts on RFE, which caused a veritable political earthquake in 1954–1955. In the 1960s, RFE became powerfully engaged in the internal situation of the ruling camp by unmasking and attacking the nationalist Partisan faction, which it viewed as a major threat to Poland. An idea cherished by Jerzy Giedroyc, editor in chief of the most important Polish émigré periodical, *Kultura*, of creating a "revisionist Free Europe" in Belgrade was a particular recognition of the radio's influence on the thinking of the Communist elites. RFE's programs were addressed primarily to those groups within the PUWP that favored liberalizing the system without departing from Marxism or from the belief in the party's leading role.[1]

It is paradoxical that the war against RFE—especially that conducted by the security apparatus—intensified during the period of relative stability of the 1960s and the first part of Edward Gierek's decade of the 1970s. The latter was most likely the longest period of social peace in the history of People's Poland, of subsiding conflicts and of broad support for the government. After an organized opposition appeared in the second half of the 1970s, the government placed its challenge of the radio on a back burner. This resembled 1956 and the period immediately following it, when the system suffered an acute crisis and took several years to regain its dominance. Whenever an internal threat disappeared or significantly diminished, the tendency would resurface to intensify the fight against this external enemy, which escaped the government's control and shattered its information monopoly. The ruling party would then attempt to increase its sway over the peoples' minds by eliminating influences it considered foreign or hostile to its system. One interpretation is that the security apparatus sought out enemies in order to maintain its ranks in a state of mobilization and to strengthen its position within the power structure. More broadly, this mechanism was a symptom of the ruling group's totalitarian tendency, even after 1956 (of course, in a less harsh form): always striving to win control over new areas of life and eliminating—or at least limiting—what it saw as antisystemic.

Andrzej Walicki, Dariusz Jarosz, and most recently Błażej Brzostek and Marcin Zaremba have argued that the paradigm of "totalitarianism" does not match the reality of post-1956 Poland. There was no more mass terror and no more all-encompassing, expansive ideology or popular mobilization aiming to implement the regime's political and ideological goals.[2] Yet if we broaden the classic definition of totalitarianism beyond concepts constructed on the foundations of the exceptional, and actually quite brief, experiences of the Third Reich and Stalinism, after 1956 we also find totalitarian mechanisms in the Polish reality, which was a system with fundamental elements rooted in the 1940s and early 1950s. These totalitarian tendencies and ambitions were still visible inside the power apparatus as late as the middle or late periods of People's Poland, the 1960s or even 1970s and 1980s.

The degree of state control over people's lives is a key category for a stable Communist system emerging from a period of terror and mass mobilization. This degree of control was far greater in Communism than in states classified as classic authoritarian regimes: the right-wing dictatorships such as those in interwar East-Central Europe (for instance, Admiral Miklós Horthy's Hungary) or Generalissimo Francisco Franco's Spain.[3] Thus, the constant efforts to limit the Western radios'—indeed, the West's—influence on the Polish population are a poignant illustration of the government's totalitarian or, for those who prefer this term, post-totalitarian ambitions, as it never put down its arms in the battle for its citizens' minds.

The obvious question is, did the Polish government's persistent efforts yield the intended weakening of RFE and its influence on Poland? Jamming certainly made it difficult to listen to foreign radio, as had the Stalinist-era persecution of those who organized group listening sessions or talked about what they had heard. But this system was never fully effective, and even at the peak of Stalinism people continued to listen to foreign stations en masse. RFE probably had its greatest victory in the mid-1950s with the influence of Józef Światło's broadcasts on the situation inside Poland. The repeated demands in 1956 to end jamming and protesters' destruction of jamming equipment in Poznań in June 1956 and in Bydgoszcz in November 1956 were a gauge of the importance of foreign broadcasts to the Poles. Indeed, the student rallies in Czechoslovakia in the spring of 1956 presented the same demands.[4]

Warsaw's subsequent efforts also failed to eliminate the radio's influence. The regime believed that it had scored a victory after its massive strike against RFE in the early 1970s. In the wake of the Czechowicz affair, Minister of Internal Affairs Franciszek Szlachcic contended that "thanks to the policies of our party, improved information systems, better outcomes of the work of the Ministry of Internal Affairs and, most important, our intelligence . . . we have contributed to the fact that for the first time in many years the sabotage centers are on the defensive."[5] The government emphasized the dramatic drop in the number of letters written to RFE from Poland, from 1,986 in the first quarter of 1971 to 279 in the second quarter and 140 in the fourth: "This decrease can be attributed largely to the propaganda action conducted in 1971 by the mass media as a result of the return to Poland of Captain A. Czechowicz and the documented uncovering of the forms and methods of RFE's sabotage activities. As a result of these political-operational efforts, the effectiveness of RFE has been weakened, the groups from which information has flown to that center have been narrowed," assessed a ministry paper in February 1972.[6]

Even if this last statement was true, these actions did not diminish RFE's long-term impact on the situation in Poland or the number of Poles willing to supply information to it. Włodzimierz Odojewski, a well-known novelist and head of RFE's Polish literary program between 1972 and 1989, created a network of more than 160 literary figures who contributed news, commentaries, and their own writing. This initiative took place after the largest propaganda campaign, which aimed to intimidate those who may have wanted to make contact with foreign organizations.[7]

The Polish government-sponsored opinion polls cited earlier show clearly that the size of RFE audiences grew as the economic crisis deepened, the public mood worsened, and political tensions mounted. And even the most carefully wrought secret police plans could do nothing about it. As far as we know, Polish intelligence also failed to recruit a single important player from within RFE's Polish Service. All the agents discussed in this book were second- or even third-tier employees. This meant that Poland's secret police never managed to win real influence over the station's programmatic line or any of its major decisions. Department I functionaries claimed that their operations bolstered antagonisms among the staff, but there is no evidence of a pivotal role.

The Ministry of Internal Affairs did help worsen the conflicts under the directorships of Jan Nowak and Zdzisław Najder, but those clashes would certainly have existed without the ministry's manipulation and operations.

One can argue that in the early 1970s, intelligence operations, combined with propaganda attacks and diplomatic interventions, did have some tangible effects, for they both deepened the mood of uncertainty among RFE's staff about the station's future and supplied ammunition to the radio's opponents (such as Senator Fulbright, who used Czechowicz's "revelations" and documents forged by the Polish secret police) and promoters of détente who regarded the radio unfavorably. The latter indeed brought about real budget cuts, significant personnel reductions, and the closing of some of the radio's field offices, which Czechowicz had attacked so fiercely as espionage outposts. But RFE itself was not closed down, as Warsaw had sought. It also cannot be denied that the large-scale disintegration and disinformation efforts of the early 1970s against Jan Nowak made both his personal life and the management of his staff difficult, since they armed his enemies in the Polish Service and ended up being one of the reasons for his departure. But even if we consider this a Security Service success, Nowak's departure was not very significant in the long term, since RFE under Nowak's successors continued to be a thorn in the Polish government's side.

The Polish Communist regime's most important goals in its battle against RFE included limiting its access to Poland and to its contacts there. Its methods included jamming, intercepting correspondence, harassing people who listened to it (in the 1950s), and, most important, persecuting those who supplied information to it. These projects were the domain of the security police and did not require difficult operations outside Poland. Yet their results were also only partly successful and were difficult to quantify, regardless of all the studies presented by the Ministry of Public Security or the Ministry of Internal Affairs. Jamming made the radio more difficult to hear, and the harassment and propaganda assaults put off some potential listeners and informants from Poland, yet at no time did the government manage to reduce the number of listeners radically (the constant pre-1956 expansion of the jamming system is evidence that there were gaps in it) or to cut RFE off from information coming from Poland. As long as the People's Republic of Poland existed, RFE fulfilled the mission for which it had been created: challenging the Communist monopoly of information.

The story of the Polish government's battle against RFE also persuasively illustrates Poland's lack of sovereignty. In 1950 it was the Soviet Council of Ministers that made the decision to jam Polish-language Western broadcasting, without consulting the Poles. The jamming system was created with Soviet specialists as supervisors. Between 1956 and 1970, RFE's Polish programs were jammed with equipment located not in Poland but in the Soviet Union and other Soviet bloc countries. Warsaw's decision to stop jamming the radio in 1987 required the Kremlin's approval.

All the countries of the Soviet bloc struggled with Western radio. The methods they used were similar: jamming, propaganda, diplomatic initiatives, and security police actions, both as intelligence operations in the West and as repressions of people at home who were in contact with the Western stations or, in some periods and in some countries, of those who merely listened. In many cases, the changes in the phases of the battle against RFE and the other broadcasters reflected the periods of liberalization and constriction in domestic politics and policies toward the West. Thus, the Gomułka government's suspension of jamming in 1956 was a feature of de-Stalinization and of opening Poland to contacts with the outside world, while stepping up the fight against RFE in the early 1960s showed the policy of "tightening the screw" domestically and limiting the Poles' contacts with the outside world. In Romania, too, interrupting the jamming of foreign radios in the 1960s was intended to demonstrate dissent from the Soviet model and to exhibit the liberal image of the local Communists. At that point, Nicolae Ceauşescu invited the director of RFE's Romanian Service for a visit, a gesture unprecedented in the history of the Soviet bloc. Remarkably, jamming was not resumed even in the 1980s, when the repressiveness of the government of "the genius of the Carpathians" went unmatched in the Communist camp. It came from Ceauşescu's interest in maintaining good relations with the West and demonstrating Romanian Communism's divergence from the Soviet model.

The absence of complex comparative studies makes it difficult to relate the different Communist countries' efforts against Western radios. The primary sources consulted for this study support the hypothesis that Poland was in the vanguard of this struggle. Poland's position owed in part to the Communist system's shallower roots and less stability there than in most of the other countries. But because of this, the ability of this outside factor to support independent antisystem thinking must have worried the government. Also, characteristic of Poland was its exceptionally strong and dynamic political émigré community, which provided a natural backdrop and support for RFE. It appears that in the 1960s and first half of the 1970s the Polish government showed the way in the war against RFE. The propaganda campaign following Andrzej Czechowicz's return to Poland was the largest undertaking of its kind in the history of the Soviet bloc and would become a model for other countries.

In the early 1970s, according to the Western opinions quoted here, Czechoslovakia came second in terms of the dynamism of its special services. This stemmed from the enormous wave of emigration that followed the crushing of the Prague Spring. After the population was pacified, the émigré community, and RFE within it, became Prague's main enemy. Yet the most drastic actions against RFE did not come from either the Polish or the Czechoslovak security services. It was the Bulgarian secret service that stood behind the murder of Georgi Markov, while the bombing of RFE's headquarters in 1981 was the work of Carlos the Jackal, who had been hired by Romania's Securitate. It was probably Romania in the 1980s that most brutally repressed people who listened to RFE. The secret police of the Communist countries (except Romania's) cooperated in actions aimed against RFE and other foreign organizations they deemed to be engaging in sabotage. They exchanged information and documents acquired through operations and coordinated their diplomatic initiatives and propaganda campaigns. The system of jamming was grounded in cross-border cooperation, and its coordination and decision making on the most important issues lay in Moscow. We know the least about any joint operations of the special services. This is an issue that remains one of the best-guarded secrets, even after the fall of communism. Perhaps one day, historians will gain access to new documents and data, which will allow them to supplement and broaden the picture painted in this book.

Notes

Introduction

1. The fullest analysis of the results of the RFE audience research can be found in Jolanta Hajdasz, "Odbiór audycji Rozgłośni Polskiej RWE w Polsce" [Reception of the RFE Polish Service programs in Poland], *Pamięć i Sprawiedliwość* 6, no. 2 (2004): 309–28; Hajdasz, *Szczekaczka, czyli Rozgłośnia Polska Radia Wolna Europa* [A Nazi street loudspeaker, or the Polish Service of Radio Free Europe] (Poznań: Media Rodzina, 2006), 249–81. The first publication to quote OBOP data was Jerzy Morawski, "Raport spod głośników" [A report from under the loudspeakers], *Spotkania*, May 21–27, 1992.

2. On RFE's own audience research, see Lechosław Gawlikowski (with Yvette Neisser Moreno), "The Audience to Western Broadcasts to Poland during the Cold War," in *Cold War Broadcasting: Impact on the Soviet Union and Eastern Europe: A Collection of Studies and Documents*, ed. A. Ross Johnson and R. Eugene Parta (Budapest and New York: Central European University Press, 2010), 121–44.

3. Wojskowe Biuro Badań Socjologicznych [Military Office of Sociological Research], "Opinie kadry zawodowej i żołnierzy zasadniczej służby wojskowej o audycjach Radia 'Wolna Europa'" [The opinions of the professional cadre and soldiers of the basic military service about the programs of Radio "Free Europe"], ed. Col. Dr. Hab. Lesław Wojtasik, Maj. Krzysztof Romanowicz, and Capt. Marian Cieślarczyk, February 1978.

4. Wojskowe Biuro Badań Socjologicznych, "Opinie kadry zawodowej i żołnierzy zasadniczej służby wojskowej o audycjach Radia 'Wolna Europa'" [The opinions of the professional cadre and soldiers of the basic military service about the programs of Radio "Free Europe"], ed. Col. Dr. Hab. Lesław Wojtasik, Lt. Col. Zygmunt Surdyk, Lt. Col. Krzysztof Romanowicz, and Capt. Marian Cieślarczyk, October 1979.

5. Wojskowe Biuro Badań Socjologicznych, "Stosunek kadry zawodowej i żołnierzy zasadniczej służby wojskowej do działalności zachodnich rozgłośni radiowych nadających program w języku polskim (badania porównawcze)" [The attitudes of the professional cadre and soldiers of the basic military service toward the activities of the Western radio stations broadcasting in Polish (a comparative study)], ed. Lt. Col. Lesław Małowiejski, September 1983.

6. Wojskowe Biuro Badań Socjologicznych, "Zasięg oddziaływania zachodnich polskojęzycznych rozgłośni radiowych na środowisko wojskowe" [The effects of the broadcasting of Polish-language radio stations on the military milieu], ed. Lt. Col. Lesław Małowiejski, August 1988.

7. Wojskowe Biuro Badań Socjologicznych, "Stosunek kadry zawodowej i żołnierzy zasadniczej służby wojskowej do działalności zachodnich rozgłośni radiowych nadających program w języku polskim (badania porównawcze)" [The attitudes of the professional cadre and soldiers of the basic military service toward the activities of the Western radio stations broadcasting in Polish (a comparative study)], ed. Lt. Col. Lesław Małowiejski, September 1983.

8. Maciej J. Drygas, "Fale w eter" [Waves into the ether], *Karta* 38 (2003): 108.

9. Ibid., 109.

10. Ibid., 115, 121.

11. Piotr Zaremba, *Młodopolacy. Historia Ruchu Młodej Polski* [The Young Poles: A history of the Young Poland Movement] (Gdańsk: Arche, 2000), 75. In June 1976, workers in several Polish cities protested against increased food prices. The authorities responded by using police force and organizing public meetings that condemned those taking part in strikes and street demonstrations.

12. Drygas, "Fale w eter," 119.

13. Renata Metzger, "Radom '76. Żebyście wiedzieli jak bili" [Radom '76: So that you will know how they beat people], *Gazeta Wyborcza*, June 23, 2006.

14. Jerzy Morawski, "Trzeci obieg towarzyszy" [The second underground of comrades], *Rzeczpospolita*, December 11, 2003.

15. Jane Curry's interview with Stanisław Ciosek, February 2003, Jane Curry Collection, Hoover Institution on War, Revolution and Peace (hereafter Hoover Institution), Palo Alto, CA.

16. Henryk Birecki, a diplomat in People's Poland who left Poland in the late 1960s, claimed that this was true. Jan Nowak-Jeziorański, *Polska z oddali. Wspomnienia* [Poland from afar: A memoir], vol. 2, *1956–1976* (Cracow: Znak, 1992), 340.

17. Author's interview with Andrzej Werblan, Warsaw, April 5, 2007.

18. Krzysztof Persak, *Sprawa Henryka Hollanda* [The case of Henryk Holland] (Warsaw: Instytut Studiów Politycznych PAN, Instytut Pamięci Narodowej, 2006), 280.

19. Nestor Ratesh, "Radio Free Europe's Impact in Romania During the Cold War," in Johnson and Parta, *Cold War Broadcasting*, 211–12.

20. Jane Curry's interview with Stanisław Ciosek, December 2003, Jane Curry Collection, Hoover Institution.

21. Archiwum Akt Nowych [Central Archive of Modern Records], Warsaw, Komitet Centralny Polskiej Zjednoczonej Partii Robotniczej [Central Committee of the Polish United Workers' Party, PZPR], 973/244, Notatka Andrzeja Wasilewskiego dla Wojciecha Jaruzelskiego [Note from Andrzej Wasilewski to Wojciech Jaruzelski], December 8, 1988; ibid., Transkrypt nasłuchu audycji Aliny Grabowskiej z 19 XI 1988 r. [Transcript of Alina Grabowska's program of November 19, 1988].

22. Jane Leftwich Curry, "Radio Free Europe in the Eyes of the Polish Communist Elite," in Johnson and Parta, *Cold War Broadcasting*, 157.

23. Władysław Bieńkowski, *Motory i hamulce socjalizmu* [Socialism's engines and brakes] (Paris: Instytut Literacki, 1968), 98–99.

Chapter 1

1. Fouad Benhalla, *La guerre radiophonique* (Paris: PUF, 1983), 33; Burton Paulu, *Radio and Television Broadcasting in Eastern Europe* (Minneapolis: University of Minnesota Press, 1974), 199.

2. Paulu, *Radio and Television Broadcasting in Eastern Europe*, 32–36; E. C. Król, *Propaganda i indoktrynacja narodowego socjalizmu w Niemczech 1919–1945. Studium organizacji, treści i technik masowego oddziaływania* [National Socialism's propaganda and indoctrination in Germany, 1919–1945: A study of the organization, contents and techniques of mass influence] (Warsaw: Instytut Studiów Politycznych PAN and Rytm, 1999), 5, 19.

3. Paulu, *Radio and Television Broadcasting in Eastern Europe*, 200.

4. Michael Nelson, *War of the Black Heavens: The Battles of Western Broadcasting in the Cold War* (Syracuse, NY: Syracuse University Press, 1997), 3.

5. Horst J. P. Bergmeier and Rainer E. Lotz, *Hitler's Airwaves: The Inside Story of Nazi Radio Broadcasting and Propaganda Swing* (New Haven, CT: Yale University Press, 1997), 22.

6. Przemysław Hauser, "Mniejszość niemiecka na Pomorzu i w Wielkopolsce w okresie międzywojennym" [The German minority in Pomerania and Greater Poland in the interwar period], in *Bydgoszcz 3–4 września 1939. Studia i dokumenty* [Bydgoszcz, September 3–4, 1939: Studies and documents], ed.Tomasz Chinciński and Paweł Machcewicz (Warsaw: Instytut Pamięci Narodowej, 2008), 54.

7. Nelson, *War of the Black Heavens*, 4–5.

8. Ibid., 6; see also Asa Briggs, *The History of Broadcasting in the United Kingdom*, vol. 3, *The War of Words, 1939–1945* (London: Oxford University Press, 1970).

9. Bergmeier and Lotz, *Hitler's Airwaves*, 22.

10. Maciej Józef Kwiatkowski, *Polskie Radio w konspiracji 1939–1944* [Polish underground radio, 1939–1944] (Warsaw: Państwowy Instytut Wydawniczy, 1989), 82–85.

11. K. R. M. Short, ed., *Western Broadcasting over the Iron Curtain* (New York: St. Martin's Press, 1986), 98.

12. Kwiatkowski, *Polskie Radio w konspiracji 1939–1944*, 33.

13. Rafał Habielski, "Kurier z Londynu" [Courier from London], *Tygodnik Powszechny* 7, February 12, 2006. For a discussion of the BBC's Polish Section, see Krzysztof Pszenicki, *Tu mówi Londyn. Historia Sekcji Polskiej BBC* [This is London: A history of the BBC Polish Section] (Warsaw: Rosner and Wspólnicy, 2009).

14. Kwiatkowski, *Polskie Radio w konspiracji 1939–1944*, 33–36.

15. Ibid., 88–90. For a discussion of Świt radio, see Tadeusz Kochanowicz, *Na wojennej emigracji. Wspomnienia z lat 1942–1944* [In wartime exile: Reminiscences from 1942–1944] (Warsaw: Książka i Wiedza, 1975); Stefan Korboński, *W imieniu Rzeczpospolitej* [In the name of the Republic] (Warsaw: Instytut Pamięci Narodowej, 2009), 218–29.

16. Ludwik Landau, *Kronika lat wojennych i okupacji* [A chronicle of the years of war and occupation], vol. 1, *Wrzesień 1939–listopad 1940* [September 1939–November 1940] (Warsaw: Państwowe Wydawnictwo Naukowe, 1962), 26.

17. Tomasz Głowiński, *O nowy porządek europejski. Ewolucja hitlerowskiej propagandy politycznej wobec Polaków w Generalnym Gubernatorstwie 1939–1945* [For

a new European order: The evolution of Nazi political propaganda for the Poles in the Generalgouvernement, 1939–1945] (Wrocław: Wydawnictwo Uniwersytetu Wrocławskiego, 2000), 51–52.

18. Kwiatkowski, *Polskie Radio w konspiracji 1939–1944*, 13.

19. Grzegorz Mazur, *Biuro Informacji i Propagandy SZP-ZWZ-AK 1939–1945* [Bureau of Information and Propaganda of the SZP-ZWZ-AK 1939–1945] (Warsaw: Instytut Wydawniczy PAX, 1987), 47–48; Kwiatkowski, *Polskie Radio w konspiracji 1939–1944*, 16.

20. Piotr Kładoczny, *Prawo jako narzędzie represji w Polsce Ludowej 1944–1956. Prawna analiza kategorii przestępstw przeciwko państwu* [The law as a tool of repression in People's Poland, 1944–1956: A legal analysis of the categories of offenses against the state] (Warsaw: Instytut Pamięci Narodowej, 2004), 357–58.

21. Robert Maciejowski, "Kara śmierci za radio" [Capital punishment for a radio], *Biuletyn Instytutu Pamięci Narodowej* 11 (2001): 22–23.

22. Kwiatkowski, *Polskie Radio w konspiracji 1939–1944*, 69–72; Tomasz Szarota, *V—jak zwycięstwo. Symbole, znaki i demonstracje patriotyczne walczącej Europy 1939–1945* [V like victory: The symbols, signs and patriotic demonstrations in fighting Europe, 1939–1945] (Warsaw: Wydawnictwa Szkolne i Pedagogiczne, 1994).

23. Frédéric Brunnquell, *Fréquence monde: Du poste colonial à RFI* (Paris: Hachette, 1991), 61–64.

24. Ibid., 59.

25. Król, *Propaganda i indoktrynacja narodowego socjalizmu*, 303–4.

26. Ibid., 290, 297–99; Nelson, *War of the Black Heavens*, 10–11.

27. Król, *Propaganda i indoktrynacja narodowego socjalizmu*, 301–2; Nelson, *War of the Black Heavens*, 8; Bergmeier and Lotz, *Hitler's Airwaves*, 99–110.

28. Bergmeier and Lotz, *Hitler's Airwaves*, 73–79.

29. Short, *Western Broadcasting over the Iron Curtain*, 99.

30. For the genesis and beginnings of the Cold War, see Herbert Feis, *From Trust to Terror: The Onset of the Cold War 1945–1950* (New York: Norton, 1970); John Lewis Gaddis, *The Cold War: A New History* (New York: Penguin Press, 2005); Melvyn Leffler and David S. Painter, *Origins of the Cold War: An International History* (New York: Routledge, 2005).

31. Alan L. Heil Jr., *Voice of America: A History* (New York: Columbia University Press, 2003), 47.

32. Jacques Semelin, *La liberté au bout des ondes: Du coup de Prague à la chute du mur de Berlin* (Paris: Belfond, 2009), 39–42.

33. Christian F. Ostermann, "The United States, the East German Uprising of 1953 and the Limits of Rollback," Cold War International History Project, Working Paper 11 (Washington, DC: Woodrow Wilson International Center for Scholars, 1994), 14.

34. José M. Faraldo, "Rewolta wnuków" [The grandchildren's rebellion], *Tygodnik Powszechny* 30, July 23, 2006.

35. Nelson, *War of the Black Heavens*, 10, 20–21.

36. Hoover Institution, Radio Free Europe/Radio Liberty, Corporate Records, box 380.1, Recent Developments in the Jamming of Western Radio Stations Broadcasting to the USSR and Eastern Europe.

37. Walter L. Hixson, *Parting the Curtain: Propaganda, Culture and the Cold War, 1945–1961* (Houndmills, UK: Macmillan, 1997), 35.

38. Paulu, *Radio and Television Broadcasting in Eastern Europe*, 36–37, 70–71. The number of radios continued to grow quickly in the Soviet Union, naturally increasing the size of potential audiences for foreign programs. In 1950 there were 3.6 million radios in the Soviet Union; in 1960, 9.7 million; and in 1970, 27.8 million.

39. Jolanta Hajdasz, *Szczekaczka, czyli Rozgłośnia Polska Radia Wolna Europa* [A Nazi street loudspeaker, or the Polish Service of Radio Free Europe] (Poznań: Media Rodzina, 2006); Jerzy Myśliński, *Mikrofon i polityka: Z dziejów radiofonii polskiej 1944–1960* [The microphone and politics: A history of Polish radio, 1944–1960] (Warsaw: Instytut Badań Literackich, 1990), 234–35.

40. Nelson, *War of the Black Heavens*, 13.

41. Habielski, "Kurier z Londynu."

42. See a comprehensive study of the history of the Polish Section of Radio France by Gabriel Garçon, *La Radio Française parle le polonais: Histoire des émissions en langue polonaise de la Radiodiffusion Française (1932–1974)* (Lille: Rayonnement culturel polonais, 1991).

43. Polish Institute and Sikorski Museum, London (hereafter IPMS), A11E/1272, Letter from Józef Potocki to Mieczysław Sokołowski, January 10, 1950; see also Krzysztof Tarka, *Emigracyjna dyplomacja. Polityka zagraniczna rządu RP na uchodźstwie 1945–1990* [The diplomacy of emigration: The foreign policy of the Polish government in exile, 1945–1990] (Warsaw: Rytm, 2003), 39–40.

44. IPMS, A11/E/1272, Letter from Potocki to Sokołowski, January 10, 1959.

45. Józef Łobodowski, "Tu mówi Madryt" [Madrid calling], *Zeszyty Historyczne* 54 (1980): 113–28.

46. IPMS, 408/156, Letter from Jan Starzewski to Zbigniew Stypułkowski, July 22, 1969.

47. "There were some short periods when we were warned about the necessity of maintaining a certain reserve or detachment in some areas. This was the case, for example, for a few weeks in the spring of this year, when this government was negotiating . . . the return of Spanish prisoners from the Soviet Union, and they recommended that we avoid direct attacks on the USSR in this period," Józef Potocki wrote in 1950 to the Foreign Ministry of the government in exile (IPMS, General Anders Collection, XLIX/1, Letter from Józef Potocki to Mieczysław Sokołowski, November 8, 1950).

48. IPMS, General Anders Collection, XX/3, Fragment of an RFE report regarding the second half of 1955, which was enclosed with a letter from Józef Potocki to General Władysław Anders, April 11, 1956.

49. See Andrzej Mania, *The National Security Council i amerykańska polityka wobec Europy Wschodniej 1945–1960* [The National Security Council and American policies toward Eastern Europe, 1945–1960] (Cracow: Wydawnictwo Uniwersytetu Jagiellońskiego, 1994); Paweł Machcewicz, "Polska i Europa Wschodnia w polityce Stanów Zjednoczonych w latach 1947–1956" [Poland and Eastern Europe in US policy in 1947–1956], presented at the XI Powszechny Zjazd Historyków Polskich [11th General Meeting of Polish Historians], *Pamiętnik* 3, part 2 (2000): 141–50.

50. Truman Library, Psychological Strategy Board, box 14, 091.412, section 1.

51. On the conception of psychological warfare and its place in US foreign policy during both World War II and the Cold War, see Robert T. Holt and Roger W. van de Velde, *Strategic Psychological Operations and American Foreign Policy* (Chicago: University of Chicago Press, 1960).

52. For a description of the Crusade for Freedom, see Richard H. Cummings, *Radio Free Europe's "Crusade for Freedom": Rallying Americans behind Cold War Broadcasting, 1950–1960* (Jefferson, NC: McFarland & Co., 2010); Józef Łaptos, "Miejsce 'krucjaty wolności' w amerykańskiej polityce wobec Europy Środkowo-Wschodniej (1949–1953)" [The Crusade for Freedom in US policy toward East-Central Europe (1949–1953)], Polska Akademia Umiejętności [Polish Academy of Learning], *Prace Komisji Środkowoeuropejskiej* 12 (2004): 103–25.

53. Semelin, *La liberté au bout des ondes*, 44.

54. A. Ross Johnson, *Radio Free Europe and Radio Liberty: The CIA Years and Beyond* (Washington, DC: Woodrow Wilson Center Press; Stanford, CA: Stanford University Press, 2010). For an analysis of the origins of the FEC and RFE, see Sig Mickelson, *America's Other Voice: The Story of Radio Free Europe and Radio Liberty* (New York: Praeger, 1983).

55. Lehman Suite and Papers, Rare Book and Manuscript Library, Columbia University, Frank Altschul Papers, Organization, 475, Policy Guidance memorandum no. 1, September 15, 1950.

56. Paweł Machcewicz, *Emigracja w polityce międzynarodowej* [Emigration in international politics], vol. 2 of *Druga Wielka Emigracja 1945–1990* [The second Great Emigration, 1945–1990] (Warsaw: Biblioteka "Więzi," 1999), 45–57.

57. Marek Rudzki, "Polska sekcja Radia Wolna Europa w Nowym Jorku" [Radio Free Europe's Polish Section in New York], *Zeszyty Historyczne* 133 (2000): 185–90.

58. Mickelson, *America's Other Voice*, 43–50.

59. Jan Nowak-Jeziorański wrote about the beginnings of his radio work in a book that I frequently refer to, *Wojna w eterze: Wspomnienia* [The war on the airwaves: A memoir] (London: Odnowa, 1986), volume 1 of his memoirs. His life under the German occupation is described in *Kurier z Warszawy* [Courier from Warsaw], which appeared in several editions abroad and in Poland. There is also much information about him in his biography by Jarosław Kurski, *Jan Nowak-Jeziorański. Emisariusz wolności* [Jan Nowak-Jeziorański: Emissary of freedom] (Warsaw: Bertelsmann Media, 2005).

60. Machcewicz, *Emigracja w polityce międzynarodowej*, 57.

61. Nowak-Jeziorański, *Wojna w eterze*, 52.

62. Hoover Institution, Stefan Korboński Papers, box 19, Letter from Stefan Korboński to the Executive Section of the Political Council, April 20, 1950.

63. Nowak-Jeziorański, *Wojna w eterze*, 46–48.

64. Hoover Institution, Stanisław Mikołajczyk Papers, box 19, Note from Stanisław Mikołajczyk on the advisory council (October 1952); ibid., Letter from Bolesław Biega to the Chief Executive Committee of the Polish Peasant Party, October 17, 1952.

65. Ibid., Polish Advisory Committee, Minutes of the First Meeting, October 16, 1952.

66. Ibid., Letter from Stefan Korboński to the Executive Section of the Political Council, April 9, 1952.

67. Ibid., Memorandum to RFE President Harold Miller, April 9, 1952.

68. *Myśl Polska*, May 15, 1952.

69. See Juliusz Mieroszewski (writing as Londyńczyk), "Głos Wolnej Polski" [The Voice of Free Poland], *Kultura* 6 (1952); Zygmunt Nagórski, Jr., "Sprawa polska w USA" [The Polish Question in the United States], *Kultura* 11 (1952); and a response from Jan Nowak and Stanisław Strzetelski in *Kultura* 1 (1953).

70. Nagórski, "Sprawa polska w USA," 12. For a study of the attitude of émigré groups to the launch of RFE's programs from Munich, see also Rafał Habielski, "Obawy i wątpliwości. Emigracja wobec inauguracji RWE" [Fears and doubts: The émigré community and RFE's inauguration," in *Pięćdziesiąt lat Rozgłośni Polskiej Radia Wolna Europa. Materiały sesji jubileuszowej* [50 years of the Polish Section of Radio Free Europe: Materials from an anniversary session], ed. Daria Nałęcz (Warsaw: Naczelna Dyrekcja Archiwów Państwowych, 2003), 64–74.

71. See, for instance, D. P., "Wolna Europa a emigracja polska" [Free Europe and the Polish émigré community], *Polityka* 42 (1959).

72. For an analysis of intelligence, see two articles by Andrzej Paczkowski in *Zeszyty Historyczne*, "Wywiad (cywilny) w PRL w 1955 r." [(Civilian) intelligence in the People's Republic of Poland in 1955] (150 [2004]: 129–53), and "Wywiad cywilny Polski komunistycznej, 1945–1989. Próba ogólnego zarysu" [Communist Poland's civilian intelligence, 1945–1989: An attempt at a general outline] (152 [2005]: 3–25). See also Leszek Pawlikowicz, *Tajny front zimnej wojny. Uciekinierzy z polskich służb specjalnych 1956–1964* [The secret front of the Cold War: Defectors from the Polish special services, 1956–1964] (Warsaw: Rytm, 2004), 50–51; Zbigniew Siemiątkowski, *Wywiad a władza. Wywiad cywilny w systemie sprawowania władzy politycznej PRL* [Intelligence and the government: Civilian intelligence in the PRP's system of exercising political power] (Warsaw: Oficyna Wydawnicza ASPA-JR, 2009), 85–87; Sławomir Cenckiewicz, *Długie ramię Moskwy. Wywiad wojskowy Polski Ludowej 1943–1991* [Moscow's long arm: The military intelligence of People's Poland, 1943–1991] (Poznań: Zysk i S-ka Wydawnictwo, 2011), 74–80.

73. Mickelson, *America's Other Voice*, 40; author's interview with James McCargar, from 1955 to 1958 a top official of the FEC, Washington, DC, March 5, 1998.

74. Author's interview with William Griffith, RFE's political adviser in Munich from 1951 to 1958, Budapest, September 26, 1996; author's interview with Paul Henze, deputy political adviser in Munich, Washington, May 7, 1998, and Stanford, CA, October 14, 2004; author's interviews with A. Ross Johnson, RFE director in 1988–1991, policy assistant for Poland from 1966 to 1969, Stanford, CA, October 13, 2004, and Washington, DC, February 2006; author's interview with John P. C. Matthews, RFE employee in the 1960s, Warsaw, October 19, 1996.

75. Nowak-Jeziorański, *Wojna w eterze*, 35, 96. See also the FEC's guidelines on the Oder-Neisse line, Eisenhower Library, C. D. Jackson Papers, box 80, NCFE-RFE-German Problem, RFE Oder-Neisse Policy, October 30, 1952.

76. On the guidelines adopted for setting up RFE's program, see Nowak-Jeziorański, *Wojna w eterze*, 69–81.

77. Kazimierz Zamorski described the early days and operation of the Research and Analysis Department and the work of RFE's outposts in his memoirs, *Pod anteną Radia Wolna Europa* [Under Radio Free Europe's antenna] (Poznań: Wydawnictwo Wers, 1995).

78. Jan Nowak-Jeziorański's archive (hereafter AJN), Memorandum to Lewis Galantiere, October 3, 1955; these views are developed further in another, undated memorandum from the same period: Remarks on Our Tactics During the "Thaw" (Liberalization of the Course) in Poland. I consulted these documents in 1998, when they were still in Nowak's home archive in Annandale, Virginia, and so I do not provide the call numbers assigned to them by the National Ossoliński Institute in Wrocław after his collection was deposited there. I do give the call numbers of other documents I read in Wrocław. Nowak-Jeziorański also wrote about the programmatic retreat and new tactics in his memoirs, *Wojna w eterze*, 221–24.

79. For more on the Voice of Free Poland program line in 1956, see Machcewicz, *Emigracja w polityce międzynarodowej*, 146–48; see also Nowak-Jeziorański, *Wojna w eterze*, 251–65.

80. Memorandum from William Griffith to Richard Condon, Policy Review of Free Hungary Programming, 23 October–23 November, December 5, 1956, in *The 1956 Hungarian Revolution: A History in Documents*, ed. Csaba Békés, Malcolm Byrne, and Janos M. Rainer (Budapest and New York: Central European University Press, 2002), 464–84. For the role of RFE's Hungarian Section and criticism of it, see Allan A. Michie, *Voices through the Iron Curtain: The Radio Free Europe Story* (New York: Dodd, Mead, 1963), 248–55; Laszlo Borhi, *Hungary in the Cold War 1945–1956: Between the United States and the Soviet Union* (Budapest and New York: Central European University Press, 2004), 282–85; Charles Gati, *Failed Illusions: Moscow, Washington, Budapest, and the 1956 Hungarian Revolt* (Washington, DC: Woodrow Wilson Center Press; Stanford, CA: Stanford University Press, 2006); Anne-Chantale Lepeuple, "Radio Europe Libre et le soulèvement hongrois de 1956," *Revue d'Histoire Moderne et Contemporaine* 47 (2000): 177–95; Nelson, *War of the Black Heavens*, 72–84; Johnson, *Radio Free Europe and Radio Liberty*, 86–118.

81. See a comparison of the programmatic lines of the Voice of Free Poland and the Voice of Free Hungary in 1956 in Paweł Machcewicz, "Radio Wolna Europa wobec wydarzeń w Polsce i na Węgrzech jesienią 1956 roku" [Radio Free Europe's approach to the events in Poland and Hungary in the autumn of 1956], in *Październik 1956. Początek erozji systemu* [October 1956: The system begins to erode], ed. Marek Jabłonowski and Stanisław Stępka (Pułtusk: Akademia Humanistyczna im. Aleksandra Gieysztora, 2007), 181–203.

82. Jan Nowak-Jeziorański in the second volume of his memoirs, *Polska z oddali. Wspomnienia* [Poland from afar: A memoir], vol. 2, *1956–1976* (Cracow: Znak, 1992), 52–53.

83. Hoover Institution, Radio Free Europe/Radio Liberty, Corporate Records, box 444.4, *RFE Broadcasting Policy Toward Poland*, August 20, 1964.

84. See the description in the second volume of Nowak-Jeziorański's memoirs, *Polska z oddali*, 52–64. For an extensive analysis of this conflict based on US documents, see Jakub Tyszkiewicz, *Otwarte okno w "żelaznej kurtynie." Polityka administracji prezydenta Eisenhowera wobec Polski (październik 1956–styczeń 1961)* [An open window in the "Iron Curtain": The Eisenhower administration's policies toward Poland (October 1956–January 1961)] (Wrocław: Wydawnictwo Uniwersytetu Wrocławskiego, 2003), 320–22.

85. Nowak-Jeziorański, *Polska z oddali*, 98–100.

86. IPMS, General Anders Collection, XXXV, Letter from Jan Nowak-Jeziorański to Władysław Anders, October 13, 1960.

87. See Nowak-Jeziorański, *Polska z oddali*, 101–8; Machcewicz, *Emigracja w polityce międzynarodowej*, 180–82; Tyszkiewicz, *Otwarte okno w "żelaznej kurtynie,"* 340–42.

88. An August 17, 1966, memorandum from Nowak to RFE director Ralph Walter can serve as an example of these efforts (Hoover Institution, Radio Free Europe/Radio Liberty, Corporate Records, box 444.4).

89. Author's interviews with William Griffith, Paul Henze, and A. Ross Johnson; see note 74.

90. In his memoirs, *Polska z oddali*, 268, Nowak-Jeziorański mistakenly gives 1963 as the beginning of RFE's campaign against the Partisans. His papers in Wrocław include scripts of programs about the Moczar group broadcast in 1962 (Zakład Narodowy im. Ossolińskich [Ossoliński National Institute], Wrocław, Jan Nowak-Jeziorański [hereafter JNJ], 37/99/3, folder "Moczar"). For a discussion of this complex and important issue for both RFE and Poland in the 1960s, see Paweł Machcewicz, "Radio Wolna Europa i 'partyzanci'" [Radio Free Europe and the "Partisans"], in *Od Piłsudskiego do Wałęsy. Studia z dziejów Polski w XX wieku* [From Piłsudski to Wałęsa: Studies in twentieth-century history of Poland] (Warsaw: Instytut Pamięci Narodowej-Instytut Studiów Politycznych Polskiej Akademii Nauk, 2008), 248–61.

91. Zakład Narodowy im. Ossolińskich, JNJ, 37/99/3, Nowak, "Factionalism in the Polish United Workers' Party," December 11, 1963.

92. Nowak-Jeziorański, *Polska z oddali*, 269.

93. Hoover Institution, Radio Free Europe/Radio Liberty, Corporate Records, box 444.4, Special Guidance on Polish "Partisans," October 2, 1963. The same folder includes RFE American management documents revealing a detachment from Nowak's views about the Partisans.

94. Thanks to the Freedom of Information Act, historians may petition the CIA for access to records concerning a specific topic of research. This author obtained some documents about the FEC and RFE to use here in this way.

95. See Johnson, *Radio Free Europe and Radio Liberty.*

96. Cord Meyer, *Facing Reality: From World Federalism to the CIA* (New York: Harper & Row, 1980), 115–18.

97. Author's interview with Paul Henze, May 7, 1998.

98. Mickelson, *America's Other Voice*, 42.

99. Sig Mickelson, a former RFE director, was the first author to use Frank Altschul's records to write openly about the ties between RFE and the Office of Policy Coordination (*America's Other Voice*, 21–22). I surveyed the documents in Frank Altschul's collection in 1998.

100. Lehman Suite and Papers, Rare Book and Manuscript Library, Columbia University, Frank Altschul Papers, Organizations, 486, NCFE, Altschul's memorandum to DeWitt C. Poole, May 23, 1950.

101. Ibid., Script writing in Washington, May 28, 1950.

102. Johnson, *Radio Free Europe and Radio Liberty*, 43.

103. Lehman Suite and Papers, Rare Book and Manuscript Library, Columbia University, Frank Altschul Papers, Organizations, 486, NCFE, Memorandum (no title and no signature), August 15, 1950.

104. Ibid., Memorandum (no title and no signature), November 1, 1950.

105. Ibid., 442, NCFE, Radio Executive Committee, July 21, 1950.

106. *Radio Free Europe: Policy Handbook*, November 30, 1951, a document I obtained from the CIA through the Freedom of Information Act.

107. Ibid.

108. Lehman Suite and Papers, Rare Book and Manuscript Library, Columbia University, Frank Altschul Papers, Organizations, 486, NCFE, Memorandum (no title and no signature), December 1, 1950.

109. See Peter Lowe, *The Korean War* (Basingstoke: Palgrave Macmillan, 2000).

110. Nowak-Jeziorański, *Wojna w eterze*, 43.

111. Ibid., 44.

112. Hoover Institution, Radio Free Europe/Radio Liberty, Corporate Records, box 254.9, Polish broadcast, Special programs, 1951–1952, Memorandum, To: C. D. Jackson, From: Ralph Walter, Subject: Special Polish Broadcast, October 3, 1951.

113. Ibid., Memorandum, To: Mr. Wamboldt, From: Mr. Mahool, July 1952. This folder also contains other documents about the "special programs" for Poland.

114. See "Operacja 'Cezary'—ubecka analiza 'gry' z WiN-em" [Operation "Cezary": The Security Service game with Freedom and Independence], annotated by Wojciech Frazik, *Zeszyty historyczne WiN-u* 15 (2001): 183–255; "Operacja 'Cezary.' Przegląd wątków krajowych" [Operation "Cezary": A review of the Polish motifs], in *"Zwyczajny resort." Studia o aparacie bezpieczeństwa 1944–1956* ["An ordinary ministry": Studies on the security apparatus, 1944–1956], ed. Kazimierz Krajewski and Tomasz Łabuszewski (Warsaw: Instytut Pamięci Narodowej, 2005), 400–436. Rafał Wnuk, "Dwie prowokacje—Piąta Komenda Zrzeszenia 'WiN' i Berg" [Two provocations: The Fifth Command of the "Freedom and Independence" Association and Berg], *Zeszyty Historyczne* 141 (2002): 71–112.

115. For a discussion of the politics of "liberation," see James. D. Marchio, "Rhetoric and Reality: The Eisenhower Administration and Unrest in Eastern Europe, 1953–1959" (PhD diss., University of Michigan, 1993); Machcewicz, "Polska i Europa Wschodnia."

116. Ostermann, "The United States, the East German Uprising of 1953 and the Limits of Rollback," 15.

117. Ibid., 15.

118. Semelin, *La liberté au bout des ondes*, 215.

119. For the origins, course, and outcomes of these events in the Soviet bloc, see Marc Kramer, "The Early Post-Stalin Succession Struggle and Upheavals in East-Central Europe: Internal-External Linkages in Soviet Policy Making," *Journal of Cold War Studies* 1, nos. 1–3 (1999).

120. Lehman Suite and Papers, Rare Book and Manuscript Library, Columbia University, Frank Altschul Papers, Organizations, 475, NCFE, Radio Free Europe, Special Guidance no. 12-A, The Opening of a New Phase, June 19, 1953.

121. Ostermann, "The United States, the East German Uprising of 1953 and the Limits of Rollback," 24.

122. The first phase of the balloon operation took place in 1951, when fliers were sent to Czechoslovakia. In 1953 they were used again, on a much larger scale; see Paweł Machcewicz, "'Operacje balonowe' 1951–1956. Przyczynek do dziejów

amerykańskiej wojny psychologicznej wobec bloku komunistycznego" ["Balloon operations," 1951–1956: A contribution to the history of American psychological warfare vis-à-vis the Communist bloc], in *Polska–Niemcy–Europa. Księga jubileuszowa z okazji siedemdziesiątej rocznicy urodzin profesora Jerzego Holzera* [Poland–Germany–Europe: A festschrift for Professor Jerzy Holzer's 70th birthday], ed. Katarzyna Karaskiewicz (Warsaw: Rytm, 2000), 345–61; Michie, *Voices through the Iron Curtain,* 130–64; Richard H. Cummings, "Balloons over East Europe: The Cold War Leaflet Campaign of Radio Free Europe," *Falling Leaf Magazine,* June 18, 1999. Cummings writes that more than 350,000 balloons carried more than 300 million fliers and brochures from 1951 to 1956.

123. For a description of the Polish "balloon action," see Machcewicz, *Emigracja w polityce międzynarodowej*, 112–22.

124. For a discussion of C. D. Jackson, see David Haight, "The Papers of CD Jackson: A Glimpse at President Eisenhower's Psychological Warfare Expert," *Manuscripts* 28, no. 1 (1976): 27–37; Robert R. Bowie and Richard H. Immerman, *Waging Peace: How Eisenhower Shaped an Enduring Cold War Strategy* (New York: Oxford University Press, 1998), 110–11.

125. Eisenhower Library, C. D. Jackson Papers, box 57, Griffith, W. E. (2), William Griffith's letter to C. D. Jackson, October 10, 1954.

126. For a discussion of US policy in 1956 and after, see Tyszkiewicz, *Otwarte okno w "żelaznej kurtynie"*; Paweł Machcewicz, "Stany Zjednoczone wobec polskiego Października 1956 roku" [The United States and the Polish October 1956], in *Polska 1944/45–1989. Studia i materiały* [Poland 1944/45–1989. Studies and materials], vol. 3 (Warsaw: Neriton, 1997), 45–61.

127. Tyszkiewicz, *Otwarte okno w "żelaznej kurtynie,"* 316; Arch Puddington, *Broadcasting Freedom: The Cold War Triumph of Radio Free Europe and Radio Liberty* (Lexington: University Press of Kentucky, 2000), 118–19.

128. Zakład Narodowy im. Ossolińskich, JNJ, 33/99/1, Special Guidance no. 29 on RFE Broadcasts to Poland, September 30, 1957.

129. Ibid., RFE Broadcasting Policy toward Poland, January 13, 1960.

130. Tyszkiewicz, *Otwarte okno w "żelaznej kurtynie"*, 327–29; Machcewicz, *Emigracja w polityce międzynarodowej*, 178–90.

131. See Nowak-Jeziorański, *Polska z oddali*, 81–101.

132. For a discussion of US policy, see Bennett Kovrig, *Of Walls and Bridges: The United States and Eastern Europe* (New York: New York University Press, 1991); Andrzej Mania, *Bridge Building. Polityka USA wobec Europy Wschodniej w latach 1961–1968* [Bridge building: US policies toward Eastern Europe in 1961–1968] (Cracow: Wydawnictwo Uniwersytetu Jagiellońskiego, 1996); Andrzej Mania, *Détente i polityka Stanów Zjednoczonych wobec Europy Wschodniej, styczeń 1969–styczeń 1981* [Détente and US policies toward Eastern Europe, January 1969–January 1981] (Cracow: Wydawnictwo Uniwersytetu Jagiellońskiego, 2003).

133. Zamorski, *Pod anteną Radia Wolna Europa*, 54–56.

134. Puddington, *Broadcasting Freedom*, 29.

135. Mickelson, *America's Other Voice*, 121–22.

136. Puddington, *Broadcasting Freedom*, 187–213; Johnson, *Radio Free Europe and Radio Liberty*, 202–21.

Chapter 2

1. For an account of the early days of RFE and Radio Madrid, see chapter 1.

2. Report by A. Zharov, Chief of the Main Directorate of Radio Communications, to the Minister of Communications of the USSR Nikolai Psurtsev, September 15, 1951, in *Cold War Broadcasting: Impact on the Soviet Union and Eastern Europe: A Collection of Studies and Documents*, ed. A. Ross Johnson and R. Eugene Parta (Budapest and New York: Central European University Press, 2010), 521–25.

3. USSR Council of Ministers Decree, October 24, 1951, in Johnson and Parta, *Cold War Broadcasting*, 526–27.

4. Minister of Public Security organizational order no. 0171 creating the Protective Service (BO) and points "K" (equipped with jamming devices). On January 17, 1955, the BO Service was folded into the Office of Allocated Communications of the Ministry of Internal Affairs, and on March 15, 1955, it was folded into the Office of Allocated Radio Communications of the Ministry of Internal Affairs, which was closed down on December 14, 1956. Aleksander Kochański, *Polska 1944–1991. Informator historyczny* [Poland 1944–1991: A historical guide], vol. 1 (Warsaw: Wydawnictwo Sejmowe, 1996), 418.

5. Archiwum Instytutu Pamięci Narodowej [Archive of the Institute of National Remembrance], Warsaw (hereafter AIPN), Ministerstwo Bezpieczeństwa Publicznego [Ministry of Public Security, hereafter MBP], 1490. This folder includes documents from the Protective Service (BO) dated 1952–1953. Unfortunately, it has been impossible to find any materials from later years.

6. AIPN, MBP, 1490, Office note, October 14, 1953.

7. AIPN, Ministerstwo Spraw Wewnętrznych [Ministry of Internal Affairs, hereafter MSW] I/4, Information about work being conducted by the Office of Allocated Radio Communications, September 9, 1955, 420–21.

8. AIPN, MBP, 1490, Skuteczność pracy Wolnej Europy za dekadę 11–20 XII 1953 [The effectiveness of Free Europe's work for the period December 11–20, 1953], 267.

9. AIPN, MBP, 1490, Meldunek no. 58 Służby BO za okres 11–20 VI 1953 [Report no. 58 from the BO Service for the period of June 11–20, 1953], 144.

10. AIPN, MSW I/4, Informacja o pracy prowadzonej przez Zarząd Wydzielonej Łączności Radiowej [Information about the work conducted by the Office of Allocated Radio Communications], September 9, 1955, 422.

11. Excerpts from Jan Panek's testimony recorded by Maciej Drygas for the film *Głos nadziei* [Voice of hope] (2003), *Karta* 38 (2003): 97–98; see also J. Maciej Drygas, "Zadudnić do zera" [To drown out completely], *Gazeta Wyborcza*, May 12, 2003.

12. AIPN, MBP, 1490, Notatka służbowa [Working note], August 19, 1953, 179–80.

13. Andrzej Paczkowski, "Jedni słuchali, inni zagłuszali" [Some listened, others jammed], *Rzeczpospolita*, May 9–10, 1992.

14. "Is dnevnika A. A. Soboleva. Zapis besedii s J. Bermanom o denezhnoi kompensatsii ukrainskim pereselentsam i komandirovanii v Polshu sovetskovo spetsyalista po radiozashchitiie," May 3, 1952, in *Sovetskii faktor v Vostochnoi Yevrope 1944–1953* [The Soviet factor in Western Europe, 1944–1953], vol. 2, *1949–1953, Dokumentii*, ed. T. V. Tsarevskaia et al. (Moscow: Rosspen, 2002), 620–21.

15. Paczkowski, "Jedni słuchali, inni zagłuszali."

16. Ibid.

17. AIPN, MBP, 1490, 94–99. A digest of listeners' letters was prepared for the Ministry of Public Security by the Radio Committee.

18. AIPN, MSW I/4. Informacja o pracy prowadzonej przez Zarząd Wydzielonej Łączności Radiowej [Information about the work of the Office of Allocated Radio Communications], September 9, 1955, 419.

19. Archiwum Akt Nowych [Central Archive of Modern Records], Warsaw (hereafter AAN), Polskiej Zjednoczonej Partii Robotniczej [Polish United Workers' Party, hereafter PZPR], 1679, Notatka dla członków Biura Politycznego KC PZPR w sprawie zagłuszania wrogich audycji radiowych (październik 1956) [Note for CC PUWP Politburo members about the jamming of hostile radio stations (October 1956)], 1.

20. AIPN, MSW I/4, 422.

21. AIPN, MBP, 1490, Notatka służbowa o wzroście wrogiej propagandy za okres od 1950 r. do obecnej chwili, marzec 1953 [Working note on the growth of hostile propaganda for the period from 1950 to the present, March 1953], 51.

22. Ibid., Skuteczność pracy za dekadę 1–10 XI 1953 r. [Effectiveness of work for the period of November 1–10, 1953], 246.

23. "Polish Proposal for Bloc-wide Coordinating of Jamming," in Johnson and Parta, *Cold War Broadcasting*, 502.

24. AIPN, MBP, 1490, Skuteczność pracy Wolnej Europy za dekadę 1–10 XI 1953 r. [Effectiveness of the work of Free Europe for the period of November 1–10, 1953], 78. The data concern "protecting" considered good, that is, totally obstructing reception. I do not cite the next category of a few to over a dozen percentage points, "sufficient protection," which probably meant making reception difficult.

25. Ibid., Skuteczność pracy za dekadę 1–10 III 1953 r. [Effectiveness of work for the period of March 1–10, 1953], 48.

26. AIPN, MSW I/4, Informacja o pracy prowadzonej przez Zarząd Wydzielonej Łączności Radiowej [Information about the work of the Office of Allocated Communications], September 9, 1955, 418.

27. AAN, PZPR, 1679, Notatka dla członków Biura Politycznego KC PZPR w sprawie zagłuszania wrogich audycji radiowych (październik 1956) [Note for CC PUWP Politburo members about the jamming of hostile radio stations (October 1956)], 3.

28. AIPN, MBP, 1490, Pismo gen. bryg. Juliusza Hibnera do ministra bezpieczeństwa publicznego gen. dyw. Stanisława Radkiewicza [Letter from Brigadier General Juliusz Hibner to Minister of Public Security Major General Stanisław Radkiewicz], May 2, 1953, 117.

29. Ibid., Pismo gen. bryg. Juliusza Hibnera do wicepremiera Piotra Jaroszewicza [Letter from Brigadier General Juliusz Hibner to Deputy Premier Piotr Jaroszewicz], August 14, 1953, 172.

30. Kochański, *Polska 1944–1991*, 1:495.

31. I found documentation for eighteen cases in which people were sentenced: one each to six-, seven-, and nine-month camp terms; six to twelve months each; one to fourteen months; one to sixteen months; three to eighteen months; and four to twenty-four months (AAN, Komisja Specjalna [Special Commission], 402, 432, 444, 446, 457, 460, 464, 497, 499, 502, 513, 516, 528, 537, 551, 558, 559).

32. AAN, Komisja Specjalna, 444.

33. Ibid., 402.
34. Ibid., 537.
35. Ibid., 499.
36. Ibid., 551.
37. Ibid., 559.
38. Ibid., 457.
39. Ibid., 441.
40. Ibid., 497.
41. Ibid., 531.
42. Ibid., 559.
43. *Komisja Specjalna do Walki z Nadużyciami i Szkodnictwem Gospodarczy 1945–1954. Wybór dokumentów* [The Special Commission for Combating Abuses and Economic Sabotage, 1945–1954: A selection of documents], ed. Dariusz Jarosz and Tadeusz Wolsza (Warsaw: Główna Komisja Badania Zbrodni Przeciwko Narodowi Polskiemu, 1995), 9; Andrzej Zaćmiński, "Przestępstwa polityczne w orzecznictwie Komisji Specjalnej do Walki z Nadużyciami i Szkodnictwem Gospodarczym 1950–1954" [Political offenses in the jurisdiction of the Special Commission for Combating Abuses and Economic Sabotage, 1950–1954], *Pamięć i Sprawiedliwość* 12, no. 1 (2008): 321–43.
44. AIPN, 014/39/107, Okólnik do szefów wojewódzkich urzędów bezpieczeństwa publicznego [Circular to the chiefs of the Provincial Offices of Public Security], October 2, 1952, 87–88.
45. Ibid.
46. Ibid., 123; see Kochański, *Polska 1944–1991*, 481. For a discussion of the persecution of people who listened to foreign radio, see Kamil Rutecki, "Wolność słowa epoki Stalina" [Freedom of speech in the Stalinist era], *Biuletyn Instytutu Pamięci Narodowej* 28, no. 5 (2003): 48–51.
47. For the regulations and the case of the lieutenant colonel, see Kochański, *Polska 1944–1991.* Kamil Rutecki discusses them in his "System zagłuszania polskich rozgłośni radiowych w PRL" [The system of jamming Polish radio stations in the People's Republic of Poland], in *Przełom w przełomie. Bydgoskie wydarzenia roku 1956* [A breakthrough within a breakthrough: The events in Bydgoszcz in 1956], ed. Alicja Paczoska-Hauke (Bydgoszcz: Urząd Miasta, 2006), 108.
48. See Zakład Narodowy im. Ossolińskich [Ossoliński National Institute], Wrocław, papers of Jan Nowak-Jeziorański (hereafter JNJ), 53/99, a 1967 paper, "Some recent examples of RFE effectiveness in Poland," including a detailed list of attacks on RFE in the first four months of the year.
49. A collection compiled by one of the most prominent editors on RFE's Polish desk is *PRL atakuje Radio "Wolna Europa." Teksty, rysunki i karykatury z prasy, radia, telewizji i wydawnictw książkowych* [The People's Republic of Poland attacks Radio Free Europe: Texts, drawings and caricatures from the press, radio, television and books], selected and with an introduction byAlina Grabowska (Wrocław: Towarzystwo Przyjaciół Ossolineum, 2002).
50. M.A.T., "Od Neues Europa do Freies Europa" [From a Neues Europa to a Freies Europa], *Express Wieczorny*, October 31, 1952.
51. SŁAW [Bolesław Wójcicki], "Dlaczego Freies Europa nazywa się Wolna Europa?" [Why is Freies Europa calling itself Wolna Europa?], *Życie Warszawy*, October 24, 1952.

52. Zakład Narodowy im. Ossolińskich, JNJ, 77/99, Wanda Odolska, "Czym cuchną pewne baloniki" [What certain balloons stink of], Radio Warsaw I, March 13, 1955, from RFE's Monitoring Department.

53. Cz. Bielan and M. Sławiński, "Mówi Radio 'Wolna Europa'" [Radio "Free Europe" speaking], *Żołnierz Polski*, November 21–27, 1952.

54. Wiesław Górnicki, "Cd. Plugawego żywota monachijskiej ladacznicy. Między Monachium a Nowym Jorkiem" [The vile life of a Munich harlot, continued: Between Munich and New York], *Dziennik Wychodźstwa*, March 3, 1955, in *PRL atakuje Radio "Wolna Europa,"* 15.

55. A.N., "W tłoku przy kasie" [Crowding around the cash register], *Trybuna Ludu*, June 4, 1952.

56. *Trybuna Ludu*, February 20, 1955, in *PRL atakuje Radio "Wolna Europa,"* 12.

57. Zakład Narodowy im. Ossolińskich, JNJ, 77/99, "Szczegóły samobójstwa Stanisława Salarka" [The specifics of Stanisław Salarek's suicide], Radio Warsaw III, April 18, 1955. The sailor's last name was rendered incorrectly when the program was transcribed.

58. Mirosław Azembski and Lucjan Wolanowski, *Czy Stanisław Talarek musiał umrzeć?* [Did Stanisław Talarek have to die?] (Warsaw: Wydawnictwo Ministerstwa Obrony Narodowej, 1955). *PRL atakuje Radio "Wolna Europa"* includes excerpts from this book on pp. 114–19.

59. Józef Prutkowski, "Radio Wolna Europa" [Radio Free Europe], *Gazeta Białostocka*, March 10–20, 1955; see *PRL atakuje Radio "Wolna Europa,"* 18–19.

60. S.K., "Nic nowego—pod ciemną gwiazdą" [There is nothing new in the dark alley], *Nowa Wieś*, December 19, 1954, in *PRL atakuje Radio "Wolna Europa,"* 11.

61. Zakład Narodowy im. Ossolińskich, JNJ, 77/99, "Odpowiedzi Fali 49" [Wave 49 responds], Radio Warsaw I, November 28, 1954. It was Tadeusz Chciuk-Celt, the author of programs on agriculture on the Voice of Free Poland, who used the radio name Michał Lasota.

62. Zakład Narodowy im. Ossolińskich, JNJ, 77/99, "Muzyka i aktualności" [Music and current events], Radio Warsaw I, May 12, 1955.

63. Michał Głowiński, "Pawiany z Monachium. PRL-owska propaganda wobec Wolnej Europy" [Baboons from Munich: The propaganda of People's Poland toward Free Europe], in *Pismak 1863 i inne szkice o różnych brzydkich rzeczach* [Hack 1863 and other sketches about various ugly things] (Warsaw: Open, 1995), 102.

64. Andrzej Paczkowski, *Trzy twarze Józefa Światły. Przyczynek do historii komunizmu w Polsce* [The three faces of Józef Światło: A contribution to the history of Communism] (Warsaw: Pruszyński i S-ka, 2009).

65. AIPN, 0298/571, vol. 2, Notatka nr 1 dotycząca ucieczki Józefa Światły [Note no. 1 concerning Józef Światło's defection], October 5, 1954.

66. Ibid., Notatka nr 2 dotycząca echa ucieczki Józefa Światły [Note no. 2 concerning the fallout from Józef Światło's defection], October 5, 1954.

67. *Aparat bezpieczeństwa w Polsce w latach 1953–1954. Taktyka, strategia, metody* [The security apparatus in Poland in 1953–1954: Tactics, strategy, methods], ed. Grzegorz Majchrzak and Andrzej Paczkowski, with an introduction by Andrzej Paczkowski (Warsaw: Instytut Pamięci Narodowej, 2004), 22–26; Andrzej Paczkowski, "Terror i kontrola. Funkcje aparatu bezpieczeństwa w systemie komunistycznym. Polska 1944–1956" [Terror and control: The functions of the security apparatus in the Communist system, Poland, 1944–1956], in *Od sfałszowanego zwycięstwa do*

prawdziwej klęski. Szkice do portretu PRL [From a sham victory to real defeat: Sketches for a portrait of the People's Republic of Poland] (Cracow: Wydawnictwo Literackie, 1999), 69–70; Andrzej Paczkowski, "Aparat bezpieczeństwa w czasach odwilży" [The security apparatus during the thaw], *Zeszyty Historyczne* 114 (1995): 3–33; Zbysław Rykowski and Wiesław Władyka, *Polska próba. Październik '56* [The Polish challenge, October '56] (Cracow: Wydawnictwo Literackie, 1989), 84–90; Paweł Ceranka, "Reperkusje ucieczki Józefa Światły w Ministerstwie Bezpieczeństwa Publicznego" [The repercussions of Józef Światło's flight for the Ministry of Public Security], in *Departament X MBP. Wzorce–struktury–działanie* [Department X of the Ministry of Public Security: Models–structures–actions], ed. Konrad Rokicki (Warsaw: Instytut Pamięci Narodowej, 2007), 206–31; Ryszard Terlecki, *Miecz i tarcza komunizmu. Historia aparatu bezpieczeństwa w Polsce 1944–1990* [Communism's sword and shield: A history of the security apparatus in Poland, 1944–1990] (Cracow: Wydawnictwo Literackie, 2009), 115–29.

68. Jan Nowak-Jeziorański, *Polska z oddali. Wspomnienia* [Poland from afar: A memoir], vol. 2, *1956–1976* (Cracow: Znak, 1992), 155–56; Alan A. Michie, *Voices through the Iron Curtain: The Radio Free Europe Story* (New York: Dodd, Mead, 1963), 137–38; Arch Puddington, *Broadcasting Freedom: The Cold War Triumph of Radio Free Europe and Radio Liberty* (Lexington: University Press of Kentucky, 2000), 61–72.

69. See a detailed discussion of the political background to the balloon action in Machcewicz, *Emigracja w polityce międzynarodowej*, 113–16.

70. Ibid., 117–19.

71. AAN, PZPR, 237/V/35, Okólnik Sekretariatu KC PZPR do egzekutyw komitetów wojewódzkich i powiatowych [Circular from the CC PUWP Secretariat to the executives of the Provincial and District Committees], February 19, 1955, 137–38.

72. Ibid., Wzmóżmy walkę z faszystowską propagandą amerykańsko-hitlerowską i z dywersją wroga [Let's intensify our battle with the American-Nazi fascist propaganda and with the enemy's sabotage], February 1955, 141–42.

73. Zakład Narodowy im. Ossolińskich, JNJ, 77/99, Odolska, "Czym cuchną pewne baloniki."

74. AIPN, Komitet do spraw Bezpieczeństwa Publicznego [Committee for Public Security, hereafter KdsBP], Pismo ppłk. Mikołaja Krupskiego, kierownika UBP m. st. Warszawy, do dyrektora Gabinetu Przewodniczącego KdsBP [Letter from Lieutenant Colonel Mikołaj Krupski, chief of the Warsaw Office of Public Security, to the director of the Office of the Chairman of the Committee for Public Security], October 26, 1955, 46; ibid., Pismo mjr. H. Trzcińskiego, zastępcy kierownika WUBP w Opolu, do dyrektora Gabinetu Przewodniczącego KdsBP [Letter from Major H. Trzciński, deputy chief of the Provincial Office of Public Security in Opole, to the director of the Office of the Chairman of the Committee of Public Security], 1955, 43; ibid., Pismo kpt. B. Kulikowskiego, zastępcy kierownika WUBP w Rzeszowie, do dyrektora Gabinetu Przewodniczącego KdsBP [Letter from Captain B. Kulikowski, deputy chief of the Provincial Office of Public Security in Rzeszów, to the director of the Office of the Chairman of the Committee of Public Security], October 29, 1955, 45; ibid., Pismo zastępcy przewodniczącego KdsBP Antoniego Alstera do sekretarza KC PZPR Jerzego Morawskiego [Letter from the deputy chairman of the Committee for Public Security Antoni Alster to the secretary of the CC PUWP Jerzy Morawski], January 17, 1956, 12.

75. AIPN, KdsBP, 247, Commentary from the *Manchester Guardian* about the Soviet demands, reprinted in the first issue of the *Wolna Europa* bulletin, dated November 1955. The folder also contains copies of brochures intercepted by the security apparatus.

76. Archiwum Ministerstwa Spraw Zagranicznych [Archive of the Foreign Ministry], Warsaw (hereafter AMSZ), Collection 9, bundle 80, vol. 971, Departament III, Notatka służbowa na temat amerykańskiej "akcji balonikowej" [A working note about the American "balloon action"], February 18, 1955, 1–3. The recipients of this note included Bolesław Bierut, Jakub Berman, and Premier Józef Cyrankiewicz.

77. Ibid., 28–32.

78. Michie, *Voices through the Iron Curtain*, 163; Puddington, *Broadcasting Freedom*, 70.

79. AMSZ, Collection 9, bundle 80, vol. 971, Depesza Adama Willmana, ambasadora w Budapeszcie [Telegram from Adam Willman, ambassador in Budapest], February 10, 1956, 19.

80. Ibid., 51.

81. The sole trace of this accident that could be found in the Committee for Public Security materials is part of a note, "Ulotki Wolnej Europy" [Free Europe's fliers] (n.d., probably October 1956): "a tragic accident took place in August of this year, when a jet plane and a balloon collided, as a result of which two pilots, Polish Army officers, died" (AIPN, KdsBP, 247, 23).

82. AMSZ, Collection 9, bundle 80, vol. 971, Depesza Henryka Bireckiego do Józefa Winiewicza [A telegram from Henryk Birecki to Józef Winiewicz], February 15, 1956, 30.

83. AMSZ, Collection 9, bundle 80, vol. 971, Notatka [Note], September 1, 1956, 53–55.

84. Adam Bromke, one of the coordinators of the Polish balloon actions, gives this as their end date. A. Bromke, List do redakcji [Letter to the editors], *Kultura* 4 (1957): 159; see also Bromke, "Towarzysze, posprzątajcie" [Comrades, clean up], *Polityka* 33 (1998).

85. Paweł Machcewicz, "Stany Zjednoczone wobec polskiego Października 1956 roku" [The United States and the Polish October 1956], in *Polska 1944/45–1989. Studia i materiały* [Poland 1944/45–1989: Studies and materials], vol. 3 (Warsaw: Neriton, 1997), 48–53; Nowak-Jeziorański, *Polska z oddali*, 251–65.

86. Puddington, *Broadcasting Freedom*, 70.

87. Władysław Kisielewski, *Od Torunia do Londynu. Podróż z przeszkodami* [From Toruń to London: A journey with obstacles] (Warsaw: Wydawnictwo Ministerstwa Obrony Nardowej, 1958), 8.

88. See Andrzej Friszke, *Życie polityczne emigracji* [The political life of the emigration], vol. 1 of *Druga Wielka Emigracja 1945–1990* [The second Great Emigration, 1945–1990], in 3 vols. (Warsaw: Więź, 1999), 147–55; Christopher Andrew and Oleg Gordievsky, *KGB: The Inside Story of Its Foreign Operations from Lenin to Gorbachev* (London: Hodder & Stoughton, 1990), 319–20; Harry Rositzke, *The CIA's Secret Operations: Espionage, Counterespionage and Covert Action* (New York: Reader's Digest Press, 1977), 169–71.

89. AIPN, 01265/508, Sprawozdanie Departamentu III MBP za rok 1952 [Report for 1952 by Ministry of Public Security Department III], March 4, 1953, 34, 40.

90. AIPN, 01265/508, Sprawozdanie Departamentu III MBP za rok 1952 [Report for 1952 by Ministry of Public Security Department III], March 4, 1953, 1.

91. AIPN, 01334/29, O działalności monachijskiej placówki Rady Politycznej, cz. 1: Na marginesie procesu ks. Józefa Lelity [About the activities of the Munich office of the Political Council, part 1: NB the trial of Father Józef Lelito], August 1953.

92. AIPN, 01227/50, Doniesienie "Pawła," Sprawa Radia Free Europe [A report from "Paweł": The case of Radio Free Europe], July 31, 1956.

93. AIPN, 0297/43, vol. 264, Informacja nr 12 dotycząca ośrodków wojny psychologicznej prowadzonej przez Stany Zjednoczone [Information no. 12 concerning the methods of psychological warfare being conducted by the United States], probably 1956.

94. Zbigniew Błażyński, *Mówi Józef Światło. Za kulisami bezpieki i partii 1940–1955* [Józef Światło speaking: Behind the scenes in the secret police and party, 1940–1955] (London: Polska Fundacja Kulturalna, 1986), 249–52.

95. AIPN, 0298/571–2, Relacja z podróży służbowej do Berlina w dniach 3–8 XII 1953 r. [Report from a work trip to Berlin on December 3–8, 1953], December 21, 1953, 1–13.

96. AIPN, 0192/594, vols. 1–5.

97. Nowak-Jeziorański, *Polska z oddali*, 361.

98. Ibid., 357, 361. Nowak-Jeziorański does write that Jabłoński was caught "at the post office as he was sending a telegram to a West German intelligence resident agent in Frankfurt am Main," but the context makes it seem that the author made a mistake and that it was actually Polish intelligence.

99. Ibid., 361.

100. Ibid., 361.

101. Zakład Narodowy im. Ossolińskich, JNJ, 41/99, Telegramy do Marka Święcickiego w Nowym Jorku, podpisane przez Jana Nowaka i Williama Griffitha [Telegrams to Marek Święcicki in New York signed by Jan Nowak and William Griffith], August 19, 1955, August 29, 1955; ibid., Odpowiedź Marka Święcickiego zawierająca opinię Światły [Marek Święcicki's reply with his opinion of Światło], September 5, 1955. Światło's last name is not mentioned in the correspondence, only his code name, "Junior," and we can guess his identity from the context.

102. AIPN, 00169/14, vols. 1–4.

103. Nowak-Jeziorański, *Polska z oddali*, 362; Zakład Narodowy im. Ossolińskich, JNJ, 41/99, "Za kulisami bezpieki i partii. Dwa oblicza Zbigniewa Brydaka" [Behind the scenes in the secret police and the party: The two faces of Zbigniew Brydak], the script of an RFE broadcast based on Brydak's account given to US intelligence. The file also contains Brydak's declaration that he had been an agent for People's Poland and information about his meeting places in Western Europe and the sums of money he received from intelligence functionaries of the Committee for Public Security.

104. *Komuniści wobec harcerstwa 1944–1950* [The Communists versus Scouting, 1944–1950], selected, edited, and with an introduction by Krzysztof Persak, vol. 11 of *Dokumenty z dziejów PRL* [Documents from the history of the People's Republic of Poland] (Warsaw: Instytut Studiów Politycznych, 1998), 110–11.

105. AIPN, 00169/14, vol. 2, Doniesienie agenturalne. Meldunek dotyczący wykonania polecenia specjalnego z dnia 15 III 1952 r. [Intelligence report. Dispatch about the fulfillment of a special task on March 15, 1952], March 19, 1952, 231–32.

106. AIPN, 00169/14, vol. 4, 175.

107. Zakład Narodowy im. Ossolińskich, JNJ, 41/99, Z. Brydak, *Harcerstwo w walce z komunizmem. Rola i losy harcerstwa w kraju* [Scouting in the struggle against Communism: The role and history of Scouting in Poland].

108. Ibid., Zbigniew Brydak's letter to Scout Master Ignacy Płonka, October 12, 1954.

109. Zakład Narodowy im. Ossolińskich, JNJ, 77/99, monitoring transcription of a program by Michalski-Brydak on Kraj Radio, Jan Nowak's legacy

110. Stefan Michalski [Zbigniew Brydak], "Berlińskie zasadzki" [Berlin traps], *Świat*, July 21, 1955.

111. Stefan Michalski [Zbigniew Brydak], "Wartownicy" [The guards], *Świat*, August 8, 1955.

112. For a discussion of the guard companies, see Czesław Brzoza, "Zapomniana armia. Polskie oddziały wartownicze w Europe (1945–1951)" [A forgotten army: The Polish guard companies in Europe (1945–1951)], *Zeszyty Historyczne* 116 (1996): 3–21.

113. Stefan Michalski [Zbigniew Brydak], "Mikrofon i szpiegowska kartoteka" [The microphone and the spies' files], *Świat*, September 4, 1955.

114. Zakład Narodowy im. Ossolińskich, JNJ, 41/99, "Za kulisami bezpieki i partii. Dwa oblicza Zbigniewa Brydaka" [Behind the scenes in the secret police and the party: The two faces of Zbigniew Brydak], program script.

115. Ibid., Brydak's case, August 30, 1955.

116. AIPN, 00169/14, vol. 4, 133.

117. Ibid., 132.

118. Ibid., Konspekt wstępny broszury o Wolnej Europie [Preliminary outline of a brochure about Free Europe], 137–40.

119. AIPN, 00169/14, vol. 5.

120. For a discussion of the repatriation campaign, see the first two volumes of *Druga Wielka Emigracja 1945–1990* [The second Great Emigration, 1945–1990]: Friszke, *Życie polityczne emigracji*, 232–41, and Machcewicz, *Emigracja w polityce międzynarodowej*, 128–41.

121. For an analysis of the role of the security apparatus in the repatriation campaign, see Sławomir Cenckiewicz, "Udział aparatu bezpieczeństwa w drugiej kampanii reemigracyjnej (1955–1957)" [The role of the security apparatus in the second reemigration campaign (1955–1957)], in *Aparat bezpieczeństwa wobec emigracji politycznej i Polonii* [The security apparatus versus political emigration and Polonia], ed. Ryszard Terlecki (Warsaw: Instytut Pamięci Narodowej, 2005), 241–83; Sławomir Cenckiewicz, "Od pierwszej reemigracji do drugiej reemigracji. Aparat bezpieczeństwa PRL wobec polskiej emigracji politycznej w latach 1944–1956," wstęp do publikacji *Polska emigracja polityczna. Informator* [From the first to the second reemigration: The security apparatus of People's Poland and Polish political emigration in 1944–1956, introduction to Polish political emigration: A guide] (Warsaw: Oficyna Wydawnicza Adiutor, 2004), v–xliv; Jerzy Lencznarowicz, "Rola Towarzystwa 'Polonia' w polityce PRL wobec Polonii w krajach zachodnich" [The role of the Polonia Association in the policies of People's Poland toward the Polonia in Western countries], *Przegląd Polonijny* 79, no. 1 (1996).

122. For a discussion of Kraj radio, see Sławomir Cenckiewicz, "Geneza, działalność i udział rozgłośni 'Kraj' w akcji reemigracyjnej (1955–1957). Przyczynek do studiów nad polityką PRL wobec emigracji i Polonii" [The origins, activity and participation of Kraj Radio in the reemigration operation (1955–1957): A contribution to the research on the policies of People's Poland toward the emigration and Polonia], *Niepodległość* 53/54 (2003–2004): 114–226; Marek Żebrowski, "Rozgłośnia spec. znaczenia (wypisy z propagandy PRL)" [A station of special significance (excerpts from the propaganda of People's Poland], *Zeszyty Historyczne* 142 (2002): 198–230; Jerzy Myśliński, *Mikrofon i polityka. Z dziejów radiofonii polskiej 1944–1960* [The microphone and politics: A history of Polish radio, 1944–1960] (Warsaw: Instytut Badań Literackich, 1990), 7–90, 295–96.

123. Cenckiewicz, "Geneza, działalność i udział rozgłośni 'Kraj,'" 205.

124. Michalski [Brydak], "Mikrofon i szpiegowska kartoteka."

125. Zakład Narodowy im. Ossolińskich, JNJ, 41/99, Re-Defection. Brydak and Counter-Brydak, August 30, 1955; ibid., The Brydak Broadcasts Create Stir in Refugee Camps of West Germany, September 6, 1955.

126. Zakład Narodowy im. Ossolińskich, JNJ, 41/99, "Za kulisami bezpieki i partii. Dwa oblicza Zbigniewa Brydaka," program script.

127. Nowak-Jeziorański, *Wojna w eterze*, 172–89.

128. Quoted in Żebrowski, "Rozgłośnia spec. znaczenia," 206–7.

129. Ibid., 213.

130. Cenckiewicz, "Geneza, działalność i udział rozgłośni 'Kraj,'" 173.

131. For contacts between Cat-Mackiewicz and the Polish secret services and his return to Poland, see Krzysztof Tarka, "'Polska jest Polską'. Powrót Stanisława Mackiewicza do kraju w czerwcu 1956 roku" ["Poland is Poland": Stanisław Mackiewicz's return to Poland in June 1956], *Zeszyty Historyczne* 150 (2004): 55–96.

132. Jerzy Giedroyc and Juliusz Mieroszewski, *Listy 1949–1956* [Letters, 1949–1956], selected and with introduction by Krzysztof Pomian; annotated and with added indexes by Jacek Krawczyk and Krzysztof Pomian (Warsaw: Czytelnik, 1999), 301; see also Krzysztof Tarka, "'Bankrut' i 'kapitulant' czy 'wybitny publicysta'? O powrocie S. Mackiewicza do Polski" [A "failure" and a "defeatist" or an "outstanding writer"? On S. Mackiewicz's return to Poland], *Zeszyty Historyczne* 151 (2005): 39.

133. Paweł Machcewicz, *Rebellious Satellite: Poland 1956* (Washington, DC: Woodrow Wilson Center Press; Stanford, CA: Stanford University Press, 2009), 104.

134. Ibid., 164–66.

135. *Centrum władzy. Protokoły posiedzeń kierownictwa PZPR. Wybór z lat 1949–1970* [The center of power: Minutes of meetings of the PUWP leadership: A selection from 1949–1970], ed. Antoni Dudek, Aleksander Kochański, and Krzysztof Persak (Warsaw: Instytut Studiów Politycznych, 2000), 224; see also Rykowski and Władyka, *Polska próba*, 267.

136. AAN, PZPR, 1679, Notatka dla członków Biura Politycznego PZPR w sprawie zagłuszania wrogich audycji radiowych [Note for PUWP Politburo members about the issue of jamming of hostile radio programs], October 1956, 3.

137. *6 lat temu . . . Kulisy polskiego Października* [Six years ago: Behind the scenes of the Polish October], ed. Jerzy Mond (Paris: Instytut Literacki, 1962), 71–72.

138. "Już nie zagłuszamy" [We have stopped jamming], *Trybuna Ludu*, November 25, 1956.

139. See Stefan Pastuszewski, *Bydgoski listopad 1956* [November 1956 in Bydgoszcz] (Bydgoszcz: Świadectwo, 1996), 14–25; Marek Rzepa, "Zagłuszaczka na Wzgórzu Dąbrowskiego" [The jammer on Dąbrowski Hill], in Paczoska-Hanke, *Przełom w przełomie,* 111–19.

140. AAN, PZPR, 1679, Pismo ministra łączności Jana Rabanowskiego do prezesa Rady Ministrów Józefa Cyrankiewicza [Letter from Minister of Communications Jan Rabanowski to the Chairman of the Council of Ministers Józef Cyrankiewicz], November 19, 1956.

141. Pastuszewski, *Bydgoski listopad 1956*, 37–39.

142. AAN, PZPR, 1679, Pismo ministra łączności Jana Rabanowskiego do prezesa Rady Ministrów Józefa Cyrankiewicza, November 19, 1956.

143. *Centrum władzy*, 224; Kochański, *Polska 1944–1991*, 639.

144. Nowak-Jeziorański, *Wojna w eterze*, 261–62.

145. Jacques Semelin, *La liberté au bout des ondes: Du coup de Prague à la chute du mur de Berlin* (Paris: Belfond, 2009), 68.

146. Nestor Ratesh, "Radio Free Europe's Impact in Romania during the Cold War," in Johnson and Parta, *Cold War Broadcasting*, 205–28.

147. Johnson and Parta, *Cold War Broadcasting*, 385.

148. Oldrich Tuma, "Broadcasting: Its Impact on Czechoslovakia" (paper presented at the Hoover Institution conference, "Cold War Broadcasting Impact," Palo Alto, CA, October, 13–15, 2004).

149. Jordan Baev, "Bulgarian Regime Countermeasures against Radio Free Europe," in Johnson and Parta, *Cold War Broadcasting*, 262.

Chapter 3

1. Henryk Dominiczak, *Organy bezpieczeństwa PRL, 1944–1990* [The security organs of the People's Republic of Poland, 1944–1990] (Warsaw: Bellona, 1997), 128, 139. A fuller account of the events of 1956 is available in Paweł Machcewicz, *Rebellious Satellite: Poland 1956* (Washington, DC: Woodrow Wilson Center Press; Stanford, CA: Stanford University Press, 2009).

2. Jan Nowak-Jeziorański, *Wojna w eterze. Wspomnienia* [The war on the airwaves: A memoir], vol. 1, *1948–1956* (London: Odnowa, 1986), 244–62; Jan Nowak-Jeziorański, *Polska z oddali. Wspomnienia* [Poland from afar: A memoir], vol. 2, *1956–1976* (Cracow: Znak, 1992), 10–21; Paweł Machcewicz, *Emigracja w polityce międzynarodowej* [Emigration in international politics], vol. 2 of *Druga Wielka Emigracja 1945–1990* [The second Great Emigration, 1945–1990] (Warsaw: Biblioteka "Więzi," 1999), 147–48. See also Machcewicz, *Rebellious Satellite.*

3. Nowak-Jeziorański, *Polska z oddali*, 22–23.

4. Archiwum Akt Nowych [Central Archive of Modern Records], Warsaw (hereafter AAN), 237/VII-2795, Notatka dotycząca spotkania części delegacji ZSP z przedstawicielami polskiej sekcji Wolnej Europy [Note about a meeting of a subgroup of the delegation of the Polish Students' Association with representatives of the Polish Section of Free Europe], April 3, 1957, 34–35. Adamski's report was also sent to the Ministry of Internal Affairs. The Security Service had information about this meeting from another, second-hand source, "an intelligence source from the territory of Belgium" (Archiwum Instytutu Pamięci Narodowej [Archive of the Institute of National Remembrance], Warsaw [hereafter AIPN], 0296/150, vol. 1).

5. AIPN, 01299/777, Linia polityczna rozgłośni Wolna Europa w Monachium w okresie od października 1956 r. do stycznia 1958 r. [The political line of Radio Free Europe in Munich in the period from October 1956 to January 1958], February 14, 1958, 5.

6. See Jakub Tyszkiewicz, *Otwarte okno w "żelaznej kurtynie." Polityka administracji prezydenta Eisenhowera wobec Polski (październik 1956–styczeń 1961)* [An open window in the "Iron Curtain": The Eisenhower administration's policies toward Poland (October 1956–January 1961)] (Wrocław: Wydawnictwo Uniwersytetu Wrocławskiego, 2003); Bennett Kovrig, *Of Walls and Bridges: The United States and Eastern Europe* (New York: New York University Press, 1991).

7. Nowak-Jeziorański, *Polska z oddali*, 13–15.

8. AIPN, 01299/777, Linia polityczna rozgłośni Wolna Europa w Monachium w okresie od października 1956 r. do stycznia 1958 r. [The political line of Radio Free Europe in Munich in the period from October 1956 to January 1958], February 14, 1958, 16.

9. Jan Nowak's archive in Annandale, Virginia (hereafter AJN), Implications of Polish Political Opinions Analysis for RFE Programming Policies [1957].

10. AIPN, 01299/789, Informacja o radiostacji Wolnej Europy w Monachium [Information about the Free Europe station in Munich], August 1, 1958, 7.

11. Wyciąg z informacji źródła "Bolek" dotyczący pracy w Wolnej Europie w Monachium Jana Kroka-Paszkowskiego [A digest of information from agent "Bolek" concerning the work at Free Europe in Munich by Jan Krok-Paszkowski] is an example of information delivered to the Security Service by a person who met with Krok-Paszkowski in Munich, November 7, 1958 (AIPN, 00231/293, vol. 2). It includes information about him, as well as about RFE's archive.

12. AIPN, 525/7, Informacja o radiostacji RWE [Information about the RFE radio station], probably 1957.

13. AIPN, Ministerstwo Spraw Wewnętrznych [Ministry of Internal Affairs, hereafter MSW], 6184, Zarządzenie ministra spraw wewnętrznych nr. 00173/58 w sprawie pracy operacyjnej Służby Bezpieczeństwa za granicą (w krajach kapitalistycznych) oraz załącznik: Wykaz obiektów i środowisk będących w zainteresowaniu operacyjnym Departamentu I MSW [Decision no. 00173/58 of the Minister of Internal Affairs about the issue of operational work of the Security Service abroad (in capitalist countries) and appendix: Listing of installations and milieus that are of operational interest to Department I of the Ministry of Internal Affairs], August 8, 1958, 109–22.

14. AIPN, 01237/432, Sprawa ewidencyjno-obserwacyjna Bogumiła Brydaka [The evidence-observation case of Bogumił Brydak], 184.

15. Nowak-Jeziorański, *Polska z oddali*, 15; Tyszkiewicz, *Otwarte okno w "żelaznej kurtynie,"* 314.

16. Paweł Ziętara, *Emigracja wobec Października. Postawy polskich środowisk emigracyjnych wobec liberalizacji w PRL w latach 1955–1957* [The émigré community and October: The attitudes of Polish émigré communities toward liberalization in People's Poland in 1955–1957] (Warsaw: LTW, 2001), 264; Jerzy Giedroyc, *Autobiografia na cztery ręce* [A four-handed autobiography], ed. Krzysztof Pomian (Warsaw: Czytelnik, 1994), 188.

17. Marcin Kula, *Paryż, Londyn i Waszyngton patrzą na Październik 1956 r. w Polsce* [Paris, London and Washington look at October 1956 in Poland] (Warsaw: Instytut Studiów Politycznych, 1992), 198.

18. Tyszkiewicz, *Otwarte okno w "żelaznej kurtynie,"* 319.

19. Ibid., 331.

20. The Polish vice minister of foreign affairs recorded their conversation in detail: Józef Winiewicz, *Co pamiętam z długiej drogi życia* [What I can remember from the long road that has been my life] (Poznań: Wydawnictwo Poznańskie, 1985), 628. For an official American record of the Gomułka-Nixon conversation with respect to RFE, see *Foreign Relations of the United States, 1958–1960*, vol. 10, pt. 2, *Eastern Europe* (Washington, DC: US Government Printing Office, 1993), 212–13.

21. Nowak-Jeziorański, *Polska z oddali*, 94–95.

22. Tyszkiewicz, *Otwarte okno w "żelaznej kurtynie,"* 335–36.

23. Ibid., 336.

24. AIPN, 01299/814, Rozmowy w sprawie przyszłości Radia Wolna Europa [Discussions about the future of Radio Free Europe], January 11, 1960.

25. Tyszkiewicz, *Otwarte okno w "żelaznej kurtynie,"* 343.

26. See Andrzej Mania, *Bridge building. Polityka USA wobec Europy Wschodniej w latach 1961–1968* [Bridge building: US policies toward Eastern Europe in 1961–1968] (Cracow: Wydawnictwo Uniwersytetu Jagiellońskiego, 1996); Tyszkiewicz, *Otwarte okno w "żelaznej kurtynie,"* 170–78; Paweł Machcewicz, "Stany Zjednoczone wobec polskiego Października 1956 roku" [The United States and the Polish October 1956], in *Polska 1944/45–1989. Studia i materiały* [Poland 1944/45–1989: Studies and materials], vol. 3 (Warsaw: Neriton, 1997), 45–61.

27. D.P., "Wolna Europa a emigracja polska" [Free Europe and the Polish emigration], *Polityka* 42 (1959).

28. Ibid. Two previous installments of the series were "Wolna Europa" [Free Europe], *Polityka* 40 (1959), and "Wolna Europa. Rzecz o metodzie zimnej wojny" [Free Europe: About the methods of the Cold War], *Polityka* 41 (1959).

29. Nowak-Jeziorański, *Polska z oddali*, 395.

30. Passent responded to a letter from me dated February 26, 2007: "In reply to your letter, for which I want to thank you, I would like to confirm that I was the author of the articles about Radio Free Europe you mention, which appeared in *Polityka* in 1959. They were actually edited materials that I had received officially via my Editors. After almost 50 years I cannot remember precisely who gave them to me, but already then their provenance had seemed unclear. Perhaps because I had not collected the materials myself and I was troubled by doubts, which I repressed, I shamefully signed them with my initials. When I think about it today, I am embarrassed; at that time I did not see it so clearly, I was a student and a beginning free-lancer at the paper." Letter dated March 6, 2007.

31. In an interview I conducted, Passent denied receiving these materials directly from the Security Service (telephone conversation of March 7, 2007). In January 1961, Lieutenant P. Adach of Section VIII of Department II (counterintelligence) of the Ministry of Internal Affairs met with Passent in the *Polityka* offices. The Security Service expected Passent to report on his meetings with US diplomats. Passent was initially registered as an operational contact, and then in 1964 as a secret collaborator. In 1970, Department II gave up on contacts with him because Passent avoided them. Adach wrote in a report about their first meeting: "The mentioned individual was certain that

I wanted to pass an article for the press through him" (AIPN, 002086/38, Raport z przeprowadzonej rozmowy z Danielem Passentem—kontaktem attaché kulturalnego ambasady USA Yale'a Richmonda [A report on an interview conducted with Daniel Passent, a contact of Yale Richmond, cultural attaché of the USA embassy], January 2, 1961). This may suggest that it was not unusual for the Security Service to relay materials directly to journalists.

32. For a description of the evolution of the PUWP leadership's policies toward intellectuals and journalists after October 1956, see Andrzej Friszke, "Kultura czy ideologia? Polityka kulturalna kierownictwa PZPR w latach 1957–1963" [Culture or ideology? The PUWP leadership's cultural policies in 1957–1963], in *Władza a społeczeństwo w PRL. Studia historyczne* [Government and society in the People's Republic of Poland: Historical studies], ed. Andrzej Friszke (Warsaw: Instytut Studiów Politycznych, 2003), 115–46.

33. Krzystof Persak, *Sprawa Henryka Hollanda* [The case of Henryk Holland] (Warsaw: Instytut Studiów Politycznych PAN and Instytut Pamięci Narodowej, 2006). The chapter titled "Odwrót od Października—dyscyplinowanie partii i prasy" [Turning away from October: The disciplining of the party and the press] contains much important information to illustrate the growth of repressive tendencies in the PUWP leadership's policies after 1956.

34. Andrzej Friszke, *Opozycja polityczna w PRL 1945–1980* [The political opposition in the People's Republic of Poland, 1945–1980] (London: Aneks, 1994), 175–76; Konrad Rokicki, *Literaci. Relacje między literatami w władzami PRL w latach 1956–1970* [The writers: Relations between writers and the authorities of People's Poland in 1956–1970] (Warsaw: Instytut Pamięci Narodowej, 2011), 159–60, 213.

35. Persak, *Sprawa Henryka Hollanda*, 302.

36. Władysław Gomułka, *Przemówienia, styczeń 1963–lipiec 1964* [Speeches, January 1963–July 1964] (Warsaw: Iskry, 1964), 89.

37. AAN, Polskiej Zjednoczonej Partii Robotniczej [Central Committee of the Polish United Workers' Party, hereafter PZPR], 1255, 83 (excerpt from a speech that was not included in the published version cited in note 36).

38. Ibid., 233–40. An excerpt from Moczar's comments is quoted in Krzysztof Lesiakowski, *Mieczysław Moczar "Mietek." Biografia polityczna* [Mieczysław Moczar "Mietek": A political biography] (Warsaw: Rytm, 1998), 224.

39. AAN, PZPR, 1255, 116.

40. Ibid., 140–41.

41. Jerzy Eisler, "Powodowani troską obywatelską" [Motivated by civic responsibility], *Tygodnik Powszechny* 11 (2004).

42. In Jerzy Eisler, *List 34* [The Letter of the 34] (Warsaw: PWN, 1993), 79.

43. "Notatka z przebiegu rozmowy I sekretarza KC PZPR tow. Władysława Gomułki z Prezydium Zarządu Głównego Związku Literatów Polskich" [Notes from a conversation between the First Secretary of the CC PUWP Comrade Władysław Gomułka and the Presidium of the Polish Writers' Union], *Zeszyty Historyczne* 153 (2005): 151–53.

44. AAN, 237/VII-21, Protokół nr 2 [Protocol no. 2], September 29, 1964, 506.

45. Eisler, *List 34*, 112–17; see also Andrzej Krajewski, "Pisarze do więzienia" [Put the writers in prison], *Rzeczpospolita*, May 2–4, 2003.

46. AIPN, 0192/72, vol. 3, Doniesienie tajnego współpracownika ps. "Ewa" [Report from the secret collaborator code-named "Ewa"], December 3, 1964, 187.

47. Nowak-Jeziorański, *Polska z oddali*, 148.

48. AIPN, 0665/176, Informacja ministra spraw wewnętrznych wygłoszona na naradzie sekretarzy propagandy komitetów wojewódzkich PZPR [Information from the minister of internal affairs presented at a meeting of propaganda secretaries of the PUWP provincial committees], 1971, 5.

49. Aleksandra Ziółkowska, *Proces Melchiora Wańkowicza 1964* [The trial of Melchior Wańkowicz, 1964] (Warsaw: Nowe Wydawnictwo Polskie, 1990), 38–39.

50. Nowak-Jeziorański, *Polska z oddali*, 152.

51. AIPN, 01265/1503, Informacja nr 06 dotycząca Melchiora Wańkowicza [Information no. 06 concerning Melchior Wańkowicz], January 7, 1965.

52. AIPN, 0296/150, vol. 1, Niektóre zagadnienia wrogiej antypaństwowej działalności politycznej [Some issues of hostile antistate political activity], June 26, 1963, 72–73.

53. AIPN, MSW II, 835, Report on the situation in Poland, probably written by the office of the minister of internal affairs, n.d., no author.

54. AIPN, 0296/150, vol. 2, Skutki dywersji polityczo-ideologicznej, jakie ostatnio występują w kraju [Consequences of political-ideological sabotage that have recently occurred in Poland], September 10, 1968, 337.

55. AIPN, 0296/150, vol. 1, Zwalczanie przejawów dywersji ideologiczno-politycznej [Combating the symptoms of ideological-political sabotage], n.d., 208.

56. AIPN, 01256/522, Departament III, Sprawozdanie z wyników pracy za rok 1965 [Department III, Report on work outcomes for 1965], January 1966, 56.

57. AIPN, 0296/150, t. 1, Dywersja ideologiczno-polityczna (tezy) [Ideological-political sabotage (theses)], May 1966, 239.

58. AIPN, 01256/522, Departament III, Sprawozdanie z wyników pracy za rok 1965 [Department III, Report on work outcomes for 1965], January 1966, 66.

59. See, for instance, AIPN, MSW II, 327, Stenogram z krajowej narady aktywu kierowniczego resortu spraw wewnętrznych na temat: "Aktualne problemy bezpieczeństwa w kraju" [Transcript of the national conference of the leadership activists of the Ministry of Internal Affairs entitled "Current security problems in Poland"], June 7, 1966, 20; AIPN, MSW II, Gabinet Ministra [Minister's Office], 837, Ocena zagrożenia wewnętrznego PRL pod względem bezpieczeństwa i porządku publicznego [An assessment of the internal threat to the People's Republic of Poland in terms of public security and order], October 14, 1969, 10.

60. AIPN, 0296/150, vol. 2, Dywersja ideologiczno-polityczna—tezy [Ideological-political sabotage: Theses], October 1967, 144–45.

61. Jerzy Eisler, *Polski rok 1968* [The Polish year 1968] (Warsaw: Instytut Pamięci Narodowej, 2006), 225; text of flier in *Wydarzenia marcowe 1968* [The March events of 1968] (Paris: Instytut Literacki, 1969), 139.

62. Eisler, *Polski rok 1968*, 280–81; text of flier in *Polskie przedwiośnie. Dokumentów marcowych tom II* [Poland's early spring: Volume 2 of the March documents] (Paris: Instytut Literacki, 1969), 59–61.

63. AIPN, 01265/1507, Hasła wysuwane w czasie ekscesów w ulotkach [Slogans conveyed on fliers during the events of excess].

64. Eisler, *Polski rok 1968*, 397.

65. Ibid., 299.

66. Ibid., 420. Text of appeal in *Wydarzenia marcowe 1968*, 94–95.

67. AIPN, 0296/150, vol. 1, Zwalczanie przejawów dywersji ideologiczno-politycznej [Combating the symptoms of ideological-political sabotage], n.d., 208.

68. Ibid., Przejawy dywersji ideologiczno-politycznej z zagranicy na kraj, 1963 r. [Signs of ideological-political sabotage from abroad to Poland, 1963], 109.

69. Jan Nowak-Jeziorański writes about this in *Polska z oddali*, 261–65, but without giving the names of his informants. He did reveal them in a TV program in Jerzy Diatłowicz's series *Rzeczpospolita i Pół.*

70. AIPN, 01299/358, Notatka informacyjna dotycząca ujawnionych kontaktów z Rozgłośnią Polską RWE [Informational note about the uncovered contacts with the Polish Section of RFE], July 21, 1962, 9–10.

71. Mieczysław F. Rakowski, *Dzienniki polityczne 1958–1962* [Political diaries, 1958–1962] (Warsaw: Iskry, 1998), 403–4.

72. AIPN, 0296/150, vol. 2, Notatka dotycząca zamierzeń ośrodków dywersji politycznej i ideologicznej w działalności przeciw PRL [Note on the intentions of political and ideological sabotage centers in their activities aimed against the People's Republic of Poland], January 1969, 375.

73. AIPN, 10299/842, Informacja dotycząca współdziałania organizacji syjonistycznych z podstawowymi ośrodkami dywersji—RWE i "Kulturą" [Information on the cooperation between Zionist organizations and the basic sabotage centers, RFE and *Kultura*], July 21, 1969, 1–2.

74. AIPN, 00221/2, Odpis-wyciąg z notatki "Juliusza" z dnia 15 IX 1969 r. ze spotkania z "Kondorem" [Transcription, excerpts of a note by "Juliusz" dated September 15, 1969 from a meeting with "Kondor"], 14.

75. AAN, 237/V-707, Działalność w zakresie propagandy zagranicznej, wojny psychologicznej i dywersji ideologicznej imperializmu oraz nasze przeciwdziałanie [Imperialism's activity in the sphere of foreign propaganda, psychological warfare and ideological sabotage and our counteractions], June 1966, 5.

76. Ibid., 28–30, 73.

77. Ibid., 46–47.

78. Zbigniew Chomicz, *75 lat Polskiego Radia. Kalendarium 1925–2000* [Seventy-five years of Polish Radio: A chronology, 1925–2000] (Warsaw: Polskie Radio, 2000), 79.

79. Jerzy Małczyński, *Byliśmy pierwsi. 45 lat temu Rozgłośnia Harcerska nadała pierwszą audycję* [We were first: Forty-five years ago, Scout Radio broadcast its first program] (Warsaw: Horyzonty, 2002), 13.

80. AAN, 237/XIX/363, Stenogram z wykładu Stefana Olszowskiego w Studium Dziennikarstwa [Transcript of Stefan Olszowski's lecture at the Journalism College], March 4, 1966, 113.

81. AAN, 237/V-707, Działalność w zakresie propagandy zagranicznej, wojny psychologicznej i dywersji ideologicznej imperializmu oraz nasze przeciwdziałanie [Imperialism's activities in the areas of foreign propaganda, psychological warfare and ideological sabotage and our counteraction], June 1966, 52.

82. Jerzy Waszczuk, beginning in 1968 working in the Press Office and later in the CC PUWP Secretariat, in a conversation with Jane Curry mentioned that in the late 1960s, a meeting of representatives of the Soviet bloc's parties took place in Prague at which this idea was discussed, but nothing was decided. Jane Curry, "RFE and the Polish Elite: The Fifth Branch of Government" (paper presented at the Hoover Institution

conference, "Cold War Broadcasting Impact," Palo Alto, CA, October 13–15, 2004). No documents about this issue have been found.

83. AIPN, 0296/150, vol. 1, Dane liczbowe dotyczące nasilenia oddziaływania wrogich ośrodków w latach 1963, 1964, 1965 i 1966 oraz bezpośrednich i pośrednich skutków tej działalności w kraju [Quantitative data on the strengthening of the effects of hostile centers in 1963, 1964, 1965, and 1966 and the direct and indirect effects of this activity in Poland], 227; AIPN, 0296/150, vol. 3, Dane liczbowe dotyczące nasilenia oddziaływania wrogich ośrodków w latach 1967–1969 oraz bezpośrednich i pośrednich skutków tej działalności w kraju [Quantitative data on the increase of the effects of hostile centers in 1967–1969 and the direct and indirect effects of this activity in Poland], April 1970, 4.

84. AIPN, 01265/1504, Informacja Departamentu III MSW dla KC PZPR, Informacja dotycząca kontaktów obywateli PRL z wrogimi ośrodkami, przejawów wrogiej propagandy, ujawnienia faktu kradzieży i prób przemycenia do Włoch cennych zbiorów muzealnych [Information from Department III of the Ministry of Internal Affairs for the CC PUWP, Information concerning contacts between citizens of the People's Republic of Poland with hostile centers, manifestations of hostile propaganda and the uncovering of the fact of thefts and attempts to smuggle precious museum collections to Italy], November 10, 1966.

85. AAN, 237/XIX/300, Notatka o obecnej sytuacji oraz najpilniejszych potrzebach inwestycyjnych w bazie technicznej radia i telewizji [Note on the current situation and the most urgent investment needs in the technical base of radio and television], October 1968, 31.

86. AAN, 237/XIX/363, Stenogram z wykładu Stefana Olszowskiego w Studium Dziennikarstwa [Transcript of Stefan Olszowski's lecture in the Journalism Program], March 4, 1966, 87.

87. AAN, 237/XIX/363, Notatka ze spotkania kierownika Biura Prasy KC PZPR Stefana Olszowskiego z przedstawicielami Klubu Dziennikarzy Sportowych SDP i pism sportowych w dniu 4 XII 1965 r. [Notes from a meeting between the head of the CC PUWP Press Office, Stefan Olszowski, and representatives of the Sports Reporters Club of the Polish Journalists' Association and of sports magazines on December 4, 1965], 38–39.

88. AAN, 237/III/48, VIII Plenum KC PZPR 16–17 V 1967 r. [Eighth Plenum of the CC PUWP, May 16–17, 1967], O aktualnych zadaniach w pracy politycznej partii [Concerning the current tasks in the party's political work], 441–42.

89. Ibid., 22.

90. Ibid., 64.

91. Ibid., 93.

92. Ibid., 184–88, 311–12.

93. AIPN, 01256/522, Departament III, Sprawozdanie z wyników pracy za rok 1965 [Report on work outcomes for 1965], January 1966, 58–59.

94. AIPN Wr, 053/1586, vol. 5, Informacja o wynikach przeprowadzonego rozpoznania problemu słuchania wrogich rozgłośni radiowych na terenie województwa wrocławskiego [Information on the results of an inquiry into the problem of listening to hostile radio stations in Wrocław Province], July 1965, 1–27.

95. AIPN Łd, 10/525, 139–45.

96. For the results of OBOP studies, see Jolanta Hajdasz, "Odbiór audycji Rozgłośni Polskiej RWE w Polsce" [Reception of programs of RFE's Polish Section in Poland], *Pamięć i sprawiedliwość* 6, no. 2 (2004): 312–13. Jerzy Morawski also wrote about OBOP's research in his reporter's book, *Głosy z Monachium* [Voices from Munich] (Warsaw: Interpress, 1993), 159–64.

Lechosław Gawlikowski, deputy director of RFE's Polish Service, believes that OBOP's data were too low by at least a dozen or so percentage points. He bases his view on an analysis of the questionnaires (which yielded lower figures when those polled spontaneously listed the foreign radio stations they listened to, and higher ones when the pollsters asked directly whether they listened to RFE) and OBOP's internal documents. According to Gawlikowski, the latter show traces of audience figures for foreign radio stations being intentionally lowered. The latter hypothesis is dubious since the OBOP study results were confidential, intended primarily for party and state leaders. Gawlikowski believes that research conducted by the Military Political Academy also points to higher listenership among officers and soldiers in the late 1970s and early 1980s, as do studies conducted by RFE's Audience and Public Opinion Research Department (Lechosław Gawlikowski [with Yvette Neisser Moreno], "The Audience to Western Broadcasts to Poland during the Cold War," in Johnson and Parta, *Cold War Broadcasting*, 121–44).

97. AIPN, 0296/150, vol. 1, Przejawy dywersji ideologiczno-politycznej z zagranicy na kraj, 1963 r., 107.

98. AIPN, 01265/481, Departament I [Department I], Sprawozdanie za rok 1963 [Report for 1963], 7.

99. AIPN, 0296/150, vol. 1, Przejawy dywersji ideologiczno-politycznej z zagranicy na kraj, 1963 r., 115–17.

100. Andrzej Friszke, *Życie polityczne emigracji* [The political life of emigration], vol. 1 of *Druga Wielka Emigracja 1945–1990* [The second Great Emigration, 1945–1990], in 3 vols. (Warsaw: Więź, 1999), 287, 320–21; Krzysztof Tarka, "Jest tylko jedna Polska. Bolesław Świderski—emigrant w służbie Polski Ludowej" [There is only one Poland: Bolesław Świderski, an émigré serving People's Poland], *Pamięć i Sprawiedliwość* 11, no. 1 (2007): 273–308.

101. Persak, *Sprawa Henryka Hollanda*, 217.

102. Krzysztof Tarka, "Między emigracją a krajem. Witold Olszewski i paryskie 'Horyzonty'" [Between the émigré community and Poland: Witold Olszewski and the Paris *Horyzonty*], *Zeszyty Historyczne* 154 (2005): 102–52.

103. Jędrzej Giertych, "Położenie Polski w świecie" [Poland's situation in the world], *Horyzonty* 123 (1966).

104. AIPN, 0296/150, vol. 1, Przejawy dywersji ideologiczno-politycznej z zagranicy na kraj, 1963 r., 117.

105. AIPN, 0397/330, Dywersja ideologiczno-polityczna przeciwko krajom obozu socjalistycznego [Ideological-political sabotage against the countries of the socialist camp], November 30, 1963, 37.

106. AIPN, MSW II, 589, Kierunki pracy i zadania SB na rok 1964 [The Security Service work streams and tasks for 1964], December 23, 1963, 84.

107. AIPN, MSW II, 30158, Sprawozdanie z pracy Służby Bezpieczeństwa MSW za okres 1 I 1962–1 IX 1963 [Report on the work of the Security Service of the Ministry of Internal Affairs for the period January 1, 1962–September 1, 1963], October 1963, 22.

108. AIPN, 01265/521, Departament III, Sprawozdanie z wyników pracy za rok 1964 [Report on the outcomes of work for 1964], 39. The distribution is somewhat different in the category of cases of operational investigation. Prevalent in the 536 cases are those concerning "enemy written propaganda (308) and hostile and harmful activity in the national economy (89)." No figure appears for contacts with foreign-instigated "sabotage." An "operational verification" was intended to obtain "initial information and materials about hostile activity," while an "operational investigation" was conducted in cases where "antistate criminal activity" had already been determined. Security Service operational instructions are given in *Instrukcje pracy operacyjnej aparatu bezpieczeństwa 1945–1989* [Instructions for operational work of the security apparatus, 1945–1989], ed. and with an introduction by Tadeusz Ruzikowski (Warsaw: Instytut Pamięci Narodowej, 2004), 111–13.

109. AIPN, MSW II, Gabinet Ministra [Minister's Office], 48, Tematy informacji opracowywanych przez jednostki Służby Bezpieczeństwa MSW i KGMO [Information topics developed by units of the Security Service of the Ministry of Internal Affairs and Headquarters of the Citizens' Militia], 6.

110. Just one folder, labeled "Pomocnicy" (Assistants), contains descriptions of dozens of such cases from many provinces for 1970–1972 (AIPN, 0140/4, Materiały dotyczące autorów listów wysyłanych do Radia Wolna Europa [Materials about the authors of letters written to Radio Free Europe]). The arrest in Cracow of Kazimierz Chałupnik, "suspected of sending letters slandering members of the CC to Radio Free Europe," is an example of such a case from an earlier period (AIPN, 01265/1549, Informacja na podstawie sprawozdań kwartalnych Wydziału III SB przy KWMO w Krakowie [Information based on quarterly reports from Section III of the Security Service in the Provincial Headquarters of the Citizens' Militia in Cracow], February 10, 1959).

111. Documents from the Cracow Security Service may serve as an example of such activity. AIPN Kr, 08/117, vol. 2.

112. AIPN, 01256/522, Departament III [Department III], Sprawozdanie za rok 1965 [Report for 1965], 60–62.

113. AIPN, 01428/3, Pismo dyrektora Departamentu I Witolda Sienkiewicza do dyrektora Departamentu III Zbigniewa Paszkowskiego [Memorandum from Director of Department I Witold Sienkiewicz to Director of Department III Zbigniew Paszkowski], January 14, 1959, 133.

114. Ibid., Pismo dyrektora Departamentu III Zbigniewa Paszkowskiego do dyrektora Departamentu I Witolda Sienkiewicza [Memorandum from Director of Department III Zbigniew Paszkowski to Director of Department I Witold Sienkiewicz], January 26, 1959, 132.

115. AIPN, MSW II, 589, Niektóre zagadnienia pracy operacyjnej w latach 1963–1964 [Some issues in operational work in 1963–1964], May 7, 1963, 56.

116. AIPN, 01265/521, Departament III [Department III], Sprawozdanie za rok 1964 [Report for 1964], 5.

117. AIPN, 0397/330, Dywersja ideologiczno-polityczna przeciwko krajom obozu socjalistycznego, November 30, 1963, 37.

118. AIPN, 0296/150, vol. 1, Przejawy dywersji ideologiczno-politycznej z zagranicy na kraj, 1963 r., 107.

119. AIPN, 01265/483, Departament I [Department I], Sprawozdanie za rok 1965 [Report for 1965], 5.

120. Ibid., Sprawozdanie za rok 1964 [Report for 1964], 5.

121. Andrzej Stefanowski, "Orędownik 'Free Europe'" [The "Free Europe" emissary], *Nasz Znak* 141/142, nos. 2/3 (1964); Juliusz Mieroszewski's article: Londyńczyk, "Kto uprawia ideologiczną dywersję?" [Who practices ideological sabotage?], *Kultura* (Paris) 195/196, nos. 1/2 (1964).

122. Janusz Kolczyński, "Mechanizm ideologicznej dywersji" [The mechanism of ideological sabotage], *Kultura* (Warsaw), November 24, 1963; Kolczyński, "Wolna Europa" [Free Europe] (parts 1 and 2), *Kultura* (Warsaw), December 1, 1963, and December 8, 1963; Kolczyński, *Dywersja* [Sabotage] (Warsaw: Iskry, 1964); Kolczyński, *Wolna Europa* [Free Europe] (Warsaw: Ministerstwo Obrony Narodowej, 1969).

123. About the creation of the East-West Center, see AIPN, MSW II, 31148, Notatka informacyjna [Informational note], November 10, 1965, 1.

124. AAN, 237/XXXI/16, Notatka Wydziału Propagandy i Agitacji KC PZPR [Note from the Department of Propaganda and Agitation of the CC PUWP], 1971, no author.

125. Nowak-Jeziorański, *Polska z oddali*, 383–413.

126. Paweł Piotrowski, "Struktury Służby Bezpieczeństwa MSW" [The structure of the Security Service of the Ministry of Internal Affairs], *Pamięć i Sprawiedliwość* 3, no. 1 (2003): 59–60.

127. AIPN, 01748/162, Zarządzenie nr 0019 dyrektora Departamentu I MSW w sprawie pracy i struktury organizacyjnej Inspektoratu "I" Departamentu I MSW [Decision no. 0019 of the director of Department I of the Ministry of Internal Affairs about the work and organizational structure of Inspectorate "I" of Department I of the Ministry of Internal Affairs], January 15, 1971, 65–66. Andrzej Paczkowski, who found this document in the Institute of National Remembrance archive, has determined that Inspectorate "I" existed already in February 1969.

128. AIPN, 0365/104, vol. 1, Zadania Departamentu III wynikające z uchwał VI Zjazdu PZPR i krajowej narady resortu spraw wewnętrznych [Department III tasks stemming from the resolutions of the 6th Conference of the PUWP and a national meeting of the Ministry of Internal Affairs], February 1972, 718; see Dominczak, *Organy bezpieczeństwa PRL 1944–1990*, 241.

The director of Department III, Colonel Stanisław Morawski, gave a detailed account of the tasks assigned to group "D," which were related largely to actions conducted against the "centers of political-ideological sabotage" and the émigré community during the ministry's meeting in April 1972. "Przygotowywanie materiałów do publikacji w kraju lub kolportażu w określonych środowiskach na Zachodzie w celu demaskowania wrogich ośrodków i osób z nimi związanych; przygotowywanie materiałów dezinformacyjnych z dziedziny polityczno-ekonomicznej w celu przekazania przeciwnikowi" [The preparation of materials for publication in Poland or distribution in specific milieus in the West in order to unmask enemy organizations and persons connected to them; the preparation of disinformation materials on political-economic topics with the goal of giving them to the adversary] (AIPN, 0365/104, vol. 2, Paper for the national meeting, April 17–18, 1972, 70–71).

129. Protocol for missing Inspectorate "I" documents in file AIPN, 01746/3. It should be noted that no documents of group "D," charged with Church affairs within Department IV, which was also active at this time, have been found either (Marek Lasota, "O raporcie sejmowej komisji poświęconym Samodzielnej Grupie 'D' w

MSW" [The report of the Sejm commission devoted to the Self-Contained Group "D" in the Ministry of Internal Affairs], *Biuletyn Instytutu Pamięci Narodowej* 24, no. 1 (2003): 27–36).

130. "Monachijska menażeria," n.d., no place of publication, archive of Institut Littéraire in Maisons-Laffitte.

131. Zakład Narodowy im. Ossolińskich (Ossoliński National Institute), Jan Nowak-Jeziorański papers (herafter JNJ), 41/99, Memorandum do Ralpha Waltera [A memorandum to Ralph Walter], January 10, 1969.

132. Nowak-Jeziorański, *Polska z oddali*, 353.

133. Zakład Narodowy im. Ossolińskich, JNJ, 41/99, Notatka [Note], November 1969.

134. AIPN, 0296, vol. 2, Notatka [Note], June 13, 1960, 5.

135. Ibid., Materiały na konferencję moskiewską [Materials for the Moscow conference], 67.

136. Ibid., 87.

137. Ibid., 90.

138. Ibid., 72.

139. AIPN, 0296, vol. 2, Wyciąg z notatki z przeprowadzonych rozmów w dniu 16 i 17 czerwca 1960 r. w sprawie koordynacji przedsięwzięć wywiadowczych między Komitetem Bezpieczeństwa Państwowego ZSRR i MSW PRL [Excerpts from a note on discussions conducted on June 16 and 17, 1960, on the issue of coordinating espionage undertakings between the Committee of State Security of the USSR and the Ministry of Internal Affairs of the People's Republic of Poland], 11.

140. Ibid., Notatka dotycząca problemów proponowanych do omówienia na spotkaniu kierownictwa MSW PRL z kierownictwem Komitetu Bezpieczeństwa Państwowego przy Radzie Ministrów Ukraińskiej Socjalistycznej Republiki Radzieckiej w Kijowie [Note on issues proposed for discussion in a meeting of the leadership of the Ministry of Internal Affairs of the People's Republic of Poland and the leadership of the Committee of State Security of the Council of Ministers of the Ukrainian Soviet Socialist Republic in Kiev, March 20, 1965, 99.

141. Ibid., Problemy na spotkanie z wiceministrem ZSRR [Issues for a meeting with the vice-minister of the USSR], May 1966, 104.

142. Ibid., Uwagi i propozycje Departamentu III w zakresie współpracy Służby Bezpieczeństwa MSW PRL z organami Komitetu Bezpieczeństwa Państwowego ZSRR [Remarks and proposals from Department III in the sphere of cooperation between the Security Service of the Ministry of Internal Affairs of the People's Republic of Poland and the organs of the Committee of State Security of the USSR], May 1967, 121.

143. Ibid., 123.

144. Ibid., 127–28.

145. AIPN, 0296, vol. 2, Uwagi i propozycje Departamentu III w zakresie współpracy Służby Bezpieczeństwa MSW PRL z organami MSW ZSRR [Remarks and proposals from Department III in the area of cooperation between the Security Service of the Ministry of Internal Affairs of the People's Republic of Poland and the organs of the Ministry of Internal Affairs of the USSR], February 28, 1969, 183–95.

146. Ibid., Protokół z rozmów pomiędzy delegacjami MSW PRL i Komitetu Bezpieczeństwa Państwowego przy Radzie Ministrów ZSRR [Minutes of discussions

between the delegations of the Ministry of Internal Affairs of the People's Republic of Poland and the Committee of State Security of the Council of Ministers of the USSR], March 10–15, 1969, 197–202.

147. Ibid., Dwuletni plan realizacji postanowień zawartych w protokole z rozmów delegacji MSW PRL i KBP przy Radzie Ministrów ZSRR [A two-year plan for implementing resolutions listed in the minutes of the discussions between the delegations of the Ministry of Internal Affairs of the People's Republic of Poland and the Committee of State Security of the Council of Ministers of the USSR], July 26, 1969, 205–13.

148. Ibid., Pismo J. Skomorochina do Stanisława Kończewicza [Letter from Y. Skoromokhin to Stanisław Kończewicz], October 24, 1969, 238.

149. For a discussion of Michał Goleniewski's work for the CIA and its effects on the work of Department I of the Ministry of Internal Affairs, see Leszek Pawlikowicz, *Tajny front zimnej wojny. Uciekinierzy z polskich służb specjalnych PRL 1956–1964* [The secret front of the Cold War: Defectors from the Polish special services, 1956–1964] (Warsaw: Rytm, 2004), 215–301.

150. Approaches to RFE Employees, November 27, 1967. A former head of RFE security, Richard Cummings, gave me this document. Cummings quoted from it in a paper he gave at a June 2005 conference in Warsaw, "The Communist Security Apparatus in East-Central Europe in 1944/45–89."

151. AIPN, 01168/422, Pismo Jerzego Lovella [Jerzy Lovell's paper], November 9, 1951, pages numbered irregularly.

152. Ibid., Raport o zatwierdzenie dokonania werbunku [Report about permission to perform recruitment], May 17, 1952.

153. Ibid. This file contains documents about Lovell's role in the attempts to recruit his brother-in-law, Chciuk's arrest in 1946, and information that Chciuk gave the Ministry of Public Security.

154. Letter from Wojciech Frazik to the author, October 9, 2006. Frazik is writing a biography of Wacław Felczak that describes in detail Chciuk's story; see also Frazik, "Kamień rzucony na szaniec. Wacław Felczak 1916–1993" [A sacrifice: Wacław Felczak 1916–1993], in *Węgry—Polska w Europie Środkowej. Historia—literatura. Księga pamiątkowa ku czci profesora Wacława Felczaka* [Hungary–Poland in Central Europe: History–literature: A festschrift for Professor Wacław Felczak], ed. Antoni Cetnarowicz, Csaba G. Kiss and Istvan Kovacs (Cracow: Instytut Historii Uniwersytetu Jagiellońskiego, 1997).

155. AIPN, 00168/422, Źródło: "Tokarz" [Source: "Tokarz"], January 12, 1960.

156. Ibid., Notatka końcowa [Concluding note], July 24, 1972.

157. AIPN, 01069/274, Źródło: "Franek," Doniesienie agenturalne [Source: "Franek": An operative's statement], January 7, 1958, 77–79.

158. Ibid., Źródło: "Włodek," Doniesienie nr XII/21/23 [Source: "Włodek": Statement no. XII/21/23], June 19, 1963, 156–60.

159. Ibid., Raport dotyczący wykorzystania TW "Michał" w czasie jego pobytu za granicą PRL do przeprowadzenia rozmów sondażowych z rozpracowywanymi figurantami: Zygmuntem Michałowskim i Jerzym Giedroyciem [Report on using secret collaborator "Michał" during his trip outside the People's Republic of Poland to conduct interviews with targets under investigation, Zygmunt Michałowski and Jerzy Giedroyc], September 19, 1970, 246–48.

160. Marek Lasota, *Donos na Wojtyłę. Karol Wojtyła w teczkach bezpieki* [Informing on Wojtyła: Karol Wojtyła in secret police files] (Cracow: Znak, 2006), 218–19.

161. AIPN, 00170/438, Notatka operacyjna na podstawie materiałów archiwalnych Wydziału II Biura "C" MSW nr 10651/I i 35191/II [Operational note based on archival materials of Section II of Office "C" of the Ministry of Internal Affairs nos. 10651/I and 35191/II], June 24, 1974, 55.

162. AIPN, 01069/274, Odpis doniesienia "Witolda." Notatka dotycząca spotkania z Zygmuntem Michałowskim oraz wyjazdy wraz z nim i Anglikiem Herbertem Auberonem na Sardynię w dniu 17 i 18 września br. [Copy of report from "Witold": Note concerning meeting with Zygmunt Michałowski and trips to Sardinia with him and the Englishman Herbert Auberon [Auberon Herbert—trans. note] on September 17 and 18 of this year], September 19, 1963, 180–87.

163. Ibid., 187.

164. AIPN, 00170/438, Notatka operacyjna na podstawie materiałów archiwalnych Wydziału II Biura "C" MSW nr 10651/I i 35191/II [Operational note based on archival materials of Section II of Office "C" of the Ministry of Internal Affairs nos. 10651/I and 35191/II], June 24, 1974, 5.

165. AIPN, 01069/274, Postanowienie o zakończeniu i przekazaniu sprawy do archiwum Departamentu I [Decision to terminate the case and store it in the Department I archive], October 23, 1973, 16.

166. Andrzej Czechowicz, *Siedem trudnych lat* [Seven difficult years] (Warsaw: Wydawnictwo Ministerstwa Obrony Narodowej, 1974), 154.

167. AIPN, 01069/274, Raport dotyczący przedsięwzięć operacyjnych w sprawie "Posłaniec" [Report concerning operational undertakings in the case of "Posłaniec"], October 14, 1963, 10.

168. AIPN, 01299/358, Notatka informacyjna dotycząca ujawnionych kontaktów z Rozgłośnią Polską RWE, July 21, 1962, 9.

169. AIPN, 0296/150, Notatka ppłk. Stefana Mikołajskiego, zastępcy naczelnika Wydziału I Departamentu III [Note from Lieutenant Colonel Stefan Mikołajski, deputy head of Section I of Department III], January 31, 1963, 70–71.

170. I have described the circumstances of the recruitment and details of collaboration in an article, "Teczka 'Fondy,' czyli o początkach penetracji agenturalnej Radia Wolna Europa" ["Fonda's" file, or the beginnings of the espionage infiltration of Radio Free Europe], in *Władza a społeczeństwo w PRL. Studia historyczne* [Government and society in the People's Republic of Poland: Historical studies] (Warsaw: Instytut Studiów Politycznych, 2003), 175–96. Materials about "Fonda" can be found in the Institute of National Remembrance archive on microfilm 00221/1.

171. See file about Mieczysław Lach, who worked for the Ministry of Internal Affairs from 1968 as "Kumor" (AIPN, 00221/7).

172. AIPN, 00221/1, Raport TW "Fonda" [Report from Secret Collaborator "Fonda"], manuscript.

173. AIPN, 00221/1, Raport z rozmowy werbunkowej przeprowadzonej z Jerzym Bożekowskim w dniach 15, 16, 17 XI 1963 r. w Wiedniu [Report on recruitment discussion conducted with Jerzy Bożekowski on November 15, 16, and 17, 1963, in Vienna], 7.

174. Sig Mickelson, *America's Other Voice: The Story of Radio Free Europe and Radio Liberty* (New York: Praeger, 1983), 5–9.

175. Kolczyński, *Wolna Europa*, 183.

176. See Kazimierz Zamorski's memoir, *Pod anteną Radia Wolna Europa* [Under Radio Free Europe's antenna] (Poznań: Wydawnictwo Wers, 1995).

177. AIPN, 00221/5, Notatka kpt. S. Markiewicza dotycząca Kazmierza Zamorskiego [Note from Captain S. Markiewicz about Kazimierz Zamorski], March 9, 1964.

178. Ibid., Raport płk. Zbigniewa Mikołajewskiego i płk. Zbigniewa Siekielewskiego dotyczący przedsięwzięć operacyjnych w sprawie krypt. "Morski" [Report by Colonel Zbigniew Mikołajewski and Colonel Zbigniew Siekielewski about the operational actions in the case code-named "Morski"], July 29, 1975.

179. For a discussion of the attempts to convince Zamorski to work for the Ministry of Internal Affairs, see Konrad Rokicki and Robert Spałek, "Donos z Monachium" [Report from Munich], *Wprost* 19, May 2, 2002.

180. See the corresponding section in "Wolna Europa (2)" [Free Europe (2)], *Kultura* (Warsaw) 25 (1963); Kolczyński, *Dywersja*, 51.

181. Kolczyński, *Dywersja*, 143. Compare the same section in Kolczyński's article, "Pour le roi de Prusse," pt. 5, *Kultura* (Warsaw) 19 (1964).

182. Machcewicz, "Teczka 'Fondy,'" 191–95.

183. AIPN, 01703/100, Akta osobowe Andrzeja Czechowicza [Personnel files of Andrzej Czechowicz], 39–40.

184. Ibid., 34.

185. This was the version he gave in conversations with Ewa Berberyusz, "Jednorazowo zużyty" [Disposable after a single use], *Tygodnik Powszechny* 32 (1990), and in 1992 with Kazimierz Zamorski, *Pod anteną Radia Wolna Europa*, 183. In Jerzy Diatłowicki's program, "Tajny agent," aired on Polish television as part of the series *Rzeczpospolita Druga i Pół* [The Second-and-a-Half Republic], he did not actually talk about blackmail but generally confirmed the circumstances of his recruitment as described earlier to Berberyusz and Zamorski. He presented a similar if less detailed version to Jerzy Morawski in the early 1990s (*Głosy z Monachium*, 195).

186. In his memoirs, Jan Nowak describes a situation that may have constituted an attempt to kidnap him. It occurred in Helsinki, where Nowak was attending a youth festival in which delegations from Communist countries were also taking part (*Polska z oddali*, 395–96).

187. Account by Andrzej Czechowicz, December 5, 2005, tape recordings in the author's possession. I also used what he told Jane Curry and A. Ross Johnson in July 2004 (Hoover Institution, Jane Curry Collection).

188. AIPN, 0665/176, Informacja ministra spraw wewnętrznych wygłoszona na naradzie sekretarzy propagandy komitetów wojewódzkich PZPR [Account by the minister of internal affairs given at a meeting of the propaganda secretaries of the PUWP provincial committees], 1971, 6.

189. The largest collection of reports and index cards from the RFE archive obtained by Czechowicz can be found in the Institute of National Remembrance archive, AIPN 02011/1108; 02011/1109.

190. This is not spelled out anywhere, but the beginning of this case is tied to information provided by agent "Gama," who worked for RFE's Polish Service. The documents repeatedly stress the need to keep the agent under cover and to protect him. According to my research, prior to Koryzma's recruitment, Czechowicz was the only agent inside the Polish Section. By then, the connection to "Fonda," Jerzy Bożekowski, had been suspended.

191. AIPN, 01263/141, Wyciąg z informacji źródła "Gama" [Extracts from information provided by "Gama"], December 29, 1965, no author.

192. Ibid., Notatka w sprawie krypt. "Kamera" [Note on the case code-named "Kamera"], April 17, 1973.

193. Ibid., Raport ze spotkania z agentem ps. "Kamera" odbytego w dniach 2–3 XII i 18 XII 1967 r. [Report on meetings with agent "Kamera" that took place on December 2–3 and December 18, 1967].

194. Ibid., Notatka w sprawie krypt. "Kamera" [Note on the case code-named "Kamera"], April 17, 1973.

195. Ibid., Raport ze spotkania z agentem ps. "Kamera" odbytego w dniach 2–3 XII i 18 XII 1967 r. [Report on meetings with agent "Kamera" that took place on December 2–3 and December 18, 1967].

196. Ibid., Raport ze spotkania z agentem ps. "Kamera" odbytego w dniach 27–28 I i 6 II 1968 r. [Report on meetings with agent "Kamera" that took place on January 27–28 and February 6, 1968].

197. Ibid., Raport ze spotkania z agentem ps. "Kamera" odbytego w dniach 2–3 XII i 18 XII 1967 r. [Report on meetings with agent "Kamera" that took place on December 2–3 and December 18, 1967].

198. Ibid., Notatka w sprawie krypt. "Kamera" [Note on the case code-named "Kamera"], April 17, 1973.

199. Ibid., Charakterystyka sprawy agenta ps. "Kamera" [The characteristics of the case of agent "Kamera"], May 2, 1968.

200. Ibid., Raport ze spotkania z agentem ps. "Kamera" odbytego w dniach 27–28 I i 6 II 1968 r. [Report on meetings with agent "Kamera" that took place on January 27–28 and February 6, 1968].

201. Ibid., handwritten note at the bottom of a document titled "Charakterystyka sprawy agenta 'Kamera'" [Characteristics of the case of agent "Kamera"].

202. Czechowicz, *Siedem trudnych lat*, 159.

203. AIPN, 02221/7, Raport z werbunku "Kumora" [Report on the recruitment of "Kumor"], May 11, 1968, 8.

204. Ibid., Notatka końcowa do tomu nr 1560 teczki pracy agenta "Kumor" [Summary note for volume no. 1560 of the working file for agent "Kumor"], 14–15.

205. Ibid., Notatka o agencie ps. "Kumor" za okres 11 V 1968–31 VIII 1974 r. [Note on agent "Kumor" for the period May 11, 1968–August 31, 1974], 21–22.

206. Ibid., 26.

207. Mieczysław Lach and Zdzisław Uberman, *Ufam ci Kilroy* [I trust you, Kilroy] (Warsaw: Krajowa Agencja Wydawnicza, 1983).

208. AIPN, 01136/247, Raport dotyczący przeprowadzenia rozmów werbunkowych z "Hilem" [Report about conducting recruitment conversations with "Hil"], December 7, 1966, no author.

209. Ibid., Notatka Stefana Jakobsa [Note from Stefan Jakobs], March 8, 1967.

210. Ibid., Notatka dotycząca informacji przekazanej w Wiedniu w styczniu 1967 r. [Note about information supplied in Vienna in January 1967], June 22, 1967.

211. Ibid., Odczyt z taśmy magnetofonowej nagranej na procesie Stefana Jakobsa w Wiedniu 28 II 1967 r. [Transcript from tape recording made at Stefan Jakobs's trial in Vienna on February 28, 1967].

212. Ibid. Notatka służbowa dotycząca sprawy "Hila" [Work note on the case of "Hil"], April 2, 1969.

213. Ibid., Postanowienie o zakończeniu i przekazaniu sprawy do archiwum Departamentu I [Decision to finish and file the case in the Department I archive], October 23, 1970.

214. Kazimierz Zamorski has written about Dr. Wawrzyńczyk's case (*Pod anteną Radia Wolna Europa*, 151–58). For his contacts with *Kultura*, see Małgorzata Ptasińska-Wójcik, "Inwigilacja Instytutu Literackiego przez Służbę Bezpieczeństwa w czasach Gomułki" [The surveillance of Instytut Literacki by the Security Service in the Gomułka era], in *Aparat bezpieczeństwa wobec emigracji politycznej i Polonii* [The security apparatus versus political emigration community and Polonia] (Warsaw: Instytut Pamięci Narodowej, 2005), 173–74.

215. "Oświadczenie dr. St. Wawrzyńczyka" [Statement by Dr. S. Wawrzyńczyk], *Trybuna Ludu*, September 17, 1967.

216. Kolczyński, "Wokół sprawy dr. Wawrzyńczyka. Dywersyjne zabiegi" [The case of Dr. S. Wawrzyńczyk: The saboteurs' ministrations], *Przekrój*, October 1, 1967.

217. AIPN, 01299/452, Notatka informacyjna dotycząca niedopuszczenia do wykorzystania dr. Stanisława Wawrzyńczyka w kampanii propagandowej RWE i paryskiej "Kultury" [Informational note about not allowing Dr. Stanisław Wawrzyńczyk to be used in a propaganda campaign by RFE and the Paris *Kultura*], September 1, 1967.

218. AIPN, MSW II, 31395, Sprawa dr. Stanisława Wawrzyńczyka [The case of Dr. Stanisław Wawrzyńczyk].

219. Zamorski, *Pod anteną Radia Wolna Europa*, 157.

220. AIPN, MSW II, 31395, Sprawa dr. Stanisława Wawrzyńczyka [The case of Dr. Stanisław Wawrzyńczyk].

221. See Paweł Machcewicz, "Kryptonim 'Medal'" [Code name "Medal"], *Rzeczpospolita*, September 18–19, 2004; the same issue of *Rzeczpospolita* published a commentary by Jan Nowak-Jeziorański, "To była zdrada" [This was treason].

222. Nowak-Jeziorański, *Wojna w eterze*, 73.

223. Author's interviews with Maciej Morawski (RFE's correspondent in Paris from 1965), July 14, 2005, and August 29, 2006. On June 21, 2005, Morawski wrote in a letter to the author about the conflict within the Polish desk: "Sometime around '66 or '67, conflicts over, on the one hand, attitudes toward Moczar and, on the other hand, the party revisionists became amplified within our radio team. I remember a meeting in a forest hotel near Munich . . . during which Józef Ptaczek thoroughly disparaged our [that is, the radio's] hostile attitude toward Moczar. Later, during a meal, some members of the staff 'jokingly' criticized me for excessively loving the 'revisionists-Zionists.' . . . Aleksandra Stypułkowska emphatically censured Moczar. This was very important, since her anti-Moczar arguments appealed to the members of the staff of the so-called nationalist orientation. . . . Powerful, though externally almost invisible, breaks within the staff occurred in '68. Trościanko and a certain number of other people condemned the 'dialogue, cooperating with' victims of the so-called anti-Zionist purges who were now in the West. Trościanko and his friends told tales about Stalinist-era criminals covered in Polish blood, or about these criminals' children. . . . One could sense that to some extent they judged the 'Polish secret policemen' less harshly, calling them 'native Polish secret policemen.'"

Jan Nowak-Jeziorański also discusses the differences of opinion among the radio staff concerning the Partisans, though very briefly (*Polska z oddali*, 281). Józef Ptaczek spoke to Jerzy Morawski about the conflict over the take on the Partisans. He mentioned Jan Krok-Paszkowski as someone who shared his views (Morawski, *Głosy z Monachium*, 39).

224. For the structure and mission of the Military Internal Service, see Paweł Piotrowski, "Wojskowa Służba Wewnętrzna 1957–1989" [The Military Internal Service, 1957–1989], *Biuletyn Instytutu Pamięci Narodowej* 6 (2002): 34–39. In the 1980s the Military Internal Service worked on both the legal and underground Solidarity and other opposition organizations, which also obviously lay outside its responsibilities as defined by law.

225. AIPN, 01069/139, Notatka końcowa dotycząca Wiktora Trościanki [Concluding note about Wiktor Trościanko], October 30, 1973, 19–21. There is no information in Trościanko's file about the first meeting in 1966, which allegedly included Dargas.

226. Friszke, *Życie polityczne emigracji*, 302–5, 357–59.

227. Tarka, "Między emigracją a krajem", 148.

228. Tadeusz Bielecki, "W oparciu o własne siły" [With one's own forces], *Myśl Polska* 11/12, 1968.

229. Antoni Dargas, "W obliczu przemian w kraju" [In view of the changes in Poland], *Myśl Polska* 11/12, 1968.

230. AIPN, 01069/139, Raport dotyczący spotkania z "Mentorem" w dniach 25–26 V 1969 r. w Austrii [Report on the meeting with "Mentor" on May 25–26, 1969 in Austria], May 30, 1969, 100–103; ibid., Raport płk. Edwarda Poradki i ppłk Stanisława Stępnia dla szefa WSW gen. Teodora Kufla [Report from Colonel Edward Poradko and Lieutenant Colonel Stanisław Stępień for General Teodor Kufel, head of the Internal Military Service], May 30, 1969, 104–24.

231. Ibid., Raport ramowy dotyczący spotkania z "Mentorem" odbytego w dniach 6–8 IV 1969 r. w Austrii [Framework report about the meeting with "Mentor" that took place on April 6–8, 1969, in Austria], April 15, 1969, 70–76; Raport ze spotkania z "Tubą" odbytego w dniach 6–9 IV 1969 r. w Austrii [Report from the meeting with "Tuba" that took place on April 6–9, 1969, in Austria], 76–90; ibid., Informacje uzyskane od "Mentora" na spotkaniu w dniach 6–9 IV 1969 r., 18 IV 1969 [Information gained from "Mentor" in meetings on April 6–9, 1969, and April 18, 1969], 91–96.

232. Another instance when similar points of view facilitated a dialogue between some members of the émigré nationalist camp and the Ministry of Internal Affairs headed by Moczar was the earlier discussion of *Horyzonty*. Its editor in chief, Witold Olszewski, allegedly said during a meeting with Polish intelligence officers that the more Mieczysław Moczar came "under attack by international Jewish publications and Free Europe, the greater is my sympathy for him" (Tarka, "Między emigracją a krajem," 141).

233. Ibid., Informacje uzyskane od "Mentora" na spotkaniu w dniach 6–9 IV 1969 r. [Information received from "Mentor" during a meeting on April 6–9, 1969], April 18, 1969, 90.

234. Ibid., Notatka dotycząca wyników informacyjnych spotkań z "Medalem" odbytych w dniach 9–10 VIII 1971 r. w Hiszpanii [Note about the informational outcomes of meetings with "Medal" conducted on August 9–10, 1971, in Spain], August 16, 1971, 11.

235. Ibid., Raport o zezwolenie na odbycie spotkania z Wiktorem Trościanką, redaktorem RWE w Monachium [Report asking for permission to conduct a meeting with Wiktor Trościanko, RFE editor in Munich], June 28, 1971, 2–8.

236. Ibid., Notatka dotycząca wyników informacyjnych spotkań z "Medalem" odbytych w dniach 9–10 VIII 1971 r. w Hiszpanii [Note about the informational outcomes of meetings with "Medal" conducted on August 9–10, 1971, in Spain], August 16, 1971, 11.

237. Ibid., Raport dotyczący spotkania z "Mentorem" w dniach 25–26 V 1969 r. w Austrii [Report on a meeting with "Mentor" on May 25–26, 1969, in Austria], May 30, 1969, 102–3.

238. AIPN, 00221/2, 18, 27. An odd aspect of the collaboration with "Kondor" that illustrated the secret police mentality well was Kozubski's request that the agent show up for meetings dressed "properly" (ibid., 17).

239. Ibid., Raport ze spotkania z "Tubą" odbytego w dniach 6–9 IV 1969 r. w Austrii [Report on a meeting with "Tuba" on April 6–9, 1969 in Austria], April 17, 1969, 85.

240. "Kapitan Czechowicz wykonał zadanie. Fragmenty relacji Andrzeja Czechowicza dla prasy, radia i telewizji [Captain Czechowicz has fulfilled his mission: Excerpts from accounts by Andrzej Czechowicz for the press, radio and television] (Warsaw, 1971), 59.

241. AIPN, 01069/139, Notatka dotycząca wyników informacyjnych spotkań z "Medalem" odbytych w dniach 9–10 VIII 1971 r. w Hiszpanii [Note about the informational outcomes of meetings with "Medal" on August 9–10, 1971, in Spain], August 16, 1971, 11.

242. Ibid., Raport dotyczący spotkań z "Medalem" odbytych w dniach 9–10 VIII 1971 r. w Hiszpanii [Report about meetings with "Medal" on August 9–10, 1971, in Spain], August 18, 1971, 17.

243. Ibid., Notatka dotycząca wyników informacyjnych spotkań z "Medalem" odbytych w dniach 9–10 VIII 1971 r. w Hiszpanii [Note about the informational outcomes of meetings with "Medal" on August 9–10, 1971, in Spain], August 16, 1971, 9.

244. See Włodzimierz Bolecki, *Ptasznik z Wilna. O Józefie Mackiewiczu (Zarys monograficzny)* [The bird keeper of Vilna: About Józef Mackiewicz (A monographic sketch)] (Cracow: Arcana, 2007); "Zrozumieć Mackiewicza. Rozmowa z prof. Włodzimierzem Boleckim" [To understand Mackiewicz: A conversation with Professor Włodzimierz Bolecki], *Rzeczpospolita*, March 2–3, 2002.

245. AIPN, 01069/139, Notatka dotycząca wyników informacyjnych spotkań z "Medalem" odbytych w dniach 9–10 VIII 1971 r. w Hiszpanii [Note about the informational outcomes of meetings with "Medal" on August 9–10, 1971, in Spain], August 16, 1971, 9.

246. Nowak-Jeziorański, *Polska z oddali*, 383–407; Dobrosława Platt, "Pomówienia z esbeckiej fałszywki" [Defamation in Security Service forgeries], *Rzeczpospolita*, May 5, 2001. A detailed discussion of the "disinformation" operations in the 1970s aimed against Jan Nowak can be found in chapter 5.

247. Andrzej Czechowicz's letter to the author, December 22, 2005.

248. AIPN, 01069/139, Raport dotyczący spotkań z "Medalem" odbytych w dniach 9–10 VIII 1971 r. w Hiszpanii [A report about meetings with "Medal" on August 9–10, 1971, in Spain], August 18, 1971, 15.

249. Ibid., Notatka informacyjna dotycząca okoliczności wykorzystania przez Departament I MSW tajnego współpracownika szefostwa WSW "Bogdana" [Informational

note about the circumstances of Department I of the Ministry of Internal Affairs use of the secret collaborator of the leadership of the Military Internal Service "Bogdan"], August 17, 1971, 20–22.

250. For a discussion of Brycht, see Henryk Dasko, "Nie ma miłości szczęśliwej" [True love doesn't exist], *Magazyn Gazety Wyborczej*, August 19, 1999; Henryk Dasko, "Jeszcze pokażę wszystkim skurnolom" [Wait till I show all them f----], *Magazyn Gazety Wyborczej*, August 26, 1999; Andrzej Chęciński, "Życie Andrzeja Brychta" [Andrzej Brycht's life], *Życie*, May 17, 2001.

251. Marta Fik, *Kultura polska po Jałcie. Kronika lat 1944–1981* [Polish culture after Yalta: A chronicle of the years 1944–1981] (London: Polonia, 1989), 397–98.

252. Dasko, "Nie ma miłości szczęśliwej."

253. Fik, *Kultura polska po Jałcie*, 420.

254. AIPN, 00170/516, vol. 2, Informacja dotycząca Andrzeja Brychta [Information about Andrzej Brycht], August 13, 1971.

255. AAN, 237/III/48, VIII Plenum KC PZPR [8th Plenum of the CC PUWP], May 16–17, 1967, 303.

256. Andrzej Brycht, *Raport z Monachium* [A report from Munich] (Warsaw: PAX, 1968), 29–30.

257. Ibid., 41.

258. Ibid., 67–68.

259. AIPN, 00170/516, vol. 1, Notatka służbowa [Work note], December 9, 1966, no author.

260. AIPN, 00170/516, vol. 6, Doniesienie, Źródło: A. B., przyjął: Andrzej Dudziński, 26 I 1967 r. [Information, Source: A. B., recorded by: Andrzej Dudziński, January 26, 1967]; Doniesienie, Źródło: A. B., przyjął: Andrzej Dudziński, 6 II 1967 r. [Information, Source: A. B., recorded by: Andrzej Dudziński, February 6, 1967].

261. Ibid., Notatka służbowa [Work note], February 6, 1967.

262. Ibid., Notatka służbowa [Work note], May 8, 1967.

263. Ibid., Notatka służbowa [Work note], October 27, 1967.

264. Ibid., Doniesienie, Źródło: "Gerard," przyjął: Andrzej Dudziński, 4 XI 1967 r. [Information, Source: "Gerard," recorded by: Andrzej Dudziński, November 4, 1967]; Notatka informacyjna [Informational note], November 20, 1967.

265. AIPN, 00170/516, vol. 2, Notatka służbowa [Work note], March 21, 1969.

266. Ibid., Raport o wznowienie współpracy z tajnym współpracownikiem ps. "Gerard" [Report on renewing collaboration with secret collaborator code-named "Gerard"], February 8, 1971.

267. Ibid., Notatka dotycząca Andrzeja Brychta [Note about Andrzej Brycht], August 13, 1971.

268. Ibid., Notatka służbowa [Work note], August 4, 1971.

269. Andrzej Brycht, *Azyl polityczny* [Political asylum] (Łódź: Krajowa Agencja Wydawnicza, 1989), 20.

270. Morawski, *Głosy z Monachium*, 57.

271. Brycht, "Słowa z chaosu" [Words out of chaos], *Kultura* 9, no. 288 (1971).

272. AIPN, 00170/516, vol. 2, Notatka informacyjna [Informational note], August 12, 1971.

273. Ibid., Informacja dotycząca Andrzeja Brychta [information about Andrzej Brycht], August 21, 1971.

274. Ibid.
275. Ibid.
276. AIPN, 00733/85, Zadania Zarządów Sztabu Generalnego w zakresie przygotowania systemu obrony terytorium kraju [Tasks of the Directorates of the General Staff in the sphere of readying the system of defenses of Poland's territory], 71–72, 75–76.
277. AIPN, 00733/86, Sprawozdanie z działalności Zarządu II Sztabu Generalnego według stanu na dzień 1 XII 1961 r. [Report on the activities of Directorate II of the General Staff as of December 1, 1961], February 8, 1960, 4.
278. All these cases are discussed in detail in Pawlikowicz, *Tajny front zimnej wojny.*
279. AIPN, 00733/86, Sprawozdanie z działalności Zarządu II Sztabu Generalnego za rok 1959 [Report on the activities of Directorate II of the General Staff for 1959], February 8, 1960, 4.
280. Pawlikowicz, *Tajny front zimnej wojny*, 59.
281. Archiwum Instytucji Ministerstwa Obrony Narodowej [Archive of the Institutions of the Ministry of National Defense], Modlin (hereafter AIMON), 341/92/164, Biuletyn informacyjny dotyczący publikacji o Wojsku Polskim w cywilnej prasie krajowej, radio i telewizji oraz radio i prasie zagranicznej w grudniu 1958 r. [Information bulletin of publications about the Polish Army in the Polish civilian press, radio and television and in foreign radio and press for December 1958], 3–10; AIMON, 344/92/164, Biuletyn informacyjny dotyczący publikacji o Wojsku Polskim w cywilnej prasie krajowej, radio i telewizji oraz radio i prasie zagranicznej w listopadzie 1958 r. [Information bulletin of publications about the Polish Army in the Polish civilian press, radio and television and in foreign radio and press for November 1958], 167–79.
282. AIMON, 380/92/575, Niektóre zagadnienia pracy polityczno-partyjnej w systemie obrony państwa [Some issues in political-party work in the state defense system], 10.
283. Ibid., 29.
284. Ibid., 12.
285. AIMON, 514/92/392, Notatka informacyjna w sprawie kierunków oddziaływania wrogiej propagandy na nastroje wojska od 1 III do 30 VI 1964 r. [Informational note about the directions of the effects of enemy propaganda on the mood in the army from March 1 to June 30, 1964], 463–64.
286. Ibid., 467.
287. Ibid.
288. AIMON, 240/91/123, Pismo ppłk. Eugeniusza Samsela do zastępcy szefa GZP gen. W. Polańskiego [Letter from Lieutenant Colonel Eugeniusz Samsel to deputy chief of the Main Political Directorate, General W. Polański], February 6, 1967, 168.
289. AIMON, 240/91/105, Ocena pracy lektorskiej w jednostkach lotnictwa operacyjnego za rok szkoleniowy 1966/67 [An assessment of the lecturer activity in the units of operational air force for training year 1966–67], December 8, 1967, 341.
290. Ibid., Pismo szefa Oddziału Propagandy Zarządu Politycznego Pomorskiego Okręgu Wojskowego ppłk. R. Milczarka do szefa Zarządu Propagandy GZP [Letter from the head of the Department of Propaganda of the Political Directorate of the Pomeranian Military District Lieutenant Colonel R. Milczarek to the head of the Propaganda Directorate of the Main Political Directorate], October 17, 1967, 71.

291. Ibid., Sprawozdanie z rocznej pracy lektorskiej w Marynarce Wojennej w 1967 r. [Report on the year's lecturer activity in the Navy for 1967], December 28, 1967, 390.

292. AIMON, 240/91/101, Opracowanie GZP w związku z zakończeniem wojny na Bliskim Wschodzie [Main Political Directorate study related to the end of the war in the Middle East], June 24, 1967, 107.

293. AIMON, 429/92/20, Pismo szefa GZP Gen. Józefa Urbanowicza [Letter from head of the Main Political Directorate, General Józef Urbanowicz], February 1, 1968. The file also contains a list of the members of the party leadership who received the Main Political Directorate analyses.

294. AIMON, 240/91/212, Pismo zastępcy szefa GZP płk. K. Korzenieckiego do szefa GZP Józefa Urbanowicza [Letter from the deputy chief of the Main Political Directorate, Colonel K. Korzeniecki to the chief of the Main Political Directorate Józef Urbanowicz], February 12, 1970, 27.

295. Ibid., Pismo zastępcy kierownika Działu Polityczno-Obronnego KOK Stefana Olszowskiego do płk. Henryka Nowaczyka [Letter from the deputy head of the Political-Defense Department of the National Defense Committee Stefan Olszowski to Col. Henryk Nowaczyk], 34.

296. AIMON, 240/91/198, Propozycje zarządu Propagandy i Agitacji Głównego Zarządu Politycznego WP w sprawie nawiązania współpracy między MON i MSW w zakresie zwalczania dywersji ideologicznej przeciwnika [Proposal from the Propaganda and Agitation Command of the Main Political Directorate of the Polish Army for establishing cooperation between the Ministry of National Defense and the Ministry of Internal Affairs in the area of combatting the enemy's ideological sabotage], January 16, 1970, 3.

Chapter 4

1. Andrzej Friszke, *Opozycja polityczna w PRL 1945–1980* [The political opposition in the People's Republic of Poland, 1945–1980] (London: Aneks, 1994), 175–81; Andrzej Friszke, "Sprawa Hanny Rewskiej" [The Hanna Rewska case], *Zeszyty Historyczne* 117 (1996): 185–95. On the arrests and trials of Rewska and Rudzińska, see Krzysztof Persak, *Sprawa Henryka Hollanda* [The Case of Hendryk Holland] (Warsaw: Instytut Studiów Politycznych PAN and Instytut Pamięci Narodowej, 2006), 46–47; Małgorzata Ptasińska-Wójcik, "Inwigilacja Instytutu Literackiego przez Służbę Bezpieczeństwa w czasach Gomułki" [The surveillance of Instytut Literacki by the Security Service in the Gomułka era], in *Aparat bezpieczeństwa wobec emigracji politycznej i Polonii* [The security apparatus versus political emigration community and Polonia] (Warsaw: Instytut Pamięci Narodowej, 105–84; Konrad Rokicki, *Literaci. Relacje między literatami w władzami PRL w latach 1956–1970* [The writers: Relations between writers and the authorities of People's Poland in 1956–1970] (Warsaw: Instytut Pamięci Narodowej, 2011), 212.

2. Ptasińska-Wójcik, "Inwigilacja Instytutu Literackiego," 130.

3. Jerzy Jaruzelski, *Stanisław Cat-Mackiewicz 1896–1966. Wilno–Londyn–Warszawa* [Stanisław Cat-Mackiewicz 1896–1966: Vilna–London–Warsaw] (Warsaw: Czytelnik, 1987), 304–6.

4. See Władysław Bartoszewski, *Warto być przyzwoitym. Teksty osobiste i nieosobiste* [Being decent is worth it: Personal and impersonal texts] (Poznań: W drodze, 1990), 35–117; Andrzej Friszke, "Władysław Bartoszewski—szkic do portretu" [Władysław Bartoszewski, a sketch for a portrait], in *Prawda i pojednanie: W 80. rocznicę urodzin Władysława Bartoszewskiego* [Truth and reconciliation: On Władysław Bartoszewski's 80th birthday], ed. Jan Barcz (Warsaw: Rytm, 2002), 619–42.

5. Archiwum Instytutu Pamięci Narodowej [Archive of the Institute of National Remembrance], Warsaw (hereafter AIPN), 0141/8, vol. 8, Wniosek o założenie sprawy rozpracowania operacyjnego [Request to open a case of operational investigation], February 21, 1963, 4.

6. Author's interview with Władysław Bartoszewski, October 30, 2005. Bartoszewski also spoke about his meeting with Tadeusz Żenczykowski and his work for RFE in an extended interview with Michał Komar: *Władysław Bartoszewski. Skąd pan jest? Wywiad rzeka* [Władysław Bartoszewski: Where do you come from? An extended interview] (Warsaw: Świat książki, 2006), 198–203, 228–30; see also Bartoszewski's statement in *Pięćdziesiąt lat Rozgłośni Polskiej Radia Wolna Europa, materiały sesji jubileuszowej* [Fifty years of the Polish Section of Radio Free Europe: Materials from a commemorative session], ed. Daria Nałęcz (Warsaw: Naczelna Dyrekcja Archiwów Państwowych, 2003), 89–93.

7. "Metody i praktyki bezpieki w pierwszych latach dwudziestolecia" [Secret police methods and practices in the first 20 years of the Communist state], *Na antenie* 39/40 (1966) (an insert in *Wiadomości*).

8. "Pół wieku życia w teczkach opisane, Opowieści prof. Władysława Bartoszewskiego wysłuchał Krzysztof Burnetko" [Half a century of a life as described in files: Professor Władysław Bartoszewski's tales, as heard by Krzysztof Burnetko], *Tygodnik Powszechny* 7 (2002).

9. Author's interview with Władysław Bartoszewski, Warsaw, October 30, 2005.

10. Author's interview with A. Ross Johnson, Washington, D.C., July 24, 2007.

11. Friszke, "Władysław Bartoszewski," 631.

12. AIPN, 0148/8, vol. 7, Notatka dotycząca Danuty Bańkowskiej [Note about Danuta Bańkowska], November 29, 1966, 29.

13. Author's interview with Stanisław Salmonowicz, September 25, 2005.

14. AIPN, 0141/8, vol. 7, Notatka dotycząca Władysława Bartoszewskiego [Note about Władysław Bartoszewski], December 1, 1966, 59.

15. AIPN, 0141/8, vol. 14, Informacja [Information], October 24, 1967, 117.

16. AIPN, 0141/8, vol. 6, Plan czynności operacyjnych w sprawie ustalenia autora wrogich informacji wysyłanych za granicę [Plan of operational tasks aimed at establishing the author of hostile information being sent abroad], October 29, 1966, 63–67; ibid., Notatka dotycząca Witolda Lisa-Olszewskiego [Note about Witold Lis-Olszewski], October 24, 1966, 18–21.

17. To read more about the repressions of Szymon Szechter and Nina Karsov, see Karsov and Szechter, *Nie kocha się pomników* [No one loves monuments] (Lublin: Oficyna im. Józefa Mackiewicza, 1987); see also Rokicki, *Literaci*, 400–402.

18. AIPN, 0141/8, vol. 6, Plan przedsięwzięć operacyjno-śledczych [Plan of operational-investigative undertakings], September 1966, 11–15.

19. Ibid., Szczegółowy zapis rozmów prowadzonych w mieszkaniu Szymona Szechtera (źródło "Fałszerz"—kryptonim podsłuchu pokojowego) [Detailed record of

conversations conducted in Szymon Szechter's apartment (source: "Fałszerz," code name for a room bug)], 85–91.

20. Ibid., Plan wstępnych przedsięwzięć operacyjnych do sprawy rozpracowania operacyjnego krypt. "Olcha" [Plan of initial operational undertakings in the case of the operational investigation code-named "Olcha"], December 2, 1966, 26–33. For the trials of Karol Głogowski, Mieczysław Zawistowski, and Łukasz Pleśnar, see Bogusław Mazur, *Ruch Wolnych Demokratów. Geneza, program i działalność w oświetleniu źródłowym (1956–1981)* [The Movement of Free Democrats: Genesis, program and activities in light of sources (1956–1981)] (Opole: Wydawnictwo Alternatywy Demokratycznej, 1986), 21–25; Friszke, *Opozycja polityczna w PRL 1945–1980*, 227.

21. AIPN, 0141/8, vol. 6, Nasłuchy radiowe [Radio monitoring], December 3, 1966, 21–24.

22. AIPN, 0148/8, vol. 7, Notatka służbowa dotycząca przeprowadzenia w dniu 13 III br. w czasie odprawy celnej na lotnisku Okęcie rewizji osobistej i kontroli bagażu redaktora Interpressu Jana Zaborowskiego [Office note concerning the body search and baggage inspection of Interpress editor Jan Zaborowski on March 13 of this year during a customs inspection at Okęcie airport], March 24, 1967, 75–78.

23. Letter from Władysław Bartoszewski to the author, February 19, 2006.

24. AIPN, 0148/8, vol. 7, Notatka służbowa [Office note], May 14, 1967, 81–83; AIPN, 0148/8, vol. 5, Plan przedsięwzięć operacyjnych w sprawie krypt. "Olcha" [Plan of operational undertakings in the case code-named "Olcha"], May 30, 1967, 44–54.

25. Letter from Władysław Bartoszewski to the author, February 19, 2006.

26. AIPN, 0148/8, vol. 6, Uzasadnienie celowości przedłużenia eksploatacji techniki operacyjnej w obiekcie krypt. "Bańka" [Justification of the reason for extending the use of operational technology in the "Bańka" site], January 2, 1968, 32–33; ibid., Raport o zezwolenie na dokonanie pozyskania [Report for requesting permission to execute a requisition], February 12, 1968, 41–45; ibid., Notatka [Note], March 6, 1969, 51; AIPN, 0148/8, vol. 14, Plan przedsięwzięć operacyjnych w sprawie krypt. "Olcha" [Plan of operational undertakings in the case code-named "Olcha"], February 17, 1969, 131; ibid., Analiza sprawy operacyjnego rozpracowania "Olcha" [An analysis of the case of the "Olcha" operational investigation], July 29, 1970, 160.

27. AIPN, 0148/8, vol. 6, Reperkusje w środowisku adwokackim rewizji przeprowadzonych w dniu 20 XI 1967 r. w mieszkaniach adwokatów Siły-Nowickiego i Lisa-Olszewskiego [Repercussions of the searches conducted on November 20, 1967 in the apartments of the lawyers Siła-Nowicki and Lis-Olszewski in lawyers' circles], November 28, 1967, 57–59.

28. Ibid., Wykaz materiałów zakwestionowanych u Władysława Siły-Nowickiego podczas rewizji domowej dokonanej w dniu 20 listopada [List of questionable materials at Władysław Siła-Nowicki's during a house search conducted on November 20], November 22, 1967, 195–203.

29. Ibid., Notatka służbowa [Office note], March 19, 1968, 60–61.

30. Ibid., Postanowienie o przedstawieniu zarzutów [Decision on filing charges], 166.

31. Ibid., Protokół przesłuchania podejrzanego [Record of interrogation of the suspect], December 11, 1967, 146–47; ibid., Protokół przesłuchania podejrzanego [Record of interrogation of the suspect], December 13, 1967, 136–40; ibid., Protokół przesłuchania podejrzanego [Record of interrogation of the suspect], December 14, 1967, 143–45; ibid., Protokół przesłuchania podejrzanego [Record of interrogation of the suspect], December 19, 1967, 154–56; ibid., Protokół przesłuchania podejrzanego

[Record of interrogation of the suspect], January 12, 1968, 174–77; Protokół przesłuchania podejrzanego [Record of interrogation of the suspect], January 22, 1968, 178–80; Protokół przesłuchania podejrzanego [Record of interrogation of the suspect], January 23, 1968, 184–89; ibid., Protokół przesłuchania podejrzanego [Record of interrogation of the suspect], January 24, 1968, 190–92; ibid., Protokół przesłuchania podejrzanego [Record of interrogation of the suspect], February 1, 1968, 167–70.

32. AIPN, 0148/8, vol. 14, Plan przedsięwzięć operacyjnych w sprawie krypt. "Olcha" [Plan of operational undertakings in the "Olcha" case], February 17, 1969, 132.

33. "'Bartek' is to go to the GDR on a private trip on April 5 of this year. The GDR's Security Service has been notified about this and asked to handle 'Bartek' with observation and operational methods," ibid., 81.

34. Ibid., Notatka dotycząca Ewy Drężepolskiej [Note about Ewa Drężepolska], August 14, 1970, 17–22.

35. As told to the author by Władysław Bartoszewski, October 30, 2005. Documents confirm this in at least one case. The Bartoszewskis' housekeeper, who had been with them for many years, fought off the Security Service's approaches in 1967, claiming poor health and a psychological breakdown. "In our conversation, she asked to be freed of the obligation to collaborate because she 'would not survive it,' and stated that she 'has had enough of Warsaw' and is planning to move to the countryside, where her brother-in-law will get her a job as a saleswoman" (AIPN, 0148/8, vol. 8, Notatka służbowa [Office note], December 22, 1967, 13–14). Her case is an eloquent and optimistic example of a simple person's moral instincts and invincibility.

36. AIPN, 0141/5, vol. 1, Notatka [Note], December 4, 1970, 195.

37. AIPN, 0148/8. vol. 14, Analiza sprawy operacyjnego rozpracowania krypt. "Olcha" [An analysis of the operational investigation code-named "Olcha"], July 29, 1970, 161.

38. AIPN, 0148/8, vol. 7, Notatka [Note], March 24, 1969, 110.

39. AIPN, 0148/8, vol. 14, Plan przedsięwzięć operacyjnych w sprawie krypt. "Olcha" [Plan of operational undertakings in case code-named "Olcha"], February 17, 1969, 138.

40. Ibid., Analiza sprawy operacyjnego rozpracowania krypt. "Olcha" [An analysis of the case of the operational investigation code-named "Olcha"], July 29, 1970, 165–66.

41. Ibid., Plan przedsięwzięć operacyjnych do sprawy rozpracownia operacyjnego krypt. "Pewnik" [Plan of operational undertakings in the operational investigation of the case code-named "Pewnik"], June 12, 1970, 121–46.

42. Author's interview with Stanisław Salmonowicz, September 28, 2005.

43. AIPN, 0141/5, vol. 1, Tezy do przesłuchań niżej wymienionych osób [Theses for interrogating persons listed below], 44–46.

44. AIPN, 0148/8, vol. 14, Informacja dotycząca współpracy Władysława Bartoszewskiego z rozgłośnią radiową Wolnej Europy [Information about Władysław Bartoszewski's cooperation with the Free Europe radio station], August 25, 1971, 297.

45. Author's interview with Stanisław Salmonowicz, September 28, 2005; Władysław Bartoszewski's account, October 30, 2005.

46. AIPN, 0141/5, vol. 1, Plan realizacji sprawy krypt. "Olcha" [Plan of implementation of the case code-named "Olcha"], September 25, 1970, 40–42.

47. Ibid., Zestaw materiałów uzyskanych w toku postępowania przeciwko grupie współpracowników Rozgłośni Polskiej Radia Wolna Europa [Collection of materials acquired in the course of the investigation against a group of collaborators of the Polish Service of Radio Free Europe], 142–59; AIPN, 0141/8, vol. 8, Odpis instrukcji zakwestionowanej u Ewy Drężepolskiej [Copy of instructions found at Ewa Drężepolska's], 208–9.

48. AIPN, 0141/5/ vol. 8, Meldunek o przedstawieniu zarzutów i zastosowaniu aresztu tymczasowego w sprawie nr. S-18/70 Prokuratury Wojskowej dla miasta stołecznego Warszawy II.2.Ds. 20/70 [Report on the filing of charges and implementing temporary arrest in case no. S-18/70 of the Military Prosecutor's Office for the capital city of Warsaw II.2.Ds. 20/70], October 5, 1970, 226–28.

49. Several dozen reports from prison informants using code names "Janek," "Piotr," "Ewa," and "Skryba" can be found in file number AIPN, 0141/5, vol. 7, 220–319. Salmonowicz, in a conversation with the author and a written statement appended to the documents he obtained from the Institute of National Remembrance as a "wronged" person, argues that the reports by prison informant "Janek" are forgeries made by the Security Service. According to Salmonowicz, "the S[ecurity] S[ervice] needed evidence that would be easier to present in court than information gained through operations, which it did not want to reveal ("Uwagi figuranta do teczek SB na jego temat" [Remarks by a target on his Security Service files], July 2004, typed text given the author by Salmonowicz). Salmonowicz points out many inaccuracies or actual mistakes in his own and his father's biographies in "Janek's" reports, as well as facts that the agent simply could not have known. It is impossible to get to the bottom of this case. Why would the secret police forge prison informants' reports, when such materials were strictly operational and not supposed to be used in court?

50. AIPN, 0141/5, vol. 7, Doniesienie [Report], no. 2231/70, 1555.

51. The surviving documentation does not include minutes of Salmonowicz's testimony. But they are discussed in Ministry of Internal Affairs (AIPN, 0141/5, vol. 1, k. 186) and Prosecutor's Office materials (AAN [Archiwum Akt Nowych (Central Archive of Modern Records), Warsaw], Prokuratura Generalna [Prosecutor General's Office], 15/40, 50, 102).

52. Author's interview with Stanisław Salmonowicz, September 28, 2005.

53. File AIPN, 0141/8, vol. 13 includes minutes of interrogations. Comparing them with the prison informants' reports allows us to reconstruct the details of the secret police method of gradually extracting testimony of importance to the investigation and the planned trial from the people who are being interrogated. For interrogations of Bartoszewski, see AIPN, 0141/5, vol. 1, Notatka służbowa dotycząca Władysława Bartoszewskiego [Office note about Władysław Bartoszewski], October 28, 1970, 139–41.

54. AIPN, 0.141/8, vol. 13, Notatka [Note], October 23, 1970, 1–3.

55. Ibid., 22–31.

56. AAN, Prokuratura Generalna [Prosecutor General's Office], 15/40, Notatka z dotychczasowych ustaleń w sprawie II.2.Ds.20/70 przeciwko Stanisławowi Salmonowiczowi, Ewie Marii Drężepolskiej i Danucie Marii Bańkowskiej, podejrzanych z art. 132 kk [Note from the conclusions reached so far in case II.2.Ds.20/70 of Stanisław Salmonowicz, Ewa Maria Drężepolska and Danuta Maria Bańkowska, suspects according to Article 132 of the Criminal Code], November 24, 1970, 30.

57. "Pół wieku życia w teczkach opisane."

58. Stefan Kisielewski, *Dzienniki* [Diaries] (Warsaw: Iskry, 1997), 483–84.

59. AIPN, 0141/5, vol. 1, Plan dalszych czynności operacyjno-śledczych w sprawie nr S-18/70 przeciwko Stanisławowi Salmonowiczowi i innym podejrzanym z art. 132 kk [Plan of further operational-investigative actions in case no. S-18/70 against Stanisław Salmonowicz and other suspects according to Article 132 of the Criminal Code], October 14, 1970, 58.

60. AIPN, 0141/8, vol. 7, Informacja [Information], October 26, 1970, 198.

61. Ibid., k. 267.

62. Author's interview with Władysław Bartoszewski, October 30, 2005.

63. Kisielewski, *Dzienniki*, 497.

64. AIPN, 0148/8, vol. 14, Doniesienie [Report], November 4, 1970, 212.

65. Author's interview with Władysław Bartoszewski and reports from secret collaborators in the files for this case.

66. AIPN, 0141/8, vol. 14, Plan rozmowy z Władysławem Bartoszewskim [Plan for a conversation with Władysław Bartoszewski], January 5, 1971, 262.

67. Ibid., 263–64.

68. Ibid., Notatka służbowa [Office note], January 22, 1971, 266.

69. Ibid., 266–67.

70. Ibid., 269–70.

71. AIPN, 0141/8, vol. 8, Plan przedsięwzięć operacyjnych w sprawie krypt. "Olcha" [Plan of operational undertakings in the "Olcha" case], February 12, 1971, 278–80.

72. Ibid., Notatka z rozmowy z Władysławem Bartoszewskim [Note from a conversation with Władysław Bartoszewski], March 15, 1971, 271–72.

73. Author's interview with Andrzej Czechowicz, December 5, 2005.

74. AIPN, 02011/80, part 1 (1), Doniesienie agenta "Romusa" [Report from agent "Romus"], December 28, 1970, 274.

75. AIPN, 0148/8, vol. 14, untitled note, April 2, 1971, 279.

76. Ibid., 280.

77. Ibid., 281–82.

78. Jan Nowak-Jeziorański wrote about this at length in his memoirs from his work at the radio, *Polska z oddali. Wspomnienia* [Poland from afar: A memoir], vol. 2, *1956–1976* (Cracow: Znak, 1992), 383–407; see also chapter 5 of this book.

79. Indefatigable secret collaborator "A-Wiktor" discussed the circumstances of finding this envelope and reactions among journalists in his report, AIPN, 0148/8, vol. 12, July 12, 1972, 2586.

80. AIPN, 0141/6, vol. 2, Oświadczenie [Declaration], May 6, 1972, 11–12. Also enclosed are the main letter (10) and the letter from "Kazik" to "Jureczek" (9).

81. AIPN, 0141/6, vol. 1, Pismo Władysława Bartoszewskiego do prokuratora generalnego PRL [Letter from Władysław Bartoszewski to the Prosecutor General of the People's Republic of Poland], July 25, 1972, 14–15.

82. AIPN, 0146/6, vol. 2, Sprawozdanie z przeprowadzonych badań podpisów i pisma maszynowego [Report from the performed analysis of signatures and typewritten text], October 12, 1972, 48-51.

83. Ibid., Postanowienie o wszczęciu dochodzenia [Decision to start the investigation], December 4, 1972, 52. Minutes of interrogations can be found in the same folder.

84. Ibid., Plan czynności sprawdzających w sprawie sfałszowania podpisu Władysława Bartoszewskiego [Plan to assess the actions in the case of the forgery of Władysław Bartoszewski's signature], October 2, 1972, 5–9.

85. AIPN, 0141/6, vol. 1, Notatka [Note], October 27, 1972, 6.

86. Friszke, *Opozycja polityczna w PRL 1945–1980,* 255–63.

87. AAN, Prokuratura Generalna [Prosecutor General's Office], 15/40, Notatka dotycząca śledztwa Prokuratury Wojewódzkiej dla m. st. Warszawy w sprawie II.2.Ds. 20/70 przeciwko Władysławowi Bartoszewskiemu i innym z art. 132 kk [Note concerning the investigation by the Provincial Prosecutor's Office for Warsaw in case 11.2.Ds 20/70 against Władysław Bartoszewski and others according to Article 132 of the Criminal Code], January 6, 1972, 49–52.

88. Ibid., Notatka kpt. Hipolita Starszaka z Biura Śledczego MSW [Note from Captain Hipolit Starszak of the Investigations Bureau of the Ministry of Internal Affairs], January 4, 1971, 55–57; ibid., Pismo dyrektora Departamentu II Prokuratury Generalnej P. Hachulskiego do prokuratora generalnego PRL Kazimierza Kosztirki [Letter from director of Department II of the Prosecutor General's Office, P. Hachulski to the Prosecutor General of the People's Republic of Poland Kazimierz Kosztirko], January 6, 1971, 58; ibid., Odręczna notatka zastępcy prokuratora generalnego Henryka Cieśluka z rozmowy z dyrektorem Biura Śledczego MSW Józefem Chomętowskim [Handwritten note from Deputy Prosecutor General Henryk Cieśluk about a conversation with Director of the Investigations Bureau of the Ministry of Internal Affairs Józef Chomętowski], 72.

89. AIPN, 0141/8, vol. 14, Notatka dotycząca Władysława Bartoszewskiego [Note about Władysław Bartoszewski], January 1971, 258.

90. AAN, Prokuratura Generalna [Prosecutor General's Office], 15/40, Pismo Stanisława Salmonowicza do prokuratora generalnego [Letter from Stanisław Salmonowicz to the prosecutor general], June 12, 1971, 94–95.

91. Ibid., Notatka dotycząca załatwienia sprawy II.2.Ds, 20/70 przeciwko Stanisławowi Salmonowiczowi, Ewie Marii Dreżepolskiej, Danucie Bańkowskiej i Władysławowi Bartoszewskiemu, podejrzanym z art. 132 kk [Note from the resolution of case II.2.Ds. 20/70 of Stanisław Salmonowicz, Ewa Maria Dreżepolska, Danuta Bańkowska and Władysław Bartoszewski, suspects on the basis of Article 132 of the Criminal Code], August 11, 1971, 102–3.

92. Ibid., Pismo dyrektora Departamentu II Prokuratury Generalnej P. Hachulskiego do zastępcy prokuratora generalnego Henryka Cieśluka [Letter from Director of Department II of the Prosecutor General's Office P. Hachulski to Deputy Prosecutor General Henryk Cieśluk], September 14, 1971, 108–9.

93. Ibid., W sprawie śledztwa przeciwko Władysławowi Bartoszewskiemu, Stanisławowi Salmonowiczowi, Danucie Bańkowskiej i Ewie Dreżepolskiej [On the investigation against Władysław Bartoszewski, Stanisław Salmonowiczow, Danuta Bańkowska and Ewa Dreżepolska], September 17, 1971, 112–14.

94. Ibid., Postanowienie o umorzeniu śledztwa [Decision to terminate the investigation], 189.

95. Ibid., Pisma Stanisława Stommy [Letters from Stanisław Stomma], February 2, 1971, 194; March 31, 1971, 200.

96. *The Black Book of Polish Censorship,* trans. and ed. Jane Curry (New York: Vintage Books, 1984), 391.

97. Juliusz Wiktor Gomulicki, *Wiedza o książce. Bibliografia. Encyklopedie. Słowniki. Varia* [Knowledge about books: Bibliography. Encyclopedias. Dictionaries. Miscellaneous] (Warsaw: Państwowy Instytut Wydawniczy, 1977), 384–85. Bartoszewski

owns the publisher's copy of the book in which the censors noted the words they questioned by hand.

98. Author's interview with Władysław Bartoszewski, October 30, 2005.

99. Author's interview with Stanisław Salmonowicz, September 28, 2005.

100. Author's interview with Władysław Bartoszewski, October 30, 2005.

101. AAN, Prokuratura generalna [Prosecutor General's Office], 15/40, Pismo dyrektora departamentu II Prokuratury Generalnej P. Hachulskiego do zastępcy prokuratora generalnego Henryka Cieśluka [Letter from Director of Department II of the Prosecutor General's Office P. Hachulski to Deputy Prosecutor General Henryk Cieśluk], September 14, 1971, 109.

102. AIPN, 01048/53, J. Łabęcki, J. Podolski, "Streszczenie sprawy operacyjnego rozpracowania kryptonim 'Kanał'" [Summary of the case of operational investigation codenamed "Kanał"], Department of Professional Training and Development of the Ministry of Internal Affairs (Warsaw, 1973). Some details, including names, were changed.

103. AIPN, 0968/227, personnel file of Janusz Łabęcki.

104. For a discussion of the "D" cells, see Marek Lasota "O raporcie sejmowej komisji poświęconym Samodzielnej Grupie 'D' w MSW" [About the report of the Sejm commission devoted to self-managing group 'D' in the Ministry of Internal Affairs], *Biuletyn Instytutu Pamięci Narodowej* 24, no. 1 (2003): 27–36.

105. Friszke, *Opozycja polityczna w PRL 1945–1980*, 251–54; Bartosz Kaliski, "Przerzut od Giedroycia" [Smuggling things from Giedroyc], *Karta* 40 (2004): 99–131; Bartosz Kaliski, "Proces Taterników" [The trial of the Mountaineers], *Zeszyty Historyczne* 121 (1997): 89–97.

Chapter 5

1. It was either Andrzej Broel-Plater or Emanuel Plater.

2. Archiwum Akt Nowych [Central Archive of Modern Records], Warsaw (hereafter AAN), 237/III/61, Stenogram VIII Plenarnego posiedzenia Komitetu Centralnego PZPR w dniach 6 i 7 II 1971 r. [Stenographic record of the 8th plenary session of the Central Committee of the PUWP on February 6–7, 1971], 371–72.

3. AAN, 237/III/62, vol. 2, 36–37.

4. AAN, 237/XI/298, Notatka z narady I sekretarzy komitetów wojewódzkich PZPR z udziałem Sekretariatu KC w dniu 18 XI 1971 r. [Note from a meeting of the first secretaries of the provincial committees of the PUWP with the participation of the CC Secretariat on November 18, 1971], 54.

5. AAN, 237/I/88, Stenogram VI Zjazdu PZPR [Stenographic record of the 6th Congress of the PUWP], December 8, 1971, 114–15.

6. AAN, 237/XIX/349, 146-47, n.d., but the contents suggest that it was written in December 1970, or perhaps in January 1971.

7. Archiwum Instytucji Ministerstwa Obrony Narodowej [Archive of the Institutions of the Ministry of National Defense], Modlin (hereafter AIMON), 240/91/238, Autoryzowany stenogram wykładu ministra Franciszka Szlachcica "Charakterystyka aktualnej sytuacji politycznej w kraju z uwzględnieniem postaw różnych środowisk" [Authorized stenographic record of a lecture by Minister Franciszek Szlachcic on "The characteristics of the current political situation in Poland, taking into account the attitudes of various social groups"], delivered on April 27, 1971, at an ideological-theoretical

conference of the leadership cadre of the armed forces of the People's Republic of Poland, 116.

8. AAN, Polskiej Zjednoczonej Partii Robotniczej [Polish United Workers' Party, hereafter PZPR], XIB/229, Meldunek Departamentu I MSW [Report from Department I of the Ministry of Internal Affairs (Ministerstwo Spraw Wewnętrznych)], January 5, 1971, 6.

9. Ibid., Meldunek [Report], March 8, 1971, 8.

10. AAN, PZPR, XIB/235, Meldunek Departamentu I MSW [Report from Department I of the Ministry of Internal Affairs], March 31, 1971, 1–2.

11. AAN, PZPR, XXXI/16, Notatka [Note], unsigned, n.d.; its contents make it appear to have been written in early 1971.

12. AIMON, 240/91/243, Załącznik do koncepcji uruchomienia środków przeciwdziałania dywersji ideologiczne [Appendix to the concept of mobilizing the means to counteract ideological sabotage], February 24, 1971, 20–39.

13. AAN, 237/VII/31, Protokół nr 41 posiedzenia Sekretariatu KC w dniu 3 VI 1971 r. [Minutes no. 41 from a meeting of the CC Secretariat on June 3, 1971], 402.

14. Ibid., Wniosek o powołanie zespołu koordynującego kierunki, metody i środki zwalczania wrogiej propagandy [Motion to create a team to coordinate the directions, methods and means of combating hostile propaganda], 409.

15. Author's interview with Andrzej Werblan, April 5, 2007. Werblan argues that the team was organized by Stefan Olszowski, who as CC secretary was responsible for ideological affairs, and Janusz Kolczyński, director of the East-West Center. Their motivation was to strengthen their positions in the CC apparatus.

16. AAN, 237/XXXII/59, Informacja o działalności Ośrodka Badania Stosunków Wschód-Zachód [Information about the activities of the Center for the Study of East-West Relations], July 6, 1972, n.p. In 1984, ninety-five people were employed by the Institute for the Study of the Contemporary Problems of Capitalism (AAN, 237/VII/70, Ocena działalności Instytutu Badania Współczesnych Problemów Kapitalizmu RSW "Prasa-Książka-Ruch" w Warszawie [An evaluation of the work of the Institute for the Study of the Contemporary Problems of Capitalism of the "Press-Book-Movement" Workers' Publishing Cooperative in Warsaw], January 1985, 172).

17. Centralne Archiwum Ministerstwa Spraw Wewnętrznych [Central Archive of the Ministry of Internal Affairs], Warsaw (hereafter CAMSWiA), Urząd Rady Ministrów—Biuro Prasowe Rządu [Office of the Council of Ministers—Government Press Office, hereafter URM/BPR], 561, Notatka w sprawie zagłuszania audycji polskojęzycznych Głosu Ameryki, BBC i Radia Wolna Europa [Note on the jamming of Polish-language programs by the Voice of America, BBC, and Radio Free Europe].

18. AIMON, 240/91/243, Załącznik do koncepcji uruchomienia środków przeciwdziałania dywersji ideologicznej [Enclosure to the conception of launching measures of counteracting ideological sabotage], February 25, 1971, 32–33.

19. AIMON, 240/91/243, Notatka dotycząca oceny skuteczności zakłócania audycji rozgłośni radiowej Wolna Europa [Note about an assessment of the effectiveness of jamming programs of the Free Europe radio station], April 13, 1971, 77–78.

20. Ibid.

21. CAMSWiA, URM/BPR, 561, Notatka w sprawie zagłuszania audycji polskojęzycznych Głosu Ameryki, BBC i Radia Wolna Europa [Note on the jamming of Polish-language programs by the Voice of America, BBC, and Radio Free Europe].

22. Author's interview with an officer cadet who had served in Lidzbark Warmiński (name withheld), November 24, 2005.

23. It has not been possible so far to find documents in Polish archives that would permit a detailed reconstruction of the jamming system in the 1970s and 1980s. Rimantas Pleikys, Lithuania's minister of communications and computer science from 1996 to 1998, wrote about it in his book, *Jamming* (Vilnius, 2001), whose section on Poland also appeared in Polish in *Świat Radio* 1 (2003). I have reservations about this book since it was self-published, has many mistakes, and often gives no sources (it has no notes). For a discussion of jamming, see also Marek Henzler, "Radio trzeszcząca Europa" [Radio creaking Europe], *Polityka* 18 (2002); Jacek Maziarski, "Zagłuszanie" [Jamming], *Nowe Państwo* 51 (2000); and Kamil Rutecki, *System zagłuszania polskich rozgłośni radiowych w PRL* [The system of jamming Polish radio stations in the People's Republic of Poland], in *Przełom w przełomie. Bydgoskie wydarzenia roku 1956* [A breakthrough within a breakthrough: The events in Bydgoszcz in 1956], ed. Alicja Paczoska-Hauke (Bydgoszcz: Urząd Miasta, 2006), 109–10.

24. AIPN, 0665/176, Informacja ministra spraw wewnętrznych wygłoszona na naradzie sekretarzy propagandy komitetów wojewódzkich PZPR [Information from the minister of internal affairs given at a meeting of the propaganda secretaries of the PUWP provincial committees], 1971, 5–6.

25. AIMON, 240/91/243, Załącznik do uruchomienia środków przeciwdziałania dywersji ideologicznej [Enclosure to launch means of counteracting ideological sabotage], February 25, 1971, 20–39.

26. AIMON, 240/91/238, Autoryzowany stenogram wykładu ministra Franciszka Szlachcica "Charakterystyka aktualnej sytuacji politycznej w kraju z uwzględnieniem postaw różnych środowisk" wygłoszonego 27 IV 1971 r. na konferencji ideowo-teoretycznej kierowniczej kadry sił zbrojnych PRL [Authorized transcript of a lecture by Minister Franciszek Szlachcic about "The characteristics of the current political situation in Poland, taking into account the positions of various social groups," given on April 27, 1971, at an ideological-theoretical conference of the leadership cadre of the armed forces of the People's Republic of Poland], 117.

27. "Sukces polskiego wywiadu" [A success of Poland's intelligence], *Trybuna Ludu*, March 9, 1971.

28. AAN, 237/XIX-166, Ocena kampanii prasowej w związku z powrotem kpt. Andrzeja Czechowicza [An assessment of the press campaign related to the return of Captain Andrzej Czechowicz], 1–8.

29. See Jerzy Diatłowicki's television program, *Tajny agent* [Secret agent].

30. AIPN, 002086/55, Wniosek o zaniechanie współpracy z tajnym współpracownikiem [Motion to abandon the association with a secret collaborator], July 14, 1965, 245.

31. AIPN, 00221/7, Notatka końcowa do tomu nr 1560 teczki pracy agenta "Kumor" [Concluding note to volume no. 1560 of the working file of agent "Kumor"], August 15, 1974, 15.

32. See the series of articles about Czechowicz by Bohdan Roliński in *Trybuna Ludu*, March 11, 12, 13, and 14, 1971.

33. AIPN, 0665/176, Informacja ministra spraw wewnętrznych wygłoszona na naradzie sekretarzy propagandy komitetów wojewódzkich PZPR [Information from the minister of internal affairs presented at a meeting of the propaganda secretaries of the PUWP provincial committees], 1971, 6–7.

34. The most important documents associated with Czechowicz can be found in the Institute of National Remembrance archive on microfilms (IPN 02011/1108 and IPN 02011/1109). They were discovered only after the Polish edition of this book was published in 2007. In that edition, I left open the question: had Czechowicz been able to find the names of RFE's informants in Poland or was Communist propaganda bluffing? I would like to thank Dr. Władysław Bułhak for pointing out these files to me.

35. Andrzej Czechowicz, *Siedem trudnych lat* [Seven difficult years] (Warsaw: Ministerstwo Obrony Narodowej, 1974), 237, 243–44.

36. AIPN, 02011/1108, part 1, Pismo ppłk Zygmunta Orłowskiego do ppłk Bolesława Żeleńskiego [Letter from Lieutenant Colonel Zygmunt Orłowski to Lieutenant Colonel Bolesław Żeleński], March 23, 1971, 1261.

37. AIPN, 02011/1108, part 2, Pismo ppłk S. Szymczykiewicza do ministra spraw wewnętrznych [Letter from Lieutenant Colonel S. Szymczykiewicz to the minister of internal affairs], May 3, 1971, 1356.

38. Jan Nowak-Jeziorański, *Polska z oddali. Wspomnienia* [Poland from afar: A memoir], vol. 2, *1956–1976* (Cracow: Znak, 1992), 360.

39. AAN, PZPR, Wydział Kultury [Culture Department], 4, Notatka z rozmowy z Wacławem Kubackim [Note from a conversation with Wacław Kubacki], April 1971, 7–9.

40. Zakład Narodowy im. Ossolińskich [Ossoliński National Institute], Wrocław, Collection of Jan Nowak-Jeziorański (hereafter JNJ), 38/99/2. This file is devoted in its entirety to General Moczar and contains an alleged opinion from a *Trybuna Ludu* reporter: "Podkowiński Marian calls him an ordinary shit." It may be that this statement upset Moczar and his people at the ministry so much that in 1971 they decided to take revenge on Podkowiński by gossiping that he talked with RFE.

41. Letter from Andrzej Czechowicz to the author, December 22, 2005.

42. Jerzy Kudaś-Bronisławski said this on Jerzy Diatłowicki's television program *Tajny agent*, as well as to the journalist Jerzy Morawski. Czechowicz himself confirmed it (Jerzy Morawski, *Głosy z Monachium* [Voices from Munich] [Warsaw: Interpress, 1993], 194, 196). Mieczysław Rakowski noted in his diary in October 1971 that there were rumors about Widy-Wirski serving as a liaison between Kliszko and RFE (*Dzienniki polityczne 1969–1971* [Political diaries, 1969–1971] [Warsaw: Iskry, 2001], 472).

43. Author's interviews with Jan Nowak-Jeziorański (August 18, 2004), Maciej Morawski (August 29, 2006), and Zygmunt Michałowski (November 4, 2005). In the same account, Maciej Morawski revealed that Tadeusz Parczewski met in Paris with Witold Trąmpczyński, who was the Polish minister of foreign trade from 1956 to 1968.

44. AIPN, 01251/284.

45. Nowak-Jeziorański, *Polska z oddali,* 360.

46. Rakowski, *Dzienniki polityczne 1969–1971,* 385.

47. "Kapitan Andrzej Czechowicz wykonał zadanie. Rozpoznanie ośrodków antypolskiej dywersji. Relacja oficera polskiego wywiadu o działalności 'Wolnej Europy' [Captain Andrzej Czechowicz has performed his mission: Identifying the methods of anti-Polish sabotage: An account by a Polish intelligence officer about Free Europe's activity], *Trybuna Ludu*, March 11, 1971.

48. "Kapitan Andrzej Czechowicz wykonał zadanie," 82–83.

49. Ibid., 112–14.

50. Ibid., 21.

51. AIPN, 02011/1108, part 2, Plan kampanii prasowo-propagandowej w związku z powrotem kpt. Andrzeja Czechowicza [Plan for a press-propaganda campaign related to the return of Captain Andrzej Czechowicz], March 15, 1971, 406.

52. Zakład Narodowy im. Ossolińskich, JNJ, 41/99, Notatka z rozmów z szeregiem kolegów [Note about conversations with numerous colleagues], March 9–10, 1971.

53. Petr Cajthaml, "Minařik i Czechowicz—propaganda sukcesu wywiadów komunistycznych [Minařik and Czechowicz, the propaganda of success by the Communist special services], in *Między przymusową przyjaźnią a prawdziwą solidarnością. Czesi–Polacy–Słowacy 1938/39–1945–1989* [Between forced friendship and real solidarity: Czechs–Poles–Slovaks, 1938/39–1945–1989], ed. Petr Blažek, Paweł Jaworski, and Łukasz Kamiński (Warsaw: Instytut Pamięci Narodowej, 2009), 200–202; see also Arch Puddington, *Broadcasting Freedom: The Cold War Triumph of Radio Free Europe and Radio Liberty* (Lexington: University Press of Kentucky, 2000), 233–35; Prokop Tomek, *Československé bezpečnostní složky proti Rádiu Svobodná Evropa. <Objekt ALFA>* [Czechoslovak security services against Radio Free Europe: "Target ALFA"] (Prague: Úřad dokumentace a vyšestřováni zločinů komunismu, 2006), 140–46.

54. Puddington, *Broadcasting Freedom*, 235–37; A. Ross Johnson, *Radio Free Europe and Radio Liberty: The CIA Years and Beyond* (Washington, DC: Woodrow Wilson Center Press; Stanford, CA: Stanford University Press, 2010), 188–90.

55. Ion Mihai Pacepa, *Red Horizons: Chronicles of a Communist Spy Chief* (Washington, DC: Regnery Gateway, 1987), 307.

56. Puddington, *Broadcasting Freedom*, 175–86; Nowak-Jeziorański, *Polska z oddali*, 364–66.

57. Wanda Jarząbek, "Władze PRL wobec normalizacji stosunków z RFN w latach 1970–1975" [The government of the People's Republic of Poland and the normalization of relations with the Federal Republic of Germany in 1970–75], in *Rocznik Polsko-Niemiecki 2004* (Warsaw: Instytut Studiów Politycznych PAN, 2005).

58. AAN, XI B/99, Notatka z rozmowy premiera Piotra Jaroszewicza z Rainerem Barzelem przeprowadzonej 21 I 1971 r. [Note from conversation between Piotr Jaroszewicz and Rainer Barzel conducted on January 21, 1971], 134.

59. Jarząbek, "Władze PRL wobec normalizacji. stosunków z RFN."

60. AAN, 237/XI-513, Notatka z rozmów z Herbertem Wehnerem, przewodniczącym frakcji SPD w Bundestagu [Note from talks with Herbert Wehner, chairman of the SPD faction in the Bundestag], February 14, 1972, 23.

61. Zakład Narodowy im. Ossolińskich, JNJ, 45/99, *Na antenie*, March 1972.

62. Puddington, *Broadcasting Freedom,* 187–211.

63. "Kapitan Andrzej Czechowicz wykonał zadanie," *Trybuna Ludu*, March 11, 1971.

64. "Kapitan Andrzej Czechowicz wykonał zadanie," 107.

65. Ibid.

66. Sig Mickelson, *America's Other Voice: The Story of Radio Free Europe and Radio Liberty* (New York: Praeger, 1983), 130; Cord Meyer, *Facing Reality: From World Federalism to the CIA* (New York: Harper & Row, 1980), 135; Nowak-Jeziorański, *Polska z oddali*, 373.

67. "Kapitan Andrzej Czechowicz wykonał zadanie," 28.

68. AIPN, 02011/80, part 1 (3), Notatka dot. Radia Wolna Europa [Note about Radio Free Europe], March 29, 1972, 56–60.

69. AMSZ, Collection 13/78, bundle 11, Projekt *aide-mémoire* do ambasady USA [Draft of an aide-mémoire for the US embassy], April 1971, unsigned.

70. AMSZ, Collection 40/75, bundle 2, Pilna notatka z rozmowy Józefa Winiewicza z ambasadorem USA z 26 bm. [Urgent note from Józef Winiewicz's conversation with the US ambassador on the 26th of this month], May 27, 1971.

71. The Soviets reported on Brezhnev's meeting with Nixon to the leadership of the PUWP. They mentioned RFE as an item on the agenda for the Moscow talks: "In our talks with Nixon, we also brought up the issue that the vicious, mendacious propaganda that is anti-Soviet and directed against our friends and allies being conducted by American newspapers, radio and television, including such 'specialized' propaganda organs as radio Free Europe is getting in the way of the notable improvement in Soviet-American relations. We would like the USA to take steps against this. Nixon promised to take steps in this direction, but expressed the reservation that not all propaganda organs lie within his domain. But he did promise to try to make them 'remain within certain defined limits'" (AAN, XI B/115, unsigned and undated document).

72. AAN, PZPR, XIB/103, Informacja dla sekretarzy komitetów wojewódzkich o wizycie Richarda Nixona w Moskwie i Warszawie [Information for secretaries of provincial committees about Richard Nixon's visit to Moscow and Warsaw], 1972, 254.

73. Pilna notatka z rozmowy z sekretarzem stanu Williamem P. Rogersem w dniu 31 V 1972 r. [Urgent note about a conversation with Secretary of State William P. Rogers on May 31, 1972], in *Polskie dokumenty dyplomatyczne. 1972* [Polish diplomatic documents, 1972], ed. Włodzimierz Borodziej (Warsaw: Polski Instytut Spraw Międzynarodowych, 2005), 324–25.

74. Ibid., 327.

75. AAN, PZPR, XIB/104, Tezy do wystąpienia na spotkaniu I sekretarzy [Theses for a speech at a meeting of first secretaries], 1972.

76. Sprawozdanie dla Biura Politycznego z wizyty we Francji [Report for the Politburo about the visit to France], in *Polskie dokumenty dyplomatyczne. 1972*, 559.

77. Ibid.

78. Dariusz Jarosz and Maria Pasztor, "Wizyta Edwarda Gierka we Francji w październiku 1972 roku" [Edward Gierek's visit to France in October 1972], *Zeszyty Historyczne* 153 (2005): 123.

79. AAN, PZPR, XIB/106, Wystąpienie Stefana Olszowskiego na naradzie ministrów spraw zagranicznych państw-stron Układu Warszawskiego w Moskwie w dniach 15–16 I 1973 r. [Speech by Stefan Olszowski at a meeting of the foreign ministers of the countries of the Warsaw Pact in Moscow on January 15–16, 1973].

80. AIPN, 01593/619, Postanowienie o zakończeniu sprawy do archiwum Departamentu I [Decision to terminate the case for the Department I archive], May 9, 1985, 22.

81. Research was conducted in Department IV materials for 1971–1973 associated with Sweden, including documents from both headquarters and the Stockholm embassy. None mentions RFE's Stockholm office. Judging by the surviving documentation, this subject was also not raised during the visit to Sweden by Premier Piotr

Jaroszewicz on October 23–25, 1972 (AMSZ, Departament IV, Collection 27/77, bundle 3; Collection 28/77, bundle 9; AMSZ, Departament IV, Collection 45/77, bundle 8; Collection 46/77, bundle 8; AMSZ, Departament IV, Collection 47/77, bundle 10; Collection 48/77, bundle 8).

82. See also Nowak-Jeziorański, *Polska z oddali*, 418.

83. AMSZ, Gabinet Ministra, 23/77, bundle 1, Sprawozdanie z wizyty I sekretarza KC PZPR Edwarda Gierka w Stanach Zjednoczonych 8–13 X 1974 r. [Report on the visit to the United States on October 8–13, 1974, by First Secretary of the CC PUWP Edward Gierek], in *Polskie dokumenty dyplomatyczne. 1974* [Polish diplomatic documents: 1974], ed. Aleksander Kochański and Mikołaj Morzycki-Markowski (Warsaw: Polski Instytut Spraw Międzynarodowych, 2007), 201.

84. AAN, 237/XIX-166, Ocena kampanii prasowej w związku z powrotem kpt. Andrzeja Czechowicza [An evaluation of the press campaign related to the return of Captain Andrzej Czechowicz], July 1971, 1–8.

85. AAN, 237/XIX-166, Analiza przebiegu, reakcji krajowych i zagranicznych oraz rezultatów akcji związanej z powrotem kpt. Andrzeja Czechowicza [An analysis of the course, Polish and foreign reactions and results of the operation related to the return of Captain Andrzej Czechowicz], July 15, 1971, 12–25.

86. AIPN, 02011/80, part 1 (2), Informacja KBP ZSRR [Information from the Committee for State Security of the USSR – KGB], August 24, 1971, 364.

87. Author's interview with Andrzej Czechowicz, December 5, 2005. Czechowicz refused to give the journalist's name. We can only guess that he was one of the group of people mentioned in this book who were most involved in the propaganda campaign against "hostile sabotage" and directly involved in the Czechowicz campaign.

88. Czechowicz, *Siedem trudnych lat*, 149–52.

89. Letter from Czechowicz to the author, December 22, 2005.

90. Author's interview with Czechowicz, December 5, 2005.

91. Zakład Narodowy im. Ossolińskich, JNJ, 49/99/3-4, Objaśnienie [Explanation]; Nowak-Jeziorański, *Polska z oddali*, 401–2.

92. AIPN, 0259/81, Protokół przesłuchania podejrzanego [Protocol of interrogation of the suspect], August 11, 1948, 320.

93. Jarosław Kurski, *Jan Nowak-Jeziorański. Emisariusz wolności* [Jan Nowak-Jeziorański: Emissary of freedom] (Warsaw: Bertelsmann Media, 2005), 45–46; Jan Nowak, *Courier from Warsaw* (Detroit, MI: Wayne State University Press, 1982), 66; Nowak, *Polska z oddali*, 402–3.

94. Waldemar Grabowski, "Kalkstein i Kaczorowska w świetle akt UB" [Kalkstein and Kaczorowska in light of Security Service documents], *Biuletyn Instytutu Pamięci Narodowej* 8/9 (2004): 87–100.

95. Extensive documentation about Kassner-Kaszubowski survives (AIPN, 01251/202). It includes letters to the authorities from people living in Pomerania who remembered him from the war and demanded that he be put on trial. See also Andrzej Gąsiorowski, *Jan Kaszubowski i służby specjalne. Gestapo, Smiersz, UB . . .* [Jan Kaszubowski and the special services: Gestapo, Smersh, UB . . .] (Gdańsk: Polnord, 2008).

96. Zakład Narodowy im. Ossolińskich, JNJ, 49/99/3-4, Explanation.

97. Nowak-Jeziorański, *Polska z oddali*, 403.

98. Dobrosława Platt ("Pomówienia z esbeckiej fałszywki" [Defamation in Security Service forgeries], *Rzeczpospolita*, May 5, 2005) has written about this extensively.

99. Copy of the "document" in Jan Nowak's papers (Zakład Narodowy im. Ossolińskich, JNJ, 45/99).

100. Materials about Andrzej Smoliński can be found in the Institute of National Remembrance archive, in folder AIPN 00221/4.

101. The analysis conducted by German police is discussed in Hans Fischer's letter of January 3, 1975, to RFE's director Ralph Walter (Zakład Narodowy im. Ossolińskich, JNJ, 49/99/3-4). Its Polish translation is in another folder of Nowak's papers (JNJ, 54/99/3, Wyniki wstępnej ekspertyzy dotyczącej dokumentu rozsyłanego anonimowo z terenu Niemiec Zachodnich w sprawie Jana Nowaka [Outcome of a preliminary expert opinion of the anonymous document about Jan Nowak mailed in West Germany]; see Platt, "Pomówienia z esbeckiej fałszywki."

102. Zakład Narodowy im. Ossolińskich, JNJ, 54/99/2, 54/99/3. Both folders include forged documents and correspondence about them.

103. Zakład Narodowy im. Ossolińskich, JNJ, 49/99/1, List Jana Nowaka do Stefana Korbońskiego [Letter from Jan Nowak to Stefan Korboński], September 24, 1974; ibid., Notatka [Note]; ibid., Listy Jana Nowaka do Tadeusza Zawadzkiego-Żenczykowskiego [Letters from Jan Nowak to Tadeusz Zawadzki-Żenczykowski], October 19, 1974, January 21, 1975; JNJ, 49/99/3-4, List Andrzeja Chileckiego do Jana Nowaka [Letter from Andrzej Chilecki to Jan Nowak], February 8, 1975.

104. Translation of the article in Nowak's papers (Zakład Narodowy im. Ossolińskich, JNJ, 49/99/2).

105. Nowak wrote about the relations between Ostoja-Starzewski and Sitko and Sokolnicki in a letter to the premier of the government in exile in London, Alfred Urbański, on January 4, 1975 (Zakład Narodowy im. Ossolińskich, JNJ, 54/99).

106. Andrzej Friszke, *Życie polityczne emigracji* [The political life of emigration], vol. 1 of *Druga Wielka Emigracja 1945–1990* [The second Great Emigration, 1945–1990], in 3 vols. (Warsaw: Więź, 1999), 419–22.

107. Krzysztof Tarka, "Prowokator 'Mikron'—Juliusz Sokolnicki" [Provocateur "Mikron," Juliusz Sokolnicki] *Zeszyty Historyczne* 157 (2006): 101–12.

108. Former agent and Security Service officer Andrzej Czechowicz has continued to support them in public, as did President of the Polish American Congress Edward Moskal, who died in 2005 (*Gazeta Wyborcza*, June 19, 2001). In 2005, right-wing League of Polish Families city council members opposed giving Jan Nowak-Jeziorański's name to an elementary school in Łódź, citing these wartime allegations (Violetta Gnacikowska and Marcin Markowski, "LPR nie chce w szkole Kuriera" [The League of Polish Families doesn't want the Courier in school], *Gazeta Wyborcza*, May 24, 2005). In 2006 League of Polish Families councilman Antoni Gut gave the same reason for opposing naming Nowak-Jeziorański the patron of a Warsaw secondary school (Dominika Dziobkowska, "Ołtarz dla ofiar, których nie było" [An altar for the victims who didn't exist], *Gazeta Wyborcza*, March 15, 2006). *Myśl Polska*, a National Party paper, and other publications of the far-right nationalist movement regularly support the allegations against Nowak. Among the writings on the subject are Adam Hojda, "Rzekome fałszywki na temat Jana Nowaka-Jeziorańskiego" [Alleged forgeries about Jan Nowak-Jeziorański], *Myśl Polska* 22/23, May 29–June 5, 2005; and

Andrzej Czechowicz himself, "Prawda o RWE i Janie Nowaku" [The truth about RFE and Jan Nowak], *Myśl Polska* 9, February 27, 2005; see also the series of articles in the periodical published by Leszek Bubel, *Tylko Polska* 45, 46, 47, and 48, 2003; 37 and 38, 2003). One of Czechowicz's articles in *Tylko Polska* was titled "Kurier Mossadu" [Courier from the Mossad], and the editors wrote the following introduction to it: "The editors of *Tylko Polska* came up with this title, which in our opinion is most fitting for the life story of the senile Semite Nowak. He is a cunning psycho, whose services the Polish Yid-media are happy to use. He is vermin and a buffoon. We have been trying for a long time, with Andrzej Czechowicz's help, to remove him from mixing things up in our compatriots' heads" (*Tylko Polska* 48, 2003).

109. Zakład Narodowy im. Ossolińskich, JNJ, 54/99/1.

110. Author's interview with Maciej Morawski, August 29, 2006.

111. "Z teki Jana Nowaka" [From Jan Nowak's file], *Życie Warszawy*, February 4–5, 1973. Copies of this letter can be found in the Jan Nowak-Jeziorański Collection (Zakład Narodowy im. Ossolińskich, JNJ, 49/99/3-4) and in the Ministry of Foreign Affairs archive (AMSZ, Department IV, 28/76, W-10).

112. Zakład Narodowy im. Ossolińskich, JNJ, 44/99. Memorandum from Jan Nowak to Ralph Walter, June 21, 1973, with an appended clipping from the *Congressional Record*, a statement of explanations about the forged letters by RFE director Walter. See also Janusz Wróbel, *Polonia Chicagowska w dobie "Solidarności" 1980–1989* [The Chicago Polonia in the Solidarity era, 1980–1989] (Łódź: Instytut Pamięci Narodowej, 2012), 117–18.

113. Zakład Narodowy im. Ossolińskich, JNJ, 45/99, Memorandum Concerning Covert Operations against RFE; ibid., 45/99, Note; Nowak-Jeziorański, *Polska z oddali*, 383–407; Alina Grabowska, "Fałszywki PRL" [Forgeries of People's Poland], in *Pięćdziesiąt lat Rozgłośni Polskiej Radia Wolna Europa. Materiały sesji jubileuszowej* [Fifty years of the Polish Section of Radio Free Europe: Materials from an anniversary session], ed. Daria Nałęcz (Warsaw: Naczelna Dyrekcja Archiwów Państwowych, 2003), 75–81.

114. Author's interview with Maciej Morawski, August 29, 2006.

115. AIPN, 0665/174, "Kierunki działania resortu spraw wewnętrznych w roku 1972. Materiały z narady krajowej 7 I 1972 r." [Directions of action of the ministry of internal affairs in 1972: Materials from a national conference, January 7, 1972], 25.

116. AIPN, 0365/104, vol. 1, Referat na naradę krajową (17–18 IV 1972 r.) [Presentation for the national meeting (April 17–18, 1972)], "Podstawowe zadania pionu III w świetle obowiązujących nowych dokumentów oraz dyrektyw kierownictwa partyjno-rządowego" [Basic tasks for Department III in view of the new documents that are in force and directives from the party-government leadership], 263–263a, 322.

117. AIPN, 0141/8, vol. 11, 281–82.

118. Simon Wiesenthal, *Justice, Not Vengeance* (New York: Grove Weidenfeld, 1989), 208; Nowak-Jeziorański, *Polska z oddali*, 408. The following judgment on Wiesenthal was uttered by the director of the Commission for the Prosecution of Nazi Crimes, Czesław Pilichowski, in October 1969: "Beginning in late 1966, and especially from June 1967, i.e., after Israel's aggression against the Arab states, Wiesenthal, influenced by and tied to international Zionist organizations . . . shifted the work of the Documentation Center he leads from the problem of pursuing Nazi criminals to waging war on alleged anti-Semitism in the countries of the socialist camp. . . . In my view,

the question of the anti-Polish and anticommunist activities of Wiesenthal and his Documentation Center in Vienna calls for a response and for pointing out the falsehoods with which he operates" (AAN, 237/XIX/351, Notatka w sprawie antypolskiej i antykomunistycznej działalności inż. Szymona Wiesenthala, kierującego Centrum Dokumentacji Żydowskiej Związku Ofiar Hitleryzmu [Note on the question of the anti-Polish and anticommunist activity of engineer Simon Wiesenthal, who directs the Jewish Documentation Center of Victims of Nazism]).

119. Wacław Szafrański, *W sieci Szymona Wiesenthala* [In Simon Wiesenthal's net] (Warsaw: Wydawnictwo Ministerstwa Obrony Narodowej, 1972), 161–62.

120. Nowak-Jeziorański, *Polska z oddali*, 409.

121. AIPN, 01419/161; AIPN, 01069/247.

122. Zakład Narodowy im. Ossolińskich, JNJ, 45/99, *Na antenie*, April 1975; Zakład Narodowy im. Ossolińskich, JNJ, 54/99, List of "dirty tricks" not mentioned in Bittman's book, March 21, 1975. For Josef Frolik and the information he gave about the activities of the Communist special services, see Christopher Andrew and Oleg Gordievsky, *KGB: The Inside Story of Its Foreign Operations from Lenin to Gorbachev* (London: Hodder & Stoughton, 1990), 429–35. Josef Frolik published a book in the West in which he described his work for the Czechoslovak secret police and his "desertion," *The Frolik Defection* (London: Corgi Books, 1975).

123. Zakład Narodowy im. Ossolińskich, JNJ, 54/99, List of "dirty tricks" not mentioned in Bittman's book, March 21, 1975.

124. Ibid., JNJ, 45/99, Memorandum from David Grozier to Ralph Walter, April 22, 1975.

125. AIPN, MSW II, 111. Posiedzenie kierownictwa [Leadership session], November 17, 1972, 128. The shortened protocol of the Politburo session did not record Gierek's instructions (AAN, 237/V-109, Protokół nr. 49 z posiedzenia Biura Politycznego i prezydium rządu [Protocol no. 49 of the session of the Political Bureau and the government Presidium], November 16, 1972, 347–52).

126. AIPN, MSW II, Gabinet Ministra [Minister's Office], 61, Protokół nr 014/71 z posiedzenia kolegium MSW [Protocol no. 014/71 of Ministry of Internal Affairs leadership], September 14, 1971, 46.

127. AIPN, 0296/150, vol. 3, Niektóre formy i metody antysocjalistycznej działalności w Polsce i jej zwalczanie [Some forms and methods of antisocialist activity in Poland and combating it], October 6, 1972, 167.

128. AAN, 237/XI-300, Referat "Aktualne problemy pracy ideologiczno-propagandowej w naszych stosunkach z zagranicą" wygłoszony przez Jana Szydlaka, członka Biura Politycznego i sekretarza KC PZPR na naradzie krajowego i zagranicznego frontu ideologicznego w Warszawie [A paper, "Current issues in the ideological-propaganda work in our relations with foreign countries," delivered by Jan Szydlak, member of the Politburo and secretary of the CC PUWP, at a meeting of the Polish and foreign ideological front in Warsaw], March 25, 1974, 147.

129. AIPN, 0296/56, vol. 6, Materiały z sympozjum na temat aktualnego zagrożenia kraju dywersją ideologiczno-polityczną oraz sposobów jej przeciwdziałania, Warszawa 1975 [Materials from a symposium about the current threat of ideological-political sabotage to our country and ways to counter it]; AAN, PZPR, Wydział Zagraniczny, 850/35, Informacja o wielostronnej współpracy w dziedzinie pracy ideologicznej i propagandy zagranicznej [Information about the multilateral cooperation in the area

of ideological work and foreign propaganda], materials have not been sorted and there are no page numbers.

130. Report to Politburo and Politburo Resolution on Fight against "Imperialist Propaganda," May 22, 1973, in Johnson and Parta, *Cold War Broadcasting*, 368–78.

131. AIPN, 0296/257, vol. 2, Notatka dotycząca niektórych tendencji w taktyce dywersji ideologicznej państw imperialistycznych przeciwko ZSRR opracowana na podstawie materiałów za rok 1974 [Note about some tendencies in the tactics of ideological sabotage of the imperialist countries against the USSR developed on the basis of materials for 1974], February 20, 1975.

132. There is very extensive documentation about the seminar, mostly papers presented by the delegations (AIPN, 0296/132, vols. 1–6; AIPN, 0296/133, vols. 1–3).

133. AIPN, 0296/56, vol. 6, Materiały z sympozjum na temat aktualnego zagrożenia kraju dywersją ideologiczno-polityczną oraz sposobów jej przeciwdziałania [Materials from a symposium on the subject of the current state of threat from ideological-political sabotage and the political-operational system of response], Warsaw, 1975.

134. AIPN, 00221/4, Notatka służbowa [Office note], June 17, 1974, 39.

135. Ibid.

136. AIPN, 00221/7, Notatka [Note], August 25, 1974.

137. AIPN, 00221/4, Raport dotyczący werbunku bądź ściągnięcia do kraju agenta wywiadu amerykańskiego w RWE ps. "Kryza" [Report on recruiting or bringing back to Poland an American intelligence agent at RFE code name "Kryza"], March 20, 1974, 33.

138. Ibid., 33.

139. Ibid., 34.

140. Draft of a PAP press release about the Smolińskis, AIPN, 00221/4, 46; Lach, AIPN, 02221/7, 52. They were published in the newspapers on September 1, 1974, and November 24, 1974 (*PRL atakuje*, 34–36).

141. AIPN, 00221/7, Omówienie do komunikatu PAP [Comments on the PAP press release], 53.

142. AIPN, 00221/5, Projekt rozmowy z K[azimierzem] Z[amorskim] [Plan for a conversation with K{azimierz} Z{amorski}], February 14, 1975, 86; AIPN, 01263/597, Raport dotyczący zorganizowania wyjazdu operacyjnego do RFN dla kontaktu operacyjnego "Akademik" [Report on the organization of an operational trip to the FRG for the "Akademik" operational contact], October 20, 1975.

143. Author's interview with Jan Nowak-Jeziorański, July 14, 2004.

144. For a discussion of the "repatriation campaign," see Friszke, *Życie polityczne emigracji*, 232–41; Paweł Machcewicz, *Emigracja w polityce międzynarodowej* [Emigration in international politics], vol. 2 of *Druga Wielka Emigracja 1945–1990* [The second Great Emigration, 1945–1990] (Warsaw: Biblioteka "Więzi," 1999), 128–41; Cenckiewicz, "Geneza, działalność i udział rozgłośni 'Kraj,'" 114–28.

145. These were the reasons for his departure that Nowak-Jeziorański lists both in his memoirs (*Polska z oddali*, 414–35) and in the memoranda he wrote in 1975 to his American superiors (Zakład Narodowy im. Ossolińskich, JNJ, 44/99, 54/99/2, Pisma Jana Nowaka do Ralpha Waltera [Jan Nowak's memoranda to Ralph Walter] of October 8 and 9, 1975.

146. Zamorski, *Pod anteną Radia Wolna Europa*; Stefan Wysocki, *Polska z oddali —prawda z bliska* [Poland from afar, the truth from up close] (Solidarność Walcząca, Oddział Trójmiasto, 1989), unsigned.

147. Danuta Mierzanowska, *Wolna Europa i świat* [Free Europe and the world] (Cracow: Wydawnictwo Baran i Suszczyński, 1998), 132.

148. Author's interview with Andrzej Czechowicz, December 5, 2005; interview with Andrzej Czechowicz by Jane Curry and A. Ross Johnson, July 2004, Hoover Institution, Jane Curry Collection.

Chapter 6

1. See Raymond Garthoff, *Détente and Confrontation: American-Soviet Relations from Nixon to Reagan* (Washington, DC: Brookings Institution Press, 1994).

2. Andrzej Mania, *Détente i polityka Stanów Zjednoczonych wobec Europy Wschodniej. Styczeń 1969–styczeń 1981* [Détente and United States policies vis-à-vis Eastern Europe, January 1969–January 1981] (Cracow: Wydawnictwo Uniwersytetu Jagiellońskiego, 2003); Bennett Kovrig, *Of Walls and Bridges: The United States and Eastern Europe* (New York: New York University Press, 1991), 157–227.

3. See the interpretation of the Final Act of CSCE written in 1975–1976 in the CC PUWP Secretariat (Archiwum Akt Nowych [Central Archive of Modern Records], Warsaw [hereafter AAN], 237/XI/318, Wnioski dla pracy ideowo-wychowawczej w związku z nowym etapem odprężenia po zakończeniu KBWE [Conclusions for ideological-educational work relating to a new stage of détente after the conclusion of the CSCE], January 14, 1976, 42–62.

4. Ibid., 60.

5. AAN, 237/XI/318, Wzmożenie popularyzowania za granicą osiągnięć PRL [Intensifying the popularization of the PRP's achievements abroad], July 21, 1976, 219.

6. AAN, Polskiej Zjednoczonej Partii Robotniczej [Central Committee of the Polish United Workers' Party, hereafter PZPR], Wydział Pracy Ideowo-Wychowawczej, 198, Antypolska propaganda-zagrożenie dla żywotnych interesów narodu (1977) [Department of Ideological-Educational Work, 198 (unorganized materials, no page numbering), Anti-Polish propaganda: A threat to the nation's vital interests].

7. Ibid.

8. Ibid.

9. AAN, 237/XXXIV/141, Wydział Pracy Ideowo-Wychowawczej, Informacja w sprawie narady ideologicznej komitetów centralnych partii odbytej w styczniu 1976 r. w Warszawie, wygłoszona przez kierownika Wydziału Pracy Ideowo-Wychowawczej KC PZPR Wiesława Klimczaka na spotkaniu z lektorami KC [Department of Ideological-Educational Work (random materials, no page numbers), Information about the ideological conference of the central committees of the parties taking place in January 1976 in Warsaw, shared by the head of the Department of Ideological-Educational Work of the CC PUWP, Wiesław Klimczak in a meeting with CC lecturers].

10. Ibid., Protokół ustaleń grupy roboczej ds. realizacji ustaleń narad ideologicznych sekretarzy KC partii z krajów socjalistycznych [Minutes of decisions of the working group for implementing the decisions of the ideological conferences of the secretaries of the CCs of the parties from the socialist countries], November 1976.

11. Archiwum Instytutu Pamięci Narodowej [Archive of the Institute of National Remembrance], Warsaw (hereafter AIPN), 0326/486, vol. 1, Informacja dotycząca niektórych zagadnień wiążących się z udziałem polskiej ekipy na Zimowych Igrzyskach Olimpijskich [Information about certain issues relating to the participation of the Polish team in the Winter Olympics], April 8, 1976.

12. Danuta Mierzanowska, *Wolna Europa i świat* [Free Europe and the world] (Cracow: Wydawnictwo Baran i Suszczyński, 1998), 27.

13. Zygmunt Jabłoński, *Gabinet figur radiowych* [The cabinet of radio figures] (London: Pogląd, 1985), 181.

14. AAN, PZPR, 850/35, Wydział Zagraniczny (materiały nieuporządkowane, b.p.), Notatka o naradzie sekretarzy komitetów centralnych bratnich partii krajów socjalistycznych w Sofii w dniach 2–3 III 1977 r. [Foreign Department (unorganized materials, no page numbers) Note about the meeting of secretaries of the central committees of the fraternal parties of the socialist countries in Sofia on March 2–3, 1977].

15. AAN, 237/XXXIV/141, (unorganized materials, unsigned), Wspólne akcje przeciwko dywersji ideologicznej wymierzonej przeciwko krajom naszej wspólnoty [Joint actions against ideological sabotage aimed against the countries of our community], 1977.

16. AAN, 237/XIB/113, Notatka informacyjna [Information note], June 5, 1978, 112–13.

17. AAN, 237/XIB/118, O rezultatakh ofitsyalnovo vizita generalnogo sekretara CK KPSS, predsedatela Presidiuma Verkhovnogo Sovieta SSSR L. I. Brezhneva w FRG [On the outcomes of the official visit of the general secretary of the CC CPSU, Chairman of the Presidium of the Supreme Soviet, L. I. Brezhnev, in the FRG], 4–7 V s.g., 81. The Poles also raised this demand during a visit to Poland by Senator Edmund S. Muskie, chairman of the Senate Budget Committee, in 1979 (AAN, 237/XIB/119, Materiały informacyjne do wizyty senatora Edmunda S. Muskie'go [Informational materials for Senator Edmund S. Muskie's visit], April 30, 1979).

18. This "action plan" was found in Stasi materials by the office of the Federal Commissioner for the Stasi Archives and was published in *Cold War Broadcasting: Impact on the Soviet Union and Eastern Europe: A Collection of Studies and Documents*, ed. A. Ross Johnson and R. Eugene Parta (Budapest and New York: Central European University Press, 2010), 441–46.

19. This was a topic of discussion in August 1978 during a meeting in Moscow of the head of the KGB's Department V, General Filip Bobkov, with the head of Department VI of the Bulgarian Committee of State Security General Petar Stoyanov (Jordan Baev, "Bulgarian Regime Countermeasures against Radio Free Europe," in Johnson and Parta, *Cold War Broadcasting*, 263).

20. AAN, 237/XIB/113, Notatka informacyjna [Information note], June 5, 1978.

21. Author's interview with Andrzej Werblan, April 5, 2007.

22. "Action Plan," in Johnson and Parta, *Cold War Broadcasting*, 441–46.

23. A. Ross Johnson, *Radio Free Europe and Radio Liberty: The CIA Years and Beyond* (Washington, DC: Woodrow Wilson Center Press; Stanford, CA: Stanford University Press, 2010), 192–93.

24. Baev, "Bulgarian Regime Countermeasures against Radio Free Europe," 263.

25. Ibid., 266.

26. Ibid., 266–70; Christopher Andrew and Vasili Mitrokhin, *The Mitrokhin Archive and the Secret History of the KGB* (New York: Basic Books, 1999), 388–89; Richard H. Cummings, *Cold War Radio: The Dangerous History of American Broadcasting in Europe, 1950–1989* (Jefferson, NC: McFarland & Co., 2009), 58–85. The information about the KGB's help to the Bulgarian secret service is based on General Oleg Kalugin's statement made after he defected to the West.

27. Johnson, *Radio Free Europe and Radio Liberty*, 196–98; Cummings, *Cold War Radio*, 99–107; Arch Puddington, *Broadcasting Freedom: The Cold War Triumph of Radio Free Europe and Radio Liberty* (Lexington: University Press of Kentucky, 2000), 245-46.

28. The Czechoslovak section received a letter warning that "next time, Radio Free Europe will disappear from its foundations in the beautiful English Garden" (Hoover Institution, Radio Free Europe/Radio Liberty, Corporate Records, 374.1). It was signed by Minařik II, an obvious reference to the Czechoslovak agent who had worked in RFE's Czechoslovak Service and in 1976 was "pulled out" and introduced in Prague with great propaganda fanfare. The real Pavel Minařik had tried but failed to convince his superiors in Czechoslovak intelligence to stage a bomb attack on RFE's headquarters in Munich and had offered his services (A. Ross Johnson, "Soviet Bloc Intelligence Activities against Western Information Programs: The Case of Radio Free Europe and Radio Liberty" [paper presented at the conference "Intelligence in Waging the Cold War: NATO, the Warsaw Pact, and the Neutrals 1949–1990," Oslo, April 28–May 1, 2005]).

29. Nestor Ratesh, "Radio Free Europe's Impact in Romania during the Cold War," in Johnson and Parta, *Cold War Broadcasting*, 211–25; Cummings, *Cold War Radio*, 146–70.

30. Johnson, "Soviet Bloc Intelligence Activities."

31. There are Bulgarian, Czechoslovak, Hungarian, and Polish documents in the archives of the office of the Federal Commissioner for the Stasi Archives, and files obtained from the KGB in Bulgarian archives (Johnson, "Soviet Bloc Intelligence Activities"). I have not managed to find RFE-related documents from other Soviet bloc spying agencies in Polish archives. During the Budapest meeting in May 1977, the Polish Security Service representative said that following the Havana meeting in 1974, the Poles had shared information and documents about Western "sabotage" organizations with the "fraternal" services and that they had received some documents from their partners (AIPN, 0296/133, vol. 7, Wybrane zagadnienia dywersji ideologiczno-politycznej przeciwko Polsce oraz działalności antysocjalistycznej w PRL. Referat na sympozjum służb bezpieczeństwa krajów socjalistycznych [Selected issues in ideological-political sabotage against Poland and antisocialist activities in the PRP: A paper for a symposium of the security services of the socialist countries], Budapest, May 1977, 5–6).

32. AIPN, 0296/133, vol. 7, Ocena polityki państw zachodnich wobec Polski i innych krajów socjalistycznych w dziedzinie dywersji ideologicznej i politycznej [An evaluation of the policies of Western countries vis-à-vis Poland and other socialist countries in the area of ideological and political sabotage], 1977, 71–72.

33. Ibid., Zamierzenia organów wywiadowczych i propagandowych krajów imperialistycznych, skierowane na aktywizację wroga wewnętrznego i doświadczenia z pracy organów bezpieczeństwa państwowego [The plans of the intelligence and propaganda organs of the imperialist countries directed at activating the domestic enemy and experiences drawn from the work of the state security organs], 109.

34. The most important book on this subject is Paweł Sasanka, *Czerwiec 1976. Geneza, przebieg, konsekwencje* [June 1976: Genesis, developments, consequences] (Warsaw: Instytut Pamięci Narodowej, 2006).

35. AIPN, 0326/486, vol. 1, Departament III, Informacja dotycząca stanu rozpoznania zagrożeń bezpieczeństwa wewnętrznego kraju w kwietniu 1976 r. [Department III, Information about the diagnosis of the threats to the domestic security of our country in April 1976], May 3, 1976.

36. Ibid., Informacja dotycząca stanu rozpoznania zagrożeń bezpieczeństwa wewnętrznego kraju w maju 1976 r. [Information about the diagnosis of the threats to the domestic security of our country in May 1976], June 1, 1976.

37. Ibid., Informacja dotycząca nastrojów wśród pracowników Huty im. Lenina [Information on the mood of the workers at the Lenin Steelworks], May 29, 1976.

38. Jacek Kuroń, *Gwiezdny czas* [A starry time] (London: Aneks, 1991), 18.

39. Biographies of Aleksander and Eugeniusz Smolar may be found in *Opozycja w PRL. Słownik biograficzny 1956–89* [Opposition in the PRP: A biographical dictionary, 1956–89], ed. Jan Skórzyński, Paweł Sowiński, and Małgorzata Strasz (Warsaw: Ośrodek "Karta," 2006), 3:245–50.

40. Author's interview with Eugeniusz Smolar, April 5, 2007.

41. Andrzej Friszke, "Jan Józef Lipski—szkic biografii" [Jan Józef Lipski, an outline for a biography], in Jan Józef Lipski, *KOR. Komitet Obrony Robotników. Komitet Samoobrony Społecznej* [KOR: Workers' Defense Committee; Committee of Social Self-Defense] (Warsaw: Instytut Pamięci Narodowej, 2006), 62.

42. Edmund Szczesiak, *Borusewicz. Jak runął mur* [Borusewicz: How the wall fell down] (Warsaw: Oficyna Wydawnicza Volumen, 2005), 106–7.

43. AIPN, 0141/7, vol. 4, Notatka urzędowa [Official note], July 7, 1977.

44. AIPN, 0365/5, vol. 6, Departament III, Informacja dotycząca oceny sytuacji społeczno-ekonomicznej w I kwartale 1978 r. [Department III, Information regarding an evaluation of the socioeconomic situation in the first quarter of 1978], April 10, 1979.

45. Pismo Rady Warszawskiej Federacji Socjalistycznych Związków Młodzieży Polskiej do prezesa Polskiej Akademii Nauk prof. Witolda Nowackiego, [Letter from the Warsaw Council of the Federation of the Socialist Unions of Polish Youth to the chairman of the Polish Academy of Sciences, Professor Witold Nowacki], April 20, 1979, in *Opozycja demokratyczna w Polsce w świetle akt KC PZPR (1976–1980). Wybór dokumentów* [Democratic opposition in Poland in light of CC PUWP documents (1976–1980): A selection of documents], selected, edited, and with an introduction by Łukasz Kamiński and Paweł Piotrowski, preface by Wojciech Wrzesiński (Wrocław: Gajt, 2002), 243–44.

46. In October 1976, the Politburo member and CC secretary in charge of the power ministries, Stanisław Kania, vetoed the repressions of KOR members (arrests, indictments by the prosecutor's office, and a series of house searches) being planned by the Ministry of Internal Affairs. Kania argued that opting for repression would only "make this group more popular in milieus such as universities and [among] writers, and even abroad, where these days we don't have a 'good press' and we want it to write better about us" ("'Zawężona represja.' Co robić z Komitetem Obrony Robotników? Narada u Stanisława Kani 22 października 1976 r." ["Narrowed-down repressions": What is to be done with the Workers' Defense Committee? A meeting hosted by Stanisław Kania on October 22, 1976], ed. Andrzej Paczkowski and Marcin Zaremba, *Więź* 8 (2001); Friszke, "Jan Józef Lipski," 57–58. Andrzej Werblan, who as CC secretary (from 1974) was charged with learning and higher education, often took part in meetings on

strategies concerning the intelligentsia, gave the author similar reasons for the government's restraint. Werblan had participated in informal sessions organized by Stanisław Kania at the Central Committee, which included discussions about how to deal with the opposition (author's interview with Andrzej Werblan, April 5, 2007).

47. Andrzej Friszke, *Opozycja polityczna w PRL 1945–1980* [The political opposition in the People's Republic of Poland, 1945–1980] (London: Aneks, 1994), 358.

48. The copious operations documentation about KOR includes numerous transcripts from telephone bugs in Kuroń's apartment and analyses of conversations that took place with people in the West. This was the Security Service method of learning about KOR's tactics and intentions. For the Security Service actions against KOR, see Robert Spałek, "'Gracze'"—Komitet Obrony Robotników w propagandzie PRL, stereotypach oraz dokumentach Ministerstwa Spraw Wewnętrznych" ["Players": The Workers' Defense Committee in PRP's propaganda, stereotypes and Ministry of Internal Affairs documents], *Pamięć i Sprawiedliwość* 4, no. 2 (2003): 79–112.

49. Friszke, "Jan Józef Lipski," 61–62, 69.

50. Józef Tejchma, *Kulisy dymisji. Z dzienników ministra kultury 1974–1977* [Secrets of a resignation: From the diaries of the minister of culture, 1974–1977] (Cracow: Cracovia, 1991), 253.

51. Friszke, "Jan Józef Lipski," 71.

52. Informacja dotycząca dalszych ustaleń w sprawie głodówki studentów Politechniki Gdańskiej, 18 VI 1977 [Information about further decisions about the hunger strike of the Gdańsk Polytechnic students], in *Opozycja demokratyczna w Polsce*, 122.

53. AIPN, 0296/133, t. 7, "Wybrane zagadnienia dywersji ideologiczno-politycznej przeciwko Polsce oraz działalności antysocjalistycznej w PRL," referat na sympozjum służb bezpieczeństwa krajów socjalistycznych" ["Selected issues in ideological-political sabotage against Poland and in anti-socialist activity in the PRP," a paper for a symposium of the security services of the socialist countries], Moscow, April 1980, 253.

54. Ibid., Tezy dotyczące sympozjum przedstawicieli służb bezpieczeństwa państw socjalistycznych w Moskwie [Theses concerning a symposium for representatives of the security services of the socialist countries in Moscow], 199.

55. Andrzej Paczkowski, *Droga do "mniejszego zła." Strategia i taktyka obozu władzy. Lipiec 1980–styczeń 1982* [The road to the "lesser evil": The governing camp's strategy and tactics, July 1980–January 1982] (Cracow: Wydawnictwo Literackie, 2002), 22.

56. Protokół nr 17 z posiedzenia Biura Politycznego KC PZPR 15 sierpnia 1980 r. [Minutes no. 17 from a session of the Politburo of the CC PUWP on August 15, 1980], in *Tajne dokumenty Biura Politycznego. PZPR a "Solidarność" 1980–1981* [Classified Politburo documents: The PUWP and "Solidarity," 1980–1981], ed. Zbigniew Włodek (London: Aneks, 1992), 31.

57. Protokół nr 18 z posiedzenia Biura Politycznego KC PZPR 16 sierpnia 1980 r. [Minutes No. 18 from a session of the Politburo of the CC PUWP on August 16, 1980], in Włodek, *Tajne dokumenty Biura Politycznego*, 36.

58. Szczesiak, *Borusewicz*, 96.

59. Timothy Garton Ash, *The Polish Revolution: Solidarity* (New York: Charles Scribner's Sons: 1983), 50.

60. Piotr Zaremba, *Młodopolacy. Historia Ruchu Młodej Polski* [The Young Poles: A history of the Young Poland Movement] (Gdańsk: Arche, 2000), 404.

61. Protokół z posiedzenia Biura Politycznego KC PZPR 23 sierpnia 1980 r. [Minutes of a session of the Politburo of the CC PUWP, August 23, 1980], in Włodek, *Tajne dokumenty Biura Politycznego*, 54

62. Jolanta Hajdasz, *Szczekaczka, czyli Rozgłośnia Polska Radia Wolna Europa* [A Nazi street loudspeaker, or the Polish Service of Radio Free Europe] (Poznań: Media Rodzina, 2006), 253. These figures may at first glance seem very high, but we must remember that they included everyone who listened to RFE, whether regularly or sporadically.

63. AIPN, MSW II, 305, "Dywersja polityczno-ideologiczna i jej zwalczanie," referat na naradę przedstawicieli organów bezpieczeństwa krajów socjalistycznych w Sofii w dniach 16–22 X 1983 r. ["Political-ideological sabotage and combating it," a paper for the meeting of representatives of the security organs of the socialist countries in Sofia on October 16–22, 1983].

64. See Paczkowski, *Droga do "mniejszego zła."*

65. The files of the CC PUWP Secretariat include a detailed list of such articles appearing in various publications (AAN, 237/XI/355, Materiały publicystyczne w całości lub istotnych—obszerniejszych fragmentach podejmujące temat walki ideologicznej i działalności sił antysocjalistycznych w Polsce. Okres obserwacji: 15 VIII–28 X 1980 r. [Journalistic materials in full or as major, extensive, fragments discussing the subjects of ideological warfare and the activities of antisocialist forces in Poland. Period of observation: August 15–October 28, 1980]).

66. "Płonne rachuby," artykuł redakcyjny [Vain calculations, an editorial], *Trybuna Ludu*, September 2, 1980; Zbigniew Nowakowski, "Nieczyste intencje, dywersyjne pióra" [Bad intentions, saboteurs' pens], *Trybuna Ludu*, October 15, 1980; Ignacy Krasicki, "Kto odpowiada za podżeganie i ingerencje" [Who is responsible for incitement and interference], *Trybuna Ludu*, October 23, 1980.

67. Jan Dziadul, "Co się dzieje w hucie" [What is going on in the steelworks], *Trybuna Robotnicza*, October 1, 1980.

68. Kazimierz Kąkol, *Na szlakach dywersji* [On the trail of sabotage] (Warsaw: Wydawnictwo Związkowe CRZZ, 1971).

69. Jerzy Bronisławski [Kudaś], *Fałszywi prorocy* [False prophets] (Warsaw: Młodzieżowa Agencja Wydawnicza, 1981), 197.

70. Note from a visit to Katowice by the Soviet group with Comrade L. M. Zamyatin on January 16, 1981, in *Poland 1980–82: Internal Crisis, International Dimensions: A Compendium of Declassified Documents and Chronology of Events*, ed. Malcolm Byrne, Paweł Machcewicz, and Christian Ostermann (Washington, DC: National Security Archive, 1997) (photocopied materials prepared for a conference on the Soviet role in the Polish crisis of 1980–1981, held in Jachranka, Poland, November 1997).

71. Paczkowski, *Droga do "mniejszego zła,"* 132, 140.

72. Hoover Institution, Radio Free Europe/Radio Liberty, Corporate Records, 395.6, Memorandum from Glenn W. Ferguson, President, to Board of Directors, Radio Free Europe/Radio Liberty, January 18, 1982.

73. Hoover Institution, Radio Free Europe/Radio Liberty, Corporate Records, 380.1, Impact of Jamming on the Reception of Programs.

74. Hoover Institution, Radio Free Europe/Radio Liberty, Corporate Records, 395.6, Memorandum from Glenn W. Ferguson, President, to Board of Directors, Radio Free Europe/Radio Liberty, January 18, 1982.

75. See Paczkowski, *Wojna polsko-jaruzelska. Stan wojenny w Polsce. 13 XII 1981–22 VII 1983* [The Polish-Jaruzelski war: Martial law in Poland, December 13, 1981–July 22, 1983] (Warsaw: Prószyński i S-ka, 2006).

76. AIPN, MSW II, 305, Wystąpienie w dyskusji na naradzie przedstawicieli organów bezpieczeństwa wewnętrznego [Speech in a discussion during a meeting of representatives of internal security organs], October 1983.

77. *Polityka Stanów Zjednoczonych Ameryki wobec Polski w świetle faktów i dokumentów (1980–1983)* [United States of America policies toward Poland in light of facts and documents (1980–1983)] (Warsaw: Polski Instytut Spraw Międzynarodowych, 1984), 11.

78. AIPN, 001103/145, Protokoły z posiedzeń Zespołu Zarządu II, Protokół z 8 V1982 r. [Minutes from meetings of the Second Division, minutes of May 8, 1982].

79. Paczkowski, *Wojna polsko-jaruzelska*, 178–80.

80. Mieczysław F. Rakowski, *Dzienniki polityczne 1981–1983* [Political diaries, 1981–1983] (Warsaw: Iskry, 2004), 523. Rakowski also writes that prior to the session, the Politburo members watched "footage of May Day demonstrations." Surviving in the minutes of the Politburo meeting of May 4, 1983, is only a laconic record of Kiszczak's account of the sequence of the events on May 1 and 3 (AAN, PZPR, 1852, Protokół nr 74 z posiedzenia Biura Politycznego KC PZPR w dniu 4 V 1983 r. [Minutes no. 74 of the meeting of the Politburo of the CC PUWP on May 4, 1983], 4–8).

81. Jane Curry, "Radio Free Europe in the Eyes of the Polish Communist Elite," in Johnson and Parta, *Cold War Broadcasting*, 160.

82. Zdzisław Najder, in an interview with the author (March 14, 2007), spoke about the differences in the RFE Polish Service program line under his and Zygmunt Michałowski's managements, especially in the methods of presenting information about Solidarity and other underground organizations. Eugeniusz Smolar, who then worked in the BBC's Polish Section, also told me about the differences in the BBC's and RFE's coverage (April 5, 2007).

83. For a discussion of US policy, see Paczkowski, *Wojna polsko-jaruzelska*, 115–21; Kovrig, *Of Walls and Bridges*, 180–82.

84. *Polityka Stanów Zjednoczonych wobec Polski*, 234.

85. Ibid., 246.

86. Ibid., 182.

87. Ibid., 186.

88. Ibid., 195–215.

89. Ibid., 216-20.

90. Rakowski, *Dzienniki polityczne 1981–1983*, 208.

91. Ibid., 323.

92. Ibid., 389.

93. Ibid., 410.

94. Ibid., 445.

95. Ibid., 503.

96. AIPN, MSW II, 1026, Ocena działalności RWE [An assessment of RFE's activity], May 4, 1983, 1.

97. Ibid., Notatka o nasileniu amerykańskiej kampanii propagandowej przeciwko Polsce [Note on the intensification of the American propaganda campaign against Poland], January 29, 1982, 6–9.

98. Ignacy Krasicki, *Radio "Wolna Europa." Mocodawcy, założenia, program* [Radio "Free Europe": Patrons, principles, program] (Warsaw: Książka i Wiedza, 1982).

99. Mieczysław Lach and Zdzisław Uberman, *Ufam ci Kilroy* [I trust you, Kilroy] (Warsaw: Krajowa Agencja Wydawnicza, 1983).

100. AIPN, 01305/555, Dywersja antysocjalistyczna Zachodu wobec Polski. Materiały z konferencji naukowej zorganizowanej 1 i 2 XII 1983 r. przez Instytut I Akademii Spraw Wewnętrznych [The West's antisocialist sabotage against Poland. Materials for an academic conference organized on December 1 and 2 by the First Institute of the Academy of Internal Affairs] (Warsaw: 1984).

101. AAN, PZPR, 237/VII/67, Protokół nr 49 z posiedzenia Sekretariatu KC PZPR w dniu 12 III 1984 r. [Minutes no. 49 of the meeting of the CC PUWP Secretariat on March 12, 1984], 404.

102. Ibid., Wybrane dane. Zachodnie radiostacje nadające w języku polskim, marzec 1984 r. [Selected data: Western radio stations broadcasting in Polish, March 1984], 435.

103. Ibid., Zwalczanie wpływów dywersji ideologicznej i propagandowej na społeczeństwo polskie (kontrpropaganda) [Countering the influence of ideological and propaganda sabotage on the Polish society (counterpropaganda)], 426.

104. Ibid., Wybrane dane. Zachodnie radiostacje nadające w języku polskim, marzec 1984 r. [Selected data: Western radio stations broadcasting in Polish, March 1984], 435.

105. AIPN, MSW II, 1460, Działalność rozgłośni dywersyjnych między 30 VII a 5 VIII 1985 r. [The activity of the sabotage radio stations between July 30 and August 5, 1985], August 8, 1985.

106. Account by Renate Marsch, correspondent of the West German DPA agency, during the conference "Stan wojenny—spojrzenie po 25 latach" [Martial law, a 25-year perspective], organized by the Solidarity Center Foundation in Warsaw on December 13, 2006.

107. Centralne Archiwum Ministerstwa Spraw Wewnętrznych i Administracji [Central Archive of the Ministry of Internal Affairs and Administration], Warsaw (hereafter CAMSWiA), Urząd Rady Ministrów/Biuro Prasowe Rządu [Office of the Council of Ministers/Government Press Office; hereafter URM/BPR], 53, Informacja dotycząca opinii o udostępnianiu materiałów bibliotecznych zawartych w Biuletynie Naczelnej Redakcji Odbioru Audycji i Opracowań w Komitecie ds. Radia i TV z 20 II 1984 r. [Information about the opinion on releasing library materials contained in the Bulletin of the Main Editorial Office of the Reception of Programs and Studies about Radio and TV of February 20, 1984], February 24, 1984.

108. Ibid., Notatka służbowa w sprawie stanu zdrowia Grażyny Staniszewskiej w tymczasowym areszcie od 4 X do 23 XII 1983 r. [Official note about Grażyna Staniszewska's health when she was under temporary arrest from October 4 to December 23, 1983], March 5, 1984. Attached to the report is a handwritten note with General Jaruzelski's signature and the sentence, "Please use as needed for propaganda."

109. CAMSWiA, URM/BPR, 566, Radio Wolna Europa sekcja polska [Radio Free Europe Polish Section], J. Wilczyński, ed., August 1988.

110. CAMSWiA, URM/BPR, 96, Konferencja prasowa ministra Jerzego Urbana [Minister Jerzy Urban's press conference], January 15, 1985.

111. AIPN, 0296/73, vol. 5, no title, n. d.

112. See, for example, "Szkodliwy precedens i zła dyplomacja" [A harmful precedent and poor diplomacy], *Nowy Dziennik* (New York), January 19–20, 1985.

113. CAMSWiA, URM/BPR, 131, Konferencja prasowa ministra Jerzego Urbana [Minister Jerzy Urban's press conference], October 13, 1985.

114. See this information in Najder's papers at the KARTA Centre; this particular document could not be located in the Institute of National Remembrance archive and may have been destroyed in 1989–1990.

115. *Siedem rozmów z generałem dywizji Władysławem Pożogą, I zastępcą ministra spraw wewnętrznych, szefem wywiadu i kontrwywiadu* [Seven conversations with Major-General Władysław Pożoga, first deputy minister of internal affairs, head of intelligence and counterintelligence], interviewed by Henryk Piecuch (Warsaw: Czytelnik, 1987).

116. Najder himself and then-RFE director George Urban have written about this conflict: Zdzisław Najder, "RWE 1982–1987. Zapiski dyrektora" [RFE 1982–1987: Director's notes], *Zeszyty Historyczne* 153 (2005): 218; George Urban, *Radio Free Europe and the Pursuit of Democracy: My War within the Cold War* (New Haven, CT: Yale University Press, 1997), 99, 124–25. The coincidence of the first and last names of the Polish government spokesman and RFE director made Deputy Director of the Polish desk Andrzej Krzeczunowicz say that Najder had been caught in a "pincer squeeze by two Urbans: Warsaw's Jerzy and Munich's George" (Najder, "RWE 1982–1987," 218).

117. KARTA Centre, PRP Archive, Zdzisław Najder's personal collection, Radio Warsaw I Monitoring, February 13, 1987.

118. Ibid., Statement by Gene (Eugene) Pell, February 13, 1987.

119. See, for example, "Les joyeueses ingérences de M. Urban dans les affaires de Radio Free Europe" [Mr. Urban's happy meddling in the affairs of Radio Free Europe], *Le Monde*, February 17, 1987.

120. KARTA Centre, PRP Archive, Zdzisław Najder's personal collection, Radio Warsaw I Monitoring, March 10, 1987.

121. For a discussion of Zdzisław Najder's ties to the Security Service in the late 1950s to early 1960s and the Security Service surveillance of him after the Polish Independence Agreement (PPN) was formed, see Paweł Machcewicz and Andrzej Paczkowski, "Tajny agent" [Secret agent], *Rzeczpospolita*, October 9, 2005; idem, "Po pierwsze niepodległość" [Sovereignty first], *Rzeczpospolita*, October 15–16, 2005. The second part of the latter article is accompanied by Najder's "Rachunek sumienia" [Examination of conscience]. After his collaboration with the secret police was revealed, Najder made his first long statement about it, which was published in *Rzeczpospolita*, October 6, 1992.

122. Najder, "RWE 1982–1987," 200; Najder's collection at the KARTA Centre includes a letter from Jan Nowak-Jeziorański dated April 5, 1978, in which he suggests that Najder take the position of director of the Polish Service. "I think that you would be the ideal candidate for my successor's deputy, and after some time for a leadership position," wrote Nowak-Jeziorański. "This would open up before you a huge—and therefore important—field of activity. If I receive any sign from you that this idea may be of interest, I will use all the influence I still have to push through your candidacy."

123. AIPN, 0582/238, vol. 1, Notatka urzędowa [Official note], April 29, 1982, 4–5.

124. AIPN, 0582/238, vols. 2, 4.

125. AIPN, 0582/238, vol. 4, Protokół rozprawy głównej [Minutes of the trial], May 26, 1983, 16.

126. AIPN, 0582/238, vols. 3, 18.

127. Ibid., Sprawozdanie z przeprowadzonych badań dokumentów [Report of a study of the documents], October 4, 1982.

128. Ibid., Pismo Józefa Chomętowskiego do Naczelnej Prokuratury Wojskowej [Letter from Józef Chomętowski to the Head Military Prosecutor's Office], January 4, 1983, 151.

129. AIPN, 0582/238, vol. 4, Protokół rozprawy głównej [Minutes of the trial], May 26, 1983, 7.

130. AIPN, 0582/238, vol. 3, Opinia Instytutu Badania Współczesnych Problemów Kapitalizmu wydana w sprawie śledczej przeciwko Zdzisławowi Najderowi [Opinion of the Institute for the Study of the Contemporary Problems of Capitalism presented at the trial of Zdzisław Najder], April 1983, 272.

131. AIPN, 0582/238, vol. 4, Notatka o stanie śledztwa w sprawie Zdzisława Najdera s. Franciszka, podejrzanego o przestępstwo z art. 124 par. 1 kk [Note on the state of the investigation in the case of Zdzisław Najder, son of Franciszek, suspected of a crime against Art. 124, para. 1 of the Criminal Code], September 24, 1982, 135.

132. Ibid., Protokół rozprawy głównej [Minutes of the trial], May 26, 1983, 7–8.

133. Ibid., Wyrok w imieniu Polskiej Rzeczypospolitej Ludowej [Sentence on behalf of the People's Republic of Poland], May 28, 1983, 40–41.

134. AIPN, 514/38, vol. 5, 105–8.

135. AIPN, 514/38, vol. 2, Wniosek o wyłączenie niektórych materiałów z akt śledztwa Zdzisława Najdera i o wszczęcie odrębnego postępowania w sprawie fałszywego oskarżenia wymienionego o zbrodnie szpiegostwa (art. 249 kk) [Request to pull out certain materials from the evidence in the trial of Zdzisław Najder and to initiate separate proceedings on the question of the false accusation of the above-mentioned of the crime of espionage (Article 249 of the Criminal Code)], January 10, 1990, 221.

136. Account by Zdzisław Najder, June 15, 2005.

137. AIPN, 514/38, vol. 5, Protokół przesłuchania świadka [Protocol of witness testimony], January 5, 1990, 801.

138. AIPN, 514/38, vol. 2, Zapisek urzędowy [Official note, illegible signature, n.d.], 223.

139. Author's interview with Zdzisław Najder, June 15, 2005.

140. Najder, "RWE 1982–1987," 207. An unidentified Ministry of Internal Affairs functionary allegedly told Henryk Piecuch in 1989 about preparations to kidnap Najder from his country house in Burgundy, which had no security. Photographs of the house, which Deputy Minister of Internal Affairs Władysław Pożoga gave Piecuch and which were published in the book *Imperium służb specjalnych* [The special services empire] (Warsaw: Agencja Wydawnicza CB, 1997), were to serve as evidence of the preparations. Unfortunately, information from books by Piecuch (a former Ministry of Internal Affairs officer) that were published in the 1990s cannot be verified. The books are a hybrid of thriller-espionage and gutter literature. But it is, of course, not out of the question that some of his stories are true.

141. Jan Nowak-Jeziorański was one of the people who maintained that Najder should be extremely careful. In a letter of June 13, 1983, he advised Najder using his

own experiences: "You should not take the same route or the same car to work and back home. I also counsel you to be extremely selective with people coming from Poland and meeting with them. There is always the possibility that instead of the guest you expect someone completely different will appear. You must assume that you have one or two so-called sleeper agents among the crew, who may surface in the most unexpected way. It would be extremely naïve of you to trust those who manifest their support, their concern about you and try to win your favors and trust. This must not, but may, be an element in the game. . . . Radio mail is the most sensitive point in the building. I never sent the most confidential letters from the radio's building. I never used the radio's travel office and kept my travel plans a close secret" (KARTA Centre, PRP Archive, Zdzisław Najder's personal collection).

142. Author's interview with Zdzisław Najder, June 15, 2005.

143. Andrzej Grajewski, Paweł Machcewicz, and Jan Żaryn, report, "Sprawa o. Konrada Hejmo. Działania Służby Bezpieczeństwa przeciwko Kościołowi katolickiemu w latach 1975–1988" [The case of Father Konrad Hejmo: The actions of the Security Service against the Catholic Church in 1975–1988], May 31, 2005, available on the Institute of National Remembrance website, www.ipn.gov.pl.

144. Author's interview with Zdzisław Najder, June 15, 2005; record of conversation with Andrzej Madejczyk in Najder's diary, December 11, 1987 (Najder gave me a copy of this page).

145. Author's interview with Zdzisław Najder, June 15, 2005.

146. Najder presented his version of this conflict in the article in *Zeszyty Historyczne* quoted earlier. Lechosław Gawlikowski wrote from the point of view of Najder's opponents in "Radio Wolna Europa 1982–1987. Spojrzenie z dystansu" [Radio Free Europe 1982–1987: A look from a distance], *Zeszyty Historyczne* 158 (2006): 101–29; see also Mierzanowska, *Wolna Europa i świat*, 240-46.

147. Author's interview with Piotr Załuski, January 11 and 17, 2007; author's interview with Danuta Drzewińska, March 15, 2007.

148. Najder's papers deposited at the KARTA Centre are an important source for reconstructing the relationship between him and his American bosses. He wrote about it in *Zeszyty Historyczne* and spoke about it in a book-length interview published in 1988 (Wiktor Grotowicz and Stanisław Oleś [Piotr Załuski], *Czy Polaków stać na optymizm? Rozmowy ze Zdzisławem Najderem* [Are the Poles capable of optimism? Conversations with Zdzisław Najder] [Berlin: Pogląd, 1988], 5–33). For a discussion of the conflict from the point of view of RFE's leadership, see Urban, *Radio Free Europe and the Pursuit of Democracy*, 99, 124–25, 301.

149. Najder, "RWE 1982–1987," 225.

150. (Wicz), "'Starzy' i 'nowi' monachijczycy" ["Old" and "new" Münchners], *Trybuna Ludu*, March 4, 1986.

151. Najder, "RWE 1982–1987," 216.

152. (Czec), "Najder za bramą" [Najder is shown the door], *Express Wieczorny*, February 12, 1987.

153. The *Krokodil* article (December 1985, January and February 1986), in Polish translation, can be found in Zdzisław Najder's papers at the KARTA Centre.

154. Jerzy Morawski, "Na akt łaski nie zasługuje" [He does not deserve a pardon], *Rzeczpospolita*, May 24–25, 2003.

155. Jędrzej Giertych, *List otwarty do społeczeństwa polskiego w Kraju* [An open letter to Polish society in Poland], June 1, 1976 (printed flier); see Andrzej Friszke, *Życie polityczne emigracji* [The political life of emigration], vol. 1 of *Druga Wielka Emigracja 1945–1990* [The second Great Emigration, 1945–1990] (Warsaw: Więź, 1999), 406–7.

156. For a profile of Jędrzej Giertych and an account of the Security Service attempts to collaborate with him, see Krzysztof Tarka, "Antykomunistyczny rusofil. Jędrzej Giertych o opozycji politycznej i polityce polskiej" [An anticommunist Russophile: Jędrzej Giertych on the political opposition and Polish politics], *Zeszyty Historyczne* 159 (2007): 135–69; see also Andrzej Krajewski, "Długi cień dziadka" [A grandfather's long shadow], *Newsweek Polska*, March 4, 2007.

157. See Wojciech Czuchnowski, "Mi się tutaj podoba" [I like it here], *Gazeta Wyborcza*, March 4, 2005; Wojciech (Czuchnawski, "Giertych nie ostrzegł Michnika" [Giertych didn't warn Michnik], *Gazeta Wyborcza*, July 29, 2005; Cezary Gmyz, "Kryptonim 'Truteń'" [Code name "Parasite"], *Wprost*, June 12, 2005.

158. AIPN, 01285/3, Raport dotyczący rozmowy operacyjnej z figurantem sprawy "Maciej" [Report on the operational conversation with the object of operation "Maciej"], March 10, 1977, 31.

159. Ibid., Raport dotyczący przedsięwzięć operacyjnych w sprawie "Truteń" [Report about operations in the "Parasite" case], February 21,1977, 29.

160. In reality, he published in *Kultura* both under his real name and under a pen name. As Stefan Michnik: "Kronika czeska i słowacka" [Czech and Slovak chronicle] 7/8, 1972; 1/2 and 3, 1976; 1/2, 1977. As Karol Szwedowicz: "Kronika czeska i słowacka" [Czech and Slovak chronicle], 11, 1972; 3, 5, 7/8, 9, 10, and 11, 1973; 4, 6, 9, and 10, 1974; 3, 1975; "Kronika czeska" [Czech chronicle], 10, 1975; "Procesy czechosłowackie" [The Czechoslovak trials], 9, 1972; "Nowa wschodząca gwiazda reżimu" [The regime's new rising star], 9, 1975; "30-lecie Instytutu Józefa Piłsudskiego w Nowym Yorku" [30th anniversary of the Piłsudski Institute in New York], 12 (1973): 96–102; "Ukrainica na VII Międzynarodowym Kongresie Slawistów w Warszawie" [Ukrainica at the 8th International Slavists' Congress in Warsaw], 1/2, 1974.

161. AIPN, 01227/699, Raport dotyczący realizacji przedsięwzięć operacyjnych w sprawie "Truteń" [Report on the realization of operational undertakings in the "Parasite" case], April 20, 1977, 36.

162. Tadeusz Borowicz, "Głos rozsądku" [Voice of reason], *Narodowiec*, July 17–18, 1977; Michał Podgórski, "Kilka słów o Michniku i jego rodzinie" [A few words about Michnik and his family], *Narodowiec*, November 29, 1977.

163. Jędrzej Giertych, "Michnik," *Opoka* 15 (1978).

164. Mieczysław Szerer, "Komisja do badania odpowiedzialności za łamanie praworządności w sądownictwie wojskowym" [Commission to study the responsibility for violating legality in the military courts], *Zeszyty Historyczne* 49 (1979): 71–160.

165. *Gazeta Wyborcza* (January 22, 1999) published the Mazur Commission's report.

166. AIPN, 01285/3, Raport dotyczący przerzutu agenta ps. "Grey" [Report on the transfer of agent "Grey"], October 16, 1973, (the page numbering is not uniform in the microfilm).

167. Ibid., Plan kombinacji operacyjnej wprowadzenia agenta "Grey'a" do obiektu "Szerszenie" [Plan of an operational combination to introduce agent "Grey" into "Szerszenie" site], October 20, 1977.

168. Ibid., AIPN, 01285/3, Notatka służbowa dotycząca spotkania z agentem "Grey" [Official note on a meeting with agent "Grey"], January 13, 1978.

169. Ibid., Notatka dotycząca spotkania z agentem "Grey" [Note on meeting with agent "Grey"], October 20, 1977.

170. Ibid., Raport dotyczący spotkania z agentem "Grey", 23 lutego 1978 r. [Report on a meeting with agent "Grey," February 23, 1978], March 10, 1978.

171. Ibid., Instrukcja [Instruction], February 23, 1978.

172. Archbishop Stanisław Wielgus's statement, *Gazeta Wyborcza*, January 5, 2007.

173. Wielgus claimed in his statement that he had talked only once with Father Kirschke, and not at the radio, where he never went, but in St. Barbara's parish in Munich.

174. AIPN, 1285/3, Raport [Report], September 26, 1978, discontinuous pagination.

175. Tomasz Terlikowski discussed the contents of the documents concerning Wielgus in "Tajna historia arcybiskupa" [The archbishop's secret story], *Rzeczpospolita*, January 4, 2007.

176. AIPN, 00221/8, Raport o zezwolenie na przerzut za granicę agentów ps. "Yon" i "Panna" [Report on permission to transfer agents "Yon" and "Panna" abroad], August 23, 1982.

177. For a discussion of the Polish government's actions against Father Franciszek Blachnicki, see Andrzej Grajewski, "Oskarżony ks. Franciszek Blachnicki" [The accused, Father Franciszek Blachnicki], *Więź* 5 (2001): 112–28; Tadeusz Isakowicz-Zaleski, *Księża wobec bezpieki na przykładzie archidiecezji krakowskiej* [Priests facing the secret police, using the example of the Cracow archdiocese] (Cracow: Znak, 2007), 146–57.

178. See Grzegorz Bochenek's biographical sketch of Father Franciszek Blachnicki in *Opozycja w PRL. Słownik biograficzny 1956–89* [Opposition in the PRP: A biographical dictionary 1956–89], ed. J. Skórzyński, P. Sowiński, and M. Strasz (Warsaw: Ośrodek "Karta," 2000), 1:38–40.

179. Grajewski, *Oskarżony ks. Franciszek Blachnicki*, 127.

180. AIPN, 00221/8, Raport dotyczący duetu agenturalnego "Yon" i "Panna" [Report on the spy duo "Yon" and "Panna"], January 31, 1987.

181. Andrzej Grajewski, "Kariera Pani Dyrektor" [The Directress's Career], *Gość Niedzielny*, April 24, 2005.

182. See Jarosław Jakimczyk, "Zabójcza Panna" [Killer Miss], *Wprost*, May 29, 2005.

183. Statement from the Christian Service for the Liberation of Nations, *Pogląd* 6/7 (1988): 129.

184. Opis ucieczki Gontarczyków z RFN [Account of the Gontarczyks' escape from the FRG], in AIPN, 00221/8, Raport operacyjny w sprawie "Yon-Panna" [Operational report in the case of "Yon-Panna"], April 18, 1988.

185. Quotations from Urban's statement about RFE in the Gontarczyks' file; for the full text, see "Konferencja prasowa rzecznika rządu" [The government spokesman's press conference], *Trybuna Ludu*, April 27, 1988.

186. AIPN, 00221/8, Raport dotyczący duetu agenturalnego "Yon"-"Panna" [Report on the "Yon"-"Panna" spy duo], December 19, 1988.

187. Ibid., Notatka dotycząca koncepcji rozgrywki propagandowej wokół powrotu Gontarczyków [Note on the conception of the propaganda game involving the return of the Gontarczyks], April 29, 1988.

188. Ibid., Raport dotyczący duetu agenturalnego "Yon"-"Panna," December 19, 1988.

189. Władysław Markiewicz, "Powrót" [The return], *Polityka* 22, May 28, 1988.

190. "Ziemia obiecana. Z Jolantą i Andrzejem Gontarczykami, pracownikami ośrodka Chrześcijańskiej Służby Narodów w Karlsbergu, korespondentami Radia Wolna Europa, którzy po kilkuletnim pobycie w Republice Federalnej Niemiec powrócili niedawno do Polski, rozmawia Jacek S. Jóźwiak" [A promised land: Jacek S. Jóźwiak interviews Jolanta and Andrzej Gontarczyk, employees of the Christian Service for the Liberation of Nations in Karlsberg, who have recently returned to Poland after a few years in the Federal Republic of Germany], *Walka Młodych*, May 29, 1988.

191. AIPN, 00221/8, Raport dotyczący duetu agenturalnego "Yon"-"Panna," December 19, 1988.

192. Ibid., Notatka [Note], April 28, 1988; Notatka [Note], May 10, 1988.

193. Documents about Zygmunt Krok-Solorz in the file AIPN 00221/6; see also conversation with Zygmunt Solorz, *Życie Warszawy*, November 17, 2006; Tadeusz Witkowski, "Zygmunt Solorz w sieci służb PRL" [Zygmunt Solorz in the net of the PRP's services], ibid.; Grzegorz Majchrzak, "Zygmunt Solorz—agent z przypadku" [Zygmunt Solorz, an accidental agent], *Rzeczpospolita*, November 21, 2006.

194. AIPN, 00221/8, Notatka [Note], April 28, 1988.

195. Najder, "RWE 1982–1987," 207.

196. I had an experience that indirectly confirms Colonel Bosak's version. After a lecture about the émigré community I gave at The Polish Institute of International Affairs in 2005, a man from the audience (of mostly state administration employees) came up to me and commented on what I had said about RFE. He told me that in the 1980s he had been the resident spy in Munich, running four Ministry of Internal Affairs' agents inside RFE's Polish desk. He did not want to be interviewed or to give me his name.

197. I used documents given to me by Alina Grabowska, which this former RFE commentator had received from the Institute of National Remembrance as an "aggrieved party," an individual who had been persecuted by the Communist security apparatus. They are a part of much broader, multivolume documentation, including the operational case code name "Zachód" [the West], which focused on uncovering communications channels between Solidarity's émigré structures and the underground in Poland, and also materials about uncovering Solidarity in the Konin region (Letter from head of the sectional Office of Opening and Archiving Documents in Łódź, Rafał Leśkiewicz, June 22, 2006).

198. Author's interviews with Alina Grabowska (April 4, 2006), Piotr Załuski (January 17, 2007), Konrad Tatarowski (February 19, 2007), and Danuta and Franciszek Drzewiński (March 15, 2007).

199. Confirming it are participants Załuski, Tatarowski, and Najder himself (author's interview with Zdzisław Najder, March 14, 2007).

200. AIPN Po, 035/1284, vol. 34, Plan gry operacyjnej w sprawie obiektowej krypt. "Zachód" prowadzonej przez Wydział III Departamentu V MSW i sprawie operacyjnego rozpracowania krypt. "Układ-II" prowadzonej przez Wydział V WUSW w Koninie [Plan of the operational game for case code name "Zachód" conducted by Section III of Department V of the Ministry of Internal Affairs and case of operational inquiry

code name "Układ-II" conducted by Section V of the WUSW (Provincial Office of Internal Affairs) in Konin], June 5, 1987, 3.

201. Ibid., Informacja operacyjna TW "Bogumił" nr 6582 [Operations information by Secret Collaborator "Bogumił" no. 6582], April 7, 1987, 28. Aleksander Świeykowski no longer remembers the details of the smuggling of the mimeograph machines but confirmed in a letter to me (March 22, 2007) that it had taken place.

202. AIPN Po, 035/1284, vol. 3, Informacja o przebiegu realizacji planu gry operacyjnej w sprawie operacyjnego rozpracowania krypt. "Układ-II" nr 7575 prowadzonej przez Wydział V WUSW w Koninie [Information about the course of realization of the plan of the operational game in the case of operational inquiry code name "Układ-II" no. 7575 conducted by Section V of theWUSW (Provincial Office of Internal Affairs) in Konin], January 8, 1988, 8–9.

203. Ibid., 8.

204. Author's interview with Piotr Załuski, January 17, 2007. Załuski did not know any details about the smuggling of *Przeciek* to Poland. He gave me a full set of its issues.

205. Author's interviews with Alina Grabowska and Leszek Perth (April 4, 2006), Zdzisław Najder, Piotr Załuski, Konrad Tatarowski, and Danuta and Franciszek Drzewiński. It is possible to recreate this conflict by reading the office correspondence between Zdzisław Najder and Alina Grabowska, which is included in Najder's papers at the KARTA Centre.

206. Author's interviews with Piotr Załuski (January 17, 2007) and Konrad Tatarowski (February 19, 2007).

207. Flier given author by Piotr Załuski, author's private collection.

208. AIPN Po, 035/1284, vol. 32, Notatka służbowa dotycząca Aliny Grabowskiej [Office note concerning Alina Grabowska], June 17, 1987, 10.

209. AIPN Po, 035/1284, vol. 3, Informacja o przebiegu realizacji planu gry operacyjnej w sprawie operacyjnego rozpracowania krypt. "Układ-II" nr 7575 prowadzonej przez Wydział V WUSW w Koninie [Information on the course of realization of the plan of the operational game in the case of the operational inquiry code name "Układ-II" no. 7575 conducted by Section V of the WUSW (Provincial Office of Internal Affairs) in Konin], January 8, 1988, 8.

210. Author's interview with Danuta Drzewińska, March 15, 2007.

211. Author's interview with Piotr Załuski, January 17, 2007.

212. Author's interview with Franciszek Drzewiński, March 15, 2007.

213. Author's inteview with Józef Szaniawski, March 23, 2007.

214. Ibid.

215. AIPN, 950/210–211, Komunikat Prokuratury Generalnej [Announcement from the Prosecutor General's Office], 473–74, published on March 4, 1985, in *Trybuna Ludu*, *Żołnierz Wolności*, *Rzeczpospolita* and *Sztandar Młodych*.

216. AIPN, 0874/14, vol. 2, Notatka dotycząca szpiegowskiej działalności obywatela PRL Józefa Szaniawskiego [Note on espionage activity by a citizen of the People's Republic of Poland, Józef Szaniawski], June 19, 1985, 5

217. Author's interview with Józef Szaniawski, March 23, 2007.

218. Henryk Piecuch, *Służby specjalne atakują* [The special services on the attack] (Warsaw: Agencja Wydawnicza CB, 1996), 248.

219. Letter from Zdzisław Najder to the author, July 19, 2005.

220. Ibid.

221. Author's interview with Józef Szaniawski, March 23, 2007.

222. AIPN, 0204/633, Zasadnicze informacje i ich ocena w sprawie krypt. "Szaniec" [Fundamental information and its evaluation about the "Szaniec" case], April 28, 1975, 20.

223. Author's interview with Józef Szaniawski, March 23, 2007.

224. AIPN, 0204/633, Notatka ze spotkania z "Bajem" w dniu 27 XI 1973 r. [Note from a meeting with "Baj" on November 27, 1973], 27–28; ibid., Notatka [Note], November 22, 1973, 29.

225. Ibid., Wniosek o zakończenie sprawy operacyjnego sprawdzenia "Szaniec" [Request to terminate the "Szaniec" case of operational inquiry], November 21, 1975, 31–32.

226. Author's interview with Józef Szaniawski, March 23, 2007.

227. See, for example, Witold Bereś and Jerzy Skoczylas, *Generał Kiszczak mówi . . . prawie wszystko* [General Kiszczak tells . . . almost all] (Warsaw: BGW, 1991).

228. Author's inteview with Józef Szaniawski, March 23, 2007.

229. Ibid.

230. AIPN, 0874/14, vol. 2, List Józefa Szaniawskiego do szefa WSW gen. Edwarda Poradki [Letter from Józef Szaniawski to the head of the MIS, General Edward Poradko], October 4, 1985, 238–39.

231. In the weekly *Nie* and the daily *Gazeta Wyborcza*; see, "Józef Szaniawski prosi SB o pomoc [Józef Szaniawski asks the S(ecurity) S(ervice) for help], *Gazeta Wyborcza*, February 17, 2005.

232. Author's interview with Józef Szaniawski, March 23, 2007.

233. Józef Szaniawski, *Reduta. Polska między historią a geopolityką* [The redoubt: Poland between history and geopolitics] (Warsaw: Ex libris, 2002), 583.

234. AIPN, 0874/14, vol. 2, Pismo dyrektora Gabinetu Ministra płk. Czesława Żmudy do prokuratora Naczelnej Prokuratury Wojskowej płk. Zbigniewa Szawłowskiego [Letter from the director of the office of the Minister of Internal Affairs, Colonel Czesław Żmuda, to the prosecutor of the Head Military Prosecutor's Office, Colonel Zbigniew Szawłowski], November 13, 1985, 277–78.

235. Ibid., Protokół przesłuchania świadka [Protocol of the questioning of a witness], November 8, 1985, 264–65.

236. AIPN, 950/211, Protokół rozprawy głównej [Protocol of the trial], January 20, 1986, 551.

237. AIPN, 0874/14, t. 1–2, Uzasadnienie wyroku Sądu Warszawskiego Okręgu Wojskowego [Justification of sentence by the Warsaw Military District Court], January 29, 1986, 9.

238. Ibid., 5. In the original August 13, 1974 letter from Wiktor Trościanko, the word "cause" is capitalized. This whole excerpt is underlined by the MIS investigators (AIPN, 950/210).

239. AIPN, 950/211, Protokół rozprawy głównej [Protocol of the trial], January 21, 1986.

240. AIPN, 0874/14, vol. 1, Wyrok Sądu Warszawskiego Okręgu Wojskowego [Sentence of the Warsaw Military District Court], January 27, 1986, 3–4.

241. Author's interview with Józef Szaniawski, March 23, 2007.

242. Ibid., Wyrok Izby Wojskowej Sądu Najwyższego [Sentence of the Military Chamber of the Supreme Court], April 18, 1986, 16–18.

243. Author's interview with Józef Szaniawski, March 23, 2007.

244. AIPN, 0874/14, vol. 2, Postanowienie o odmowie warunkowego przedterminowego zwolnienia [Decision about denying a conditional pre-term release], August 17, 1989, 396.

245. Ibid., Postanowienie z 16 XII 1989 [Decision of December 16, 1989], 403.

246. Document of prisoner's release, copy of document given this author by Szaniawski.

247. AIPN, 0874/14, vol. 1, Rewizja nadzwyczajna prokuratora generalnego [Extraordinary appeal by the prosecutor general], April 19, 1990, 20–23.

248. AIPN, 0874/14, vol. 2, Pismo ministra sprawiedliwości do prokuratora generalnego [Letter from the minister of justice to the prosecutor general], May 16, 1990, 414.

249. Ibid., Pismo ministra sprawiedliwości Aleksandra Bentkowskiego [Letter from Minister of Justice Aleksander Bentkowski], May 21, 1990, 413.

250. AIPN, 0874/14, vol. 1, Wyrok Izby Wojskowej Sądu Najwyższego [Sentence of the Military Chamber of the Supreme Court], October 5, 1989, 24.

251. Author's interview with Józef Szaniawski, March 23, 2007.

252. AIPN, 0874/14, vol. 2, Pismo zastępcy naczelnego prokuratora wojskowego do Wojewódzkiego Sztabu Wojskowego w Warszawie [Letter from the head military prosecutor to the Provincial Military Staff in Warsaw], March 23, 1993, 446.

253. See Andrzej Paczkowski, "Polska 1986–1989. Od kooptacji do negocjacji" [Poland 1986–1989: From co-optation to negotiation], in *Od sfałszowanego zwycięstwa do prawdziwej klęski. Szkice do portretu PRL* [From a forged victory to real defeat: Sketches for a portrait of the People's Republic of Poland] (Cracow: Wydawnictwo Literackie, 1999), 126–87; Antoni Dudek, *Reglamentowana rewolucja. Rozkład dyktatury komunistycznej w Polsce 1988–1990* [A regulated revolution: The disintegration of the Communist dictatorship in Poland 1988–1990] (Cracow: Arcana, 2004).

254. Mieczyław F. Rakowski, *Dzienniki polityczne 1984–1986* [Political diaries 1984–1986] (Warsaw: Iskry, 2005), 434.

255. Ibid., 437.

256. AAN, 237/V/340, Zapis rozmowy przewodniczącego Rady Państwa Wojciecha Jaruzelskiego z zastępcą sekretarza stanu Johnem C. Whiteheadem [Minutes of the talks between the Chairman of the Council of State Wojciech Jaruzelski and Deputy Secretary of State John C. Whitehead], January 31, 1987, 192.

257. CAMSWiA, URM, BPR, 561, Notatka z narady w sprawie zagłuszania audycji polskojęzycznych rozgłośni Głos Ameryki, BBC i Wolna Europa [Note from a meeting on the question of jamming the Polish-language programs of Voice of America, BBC and Free Europe radios], April 17, 1987. This document mentions the beginning of March 1987 as the time the Polish government decided to end jamming. Politburo and CC Secretariat records from March 1987 do not mention jamming.

258. Ibid., Problem zagłuszania RWE i Radia Swoboda na wiedeńskiej konferencji pohelsińskiej [The issue of jamming RFE and Radio Liberty at the Helsinki review conference in Vienna], monitoring of RFE programs, June 1987.

259. Ibid., Wizyta Romana Malinowskiego w Waszyngtonie. Korespondencja Jacka Kalabińskiego [Roman Malinowski's visit to Washington. Jacek Kalabiński's correspondence], monitoring of RFE programs, June 1987.

260. Hoover Institution, RFE/RL, Corporate Records, 380.2, Memorandum of Conversation, December 17, 1987.

261. See, for example, Andrzej Jeżewski, "Opłacone chciejstwo" [Paid wishful thinking], *Żołnierz Wolności*, April 14, 1987.

262. Hoover Institution, RFE/RL, Corporate Records, 380.2, Memorandum of Conversation, December 17, 1987.

263. Hajdasz, *Szczekaczka, czyli Rozgłośnia Polska Radia Wolna Europa*, 250–76.

264. Marek Łatyński, *Ogród Angielski 1. Wspomnienia z Radia Wolna Europa* [English Garden 1: A memoir about Radio Free Europe] (Lublin: Wydawnictwo UMCS, 1997), 22, 66.

265. Documents concerning the different Soviet bloc countries' termination of jamming can be found at the Hoover Institution (RFE/RL, Corporate Records, 380.2).

266. Dudek, *Reglementowana rewolucja*, 124–25.

267. AIPN, MSW II, 3946, Analiza dywersyjnego oddziaływania propagandowego zachodnich rozgłośni polskojęzycznych w kwietniu 1988 r. [An analysis of the propaganda effects of the Western Polish-language stations in April 1988], May 5, 1988, 1–2.

268. KARTA Centre, Archive of the PRP, Zdzisław Najder's personal collection, Jerzy Urban's press conference, Polish Television, June 21, 1988, transcript of the statement by the government spokesman.

269. (Sew), "Próba prawdy" [A test of truth], *Życie Warszawy*, June 22, 1988.

270. M. Rudziński, "Czy RWE podniesie rękawicę? [Will RFE pick up the gauntlet?], *Sztandar Młodych*, June 22, 1988.

271. Andrzej Mędykowski, "Do Radia 'Wolna Europa.' Brońcie swoich racji, jeśli je macie" [To Radio "Free Europe": Defend your positions, if you can], *Żołnierz Wolności*, June 22, 1988.

272. Łatyński, *Ogród Angielski 1.*, 164.

273. Ibid., 168.

274. "Dialog z kim?" [A dialogue with whom?], *Dziennik Polski*, June 27, 1988.

275. KARTA Centre, PRP Archive, Zdzisław Najder's personal collection, Gene Pell's letter to Jerzy Urban, August 11, 1988; see CAMSWiA, URM/BPR, 568, Polish translation of the letter.

276. CAMSWiA, URM/BPR, 568, Pismo Jerzego Urbana do Wojciecha Jaruzelskiego [Jerzy Urban's letter to Wojciech Jaruzelski], July 9, 1988.

277. Ibid., Notatka o projekcie wyjazdu Jerzego Urbana do RWE oraz zaproszenia publicystów RWE do Warszawy [Note on Jerzy Urban's planned trip to RFE and invitations to RFE commentators to Warsaw], July 18, 1988.

278. Ibid., Projekt odpowiedzi Jerzego Urbana do Gene'a Pella [Draft reply from Jerzy Urban to Gene Pell], July 18, 1988.

279. Ibid., Pismo Jerzego Urbana do Wojciecha Jaruzelskiego [Letter from Jerzy Urban to Wojciech Jaruzelski], July 20, 1988.

280. "Konferencja prasowa rzecznika rządu" [Government spokesman's press conference], *Rzeczpospolita*, August 10, 1988.

281. CAMSWiA, URM/BPR, 568, Pismo Jerzego Urbana do Gene'a Pella [Letter from Jerzy Urban to Gene Pell], September 13, 1988.

282. Łatyński, *Ogród Angielski 1*, 219.

283. CAMSWiA, URM/BPR, 568, Pismo ministra spraw zagranicznych Tadeusza Olechowskiego do sekretarza KC PZPR Stanisława Cioska [Letter from Foreign Minister Tadeusz Olechowski to CC PUWP Secretary Stanisław Ciosek], May 23, 1988.

284. "Do Warszawy mogę jechać jutro. Z Markiem Łatyńskim, dyrektorem Rozgłośni Polskiej RWE, rozmawia Bogusław Sonik" [I am ready to go to Warsaw tomorrow: Bogusław Sonik interviews Marek Łatyński, director of RFE's Polish Service], *Tygodnik Powszechny*, June 25, 1989.

285. Łatyński, *Ogród Angielski 1*, 227, 233.

286. "Rezygnacja. Rozmowa ze Zdzisławem Najderem, byłym dyrektorem sekcji polskiej Radia Wolna Europa" [Resignation: An interview with Zdzisław Najder, former director of the Polish Section of Radio Free Europe], *Polityka*, August 12, 1989.

287. Kurski, *Jan Nowak-Jeziorański*, 298.

288. AIPN, MSW II, 3946, Analiza oddziaływania propagandowego zachodnich rozgłośni polsko-języcznych w sierpniu 1989 r. [An analysis of the propaganda effects of Western Polish-language radio stations in August 1989], September 5, 1989, 8–14.

289. Łatyński, *Ogród Angielski 1*, 259.

290. AIPN, 01746/3, Protokół brakowania akt nr 126 [Log of destroyed files No. 126], January 4, 1990, 1. The same file includes a record of all the listed materials of Department I of the Ministry of Internal Affairs as destroyed.

Conclusion

1. Janusz Korek, *Paradoksy paryskiej "Kultury." Ewolucja myśli politycznej w latach 1947–1980* [The paradoxes of the Paris *Kultura:* The evolution of political thought in 1947–1980] (Stockholm: Almqvist & Wiksell International, 1998); Barbara Toruńczyk, *Rozmowy w Maisons-Laffitte 1981* [Conversations at Maisons-Laffitte, 1981] (Warsaw: Fundacja Zeszytów Literackich, 2006), 133–34.

2. Andrzej Walicki, *Marksizm i skok do królestwa wolności. Dzieje komunistycznej utopii* [Marxism and the leap to the kingdom of freedom: A history of the Communist utopia] (Warsaw: PWN, 1996); Dariusz Jarosz, *Polacy a stalinizm. 1948–1956* [The Poles and Stalinism, 1948–1956] (Warsaw: Instytut Historii PAN, 2000), 228–30; Dariusz Jarosz, "O polskim stalinizmie—polemicznie" [About Polish Stalinism—polemically], *Więź* 2 (2002): 100–12; Błażej Brzostek and Marcin Zaremba, "Polska 1956–1976: W poszukiwaniu paradygmatu" [Poland 1956–1976: In search of a paradigm], *Pamięć i Sprawiedliwość* 10, no. 2 (2006): 29; see also the opinions of a dozen historians, sociologists, and politicians in a debate about using the term "totalitarianism" for the People's Republic of Poland published in *Przegląd Polityczny* 79/80 (2006).

3. See, for example, Janusz Żarnowski, ed., *Dyktatury w Europie Środkowo-Wschodniej 1918–1939* [Dictatorships in East-Central Europe, 1918–1939] (Wrocław: Zakład Narodowy im. Ossolińskich, 1973); Javier Tussel, *La dictadura de Franco* (Madrid: Alianza Editorial, 1988).

4. Muriel Blaive, *Une destalinization manquée. Tchécoslovaquie 1956* (Brussels: Éditions Complexes, 2005), 49; John P. C. Matthews, *Tinderbox: East-Central Europe*

in the Spring, Summer and Early Fall of 1956 (Tucson, AZ: Fenestra Books, 2003), 61.

5. AIPN, MSW II, 380, Wystąpienie ministra spraw wewnętrznych gen. bryg. Franciszka Szlachcica w pierwszym dniu narady na temat "Sprawy kadrowe w resorcie spraw wewnętrznych" [Speech by Minister of Internal Affairs Brigadier General Franciszek Szlachcic on the first day of the meeting, "Cadre Issues in the Ministry of Internal Affairs"], September 15, 1971, 95.

6. AIPN, 0296.150, vol. 3, Informacja dotycząca korespondencji kierowanej do RWE [Information about correspondence directed to RFE], February 29, 1972, 118.

7. "Włodzimierz Odojewski, Literacka konspira, rozmawiał Bronisław Tumiłowicz" [Włodzimierz Odojewski, a literary conspiracy, in conversation with Bronisław Tumiłowicz], *Przegląd*, January 18, 2004.

Bibliography

Archival Sources

Archiwum Akt Nowych (Central Archive of Modern Records), Warsaw

Komitet Centralny Polskiej Zjednoczonej Partii Robotniczej (Central Committee of the Polish United Workers' Party)

Komisja Specjalna do Walki z Nadużyciami i Szkodnictwem Gospodarczym (Special Commission for Combating Economic Abuses and Sabotage)

Archiwum Instytutu Pamięci Narodowej (Archive of the Institute of National Remembrance), Warsaw

Ministerstwo Bezpieczeństwa Publicznego (Ministry of Public Security)

Komitet do spraw Bezpieczeństwa Publicznego (Committee for Public Security)

Ministerstwo Spraw Wewnętrznych (Ministry of Internal Affairs)

Zarząd II Sztabu Generalnego Ministerstwa Obrony Narodowej (Directorate II of the General Staff of the Ministry of National Defense)

Wojskowa Służba Wewnętrzna (Military Internal Service)

Naczelna Prokuratura Wojskowa (Chief Military Prosecutor's Office)

Centralne Archiwum Ministerstwa Spraw Wewnętrznych (Central Archive of the Ministry of Internal Affairs), Warsaw

Urząd Rady Ministrów—Biuro Prasowe Rządu (Office of the Council of Ministers—Government Press Office)

Archiwum Instytucji Ministerstwa Obrony Narodowej (Archive of the Institutions of the Ministry of National Defense), Modlin

Główny Zarząd Polityczny Sztabu Generalnego (Main Political Directorate of the General Staff of the Ministry of National Defense)

Wojskowe Biuro Badań Socjologicznych (Military Office of Sociological Research), Rembertów
Opracowania Instytutu Badań Społecznych Wojskowej Akademii Politycznej (Reports of the Institute of Social Research of the Military Political Academy)

Archiwum Ministerstwa Spraw Zagranicznych (Archive of the Foreign Ministry), Warsaw
Departments III and IV
The Minister's Office

Zakład Narodowy im. Ossolińskich (Ossoliński National Institute), Wrocław
Jan Nowak-Jeziorański Collection

Ośrodek "Karta" (KARTA Centre), Warsaw
Personal collection of Zdzisław Najder

Polish Institute and Sikorski Museum, London
General Anders Collection

Hoover Institution on War, Revolution and Peace, Stanford University
Radio Free Europe/Radio Liberty, Corporate Records
Stanisław Mikołajczyk Papers
Stefan Korboński Papers
Jane Curry Collection

National Archives, College Park, Maryland
Department of State
National Security Council

Truman Library, Independence, Missouri
Psychological Strategy Board

Eisenhower Library, Abilene, Kansas
C. D. Jackson Papers
C. D. Jackson Records

Lehman Suite and Papers, Rare Book and Manuscript Library, Columbia University, New York
Frank Altschul Papers

Central Intelligence Agency
Documents obtained by the author through the Freedom of Information Act

Open Society Archives in Budapest
Materials of the Polish Service of Radio Free Europe

Author's Interviews, Personal Collection

Władysław Bartoszewski
Richard Cummings
Andrzej Czechowicz
Danuta Drzewińska
Franciszek Drzewiński
Lechosław Gawlikowski
Alina Grabowska
William Griffith
Paul Henze
A. Ross Johnson
John P. C. Matthews
James McCargar
Zygmunt Michałowski
Maciej Morawski
Zdzisław Najder
Jan Nowak-Jeziorański
Leszek Perth
Stanisław Salmonowicz
Eugeniusz Smolar
Józef Szaniawski
Aleksander Świeykowski
Konrad Tatarowski
Andrzej Werblan
Piotr Załuski

Published Sources

Documents

Aparat bezpieczeństwa w Polsce w latach 1953–1954. Taktyka, strategia, metody [The security apparatus in Poland in 1953–1954: Tactics, strategy, methods]. Edited by Grzegorz Majchrzak and Andrzej Paczkowski, introduction by Andrzej Paczkowski. Warsaw: Instytut Pamięci Narodowej, 2004.

The Black Book of Polish Censorship. Translated and edited by Jane Curry. New York: Vintage Books, 1984.

Centrum władzy. Protokoły posiedzeń kierownictwa PZPR. Wybór z lat 1949–1970 [The center of power: Minutes of meetings of the PUWP leadership. A selection from 1949–1970]. Edited by Antoni Dudek, Aleksander Kochański, and Krzysztof Persak. Warsaw: Instytut Studiów Politycznych, 2000.

Departament X MBP. Wzorce–struktury–działanie [Department X of the Ministry of Public Security: Models–structures–actions]. Edited by Konrad Rokicki. Warsaw: Instytut Pamięci Narodowej, 2007.

Foreign Relations of the United States, 1958–1960. Vol. 10, pt. 2, *Eastern Europe*. Washington, DC: US Government Printing Office, 1993.

Gomułka, Władysław. *Przemówienia, styczeń 1963–lipiec 1964* [Speeches, January 1963–July 1964]. Warsaw: Iskry, 1964.

The Hidden History of Hungary 1956: A Compendium of Declassified Documents, edited by Csaba Békés, Malcolm Byrne, and Christian Ostermann. Washington, DC, and Budapest, 1996 (photocopy).

Instrukcje pracy operacyjnej aparatu bezpieczeństwa 1945–1989 [Instructions for operational work of the security apparatus, 1945–1989], edited and with an introduction by Tadeusz Ruzikowski. Warsaw, 2004.

Komisja Specjalna do Walki z Nadużyciami i Szkodnictwem Gospodarczym 1945–1954. Wybór dokumentów [Special Commission for Combating Abuses and Economic Sabotage, 1945–1954: A selection of documents]. Edited and with an introduction by Dariusz Jarosz and Tadeusz Wolsza. Warsaw: Główna Komisja Badania Zbrodni Przeciwko Narodowi Polskiemu, 1995.

Komuniści wobec harcerstwa 1944–1950 [The Communists versus Scouting, 1944–1950]. Selected, edited, and with an introduction by Krzysztof Persak. Vol. 11 of *Dokumenty do dziejów PRL* [Documents from the history of the People's Republic of Poland]. Warsaw: Instytut Studiów Politycznych, 1998.

The 1956 Hungarian Revolution: A History in Documents. Edited by Csaba Békés, Malcolm Byrne, and Janos M. Rainer. Budapest and New York: Central European University Press, 2002.

"Operacja 'Cezary'—ubecka analiza 'gry' z WiN-em" [Operation "Cezary": The Security Service game with Freedom and Independence]. Annotated by Wojciech Frazik. *Zeszyty Historyczne WiN-u* 15 (2001): 183–255.

Opozycja demokratyczna w Polsce w świetle akt KC PZPR (1976–1980). Wybór dokumentów [The democratic opposition in Poland in light of CC PUWP documents (1976–1980): Selected documents]. Selected, edited, and with an introduction by Łukasz Kamiński and Paweł Piotrowski, preface by Wojciech Wrzesiński. Wrocław: Gajt, 2002.

Poland 1980–82: Internal Crisis, International Dimensions. A Compendium of Declassified Documents and Chronology of Events. Edited by Malcolm Byrne, Paweł Machcewicz, and Christian Ostermann. Washington, DC: National Security Archives, 1997 (photocopy).

Polityka Stanów Zjednoczonych Ameryki wobec Polski w świetle faktów i dokumentów (1980–1983) [United States of America policies toward Poland in light of facts and documents (1980–1983)]. Warsaw: Polski Instytut Spraw Międzynarodowych, 1984.

Polska w dokumentach z archiwów rosyjskich 1949–1953 [Poland in documents from Russian archives, 1949–1953]. Selected and edited by Aleksander Kochański. Warsaw: Instytut Studiów Politycznych PAN, 2000. Vol. 12 of *Dokumenty do dziejów PRL* [Documents from the history of the People's Republic of Poland].

Polskie dokumenty dyplomatyczne. 1972 [Polish diplomatic documents, 1972], edited by Włodzimierz Borodziej. Warsaw: Polski Instytut Spraw Międzynarodowych, 2005.

Polskie dokumenty dyplomatyczne. 1974 [Polish diplomatic documents, 1974]. Edited by Aleksander Kochański and Mikołaj Morzycki-Markowski. Warsaw: Polski Instytut Spraw Międzynarodowych, 2007.

Polskie przedwiośnie: Dokumentów marcowych tom II [Poland's early spring: Volume 2 of the March documents]. Paris: Instytut Literacki, 1969.

"Raport komisji Mazura" [Report of the Mazur Commission]. *Gazeta Wyborcza*, January 22, 1999.

Sawicki, Jacek Z. "Wojna z bigbitem" [The war with big beat]. *Zeszyty Historyczne* 152 (2005).

6 lat temu . . . Kulisy polskiego Października [Six years ago: Behind the scenes of the Polish October]. Edited by Jerzy Mond. Paris: Instytut Literacki, 1962.

Sovetskii faktor w Vostochnoj Yevrope 1944–1953 [The Soviet factor in Western Europe, 1944–1953]. Vol. 2, *1949–1953. Dokumentii.* Edited by T. V. Tsarevskaia et al. Moscow: Rosspen, 2002.

Tajne dokumenty Biura Politycznego: PZPR a "Solidarność" 1980–1981 [Classified Politburo documents: The PUWP and "Solidarity," 1980–1981]. Edited by Zbigniew Włodek. London: Aneks, 1992.

Wydarzenia marcowe 1968 [The March 1968 events]. Paris: Instytut Literacki, 1969.

"'Zawężona represja.' Co robić z Komitetem Obrony Robotników? Narada u Stanisława Kani 22 października 1976 r." ["Narrowed-down repressions": What is to be done with the Workers' Defense Committee? A meeting hosted by Stanisław Kania on October 22, 1976]. Edited by Andrzej Paczkowski and Marcin Zaremba. *Więź* 8 (2001).

Newspapers and Periodicals (Poland and Emigration)

Dziennik Polski i Dziennik Żołnierza
Express Wieczorny
Horyzonty
Kultura (Paris)
Kultura (Warsaw)
Myśl Polska
Na Antenie
Narodowiec

Nasz Znak
Opoka
Polityka
Przekrój
Sztandar Młodych
Świat
Trybuna Ludu
Trybuna Robotnicza
Tygodnik Powszechny
Walka Młodych
Żołnierz Wolności
Życie Warszawy

Propaganda Publications, Reportage, Literature

Azembski, Mirosław, and Lucjan Wolanowski. *Czy Stanisław Talarek musiał umrzeć?* [Did Stanisław Talarek have to die?]. Warsaw: Wydawnictwo Ministerstwa Obrony Narodowej, 1955.

Bronisławski, Jerzy [Kudaś]. *Fałszywi prorocy* [False prophets]. Warsaw: Młodzieżowa Agencja Wydawnicza, 1981.

Brycht, Andrzej. *Azyl polityczny* [Political asylum]. Łódź: Krajowa Agencja Wydawnicza, 1989.

———. *Raport z Monachium* [A report from Munich]. Warsaw: PAX, 1968.

Czechowicz, Andrzej. *Siedem trudnych lat* [Seven difficult years]. Warsaw: Wydawnictwo Ministerstwa Obrony Narodowej, 1974.

Kapitan Czechowicz wykonał zadanie. Fragmenty relacji Andrzeja Czechowicza dla prasy, radia i telewizji [Captain Czechowicz fulfilled his mission: Excerpts from Andrzej Czechowicz's accounts for radio and television]. Warsaw: MON, 1971.

Kąkol, Kazimierz. *Na szlakach dywersji* [On the trail of sabotage]. Warsaw: Wydawnictwo Związkowe, 1971.

Kolczyński, Janusz. *Dywersja* [Sabotage]. Warsaw: Iskry, 1964.

———. *Wolna Europa* [Free Europe]. Warsaw: Ministerstwo Obrony Narodowej, 1969.

Krasicki, Ignacy. *Radio "Wolna Europa." Mocodawcy, założenia, program* [Radio "Free Europe": Patrons, principles, program]. Warsaw: Książka i Wiedza, 1982.

Lach, Mieczysław, and Zdzisław Uberman. *Ufam ci Kilroy* [I trust you, Kilroy]. Warsaw: Krajowa Agencja Wydawnicza, 1983.

Monachijska menażeria, no date or place of publication, archive of Instytut Literacki in Maisons-Laffitte.

PRL atakuje Radio "Wolna Europa." Teksty, rysunki i karykatury z prasy, radia, telewizji i wydawnictw książkowych [The People's Republic of Poland attacks Radio Free Europe: Texts, drawings and caricatures from the press, radio, television and books]. Selected and with an introduction by Alina Grabowska. Wrocław: Towarzystwo Przyjaciół Ossolineum, 2002.

Szafrański, Wacław. *W sieci Szymona Wiesenthala* [In Simon Wiesenthal's net]. Warsaw: Wydawnictwo Ministerstwa Obrony Narodowej, 1972.

Diaries, Letters, Memoirs

Bartoszewski, Władysław. *Warto być przyzwoitym. Teksty osobiste i nieosobiste* [Being decent is worth it: Personal and impersonal texts]. Poznań: W drodze, 1990.

Bereś, Witold, and Jerzy Skoczylas. *Generał Kiszczak mówi . . . prawie wszystko* [General Kiszczak tells . . . almost all]. Warsaw: BGW, 1991.

Błażyński, Zbigniew. *Mówi Józef Światło. Za kulisami bezpieki i partii 1940–1955* [Józef Światło speaking: Behind the scenes in the secret police and party, 1940–1955]. London: Polska Fundacja Kulturalna, 1986.

Drygas, Maciej J. *Fale w eter* [Waves into the ether]. *Karta* 38 (2003): 94–121.

———. "Zadudnić do zera" [To drown out completely]. *Gazeta Wyborcza*, May 12, 2003.

Frolik, Josef. *The Frolik Defection*. London: Leo Cooper, 1975.

Gawlikowski, Lechosław. "Radio Wolna Europa 1982–1987. Spojrzenie z dystansu" [Radio Free Europe, 1982–1987: A look from a distance]. *Zeszyty Historyczne* 158 (2006): 101–29.

Giedroyc, Jerzy. *Autobiografia na cztery ręce* [A four-handed autobiography]. Edited by Krzysztof Pomian. Warsaw: Czytelnik, 1994.

Giedroyc, Jerzy, and Juliusz Mieroszewski. *Listy 1949–1956* [Letters 1949–1956]. Selected and with an introduction by Krzysztof Pomian, annotated and with added indexes by Jacek Krawczyk and Krzysztof Pomian. Warsaw: Czytelnik, 1999.

Grotowicz, Wiktor, and Stanisław Oleś [Piotr Załuski]. *Czy Polaków stać na optymizm? Rozmowy ze Zdzisławem Najderem* [Are the Poles capable of optimism? Conversations with Zdzisław Najder]. Berlin: Pogląd, 1988.

Jabłoński, Zygmunt. *Gabinet figur radiowych* [The cabinet of radio figures]. London: Pogląd 1985.

Jan Nowak-Jeziorański. Głos wolnej Europy [Jan Nowak-Jeziorański: The voice of a free Europe]. Selected and edited by Barbara Toruńczyk. Warsaw: Fundacja Zeszytów Literackich, 2005.

Karsov, Nina, and Szymon Szechter. *Nie kocha się pomników* [No one loves monuments]. Warsaw: Oficyna im. Józefa Mackiewicza, 1987.

Kisielewski, Stefan. *Dzienniki* [Diaries]. Warsaw: Iskry, 1997.

Kisielewski, Władysław. *Od Torunia do Londynu. Podróż z przeszkodami* [From Toruń to London: A journey with obstacles]. Warsaw: Wydawnictwo Ministerstwa Obrony Narodowej, 1958.

Kobyliński, Anatol. *Wędrówki Pana Anatola* [Mr. Anatol's wanderings]. Warsaw: Agawa, 1996.

Kochanowicz, Tadeusz. *Na wojennej emigracji: Wspomnienia z lat 1942–1944* [In wartime exile: Reminiscences from 1942–1944]. Warsaw: Książka i Wiedza, 1975.

Komar, Michał. *Władysław Bartoszewski. Skąd pan jest? Wywiad rzeka* [Władysław Bartoszewski: Where do you come from? An extended interview]. Warsaw: Świat Książki, 2006.

Korboński, Stefan. *W imieniu Rzeczypospolitej* [In the name of the Republic]. Warsaw: Instytut Pamięci Narodowej, 2009.

Kuroń, Jacek. *Gwiezdny czas* [A starry time]. London: Aneks, 1991.

Landau, Ludwik. *Kronika lat wojny i okupacji* [A chronicle of the years of war and occupation]. Vol. 1, *Wrzesień 1939–listopad 1940* [September 1939–November 1940]. Warsaw: Państwowe Wydawnictwo Naukowe, 1962.

Łatyński, Marek. *Ogród Angielski 1. Wspomnienia z Radia Wolna Europa* [English Garden 1: A memoir about Radio Free Europe]. Lublin: Wydawnictwo UMCS, 1997.

Łobodowski, Józef. "'Tu mówi Madryt'" ["Madrid calling"]. *Zeszyty Historyczne* 54 (1980): 113–28.

Małczyński, Jerzy. *Byliśmy pierwsi. 45 lat temu Rozgłośnia Harcerska nadała pierwszą audycję* [We were first: Forty-five years ago Scout Radio broadcast its first program]. Warsaw: 2002.

Meyer, Cord. *Facing Reality: From World Federalism to the CIA*. New York: Harper & Row, 1980.

Mierzanowska, Danuta. *Wolna Europa i świat* [Free Europe and the world]. Cracow: Wydawnictwo Baran i Suszczyński, 1998.

Moja Jerozolima, mój Izrael. Władysław Bartoszewski w rozmowie z Joanną Szwedowską [My Jerusalem, my Israel: Władysław Bartoszewski in conversation with Joanna Szwedowska]. Warsaw: Rosner & Wspólnicy, 2004.

Najder, Zdzisław. "RWE 1982–1987. Zapiski dyrektora" [RFE 1982–1987: Director's notes]. *Zeszyty Historyczne* 153 (2005).

Nowak-Jeziorański, Jan. *Courier from Warsaw*. Detroit, MI: Wayne State University Press, 1982.

———. *Polska z oddali. Wspomnienia* [Poland from afar: A memoir]. Vol. 2, *1956–1976*. Cracow: Znak, 1992.

———. "To była zdrada" [It was a betrayal]. *Rzeczpospolita*, September 18–19, 2004.

——— *Wojna w eterze: Wspomnienia* [The war on the airwaves: A memoir]. Vol. 1, *1948–1956*. London: Odnowa, 1986.

"Oświadczenie abp. Stanisława Wielgusa" [Statement by Archbiship Stanisław Wielgus]. *Gazeta Wyborcza*, January 5, 2007.

Pacepa, Ion. *Red Horizons: Chronicles of a Communist Spy Chief.* Washington, DC: Regnery Gateway, 1987.

Pół wieku w teczkach opisane. Opowieści prof. Władysława Bartoszewskiego wysłuchał Krzysztof Burnetko [Half a century of a life as described in files: Professor Władysław Bartoszewski's tales, as heard by Krzysztof Burnetko]. *Tygodnik Powszechny*, February 17, 2002.

Pszenicki, Krzysztof. *Tu mówi Londyn. Historia Sekcji Polskiej BBC* [This is London: A History of the BBC Polish Section]. Warsaw: Rosner and Wspólnicy, 2009.

Rakowski, Mieczysław F. *Dzienniki polityczne 1958–1962* [Political diaries, 1958–1962]. Warsaw: Iskry, 1998.

———. *Dzienniki polityczne 1963–1966* [Political diaries 1963–1966]. Warsaw: Iskry, 1999.

———. *Dzienniki polityczne 1967–1968* [Political diaries 1967–1968]. Warsaw: Iskry, 1999.

———. *Dzienniki polityczne 1969–1971* [Political diaries, 1969–1971]. Warsaw: Iskry, 2001.

———. *Dzienniki polityczne 1981–1983* [Political diaries, 1981–1983]. Warsaw: Iskry, 2004.

———. *Dzienniki polityczne 1984–1986* [Political diaries, 1984–1986]. Warsaw: Iskry, 2005.

———. *Dzienniki polityczne 1987–1990* [Political diaries, 1987–1990]. Warsaw: Iskry, 2005.

Rudzki, Marek. "Polska sekcja Radia Wolna Europa w Nowym Jorku" [Radio Free Europe's Polish Section in New York]. *Zeszyty Historyczne* 133 (2000): 185–90.

Siedem rozmów z generałem dywizji Władysławem Pożogą I zastępcą ministra spraw wewnętrznych, szefem wywiadu i kontrwywiadu, rozmawiał Henryk Piecuch [Seven conversations with Major-General Władysław Pożoga, first deputy minister of internal affairs, head of intelligence and counterintelligence, interviewed by Henryk Piecuch]. Warsaw: Czytelnik, 1987.

Staśko, Marek. "Dom przy Ogrodzie Angielskim, czyli Radio Wolna Europa od frontu i od tyłu" [The building at English Garden, or Radio Free Europe from front and back]. Unpublished manuscript.

Szaniawski, Józef. *Reduta: Polska między historią a geopolityką* [The redoubt: Poland between history and geopolitics]. Warsaw and Chicago: Ex libris, 2002.

Szczesiak, Edmund. *Borusewicz. Jak runął mur* [Borusewicz: How the wall fell down]. Warsaw: Oficyna Wydawnicza Volumen 2005.

Szerer, Mieczysław. "Komisja do badania odpowiedzialności za łamanie praworządności w sądownictwie wojskowym" [Commission to study the responsibility for violating legality in the military courts]. *Zeszyty Historyczne* 149 (1979).

Tejchma, Józef. *Kulisy dymisji. Z dzienników ministra kultury 1974–1977* [Secrets of a resignation: From the diaries of the minister of culture, 1974–1977]. Cracow: Cracovia, 1991.

Toruńczyk, Barbara. *Rozmowy w Maisons-Laffitte, 1981* [Conversations at Maisons-Laffitte, 1981]. Warsaw: Fundacja Zeszytów Literackich, 2006.

Urban, George. *Radio Free Europe and the Pursuit of Democracy: My War within the Cold War*. New Haven, CT: Yale University Press, 1997.

Wiesenthal, Simon. *Justice, Not Vengeance*. New York: Grove Weidenfeld, 1989.

Winiewicz, Józef. *Co pamiętam z długiej drogi życia* [What I can remember from the long road that has been my life]. Poznań: Wydawnictwo Poznańskie, 1985.

Włodzimierz Odojewski, Literacka konspira, rozmawiał Bronisław Tumiłowicz [Włodzimierz Odojewski, a literary conspiracy, in conversation with Bronisław Tumiłowicz]. Przegląd, January 18, 2004.

Wspomnienia pracowników Rozgłośni Polskiej Radia Wolna Europa [Reminiscences of some employees of the Polish section of Radio Free Europe]. Edited by Alina Grabowska. Warsaw: Oficyna Wydawniczar RYTM, 2002.

Wysocki, Stefan. *Polska z oddali—prawda z bliska* [Poland from afar: The truth from up close]. Solidarność Walcząca, oddział Trójmiasto, 1989.

Zamorski, Kazimierz. *Pod anteną Radia Wolna Europa* [Under Radio Free Europe's antenna]. Poznań: Wydawnictwo Wers, 1995.

Books and Articles

Andrew, Christopher, and Oleg Gordievsky. *KGB: The Inside Story of Its Foreign Operations from Lenin to Gorbachev*. London: Hodder & Stoughton, 1990.

Andrew, Christopher, and Vasili Mitrokhin. *The Mitrokhin Archive and the Secret History of the KGB*. New York: Basic Books, 1999.

Ash, Timothy Garton. *The Polish Revolution: Solidarity*. New York: Charles Scribner's Sons, 1983.

Baev, Jordan. "Bulgarian Regime Countermeasures against Radio Free Europe." In *Cold War Broadcasting: Impact on the Soviet Union and Eastern Europe; A Collection of Studies and Documents*, edited by A. Ross Johnson and R. Eugene Parta, 259–74. Budapest and New York: Central European University Press, 2010.

Benhalla, Fouad. *La guerre radiophonique*. Paris: PUF, 1983.

Berberyusz, Ewa. "Jednorazowo zużyty" [Disposable after a single use]. *Tygodnik Powszechny* 32 (1990).

Bergmeier, Horst J. P., and Rainer E. Lotz. *Hitler's Airwaves: The Inside Story of Nazi Radio Broadcasting and Propaganda Swing*. New Haven, CT: Yale University Press, 1997.

Bieńkowski, Władysław. *Motory i hamulce socjalizmu* [Socialism's engines and brakes]. Paris: Instytut Literacki, 1968.

Blaive, Muriel. *Une déstalinisation manquée: Tchécoslovaquie 1956*. Brussels: Éditions Complexes, 2005.

Blažek, Petr, Paweł Jaworski, and Łukasz Kamiński, eds. *Między przymusową przyjaźnią a prawdziwą solidarnością. Czesi–Polacy–Słowacy 1938/39–1945–1989* [Between forced friendship and real solidarity: Czechs–Poles–Slovaks, 1938/39–1945–1989]. Warsaw: Instytut Pamięci Narodowej, 2009.

Bochenek, Grzegorz. "Ks. Franciszek Blachnicki" [Father Franciszek Blachnicki]. In *Opozycja w PRL. Słownik biograficzny 1956–89* [Opposition in the PRP: A biographical dictionary 1956–89]. Edited by J. Skórzyński, P. Sowiński, and M. Strasz, 1:38–40. Warsaw: Ośrodek "Karta," 2000.

Bolecki, Włodzimierz. *Ptasznik z Wilna. O Józefie Mackiewiczu (Zarys monograficzny)* [The bird keeper of Vilna: About Józef Mackiewicz (A monographic sketch)]. Cracow: Arcana, 2007.

Borhi, Laszlo. *Hungary in the Cold War 1945–1956: Between the United States and the Soviet Union*. Budapest and New York: Central European University Press, 2004.

Bowie, Robert R., and Richard H. Immerman. *Waging Peace: How Eisenhower Shaped an Enduring Cold War Strategy*. New York: Oxford University Press, 1998.

Briggs, Asa. *The History of Broadcasting in the United Kingdom*. Vol. 3, *The War of Words, 1939–1945*. London: Oxford University Press, 1970.

Bromke, Adam. List do redakcji [Letter to the editors]. *Kultura* 4 (1957): 159.

———. *Towarzysze, posprzątajcie* [Clean up, comrades]. *Polityka* 33, August 15, 1998.

Brunnquell, Frédéric. *Fréquence monde: Du poste colonial à RFI*. Paris: Hachette, 1991.

Brzostek, Błażej, and Marcin Zaremba. "Polska 1956–1976. W poszukiwaniu paradygmatu" [Poland 1956–1976: In search of a paradigm]. *Pamięć i Sprawiedliwość* 10, no. 2 (2006).

Brzoza, Czesław. "Zapomniana armia. Polskie oddziały wartownicze w Europie (1945–1951)" [A forgotten army: The Polish guard companies in Europe (1945–1951)]. *Zeszyty Historyczne* 116 (1996): 3–21.

Cajthaml, Petr. "Minařik i Czechowicz—propaganda sukcesu wywiadów komunistycznych" [Minařik and Czechowicz: The propaganda of success by the Communist special services]. In *Między przymusową przyjaźnią a prawdziwą solidarnością. Czesi–Polacy–Słowacy 1938/39–1945–1989* [Between forced friendship and real solidarity: Czechs–Poles–Slovaks, 1938/39–1945–1989], edited by Petr Blažek, Paweł Jaworski, and Łukasz Kamiński. Warsaw: Instytut Pamięci Narodowej, 2009.

Cenckiewicz, Sławomir. *Długie ramię Moskwy. Wywiad wojskowy Polski Ludowej 1943–1991* [Moscow's long arm: The military intelligence of People's Poland, 1943–1991]. Poznań: Zysk i S-ka Wydawnictwo, 2011.

———. "Geneza, działalność i udział rozgłośni 'Kraj' w akcji remigracyjnej (1955–1957). Przyczynek do studiów nad polityką PRL wobec emigracji i Polonii" [The origins, activity and participation of Kraj radio in the reemigration operation (1955–1957): A contribution to the research on the policies of People's Poland toward the emigration and Polonia]. *Niepodległość* 53/54 (2003–2004): 114–226.

———. "Od pierwszej reemigracji do drugiej reemigracji. Aparat bezpieczeństwa PRL wobec polskiej emigracji politycznej w latach 1944–1956," wstęp do publikacji *Polska emigracja polityczna. Informator* [From the first to the second reemigration: The security apparatus of People's Poland and Polish political emigration in 1944–1956, introduction to Polish political emigration: A guide]. Warsaw: Oficyna Wydawnicza Adiutor, 2004.

———. "Udział aparatu bezpieczeństwa w drugiej kampanii reemigracyjnej (1955–1957)" [The role of the security apparatus in the second reemigration campaign (1955–1957)]. In *Aparat bezpieczeństwa wobec emigracji politycznej i Polonii* [The security apparatus versus political emigration and Polonia], edited by Ryszard Terlecki. Warsaw: Instytut Pamięci Narodowej, 2005).

Ceranka, Paweł. "Reperkusje ucieczki Józefa Światły w Ministerstwie Bezpieczeństwa Publicznego" [The repercussions of Józef Światło's flight for the Ministry of Public Security]. In *Departament X MBP. Wzorce–struktury–działanie* [Department X of the Ministry of Public Security: Models–structures–actions], edited by Konrad Rokicki, 206–31. Warsaw: Instytut Pamięci Narodowej, 2007.

Chęciński, Andrzej. "Życie Andrzeja Brychta" [Andrzej Brycht's life]. *Życie*, May 17, 2001.

Chomicz, Zbigniew. *75 lat Polskiego Radia. Kalendarium 1925–2000* [Seventy-five years of Polish Radio: A chronology, 1925–2000]. Warsaw: Polskie Radio, 2000.

Cummings, Richard H. "Balloons over East Europe: The Cold War Leaflet Campaign of Radio Free Europe." *Falling Leaf Magazine*, June 18, 1999.

———. *Cold War Radio: The Dangerous History of American Broadcasting in Europe, 1950–1989*. Jefferson, NC: McFarland & Co., 2009.

———. *Radio Free Europe's "Crusade for Freedom": Rallying Americans behind Cold War Broadcasting, 1950–1960*. Jefferson, NC: McFarland & Co., 2010.

Curry, Jane Leftwich. "Radio Free Europe in the Eyes of the Polish Communist Elite." In *Cold War Broadcasting: Impact on the Soviet Union and Eastern Europe; A Collection of Studies and Documents*, edited by A. Ross Johnson and R. Eugene Parta, 147–68. Budapest and New York: Central European University Press, 2010.

———. "RFE and the Polish Elite: The Fifth Branch of Government." Paper presented at the Hoover Institution conference, "Cold War Broadcasting Impact," Palo Alto, CA, October 13–15, 2004.

Czuchnowski, Wojciech. "Giertych nie ostrzegł Michnika" [Giertych didn't warn Michnik]. *Gazeta Wyborcza*, July 29, 2005.

———. "Mi się tutaj podoba" [I like it here]. *Gazeta Wyborcza*, March 4, 2005.

Dasko, Henryk. "Jeszcze pokażę wszystkim skurnolom" [Wait till I show all them f----]. *Magazyn Gazety Wyborczej*, August 26, 1999.

———. "Nie ma miłości szczęśliwej" [True love doesn't exist]. *Magazyn Gazety Wyborczej*, August 19, 1999.

"Do Warszawy mogę jechać jutro. Z Markiem Łatyńskim, dyrektorem Rozgłośni Polskiej RWE, rozmawia Bogusław Sonik" [I am ready to go to Warsaw tomorrow: Bogusław Sonik interviews Marek Łatyński, director of RFE's Polish Service]. *Tygodnik Powszechny*, June 25, 1989.

Dominiczak, Henryk. *Organy bezpieczeństwa PRL 1944–1990* [The security organs of the People's Republic of Poland, 1944–1990]. Warsaw: Bellona, 1997.

Dudek Antoni. *Reglamentowana rewolucja. Rozkład dyktatury komunistycznej w Polsce 1988–1990* [A regulated revolution: The disintegration of the Communist dictatorship in Poland, 1988–1990]. Cracow: Arcana, 2004.

Dziadul, Jan. "Co się dzieje w hucie" [What is going on in the steelworks]. *Trybuna Robotnicza*, October 1, 1980.

Eisler, Jerzy, *List 34* [The Letter of the 34]. Warsaw: PWN, 1993.

———. *Marzec 1968. Geneza, przebieg, konsekwencje* [March 1968: Genesis, course, consequences]. Warsaw: PWN, 1991.

———. *Polski rok 1968* [The Polish year 1968]. Warsaw: Instytut Pamięci Narodowej, 2006.

———. "Powodowani troską obywatelską" [Motivated by civic responsibility]. *Tygodnik Powszechny* 11 (2004).

Faraldo, José M. "Rewolta wnuków" [The grandchildren's rebellion]. *Tygodnik Powszechny* 30, July 23, 2006.

Feis, Herbert. *From Trust to Terror: The Onset of the Cold War 1945–1950.* New York: Norton, 1970.

Fik, Marta. *Kultura Polska po Jałcie. Kronika lat 1944–1981* [Polish culture after Yalta: A chronicle of the years 1944–1981]. London: Polonia, 1989.

Frazik, Wojciech. "Kamień rzucony na szaniec. Wacław Felczak 1916–1993" [A stone thrown at the rampart: Wacław Felczak 1916–1993]. In *Węgry – Polska w Europie Środkowej. Historia – literature: Księga pamiątkowa ku czci profesora Wacława Felczaka* [Hungary–Poland in Central Europe: History–literature; A festschrift for Professor Wacław Felczak], edited by Antoni Cetnarowicz, Saba G. Kiss, and Istvan Kovacs. Cracow: Instytut Historii Uniwersytetu Jagiellońskiego, 1997.

Friszke, Andrzej. "Jan Józef Lipski—szkic biografii" [Jan Józef Lipski, an outline for a biography]. In J. J. Lipski, *KOR. Komitet Obrony Robotników. Komitet Samoobrony Społecznej* [KOR: Workers' Defense Committee: Committee of Social Self-Defense]. Warsaw: Instytut Pamięci Narodowej, 2006.

———. "Kultura czy ideologia? Polityka kulturalna kierownictwa PZPR w latach 1957–1963" [Culture or ideology? The PUWP leadership's cultural policies in 1957–1963]. In *Władza a społeczeństwo w PRL. Studia historyczne* [Government and society in the People's Republic of Poland: Historical studies]. Warsaw: Instytut Studiów Politycznych, 2003.

———. *Opozycja polityczna w PRL 1945–1980* [The political opposition in the People's Republic of Poland, 1945–1980]. London: Aneks, 1994.

———. "Sprawa Hanny Rewskiej" [The Hanna Rewska case]. *Zeszyty Historyczne* 117 (1996): 185–95.

———. "Władysław Bartoszewski—szkic do portretu" [Władysław Bartoszewski, a sketch for a portrait]. In *Prawda i pojednanie. W 80. rocznicę urodzin Władysława Bartoszewskiego* [Truth and reconciliation: On Władysław Bartoszewski's 80th birthday], edited by Jan Barcz. Warsaw: Rytm, 2002.

———. *Życie polityczne emigracji* [The political life of emigration]. Vol. 1 of *Druga Wielka Emigracja 1945–1990* [The second Great Emigration, 1945–1990], in 3 vols. Warsaw: Więź, 1999.

Gaddis, John Lewis. *The Cold War: A New History*. New York: Penguin Press, 2005.

———. *Strategies of Containment: A Critical Appraisal of Postwar American National Security Policy*. New York: Oxford University Press, 1982.

Garçon, Gabriel. *La Radio Français parle le polonais: Histoire des émissions en langue polonaise de la Radiodiffusion Française (1932–1974)*. Lille: Rayonnement culturel polonais, 1991.

Garthoff, Raymond. *Détente and Confrontation: American-Soviet Relations from Nixon to Reagan*. Washington, DC: Brookings Institution Press, 1994.

Gąsiorowski, Andrzej. *Jan Kaszubowski i służby specjalne. Gestapo, Smiersz, UB . . .* [Jan Kaszubowski and the special services: Gestapo, Smersh, UB . . .]. Gdańsk: Polnord, 2008.

Gati, Charles. *Failed Illusions: Moscow, Washington, Budapest, and the 1956 Hungarian Revolt*. Washington, DC: Woodrow Wilson Center Press; Stanford, CA: Stanford University Press, 2006.

Gawlikowski, Lechosław (with Yvette Neisser Moreno). "The Audience to Western Broadcasts to Poland During the Cold War." In *Cold War Broadcasting: Impact on the Soviet Union and Eastern Europe; A Collection of Studies and Documents*, edited by A. Ross Johnson and R. Eugene Parta, 121–44. Budapest and New York: Central European University Press, 2010.

Giertych, Jędrzej. *List otwarty do społeczeństwa polskiego w Kraju* [An open letter to Polish society in Poland]. June 1, 1976. Printed flier.

———. "Położenie Polski w świecie" [Poland's situation in the world]. *Horyzonty* 123 (1966).

Głowiński, Michał. "Pawiany z Monachium. PRL-owska propaganda wobec Wolnej Europy" [Baboons from Munich: The propaganda of People's Poland toward Free Europe]. In *Pismak 1863 i inne szkice o różnych brzydkich rzeczach* [Hack 1863 and other sketches about various ugly things]. Warsaw: Open, 1995.

Głowiński, Tomasz. *O nowy porządek europejski. Ewolucja hitlerowskiej propagandy politycznej wobec Polaków w Generalnym Gubernatorstwie 1939–1945* [For a new European order: The evolution of Nazi political propaganda for the Poles in the Generalgouvernement, 1939–1945]. Wrocław: Wydawnictwo Uniwersytetu Wrocławskiego, 2000.

Gmyz, Cezary. "Kryptonim 'Truteń'" [Code name "Parasite"]. *Wprost*, June 12, 2005.

Gomulicki, Juliusz Wiktor. *Wiedza o książce. Bibliografia. Encyklopedie. Słowniki. Varia* [Knowledge about books: Bibliography. Encyclopedias. Dictionaries. Miscellaneous]. Warsaw: Państwowy Instytut Wydawniczy, 1977.

Grabowska, Alina. "Fałszywki PRL" [Forgeries of People's Poland]. In *Pięćdziesiąt lat Rozgłośni Polskiej Radia Wolna Europa. Materiały sesji jubileuszowej* [Fifty years of the Polish section of Radio Free Europe: Materials from an anniversary session], edited by Daria Nałęcz, 75–81. Warsaw: Naczelna Dyrekcja Archiwów Państwowych, 2003.

Grabowski, Waldemar. "Kalkstein i Kaczorowska w świetle akt UB" [Kalkstein and Kaczorowska in light of Security Service documents]. *Biuletyn Instytutu Pamięci Narodowej* 8–9 (2004): 87–100.

———. *Polska Agencja Telegraficzna 1918–1991* [The Polish Telegraphic Agency 1918–1991]. Warsaw: Polska Agencja Prasowa, 2005.

Grajewski, Andrzej. "Kariera Pani Dyrektor" [The Directress's Career]. *Gość Niedzielny*, April 24, 2005.

———. "Oskarżony ks. Franciszek Blachnicki" [The accused, Father Franciszek Blachnicki]. *Więź* 5 (2001).

Grajewski, Andrzej, Paweł Machcewicz, and Jan Żaryn. "Sprawa o. Konrada Hejmo. Działania Służby Bezpieczeństwa przeciwko Kościołowi katolickiemu w latach 1975–1988" [The case of Father Konrad Hejmo: The actions of the Security Service against the Catholic Church in 1975–1988], May 31, 2005. Institute of National Remembrance, Warsaw, www.ipn.gov.pl.

Habielski, Rafał. "Kurier z Londynu" [Courier from London]. *Tygodnik Powszechny* 7, February 12, 2006.

———. "Obawy i wątpliwości. Emigracja wobec inauguracji RWE" [Fears and doubts: The émigré community and RFE's inauguration]. In *Pięćdziesiąt lat Rozgłośni Polskiej Radia Wolna Europa. Materiały sesji jubileuszowej* [Fifty years of the Polish Service of Radio Free Europe: Materials from an anniversary session], edited by Daria Nałęcz. Warsaw: Naczelna Dyrekcja Archiwów Państwowych, 2003.

Haight, David. "The Papers of CD Jackson: A Glimpse at President Eisenhower's Psychological Warfare Expert." *Manuscripts* 28, no. 1 (1976).

Hajdasz, Jolanta. "Odbiór audycji Rozgłośni Polskiej RWE w Polsce" [Reception of programs of RFE's Polish Section in Poland]. *Pamięć i Sprawiedliwość* 6, no. 2 (2004): 309–28.

———. *Szczekaczka, czyli Rozgłośnia Polska Radia Wolna Europa* [A Nazi street loudspeaker, or the Polish Service of Radio Free Europe]. Poznań: Media Rodzina, 2006.

Hajdasz, Jolanta, and Agata Ławniczak. *Polak z oddali. Jan Nowak-Jeziorański w Poznaniu i nie tylko* [A Pole from afar: Jan Nowak-Jeziorański in Poznań and not only]. Poznań: Wydawnictwo Miejskie, 2000.

Hauser, Przemysław. "Mniejszość niemiecka na Pomorzu i w Wielkopolsce w okresie międzywojennym" [The German minority in Pomerania and Greater Poland in the interwar period]. In *Bydgoszcz 3–4 września 1939. Studia i dokumenty* [Bydgoszcz, September 3-4, 1939: Studies and documents], edited by Tomasz Chinciński and Paweł Machcewicz. Warsaw: Instytut Pamięci Narodowej, 2008.

Heil, Alan L., Jr. *Voice of America: A History*. New York: Columbia University Press, 2003.

Henzler, Marek. "Radio trzeszcząca Europa" [Radio creaking Europe]. *Polityka* 18 (2002).

Hixson, Walter L. *Parting the Curtain: Propaganda, Culture and the Cold War, 1945–1961*. Houndsmills, UK: Macmillan, 1997.

Holt, Robert T., and Roger W. van de Velde. *Strategic Psychological Operations and American Foreign Policy*. Chicago: University of Chicago Press, 1960.

Isakowicz-Zaleski, Tadeusz. *Księża wobec bezpieki na przykładzie archidiecezji krakowskiej*, [Priests facing the secret police, using the example of the Cracow archdiocese]. Cracow: Znak 2007.

Jakimczyk, Jarosław. "Zabójcza Panna" [Killer Miss]. *Wprost*, May 29, 2005.

Januszewski, Radosław, and Jan Strękowski. "Komandosi zimnej wojny." *Rzeczpospolita*, part I, April 20–21, 2002; part II, April 27–28, 2002; part III, May 2–3, 2002.

Jarosz, Dariusz. "O polskim stalinizmie—polemicznie" [About Polish Stalinism —polemically]. *Więź* 2 (2002).

———. *Polacy a stalinizm. 1948–1956* [The Poles and Stalinism, 1948–1956]. Warsaw: Instytut Historii PAN, 2000.

Jarosz, Dariusz, and Maria Pasztor. "Wizyta Edwarda Gierka we Francji w październiku 1972 roku" [Edward Gierek's visit to France in October 1972]. *Zeszyty Historyczne* 153 (2005).

Jaruzelski, Jerzy. *Stanisław Cat-Mackiewicz 1896–1966. Wilno–Londyn–Warszawa* [Stanisław Cat-Mackiewicz, 1896–1966: Vilna–London–Warsaw]. Warsaw: Czytelnik, 1987.

Jarząbek, Wanda. "Władze PRL wobec normalizacji stosunków z RFN w latach 1970–1975" [The government of the People's Republic of Poland and the normalization of relations with the Federal Republic of Germany in 1970–1975]. In *Rocznik Polsko-Niemiecki 2004*. Warsaw: Instytut Studiów Politycznych PAN, 2005.

Johnson, A. Ross. *Radio Free Europe and Radio Liberty: The CIA Years and Beyond*. Washington, DC: Woodrow Wilson Center Press; Stanford, CA: Stanford University Press, 2010.

———. “Soviet Bloc Intelligence Activities against Western Information Programs: The Case of Radio Free Europe and Radio Liberty.” Paper presented at the conference “Intelligence in Waging the Cold War: NATO, the Warsaw Pact, and the Neutrals 1949–1990,” Oslo, April 28–May 1, 2005.

Johnson, A. Ross, and R. Eugene Parta, eds. *Cold War Broadcasting: Impact on the Soviet Union and Eastern Europe; A Collection of Studies and Documents*. Budapest and New York: Central European University Press, 2010.

Kaliski, Bartosz. “Proces Taterników” [The trial of the Mountaineers]. *Zeszyty Historyczne* 121 (1997): 89–97.

——— “Przerzut od Giedroycia” [Smuggling from Giedroyc]. *Karta* 40 (2004): 99–131.

Kamiński, Łukasz. “Od ‘Wolnej Europy’ do wolnej Polski” [From Free Europe to free Poland]. *Tygodnik Powszechny*, May 5, 2002.

Karaskiewicz, Katarzyna, ed. *Polska–Niemcy–Europa. Księga jubileuszowa z okazji siedemdziesiątej rocznicy urodzin profesora Jerzego Holzera* [Poland–Germany–Europe: A festschrift for Professor Jerzy Holzer’s 70th birthday]. Warsaw: Rytm, 2000.

Kładoczny, Piotr. *Prawo jako narzędzie represji w Polsce Ludowej 1944–1956. Prawna analiza kategorii przestępstw przeciwko państwu* [The law as a tool of repression in People’s Poland, 1944–1956: A legal analysis of the categories of offenses against the state]. Warsaw: Instytut Pamięci Narodowej, 2004.

Kochański, Aleksander. *Polska 1944–1991. Informator historyczny* [Poland 1944–1991: A historical guide]. Vol. 1. Warsaw: Wydawnictwo Sejmowe, 1996.

Korek, Janusz. *Paradoksy paryskiej “Kultury.” Ewolucja myśli politycznej w latach 1947–1980* [The paradoxes of the Paris *Kultura:* The evolution of political thought in 1947–1980]. Stockholm: Almqvist & Wiksell International, 1998.

Kovrig, Bennett. *Of Walls and Bridges: The United States and Eastern Europe*. New York: New York University Press, 1991.

Krajewski, Andrzej. “Długi cień dziadka” [A grandfather’s long shadow]. *Newsweek Polska*, March 4, 2007.

———. “Pisarze do więzienia” [Put the writers in prison]. *Rzeczpospolita*, May 2–4, 2003.

Krajewski, Kazimierz, and Tadeusz Łabuszewski, eds. *“Zwyczajny resort.” Studia o aparacie bezpieczeństwa 1944–1956* [“An ordinary ministry”:

Studies on the security apparatus, 1944–1956]. Warsaw: Instytut Pamięci Narodowej, 2005.

Kramer, Mark. "The Early Post-Stalin Succession Struggle and Upheavals in East-Central Europe: Internal-External Linkages in Soviet Policy Making." *Journal of Cold War Studies* 1, nos. 1–3 (1999).

Król, Eugeniusz Cezary. *Propaganda i indoktrynacja narodowego socjalizmu w Niemczech 1919–1945. Studium organizacji, treści i technik masowego oddziaływania* [National Socialism's propaganda and indoctrination in Germany, 1919–1945: A study of the organization, contents and techniques of mass influence]. Warsaw: Instytut Studiów Politycznych PAN & Rytm, 1999.

Kula, Marcin. *Paryż, Londyn i Waszyngton patrzą na Październik 1956 r. w Polsce* [Paris, London and Washington look at October 1956 in Poland]. Warsaw: Instytut Studiów Politycznych, 1992.

Kurski, Jarosław. *Jan Nowak-Jeziorański. Emisariusz wolności* [Jan Nowak-Jeziorański. Emissary of freedom]. Warsaw: Bertelsmann Media, 2005.

Kwiatkowski, Maciej Józef. *Polskie Radio w konspiracji 1939–1944* [Polish underground radio, 1939–1944]. Warsaw: Państwowy Instytut Wydawniczy, 1989.

Łaptos, Józef. *Miejsce "krucjaty wolności" w amerykańskiej polityce wobec Europy Środkowo-Wschodniej (1949–1953)* [The Crusade for Freedom in US policy toward East-Central Europe (1949–1953)]. Polska Akademia Umiejętności [Polish Academy of Learning]. *Prace Komisji Środkowoeuropejskiej* 12 (2004): 103–25.

Lasota, Marek. *Donos na Wojtyłę. Karol Wojtyła w teczkach bezpieki* [Informing on Wojtyła: Karol Wojtyła in secret police files]. Cracow: Znak, 2006.

———. "O raporcie sejmowej komisji poświęconym Samodzielnej Grupie 'D' w MSW" [The report of the Sejm commission devoted to the Self-Contained Group "D" in the Ministry of Internal Affairs]. *Biuletyn Instytutu Pamięci Narodowej* 24, no. 1 (2003): 27–36.

Leffler, Melvyn, and David S. Painter. *Origins of the Cold War: An International History*. New York: Routledge, 2005.

Lencznarowicz, Jerzy. "Rola Towarzystwa 'Polonia' w polityce PRL wobec Polonii w krajach zachodnich [The role of the Polonia Association in the policies of People's Poland toward the Polonia in Western countries]. *Przegląd Polonijny* 79, no. 1 (1996).

Lepeuple, Anne-Chantale. "Radio Europe Libre et le soulèvement hongrois de 1956." *Revue d'Histoire Moderne et Contemporaine* 47 (2000): 177–95.

Lesiakowski, Krzysztof. *Mieczysław Moczar "Mietek." Biografia polityczna* [Mieczysław Moczar "Mietek": A political biography]. Warsaw: Rytm, 1998.

Lipski, Jan Józef. *KOR. Komitet Obrony Robotników, Komitet Samoobrony Społecznej*. Warsaw: Instytut Pamięci Narodowej, 2006.

Lowe, Peter. *The Korean War*. Basingstoke, UK: Palgrave Macmillan, 2000.

Machcewicz, Paweł. *Emigracja w polityce międzynarodowej* [Emigration in international politics]. Vol. 2 of *Druga Wielka Emigracja 1945–1990* [The second Great Emigration, 1945–1990]. Warsaw: Biblioteka "Więzi," 1999.

———. "Kryptonim 'Medal'" [Code name "Medal"]. *Rzeczpospolita*, September 18–19, 2004.

———. "'Operacje balonowe' 1951–1956. Przyczynek do dziejów amerykańskiej wojny psychologicznej wobec bloku komunistycznego" ["Balloon operations," 1951–1956: A contribution to the history of American psychological warfare vis-à-vis the Communist bloc]. In *Polska–Niemcy–Europa: Księga jubileuszowa z okazji siedemdziesiątej rocznicy urodzin profesora Jerzego Holzera* [Poland-Germany-Europe: A festschrift for Professor Jerzy Holzer's 70th birthday], edited by Katarzyna Karaskiewicz. Warsaw: Instytut Studiów Politycznych PAN, 2000.

———. "Polska i Europa Wschodnia w polityce Stanów Zjednoczonych w latach 1947–1956" [Poland and Eastern Europe in US policy in 1947–1956]. Presented at the XI Powszechny Zjazd Historyków Polskich [11th General Meeting of Polish Historians]. "Pamiętnik," vol. 3, pt. 2, 141–50.

———. *Polski rok 1956* [The Polish Year 1956]. Warsaw: Mówią Wieki, 1993.

———. "Radio Wolna Europa i 'partyzanci'" [Radio Free Europe and the "Partisans"]. In *Od Piłsudskiego do Wałęsy. Studia z dziejów Polski w XX wieku* [From Piłsudski to Wałęsa: Studies in the twentieth-century history of Poland], 248–61. Warsaw: Instytut Pamięci Narodowej-Instytut Studiów Politycznych PAN, 2008.

———. "Radio Wolna Europa wobec wydarzeń w Polsce i na Węgrzech jesienią 1956 roku" [Radio Free Europe's approach to the events in Poland and Hungary in the autumn of 1956], in *Październik 1956. Początek erozji systemu* [October 1956: The system begins to erode], edited by Marek Jabłonowski and Stanisław Stępka. Pułtusk: Akademia Humanistyczna im. Aleksandra Gieysztora, 2007.

———. *Rebellious Satellite: Poland 1956*. Washington, DC: Woodrow Wilson Center Press; Stanford, CA: Stanford University Press, 2009.

———. "Stany Zjednoczone wobec polskiego Października 1956 roku" [The United States and the Polish October 1956]. In *Polska 1944/45–1989. Studia i materiały* [Poland 1944/45–1989: Studies and materials], vol. 3, 45–61. Warsaw: Neriton, 1997.

———. "Teczka 'Fondy,' czyli o początkach penetracji agenturalnej Radia Wolna Europa" ["Fonda's" file, or the beginnings of the espionage infiltration of Radio Free Europe]. In *Władza a społeczeństwo w PRL. Studia historyczne* [Government and society in the People's Republic of Poland: Historical studies]. Warsaw: Instytut Studiów Politycznych, 2003.

Maciejowski, Robert. "Kara śmierci za radio" [Capital punishment for a radio]. *Biuletyn Instytutu Pamięci Narodowej* 11 (2001): 22–23.

Majchrzak, Grzegorz. "Zygmunt Solorz—agent z przypadku" [Zygmunt Solorz, an accidental agent]. *Rzeczpospolita*, November 21, 2006.

Małczyński, Jerzy. *Byliśmy pierwsi. 45 lat temu Rozgłośnia Harcerska nadała pierwszą audycję* [We were first: Forty-five years ago, Scout Radio broadcast its first program]. Warsaw: Horyzonty, 2002.

Malewski, Jerzy [Włodzimierz Bolecki]. *Wyrok na Józefa Mackiewicza*. London: Puls, 1991.

Mania, Andrzej. *Bridge building. Polityka USA wobec Europy Wschodniej w latach 1961–1968* [Bridge Building: US policies toward Eastern Europe in 1961–1968]. Cracow: Wydawnictwo Uniwersytetu Jagiellońskiego, 1996.

———. *Détente i polityka Stanów Zjednoczonych wobec Europy Wschodniej, styczeń 1969–styczeń 1981* [Détente and US policies toward Eastern Europe, January 1969–January 1981]. Cracow: Wydawnictwo Uniwersytetu Jagiellońskiego, 2003.

———. *The National Security Council i amerykańska polityka wobec Europy Wschodniej 1945–1960* [The National Security Council and American policies toward Eastern Europe, 1945–1960]. Cracow: Wydawnictwo Uniwersytetu Jagiellońskiego, 1994.

Marchio, James D. "Rhetoric and Reality. The Eisenhower Administration and Unrest in Eastern Europe, 1953–1959." PhD diss., University of Michigan, 1993.

Markiewicz, Władysław. "Powrót" [The return]. *Polityka* 22, May 28, 1988.

Matthews, John P. C. *Tinderbox: East-Central Europe in the Spring, Summer and Early Fall of 1956*. Tucson, AZ: Fenestra Books, 2003.

Maziarski, Jacek. "Zagłuszanie" [Jamming]. *Nowe Państwo* 51 (2000).

Mazur, Bogusław. *Ruch Wolnych Demokratów. Geneza, program i działalność w oświetleniu źródłowym (1956–1981)* [The Movement of Free Democrats: Genesis, program and activities in light of sources (1956–1981)]. Opole: Wydawnictwo Alternatywy Demokratycznej, 1986.

Mazur, Grzegorz. *Biuro Informacji i Propagandy SZP-ZWZ-AK 1939–1945* [Bureau of Information and Propaganda of the SZP-ZWZ-AK, 1939–1945]. Warsaw: Instytut Wydawniczy PAX, 1987.

Metzger, Renata. "Radom '76. Żebyście wiedzieli, jak bili" [Radom '76: So that you will know how they beat people]. *Gazeta Wyborcza*, June 23, 2006.

Michie, Alan A. *Voices through the Iron Curtain: The Radio Free Europe Story*. New York: Dodd, Mead, 1963.

Mickelson, Sig. *America's Other Voice: The Story of Radio Free Europe and Radio Liberty*. New York: Praeger, 1983.

Mieroszewski, Juliusz [Londyńczyk]. "Kto uprawia ideologiczną dywersję?" [Who practices ideological sabotage?]. *Kultura* (Paris) 195/196, nos. 1/2 (1964).

Morawski, Jerzy. *Głosy z Monachium* [Voices from Munich]. Warsaw: Interpress, 1993.

———. "Na akt łaski nie zasługuje" [He does not deserve a pardon]. *Rzeczpospolita*, May 24–25, 2003.

———. "Raport spod głośników" [A report from under the loudspeakers]. *Spotkania*, May 21–27, 1992.

———. "Trzeci obieg towarzyszy" [The second underground of comrades]. *Rzeczpospolita*, December 11, 2003.

Myśliński, Jerzy. *Kalendarium polskiej prasy, radia i telewizji* [A timeline of Polish press, radio and television]. Warsaw: BEL Studio, 2004.

———. *Mikrofon i polityka. Z dziejów radiofonii polskiej 1944–1960* [The microphone and politics: A history of Polish radio, 1944–1960]. Warsaw: Instytut Badań Literackich, 1990.

Nelson, Michael. *War of the Black Heavens: The Battles of Western Broadcasting in the Cold War*. Syracuse, NY: Syracuse University Press, 1997.

Opozycja w PRL. Słownik biograficzny 1956–89 [Opposition in the PRP: A biographical dictionary, 1956–89]. Edited by Jan Skórzyński, Paweł Sowiński, and Małgorzata Strasz. 3 vols. Warsaw: Ośrodek "Karta," 2000–2006.

Ostermann, Christian F. "The United States, the East German Uprising of 1953 and the Limits of Rollback." Cold War International History Project, Working Paper 11. Washington, DC: Woodrow Wilson International Center for Scholars, 1994.

Paczkowski, Andrzej. "Aparat bezpieczeństwa w czasach odwilży" [The security apparatus during the thaw]. *Zeszyty Historyczne* 114 (1995): 3–33.

———. *Droga do "mniejszego zła." Strategia i taktyka obozu władzy. Lipiec 1980–styczeń 1982* [The road to the "lesser evil": The governing camp's strategy and tactics, July 1980–January 1982]. Cracow: Wydawnictwo Literackie, 2002.

———. "Jedni słuchali, inni zagłuszali" [Some listened, others jammed]. *Rzeczpospolita*, May 9–10, 1992.

———. *Od sfałszowanego zwycięstwa do prawdziwej klęski. Szkice do portretu PRL* [From a sham victory to real defeat: Sketches for a portrait of the People's Republic of Poland]. Cracow: Wydawnictwo Literackie, 1999.

———. *Trzy twarze Józefa Światły. Przyczynek do historii komunizmu w Polsce* [The three faces of Józef Światło: A contribution to the history of Communism]. Warsaw: Prószyński i S-ka, 2009.

——. *Wojna polsko-jaruzelska. Stan wojenny w Polsce. 13 XII 1981–22 VII 1983* [The Polish-Jaruzelski war: Martial law in Poland, December 13, 1981–July 22, 1983]. Warsaw: Prószyński i S-ka, 2006.

———. "Wywiad cywilny Polski komunistycznej, 1945–1989. Próba ogólnego zarysu" [Communist Poland's civilian intelligence, 1945–1989: An attempt at a general outline]. *Zeszyty Historyczne* 152 (2005): 3–25.

———. "Wywiad (cywilny) w PRL w 1955 r." [(Civilian) intelligence in the People's Republic of Poland in 1955]. *Zeszyty Historyczne* 150 (2004): 129–53.

Pastuszewski, Stefan. *Bydgoski listopad 1956* [November 1956 in Bydgoszcz]. Bydgoszcz: Świadectwo, 1996.

Paulu, Burton. *Radio and Television Broadcasting in Eastern Europe*. Minneapolis: University of Minnesota Press, 1974.

Pawlikowicz, Leszek. *Tajny front zimnej wojny. Uciekinierzy z polskich służb specjalnych PRL 1956–1964* [The secret front of the Cold War: Defectors from the Polish special services, 1956–1964]. Warsaw: Rytm, 2004.

Persak, Krzysztof. *Sprawa Henryka Hollanda* [The case of Henryk Holland]. Warsaw: Instytut Studiów Politycznych PAN and Instytut Pamięci Narodowej, 2006.

Pięćdziesiąt lat Rozgłośni Polskiej Radia Wolna Europa, materiały sesji jubileuszowej [Fifty years of the Polish section of Radio Free Europe: Materials from a commemorative session]. Edited by Daria Nałęcz. Warsaw: Naczelna Dyrekcja Archiwów Państwowych, 2003.

Piecuch, Henryk. *Imperium służb specjalnych* [The empire of the special services]. Warsaw: Agencja Wydawnicza CB, 1997

———. *Służby specjalne atakują* [The special services on the attack]. Warsaw: Agencja Wydawnicza CB, 1996.

Piotrowski, Paweł. "Struktury Służby Bezpieczeństwa MSW" [The structure of the Security Service of the Ministery of Internal Affairs]. *Pamięć i Sprawiedliwość* 3, no. 1 (2003).

———. "Wojskowa Służba Wewnętrzna 1957–1989" [The Military Internal Service 1957–1989]. *Biuletyn Instytutu Pamięci Narodowej* 6 (2002): 34–39.

Platt, Dobrosława. "Pomówienia z esbeckiej fałszywki" [Defamation in Security Service forgeries]. *Rzeczpospolita*, May 5, 2001.

Pleikys, Rimantas. *Jamming*. Vilnius, 2001.

Prokop, Tomek. *Československé bezpečnostní složky proti Rádiu Svobodná Evropa. <Objekt ALFA>* [Czechoslovak security services against Radio Free Europe: "Target ALFA"]. Prague: Úřad dokumentace a vyšestřováni zločinů komunismu, 2006.

Ptasińska-Wójcik, Małgorzata. "Inwigilacja Instytutu Literackiego przez Służbę Bezpieczeństwa w czasach Gomułki" [The surveillance of Instytut Literacki by the Security Service in the Gomułka era]. In *Aparat bezpieczeństwa wobec emigracji politycznej i Polonii* [The security apparatus versus political emigration community and Polonia]. Warsaw: Instytut Pamięci Narodowej—Komisja Ścigania Zbrodni przeciwko Narodowi Polskiemu, 2005.

Puddington, Arch. *Broadcasting Freedom: The Cold War Triumph of Radio Free Europe and Radio Liberty*. Lexington: University Press of Kentucky, 2000.

Ratesh, Nestor. "Radio Free Europe's Impact in Romania during the Cold War." In *Cold War Broadcasting: Impact on the Soviet Union and Eastern Europe; A Collection of Studies and Documents*, edited by A. Ross Johnson and R. Eugene Parta, 205–28. Budapest and New York: Central European University Press, 2010.

"Rezygnacja. Rozmowa ze Zdzisławem Najderem, byłym dyrektorem sekcji polskiej Radia Wolna Europa" [Resignation: An interview with Zdzisław Najder, former director of the Polish section of Radio Free Europe]. *Polityka*, August 12, 1989.

Rokicki, Konrad. *Literaci. Relacje między literatami w władzami PRL w latach 1956–1970* [The writers: Relations between writers and the authorities of People's Poland in 1956–1970]. Warsaw: Instytut Pamięci Narodowej, 2011.

———. "Służba Bezpieczeństwa wobec inteligencji twórczej od Października '56 do Marca '68" [The Security Service versus the creative intelligentsia from October '56 to March '68]. *Pamięć i Sprawiedliwość* 10, no. 2 (2006).

Rokicki, Konrad, and Robert Spałek. "Donos z Monachium" [Report from Munich]. *Wprost* 19, May 2, 2002.

Rositzke, Harry. *The CIA's Secret Operations: Espionage, Counterespionage and Covert Action*. New York: Reader's Digest Press, 1977.

Rutecki, Kamil. "System zagłuszania polskich rozgłośni radiowych w PRL" [The system of jamming Polish radio stations in the People's Republic of Poland]. In *Przełom w przełomie. Bydgoskie wydarzenia roku 1956* [A breakthrough within a breakthrough: The events in Bydgoszcz in 1956], edited by Alicja Paczoska-Hauke. Bydgoszcz: Urząd Miasta, 2006.

———. "Wolność słowa epoki Stalina" [Freedom of speech in the Stalinist era]. *Biuletyn Instytutu Pamięci Narodowej* 28, no. 5 (2003): 48–51.

Rykowski, Zdzisław, and Wiesław Władyka. *Polska próba. Październik '56* [The Polish challenge: October '56]. Cracow: Wydawnictwo Literackie, 1989.

Sasanka, Paweł. *Czerwiec 1976. Geneza, przebieg, konsekwencje* [June 1976: Genesis, developments, consequences]. Warsaw: Instytut Pamięci Narodowej, 2006.

Semelin, Jacques. *La liberté au bout des ondes: Du coup de Prague à la chute du mur de Berlin.* Paris: Belfond, 2009.

Short, K. R. M., ed. *Western Broadcasting over the Iron Curtain.* New York: St. Martin's Press, 1986.

Siemiątkowski, Zbigniew. *Wywiad a władza. Wywiad cywilny w systemie sprawowania władzy politycznej PRL* [Intelligence and the government: Civilian intelligence in the PRP's system of exercising political power]. Warsaw: Oficyna Wydawnicza ASPA-JR, 2009.

Skalski, Ernest. "Radio, które wygrało" [The radio that won]. *Gazeta Wyborcza*, May 2–3, 2002.

Spałek, Robert. "'Gracze'—Komitet Obrony Robotników w propagandzie PRL, stereotypach oraz dokumentach Ministerstwa Spraw Wewnętrznych" ["Players": The Workers' Defense Committee in the PRP's propaganda, stereotypes and Ministry of Internal Affairs documents]. *Pamięć i Sprawiedliwość* 4, no. 2 (2003): 79–112.

Stępniak, Władysław, ed. *Wokół Rozgłośni Polskiej Radia Wolna Europa* [On the Polish Service of Radio Free Europe]. Warsaw: Naczelna Dyrekcja Archiwów Państwowych, 2002.

Szarota, Tomasz. *V—jak zwycięstwo. Symbole, znaki i demonstracje patriotyczne walczącej Europy 1939–1945* [V like victory: The symbols, signs and patriotic demonstrations in fighting Europe, 1939–1945]. Warsaw: Wydawnictwa Szkolne i Pedagogiczne, 1994.

Tarka, Krzysztof. *Antykomunistyczny rusofil. Jędrzej Giertych o opozycji politycznej i polityce polskiej* [An anti-Communist Russophile: Jędrzej Giertych on the political opposition and Polish politics]. *Zeszyty Historyczne* 159 (2007): 135–69.

———. "'Bankrut' i 'kapitulant' czy 'wybitny publicysta'? O powrocie S. Mackiewicza do Polski" [A "failure" and a "defeatist" or an "outstanding writer'? On S. Mackiewicz's return to Poland]. *Zeszyty Historyczne* 151 (2005).

———. *Emigracyjna dyplomacja. Polityka zagraniczna rządu RP na uchodźstwie 1945–1990* [The diplomacy of emigration: The foreign policy of the Polish government in exile, 1945–1990]. Warsaw: Rytm, 2003.

———. "Jest tylko jedna Polska. Bolesław Świderski—emigrant w służbie Polski Ludowej" [There is only one Poland: Bolesław Świderski, an émigré serving People's Poland]. *Pamięć i Sprawiedliwość* 11, no. 1 (2007).

———. "Między emigracją a krajem. Witold Olszewski i paryskie 'Horyzonty'" [Between the émigré community and Poland: Witold Olszewski and the Paris *Horyzonty*]. *Zeszyty Historyczne* 154 (2005): 102–52.

———. "'Polska jest Polską.' Powrót Stanisław Mackiewicza do kraju w czerwcu 1956 roku" ["Poland is Poland": Stanisław Mackiewicz's return to Poland in June 1956]. *Zeszyty Historyczne* 150 (2004): 55–96.

———. "Prowokator 'Mikron'—Juliusz Sokolnicki" [Provocateur "Mikron," Juliusz Sokolnicki]. *Zeszyty Historyczne* 158 (2006): 101–12.

Terlecki, Ryszard. *Miecz i tarcza komunizmu. Historia aparatu bezpieczeństwa w Polsce 1944–1990* [Communism's sword and shield: A history of the security apparatus in Poland, 1944–1990]. Cracow: Wydawnictwo Literackie, 2009.

Terlikowski, Tomasz. "Tajna historia arcybiskupa" [The archbishop's secret story]. *Rzeczpospolita*, January 4, 2007.

Tuma, Oldrich. "Broadcasting: Its Impact on Czechoslovakia." Paper presented at the Hoover Institution conference, "Cold War Broadcasting Impact," Palo Alto, CA, October 13–15, 2004.

Tussel, Javier. *La dictadura de Franco*. Madrid: Alianza Editorial, 1988.

Tyszkiewicz, Jakub. *Otwarte okno w "żelaznej kurtynie." Polityka administracji prezydenta Eisenhowera wobec Polski (październik 1956–styczeń 1961)* [An open window in the "Iron Curtain": The Eisenhower administration's policies toward Poland (October 1956–January 1961)]. Wrocław: Wydawnictwo Uniwersytetu Wrocławskiego, 2003.

Walicki, Andrzej. *Marksizm i skok do królestwa wolności. Dzieje komunistycznej utopii* [Marxism and the leap to the kingdom of freedom: A history of the Communist utopia]. Warsaw: PWN, 1996.

———. *Polskie zmagania z wolnością* [The Polish struggles with freedom]. Cracow: Universitas, 2000.

Witkowski, Tadeusz. "Zygmunt Solorz w sieci służb PRL" [Zygmunt Solorz in the net of the PRP's services]. *Życie Warszawy*, November 17, 2006.

Wnuk, Rafał. "Dwie prowokacje—Piąta Komenda Zrzeszenia 'WiN' i Berg" [Two provocations, the Fifth Command of the "Freedom and Independence" Association and Berg]. *Zeszyty Historyczne* 141 (2002): 71–112.

Wróbel, Janusz. *Polonia Chicagowska w dobie "Solidarności" 1980–1989* [The Chicago Polonia in the Solidarity era 1980–1989]. Łódź: Instytut Pamięci Narodowej, 2012.

Zaćmiński, Andrzej. "Przestępstwa polityczne w orzecznictwie Komisji Specjalnej do Walki z Nadużyciami i Szkodnictwem Gospodarczym (1950–1954)" [Political offenses in the jurisdiction of the Special Commission for Combating Abuses and Economic Sabotage (1950–1954)]. *Pamięć i Sprawiedliwość* 12, no. 1 (2008): 321–43.

Zaremba, Piotr. *Młodopolacy. Historia Ruchu Młodej Polski* [The Young Poles: A history of the Young Poland Movement]. Gdańsk: Arche, 2000.

Żarnowski, Janusz, ed. *Dyktatury w Europie Środkowo-Wschodniej 1918–1939* [Dictatorships in East-Central Europe, 1918–1939]. Wrocław: Zakład Narodowy im. Ossolińskich, 1973.

Żebrowski, Marek. "Rozgłośnia spec. znaczenia (wypisy z propagandy PRL)" [A station of special significance (excerpts from the propaganda of People's Poland)]. *Zeszyty Historyczne* 142 (2002): 198–230.

Ziętara, Paweł. *Emigracja wobec Października. Postawy polskich środowisk emigracyjnych wobec liberalizacji w PRL w latach 1955–1957* [The émigré community and October: The attitudes of Polish émigré communities toward liberalization in People's Poland in 1955–1957]. Warsaw: LTW, 2001.

Ziółkowska, Aleksandra. *Proces Melchiora Wańkowicza 1964* [The trial of Melchior Wańkowicz, 1964]. Warsaw: Nowe Wydawnictwo Polskie, 1990.

"Zrozumieć Mackiewicza. Rozmowa z prof. Włodzimierzem Boleckim" [To understand Mackiewicz: A conversation with Prof. Włodzimierz Bolecki]. *Rzeczpospolita*, March 2–3, 2002.

Index

AAN. *See* Archiwum Akt Nowych (Central Archives of Modern Records)
Academy of Internal Affairs, 242
Adamski, Wiesław, 82, 311*n*4
Adenauer, Konrad, 65, 77
adversarial centers, 69
AIPN. *See* Instytutu Pamięci Narodowej
Altschul, Frank, 10, 36, 37, 38–39, 299*n* 99
Anders, Władysław, 33
Andropov, Yuri, 118
Animal Farm (Orwell), 64
"Anti-Polish Propaganda: A Threat to the Nation's Vital Interests" (Bureau of Ideological-Educational Work), 219–20
anti-Semitism and anti-Zionism: in anti-RFE propaganda, 61, 98–99; anti-Zionist campaign (March 1968), 139; against Bartoszewski, 170–71; Czechowicz's, 193; at Internal Affairs Ministry, 129; in *Monachijska menażeria*, 114–15; in Russia, 55; in *Siedem trudnych lat*, 203
archival research sources, 8–11
Archiwum Akt Nowych (AAN, Central Archives of Modern Records), 8
Archiwum Instytut Pamięci Narodowej. *See* Institute of National Remembrance
Association of Polish Librarians, 171
athletic competitions, radio reporting on, 102
audience size (for RFE), 3–4, 104, 105, 233, 242, 276
Auschwitz concentration camp, 64, 174
Austria, 17, 66, 129, 135, 223; jamming attempts by, 19
Austrian Cultural Institute, 163, 165
"A-Wiktor" (intelligence collaborator), 170, 172, 173
Azyl polityczny (*Political asylum*, Brycht), 151

Babiuch, Edward, 232
Badowski, Kazimierz, 160
"Baj" (Jerzy Barszczewski), 269
balloon operations (balloon war), 41, 63–67, 300*n*122
Bańkowska, Danuta: charges against, 231; Operation Olcha and, 159, 161, 163–64, 167, 169–70, 177, 179
"Bar" (Stefan Jakobs), 134–35
Barański, Marek, 271
Bardonowa, Wiesława, 230–31
Barszczewski, Jerzy ("Baj"), 269
Bartoszewski, Władysław ("Bonza," "Szatan," "Bartek"), 30, 178, 209, 231, 272, 334*n*35. *See also* Operation Olcha
Barzel, Rainer, 196
BBC. *See* British Broadcasting Corporation

Beam, Jacob, 43, 85
Bednarz, Wiesław, 261
Behind the Scenes in the Secret Police and the Party (Światło, RFE brochures), 61–62, 64
Bentkowski, Aleksander, 273
Berg affair, 77, 271–72
"The Berlin Traps" (Brydak), 73
Berman, Jakub, 48, 70
Bialer, Seweryn, 64
BIB. *See* Board for International Broadcasting
Bielecki, Tadeusz, 139
Bieńkowski, Władysław, 8
Bierut, Bolesław, 48, 62
Birecki, Henryk, 115
Bisztyga, Jan, 278
Blachnicki, Franciszek, 258–59
Błyskawica (Lightning) radio station, 15
BND. See Bundesnachrichtendienst
Board for International Broadcasting (BIB), 197, 275–76, 281
Bochnia, persecution of listeners to Western radio in, 52
Bodeński, Lesław, 23
"Bogdan" (military intelligence agent), 144
"Bogumił" (Polish agent), 262–66
border issue (Oder-Neisse line), 27–28, 32–33, 58
Borowicz, Tadeusz, 255
Borusewicz, Bogdan, 228, 232
Bosacki, Henryk, 262
Bosak, Henryk, 251
Bożekowski, Jerzy ("Fonda"), 124–28, 131
Brandt, Willy, 76
Bratkowski, Stefan, 270
Brest negotiations, radio broadcasts during, 13
Brezhnev, Leonid, 198, 222, 343*n*71
Britain: foreign-language broadcasts, 14; jamming by, 19
British Broadcasting Corporation (BBC): foreign-language programming, 14, 18, 19; German Service, 17; importance during World War II, 15; jamming of, 78; listenership, 4, 20; popularity, 45; signature tune of, 16
Brown, James, 248
Brycht, Andrzej ("Gerard"), 145–51; *Azyl polityczny* (*Political asylum*), 151; *Dancing w kwaterze Hitlera* (*A ball in Hitler's headquarters*), 145; "Föhn" ("Fen"), 150; *Raport z Monachium* (*A report from Munich*), 145, 147, 148, 150
Brydak, Bogumił, 84–85
Brydak, Zbigniew (Stefan Michalski), 70–75, 76; "The Berlin Traps," 73
Bryn, Jerzy, 152
Brzostek, Błażej, 285
Buckley, James, 205
Budzyński, Wiktor, 74
building bridges policy, 43, 99
Bulgaria: anti-RFE campaign, participation in, 224, 289; jamming by, 47, 81
Bundesnachrichtendienst (West German intelligence, BND), 251
Bureau of Information and Propaganda of the Central Command of the Union for Armed Struggle (later, of the Home Army, ZWZ-AK), 16
Bydgoszcz, jamming stations and equipment in, 4, 79, 80

Campaign of Truth (Truman), 19
Captain Czechowicz Fulfilled His Mission (Czechowicz), 201
Captain Pavel Minařik: The Spy Returns (book), 194
Carbonnel, Éric de, 85
card catalog (Research and Analysis Department archives), 29
"Carlos the Jackal" (Ilich Ramirez Sanchez), 224, 289
Carter, Jimmy, 43, 235
Case, Clifford, 44, 196, 205
Catholic Church, actions against, 191
Cat-Mackiewicz, Stanisław, 77–78, 156, 216
CC. *See* Central Committee (of PUWP)
Ceauşescu, Nicolae, 195, 225, 288

Celt, Marek (Tadeusz Chciuk, Michał Lasota), 120–21
censorship, 88, 171, 178–79
Center for Press Documentation, PAP, 269
Center for Public Opinion Research (Ośrodek Badania Opinii Publicznej, OBOP), 3, 105–6, 233
Center for the Study of East-West Relations (Ośrodek Wschód-Zachód, East-West Center, later Institute for the Study of the Contemporary Problems of Capitalism), 112, 185–86, 220, 248
Central Archives of Modern Records. *See* Archiwum Akt Nowych
Central Committee (of PUWP): balloon operations, response to, 64; Brycht, actions against, 149; Information Department, 242; plenums, 31, 41, 66, 89–90, 93, 100, 102–3, 113, 146, 181–82, 238; Press Office, 10, 183–84, 187, 201–2, 280; Propaganda and Agitation Department, 184–85, 187; on RFE, 183–84; RFE transcripts for, 7; sabotage, coordinated battle against, 185; sabotage radio stations, reports on, 242–43; Secretariat, 185, 219, 242; Social Sciences Academy, 243
Central Intelligence Agency (CIA, US): documents from, 10; FEC funding and oversight by, 22–23, 26, 68; RFE, relationship with, 35–37, 43–44, 196–97; supposed control of RFE by, 193, 271
Central Military Archive, 10
Cezary (Public Security Ministry operation), 67–68
Chciuk, Tadeusz (Marek Celt, Michał Lasota), 120–21
Chilecki, Andrzej ("Hil"), 134–35, 206
Chomętowski, Józef, 169, 248
Christian Service for the Liberation of Nations, 258, 259
Chronicle of the Years of War and Occupation (Landau), 16
Chrzanowski, Wiesław, 158
CIA. *See* Central Intelligence Agency
Ciastoń, Władysław, 233, 236
Cibor, Tadeusz, 92, 248
Ciesielski, Henryk, 55
Cieśluk, Henryk, 177–78
Ciosek, Stanisław, 7
Clay, Lucius, 19
clergy, reactionary, 61, 68
coded messages, sent by RFE, 38–39
Cohn, Ludwik, 172
Cold War, 21–44; anti-radio station actions as East-West confrontation, 283; anti-Stalinist thaw (1956), 30–31, 82–85, 88–90; beginnings of foreign-language radio broadcasting during, 18–21; birth of RFE, 21–23; broadcasting as main front in, 1; CIA, RFE's relationship with, 35–37, 43–44; policy handbook, 37–39; propaganda offensive and psychological warfare, 39–42; RFE's Polish Desk, early days of, 23–30; RFE's Polish Desk, guidelines for, 42–43; RFE's Polish Desk, oversight of, 31–34
collaboration, threats against, 267
collective listening, to Western radio stations, 51–57
Commission for the Prosecution of Nazi Crimes, 346–47*n*118
Committee for National Defense, Political-Defense Department, 155
Committee for Public Safety, 65
Committee for Public Security. *See* Public Security Ministry
Committee for the Defense of Workers. *See* Komitet Obrony Robotników
Committee of State Security (Bulgaria), 224
Committee on Radio Broadcasting Policy, 42
Communications Ministry, 186, 274
Communist and Workers' Party Central Committee (CC) secretaries, 220
Communist bloc. *See* Soviet (Communist) bloc

Communist elite, anticommunist political émigrés, contacts with, 190
Communist International, 14
Communist Party of Poland (KPP). *See* Polish United Workers' Party
Communist Party of the Soviet Union (CPSU), 64
Conference on Security and Cooperation in Europe (CSCE), 218–20
Congress (US): criticisms of RFE, 196–97; RFE, actions on, 214
containment doctrine, 22
Council of Ministers (USSR), 46, 239–40, 287
Council of the National and Foreign Ideological Front (PUWP), 212
counterintelligence. *See* Internal Affairs Ministry, Department II
counterpropaganda, 239–46
Counterpropaganda Unit, 242
CPSU. *See* Communist Party of the Soviet Union
Cracow, popular unrest in, 80
Crusade for Freedom, 23
CSCE. *See* Conference on Security and Cooperation in Europe
CSRS (Czechoslovak Socialist Republic). *See* Czechoslovakia
Cummings, Richard, 268
Curry, Jane, 8, 316*n*82
Cyprus crisis, 19
Cyrankiewicz, Józef, 80, 90–91
Czapla, Jan, 182
Czarnecki, Marian, 168
Czechoslovak Service (RFE), 27–28, 194–95, 224–25, 351*n*28
Czechoslovakia (Czechoslovak Socialist Republic, CSRS): Abwehr and Gestapo archives, use of, 210–11; balloon operations in, 41, 63, 65–66; BBC listenership in, 20; Czechowicz campaign and, 201; jamming by, 46, 47, 81, 187; Operation Pająk, participation in, 224; propaganda campaigns in, 194–95; special services, dynamism of, 288–89; street protests in (1953), 40
Czechowicz, Andrzej: at Academy of Internal Affairs conference, 242; on American guard companies, 73; on anti-Nowak documents, 10, 345*n*108; *Captain Czechowicz Fulfilled His Mission*, 201; on Koryzma, 132–33; MIA report on, 184; on Michałowski, 123; military-civilian cooperation in campaign against, 155; on Nowak's departure from RFE, 217; Operation Olcha and, 173–74; Poland, return to, 119; propaganda attacks related to, 187–95, 197–98, 201–3, 286; public disclosures of, propaganda response to, 29; on RFE, 193; spying by, 128–30; on Stypułkowska, 142; Szaniawski case, testimony in, 271–72; on Widy-Wirski, 341*n*42. See also *Siedem trudnych lat*
Czyrek, Józef, 7

Dajczgewand, Józef, 148
Dancing w kwaterze Hitlera (*A ball in Hitler's headquarters*, Brycht), 145
Dankowski, Henryk, 264
Dargas, Antoni, 139–40, 152
Dawn (Świt) radio station, effectiveness of, 15
death sentences, for radio ownership, 16, 17
de Gaulle, Charles, 17
Dehnel-Szyc, Małgorzata, 248
Department I, II, III. See Internal Affairs Ministry, *individual departments*
Department VII, Department X. See Public Security Ministry, *individual departments*
Department of Ideological-Educational Work (CC PUWP), 219–20
Department of Propaganda and Agitation (CC PUWP), 64, 184–85, 187
de-Stalinization movement (1956), 30–31, 78, 82–85, 88–90, 212
détente, fight against sabotage and, 211–16
Deutsche Hörer! (radio program), 17
Deutsche Welle (radio station), popularity of, 20

"D" Group of Special Tasks, 179
dictatorships, nature of, 283
diplomatic offensive, against RFE, 198
Directorate I, General Staff of the Polish Army, 152
Directorate II, General Staff of the Polish Army, 144, 151–52, 236–37
disintegration and disinformation campaigns, 9, 112–13, 179, 203–11, 287
Doctors' Plot, 55
doctrine of softening, 99
Dollfuss, Engelbert, 19
Dominik, Julian, 52
Dreżepolska, Ewa, 159, 165, 167–69, 177, 179, 231
Drygas, Maciej, 5, 47
Drzewiński, Franciszek and Danuta, 263, 264, 265
Dub, Władysław, 53
Dudziński, Andrzej, 147, 149, 247
Dulles, Allen, 22–23
Dulles, John Foster, 85–86
Durkee, William P., 36
Dwojak, Feliks, 75
Dywersja (*Sabotage*, Kolczyński), 112
Dziadul, Jerzy, 233
Dziennik Polski (émigré newspaper), on Urban, 277
Dziennik Radiowy (Radio Daily), as information source, 16
Dzienniki polityczne 1958–1962 (*Political diaries 1958–1962*, Rakowski), 8, 97–98, 192, 238–39, 274

East Germany. *See* German Democratic Republic
East-West Center (Ośrodek Wschód-Zachód, Center for the Study of East-West Relations, later Institute for the Study of the Contemporary Problems of Capitalism), 112, 185–86, 220, 248
"The Effects of the Main Ideological-Political Sabotage Centers on Poland" (security document), 117
Eisenhower, Dwight, 11, 40
Eisenhower, Milton S., 198
Eisler, Jerzy, 95
émigrés: Communist elite, contacts with, 190; from Czechoslovakia, 211; government subsidies for publications of, 107; military intelligence operations against, 151–52; Polish government in exile, 15, 21, 26; portrayals of, in propaganda, 146–47; repatriation campaign, 75–78; reports on political activities of, 186; RFE, texts attacking, 254; RFE as station of, 23; RFE's relationship with, 24–26, 31; Scouting movement, 72; spy operations among, 135; strength of community of, 288; struggle over, 77. See also *Kultura*
Erdman, Marta, 92–93
Der Europäische Osten (monthly), 127
evil, RFE as symbol of, 61–62
Express Wieczorny (newspaper): anti-RFE propaganda in, 57; on Najder, 245, 253

False Prophets (Kudaś-Bronisławski), 233–34
family reunification program, 66
Features and News from behind the Iron Curtain (bulletin), 210
FEC. *See* Free Europe Committee
Federal Republic of Germany (FRG, West Germany): as threat to Poland, 139; balloon operations and, 65, 66; Brycht on, 146; importance to RFE, 27; Oder-Neisse border, recognition of, 33; Office for the Protection of the Constitution, 266; *Ostpolitik*, 195–97; Poland, relations with, 125; West German intelligence service, 251
Fejgin, Anatol, 63, 70
Felczak, Wacław, 121
Fifth Command of Freedom and Independence. *See* Wolność i Niezawisłość (Freedom and Independence) movement

Fikus, Dariusz, 270
Filipski, Ryszard, 145
Final Act (of CSCE), 218–20
final years of RFE. *See* last years of RFE
Flak, Sylwester, 248, 249, 250
Florczak, Zbigniew, 77
flying universities, 229
"Föhn" ("Fen," Brycht), 150
"Fonda" (Jerzy Bożekowski), 124–28, 131
Foreign Affairs Ministry, 43, 66, 85–86, 220
foreign policy: radio broadcasting as instrument of, 13–18; RFE and, 195–201
foreign radio stations. See *names of individual radio stations (e.g., Radio Madrid)*
foreign sabotage: CC PUWP report on, 184–85; Czapla on, 182; government discussions of, 102, 117–18, 183; information-propaganda actions against, 112; institutions fighting, during Gierek era, 185–86; MIA fight against, 107–8; military institutions' fight against, 151; penalties for contact with centers of, 240; plans for fighting, 187; Security Service Unit on, 93–94
forgeries: against Najder, 250; against Nowak and RFE, 208; in Operation Olcha, 170, 175–76; postwar, 206, 207–8; against Wiesenthal, 210
"The Four Faces of Agent X" (*Krokodil*), 253
Fourth Program, 100, 103
Frąckowiak, Halina, 270, 272
France: foreign-language broadcasts, 14; radio broadcasts to Iron Curtain countries, 21
Franco, Francisco, 19, 285
"Franek" (Krzysztof Michałowski, "Włodek," "Michał"), 121–22
Frank, Hans, 16
"Freda" (RFE pollster and spy), 133, 215
Freedom. *See* Radio Liberty
Freedom and Independence (Wolność i Niezawisłość) movement. *See* Wolność i Niezawisłość (Freedom and Independence) movement
Freedom of Information Act, 299*n*94
Free Europe. *See* Radio Free Europe
Free Europe Committee (FEC): balloon actions by, 63; Brydak's allegations against, 76; CIA, relationship with, 35–37, 68; creation of, 22–24; founders, characteristics of, 35–36; Giertych on, 107; operational freedom of, 26–27. *See also* Radio Free Europe (RFE)
Freies Europa. *See* Radio Free Europe
FRG. *See* Federal Republic of Germany
Friszke, Andrzej, 230
Frolik, Josef, 210
Fulbright, J. William, 44, 197–98, 208, 287

Galantiere, Lewis, 30
"Gama" (intelligence agent), 130
Gancwajch, Abram, 210
Garstka, Wojciech, 259–60
Gawlikowski, Lechosław, 49, 264, 318*n*96
Gazeta Białostocka (newspaper), anti-RFE propaganda in, 60
Gdańsk shipyard strike, 232
GDR. *See* German Democratic Republic
General Staff of the Polish Army. *See* Directorate II
Georgescu, Emil, 225
German Democratic Republic (GDR, East Germany): Czechowicz campaign and, 201, 202; Poland, border with, 27–28, 32–33, 58; RIAS success in, 18–19; secret police (Stasi), 70, 164, 213, 223, 224; uprising in (June 1953), US passivity toward, 40
German expellee organizations, 206–7
German refugee camps, 193
German Service (BBC), 17
Germany: foreign-language broadcasts by, 14; radio, use for propaganda, 13; RFE, attitude toward, 124–25; RFE as

serving interests of, 57. *See also* Federal Republic of Germany; German Democratic Republic; Third Reich
Gestapo agents and informers, 204–5
Gheorghiu-Dej, Gheorghe, 7
Giedroyc, Jerzy, 78, 110, 116, 151, 180, 284
Gierek, Edward, and regime of: Czechowicz campaign witch hunts and, 192; foreign sabotage, response to plan for fighting, 188; on Gdańsk shipyard strike, 232; Krasicki's criticisms of, 241; MIA reports for, on RFE dangers, 184; Moczar on, 182; Nowak kidnapping, actions on plans for, 129; Operation Olcha, impact on, 176–77; Paris visit, 199–200; on sabotage centers, fight against, 211
Gierek era, 181–217; conclusions on, 216–17; Czechowicz-related propaganda attacks, 187–95, 197–98, 201–3; détente and fight against sabotage, 211–16; disinformation campaigns, 203–11; foreign policy, RFE and, 195–201; ideological sabotage, continued fight against, 181–87; summary of, 284–85
Giertych, Jędrzej, 107, 139, 254–56
Giertych, Maciej, 254
Głogowski, Karol, 160, 163
Glonek, Andrzej, 270
Główczyk, Jan, 274
Głowiński, Michał, 61
Główny Zarząd Polityczny Wojska Polskiego. *See* Main Political Directorate, General Staff of the Polish Army
Goebbels, Joseph, 14
Goerlich, Joachim, 206
Golde, Anna, 204–5
Golde, Kazimierz, 77
Goleniewski, Michał, 120, 123–24
Gomulicki, Juliusz W., 178–79
Gomułka, Władysław: at Eighth CC PUWP Plenum (October 1956), 66–67, 102–3; Holland case and, 89, 90; on jamming, 78–79; Khrushchev's reprimand of, 89; Letter of the 34 and, 91; RFE, criticisms of, 86; RFE monitoring materials for, 7; on Słonimski, 91–92; Światło and, 62; on West, ideological confrontation with, 89–90. *See also* Gomułka era
Gomułka era, 82–155; Brycht's activities against RFE, 145–51; jamming during, 186; KGB, cooperation with, 115–19; Letter of the 34, 90–92; MIA large-scale operations, 106–15; MIA programs combating RFE, 99–103; Polish Army's intelligence activities, 151–55; Polish enemies, portrayals of, 93–99; public opinion research, 103–6; semi-thaw (1956), 82–85; spy operations, 119–37; summary of, 288; thaw, end of, 88–90; Trościanko case, 137–44; US-Polish relations, RFE as rusty nail in, 85–88
Gontarczyk, Andrzej and Jolanta ("Yon" and "Panna"), 258–61, 277, 362*n*190
Gorbachev, Mikhail, 7, 273
Górnicki, Wiesław, 59
Górski (secret Internal Affairs Ministry collaborator), 85
government (Poland). *See* Poland and Polish government
Government Press Spokesman's Office. *See* Press Office of Central Committee of PUWP
Grabowska, Alina, 7, 252, 264–66, 362*n*197
Grabski, Tadeusz, 239
gradualism, 41–43
Griffith, William, 27, 31, 39, 41, 74
Grot-Rowecki, Stefan, 205
Group "D," Department III, Internal Affairs Ministry, 113, 208–9, 320*n*128, 320*n*129
Grzędziński, January, 156, 161
"Guards" (Brydak), 73
Guzik, Leszek, 213, 214–15

Haczewski, Ireneusz, 5
Hanke, Hugo, 216

Hass, Ludwik, 160
Hejmo, Konrad, 251
Helsinki Accords (Final Act of CSCE), 218–20
Henze, Paul, 36
Herter, Christian, 86
Hibner, Juliusz, 50–51
"Hil" (Chilecki, Andrzej), 134–35
historians: reporters, comparison with, 12; work of, 9–10
"The History of the Sins of Stanisław Mikołajczyk" ("Dzieje grzechu St. Mikołajczyka," MIA brochure), 111
Hoffman, Emil, 224
Holland, Henryk, 89
Horthy, Miklós, 285
Horyzonty (Olszewski and Giertych), 107, 139
Hungary (Hungarian Socialist Republic, HSR): balloon operations in, 41, 63, 66; ideological sabotage, fight against, 212; jamming by, 46, 47, 81; Soviet invasion of (October 1956), 31–32
hunger strikes, 231
Husák, Gustáv, 211

I Chose the Truth (Bialer), 64
ideological sabotage (ideological subversion): fight against, 1–2, 181–87; Gierek's administration on, 181; ideological-political sabotage, 93–94; MIA on, 106; military training devoted to, 154; Zamyatin on, 235. *See also* propaganda; psychological warfare
"Imperialism's Activities in the Areas of Foreign Propaganda, Psychological Warfare and Ideological Sabotage and Our Counteraction" (interagency security committee report), 99–101
individuals listening to Western radio. *See* listeners of Western radio
infiltrations of RFE, attempted, 70–75
Information office (CC PUWP), 242
information sources (for RFE), 28–30, 36–37, 190–91, 227–28
Innsbruck Winter Olympics, 220–21
Inspectorate "I" (MIA), 113, 208–9
"The Inspirational Role of the Centers of Sabotage in Programming Opposition Activity in the PRP" (Czechowicz and Kopczyk), 242
Institute for the Study of the Contemporary Problems of Capitalism. *See* East-West Center
Institute of Social Research of the Military Political Academy (Instytut Badań Społecznych Wojskowej Akademii Politycznej), 3
Instytut Badania Współczesnych Problemów Kapitalizmu (Institute for the Study of the Contemporary Problems of Capitalism, formerly East-West Center), 112, 185–86, 220, 248
Instytut Badań Społecznych Wojskowej Akademii Politycznej (Institute of Social Research of the Military Political Academy), 3
Instytut Pamięci Narodowej (Institute of National Remembrance, IPN): archive of (Archiwum Instytutu Pamięci Narodowej, AIPN), 8–9; Brydak case documents in, 71; Czechowicz documents in, 130, 190, 191; intelligence operations documents in, 69; Kassner documents in, 204; note on Fulbright's staff, discussions with, 198; Operation Olcha files in, 166; reserved collection, 254
intellectuals, government actions against, 180
intelligence operations, against RFE, initiation of, 67–70
Inter-Factory Strike Committee, 232
Internal Affairs Ministry (Secret Service, Security Service): anti-Semitism at, 129, 140–41; Brycht's emigration to Belgium, response to, 150–51; Czechowicz-related

propaganda campaign, 187, 202–3; document shredding by, 281–82; on foreign sabotage, goals and methods of, 96–97; forgeries by, 208–9, 335*n*49; Inspectorate "I," 113, 208–9; interrogation methods, 335*n*53; jamming, participation in, 48; KGB, cooperation with, 115–19; large-scale operations of, 106–15; listeners to foreign radio, reactions to, 55; as listeners to RFE, 6; military intelligence, relations with, 144; Najder trial and, 246–53; Office of Radio Communications, 48, 80; on Partisans, 97; on political system, threats to, 212; RFE, actions against, 75, 99–103, 220, 253–66, 362*n*196; RFE Research and Analysis Department, actions against, 29; on RFE war against Moczar, 34; Światło affair and, 63; symposium on ideological sabotage, 213; top leaders, influence over, 93; vigilance against collective listening to Western radio, 56

Internal Affairs Ministry, studies and research by: Bartoszewski, report on, 160; foreign centers, study of, 93–94, 106; opinion polls on foreign radio listeners, 103–6; on RFE, 84, 86–87, 281

Internal Affairs Ministry, Department I (foreign intelligence): anti-Semitism of, 98–99; articles planted by, 234; Czechowicz campaign, involvement with, 202; offensive actions, move to, 209; Operation Olcha, role in, 173; plan to fight RFE (1974), 213–14; psychological warfare, activities regarding, 106–7; RFE, reports on, 83–85, 184; on RFE's Stockholm bureau, 200; sabotage, role in fight against, 108, 110–11; Section III, 108, 134; Section IV, 108, 119, 172–73; Section VIII (later Section XI), 106, 108, 113; spies within, 120; spy operations by, 124, 127; Szaniawski case and, 269; Trościanko-Dargas case, involvement with, 152

Internal Affairs Ministry, Department II (counterintelligence), 109, 124, 147–49, 189, 269

Internal Affairs Ministry, Department III (combating internal political opponents): foreign interference, reports on, 94–95; Group "D," 113, 208–9, 320*n*128, 320*n*129; KGB, work with, 117–19; offensive actions, move to, 209; operation Cezary and, 67–68; Operation Olcha, role in, 161, 163–66, 171–74; reports by, 226–27, 229, 231; sabotage, role in fight against, 108–10; Section II, 176; spy operations by, 124; on student revolt slogans, 95–96

Internal Forces, 50–51. *See also* Protective Service

Intern-Informationen (neo-Nazi publication), attacks on Nowak in, 207

"Ionescu" (Romanian agent), 195

IPN. *See* Instytut Pamięci Narodowej

"Issues for a Meeting with the Vice-Minister of the USSR" (security document), 117

Italy, use of radio broadcasts for propagandizing, 14

I trust you, Kilroy. See Ufam ci Kilroy

"Ivan" (Bulgarian agent), 224

Izvestia (newspaper), Hoffman article in, 224

Jabłoński (Security Service agent), 70

Jackson, C. D., 35, 41

Jakobs, Stefan ("Bar"), 134–35

jamming: costs of, 49, 284; end of (1988), 274–76; by Germany, of Soviet broadcasts, 14; under Gierek regime, 186–87; impact of, 285–86; jamming stations and equipment, destruction of (1956), 4, 78, 79–80; Main Political Directorate on, 153; by Poland, 21, 45–50, 81; by Soviet Union, 19, 235;

jamming (*continued*)
stationary jamming centers (K points), 47; by Third Reich, 17, 19; UN censure of, 19
Jamming (Pleikys), 340*n*23
Janek Krasicki Silver Medal, 145
Jankiewicz, Edward, 122
Janusz, Kazimierz, 227
Jarosz, Dariusz, 285
Jaroszewicz, Piotr, 87, 196, 343–44*n*81
Jaruzelski, Wojciech: Gierek team, criticism of, 233; Hitler, comparison with, 243–44; new propaganda strategy, 273–74; RFE programs, attention to, 7–8; Urban's anti-RFE plan and, 278, 279–80; US policies, protests against, 237–38; on Wałęsa, 239; Whitehead and, 274
Jarząbek, Wanda, 195–96
Jegliński, Anatol, 47, 48
Jewish Documentation Center, 210
Jeziorański, Zdzisław. *See* Nowak, Jan
Johnson, A. Ross, 35, 37, 281
Josten, Josef, 210
Jóźwiak, Jacek S., 260

Kaczmarek, Czesław, 122
Kaczorowska, Blanka, 205
Kąkol, Kazimierz, 234
Kalkstein, Ludwik, 205
Kalugin, Oleg, 350*n*26
"Kamera" (Janusz Koryzma), 130–33
Kania, Stanisław, 169, 352–53*n*46
Karpiński, Jakub, 180, 260
Karsov, Nina, 161, 163
Kassner, Alfred, 204–5
Kassner, Johann, 143–44, 203–4, 205, 207
Kassner-Kaszubowski, Johannes, 205, 344*n*95
Katelbach, Tadeusz, 110
Katyń massacre, 8, 137
Kennan, George, 22, 35
Kępa, Józef, 169
KGB, 115–19, 165, 195, 203, 212–13, 224
Khrushchev, Nikita, 64, 89
Kirschke, Tadeusz, 159, 206, 256, 258
Kisielewski, Stefan, 166, 170
Kisielewski, Władysław, 67
Kissinger, Henry, 200–201, 221
Kiszczak, Czesław, 237, 270, 281
Kliszko, Zenon, 97, 103, 192
Kloss, Captain (fict.), 194
Kobyliński, Stanisław, 53–54
Kochański, Aleksander, 57
Kołakowski, Leszek, 149
Kolczyński, Janusz: actions against RFE, 278; articles against RFE, 111, 112, 234; book on RFE, 126–27; Czechowicz, radio program on, 188; foreign sabotage, leader in fight against, 185–86; at Sixth PUWP Congress, 183; on Wawrzyńczyk, 136; Werblan on, 339*n*15
Kołodziejski, Zdzisław, 271
Komisja Specjalna do Walki z Nadużyciami i Szkodnictwem Gospodarczym (Special Commission for Combating Economic Abuses and Sabotage), 9, 52, 55
Komitet Obrony Robotników (Committee for the Defense of Workers, KOR), 7, 227, 230, 231, 233, 352*n*46, 353*n*48
"Kondor" (intelligence agent), 98–99, 142
Konic, Andrzej, 194
"Konrad" (intelligence agent), 135
Kopczyk, Henryk, 242
KOR. *See* Komitet Obrony Robotników
Korboński, Stefan, 10, 25–26
Korczyński, Grzegorz, 209–10
Koryzma, Janusz ("Kamera"), 130–33
Kościół, lewica, dialog (*The Church, the Left, a dialogue*, Michnik), 255
Kosior-Zbierska, Eleonora, 5
Kostov, Vladimir, 224
Kostrzewa, Henryk, 273
Kostrzewski, Andrzej, 5
Kosztirko, Kazimierz, 177–78
Kowalewski, Janusz, 206
Kowalska, Anka, 227

Kowalski, Jerzy, 272
Kowalski, Stanisław, 6–7
Kozdra, Władysław, 103
Kozłowski, Maciej, 180
Kozubski, Czesław, 132, 142
K points (stationary jamming centers), 47
KPP (Communist Party of Poland). *See* Polish United Workers' Party
Kraj (Our country) Polish radio channel: Brydak's appearance on, 72; repatriation campaign and, 75–76; on RFE, 77
Krall, Hanna, 90
Krasicki, Ignacy ("Witold," assumed alias of Wacław Szafrański), 122–23, 189, 210, 233, 240–41
Kraśko, Wincenty, 169
Kremlin. *See* Soviet Union
Krokodil (Soviet periodical), on Najder, 253
Krok-Paszkowski, Jan, 138, 327*n*223
Krok-Solorz, Zygmunt, 261–62
Król, Jan, 54–55
Kronika (émigré publication), Polish subsidization of, 107, 234
Kruczkowski, Adam, 103
Krupski, Mikołaj, 137
"Kryza" (Andrzej Smoliński), 206, 214–15, 269
Krzeczunowicz, Andrzej, 357*n*116
Kubacki, Wacław, 191
Kubat, Stanisław, 257–58
Kuczyński, Waldemar, 260
Kudaś-Bronisławski, Jerzy, 188–89, 233–34, 341*n*42
Kufel, Teodor, 140
kulaks (rich farmers), 61
Kulik, Ewa, 227
Kultura (émigré publication, Paris): anti-Semitic portrayal of, 98; Brycht and, 145, 150; Cat-Mackiewicz and, 78; Florczak on, 77; Main Political Directorate on, 153; MIA articles in, 112; Mountaineers and, 180; RFE, criticisms of, 26; Wawrzyńczyk on, 136; writers punished for contact with, 156
"Kumor" (Mieczysław Lach), 133–34, 189, 214–15, 241–42, 269
Kun, Béla, 13
Kuroń, Grażyna, 227
Kuroń, Jacek, 103, 227, 229, 230–31
Kwatera Radiowa (Radio Headquarters), 16

Łabęcki, Janusz, 171–73, 179
labor camps, 2, 52, 56, 70
Lach, Mieczysław ("Kumor"), 133–34, 189, 214–15, 241–42, 269
"Lakar" (Andrzej Madejczyk), 251, 268
Landau, Ludwik, 16
Lange, Oskar, 97
Lasota, Marek, 122
Lasota, Michał (Marek Celt, Tadeusz Chciuk), 120–21
last years of RFE, 218–82; counter-propaganda and, 239–43; Final Act of CSCE, RFE vs., 218–20; martial law and normalization, 235–39; MIA operations during, 253–66; Najder trial, 246–53; opposition movements, period of, 226–35; overview, 44; People's Republic of Poland, final years of, 273–83; Soviet bloc cooperation against RFE, 220–26; Szaniawski arrest and trial, 266–73; Urban, RFE vs., 243–46
Łatyński, Marek, 280–81
League of Polish Families, 345*n*108
Lechoń, Jan, 24
legal community, Bartoszewski and, 160–62
Leipzig meeting of Soviet bloc countries, 222, 223
"Let Poland Be Poland" (US TV program), 240
Letter of the 10 (counter-protest letter), 91
Letter of the 34 (protest letter), 90–92, 94
Letter to a Communist (RFE program), 28
Lewinówna, Zofia, 157
Lidzbark Warmiński, popular unrest in, 80

Lightning (Błyskawica) radio station, 15
Lipski, Jan Józef, 158, 230–31
Lis, Bogdan, 240
Lis-Olszewski, Witold, 158, 159, 161–64
listeners of Western radio: harassment of, 51–57; research on, 103–6; RFE listenership, 3–4, 104, 105, 233, 242, 276
literary programs (on RFE), 286
Łobodowski, Józef, 21
Łódź secret police, research by, 105
Loga-Sowiński, Ignacy, 98
Lovell, Jerzy ("Tokarz"), 120–21
Ludwiczak, Stanisław, 261, 263
Łukaszewicz, Jerzy, 204, 213

Macedoński, Adam, 6
Machcewicz, Paweł, research sources, 8–12
Machine Industry Ministry, 51
Mackiewicz, Józef, 143, 234
Madejczyk, Andrzej ("Lakar"), 251, 268
Main Political Directorate, General Staff of the Polish Army (Główny Zarząd Polityczny Wojska Polskiego): Czechowicz-related propaganda campaign, 187–88; hostile radio stations, weekly analyses of, 155; on jamming, success of, 186–87; on listening to enemy radio stations, 56–57; plan against RFE and (1976), 220; propaganda activities by, 152–54; records of, 10; sabotage, plans for coordinated battle against, 185
Makowski, Aleksander, 278
Malenkov, Georgi, 62
Malinowski, Roman, 275
Marak, Erwin, 211
Marchwiński, Janusz, 150
Marek, Karol, 127
Marin, Yuri, 194–95
Markiewicz, Andrzej, 156
Markiewicz, Wojciech, 260
Markov, Georgi, 224, 289
martial law and normalization, 235–39
Matacz, Zbigniew, 272
Mazewski, Alojzy, 277
Mazowiecki, Tadeusz, 281
Mazur, Staszek, 6
Mazur Commission, 256
Mazurek, Janusz, 254, 257
"Medal." *See* Trościanko, Wiktor
Meehan, Francis J., 238
"Mentor." *See* Trościanko, Wiktor
Meyer, Cord, 36
Mężydło, Antek, 228
MIA. *See* Internal Affairs Ministry
"Michał" (Krzysztof Michałowski, "Włodek," "Franek"), 121–22
Michalczak, Janusz, 272
Michałowski, Krzysztof ("Włodek," "Franek," "Michał"), 121–22
Michałowski, Zygmunt ("Posłaniec"): Kirschke, search for replacement for, 256; on Kliszko, alleged contact with, 192; retirement of, 246; RFE director, appointment as, 217; Security Services's actions against, 121–24; as supposed CIA agent, 271; Szaniawski and, 268
Michalski, Stefan (Zbigniew Brydak), 70–75
Michnik, Adam, 95, 229, 230–31, 255
Michnik, Stefan (Karol Szwedowicz), 255–56
"Michnik" (Giertych), 255
"The Microphone and the Files" (Brydak), 73
Mieczkowska, Jadwiga (Aleksandra Stypułkowska), 142–43, 326*n*223
Mieczysław Lepecki Prize, 178
Mielke, Erich, 70
Mieroszewski, Juliusz, 78, 111–12
Mierzanowska, Danuta, 217
Mijal, Kazimierz, 103
Mikołajczyk, Stanisław, 10, 25, 68, 111, 121, 143–44
Mikołajewski, Zbigniew, 140–41
Mikołajska, Halina, 227
Milewicz, Ewa, 227
Milewski, Mirosław, 214, 225–26
Military Anticommunist Organization, 95

Military Internal Service (MIS, Wojskowa Służba Wewnętrzna), 138, 140, 152, 266–73
Military Office of Sociological Research, 4, 10
Miller, Jan Nepomucen, 156, 160
Minařík, Pavel, 194–95, 351*n*28
Minařík II (pseud.), 351*n*28
Ministries. *See names of individual ministries*
Mitzner, Zbigniew, 77
mobile jamming units, 47
Moczar, Mieczysław: Czechowicz's attitude toward, 194; Olszewski on, 327*n*232; Operation Olcha and, 169; Podkowiński as source of information about, 192; positions held by, 34; RFE, attacks on, 90; RFE, interest in, 181–82, 239. *See also* Partisans
Moczulski, Leszek, 228
Modzelewski, Karol, 103
Monachijska menażeria (*The Munich menagerie*, disinformation brochure), 113–15
Monat, Paweł, 152
Moosmann, André (Radio France), 20
Morawski, Jerzy, 253
Morawski, Kajetan, 20
Morawski, Maciej, 192, 200, 208, 280, 326*n*223
Morawski, Stanisław, 320*n*128
"Morski" (Kazimierz Zamorski), 29, 44, 126–27, 135–36, 137, 217
Moscow Olympics, 222
Moskal, Edward, 345*n*108
Mountaineers, 180
"Munich baboons" (RFE staff), in anti-RFE propaganda, 61
Munich Olympics, 221
Munich radio station. *See* Radio Free Europe
Music and Current Events (*Muzyka i aktualności*, radio program): anti-RFE propaganda in, 61; Brydak's appearance on, 72
Muskie, Edmund S., 350*n*17
Muzyczka, Ludwik, 159
Muzyka i aktualności. See *Music and Current Events*
Myśl Polska (Polish exile periodical), RFE, criticisms of, 26

Na antenie (*On the air*, RFE publication), 158
Nagórski, Zygmunt, 26
Nagy, Imre, 31
Najder, Zdzisław: archive of, 10–11, 244–45; as author for *Przeciek*, 264; dismissal of, 245–46, 252; Grabowska and, 264–65; kidnapping of, plans for, 358*n*140; Michałowski, differences from, 355*n*82; Nowak's cautions for, 358–59*n*141; Nowak's support for candidacy of, 357*n*122; RFE under, 237; staff conflicts with, 244, 251–52, 264–65, 287; as supposed CIA agent, 271; Szaniawski case and, 268, 272; trial of, 246–53
"Najder Is Shown the Door" (*Express Wieczorny* article), 245, 253
Narodowiec (émigré newspaper), on Michnik, 255
Na szlakach dywersji (*On the trail of sabotage*, Kąkol), 234
Nasz Znak (émigré publication): government subsidy of, 107, 234; Stefanowski article in, 111
National Archives (US), 11
National Broadcasting Company, 17
National Council of the Patriotic Movement for National Rebirth (Patriotyczny Ruch Odrodzenia Narodowego, PRON), 237–38
National Defense Ministry, 60, 210
National Democratic Party, 26
National Party, 139–40
National Security Council (US), 22, 40–41
Natolin (conservative Stalinist PUWP faction), 83
Natorf, Włodzimierz, 275
"Nawrócony" (Zbigniew Sołuba, "Zbyszewski"), 189, 191

Népszabadság (Hungarian Socialist Workers' Party daily), Czechowicz campaign and, 201
Netherlands, foreign-language broadcasts by, 14
New Poland's Army, 226–27
The New Statesman and Nation (weekly magazine), as alleged conduit for instructions to RFE, 59
New York bureau (FEC), 24
Nixon, Richard, 86, 87, 198, 200, 343*n*71
Nowak, Jan (born Zdzisław Jeziorański): broadcast of speech excerpts, 261; Czechowicz on, 132–33, 193; influence on RFE, 24, 34, 217; information sources, contacts with, 29–30; Internal Affairs Ministry on, 84; Kassner on, 143; listeners' memories of, 5; Oder-Neisse border issue and, 27, 33; Operation Olcha and, 173, 175; personal archives of, 10–11; Poland, return to, 281; Polish Students' Association delegation, meeting with, 82–83; *Polityka* on, 88; problems faced by, 24–25; programmatic memorandum (1957), 84; program retreat, organization of, 30; resignation, 216, 287; RFE oversight, resistance to, 32; scripts of, 299*n*90; security concerns, 115; staff conflicts under, 287; work during World War II, 205; writings of, 296*n*59
Nowak, Jan, attacks on: allegations against, 114, 115, 345*n*108; kidnapping of, plans for, 129, 324*n*186; MIA campaign to malign, 174; portrayal as collaborationist, 203–8
Nowak, Jan, personal relationships: Bartoszewski and, 159; Kliszko and, 192; Mackiewicz and, 143; Moczar, decision to attack, 97; Najder and, 357*n*122, 358–59*n*141; Szaniawski and, 268; Trościanko and, 137, 141–42, 143, 203; Urbański, letter to, 345*n*105; Zamorski, relations with, 127
Nowak, Jan, views of: on balloon operations, 41, 63–64; on Brydak case, 74; on code messages, 39; on disinformation campaign, 112–13; on émigrés, working with, 25; on Jabłoński, capture of, 308*n*98; on Kassner, 204; on Letter of the 34, effects of, 92; on Nixon, 86; on probable influence of free radio stations in Soviet Union, 30; on RFE, attempted infiltrations of, 70–72; on RFE's adversaries, 43; on RFE Stockholm bureau, 200; on Voice of Free Poland, name change for, 31–32
Nowak, Krzysztof, 6
Nowakowski, Tadeusz, 147, 221
Nowa Wieś (newspaper), anti-RFE propaganda in, 60

Oblicze Tygodnia (émigré publication), government subsidy of, 107, 234
OBOP. See Ośrodek Badania Opinii Publicznej (Center for Public Opinion Research)
occupied Poland, listening to foreign radio in, 15–16
Ociepka, Wiesław, 209
"Odebrano mi Polskę" ("They have taken Poland away from me," Żytomirski), 164
Oder-Neisse border issue, 27–28, 32–33, 58
Odojewski, Włodzimierz, 286
Odolska, Wanda, 58, 65
Odwrotna strona medalu (*The other side of the coin*, RFE program), 137, 158
Office of Criminal Affairs, Headquarters of the Citizens' Militia, 247
Office of the Federal Commissioner for the Stasi Archives (Germany), 9
Office of Policy Coordination (CIA), 36
Office of Radio Communications, Internal Affairs Ministry, 48, 80
Olcha. *See* Operation Olcha
Olszewski, Witold, 107, 139, 161, 327*n*232

Olszowski, Stefan: analysis of Soviet press, order for analysis of, 267; French foreign minister, discussion with, 199–200; Operation Olcha and, 169; on Polish Radio's Fourth Program, 103; political marginalization of, 185; on problem of foreign radio stations, 102; at Sixth PUWP Congress, 183; US, accusations against, 238; US Secretary of State, meeting with, 198–99; Werblan on, 339*n*15
"On Their Knees: A Study of Today's Emigration" (Gontarczyks), 261
Onyszkiewicz, Wojciech, 228–29
"Open Letter to Polish Society in Poland" (Giertych), 254
"Open letter to the Party" (Kuroń and Modzelewski), 103
Operation Bonza (Big Shot), 157
Operation "Nord," 224
Operation Olcha, 156–80; arrests in, 166–67; Bartoszewski, actions against, 169–76; Bartoszewski, contact with RFE, 157–60; Bartoszewski, surveillance of, 164–66; conclusions on, 180; final disposition of, 176–79; investigations during, 168–69; legal community as information source for RFE, 160–62; overview, 156–57; smuggling routes, search for, 162–64
Operation Pająk (Spider), 223, 224
Operation Spotlight, 64
Opoka (periodical), article on Michnik, 255
opposition movements, period of, 226–35
origins of RFE, 13–18
Orwell, George, 64
Orzeł Biały (Sanacja newspaper), anti-RFE propaganda in, 59
Osek, Józef, 173–74
Ośrodek Badania Opinii Publicznej (OBOP, Center for Public Opinion Research), 3, 105–6, 233
Ośrodek Wschód-Zachód. *See* East-West Center
Ostermann, Christian F., 40
Ostoja-Starzewski, Aleksander, 206
Ostrowski, Kazimierz, 158, 159
Our country (Kraj) Polish radio channel: Brydak's appearance on, 72; repatriation campaign and, 75–76; on RFE, 77
Ozór, Władysław, 55

Pacepa, Ion, 195
Pachowski, Jarosław, 278
Paczkowski, Andrzej, 48–49
Pampuch-Brońska, Wanda, 70, 127
Pancer, Maria, 169, 177–78
PAP (Polish Press Agency), 7, 215, 266–69
Parczewski, Tadeusz, 192, 341*n*43
Paris *Kultura*. See *Kultura*
Partisans, 34, 97, 138, 145, 181, 326*n*223
Passent, Daniel, 88, 313*n*30, 313*n*31
Patriotyczny Ruch Odrodzenia Narodowego (Patriotic Movement for National Rebirth, PRON), 237–38
Paweł (Public Security Ministry agent), 69
Pawłowicz, Karol, 172, 173–74
PAX (Catholic pro-Communist group), 64, 129, 145, 156
Pell, Gene, 245, 277–78, 279, 280
People's Republic of Poland. *See* Poland and Polish government
Persak, Krzysztof, 89
personal accounts, as research sources, 11–12
photocopying machines, 265
Piasecki, Bolesław, 64, 129–30
Piecuch, Henryk, 245, 268, 358*n*140
Piętek, Henryk, 160, 212
Pleikys, Rimantas, 340*n*23
Pobóg-Malinowski, Piłsudskiite Władysław, 20
Podgórski, Michał, 255
Podkowiński, Marian, 69, 191–92
Podolski, Jerzy, 179

Poland and Polish government (Polish Communist regime, People's Republic of Poland, PRP): anticommunist underground, communications with, 39; balloon operations, response to, 64–65, 66; Communist system in, 2; destalinization movement (1956), 30, 78; enemies of, portrayals of, 93–99; exile community, views on, 1; final years of, 273–83; foreign broadcasts in, popularity of, 20; FRG, relations with, 125; Germans in, radio broadcasts to, 14; Germany, border with, 27–28, 32–33, 58; jamming by, 21, 45–50; openness toward West, efforts against, 2; People's Republic, final years of, 273–82; radios in, 20; RFE, criticisms of, 26; RFE, information obtained from, 6; RFE and Voice of Free Poland as enemy of, 49, 73, 219; RFE's popularity, research on, 2–3; security apparatus of, during post-Stalinist period, 178; sovereignty, lack of, 287–88; Soviet Union, relations with, 46, 139; Stalinism in, factors influencing end of, 62; US, normalization of relations with, 274; Western Europe, limitations on operations in, 26. *See also* Foreign Affairs Ministry; Internal Affairs Ministry; Stalinist era; *entries beginning "Polish"*
Połeć, H., 246
policy guidelines (RFE), 37–39, 42
Polish Army (military): anti-RFE propaganda in publications of, 58; Directorate I, General Staff, 152; Directorate II, General Staff, 144, 151–52, 236–37; intelligence activities, 144, 151–55; listening to foreign radio stations by members of, 56–57, 153–54; Military Internal Service, 138, 152, 266–73; Military Office of Sociological Research, 4, 10; RFE, audience research on, 3–4; Section III, Directorate I, General Staff, 152. *See also* Main Political Directorate
Polish Committee of National Liberation, 16
Polish Communist regime. *See* Poland and Polish government
Polish Communists, Khrushchev's reprimands of, 89
Polish Desk (RFE). *See* Polish Service of Radio Free Europe
Polish episcopate, offensive against, 145
Polish government in exile, 15, 21, 26
Polish Independence Agreement. See Polskie Porozumienie Niepodległościowe
Polish Institute (London), 10
Polish Institute of International Affairs. *See* East-West Center
Polish intelligence. *See* Internal Affairs Ministry
Polish National Democratic Committee, 25
Polish October (thaw, 1956), 30–31, 82–85, 88–90
Polish Peasant Party. *See* Polskie Stronnictwo Ludowe
Polish PEN Club, 178
Polish Press Agency (PAP), 7, 188, 215, 266–69
Polish Radio: Brydak programs on, 72; Fourth Program, 100, 103; jamming of RFE by, 187; signal strength of, 101–2
Polish Scouting Association, 71–72
Polish Section (BBC), 20
Polish Section (Radio France), 20–21
Polish Section (Radio Madrid), 21
Polish Service of Radio Free Europe (previously Voice of Free Poland): beginnings of, 23–30; guidelines for, 42–43; Koryzma suit against, 131–32; models for, 15; name change, 31–32; oversight of, 31–34; Partisans, programs on, 34; program line differences in, 355*n*82; size of, 20; spies in, 114, 262, 362*n*196; staff conflicts within, 216–17, 244, 251–52, 277–78, 287; *Ufam ci Kilroy* on, 241–42. *See also* Czechowicz,

Andrzej; Najder, Zdzisław; Nowak, Jan; Voice of Free Poland
Polish Students' Association, 82–83
Polish United Workers' Party (PUWP, formerly Polish Workers' Party): archive of, 8–9; Council of the National and Foreign Ideological Front, 212; elite of, RFE influence on, 8; enemies, focus on, 1; factions of, 83; plans against RFE, 1–2, 220, 222; post–October 1956 policies, 88; pressure against RFE, 43; RFE, views on, 181; RFE's views on, 83; ritualistic enemies of, 183. *See also* Central Committee (of PUWP); Partisans
Polish Workers' Party (PPR, later PUWP), 83
Politburo, 7, 102–3
political activists, RFE as support for, 6
Political Council (Rada Polityczna), 24, 25–26
political crises, impact on RFE listenership, 4–5
Political-Defense Department, Committee for National Defense, 155
political emigration, methods of fighting, 215–16
political police. *See* Public Security Ministry
political prisoners, release of, 273
Polityka (PUWP news magazine): anti-RFE articles in, 88; on Gontarczyks, 260–61; Najder interview in, 281
Polonia Association for the Development of Relations with Poles Abroad, 75
Polskie Porozumienie Niepodległościowe (PPN, Polish Independence Agreement), 245, 246
Polskie Stronnictwo Ludowe (PSL, Polish Peasant Party), 1, 25, 111, 157
Pomeranian Military District, 154
Pomorski, Wacław, 136
Pompidou, Georges, 199
Poncet, Władysław, 271
Po prostu (weekly): closing of, 88; delegation from, meeting with Nowak, 82–83
Poradko, Edward, 270
"Posłaniec." *See* Michałowski, Zygmunt
Postal Service and Telegraphs Ministry, 47
Postoł, Jan, 183
Potocki, Józef, 21, 295*n*47
Potsdam Conference, 27
"Powrót kapitana" ("The Captain Returns," radio program), 188
Poznań, jamming stations and equipment in, 4, 78, 80
Pożoga, Władysław, 245, 259, 268, 358*n*140
PPN. *See* Polskie Porozumienie Niepodległościowe
PPR (Polish Workers' Party, later PUWP), 83
Prądnik concentration camp, 174
Prague (as Czechoslovakia). *See* Czechoslovakia
Prague meeting of Soviet bloc countries, 222–23
Pravda (Soviet newspaper), on Blachnicki, 258
preemptive censorship, 32
Presidium, resolution of limited range radios, production of, 51
Press Office of Central Committee of PUWP, 10, 183–84, 187, 201–2, 280
price rises, strikes against, 276
prison screws, 6–7
private radios. *See* radios
PRON. *See* Patriotyczny Ruch Odrodzenia Narodowego
Pronobis, Witold, 263, 264
propaganda: anti-German, 145; anti-RFE, anti-Semitism in, 61, 98–99; Cold War propaganda offensive and psychological warfare, 39–42; counterpropaganda, 239–46; Czechowicz-related campaigns, 187–95, 197–98, 201–3; depictions of RFE in, 35; on Gontarczyks, 259–60; Jaruzelski's new strategy on, 273–74;

propaganda (*continued*)
propaganda attacks during martial law, 235; Public Security Ministry on struggle against, 56; punishments for dissemination of, 55–56; radio broadcasting as instrument of, 13–18; against reactionary clergy, 61; RFE, attacks on, 35, 57–62; against sabotage centers, 146–47; Smoliński- and Lach-related campaigns, 214–15; against Światło, 60; against Voice of Free Poland, 58–59; whispered propaganda, 52, 303*n*31. *See also* ideological sabotage; psychological warfare
Propaganda and Agitation Department, CC PUWP, 184–85, 187
Prosecutor General's Office, 267
Protective Service, 46, 48
Provincial Prosecutor's Office (Warsaw), on Bartozcweski, 176–77
PRP (People's Republic of Poland). *See* Poland and Polish government
Prutkowski, Józef, 60
Przeciek (*Leak*, Załuski and Tatarowski), 263–64
Przygodzki, Jerzy, 272
PSL. *See* Polskie Stronnictwo Ludowe
Psychological Strategy Board (US), 40–41
psychological warfare and propaganda offensive, 22, 39–42. *See also* ideological sabotage; propaganda
Pszon, Mieczysław, 158
Ptaczek, Józef, 115, 138, 268, 271, 272, 326*n*223
Ptasiński, Jan, 146
Public Security Ministry (later Committee for Public Security): Brydak report for, 72, 74; Department VII, 121; Department X, 62; dissolution of, 48, 63, 82; hostile programming, methods of fighting, 50–51; jamming, statistics on, 49; Kassner, documents on, 204; operation Cezary, 67–68; on radio transmission centers, 46–47; repatriation campaign and, 75; on struggle against hostile propaganda, 56; Światło affair and, 63; on US psychological warfare centers, 69
Pudysz, Zdzisław, 247
Puławy (liberal anti-Stalinist PUWP faction), 34, 83
Putrament, Jerzy, 90
PUWP. *See* Polish United Workers' Party
Pyjas, Stanisław, 228–29, 230

Rabanowski, Jan, 80
Raczyński, Edward, 15
Raczyński, Paweł, 200
Rada Polityczna (Political Council), 24, 25–26
Radio Ankara, 20
radio broadcasting: as instrument of foreign policy and propaganda, 13–18; as main front in Cold War, 1. *See also* Radio Free Europe
radio centers, plan for construction of, 101
Radio Daily. See *Dziennik Radiowy*
Radio Executive Committee, 37
Radio France, 20–21, 72, 78
Radio Free Europe (RFE): actions against, summary of, 287; broadcasts, importance of content of, 1, 4–5; conclusions on, 283–89; criticisms of, 43; Czechoslovak Service, 27–28, 194–95, 224–25, 351*n*28; early perceptions of, 45; first Polish programming, 45; genesis of, 13–18; during Gierek era, 181–217; goal of, 83; during Gomułka era, 82–155; and Hungarian uprising (October 1956), 31–32; last years of, 218–82; listenership, 3–4, 104, 105, 233, 242, 276; numbers of programs of, 101; objectives of, 23; Operation Olcha and, 156–80; origins and place in Cold War, 13–44; overview, 1–8; perceptions of, in Poland, 26; Polish government, primary adversary to, 2, 49, 73; political nature of, 276; popularity, 104, 105, 233; Research and Analysis Department, 28–29, 43, 84,

126–27, 211; research sources for, 8–12; Romanian Service, 7, 288; security at, 131; during Stalinist era, 45–81. *See also* Polish Service of Radio Free Europe; Voice of Free Poland
"Radio Free Europe" (Prutkowski), 60
Radio Free Europe and Radio Liberty: The CIA Years and Beyond (Johnson), 35
Radio Free Europe: Policy Handbook (Radio Executive Committee), 37–38
Radio Headquarters (Kwatera Radiowa), 16
Radio in the American Sector (RIAS), 18–19, 40
Radio Liberty (RL, formerly Radio Liberation), 44, 74, 102, 194–95, 197, 221–22
Radio Madrid, 20, 21, 45, 46
Radio Moscow, 13
Radio Polskie, 15
radios: confiscation of, 15–16, 17–18; in Poland, numbers of, 50; with reduced range of frequencies, production of, 50–51; in Soviet Union, 295*n*38
radio stations: Polish, as competition to RFE, 100; socialist anti–Free Europe radio station, 101. *See also* Free Europe Committee; jamming; Radio Free Europe; Voice of America; *entries beginning "Radio"*
Radio Youth Weekly (radio program), 243
Radkiewicz, Stanisław, 50–51, 56, 63
Rakowski, Mieczysław: diary as source of information on RFE, 238–39; *Dzienniki polityczne* (*Political diaries*), 8, 97; marriage, 162; on MIA witch hunt, 192, 341*n*42; on political prisoners, 274; on RFE's attention to Partisans, 97–98
Ramparts (student magazine), 44
Rapacki, Adam, 7, 66, 85–86, 97
Raport z Monachium (*A report from Munich*, Brycht), 145, 147, 148, 150
reactionary clergy, 61, 68
Reagan, Ronald, and administration of, 43, 237, 240
receivers with reduced range of frequencies, production of, 50–51
Recovered Territories, 58, 74, 146
refugees, 69, 76, 193. *See also* émigrés
repatriation campaign, 75–78, 215–16
replacement concept, for RFE, 102
reporters, comparison with historians, 12
Republic of Poland, 207
Research and Analysis Department (RFE), 28–29, 43, 84, 126–27, 211
resistance movements (World War II), importance of foreign programs to, 16–17
Rettinger, Józef, 121
RFE. *See* Radio Free Europe
Rheinischer Merkur (newspaper), on Nowak, 206
RIAS. *See* Radio in the American Sector
RL. *See* Radio Liberty
Rogers, William P., 198–99
Roliński, Bohdan, 197
Romania: anti-RFE actions by, 224–25; Ceauşescu's jealousy, 195; jamming by, 19, 47, 81, 288; radio broadcasts to, jamming of, 46; radio listeners, actions against, 289; RFE monitoring transcripts for government of, 7
Romanian Service (RFE), 7, 288
Roszkowski, Janusz, 266
Różański, Józef (Jacek), 63
Rozmarek, Karol, 33
Ruch (underground organization), 176
Rudzińska, Anna, 89, 156
Rusinek, Kazimierz, 209
Russia, 13, 205; anti-Semitic campaign in, 55. *See also* Soviet Union
Rybacki, Z., 150–51
Rybicki, Józef, 176
Rykowski, Zbysław, 280
Ryszka, Franciszek, 244

sabotage: détente and fight against, 211–16; plans for coordinated battle against, 185; propaganda against, 146–47; against RFE, 125–26.

sabotage (*continued*)
See also foreign sabotage; ideological sabotage; propaganda; psychological warfare
Salmonowicz, Stanisław, 159–60, 165–69, 177, 179, 231, 335*n*49
Samodzielna Sekcja I (Self-Contained Section I), 113
Samsel, Eugeniusz, 154
Samulski, Aleksander, 53–54
Sanchez, Ilich Ramirez ("Carlos the Jackal"), 224, 289
Sapieha, Paul (Paweł), 39
"Scenes from Ambiances" (Brydak), 75
Schumann, Maurice, 199–200
Schwarz, Mieczysław, 125–27
Scout Radio, 100–101
Scouts (Polish Scouting Association), 71–72
Secretariat of the CC PUWP, 185, 219, 242
secret police. *See* Internal Affairs Ministry
Secret Service. *See* Internal Affairs Ministry
Section II, Department III, Internal Affairs Ministry, 176
Section III, Department I, Internal Affairs Ministry, 108, 134
Section III, Directorate I, General Staff of the Polish Army, 152
Section IV, Department I, Internal Affairs Ministry, 108, 119, 172–73
Section VIII, Department I, Internal Affairs Ministry (later Section XI), 106, 108, 113
Securitate (Romania), 225
security police. *See* Internal Affairs Ministry
Security Service. *See* Internal Affairs Ministry
Sejm (parliament), 85, 105, 231, 239
Self-Contained Section I (Samodzielna Sekcja I), 113
Sellin, Jarosław, 232
Semelin, Jacques, 23
semi-thaw, during Gomułka era, 82–85
sentences, for whispered propaganda, 52, 303*n*31
Service for Poland's Victory (Służba Zwycięstwu Polski), 16
Seven difficult years. See *Siedem trudnych lat*
show trials, 92–93, 249, 270
Siedem trudnych lat (*Seven difficult years*, memoirs, Czechowicz): anti-Zionism of, 203; construction of, 203–4; Operation Olcha and, 174; propagandistic nature of, 114, 123, 132–33, 143–44, 146, 155; RFE informant records in, 190, 193
signal jamming. *See* jamming
Sikorski Museum (London), 10
Siła-Nowicki, Władysław, 161, 163, 164
Sitko, Karol, 206
Six-Day War, 154–55
Sixth PUWP Congress (December 1971), 183
Skalnik, Kurt, 158, 162–63, 165
Skorupiński, Mieczysław, 152
Śliwicki, Zygmunt, 174
Słonimski, Antoni, 91–92, 166
Służba Zwycięstwu Polski (Service for Poland's Victory), 16
Small Criminal Code (1946), 52
Śmiech, Romuald, 160
Śmigiel, Staszek, 228
Smolar, Aleksander, 227, 260
Smolar, Eugeniusz, 227–28, 355*n*82
Smoliński, Andrzej ("Kryza"), 206, 214–15, 269
Śniady, Jacek (pseud. of Jerzy Szyszko-Bohusz), 59, 90, 146
Sobolev, Arkadii, 48
socialism, imperialist weapons against, 153
socialist anti–Free Europe radio station, 101
Social Sciences Academy (CC PUWP), 243
Society for Educational Courses. *See* Towarzystwo Kursów Naukowych
Sofia meeting of Soviet bloc countries, 221–22, 223

Sokolnicki, Juliusz, 207
Sokorski, Włodzimierz, 103, 183
Soldiers' Song Festival (Kołobrzeg), 270
Solidarity, 4, 6, 43, 232, 233, 235–36, 252, 258, 362*n*197
Sołuba, Zbigniew ("Nawrócony," "Zbyszewski"), 189, 191
Soviet (Communist) bloc: anti-sabotage campaigns, participation in, 289; cooperation against RFE, 132, 220–26; Czechowicz campaign and, 201–3; information control in, 283; jamming by, 45–50, 80–81, 187, 275, 276; security cooperation within, 116; seminar on ideological sabotage, 213; spy agencies, documents from, 351*n*31; US policies toward, 40–41; Western radio, actions against, 288. See also *individual countries*
Soviet Union (USSR): allies, relations with, 46; anti-RFE campaign, participation in, 199; anti-Semitic campaign in, 55; balloon operations, response to, 65; Final Act of CSCE and, 218; Hungary, intervention in, 31; ideological sabotage against, 212–13; jamming by, 19, 45–46, 235, 274–75, 287–88; Poland, relations with, 139; propagandizing, using radio broadcasts, 13, 14; radios in, 19, 295*n*38; repatriation campaign and, 75, 77. *See also* Communist Party of the Soviet Union
Spain: jamming attempts by, 19; Polish government in exile, recognition of, 21
Special Commission for Combating Economic Abuses and Sabotage (Komisja Specjalna do Walki z Nadużyciami i Szkodnictwem Gospodarczym), 9, 52, 55
Special Guidelines (RFE), 34
special undertakings, description of, 226
sports, 102, 220–22
spy operations, 119–37; against Chciuk, 120–21; against Michałowski, 121–24; overview, 119–20; use of RFE employees' family and friends in, 120; using Bożekowski, 124–28, 131; using Chilecki, 134–35; using Czechowicz, 128–30; using Koryzma, 130–33; using Lach, 133–34; Wawrzyńczyk and, 135–37
staff conflicts (at RFE), 244, 251–52, 277–78, 287
Stalinist era, 45–81; attempted infiltrations of RFE, 70–75; balloon war, 63–67; Communist propaganda attacks, 57–62; conclusions on, 78–81; individuals listening to Western radio, harassment of, 51–57; intelligence operations, initiation of, 67–70; receivers with reduced range of frequencies, production of, 50–51; repatriation campaign, 75–78; signal jamming by Soviet bloc, 45–50; Światło revelations and, 62–63
Staniszewska, Grażyna, 243
Staniszewski, Stefan, 275–76, 278
Stasi (East German intelligence service). *See* German Democratic Republic
State Department (US): FEC and, 26, 35; limitations on, 22–23; on the Partisans, 34; pressure on RFE, 41–42; RFE, oversight of, 32, 43; on Rozmarek speech, transmission of, 33; Vatican, discussions with, 87
stationary jamming centers (K points), 47
Stawka większa niż życie (*Stakes higher than life itself*, TV show), 194
Stefanowski, Andrzej, 111
Stepaczenko, Jerzy, 52
Stockholm bureau (RFE), 200
Stomma, Stanisław, 178
street demonstrations and strikes, 95–96, 237–38, 276–77. *See also* workers' protests
Strzetelski, Stanisław, 23–24
student revolt (1968), 95–96
Student Solidarity Committee (Cracow), 228–29
Stypułkowska, Aleksandra (Jadwiga Mieczkowska), 142–43, 326*n*223

Sweden, RFE Stockholm bureau, 200
Świat (periodical), Brydak articles in, 73, 76
Światło, Józef: assertions on travel, 70; Brydak case and, 71; importance of revelations by, 6, 284, 286; propaganda against, 30, 60; RFE programs by, 26, 45, 62–63
Świdlicki, Andrzej, 264
Świeykowski, Aleksander, 263–64
Świtała, Kazimierz, 118, 167
Świtalski, Grzegorz, 52–53
Świtalski, Włodzimierz, 53
Świt (Dawn) radio station, effectiveness of, 15
Szafrański, Wacław (believed to be Ignacy Krasicki, "Witold"), 122–23, 189, 210, 233, 240–41
Szaniawski, Józef, 266–73
"Szaniec" (operational inquiry code), 269
Szarzyńska-Rewska, Hanna, 89, 156
Szawłowski, Zbigniew, 272
Szczepański, Maciej, 252
Szczuka, Stanisław, 161
Szechter, Szymon, 161, 163
Szerer Commission report, 256
Szlachcic, Franciszek: on Czechowicz, reports from, 130; Czechowicz campaign and, 188, 189–90, 204; on RFE, flow of information to, 92; on RFE's role in workers' protests, 184; on sabotage centers, 286
Szlajfer, Henryk, 95, 148
Sznajder, Franciszek, 268
Szpakowska, Małgorzata, 180
Szpet, Zygmunt, 54
Szpilki (satirical weekly), 243
Sztandar Młodych (newspaper), on RFE, 277
Szutenbach, Lech, 54
Szwedowicz, Karol (Stefan Michnik), 255–56
Szydlak, Jan, 169, 212, 220
Szymborski, Krzysztof, 180
Szyszko-Bohusz, Jerzy (Jacek Śniady), 59, 90, 146
Tadeusz Kościuszko station, 14–15
Talarek, Stanisław, 59–60
Tarka, Krzysztof, 107, 207
Tatarkówna, Michalina, 90
Tatarowski, Konrad, 263, 264
Teatr Jednego Aktora, 145
Tejchma, Józef, 231
telephone bugs, 353*n*48
Ten jest z Ojczyzny mojej. Polacy z pomocą Żydom 1939–1945 (*He is my neighbor: The Poles who came to the Jews' rescue, 1939–1945*, Bartoszewski and Lewinówna), 157
thaw (Polish October, 1956), 30–31, 82–85, 88–90
"Theses for the speech for the trial of Zdzisław Najder" (anonymous document), 249–50
third basket (of Final Act of CSCE), 218–19
Third of May holiday, 5
Third Regiment of Radio Interference, 187
Third Reich, 14, 17–18, 19
Tito, Josip Broz, 28
totalitarian regimes, 13–14, 285
Towarzystwo Kursów Naukowych (TKN, Society for Educational Courses), 229–30
Traciłowski, M., 265
Trąmpczyński, Witold, 341*n*43
tribunal, against RFE and RL, 223
Trojan, Henryk, 152
Trojanowski, Wojciech, 221
Trościanko, Wiktor ("Medal," "Tuba," "Mentor"): Brycht on, 146; Jabłoński and, 70; material for radio programs of, 158; military intelligence, work with, 137–44, 152; *Monachijska menażeria* on, 115; Morawski on, 326*n*223; on national Communism, 34; Nowak, allegations against, 203–4; Szaniawski case and, 268, 271, 272
Trotskyites, trial of, 160–61
Truman, Harry, 11, 19

Trybuna Ludu (PUWP daily): on jamming, end of, 79; on RFE staff conflicts, 252; Urban's story in, 244; on Voice of Free Poland, 59; on Wawrzyńczyk, 136
"Tuba." *See* Trościanko, Wiktor
Tumanov, Oleg, 194–95
Tworkowska, Maria, 180
Tygodnik Polski (émigré publication): Operation Olcha and, 160–61; publisher of, 107
Tygodnik Powszechny (Catholic weekly), Bartoszewski and, 158
Tylko Polska (newspaper), on Nowak, 346*n*108
Tyszkiewicz, Michał, 59

Uberman, Zdzisław, 242
Ufam ci Kilroy (*I trust you, Kilroy*, Lach and Uberman), 134, 241–42
UN General Assembly, 19, 238
Union of Journalists, 26
Union of Socialist Polish Youth. *See* Związek Socjalistycznej Młodzieży Polskiej
United States: Communist bloc, policies toward, 40–41; intrawar foreign-language radio broadcasts, 14; Oder-Neisse border issue and, 27, 33, 73–74; overseas programming, during World War II, 15; Poland, relations with, 85–88, 274; Soviet satellites, policy toward, 22. *See also* Central Intelligence Agency; State Department
University of Warsaw, 95, 101, 103, 148–49
Urban, Jerzy, 10, 243–46, 259, 277–80
USSR. *See* Soviet Union

Vatican: discussions with US State Department on RFE, 87; radio station in, 14, 20
Vienna, spy operations in, 135–37
Voice of America (VOA): Brydak and, 72; frequencies for Russian-language programs, 19; initiation of, 15; jamming of, 46, 78; listenership, size of, 4, 276; popularity of, 3, 20; reductions to, after World War II, 18; as State Department constituent, 22
Voice of Free Czechoslovakia, 27–28
Voice of Free Hungary, 31
Voice of Free Poland (later Polish Service of Radio Free Europe): borders, discussions of, 27–28; Brydak and, 72, 74–75; on Poles in Soviet Union, 77; as primary adversary to Polish government, 49, 73; propaganda against, 58–59; Public Security Ministry's information on, 68; reputation and credibility of, 30; RFE's use of name, 26. *See also* Polish Service of Radio Free Europe
Volksstimme (newspaper), Hoffman article in, 224
V (for victory) symbol, 16–17

Wagner, Karol, 21
Wajda, Andrzej, 7–8
Wałęsa, Lech, 239
Walicki, Andrzej, 285
Walka Młodych (weekly), on Gontarczyks, 260
Walter, Ralph, 345*n*101, 346*n*112
Wańkowicz, Melchior, 92–93, 160, 178, 216, 248
Warsaw (as Poland). *See* Polish government
Warsaw Command, Citizens' Militia, 175–76
Warsaw Uprising (1944), 15
Warsaw Pact countries: broadcasting within Poland by, 100; foreign ministers meeting, 200. *See also* Soviet (Communist) bloc
Warsaw Polytechnic, 96
Warsaw Radio: anti-RFE propaganda in, 61; Nowak speech, broadcast of excerpts of, 261; on RFE, 59–60
Warsaw's 1,859 days (*1859 dni Warszawy*, Bartoszewski), 178, 272
Washington (as US). *See* United States
Wasilewski, Andrzej, 7–8

Waszczuk, Jerzy, 316*n*82
Wave 49 (radio program), anti-REF propaganda on, 61
Wawrzyńczyk, Stanisław, 135–37
Wehner, Herbert, 196
Werblan, Andrzej, 7, 169, 185, 223, 339*n*15, 352–53*n*46
"the West" ("Zachód," operational case code name), 362*n*197
Western radio, harassment of people listening to, 51–57
West German intelligence. *See* Bundesnachrichtendienst
West Germany. *See* Federal Republic of Germany
whispered propaganda, 52, 303*n*31
Whitehead, John C., 274
"Who Is Responsible for the Incitement and Interference" (Krasicki), 233
"Whom do you support?" (Internal Affairs Ministry), 95
Wiadomości (émigré publication), writers punished for contact with, 156
Wiatr, Mieczysław, 272
Widy-Wirski, Feliks, 191, 192, 341*n*42
Wielgus, Stanisław ("Grey"), 256–58, 261
Wierzyński, Kazimierz, 24
Wiesenthal, Simon, 209–10, 346–47*n*118
Wiłkomirska, Wanda, 162–63
Willman, Adam, 196
WiN. *See* Wolność i Niezawisłość (Freedom and Independence) movement
Wirpsza, Witold, 148
Wisner, Frank, 36
"Witold" (Ignacy Krasicki, assumed alias of Wacław Szafrański), 122–23, 189, 210, 233, 240–41
"Włodek" (Krzysztof Michałowski, "Franek," "Michał"), 121–22
Wojskowa Służba Wewnętrzna (Military Internal Service), 138, 152, 266–73
Wojtecki, Jerzy, 239
Wolna Europa (Free Europe, bulletin), 64
Wolność i Niezawisłość (Freedom and Independence) movement, 22, 39, 67, 157
workers' protests: (1970), 181, 182, 183, 184, 190; (1976), 226, 292*n*11; (1980), 232. *See also* street demonstrations and strikes
World War II, foreign propaganda by radio, effects on, 14–16
Woroszylski, Wiktor, 148
Writers' Union, 91
Wróblewicz, Henryk, 98–99, 215
Wrocław Security Office, research by, 104–5
W sieci Szymona Wiesenthala (*In Simon Wiesenthal's net*, Szafrański), 210
Wyka, Kazimierz, 166
Wysocki, Stefan, 217
Wyszyński, Stefan, 62, 191

youth groups, conspiratorial, 94–95
Yugoslavia, as model for Poland, 28

Zaborowski, Jan, 162
"Zachód" ("the West," operational case code name), 362*n*197
Zagadnienia istotne (*The real issues*, Piasecki), 64
Zakrzewski, Tadeusz, 278
Zaleski, Wojciech, 21
Załuski, Piotr, 263, 264, 265–66
Zamorski, Kazimierz ("Morski"), 29, 44, 126–27, 135–36, 137, 217
Zamyatin, Leonid, 234–35
Zaremba, Marcin, 285
Zaremba, Paweł, 215
Zaremba, Piotr, 6
Zaremba, Zygmunt, 205
Zawadzki, Tadeusz. *See* Żenczykowski, Tadeusz
"Zbyszewski" (Zbigniew Sołuba, "Nawrócony"), 189, 191
Żenczykowski, Tadeusz (known as Zawadzki): allegations against, 114, 115; Bartoszewski and, 158, 159, 179; Cat-Mackiewicz on, 77; information sources, contacts with, 30;

intelligence report on, 69; Nowak, support for, 206; Operation Olcha and, 159–60, 163, 165–68, 173–75
Zeszyty Historyczne (periodical), Szerer Commission report in, 256
Zharov, A., 45–46
Zionism and Zionists, 140, 144, 155. *See also* anti-Semitism and anti-Zionism
Żmuda, Czesław, 271
"Znicz" (alleged Home Army officer), 170–71
Żołnierz Wolności (military newspaper): anti-RFE propaganda in, 58; on Blachnicki, 258; on RFE, 277
Związek Socjalistycznej Młodzieży Polskiej (Union of Socialist Polish Youth, ZSMP), 3–4
Życie Warszawy (newspaper): anti-Nowak forgeries in, 208; anti-RFE propaganda in, 57; on test of truth for RFE, 277
Żytomirski, Eugeniusz, 164

COLD WAR

INTERNATIONAL HISTORY

PROJECT SERIES

James G. Hershberg
series editor

Battleground Africa
Cold War in the Congo, 1960–1965
By Lise Namikas

The Soviet Cuban Missile Crisis
Castro, Mikoyan, Kennedy, Khrushchev, and the Missiles of November
By Sergo Mikoyan. Edited by Svetlana Savranskaya

Divided Together
The United States and the Soviet Union in the United Nations, 1945–1965
By Ilya V. Gaiduk

Marigold
The Lost Chance for Peace in Vietnam
By James G. Hershberg

After Leaning to One Side
China and Its Allies in the Cold War
By Zhihua Shen and Danhui Li

The Cold War in East Asia, 1945–1991
Edited by Tsuyoshi Hasegawa

Stalin and Togliatti
Italy and the Origins of the Cold War
By Elena Agarossi and Victor Zaslavsky

A Distant Front in the Cold War
The USSR in West Africa and the Congo, 1956–1964
By Sergey Mazov

Connecting Histories
Decolonization and the Cold War in Southeast Asia, 1945–1982
Edited by Christopher E. Goscha and Christian F. Ostermann

Rebellious Satellite: Poland 1956
By Paweł Machcewicz

Two Suns in the Heavens
The Sino-Soviet Struggle for Supremacy, 1962–1967
By Sergey Radchenko

The Soviet Union and the June 1967 Six-Day War
Edited by Yaacov Ro'i and Boris Morozov

Local Consequences of the Global Cold War
Edited by Jeffrey A. Engel

Behind the Bamboo Curtain
China, Vietnam, and the World beyond Asia
Edited by Priscilla Roberts

Failed Illusions
Moscow, Washington, Budapest, and the 1956 Hungarian Revolt
By Charles Gati

Kim Il Sung in the Khrushchev Era
Soviet-DPRK Relations and the Roots of North Korean Despotism, 1953–1964
By Balázs Szalontai

Confronting Vietnam
Soviet Policy toward the Indochina Conflict, 1954–1963
By Ilya V. Gaiduk

Economic Cold War
America's Embargo against China and the Sino-Soviet Alliance, 1949–1963
By Shu Guang Zhang

WOODROW WILSON CENTER PRESS
STANFORD UNIVERSITY PRESS